Recent Studies
in Early Christianity

A Collection of Scholarly Essays

Series Editor

Everett Ferguson

A GARLAND SERIES

Series Contents

History, Hope, Human Language, and Christian Reality

Edited with an introduction by
Everett Ferguson

GARLAND PUBLISHING, INC.
A MEMBER OF THE TAYLOR & FRANCIS GROUP
New York & London
1999

Library of Congress Cataloging-in-Publication Data

History, hope, human language, and Christian reality / edited, with
  introductions by Everett Ferguson.
     p. cm. — (Recent studies in early Christianity ; 6)
     Includes bibliographical references.
     ISBN 0-8153-3338-2 (alk. paper)
     1. Theology, Doctrinal—History—Early church, ca. 30–600.
    2. Church history—Primitive and early church, ca. 30–600.
I. Ferguson, Everett, 1933– . II. Series.
BT25.H57 1999
270.1—dc21   99-23039
                                              CIP

Printed on acid-free, 250-year-life paper
Manufactured in the United States of America

Contents

Series Introduction

Garland published in 1993 *Studies in Early Christianity: A Collection of Scholarly Essays*, an eighteen-volume set of classic articles on the early history of Christianity. The present set of six volumes, *Recent Studies in Early Christianity*, continues that first series by selecting articles written during the last decade. The chronological scope is the same, the first six centuries of the common era. The arrangement once more is topical but with a conflation and realignment of topics to fit the smaller number of volumes. The present series of essays will serve as an important supplement for those who possess the first series. For those without the first series, it will introduce key areas of research and debate on the early history of Christianity.

The growing academic interest in Christianity during its early centuries, as noted in the series introduction to *Studies in Early Christianity*, has greatly accelerated. There has been a proliferation of studies during the last decade on the subject of Christianity in late antiquity. The very popularity of the designation "late antiquity" says something about the current intellectual climate in which these studies arise: a shift from a primary emphasis on Christianity itself to the larger cultural setting of which it was a part, a shift from doctrinal studies to the church as a social institution, and a shift from concern for orthodoxy to the popular religious attitudes and expressions.

The increased study of this period finds expression in more doctoral students, record membership in professional organizations, like the North American Patristics Society and the Association internationale d'études patristiques, and large attendance at the International Conferences on Patristic Studies in Oxford (August 16-21, 1999, marks the thirteenth of these meetings that occur every four years), in addition to participation in specialized conferences on Origen, Gregory of Nyssa, Augustine, and others. Expanded literary productivity is evidenced by new journals (*The Journal of Early Christian Studies*, edited by Elizabeth Clark and Everett Ferguson, a continuation of *The Second Century*; *Zeitschrift für Antikes Christentum/Journal of Ancient Christianity*, edited by H.C. Brennecke and C. Markschies), new reference works (*The Encyclopedia of Early Christianity* [New York: Garland], edited by Everett Ferguson, first edition in 1990, second and greatly expanded edition in 1997, paperback edition 1998; *The Encyclopedia of the Early Church* [New York: Oxford University Press, 1992], English translation of *Dizionario Patristico e di Antichità Cristiane*, edited by Angelo Di Berardino), and substantial scholarly monographs in the field.

In some ways the selection of articles for six volumes on a decade of scholarship is more difficult than eighteen volumes on a century: We do not have the perspective of time to judge what is of enduring worth. Although some of these pieces will no doubt become classics, the guiding principle in selection has been to point to areas that are drawing the greatest attention. Some subjects have become virtually independent subdisciplines in the study of religion in late antiquity. This is notably true of Gnosticism, although the very term is under attack as a proper category.

The six volumes of this collection of scholarly essays take up the following broad topics: (1) the social setting of the early church, with attention to such matters as women, family, friendship, funerary practices, education, and slavery; (2) the political, cultural, and religious setting of early Christianity in relation to Romans, Greeks, and Jews; (3) the internal development of the church as it recognized its canon of scriptures, interpreted those scriptures, defined its confession of faith, and articulated standards of conduct; (4) the diversity — geographical, doctrinal, disciplinary — that counterbalanced the efforts to achieve a unified orthodoxy; (5) the many expressions of devotion and spirituality that both nourished and manifested faith; and (6) the varied ways in which early Christians wrestled with the limitations of historical existence and human language yet voiced their hopes for another and better world.

These topics represent the emphases in the modern study of early Christianity: social history and the application of the social sciences to the understanding of the historical texts, women's concerns and gender issues, Christians' relations with their Jewish and pagan neighbors, variety in early Christianity (especially fueled by the Nag Hammadi texts but not exclusively so), types of asceticism, literary forms and criticism, and Christianity's relationship to late antiquity and the transition to the medieval world. Some themes long present in the study of early Christianity continue to gain attention: the creedal definition of the faith, the causes and effects of persecution, different approaches to the interpretation of the Bible, forms of worship and spirituality, Christian morality, and the Christian hope.

One person's judgment and one small set of essays cannot do full justice to the rich flowering of studies in the field of early Christianity. We can only point to the areas of emphasis and call attention to some significant studies. These studies will lead teachers and students into the larger field and, we hope, spark their interest in pursuing some of these questions and related matters more extensively, thereby enlarging the number of researchers in a field not only intellectually challenging but also spiritually significant.

Volume Introduction

Contemporary intellectual trends that are grouped under the heading of "postmodernism" call into question the ways of doing history that have prevailed since the Enlightenment. In view of modern theories of language and perspectives on reality, is it possible to do history? Several articles in the last decade have tackled philosophical and practical questions pertaining to the historiography of the early Christian movement. The first set of articles chosen for reprint represent some of the recent examinations of early Christian views of history.

The volume opens with a general discussion of the current intellectual scene, Frederick W. Norris's presidential address to the North American Patristic Society, that explores the recent changes in historiography, what these mean for reading patristic texts within an interpretative community, and the need for a forum where those of different viewpoints can talk with one another. Then Rachel Moriarity takes a look at the developing historical consciousness in the early church.[1] Peter Kaufman examines one early thinker who was not a historian, Tertullian, for the implicit views on history involved in his attitudes on heresy and the unfolding interpretation of revelation. As early Christian historians wrote of the Christian past, they preserved important comments on their own times as well.[2] Christian theology offered distinctive perspectives on the nature of history (Eno).[3] The patristic thinker who had the most profound influence on the western writing and philosophy of history was Augustine.[4] When one thinks of history and Augustine, attention immediately turns to his *City of God*, but this is not the only place where questions of history are explored in depth by the great North African. One of the leading European interpreters of patristic thought, Basil Studer, examines the relation of history and faith in one of Augustine's major theological writings, *On the Trinity*.

According to Christian faith, history ends in the fulfillment of hope. The second set of papers in this collection deals with some classic elements of the Christian eschatological hope — the millennium, resurrection, destiny of the soul, and divine predestination. The approach of a new millennium in the western calendar raises interest in eschatological speculation about the return of Christ and a literal millennial reign by Christ on earth, a view espoused by several prominent early Christian thinkers, notably Irenaeus.[5]

Perhaps of less momentary excitement but of more lasting concern in Christian thought are questions about death, the state of the departed, and the nature of the resurrection body and of the soul. The ancient world envisioned a close connection between the living and the deceased.[6] Origen's speculations on the human soul and the resurrection were a ferment in early Christian thinking. Two approaches to his thought are represented in this collection (Edwards and Hennessey).[7] Caroline Bynum has been an influential figure in interpreting how Christian thought about the human body and its resurrection in late antiquity continued to play itself out in the Middle Ages. Leo the Great represented an early effort to prune the Augustinian doctrines of grace and predestination of their deterministic elements and to integrate them into the church's traditional theology (Barclift, "Predestination and Divine Foreknowledge").

Part of the postmodernist outlook is fueled by questions pertaining to the nature and functions of language. Reflection on the nature of human language was not foreign to early Christian thinkers, and the church fathers recognized the accommodative nature of human language as a vehicle of divine revelation.[8] As with the biblical affirmation that "the Word became flesh" in Jesus Christ, so Christians recognized that the divine revelation must be expressed within the limitations of language and that this made all the more necessary a concern with literacy and education. On this subject, as on so much else in Christian thought, Irenaeus was an early pioneer (Richard Norris), and Augustine a subtle and profound elaborator (C. Ando).

Leo the Great is once more taken as an example, this time of how doctrine had to be accommodated to language, traditional thought, and the changing currents of debate (Barclift, "The Shifting Tones of Leo the Great's Christological Vocabulary"). The church has often played an important role in advancing literacy, where this was not present in societies to which the gospel was brought. It took this role in western history at the time when the institutions that had been responsibile for the functions of preserving ancient learning and promoting education were collapsing (Ferreiro). The divine word came to be communicated not only in speech and writing but also in artistic images (Cameron, one of the most creative interpreters of Christianity in the context of late antiquity). With the acceptance of art within the churches came theological reflection on the meaning and uses of those images (Chazelle).

The reality of Christian living in the complex Mediterranean world of late antiquity is represented in the careers of some prominent churchmen of the fourth century — Hilary of Poitiers and Ambrose — and one key figure in the transmission of the values of that ancient world to medieval Britain — the Venerable Bede. Factors in the selection of these figures include, in addition to the presence of significant studies about them, their absence from *Studies in Early Christianity* and from the present series, *Recent Studies in Early Christianity*, a balancing of a perhaps heavier attention to Greek figures in other volumes, and their importance in illustrating themes from this volume and other volumes in the series. Both Hilary of Poitiers and Ambrose have been given major study by Dan Williams. Hilary was a central figure in the Arian controversy of the fourth century, intimately involved in the church-state tensions of that conflict. Ambrose as bishop of Milan had more to do with orthodoxy's triumph over paganism and Arianism in the West than did the bishop of Rome, but this was not easy or as clear-cut as appears on the surface.[9] Note should also be taken of Jerome, the most learned man in the Latin West. His bitter polemics against those who disagreed with him and his contradictions in character should not drown out the influence his positions on asceticism, virginity, and the saints had on western piety and his Bible translation (Vulgate) and commentaries had on Latin Bible scholarship, including his recognition of Jewish interpretations and defense of the Hebrew Bible.[10] Bede holds a special interest as one of the last of the fathers, an Englishman, and a scholar in Greek, one of the most learned men in the West after Jerome. Kelly brings him attention in an attractive way.

Notes

[1] One facet of that, phrased in modern terms, is examined by Wolfram Kinzig, "The Idea of Progress in the Early Church until the Age of Constantine," *Studia Patristica* 24 (1993):119–34.

[2] J.H.W.G. Liebeschutz, "Ecclesiastical Historians on Their Own Times," *Studia Patristica* 24 (1993): 151–63.

[3] Alden A. Mosshammer, "Historical Time and the Apokatastasis according to Gregory of Nyssa," *Studia Patristica* 27 (1993):70–93.

[4] A narrow segment of that influence is studied by Alfred Schindler, "Augustine and the History of the Roman Empire," *Studia Patristica* 22 (1989):326–36.

[5] Christopher R. Smith, "Chiliasm and Recapitulation in the Theology of Irenaeus," *Vigiliae Christianae* 48 (1994):313–31.

[6] Eoin de Bhaldraithe, "*Oblationes pro defunctis*: What Did Tertulian Mean?" *Studia Patristica* 20 (1989):346–51.

[7] The latter has written also on "Gregory of Nyssa's Doctrine of the Resurrection Body," *Studia Patristica* 22 (1989):28–34.

[8] For an earlier consideration of this question, Frances Young, "The God of the Greeks and the Nature of Religious Language," in William R. Schoedel and Robert L. Wilken, eds., *Early Christian Literature and the Classical Tradition: in honorem Robert M. Grant* (Paris: Beauchesne, 1980), pp. 45–74.

[9] Ivor J. Davidson, "Ambrose's *De Officiis* and the Intellectual Climate of the Late Fourth Century," *Vigiliae Christianae* 49 (1995):313–33, argues that Ambrose aimed to transform Cicero for Christian purposes, a project that set the program for western medieval culture.

[10] Stefan Rebenich, "Jerome: The 'Vir Trilinguis' and the 'Hebraica Veritas,'" *Vigiliae Christianae* 47 (1993):50–77.

Black Marks on the Communities' Manuscripts[1]

FREDERICK W. NORRIS

Next year is the twenty-fifth anniversary of the North American Patristic Society's birth; we will celebrate it in Oxford. Twenty-five years ago Michael McHugh and Robert Sider planned the first NAPS conference which was held in New York at the December, 1970 national meeting of the American Philological Society. Bruce Metzger, Luitpold Wallach and Louis Swift were added to the steering committee at that meeting.[2] Swift, during 1972, began to publish a newsletter called *Patristics* which kept the circle of nearly two hundred in contact with each other's research. In 1981 at the suggestion of Joseph Kelly the newsletter emerged as a review which concentrated on longer notices of important books. That same year our first independent international meeting was held here at Loyola University of Chicago. During 1986 the "Patristic Monograph Series," formerly supported by the Philadelphia Patristic Foundation, became an organ of our society. Published by Mercer University Press, it offers typeset, hardbound technical studies for a reasonable price. Joseph Lienhard now serves as its editor. The first edition of the *Encyclopedia of Early Christianity* appeared in 1990, commended by this society and the American Society of Church History, and written primarily by our members. A second edition is scheduled for 1995. Less than two years ago the work of many, but particularly

1. 1994 NAPS Presidential Address. Thanks are due to a circle at Emmanuel School of Religion and Milligan College who discussed drafts of this address with me. Two former students deserve special mention, Robert Parsley and Philip Kenneson. Through the latter I received approval to read a manuscript written by A. K. M Adam of Princeton Theological Seminary, a deconstructionist approach to New Testament studies.
2. Michael McHugh, "The North American Patristic Society: Retrospect and Prospect," *Classical Folio* 25 (1971): 5–8. Official incorporation of the society was granted 17 December 1973 by the state of Kentucky.

Journal of Early Christian Studies 2:3, 443–466 © 1994 The Johns Hopkins University Press.

of Elizabeth Clark, Everett Ferguson and Patout Burns, led to the *Journal of Early Christian Studies* which has absorbed the book review function of *Patristics* and continues the efforts of *Second Century*. The journal has over eleven hundred subscribers, the society nearly five hundred fifty members. According to guild standards, we have matured. That maturing has brought lively debates about who we are and what we shall become.

There have been changes. Some things we and colleagues in our fields of inquiry have been we no longer can be. In the 1970s when NAPS was imbedded within an historical philological society, the Rankian ideal was still in vogue. The goal was to describe what had actually happened, to let the text and its author speak unencumbered by our concerns. That was the way we had been educated. We were not alone. Averil Cameron rightly claims that this type of historicism has dominanted the field of ancient history up through the 1980s.[3] A survey of the research projects mentioned in *Patristics* during the 1970s or the reviews of the 1980s would not controvert her opinion. Few of us understood how much the land had shifted or consistently articulated the lessons of caution we had learned.

Today we seldom defend our work as neutral or totally objective. Philosophically, the distanced, dispassionate study of texts has been an ideal, but it is a battered one. Well before 1970 Ludwig Wittgenstein had made his dramatic shift away from the *Tractatus*, so admired by the Vienna circle of logical positivists, and gave us the remarkable later writings that explore meaning as use and the practice of language games.[4] Opponents of logical positivism had warned that the major definition of the school could not pass its own test. The statement that only tautologies and sentences subject to empirical verification have meaning is on that very ground meaningless because it is neither a tautology nor an empirically testable claim. The invigorating dream of doing away with aesthetics, ethics, religion and other realms of discourse as utter nonsense was fading. In writing his history of philosophy, A. J. Ayer, positivism's most brilliant English-speaking advocate, himself noted that the effort had failed.[5] Members of this society may have felt or even now feel the loss of older historicism's

3. Averil Cameron (ed.), *History as Text: The Writing of Ancient History* (Chapel Hill, NC: The University of North Carolina Press, 1989), introduction.
4. See particularly his *Philosophical Investigations*, trans. by G. E. M. Anscombe, 3rd ed. (Oxford: Basil Blackwell, 1967), the student notes published as *The Lectures and Conversations on Aesthetics, Psychology and Religious Belief*, ed. by Cyril Barrett (Oxford: Basil Blackwell, 1966) and *On Certainty*, ed. by G. E. M. Anscombe and G. H. von Wright (Oxford: Basil Blackwell, 1969).
5. Compare A. J. Ayer's treatment of logical positivism in his *Language, Logic and Truth* (London: V. Gollancz, Ltd., 1936) with his *Philosophy in the Twentieth Century* (New York: Random, 1982), 108–141.

philosophical underpinnings as either freeing or threatening. But both Cartesian and Kantian foundationalism are gone.[6]

Part of the broader philosophical shift is reflected even in mathematics. Nearly fifteen years ago Morris Kline, the renowned historian, wrote *Mathematics: The Loss of Certainty*[7] in which he demonstrated that the one science which has been the model of concrete objectivity itself includes important uncertainties. Mathematics is wonderfully precise in some areas and does allow physicists, among others, to think about things that they can hardly express in language. But it is not the consistent whole that the Enlightenment had hoped it would be. Euclidean geometry and two types of non-Euclidean geometry developed in the eighteenth century give us three descriptions of the universe, each of which has explanatory power, confirmation in nature, and yet strikingly, is inconsistent with the other two. Kurt Gödel's paper on undecidability over sixty years ago demonstrated that no logical system could enfold both completely and consistently all the true statements of simple arithmetic. Completeness means inconsistency; consistency means incompleteness.[8]

These background claims about objectivity and certainty may seem unusual, if not downright odd. But they exist. At least the bulk of early Christian studies does not reflect the mathematical plague of some sociology: that is, if it can be expressed statistically, it has the strongest claim to truth. So many of our sources have been lost that all our statistics are skewed. We often have to deal with "lies" and "damned lies," but we do not have the data to depend upon statistics.

We may appreciate the physicist Stephen Hawking's sense that the principle of ultimate ignorance in the universe, represented by black holes, is itself limited. Although much of what we would like to know about black holes is impossible, some information does seep out. Hawking calls himself a realist who recognizes that "we do not know what reality is independent of a theory" and yet he believes that a unified theory of reality is just

6. John Milbank, *Theology & Social Theory: Beyond Secular Reason*, Signposts in Theology (Oxford: Basil Blackwell, 1990), more fully than anyone else shows both how bankrupt foundationalism is and what can still be most interestingly funded. Robert Audi, *Belief, Justification & Knowledge: An Introduction to Epistemology* (Belmont, CA: Wadsworth Publishing Company, 1988) supports a type of foundationalism.

7. Morris Kline, *Mathematics: The Loss of Certainty* (New York: Oxford University Press, 1980).

8. See Morris Kline, *Mathematical Thought from Ancient to Modern Times* (New York: Oxford University Press, 1971 [paperback edition, 1990]), particularly volume 3, for a description of the differing geometries and Gödel's work. Ernest Nagel and James R. Newman, *Gödel's Proof* (New York: New York University Press, 1958) provide a readable introduction to Gödel's papers on undecidability and a warning that his efforts do not destroy rationality.

around the corner. People who state their beliefs encourage me, even if theirs are not mine. But I suspect that few of us, certainly not I, know what to do with his insistence that contemporary physics demands true but multiple histories of the universe and something called imaginary time which operates at right angles from real time.[9] Historians are puzzled by such things.

Thomas Kuhn's arguments about paradigms,[10] however, inform many students of early Christian literature, although the critiques of his position by Stephen Toulmin and Paul Feyerabend[11] among others, seldom receive much attention. Even the so-called hard sciences are formed by communities who put forward questions which are not clearly demanded by an apparently objective look at data, but which are shaped by the theories which their guilds have accepted. When those paradigms shift, greatly different questions are asked of the same experiments with startlingly different conclusions.

Karl Popper attempted to stop the leak in the dike when positivism failed; he demanded that statements at least be open to falsification. But his ideal also has significant holes.[12] Modern readings of various university disciplines pointed out the problems with objectivity well before the flowering of postmodernism.[13] Of course, discoveries of different data may push those within an older paradigm to argue for a change of model as Toulmin insists,[14] but for those of us in this society with its textual orienta-

9. His stunningly popular *A Brief History of Time* (New York: Bantam Books, 1986) made those claims. He has offered further popular exposition in his *Black Holes and Baby Universes and Other Essays* (New York: Bantam Books, 1993). The quotation is from his essay, "My Position," *Black Holes*, 44.

10. Thomas Kuhn, *The Structure of Scientific Revolutions*, 2nd ed., enlarged (Chicago: The University of Chicago Press, 1970).

11. Stephen Toulmin, *Human Understanding* (Oxford: Clarendon Press, 1976), particularly chapter 2. Paul Feyerabend, *Against Method* (London: New Left Books, 1975). Also see *Criticism and the Growth of Knowledge*, ed. by Imre Lakatos and Alan Musgrave (London: Cambridge University Press, 1970).

12. Karl Popper, *The Logic of Scientific Discovery* (London: Hutchinson, 1959). Thomas Kuhn, "Logic of Discovery or Psychology of Research?" *Criticism and the Growth of Knowledge*, ed. by Imre Lakatos and Alan Musgrave (Cambridge: Cambridge University Press, 1970), 1–23 and Paul Feyerabend, *Against Method* attack Popper's views. But Gunnar Anderson, "Naive and Critical Falsificationism," *In Pursuit of Truth*, ed. by Paul Levinson (Atlantic Highlands, NJ: Humanities Press, 1982), 50–63 finds them still helpful for scientific research because they are neither positivist nor conventionalist.

13. Sketches of cultural anthropology, linguistics, sociology—any number of university disciplines—would point up similar sets of problems.

14. Stephen Toulmin, *Human Understanding*, 98–117.

tion, new materials—texts previously unknown, newly discovered old coins or even the burgeoning growth of archaeological evidence which has discipline-shattering consequences—are not appropriated as quickly or as frequently as they should be. We have had difficulty getting papers concerning art and archaeology on the program of this conference. I do not remember a numismatics paper. What we major in are shifting views taken from other fields of inquiry which we bring back to the old texts in order to create lively questions.

NAPS, born in philology, still has roots within it. We expect presentations at this meeting to be given by those who can read and translate with some competence the texts they treat. Greek, Latin, Syriac and Coptic are tools often expected of members within our guild. The command of other languages is honored. But it is not clear to me that some of those who have created the newer paradigms impinging on our fields understand the need for these skills.

The levels of philological study continue to fall in North American education. (I suspect that the largest reason is the loss even of Latin in the high-school curriculum and the absence of Greek for decades because parents and educators do not believe their study prepares young people for the real world.) It was easier to insist on careful investigation of the black marks on the page when it was assumed that, once they were deciphered, we had the text's content, the author's intent, in our pockets. Close exegesis of Augustine meant finding out precisely what he intended. Does the deficiency of the old Rankian, old historicist ideal demand that we can no longer cogently argue for the close study of texts?

I think not. Even some influenced by deconstruction suggest that texts at the least offer resistance, if they are not actually part of the constraints on meaning. We do not enlist deconstructionists who have no knowledge of the basic ancient languages for the investigation of sites being excavated or for the cataloguing of ancient libraries with the hope of finding new texts. Hand them an inscription, a legible coin or a newly discovered manuscript and they are of no assistance. They can't read. Deconstructive readings of texts in any other language are dependent at the initial level on having the black marks translated into the deconstructionist's tongue. There are texts in NAPS, not in the sense of E. D. Hirsch that "verbal meaning is determinative, . . . an entity which always remains the same from one moment to the next,"[15] and not only in the sense of Stanley Fish, i.e., that "one means by text the structure of meaning that is obvious and inescapable

15. E. D. Hirsch, *Validity in Interpretation* (New Haven, CT: Yale University Press, 1967), 46.

from the perspective of whatever interpretive assumptions happen to be in force."[16]

Where shall we look for clarification of these issues? Hollywood seems uninterested in our questions. Furthermore, John Cleese, the British humorist of Monty Python fame, is not regarded as a philosophical guide contributing to discussions about texts and communities. If he has any authorial intent it is to make us laugh. But his advice from the movie, *A Fish Called Wanda*, uttered by Jamie Lee Curtis as a complaint about the stupidity of Kevin Klein's character, might well be taped to the doors of our Deans. I quote: "Aristotle was not Belgian. The central teaching of Buddhism is not 'Every man for himself.' The London Underground is not a political movement. These are mistakes, Otto. I looked them up." When Stanley Fish's poetry class studied a list of authors to be read by the previous class and made a poem out of them, he may have been given the most interesting example for making his particular point. A list of names without verbs or any other relational black marks may be shifted with more ease than full sentences and paragraphs. Some of the moves his students made were delightful.[17] But John Cleese might have replied, "It's a mistake, Stanley. Listen to Wanda."

Frances Young, a British colleague, offers a promising analogy in her book *Virtuoso Theology: The Bible and Interpretation*.[18] She suggests that interpreting texts is like the art of musical performance. A musician who follows a piece of music cannot play just any notes or just any rhythms. The reason for musical notation is to give the composer a strong hand in what the performer does. To press her metaphor, Bach is not Mozart; Duke Ellington is not Johnny Cash. They can be distinguished.

Yet any lover of music knows that there are wooden players, those who get the notes and the rhythms right but do not offer a creative performance. The performer, although constrained by the notation, is deeply involved in the performance. Her or his sense of the music is informed by

16. Stanley Fish, *Is There a Text in This Class? The Authority of Interpretive Communities* (Cambridge, MA: Harvard University Press, 1980), vii.

17. Fish, "How to Recognize a Poem When You See One," *Is There a Text?* 322–337.

18. Frances Young, *Virtuoso Theology: The Bible and Interpretation* (Cleveland, OH: Pilgrim Press, 1992) previously published under the title *The Art of Performance: Towards a Theology of Holy Scripture* (London: Darton, Longman and Todd, 1990). She attacks structuralism, particularly pp. 6–12, outside her major analogy and insists that "the aim of biblical criticism to ascertain the original form of the text and the original intention of the author is not to be despised." I have no doubt that such would be her advice for the interpretation of other early Christian literature. For those in our society, her volume is perhaps most interesting when she uses early Christian writers as examples of how Scripture was interpreted.

years of training in the appropriate repertoire and is attuned to the audience.

There are still studies within our fields of inquiry which are based on paying attention to the notes and the rhythms. They depend upon the close reading of often overlooked materials which shift small conclusions or large generalizations. Inscriptions, coin hoards, other such discoveries may move us to change our minds.[19] For example, the older claim of some scholars that paganism was dying rapidly in the fourth century, finished off by Theodosius' laws, has been challenged piecemeal for specific localities. Julian's story of rushing to Daphne's temple of Apollo to celebrate a great festival, only to find a solitary priest ready to sacrifice a lone goose, offers strong support for the generalization.[20] But Frank Trombley's magisterial work, *Hellenic Religion and Christianization*, demonstrates from scattered sources that pagans defiantly went underground and, although weakened, persisted. Christianization was a fascinating popular process that took different shapes in different locales at different times; pagan worship secretly went on well into the sixth century and beyond. Reading inscriptions and regularly ignored hagiographic texts will continue to inform and challenge our claims. I would be hesitant to use the term "empirical fact" as forcefully as Trombley does. He could learn from fuller deliberations about views of history, but I find the arguments which he so carefully mounts persuasive. He grinds an axe in order to help us fell a dead tree that looks like a live possibility only because it is so large and we sometimes think we may still be in the midst of winter.[21]

19. The description of Paul of Samosata, bishop of Antioch, as a high-level bureaucrat in the governmental structure of Zenobia is no longer tenable since a coin hoard shows that Zenobia never controlled the Antiochene mint and thus most probably never ruled Antioch. A study of Roman bureaucracy then offers a background for the charges against him. See my "Paul of Samosata: *Procurator Ducenarius*," *The Journal of Theological Studies* n.s. 35 (1984): 50–70. But Virginia Burrus, "Rhetorical Stereotypes in the Portrait of Paul of Samosata," *Vigiliae Christianae* 43 (1989): 215–225 on other grounds has suggested that all the heretical charges are fallacious, not reflective of Paul's actual political or social context. No unadorned "empirical facts" decide the issue. A look at the web of arguments will be persuasive or not.

20. Julian, *Misopogon* 361D–362B, *The Works of the Emperor Julian*, trans. by W. C. Wright, The Loeb Classical Library (Cambridge, MA: Harvard University Press, 1913), 486, 488.

21. Frank R. Trombley, *Hellenic Religion and Christianization, c. 370–529*, Religions in the Graeco-Roman World, formerly Études préliminaires aux religions orientales dans l'empire romain, vols. 115/1 & 2 (Leiden: E. J. Brill, 1993). As an example of his need to sharpen some arguments, he claims that "the historicity and priority of the Greek recension of Mark the Deacon's narrative" is an "empirical fact" (vol. 1, 243). But he requires an appendix of large proportions (246–282) to make the case. He argues

The black marks must receive their due; yet they do not reign supreme. Frances Young's use of musical performance as an analogy for the interpretation of texts may be most important because it emphasizes not only the composer's notation but also the creativity of the performer, the importance of the repertoire and the place of the audience. The emphasis on written pitch and rhythm is the weakest part of the analogy. Musical notation is less complicated than language. But even that simplicity does not mean that every note written on the page will be performed at the same pitch or with the same relationship to other notes. Various tonal scales provide standards in different cultures; within the same culture instruments have been tuned to a different primary note. Notation of jazz for many instruments or writing down blues, Cajun or country fiddle and guitar playing may be very difficult if not impossible. Some of the best classical performances include grace notes never written or added in parentheses. Every cadenza is an unwritten improvisation which depends upon the virtuoso.[22]

Language is also not as deeply embedded in the widest public domain as Young sometimes claims,[23] at least not in the sense that its meaning is the property of all. She herself says that lexical or

> philological constraints are themselves subject to the constraints of the rationality operative in the cultural context within which interpretation takes place. Doctrine can only be read from the Bible within the closed world of the Church's Salon, and even there the context in terms of the rationality operative at any one time has been subject to radical shifts over the centuries.[24]

Wittgenstein struggled with language games, particularly in regard to religion. He insisted that language about religion could make sense. It was not an area of nonsense as the logical positivists had proposed,[25] but people had to be initiated into it. Not every human being from any inter-

---

convincingly, but there is no bold, obvious empirical character in the Greek recension that overpowers all other claims. He attacks the assumptions, presumptions and readings of others. Well done, but not "empirical fact" in any strong sense.

22. In her chapter on "Improvisation and Inspiration," Young, *Virtuoso Theology,* 160–186 well develops this understanding of the cadenza.

23. Young, *Virtuoso Theology,* 10, 99, 106.

24. *Ibid.,* 128.

25. For an overview see Cyril Barrett, *Wittgenstein on Ethics and Religious Belief* (Oxford: Basil Blackwell, 1991). In *Culture and Value* (Oxford: Basil Blackwell, 1980), 73, Wittgenstein says "An honest religious thinker is like a tightrope walker. He almost looks as though he were walking on nothing but air. His support is the slenderest imaginable. And yet it is possible to walk on it."

pretive community could read it neutrally and understand quickly and easily what it was.

We must recognize the way in which paradigms that influence, even determine, our investigations are formed through our participation in various communities. The strongest difference between the old and the new in patristics is not whether theology or history will provide the interpretive frame. Theology is not singularly some kind of theosophy which deforms our work; intellectual, social, economic, political and cultural histories do not necessarily provide clearly better readings of our sources.[26] What is crucial is how we, who work so hard on the close reading of texts, can use that study to teach ourselves how much the paradigms of our controlling communities form the conclusions we reach. What we need in our fields of inquiry are people who "combine a methodological self-consciousness with an obvious delight in the careful reading of complex texts," people who know that "objectivity is not in any pure form a possibility" but at the same time have no desire "to look at the past with the willful intention of seeing [in it their] own prejudices and concerns."[27] The so-called "new historicism" offers remarkable insight, although parts of its varied perceptions are questionable. We need not give up on the historical-critical task just because we recognize that we have a location within interpretive communities.[28] Even Gertrude Himmelfarb,

---

26. Elizabeth Clark, "The State and Future of Historical Theology: Patristic Studies," *In Memory of Wilhelm Pauck (1901–1981): Memorial Notices, Liturgical Pieces, Essays and Addresses*, ed. by David Lotz, Union Papers No. 2 (New York: Union Theological Seminary, 1982), 46–56, reprinted in *Ascetic Piety and Women's Faith*, Studies in Women and Religion 20 (Lewiston, NY: Edwin Mellen Press, 1986), 3–12 expresses a clear and decidedly different approach from the one represented here. The study, however, that underlies her brilliant book, *The Origenist Controversy: The Cultural Construction of an Early Christian Debate* (Princeton: Princeton University Press, 1992), 7, led her to "signal [her] chastened reconsideration of the importance of both theology and an ascetic spirituality for the controversy." The power of the volume comes from its blending of different and persuasive approaches to the materials.

27. Jean E. Howard, "The New Historicism in Renaissance Studies," *English Literary Renaissance* 16 (1986): 31–32, 43.

28. Howard, *ibid.*, 32–41 looks critically and in some detail at the work of Stephen Greenblatt and Louis Montrose, but she mentions eleven other authors and three journals which, from her perspective, reflect this view in Renaissance studies. *Poststructuralism and the Question of History*, ed. by Derek Attridge, Geoff Bennington, and Robert Young (Cambridge: Cambridge University Press, 1987) is a helpful introduction. The essays by Hayden White, "New Historicism: A Comment" and Stanley Fish, "The Young and the Restless," in another good collection, *The New Historicism*, ed. by H. Aram Veesner (New York: Routledge, 1989), 293–316, point out specific problems in the approaches of some new historicists. (Fish's article is reprinted in

who rightly rails against postmodernists who cannot decide if the Holocaust happened or if the Nazi involvements of de Man and Heidegger mean anything, warns that "every historical work is necessarily imperfect, tentative, and partial (in both senses of the word)." Such views of history are not new.[29]

A number of our colleagues in ancient history understand that positivistic readings are anachronisms. Ancient historians did not write positivistic history, even if their names were not all Eusebius or Procopius.[30] Two recent works by Averil Cameron, *History as Text* and *Christianity and the Rhetoric of Empire*, are good examples of how we can break loose to offer interesting studies of the materials we investigate. The shadow of Arnaldo Momigliano's old historicism still hovers over the first volume with its worry that there is no objective history and that there is only a rhetorical stance for the historian, but the second is further along into the contemporary setting.[31]

There's No Such Thing as Free Speech and It's a Good Thing, Too [Oxford: Oxford University Press, 1994], 243–256.) The contribution of John D. Schaeffer, "The Use and Misuse of Giambattista Vico: Rhetoric, Orality and Theories of Discourse," in *The New Historicism*, 89–101 is dramatically enlightening for those in early Christian studies who have studied ancient rhetoric and its use by early theologians.

29. See her *On Looking into the Abyss: Untimely Thoughts on Culture and Society* (New York: Alfred A. Knopf, 1994), particularly "On Looking into the Abyss," 3–26 and "Postmodernist History," 131–161. The quotation is the last clause in a paragraph (134–135) which reads: "Historians, ancient and modern, have always known what postmodernism professes to have discovered—that any work of history is vulnerable on three counts: the fallibility and deficiency of the historical record on which it is based; the fallibility and selectivity inherent in the writing of history; and the fallibility and subjectivity of the historian. As long as historians have reflected upon their craft, they have known that the past cannot be recaptured in its entirety, if only because the remains of the past are incomplete and are themselves part of the present. They have also known that the writing of history necessarily entails selection and interpretation, that there is inevitable distortion in the very attempt to present a coherent account of an often inchoate past, that, therefore, . . ."

While I was in grammar school I saw my father's Brownie camera pictures of Dachau and watched him shudder as he told their stories. I remain passionately disturbed by the responses of some postmodernists to the Holocaust.

30. See particularly the collection of essays in *Reading the Past in Late Antiquity*, ed. by Graeme Clarke (Ruschcutters Bay, Australia: Australian National University Press, 1990).

31. The dedication of *History as Text: The Writing of Ancient History*, ed. by Averil Cameron, includes the phrase "and in memory of Arnaldo who would not have liked it," the book I assume. The introduction, p. 10, says that the volume "is far from claiming that history can never be objective, that history is nothing but rhetoric, or that there is no distinction between good and bad works of history." Her *Christianity and the*

I do not think we can effectively make a text say anything we like. Stanley Fish has spent much of his time insisting that "anything we like" is not possible. From many vantage points he shows how there are constraints on meaning.[32] He is a close reader of Milton.[33] Most deconstructionists and new historicists read texts carefully. But their point and ours must be that communal commitments do create different projects. Or to put it another way, the attempt to rely on the black marks alone should teach us that totally objective, distanced reading is an impossible goal.

As we construe them, our projects demand that we be able to read the primary languages. When you first learned Greek grammar you were probably struck by how much more precise the Greek black marks were than the English ones. Intricate conditional statements, at least five cases, a style in which all word order does not have to portray sense: those features were impressive.

Yet a good linguist would point out that each language does some tasks better and some tasks worse than the language chosen for comparison. Gregory Nazianzen was wrong to insist that no one could construct theology in Latin because the Roman tongue was too barbaric.[34] Greek has its own significant ambiguities. We were taught historic presents, subjective and objective genitives, and other anomalies as if they could be solved by closer attention to forms. Our textbooks pointed out that the same forms were employed for middle and passive voice in some tenses, but seldom mentioned that as a result, those black marks were sometimes confusing.[35] Yet when we began to read, we noticed that making the choices about which rules applied was not a neutral, mechanical process, but one that demanded interpretive decisions. We earlier thought that context was the determiner; once again the rule of the black marks, now as a collective. We often found, however, that what we call context is influenced not only by the piece of literature itself, or by what we know of the times, but also by

---

Rhetoric of Empire (Berkeley, CA: University of California Press, 1990) does not find a place for objectivity in history.

32. Stanley Fish, *Doing What Comes Naturally: Change, Rhetoric, and the Practice of Theory in Literary and Legal Studies* (Durham, NC: Duke University Press, 1989), particularly in chapters 2–7, argues for various kinds of constraints on meaning.

33. See his classic *Surprised by Sin: The Reader in "Paradise Lost"* (Berkeley: University of California Press, 1971) and his look at present Milton studies in "Milton's Career and the Career of Theory," in *There's No Such Thing as Free Speech*, 257–266.

34. *Or.* 21.35, *Grégoire de Nazianze: Discours 20–23*, SC 270, ed. by Justin Mossay with Guy Lafontaine (Paris: Les Éditions du Cerf, 1980), 186.

35. For Koine Greek see Stanley E. Porter, *Idioms of the Greek New Testament* (Sheffield: JSOT Press, 1992), 72–73.

454 JOURNAL OF EARLY CHRISTIAN STUDIES

the deep commitments we have as readers. It is no accident that the teaching of grammar in the ancient world was aligned with the teaching of rhetoric, the art of persuasion, which itself employed various branches of philosophy. In his *Theological Orations* Gregory Nazianzen attacks his opponents at the level of grammar. On occasion those attacks appear to be fair and obvious to some readers, particularly a postmodern reader who knows Wittgenstein well.[36] But they are always a part of Nazianzen's strong belief that his antagonists are demeaning the faith. He is no neutral observer objectively stating his case. His grammatical arguments appear in invective designed to flay his opponents alive. Even grammar is set within larger interpretive frames.

We learn the force of these problems best by paying attention to the black marks, as well as focusing on contemporary philosophical and literary backgrounds. The insights of new historicist or deconstructionist readings make better sense when you have worked long and hard at creating a critical text and translating it. Yet some doctoral programs no longer teach epigraphy and paleography; a distressing number of new Ph.D.s have never looked at a manuscript, even in microform, unless by some quirk their dissertations are connected with a new manuscript find. There are, however, manuscripts which have not yet been made a part of our critical texts.[37] The possible openings into eastern Europe and Russia make the training of manuscript readers a priority. For example, one of the best manuscripts of John Chrysostom's commentary on Matthew has been in Cracow; it may now be accessible. Our European colleagues will doubtless move into these areas, but the opportunities are too great for their numbers alone. It is also not certain that those creating critical texts have learned the contemporary paradigms that form part of the significant debates within our society.

Critical texts and translations, which still loom large in European study of early Christianity, are not a large part of what members of our society

36. See my comments particularly on the Theologian's Orations 29 and 30 in *Faith Gives Fullness to Reasoning: A Commentary on Gregory Nazianzen's "Theological Orations,"* intro. and commentary by Frederick W. Norris, trans. by Lionel Wickham and Frederick Williams, Supplements to *Vigiliae Christianae* 13 (Leiden: E. J. Brill, 1991), 132–182 and my "Theology as Grammar: Gregory Nazianzen and Ludwig Wittgenstein," *Arianism after Arius,* ed. by Michel Barnes and Daniel H. Williams (Edinburgh: T. & T. Clark, 1993), 237–249.
37. The masterful European text critical project on the corpus of Gregory Nazianzen under the auspices of the Görres Gesellschaft shows what a massive task such an undertaking is. Justin Mossay, "Ver une édition critique de Grégoire de Nazianze," *Revue d'histoire de ecclésiastique* 40 (1979): 629 estimated that there are between 1,200 and 1,500 Greek manuscripts as well as versions in Armenian, Georgian, Coptic, Syriac and Arabic.

and our North American colleagues produce because our manuscript reading skills have diminished. The GCS series, overseen by Harnack and Mommsen in an old historicist milieu, has recently suffered under the pressures of East German cultural priorities. Now the series is within united Germany, but we do not know if it will recover. The French SC series flourishes. Again these series may be tied in individual cases to an old historicist sense of textual study—we will get back to precisely what Ambrose meant—but the production of texts and translations is not a project which only objectivists may enter. The SBL and the AAR have text and translation series; the ACW series is beginning one. Much still needs to be done.

There are also quite interesting studies to be undertaken in the area outside creating critical texts but inside studying textual variants. Bart Ehrman in his book, *The Orthodox Corruption of Scripture*, has investigated the relationship between different manuscript readings and the Christological commitments of unnamed scribes in second- and third-century Christianity. He has asked, what is the import of certain textual variants of Christian scripture for the understanding of doctrinal development?[38] His effort is based on text-critical methods long employed by classicists and Biblical scholars for the study of manuscripts. He concludes that important New Testament Christological verses were read by scribes from within the theological confessions of their communities. They changed the texts to clarify the readings they "knew" were already the point of the texts.

Ehrman's cases are at their best when he can show that the corrections are in the margins of existing manuscripts. They also appear strong when "the original reading," defined through the accepted principles of textual study, seems unquestionable. His volume is flawed, however, because he has not yet dislodged himself from the more positivistic sense of textual

38. Bart Ehrman, *The Orthodox Corruption of Scripture: The Effect of Early Christological Controversies on the Text of the New Testament* (Oxford: Oxford University Press, 1993). At times Ehrman is also deceived by not looking thoroughly at our lexica. For instance, in discussing Matthew 1:18, pp. 75–77, he says that "the earliest and best manuscripts" read *genesis*, "beginning" rather than the *gennesis*, "birth" of "a large number of witnesses." This is evidence not of "simple coincidence" but of "orthodox corruption." Yet G. W. H. Lampe, *A Patristic Greek Lexicon* (Oxford: Clarendon Press, 1961), 310–313 notices how patristic authors and those who copied their texts often used *genetes* "created" and *gennetes* "begotten" interchangeably. Those who read patristic literature become accustomed to this unexpected phenomenon and do not attribute to it some significant meaning. It is difficult to prove intentional "corruption" of Mt. 1:18 by orthodox scribes when orthodox theologians seem to have framed anti-Arian polemic with the occasional substition of *genetes* for *gennetes*, a "mistake" that supported Arian positions.

studies. Ehrman knows contemporary literary theory and uses his key word "corruption" in an ironic sense. But we can only demonstrate that a text has been corrupted if we are certain that our methods can lead us to know what the incorrupt text had been. Ehrman offers little criticism of the principles for establishing "the" original reading. Yet there are at least three schools of textual study, some which follow prioritized rules almost slavishly and some which produce eclectic texts marked by different weighting of rules in different contexts. These schools do not apply the same principles in the same places. Shared methods do not lead to the same results. With some regularity Ehrman himself stands against the United Bible Society's readings of Scriptural texts. Finding the "original text" is not as objective a search as Ehrman seems to suppose; a series of judgments are involved.

The clash of textual positivism, social history and literary theory makes the book extremely interesting even though flawed. Reading a text in antiquity ordinarily meant reading aloud a manuscript usually without word divisions or punctuation marks and correcting the errors as one went along. Sometimes readers compared manuscripts; sometimes they had only one exemplar. But each reader always expected errors. The printing press was what impressed us with uniformity of spelling and grammar in copies of texts. No early Christian theologian ever had that cancerous luxury. The texts we now study were then in flux at the level of the black marks because those black marks were created by scribes who themselves belonged to worshipping communities and by readers who knew that the words or letters were not always correct. Why call their changes "corruption" even in an ironic way, when the scribes themselves did not think that they had in their hands "incorrupt" texts? Perhaps they are among the most "honest" readers of antiquity because they wrote down what they "knew" the text said. When Ehrman compares the scribes' readings with what postmodern theorists have taught us about reading, his sense of things appears better, but he resists such insights at the level of defining the "original reading." There is, however, little reason to suggest that we can do manuscript study on a positivistic level while at the same time we do interpretive studies on a postmodern level.[39]

39. George Lindbeck in a review essay of the festschrift offered to Karlfried Froehlich, *Biblical Hermeneutics in Historical Perspective*, ed. by Mark S. Burrows and Paul Rorem (Grand Rapids, MI: Eerdmans, 1991) in *Modern Theology* 10 (1994): 106 notes that Ehrmann's article, "The Text of Mark in the Hands of the Orthodox," does not connect his observations about the textual variants with his comments on deconstructive literary theory. That article apparently was part of Ehrman's study for the present volume.

Of course the authors we regularly investigate did read and make corrections. They also compared manuscripts and translations. All ancient readers expected problems and solved them as they appeared. Augustine's *De doctrina Christiana* indicates how he compared various texts and translations, but he always thought that his rule of faith, even more pointedly the love of neighbor and self, indicated what the meaning of the Biblical texts would be.[40] One of the most able students of manuscripts and translations, Origen, was also one of the best allegorists who read Scripture in terms of his rule of faith.[41] He never saw the correction of black marks as a task separate from reading the texts in and for the community. Yet he is often dismissed as the interpreter who most deformed the process.[42]

To restate part of my thesis, it is precisely in creating critical texts and translations that we can see ways in which new historicist and deconstructive readings are truthful. Until 1976 we studied Origen's *Peri Archon* from Paul Koetschau's 1913 critical text in the GCS. He had decided—and the English translator Butterworth followed him—to include within the text passages used by Origen's opponents to skewer the Alexandrian as a heretic.[43] So much of the *Peri Archon* is preserved only in Rufinus' Latin translation that we know we can not recover precisely what Origen said even if old historicist presuppositions form our paradigm. Was Rufinus a terrible translator who censored the text by eliminating troublesome passages or did he have a clear conscience because he thought the texts suffered from serious interpolations? Jerome, who along with other descriptions is the purest example of a junkyard dog among the fathers, provided a different translation and rabid attacks on Rufinus' work. Jerome's full translation is lost; some snippets remain. In reading the GCS text one understands that Jerome and the Council of 553 are the community which tells us who Origen was.

40. Augustine *De doctrina Christiana*, ed. by G. M. Green, CSEL 80 (Vienna: Hoelder-Pichler-Tempsky, 1963), 3–169, particularly Books II & IV.

41. Origen, *Traité des principes, I*, Preface, ed. by Henri Crouzel & Manlio Simonetti, SC 252 (Paris: Les Éditions du Cerf, 1978).

42. For a sympathetic treatment of allegory see David Dawson, *Allegorical Readers and Cultural Reason in Ancient Alexandria* (Berkeley, CA: University of California Press, 1992). The boldest statement of the case for pre-modern Biblical commentary is by David Steinmetz, "The Superiority of Pre-Critical Exegesis," *Theology Today* 37 (1980): 27–38, reprinted in *Ex Auditu* 1 (1985): 74–82.

43. *Origenes Werke, De Principiis*, ed. by Paul Koetschau, GCS 22 (Leipzig: J.C. Hinrichs, 1913). In the introduction, lxxxviii–cxxxvii, he indicates why he allows forty-three Greek fragments to correct Rufinus' translation. *Origen, On First Principles*, by G. W. Butterworth (London: SPCK, 1936; Reprint New York: Harper & Row Torchbook Edition, 1966) follows his lead.

Some contemporary scholars take seriously Rufinus' claim not to change anything without textual evidence from other pieces written by Origen. More importantly they stress that Rufinus had a sympathy for Origen's positions and a sense of their subtlety.[44] The interesting change in Origen studies is that a German edition of *Peri Archon* by Herwig Görgemanns and Heinrich Karpp[45] and the SC edition by Henri Crouzel and Manlio Simonetti[46] do not use all Jerome's translations or all the charges of Origen's opponents leading to 553. As a result we read a different Origen from the one who emerges from the "simple, objective" GCS critical text.

This is a grand example because it shows us what happens all the time, but sometimes in a way hidden from view. No critical text is unaffected by the commitments of its creators, the guilds or communities to which they belong. Görgemanns and Karpp appeal to historical, philological criteria, but their arguments rely upon a model which cannot be defended as a paradigm of absolute neutrality and distance. Crouzel's and Simonetti's picture of Origen as the Church's theologian is the controlling paradigm for their text.

None of this work has been done in a neutral vacuum. J. N. D. Kelly insisted that using Jerome's fragments and those from other of Origen's opponents was correct because the opposition on these points was so strong and widespread.[47] In one of Origen's few extant letters, which appears both in texts from Rufinus and Jerome, Origen insists that it is absurd to think the Devil will be saved. He also notes that a person whom he debated changed the transcripts of their confrontation and circulated

44. See the remarkable unpublished 1970 Yale dissertation by James Armantage, "Will the Body be Raised?" particularly p. 357. Robert Daly, "Origen," *The Encyclopedia of Early Christianity* (New York: Garland Press, 1990), 667 says "The Latin translations of Rufinus, formerly suspect, have been proven, by comparison with genuine Greek fragments, to be substantially accurate." Pierre Lardet, *L'Apologie de Jérôme contre Rufin: Une Commentaire*, Vigiliae Christianae Supplements 15 (Leiden: E.J. Brill, 1993) discusses this set of issues. The best recent discussion of the combat between Rufinus and Jerome is Elizabeth Clark, *The Origenist Controversy*, particulary 121–151, 159–193.

45. *Origenes, Vier Bücher von den Prinzipien*, ed. by Herwig Görgemanns und Heinrich Karpp, Texte zur Forschung, Bd. 24 (Darmstadt: Wissenschaftliche Buchgesellschaft, 1976). They do not employ all Koetschau's fragments. They explain their methods, pp. 46–49.

46. *Traité des principes, I–V*, ed. by Henri Crouzel and Manlio Simonetti, SC 252, 253, 368, 269 & 312 (Paris: Les Éditions du Cerf, 1978, 1980, 1984). The explanation of the choice of witnesses for the texts is in SC 252, 23–46.

47. J. N. D. Kelly, *Early Christian Doctrines*, 5th ed. (New York: Harper & Row, 1978), 473–474.

copies of the new, corrected version. That act reminded Origen of what Marcion had done ever-so-graciously for the gospels and Paul.[48] But in Kelly's view, because Origen has been accused so often of universalism, he surely held that view. Selected texts from Origen seem to teach that doctrine; we should let them stand. As historians we too often find that we have made the author we study much more consistent than our friends ever find us to be. Yet much of the so-called evidence comes from Origen's most angry antagonists.[49]

Kelly certainly offers a political reading of Origen's texts. Think of the possibilities for your career. Tenure is difficult enough to achieve. What if the rules demanded that the majority report should always be written by your enemies? After all, there are many of them and they wouldn't be angry if you weren't wrong.

This example from Origen studies is the clearest one I know which parallels the comments of Michel Foucault and Jacques Derrida about what would comprise the complete works of Friedrich Nietzsche.[50] At his death a number of Nietzsche's works were in manuscript form. They had to be edited to be published. So whose works are they? Should the retention of everything he wrote lead to saving the sentence "I have forgotten my umbrella"? Are the collected works of Nietzsche his or his editors'?

It is precisely the meticulous study of Origen, and the insistence that we not forget the state of his texts, that should lead us to recognize the good sense of at least part of what new historicists and deconstructionists want to teach us. Knowing Greek and Latin is necessary for deciphering some newly discovered text or reading old ones. But that knowledge does not create a privileged location unassailed by other considerations. Some of

---

48. Rufinus, *De alteratione librorum Origenis,* in *Tyrannii Rufini Opera* ed. by Manlio Simonetti, CCL XX (Turnholt: Brepols, 1961), 10–13 and Jerome, *Apologia contra Rufinus,* ed. by Pierre Lardet CCL LXXIX (Turnholt: Brepols, 1982), 50–54. The letter is condensed in different ways by each author but both support Origen's rejection of the Devil's salvation.

49. See my "Universal Salvation in Origen and Maximus," in *Universalism and the Doctrine of Hell: Papers presented at the Fourth Edinburgh Conference in Christian Dogmatics, 1991* (Grand Rapids, MI: Baker Book House, 1992), 35–72.

50. The interesting comments focus on whether "I have forgotten my umbrella" should be part of Nietzsche's collected works. The larger point turns on the fact that so many of Nietzsche's published pieces were in manuscript form when discovered, then edited and published by editors. Michel Foucault, "What Is An Author?" *Language, Counter-Memory, Practice,* ed. by Donald F. Bouchard, trans. by Donald F. Bouchard and Sherry Simon (Ithaca, NY: Cornell University Press, 1977) 113–138 and Jacques Derrida, *Spurs, Éperons,* trans. by Barbara Harlow (Chicago: University of Chicago Press, 1978), 122–143.

the strongest points new historicists and deconstructionists offer us are those we might be open to because of our own careful readings of texts, yet too often we are closed to their concerns because we treat our linguistic tools as shamans treat their magic; that is, if you know what we know as historical philologists, you would understand that all significant problems eventually dissolve at that level. We need to remember that our tools work because we belong to communities who teach us the importance of what those tools work on and how they are to be employed.

We sometimes have difficulty recognizing that many of the problems we uncover in studying Origen are present when we investigate other authors as well. We often circumvent them with facile confidence when we are rather sure that we "know" who those authors are, when a critical text is available in the author's language and a translation is available in our own.

Indeed, authorship of texts remains a problem. The best text course I ever had was one in which Luise Abramowski used her wide knowledge of Nestorian Syriac texts to show that the beginning sentences of many paragraphs in Leontius' treatise against the Nestorians were not statements from Leontius himself but quotations from his Nestorian opponents.[51] If her arguments are convincing, these fragments comprise the latest evidence we have in Greek for Nestorian views. Since no one had seen what she saw, most students of Leontius have had difficulty making consistent sense of his positions against Nestorians.

I think her case stands, although I am aware that her Syriac studies deeply influenced her discovery, certainly at the level of building the historical context, and probably at the level of what she was equipped to find and even the level of what she expected in a text. But distinguishing authors for various pieces, arguing about what is genuine and what is not, always raises some puzzling questions. How difficult it is to know who wrote what, particularly when we are told that forgery industries were going concerns in early Christianity. Foucault warns that the four criteria used by Jerome for determining authorship are difficult to apply.[52] Perhaps you also remain puzzled by how two generations who have grown up on the early and the late Wittgenstein and the early and the late Heidegger feel oh-so-confident in determining which works belong to a given author when

51. Luise Abramowski, "Ein nestorianischen Traktat bei Leontius von Jerusalem," *Orientalia Christiana Analecta* 221 (1983): 43–55, reprinted in *Formula and Context: Studies in Early Christianity* (London: Variorum Reprints, 1992). Pages 51–55 list the Nestorian citations she found.
52. Michel Foucault, "What Is an Author?" *Language, Counter-Memory, Practice*, 128–129. Foucault's reference is to Jerome, *Liber de viribus inlustribus*, TU 14, ed. by E. C. Richardson (Leipzig: J.C. Hinrichs, 1896).

NORRIS/BLACK MARKS   461

they are investigating other authors. What would have to be missing in the Wittgensteinian or the Heideggerian corpus for us to swear on our best principles and methods that the so-called early or late works were actually written by different people? How often is it the case that such a minimum and more is missing for the authors we study?

To return to Jerome's four criteria, pieces that refer to events after the author's death as happening during her or his lifetime present a rather strong case against the work's authenticity, unless there is evidence that those specific passages are interpolations. Should we allow a seasoned scholar to guess that such statements are interpolations or editorial redactions as the New Testament guild so often does? Second, stylistic uniformity may be a helpful distinguishing tool, but you know from your own work how much your style has changed. Who would recognize that one of your college papers and your most recently published piece were written by the same person? Third, I now have no objection to an editor organizing my works after my death on the basis of the consistency of their ideas. The problem is that I am rather certain there is no such sterling consistency there. I am not convinced I could write a coherent *Retractions*. Fourth, my reputation might also be enhanced by a strong editor who would eliminate the inferior pieces in favor of the superior ones, but I am not certain who would publish the collected works of Frederick W. Norris in one volume of eighteen pages. What I am certain of is that the editor would be making a large number of anything-but-objective decisions: superiority, consistency, style, maybe even historical date. Authorship of genuine collected works is a troublesome issue, one that does not allow us to jump out of our interpretive communities into a neutral public arena of judgment shared by all.

Translations are also subject to such prior commitments. The inexpensive rendition of Athanasius' *De Incarnatione* by an anonymous religious, introduced by words from C. S. Lewis, was once considered a prize.[53] If you always thought Athanasius was an Augustinian, it will help you make your case. We feel confident that we can sort out such mistakes with ease, but we find that our own translations of texts reflect, even embody, the structures of the interpretive communities we inhabit. Muslims know that a translation of the Qur'an is an interpretation; Christians have deferred to native speakers as the experts in translations into the mother tongues of various cultures.[54] As members of NAPS we can sort out some issues that

53. Athanasius, *The Incarnation of the Word of God*, trans. by a religious of C.S.M.V. S.Th. (New York: Macmillan, 1946).
54. Lamin Sanneh, *Translating the Message: The Missionary Impact on Culture* (Maryknoll, NY: Orbis Press, 1989) persuasively argues that Christian missionaries

19

plague translation, but we can never claim a positivistic objectivity for our efforts that puts us up over the project and out of our webs of influence.

Recognizing the ways in which interpretive communities influence our work is not an entirely negative process. It can also open us up to contemporary interests. Patristic commentary on scripture is an old concern but not necessarily a broadly shared one. Few Ph.D.s in New Testament studies are trained in, even exposed to, the history of interpretation, except as a dismissive exercise. Can anything good come before 1650? Biblical commentaries written in this century seldom make reference to works written before 1900. Sometimes they abandon any comment over twenty years old; that is part of their historical-critical paradigm. Both patristic and medieval categories of interpretation have been found wanting, but often on the grounds of so-called objective, distanced historical investigation which many if not all of us honor as deeply wounded, perhaps even mutilated. Some in this society may be interested in providing better access to scriptural interpretation by making early Christian commentaries more accessible to the academy and particularly to the Church. Such projects are in the planning.

When we investigate early Christian literature outside Scripture and its commentaries, we may be assisted by readings from other centuries. In my commentary on Nazianzen's *Theological Orations* I found the work on Gregory by Elias of Crete, a twelfth-century figure, to be one of the major influences in opening up the Theologian's writings. Elias left me with baffling references to authors whose names and works are lost. I was humbled by what I could not know. But he also alerted me to Gregory's dependence upon Aristotle and the rhetorician Hermogenes, something I could investigate. Perhaps the biggest mistake I made in my commentary was not taking the extra time to study carefully Maximus the Confessor's struggles with difficult texts in Gregory. Our reading of early Christian texts can be enhanced by tracking how they have been interpreted in previous centuries. Once we leave the old historicist paradigm behind, *Wirkungsgeschichte* grows in importance.

Perhaps the most significant insights of the new historicists and the deconstructionists go to the heart of our sense of this society. Clearly our members and those in our fields of inquiry will continue to produce literary, historical, philological, social and theological studies of the texts, art and

---

often enhanced cultures in which they lived when they recognized that only native speakers could be the final judges of effective translation. The Norse legends are still available because Bible translation projects created a language in which they could be written.

20

artifacts we investigate. No one of us can command all the various methods or look at all the data. But we must not deceive ourselves into thinking that all the members of this society are about the same projects because we have assumed that we gaze at the same objects and employ the same scientific methods. We have not suffered from the wars that have plagued various departments in universities, seminaries and colleges. We have been civil to each other, perhaps at the least because the powerbase in this society is so inconsequential. Tolerance is an Enlightenment virtue that many revere. But in some ways I would rather have us avoid the vice of tolerance which leads to silence during the discussions of papers and derisive dismissal afterwards in smaller circles of shared views. Let us in good humor go after each other's interpretations knowing that correctness, of whatever sort, lies in our communal commitments and purposes. (This address excepted of course.)

Averil Cameron notes that for some time contemporary scholars with clear commitments and purposes have been willing to make derogatory judgments about early Christian communities and their texts as superstitious, irrational, lower class, authoritarian, or sexually stunted. Yet in her view "historians are readily criticized if they show sympathy for Christianity."[55] As a deconstructionist who has pioneered reader response theory, Stanley Fish decries the loss of discussions about aesthetics and theology in Milton studies and asks how the avoidance of those issues could pass as history.[56]

John D. Schaeffer warns that the appropriation of Giambattista Vico's work by new historicsts has sometimes not mentioned Vico's reliance on religion.[57] Within the paradigms of deconstruction and new historicism there is no reason that scholars with Christian commitments and purposes should not be clear and bold about the stance from which they read the texts. At the least such a reading is one of the local varieties available. It has a defined *telos* and is set within a recognizable community. Non-Christian readings are not to be privileged because of some objective criteria. If they

55. Averil Cameron, *Christianity and the Rhetoric of Empire*, 24–29 mentions Gibbon, T. D. Barnes and de Ste. Croix.

56. Stanley Fish, "Milton's Career and the Career of Theory," *There's No Such Thing as Free Speech*, 257–266, particularly 264, notes that some new historicists have tended to dismiss those issues for the study of Milton as inconsequential. For me it seems that they still play on the ground of logical positivism.

57. John D. Schaeffer, "The Use and Misuse of Giambattista Vico: Rhetoric, Orality and Theories of Discourse," *The New Historicism*, 89–101 points out that in regard to religion Vico is quite different from Foucault. Also see his "Vico's Rhetorical Model of the Mind: *Sensus Communis* in the *De nostri temporis studiorum ratione*," *Philosophy and Rhetoric* 14 (1981): 152–167.

464 JOURNAL OF EARLY CHRISTIAN STUDIES

are privileged in the university, it is because of the university's self-understanding as an interpretive community with a distinct purpose, not because of some unassailable, neutral claim that universities tell the truth better than any other community.[58]

As a seminary professor I claim that most "patristic" texts have been written, copied and preserved by and for the Church. The view of the *sensus communis* held by Giambattista Vico,[59] which is important to new historicists and others,[60] strikes a resonating chord with those of us educated within a *sensus fidelium*. Tony Bennett's deconstructive talk of "reading formations" as another way to speak of interpretive communities[61] may be applied—with a significant twist—to a seminary. Our task in a theological school is to provide formation partially in order that those in the community might learn to read their texts. At the very least a text read in that "reading formation" is, as Stanley Fish says, "the structure of meaning that is obvious and inescapable from the perspective of whatever interpretive assumptions happen to be in force."[62] I do, however, think that both fish, Stanley and Wanda, can teach me about good and bad history. In my view the black marks on the page offer pointed suggestions about what they mean. Early Christian texts show that theology constructed within community was important for the early Church.

For my sake I seek conversations about how university departments without Christian commitment, which often find theology absent or unat-

---

58. Jonathan Culler, "Criticism and Institutions: The American University," *Post-structuralism and the Question of History*, 82–98 points up the ironic role of university politics in both supporting and denying developments in literary criticism.

59. See *The New Science of Giambattista Vico*, trans. by Max Frisch and Thomas G. Bergin (Ithaca: Cornell University Press, 1944) and his *On the Study Methods of Our Time*, trans. by Elio Gianturco (Indianapolis: Bobbs-Merrill Inc., 1965). Vico's views remind me of Gregory the Theologian. Vico taught rhetoric. He defended Aristotle's enthymemes, recognized the significance of the *sensus communis*, and insisted on the power of metaphor and poetry. All argument rests within a community and must deal with probability questions. He also attacked Descartes' view of probability as falsehood in a way reminiscent of Nazianzen's attacks on Eunomians.

60. John Schaeffer, "The Use and Misuse of Giambattista Vico: Rhetoric, Orality, and Theories of Discourse," *The New Historicism*, 89–101. Hayden White, "The Tropics of History: The Deep Structure of *The New Science*," *Giambattista Vico's Science of Humanity*, ed. by Giorgio Tagliacozze and Donald P. Verene (Baltimore, MD: Johns Hopkins University Press, 1976), 65–86. Edward Said, a maverick who turns up in new historicist and deconstructionist efforts, deals with Vico in his *Beginnings: Intention and Method* (Baltimore, MD: Johns Hopkins University Press, 1975).

61. Tony Bennett, "Texts in History: The Determinations of Readings and Their Texts," *Post-Structuralism and the Question of History*, 63–81.

62. Stanley Fish, *Is There a Text?* vii.

tractive, prepare to read these texts and make sense of them.[63] I know why in seminary we read the mothers and fathers to educate theologians and ministers. I do not know why they must be read within religious studies departments. For my seminary community they are at the core; for the religious studies department are they ever more than an exotic elective? Surely not all theological schools find the mothers and fathers of the early church at the heart of their efforts, but neither are many religious studies departments dominated by early Christian studies.

I am not displeased when the texts we concentrate on in this society are read in religious studies, classics, history or literature departments, for I often find insights in such discussions which my community did not see. Just as Christian missionaries can hear those of other religions comment on their scriptural texts with what they recognize as insight and clarity, so we theologians can listen to those outside our community talk about these texts from a different perspective. But I also have not forgotten Tertullian's forceful claim in his *De praescriptione haereticorum*:[64] the Gnostics cannot interpret Christian Scriptures because those Scriptures are not their books. His was not a gentle spirit, but his point now appears to be more than an ancient one totally dependent upon "outdated" categories of Roman law; it sounds quite postmodern.

As the importance of interpretive communities in producing, selecting, preserving, and deeply influencing the reading of—if not wholly creating the meaning of—our texts becomes clearer, even the remarkable work-in-progress of Brian Stock (which might creatively focus some of our common efforts)[65] may reveal further the deep differences among those of us within this society. We enjoy meeting together and listening as someone else tries to make sense of texts and artifacts, architecture and art. I hope that we can learn from each other. I am convinced, however, that much of what we will learn is how disparate our "reading formations" are and how much that means that we will disagree. Within my broadest Christian

63. The question of Robert Wilken's 1989 AAR–SBL Presidential Address is surely a beginning point for such discussions: "Who Will Speak *for* the Religious Traditions?" *Journal of the American Academy of Religions* 57 (1989): 699–717.

64. Tertullian, *De praescriptione haereticorum*, ed. by A. Kroymann, CSEL 70 (Vienna: Hoelder-Pichler-Tempsky, 1942), 1–58.

65. Brian Stock, *Listening for the Text: On the Uses of the Past* (Baltimore: Johns Hopkins University Press, 1990) goes well beyond his interesting *The Implications of Literacy* (Princeton: Princeton University Press, 1983). Mark Vessey suggested Stock's work to me after this address was given. Vessey's review essay "Literacy and *Litteratura*, A.D. 200–800," *Studies in Medieval and Renaissance History*, Vol. 13 (O.S., vol. 23) (New York: AMS Press, 1992), 139–160 finds Stock's recent efforts to be among the most promising. I agree.

community, some of the most interesting voices interpreting early Christian texts are Christian theologians from Africa, Asia, and Latin America. These people show that the problems with the name of our society do not stop with "patristic" but extend to "North American" as well, a problem that would not be solved by adding Europeans and their insights at the levels of theory, method or philological, historical study. These voices are creating new readings because of their varied native cultures and traditions. They are not residents of the industrial North and they are not all men. Some of them, like Mercy Amba Oduyoye, Lamin Sanneh, and Kwame Bediako,[66] make historical comments and acknowledge that their sense of what the texts mean is formed by their present commitments and their membership in specific communities. I know that it is a shared community and a shared purpose that allow those of us who are Christian theologians to hear each other well. I do not find that NAPS as a guild has that power.

But NAPS is an important quasi-public square in which we can try to talk with each other. I like to think that we shall vigorously continue the attempts.

Frederick W. Norris is the Dean E. Walker Professor of Church History and Professor of Christian Doctrine at the Emmanuel School of Religion, Johnson City, Tennessee

66. Mercy Amba Oduyoye, *Hearing and Knowing: Theological Reflections on Christianity in Africa* (Maryknoll, NY: Orbis Press, 1986) comments on the suppression of the Donatists as an aid to Muslim expansion as well as Coptic and Ethiopic indigenization and the lack of it in Nubian Churches. Lamin Sanneh, *Encountering the West: Christianity and the Global Cultural Process* (Maryknoll, NY: Orbis Press, 1993) uses Coptic and Ethiopic communities as examples of his argument about the importance of Christianity's decision to translate its Scriptures into the mother tongues of various cultures. He has a deft control of both ancient and modern views of intercultural contacts. Kwame Bediako, *Theology and Identity: The Impact of Culture upon Christian Thought in the Second Century and Modern Africa*, Regnum Studies in Mission (Oxford: Regnum Books, 1992) employs careful investigation of second-century Christianity as a penetrating model for grasping the contemporary Christian efforts in Africa. Also see the work of Naim Stifan Ateek, Itumeleng J. Mosala, Christine Amjad-Ali, Anil D. Solanki and Otele Perilini.

'THE FAITH OF OUR FATHERS':
THE MAKING OF THE EARLY CHRISTIAN PAST

by RACHEL MORIARTY

A hundred years ago, in 1895, London theatre audiences were treated to an interesting exchange on what we would now call the reception of early Church history. The play was Oscar Wilde's *The Importance of Being Earnest*, and in it the Reverend Dr Chasuble and Miss Prism are discussing marriage, not entirely hypothetically. Dr Chasuble '(with a scholar's shudder)' observes, 'The precept as well as the practice of the Primitive Church was distinctly against matrimony', and Miss Prism replies '(sententiously), That is obviously the reason why the Primitive Church has not lasted up to the present day'.[1]

In a volume devoted to 'the Church Retrospective', these disputants are significant players, for the early Church certainly has lasted up to the present day, at least in the minds of people looking for the sources of ecclesiastical Tradition and History. Dr Chasuble, for Tradition, sees the 'Primitive Church' as the self-validating reference point for its successor; Miss Prism, a good Anglican, takes a more pragmatic historical view. They are engaged in a polite version of a long-standing and still lively Christian dispute over finding models for today from the time of the Church's youth.

The Church has always based its future on its past, and the very earliest Church has had a special status as a touchstone for original faith and practice, the fresh dawn of the age of salvation. The period to which this status applies varies, but at its longest it covers the first four or five centuries, the so-called 'Undivided Church', from Pentecost to Chalcedon. Regularly in the history of churches ever since there have been moves to return again to parts of this pristine source – at the Renaissance and the Reformation, among early Nonconformists and nineteenth-century Anglo-Catholics, and in

---

[1] *The Importance of Being Earnest*, in Oscar Wilde, *Plays* (London, 1970), p. 279.

25

monastic movements, to give some examples; and arguments from 'the Fathers' have been used to defend change (for example in Cranmer's wish, which survives in the 1662 Book of Common Prayer, to restore 'the godly and decent order of the ancient Fathers'),[2] and to resist it (as in current argument against the ordination of women). Interpretations have conflicted as opponents appeal to what they call 'the New Testament Church', 'the patristic tradition', and other titles representing views of the Christian inheritance; but the notion of resort to an ancient line of tradition remains constant. Christianity demands a retrospective Church, in which perceived origins have a special authority.

This paper examines a paradox about this early Church tradition. The earliest Christians, both Jews and 'pagans', came from religious backgrounds which relied on ancient and ancestral practice (in Latin the *mores maiorum*), yet they were themselves in the opposite situation: they had no traditional past for their own practices, and had collectively rejected the past and the ancestors they were born with. The tradition we have inherited from them, however, again depends on our continuity with their past. So it seems reasonable to ask what the sources show about the way they turned their lack of history into a 'tradition' which has survived to the present day.

Can it even be suggested that early Christian historical tradition, as it has reached us from the first centuries, was at least partly composed, selected, and transmitted to help provide Christians with the past they lacked? This paper explores some aspects of that suggestion, considering some examples of how Christians presented their story, to see how they shaped a coherent inherited tradition, a kind of 'Christian Heritage Source-Pack', to match those of others and to act as a resource and a memory for later generations. These examples come from a fairly small field, mostly from apology and accounts of martyrdom, two literary forms of the first three centuries which dealt particularly with issues of

---

[2] See the Prefaces to the Prayer Books of 1549 and 1552, reprinted in, for example, *The First and Second Prayer Books of Edward VI*, Everyman Library (London and New York, 1910), pp. 3, 321; and 'Concerning the Services of the Church', section 2 in *The Book of Common Prayer, 1662*.

Christian identity, together with a few later examples; all but one are from Christian sources. The important question of the Jewish past of Christianity is not tackled in this study, but it will appear briefly later, in the course of discussion.[3]

The case begins in the relative calm of the fourth century when Eusebius, arranging his pre-Constantinian material in a new kind of retrospective edition, sets out the selection criteria for his plan for a History of the Church and reveals something of what he understands by tradition. His Christian predecessors have left records

> to admonish us on the path along which we ought to walk. We have gathered, therefore, from these whatsoever we have deemed profitable for the project in hand, and having plucked, as it were, from meadows of literature suitable passages, we shall attempt to embody them as an historical narrative: happy if we may preserve the successions from the Apostles of our Saviour. I trust that they will prove of benefit to those who are eager for the useful learning afforded by history.[4]

Two things are at once clear: Eusebius is committed to continuity with the past ('the successions'), but he expects to shape and use it for a precise purpose, to be 'useful'. He famously preserved invaluable sources, but already selection has been at work and some flowers dropped to make the structured posy of the Christian past. It is necessary to go further back to see what the surviving predecessors say, first about their own use of tradition, then about charges against Christians for rejecting their past, and finally in making a new tradition in response.

Right from the start, there is an assumption that ancestral tradition is important to credibility as a religious group.

---

[3] For comprehensive discussion of this subject, see E. P. Sanders, ed., *Jewish and Christian Self-Definition*, 3 vols (London, 1981-3) [hereafter Sanders].

[4] Eusebius, *Ecclesiastical History*, I, i [hereafter HE] in Eusebius, Bishop of Caesarea, *The Ecclesiastical History and the Martyrs of Palestine*, ed. H. J. Lawlor and J. E. L. Oulton, 2 vols (London, 1954) [hereafter Lawlor and Oulton], 1, p. 4. For Eusebius' contribution to Church history, see also Frances M. Young, *From Nicaea to Chalcedon* (London, 1983), pp. 1-21.

Christian reliance on it started, we are told, on the first day of the Church's life, when Peter, as soon as he could make himself heard over the babel of Pentecost, offered its credentials from Jewish tradition, in an address linking Christ to scriptural proof-texts about the Messiah.[5] In the second century, when personal links with Peter's time were almost gone, Irenaeus identified apostolic tradition as one of the markers of 'truth', that is, true Christianity. For him, 'The tradition of the Apostles is manifested in the entire world, and all who wish to see the truth can contemplate it readily in every church.'[6] Moreover, 'By knowledge of the truth we mean the teaching of the Apostles, and the order of the Church as established from the earliest times throughout the world.'[7]

The same stress on continuity is evident in martyrology, in this case the introduction to the story of Perpetua, a Roman matron who died at Carthage in about 202: 'The deeds recounted about the faith in ancient times were a proof of God's favour ... and they were set forth in writing precisely that honour might be rendered to God and comfort to men by the recollection of the past through the written word. Should not then more recent examples be set down?'[8]

Much later, in the fifth century, Vincent of Lérins could claim to define Catholic teaching (rather against the odds, historically) by saying, 'In the Catholic church we take care that we hold that which has been believed everywhere, always, by everyone. . . . And we shall observe this rule if we

[5] Acts 2.14-26.
[6] Irenaeus, *Against the Heresies*, III, iii, 4, in J. Stevenson, ed., *A New Eusebius*, new edn, revised W. H. C. Frend (London, 1989) [hereafter *NE*], p. 114.
[7] Irenaeus, *Against the Heresies*, IV, viii, 8, in Henry Bettenson, ed., *The Early Christian Fathers* (Oxford, 1969), p. 89.
[8] *The Martyrdom of Perpetua and Felicitas*, 1, in H. Musurillo, ed., *Acts of the Christian Martyrs* (Oxford, 1972) [hereafter Musurillo], p. 107, and introduction, pp. xxv-vi; see Stuart G. Hall, 'Women among the early martyrs', *SCH*, 30 (1993), pp. 1-21 and W. H. C. Frend, *Martyrdom and Persecution in the Early Church* (Oxford, 1965) [hereafter Frend], pp. 376-7. It seems possible that the presentation of this account, and perhaps others, was shaped to some extent by discussion on the whole question of the status of recent events in relation to the 'ancestral' past: see Rachel Moriarty, 'The claims of the past', to be published in a forthcoming vol. of Elizabeth A. Livingstone, ed., *Studia Patristica* (Papers presented at the Twelfth International Conference on Patristic Studies held in Oxford, 1995). See also n. 33 below.

follow universality, antiquity, consent.'⁹ By this time, the historical virtues of universality, antiquity, consent have become the marks of 'tradition'.

It is clear that Christians were concerned to defend themselves against charges of having no past, and that they regarded those charges as crucial to their differences from their pagan neighbours. But before looking at the defence they offered we should see how they set out the charges themselves, usually in words attributed to opponents, for this shapes our present concern for the way they presented their own case.

Clement of Alexandria, who died in about 214, and wrote, it is thought, for a general educated audience interested in Christianity, addresses an objector thus (we shall see later how he replies to him): 'But, you say, it is not reasonable to overthrow a way of life handed down to us by our forefathers.'¹⁰ Similarly, Minucius Felix, in a dialogue from 197 again aimed at an educated pagan public, makes the point more fully, in the words he gives his non-Christian character Caecilius:

> How much better it is to receive the teaching of our ancestors as the high priest of truth, to reverence the traditional religion, to worship the gods whom your parents taught you to fear before you knew them intimately, and not to pronounce judgement upon the divinities, but to believe our forefathers who, in a still uncivilized age, when the world was only just born, were thought worthy of having the gods as kindly or as kings! Thus it is that in every empire, province and city each nationality observes the ritual of its own family and worships its local divinities.¹¹

Other second-century apologists tell the same tale. Origen's *agent provocateur* Celsus maintains that not to accept the

---

⁹ Vincent of Lérins, *Commonitorium*, II, 6, quoted in J. Stevenson, ed., *Creeds, Councils and Controversies*, new edn, rev. W. H. C. Frend (London, 1989), p. 322.
¹⁰ Clement of Alexandria, *Protrepticus*, x, 89, in *NE*, p. 180. For Clement's view of history, see Raoul Mortley, 'The past in Clement of Alexandria', in Sanders, 1, pp. 186–200.
¹¹ Minucius Felix, *Octavius*, vi, 1, in *NE*, p. 177.

Emperor as divinely appointed (that is, for him, with the
authority of Jupiter) is to invite personal punishment and
disaster from Rome's enemies.[12] Elsewhere he makes the
telling point that Christian teachers persuade children not to
obey their fathers and schoolteachers, and 'urge the children
on to rebel' – a point echoed by critics of cults today.[13] The
attack on Christians as presented here had two prongs: they
were suspect on the public issue of civic loyalty and
allegiance to the Emperor (seen as empowered by God and
endorsed by ancestral practice), and on the more domestic
issue of family and parental discipline.

The charge of rejecting ancestral gods, which amounted to
'atheism', was especially associated with persecution.
Tertullian quotes the cry, 'The Christians to the lion!', as an
example of the response of the urban Roman mob to any
disaster;[14] and later Eusebius recalls the usual imperial case for
persecution: 'How can men fail to be in every way impious
and godless who have apostasized from their ancestral
gods?'[15] The end of persecution came with the collapse of this
case.

Eusebius and Lactantius, another defender of Christianity,
both recorded the text of Galerius' Edict of Toleration of 311:
'It has been our special care that the Christians too who had
left the persuasion of their forefathers should come to a better
mind. ... Instead of following those constitutions of the
ancients which peradventure their own ancestors had first
established, they were making themselves laws ...' – but
persecution failed to bring about a return to 'the institutions
of the ancients', and it now seems that any prayer is better
than none to avert national calamity. 'We therefore have
thought it right to offer our speediest indulgence, that
Christians may exist again .... It shall be their duty to pray

[12] Origen, *Contra Celsum*, viii, 67–9, in *NE*, pp. 135–6. For discussion of Celsus'
attitudes see Robert L. Wilken, *The Christians as the Romans Saw Them* (New Haven,
1984) [hereafter Wilken], pp. 94–125, and Robert M. Grant, *Greek Apologists of the
Second Century* (London, 1988), pp. 133–9; this book also covers other apologists
cited in this paper.
[13] Origen, *Contra Celsum*, iii, 55, in *NE*, p. 116.
[14] Tertullian, *Apology*, xl, 2, in *NE*, p. 158; for Tertullian see T. D. Barnes,
Tertullian: A Historical and Literary Study (Oxford, 1971).
[15] Eusebius, *Praeparatio Evangelica*, i, 2, in *NE*, p. 181 (note).

their god for our good estate, and that of the state.'[16] After more than 250 years, Christians can record that the positive value of prayer has prevailed over the negative pagan view that Christians are to be punished for rejection of the past, in its ritual and ancestral sense.

What is behind all this? The background to these Christians' accounts of the charges against them lies in an ideological base common in antiquity, where ancestral tradition was perceived as the key to securing personal, family, and political survival.[17] There is abundant evidence for this attitude in classical sources, especially among Romans, but it was common to most of the peoples over whom they ruled. Romans had always been taught that the safety of the Roman state depended on ancient customs, loyalty, and devotion to the gods, and since the time of Augustus, who died in AD 14, the view of a traditionally-based Rome marked out for a divine destiny was built into its public image and the educational system of the influential young, through writers like Virgil, Livy, and Horace, and supported by the cautious but significant introduction of a cult of the Emperor. Clearly there are elements here too of a constructed tradition, and of a mythical past based on an agenda of political expediency; but the picture depended on attitudes accepted by most of the Empire's subjects. The shared view of ancestral tradition gave it credence through-out the Empire, and a variety of ancestors, new religions, and philosophical positions did not ordinarily compromise ances-tral identity, since they were not seen as alternatives to one standard practice. As the author of the book of Acts noted, the Athenians were constantly looking for novelty, but in the speech put into Paul's mouth on the Areopagus he is careful to make the links backward from Christianity to traditional patterns of various kinds.[18]

[16] Lactantius, *On the Deaths of the Persecutors*, 34, in *NE*, p. 280; and see Eusebius, *HE*, viii, 17, 6-7, in Lawlor and Oulton, 1, p. 276, and discussion, 2, pp. 285-6.
[17] For discussion of these classical issues, see R. M. Ogilvie, *The Romans and their Gods* (London, 1979), especially pp. 112-25; A. H. M. Jones, *Augustus* (London, 1977), pp. 144-52; and especially Robin Lane Fox, *Pagans and Christians* (London, 1986). Lane Fox argues that ancestral tradition was not static, and that there was interest in change and development; see pp. 29, 258-60.
[18] Acts 17.21.

The earliest non-Jewish Christians were born into this setting, and many later ones educated into it and into its assumption that religious credibility, civic loyalty, and historical continuity went hand in hand. But if their refusal to sacrifice cut them off from the past of their neighbours, they still felt the need for a past of their own, for the sake of the development of their own religious community. There were other strands to this need: they wanted at first to establish themselves as a group who came from a variety of ancestral traditions; as they gained a history, they sought to package and circulate the record of Christian experience among their scattered communities, and eventually to lay down a shared foundation of Christian memory for later generations. Most important, they needed a past because it was their only guarantee of credible identity. As Christians present the case, their opponents did not understand their refusal to rely on the customs of their ancestors, nor their adoption of a religious culture which had no retrospective dimension. Collectively they were suspect citizens, individually they breached the sacred ties of family and the past; and under challenge and persecution they often repudiated everything that the weight of ancestral morality was supposed to sustain.

In spite of the limits of this discussion, it must be noted that Christians were challenged on their rejection of Judaism, and apologists discuss it.[19] Judaism had the edge over Christianity in the matter of ancestors, and was tolerated on this ground as a *religio licita*, a religion officially counted as acceptable. The Emperor Marcus Aurelius justified this (in our only non-Christian source) on the grounds that as a traditional Roman he 'always stood by the old places and the old ways'.[20] But after Christians and Jews separated, neither welcomed the other's immediate past, and the Christians were more struck by their differences than their similarities. In terms of scripture, spirituality, and theology the Christian Church saw itself as inseparably linked with the Old Testament past of the Jews and the early sources, notably the letter known as I Clement, work this out in detail. But this did not mean that

[19] See, for instance, Wilken, pp. 112–17, on Celsus, and Robert Markus, *Christianity in the Roman World* (London, 1974), pp. 1–26, on Tertullian and others.
[20] Marcus Aurelius, *Meditations*, i, 13; see Frend, p. 237.

Christians claimed the Jews' history as their own, nor that they mounted an ancestral case from a Jewish past. At the turn of the first century Ignatius had no time for identification with Jews, and said so decisively: 'It is outrageous to utter the name of Jesus Christ and live in Judaism',[21] though he was ready enough to claim the prophets as suitable persecuted forerunners.

Once Christians had set out their opponents' case, they gave themselves the chance to reply. They took up one of two general positions: either they assimilated the surrounding culture and drew out links to show that Christians shared the ordinary assumptions of the inhabitants of the Empire, and even accommodated these into a shared tradition; or they sharply repudiated any compromise with pagan attitudes and defied Roman authority, but redefined Christian ancestry and tradition in opposition to them. Either way, they contribute to a Christian past.

For the first strand, second-century apologetic insists that Christians regularly protested their civic decency. 'We . . . are of all people most piously and righteously disposed towards the Deity and towards your government', wrote Athenagoras to Marcus Aurelius;[22] while the anonymous author of the *Letter to Diognetus* complained of the mistreatment of Christians in spite of their exemplary conformity: 'They dwell in Greek or barbarian cities according as each one's lot has been cast, and follow the customs of the land in clothing and food, and other matters of daily life. . . . They obey the established laws, and in their own lives they surpass the laws.'[23]

This was taken further into the field of political loyalty; Christians were loyal to the Emperor and prayed for him. Tertullian claimed that 'We, on behalf of the safety of Emperors, invoke the eternal God', since the end of the world, and the suffering that will accompany it, is postponed by the peace which Rome has brought.[24] Others developed this into a more sophisticated pattern. God gives earthly

21 Ignatius, *To the Magnesians*, x, 3, in *NE*, p. 14.
22 Athenagoras, *Legatio pro Christianis*, 1, in *NE*, pp. 66–7.
23 *Letter to Diognetus*, v, 6, in *NE*, p. 55.
24 Tertullian, *Apology*, xxxii, 1; in *NE*, p. 162; and see Frend, pp. 365–80.

emperors power and glory, said Clement of Rome,[25] and the apology of Melito of Sardis presents the argument that the Church and the Empire, especially the *pax Romana*, work together for God's purposes. For him the success of the Empire is 'proof of the fact that it was for the good that our doctrine flourished alongside the Empire in its happy inception'.[26]

These passages show a presentation of history which joins Christians to the historical destiny and past of Rome, through its God-given rulers. In one sense this history divorces the Emperor from the exclusive support of the Roman state religion, but in another it unites Roman Christians again to their actual ancestors.

Some were more radical in embracing the pre-Christian past. Justin began a long tradition of claiming figures from earlier history as 'Christians before Christ', in his case the Greeks Socrates and Heraclitus, as well as non-Greeks or 'barbarians', among whom he includes Abraham; for 'those who lived with reason are Christians, even though they were thought atheists'. He was among the first to embrace as Christian the ideas and theory of Greek philosophers, who shared to some extent in the 'generative word', the *logos*: 'Whatever things were rightly said among all teachers, are the property of us Christians.'[27]

The argument Clement of Alexandria gives his opponent has already been considered (p. 9): he continues by claiming to develop and enhance ancestral tradition:

Why do we not continue to use our first food, milk? . . . Why do we increase or diminish our family property, and not keep it at the same value as when we first received it? . . . Shall we not, even at the risk of displeasing our fathers, bend our course towards the truth and seek after him who is our real father, thrusting away custom as some deadly drug?[28]

---

[25] Clement of Rome, *Letter of the Romans to the Corinthians*, lxi, in J. B. Lightfoot, *The Apostolic Fathers*, ed. J. R. Harmer (London, 1926), p. 83.
[26] Eusebius, *HE*, iv, 26,8; in *NE*, pp. 65–6, and note.
[27] Justin, *Apology*, i, 46 and ii, 13, and *NE*, pp. 61–2.
[28] Clement of Alexandria, *Protrepticus*, x, 89, in *NE*, p. 181 (see n. 10 above).

The Faith of our Fathers

For some Christians, the learned past was inescapable.
Later, Augustine reflected movingly on the power of classical
culture to inspire love and practical loyalty, and it must
always have been hard to abandon the cherished past.[29] The
wish to include the heroes of classical learning in a Christian
framework sprang not only from reason but, surely, from a
real admiration for them. Regulus, for example, a Roman
hero who kept his word to the enemy at the cost of his life, is
quoted with praise by Tertullian and Cyprian, and Augustine
sees him as the noblest Roman of them all.[30] Elsewhere,
Hermas naturally mistook the elderly woman who appears to
him in a vision, really the Church, for the pagan Sibyl.[31]
Classical language and thought, and literary and mythological models, permeate Christian writing, bringing with them,
suitably adapted, the ancestry which many Christians had
grown up with and learned to love, and offering a model of a
united tradition for a world now saved from divisions. As
ideas on classical tradition and allegorical exegesis developed,
the treasures of classical scholarship came to be identified, by
Origen, Gregory of Nyssa, and Augustine (for example),
with the spoils taken from the Egyptians by the fleeing
Hebrews at the Exodus.[32] Thus an alien past was, as it were,
hallowed by association and an Old Testament model, and
could be acknowledged as respectably as any similarly
appropriated material.

On the other hand, there is a different set of models of
repudiation of this heritage. Not surprisingly this is to be
found mainly in accounts of martyrdom. Perpetua, for
instance, a wealthy Roman matron, will not give in to her
father's pleading nor the demand of the governor, but replied
in a way that upsets every decent convention: 'Hilarianus said

[29] This theme appears especially in *City of God*: see Peter Brown, *Augustine of Hippo* (London, 1967), pp. 299–312.
[30] Augustine, *City of God*, i, 24, translated in St Augustine, *City of God*, trans. Henry Bettenson (London, 1972), p. 35.
[31] Hermas, *The Shepherd*, Vis. II, 1–4, in *NE*, pp. 51–2.
[32] Exod. 12.35–6. See discussion in Jaroslav Pelikan, *Christianity and Classical Culture* (New York, 1993), pp. 171, 187–8; and Gregory of Nyssa, *The Life of Moses*, trans. Abraham J. Malberbe and Everett Ferguson (New York, 1978), 2, 112–16, pp. 80–1, and 170–1, nn. 128–9; they also cite Origen, *Ep. ad Greg. Thaum.* (*PG* 11.88–9) and Augustine, *De Doct. Christ.* 2.40.61.

to me, "Have pity on your father's grey head – have pity on your infant son. Offer the sacrifice for the welfare of the emperors." "I will not", I retorted.'[33] Other accounts have the same kind of story, but claim a Christian pedigree with different rulers and different parents. Polycarp, the saintly Bishop of Smyrna, is invited to 'swear by the genius of Caesar, change your mind; say "away with the atheists!" ' He obeys the second (who are atheists, to a Christian?), but will not curse Christ: 'Eighty-six years have I served him, and he has done me no wrong: how then can I blaspheme my King and my God?'[34]

Others follow his example; they have their own family loyalty. Invited to name their parents, they name Christ; they are described as showing 'maternal love' to their 'brothers', 'before the Father'. One of the martyrs of Lyons, Sanctus, refuses to admit to any other identity: 'To all their questions he answered in Latin: "I am a Christian!" He kept repeating this again and again instead of giving his name, birthplace, nationality, or anything else.'[35] An apologist, Aristeides, explicitly gave Christians their ancestry: 'As for the Christians, they trace their line from the Lord Jesus Christ.'[36] In behaving scornfully to the ancestral traditions embodied in the Emperor and his religious trappings, they are all the same claiming and consolidating a shared Christian heritage, to replace the one they reject.

To conclude: these sources can be seen not simply as a set of documents revealing Christian history, but as material presented, and later selected, to make clear to later Christians the basis for relying on tradition; and to this selection was added, in explanation, the case made against Christians for not having an ancestral tradition, and their double response, to claim a tradition of their own by both accommodating and

---

[33] *The Martyrdom of Perpetua and Felicitas*, in Musurillo, pp. xvi and 115. Perpetua's story illustrates the painful need for all Christians sometimes to renounce ordinary family ties, but it may have a special significance for a female martyr, perhaps different from that of a male one. See Brent D. Shaw, 'The passion of Perpetua', in *P&P*, 139 (May, 1993), pp. 1–45, and Gillian Cloke, *This Female Man of God* (London, 1995), p. 35; and see n. 8 above.

[34] *The Martyrdom of Polycarp*, ix, 3, in *NE*, pp. 25–30.

[35] *The Martyrs of Lyons and Vienne*, in Musurillo, p. 69, and in *NE*, pp. 34–44.

[36] Aristeides, *Apology*, xv,1, in *NE*, p. 52.

renouncing the culture around them. Of the two types of source quoted, apology sets out its own case and answers it, and accounts of martyrdom fit history together with interpretation; but both convey firmly the traditions on which Christians would come to rely. They have Fathers and ancestral practices, they can define and defend them, and they expect their adherents to know what they are. This, it can be argued, did not happen by accident, but emerged as part of an exercise in teaching, recording, and packaging which went on into later centuries, even when defence was no longer necessary, and which both set Christians apart from their neighbours and united them with the best of their own past. The details and the process formed the tradition of the earliest Christianity, a tradition which still influences and shapes Churches today.

La Sainte Union College, Southampton

Tertullian on Heresy, History, and the Reappropriation of Revelation

PETER IVER KAUFMAN

Tertullian understood the apostle Paul to have suggested there would always be heretics (1 Cor. 11:19), and he presumed God had supplied scripture for their use. Without sacred literature heretics would have nothing of consequence to misread. Without contests over critical passages, there could be no winners, no losers—no heretics.[1] The difficulty, Tertullian acknowledged, was that heretics were the poorest of losers; they never conceded defeat. He advised against trying to take (or take back) scripture passage by passage. The only way to get the best of heretics and get on with the work of interpreting texts correctly was to deny heretics' right to appeal to scripture.[2] It had been supplied *for* them, but only to enable wayward expositors to identify themselves as heretics. This was Tertullian's version of "enough rope." Heretics' expositions showed others how far the expositors

The author thanks Bart Ehrman, Trent Foley, and Douglas McGaughey for reviews of preliminary drafts of this article.

1. *De praescriptionibus adversus haereses omnes* (hereafter cited as *Praes.*), 39.7. I have used texts in *Corpus Christianorum: Series Latina*, vols. 1–2 (Turnhout, 1953–1954). For Tertullian's *praescriptiones*, see Joseph K. Stirnimann, *Die praescriptio Tertullians im Lichte des römischen Rechts und der Theologie* (Freiburg, 1949), pp. 135–149; for his tactics, E. Flesseman-Van Leer, *Tradition and Scripture in the Early Church* (Assen, 1954), pp. 180–185 and Otto Kuss, "Zur Hermeneutik Tertullians," *Neutestamentliche Aufsätze: Festschrift für Prof. Josef Schmid zum 70. Geburtstag*, ed. J. Blinzler, Otto Kuss, and F. Mussner (Regensburg, 1963), pp. 140–144. Paolo Siniscalo, "Recenti studi su Tertulliano," *Rivista di storia e letteratura religiosa* 14 (1978): 396–405 and Robert D. Sider, "Approaches to Tertullian: A Study of Recent Scholarship," *The Second Century* 2 (1982): 228–260 provide bibliographical surveys. Useful bibliographical remarks as well as a general biographical introduction are available in the second edition of Timothy D. Barnes, *Tertullian: A Historical and Literary Study* (Oxford, 1985); the postscript corrects errors in the first edition (Oxford, 1971) and recommends the plural of *praescriptio*, which I have adopted also. Among other studies that take different approaches to the issues discussed here, note Gottfried Zimmermann, *Die hermeneutischen Prinzipien Tertullians* (Würzburg, 1937); Heinrich Karpp, *Schrift und Geist bei Tertullian* (Gütersloh, 1955); Jean Claude Fredouille, *Tertullien et la conversion de la culture antique* (Paris, 1972); J. E. L. Van der Geest, *Le Christ et l'Ancien Testament chez Tertullien* (Nijmegen, 1972); and particularly two recent, provocative papers: Vittorino Grossi, "A proposito della conversione di Tertulliano al Montanismo (*De pudicitia* 1.10–13)," *Augustinianum* 27 (1987): 57–70 and Renato Uglione, "La gradualità della rivelazione in Tertulliano," in *Crescita dell'uomo catechesi dei padri*, ed. Sergio Felici (Rome, 1987), pp. 133–144.

2. *Praes.*, 15.4 and 19.2–3.

Mr. Kaufman is Bowman & Gordon Gray professor of religious studies in the University of North Carolina at Chapel Hill, Chapel Hill, North Carolina.

deviated from the precious tradition originating with the apostles, and to assist those others apologists introduced a rule of faith condensing the apostles' instruction and tradition. Tertullian's several presentations of the rule of faith raise important questions; discrepancies prompt suspicion that no precise formulation or rule inspired consensus, that rules were rather makeshift. At the time, however, Tertullian obviously was more interested in another discrepancy, the one between his rule(s) expressing Christianity's incontrovertible truths and the opinions and exegesis of benighted heretics, for God provided heretics, apologists, and controversy to keep traditional or "regular" Christianity advancing on its proper course.[3] Tertullian's confidence in the advance of Christianity is the subject of this paper. How did he come by it and just how did he relate the persistence of heresy to the progress of Christianity?

Answers to the first question usually fall one of two ways. Years ago, Tertullian's confidence was attributed to his fascination with the Montanist renewal movement in North Africa. Allegedly, Tertullian came under the spell of Montanists who thought the Paraclete revealed still more about religion than church authorities cared to disclose. Ergo, prophets as recipients of the Spirit's revelations, not bishops, were the vanguards and safeguards of Christianity's advance. Echoing the apostle, Tertullian once declared he had given up "childish ways" (1 Cor. 13:11), so with some justification Vittorino Grossi likened Tertullian's reputed disavowal of rules and "regular" Christianity and his apparent adoption of Montanism, the Paraclete, and the

---

3. *Adversus Marcionem* (hereafter cited as *Marc.*), 4.5.2–4. For Tertullian's summaries see *Praes.*, 13; *De virginibus velandis* (hereafter cited as *Virg.*), 1.2–3; *Adversus Praxean* (hereafter cited as *Prax.*), 2.1–5; and Kuss, "Hermeneutik," pp. 146–150. Tertullian's stands against heresy and for doctrinal conformity are customarily cited in comments on his rules; see, for example, Flesseman-Van Leer, *Tradition*, pp. 159–173; Bergt Hägglund, "Die Bedeutung der *regula fidei* als Grundlage theologischer Aussages," *Studia Theologica* 12 (1958): 19–29, 34–44; and Joseph Moingt, S. J., *Théologie trinitaire de Tertullien*, 4 vols. (Aubier, 1966), 1:79–86. For general remarks on the issue of apostolic origins, see Sigfred Pederson, "Die Kanonfrage als historisches und theologisches Problem," *Studia Theologica* 31 (1977): especially 85–89. The most helpful and suggestive conclusions about formulations and functions of Tertullian's *regulae* are those of René Braun, *Deus Christianorum: Recherches sur le vocabulaire doctrinal de Tertullien*, 2nd ed. (Paris, 1977), pp. 446–453 and L. William Countryman, "Tertullian and the *Regula Fidei*," *The Second Century* 2 (1982): 208–227. Countryman identifies the pattern followed by instructors, accounting for consistencies and variations by associating the rules with catechesis ("oral instruction") and with "the need to innoculate the catholic people against Gnosticism." Thomas P. O'Malley, S. J., *Tertullian and the Bible* (Utrecht, 1967) reconstructs Tertullian's attitudes toward exegesis, yet also consult R. P. C. Hanson, "Notes on Tertullian's Interpretation of Scripture," *The Journal of Theological Studies*, new series 12 (1961): 273–279; Braun, *Deus Christianorum*, pp. 454–473; and J. H. Waszink, "Tertullian's Principles and Methods of Exegesis," *Early Christian Literature and the Classical Intellectual Tradition: In honorem Robert M. Grant*, ed. William R. Schoedel and Robert L. Wilken (Paris, 1979), pp. 17–31.

progress of revelation to Paul's conversion from Judaism to Christianity.[4] Lately, however, others have sifted those "childish ways" and have discovered traces of a theory of progress in Tertullian's earliest work. Jean-Claude Fredouille and Renato Uglione reach relatively the same conclusion about Tertullian's intellectual odyssey and ascribe his idealization of progress to his early and constant study of Stoicism.[5] Neither Montanist nor Stoic influence can be ruled out, yet an overlooked source of Tertullian's commitment to Christianity's advance suggests itself once we reexamine his critical practice, particularly his approach to scripture. To the extent that such a reexamination concentrates on Tertullian's efforts to substitute a defensible historical rationality of revelation for those philosophical rationalities proposed by heretics, it also addresses the second of our questions or concerns, the perplexing compatibility between the persistence of heresy and the progress of Christianity.

If we start with Tertullian's several statements about the public reading of sacred texts we might better understand why, having forbidden heretics from using scripture and having despaired of winning them over with counter-exegesis, he nonetheless insisted on striking at their interpretations with his own. As vital for catechesis as concise rules of faith would have been, Tertullian recognized that recitations from other, livelier documents were significant moments in each congregation's corporate life and worship. Critics called Christians misanthropic because they refused to attend civic assemblies, games, and spectacles. They complained that Christians were reclusive, secretive; they suspected them of sedition. Tertullian replied by explaining that pious Christians took their pleasures less spectacularly than pagans, but no less sociably. They happily and publicly gathered to sing psalms and hear their sacred texts read, sometimes by readers impersonating Old Testament prophets or New Testament evangelists and apostles. Had lectionaries from Tertullian's time survived much more could be learned and

---

4. *De pudicitia* (hereafter cited as *Pud.*), 1.10–13 and Grossi, "Della conversione," pp. 64–67. Despite the declaration, Tertullian was no schismatic (see for example, Moignt, *Théologie* 1:58–59). Claude Rambeaux, *Tertullien face aux morales des trois premiers siècles* (Paris, 1979), pp. 304–305 implies that "childish ways" may refer only to Tertullian's early agreement with the church's policy on pardons. At issue is also the character of Montanism in North Africa. Could it have been a loyal opposition within the church? Douglas Powell, "Tertullianists and Cataphrygians," *Vigiliae Christianae* 29 (1975): 38–40, 52–54 and H. Paulsen, "Die Bedeutung des Montanismus für die Herausbildung des Kanons," *Vigiliae Christianae* 32 (1978): 28–29, 37–40 offer suggestive and conditionally affirmative answers. Also consult the informative presentations in Barnes, *Tertullian*, pp. 130–142 and in two much older yet still valuable studies, Paul Monceaux, *Histoire littéraire de l'Afrique chrétienne*, 7 vols. (Paris, 1901), 1: 394–438 and Pierre Champagne de Labriolle, *La crise montaniste* (Paris, 1913). Gerald Lewis Bray, *Holiness and the Will of God: Perspectives on the Theology of Tertullian* (Atlanta, 1979), pp. 60–65 minimizes Montanist influence.

5. Fredouille, *Tertullien*, pp. 434–442 and Uglione, "Gradualità," pp. 141–144.

current scholarly disputes about canonicity and authority could be more readily settled. Still, the aim of reading and exposition—bouyant, theatrical, or spare and solemn—appears to have been to edify the faithful and perhaps to censure the unrighteous.[6] Scripture's standards for conduct were probably featured in public reading and exposition. Tertullian recommended that such standards be set in the context of scripture's revelations about God's promises and plans for creation, yet he admitted that expository effort at this level could lead to problems. Philosophically inclined interpreters never missed a chance to project their preoccupations and prejudices on the simple and straightforward accounts of Christ's ministry. Christ came to save the soul, not to speculate about its structure, yet one would not know that after hearing some Christians explain their favorite texts. They were intent on making Christianity philosophically respectable. Making Christ reasonable and respectable, however, Christian philosophers often made themselves heretics.[7]

New Testament parables, according to Tertullian, were especially susceptible to misreading. They taught valuable moral lessons, yet philosophers expected more; they hoped to learn about the origin of the soul, the character of spiritual beings, the occult meaning of every phrase. Philosophers wanted and found in (or forced on) scripture some validation for their cherished doctrines. They thus came away from the Bible more arrogantly attached to those doctrines, more foolishly infatuated with their wild imaginings (*figmenta*), and more deeply mired in their heresies.[8]

Like Irenaeus before him, Tertullian thought the Valentinians particularly culpable. They were indifferent to the parables' moral lessons and to the *prima facie* meaning of the narratives of Christ's ministry and fate. For

6. *Apologeticum* (hereafter cited as *Apol.*), 39.3; *De monogamia* (hereafter cited as *Monog.*), 12.3; *Praes.*, 36.1 ("apud quas ipsae authenticae litterae eorum recitantur sonantes vocem et repraesentes faciem"); and *De spectaculis*, 19–21. Also note *De anima*, 9.4, where Tertullian may be emphasizing correspondences between worship among the Montanists and among Christian critics of Montanism ("scripturae leguntur"). See *Tertullianus, De Anima*, ed. John Hendrik Waszink (Amsterdam, 1947), p. 169. For other observations on Tertullian's revelations about reading, consult Paul Glaue, "Die Vorlesung heiliger Schrift bei Tertullian," *Zeitschrift für die neutestamentliche Wissenschaft und die Kunde der älteren Kirche* 23 (1924): 147–149.
7. Tertullian's attitude toward philosophy can be perplexing. Philosophy was useful, even admirable (*De anima*, 20.1 on Seneca and *De pallio*, 6.2), but it was also, he said, the principal source of heresy (*Praes.*, 7.3: "haereses a philosophia subornatur"). I will stress Tertullian's appreciation of the sinister influence of philosophy, yet his sensitive handling of pagan political thought and his profound debts to classical rhetoric betoken generally positive assessments of the culture of classical antiquity. See Richard Klein, *Tertullian und das römische Reich* (Heidelberg, 1968), Robert Dick Sider, *Ancient Rhetoric and the Art of Tertullian* (Oxford, 1971), Fredouille, *Tertullien*, particularly pp. 29–35, 152–178, 307–357, and Mark S. Burrows, "Christianity in the Roman Forum: Tertullian and the Apologetic Use of History," *Vigiliae Christianae* 42 (1988): 209–235.
8. *Pud.*, 8.12.

instance, they were convinced that spiritual natures suffered neither change nor pain. Hence, they could not accept the reality of a suffering savior. Valentinians so remodeled their savior and scripture that the passion all but ended during Christ's interview with Pilate, when purportedly the *soter* or spiritual element returned to its source.[9] Tertullian claimed that reasoning of this kind required no serious response. The philosopher's *figmenta* had no place in Christianity. They were comparable to a pagan's *fabulae*, the laughable literature about gods' misadventures and interventions in daily life. The Valentinians' *soter* resembled the divine custodians whom guileless pagans appointed to preside over every human enterprise and every stage of human development. Even the unborn have celestial protectors who come and go (as the *soter* allegedly came upon and withdrew from Christ). One god attends to conception, another to birth. One custodian oversees the child's first babbling; another arrives to encourage the first words and a third to steady the child's first steps. In his *Ad nationes*, Tertullian implied that the traffic between heaven and earth must have been horrendously heavy, but he wondered why no god had been assigned to clean up a child's first filth.[10]

Tertullian asserted that superstition lay behind both pagan religions and philosophers' *figmenta*. He intimated that philosophical speculation about the ghostly, incorporeal nature of the soul derived from the silly tales of celestial custody and caretaking. Philosophers were fond of attributing substantive acts to insubstantial beings.[11] Tertullian warned Christians to steer clear of *fabulae* and *figmenta*. Athens, after all, could teach nothing to Jerusalem. Christians who tried to acquire a philosophical rationality for Christianity all but surrendered the singular story of Christ. The result, he sadly noted, was that there was little to choose between some Christians' gospels and the preposterous fables of pagan poets.[12]

A number of learned Christians, however, claimed that philosophy was the surest way to make sense of enigmatic or obscure passages in the Christian scripture. Tertullian flatly disagreed. He admitted that obscurity was something of a problem, yet he hastened to point out that philosophers' solutions strayed from scripture's meaning and caused greater difficulties. Philosophers dragged troubling passages from their contexts. They hauled hostage sentences along a backstairs route, through the schools or systems of pagan philosophy, until they imagined they found the truth that the puzzling passages figuratively expressed. For Tertullian, there were no backstairs routes from mystery to meaning: absolutely everything necessary for interpretation was on view somewhere in scripture. Problematic passages would be

9. *Adversus Valentinianos*, 6.3 and 27.2.
10. *Ad nationes* (hereafter cited as *Nat.*), 2.11; *Apol.*, 10.6–7.
11. *De anima*, 6.
12. *Praes.*, 7; *Apol.*, 47.11; and *De idolatria*, 10.1.

made plain once other, clearer, topically related statements were discovered, for God guaranteed there could be no contradiction or inconsistency in sacred literature. Perhaps isolated and uncertain phrases tempted readers to question, say, the resurrection of the flesh. Tertullian would have expositors assemble the many, direct, and incontestable references to Christ's body, Christ's resurrection, and God's promises to reward the faithful, body and soul. Obscurity in one place might lead to error, but the search for philosophical rationality and respectability, no matter how cleverly it capitalized on obscurity, could not mislead the competent Christian exegete, acquainted with the weight of evidence and familiar with the sacred texts' signifying conventions.[13]

Our illustration was not chosen arbitrarily; Tertullian considered the subject of resurrection critical. He supposed that Christianity's appeal so rested on hopes for eternal reward that vague promises—or, to be more precise, scripture's promises vaguely represented—would take a devastating toll. He found it hard to understand and impossible to forgive pagan enemies of Christianity, who believed their gods paraded in the flesh yet who refused to accept the story of Christ's incarnation, earthly virtues, and resurrection. He found it equally impossible to pardon recklessly philosophical friends of Christianity. They sedulously probed Christ's pre-existence and pondered the celestial properties of Christ's flesh. Nonetheless, they recoiled from the resurrection as from sorcery, terrified, it would seem, by anything judged unphilosophical by their ludicrous standards.[14]

Against pagan enemies and heretically philosophical "friends," Tertullian wielded scriptural assurances of Christ's incarnation, corporeality, and resurrection. Christ, he argued, entered history in the flesh—son of David, seed of Abraham. He was the savior Hebrew prophets had promised and, in turn, he promised that the flesh of his followers would be redeemed, resurrected. That promise was prefigured by the healing and saving that constituted Christ's ministry, reliably recounted in the gospels. Other New Testament documents attested to the ministry's success and reflected on its meaning. From books of Hebrew scripture, Tertullian learned of the perfect correspondence between what was foretold in the Old and fulfilled in the New Testaments. All this gave Christ's work and Christian revelation historical rationality.[15]

---

13. *De resurrectione mortuorum*, 21.2 and 27.2. On consistence see *Monog.*, 11.13 and *Pud.*, 19.3–4.
14. *De carne Christi* (hereafter cited as *Carne*), 22; *Apol.*, 21.8; and *Nat.*, 1.19.
15. *Marc.*, 4.35.14–15. Also see Zimmermann, *Prinzipien*, pp. 10–17; Fredouille, *Tertullien*, pp. 285–288 and his "Bible et apologétique," in *Le monde latin antique et la Bible*, ed. Jacques Fontaine and Charles Pietri (Paris, 1985), pp. 483–485; and Renato Uglione, "L'Antico Testamento negli scritti Tertullianei sulle seconde nozze," *Augustinianum* 22 (1982): 169–171.

Tertullian was uninterested in what philosophers might have to say about Christ's pre-existence, yet he was deeply and historically concerned with the prehistory of Christ's ministry. In other words, he insisted that the same Christ who became flesh and appeared to all with eyes to see and ears to hear appeared also beforehand to the patriarchs and prophets.[16] He argued that the incarnation fulfilled an old promise while the resurrection made a new one. Yet he stressed the connection and continuity to alert Jews to the gospel's realization of their hopes for a messiah and to thwart some heretics' plans to jettison the Old Testament. He probably wanted to outmaneuver pagans as well, for they bragged of the antiquity of their ancestral traditions. Scriptural continuities gave Christianity a more formidable ancestry than that of relatively recent Roman cults. But Tertullian also stressed continuity because it proved God's fidelity, confirmed the historical rationality or coherence of revelation, and underscored the transforming power of Christ's ministry, a power extending into his own time, transforming the lives of listeners, if only scripture's promises and continuities were properly pre-sented.[17]

Fables, in Tertullian's opinion, inspired unsustainable faith. Hence, he emphasized the historicity of scriptural stories, continuities, and characters. Christ was no apparition. His flesh neither glowed nor gave way to the touch: it was not, as some heretics claimed, phantom flesh. Christ hungered, thirsted, and wept. Tertullian labored the point that Christ took humble, even contemptible form. And Christ's humiliations and suffering (*reproba-tiones et passiones*) enacted a drama of redemption which must be reenacted in the lives of listeners who come to appreciate that one must die to live, be rejected by this world to be accepted in the next. Tertullian feared that Jews, unwilling to trade their expectations for a better one, and philosophically learned Christians, unprepared to trade their "intelligence" for a higher one, were likely to remain unaccepting and unemancipated. The Christian revela-tion offended common sense and conventional philosophy. Yet God re-warded uncommon sense and the relatively untutored perception that could ascertain God's promises, prescriptions, and consolations in the historical narratives of Christ's ministry.[18]

Tertullian's window on the war between history and philosophy offers a partisan yet provocative view. He accused philosophers of overlooking historical conditions that had affected the formulation of their purportedly timeless truths. Philosophers, for example, were delighted to draw inferences from Socrates's last thoughts on the soul's origin and fate. Tertullian charged

---

16. *Prax.*, 14.
17. *Apol.*, 6.9–10 and 21.31. Also see Burrows, "Christianity," pp. 211–214.
18. *Adversus Judaeos*, 8.2 and 14.2–3; *Carne*, 9.6–8; and *Marc.*, 5.5.9: "Quid infirmum dei fortius homine, nisi nativitas et caro dei?"

that they romanticized the circumstances surrounding their hero's imprisonment, circumstances that had hardly been conducive to clear thinking.
Socrates, after all, faced death. He was badgered by sad and solicitous friends,
distracted by efforts to suppress his own sadness at leaving his wife widowed
and his children orphaned. Tertullian, supplying those distractions, guessed
that efforts to maintain calm and composure exhausted Socrates: the distractions doubtlessly must have confused him. Tertullian also presumed that
Socrates's remarks on the soul's immortality reflected his desire to console
friends and to deprive enemies of the satisfaction of seeing their critic and his
comrades disconsolate. In the very first sentences of his De anima, Tertullian
denounced philosophers' willful ignorance of history. To recycle and rely on
the authority of Socrates' final thoughts without allowing for extenuating and
debilitating circumstances was irresponsible, but it was, Tertullian suggested,
typically philosophical—ahistorical and discreditable.[19]

Heretically philosophical Christians were just as blind. They cared nothing
about the historical contexts of their favorite scriptural passages. Tertullian
was especially upset by their constant drumming on Christ's apparent call for
curiosity: ask, seek, and knock, and you will find (Matt. 7:7). Heretics used
the injunction to justify philosophical studies, to make room for philosophy
in biblical theology. Tertullian countered that Christ's remarks did not
enjoin philosophical inquiry; they were, he said, addressed to Jews. They
were meant to encourage Jews to look more deeply into and beyond Hebrew
scripture, but that "beyond" was not boundless. Asking and seeking, faith
should not cross its own frontiers. Had heretics attended to the historical
context and coupled the passage in Matthew with the imperative to "search
the scriptures" (John 5:39), they would have understood Christ's instructions
and aborted their extrascriptural excursions. They would have found what
they should have been seeking and sought no further.[20]

Was there any better way to subvert heretical exposition and, ideally, to
encourage philosophers' self-censorship than to appeal to historical context?
Learn, Tertullian advised, about persons addressed in specific scriptural
passages: it made a great difference that the injunction to ask and seek had
been addressed to Jews, for that contextual detail restricted application. To
take another example, categorical statements about God's unity were less
likely to occasion heretical doubts about Christ's divinity if expositors recalled
that they were originally addressed to idolators. They were prohibitions
against idolatry, not advanced warnings against christology.[21] Learn, Tertullian also advised, to distinguish the special situations that had prompted
scriptural prescriptions. Christ countenanced flight during persecution (Matt.

19. De anima, 1.1–4.
20. Praes., 8 and 14.
21. Prax., 18.

10:23), but Christians should not make a general rule of that isolated utterance. Many other scriptural passages, indeed the weight of the evidence, called for steadfastness and suffering ("blessed are the persecuted").[22]

Retrieval of historical conditions was sometimes a matter of what Tertullian might have called simple induction. He complained, however, that heretics were so intent on doctoring and distorting biblical stories to fit their peculiar prejudices that the simplest contextual considerations were conveniently forgotten. Marcion was but one of the heretics in Tertullian's gallery of rogues, yet he was the one who drew the most fire. He concluded that the Old Testament and its law belonged to another era, another God. If, as is likely, he knew of it, he must have been profoundly distressed by the version of Christ's conversations with a lawyer in Luke's gospel (10:25–26) which essentially reduced his case for the law's obsolescence to rubble. How could the Old Testament be dismissed, if, as reported, the lawyer, asking about *eternal* life, received Christ's counsel to read the law? Predictably, Marcion redrafted the question; his lawyer inquired only about "the law of life," *de lege vitae*. To restore the text, Tertullian set about restoring the context, showing why Marcion's translation and omission were untenable. Any lawyer should have known the laws governing life. *De lege vitae*, lawyers were experts. Having established that, Tertullian improvised: the lawyer in Luke, he figured, must have heard that Christ had raised the dead. Naturally, he had been intrigued by such an extraordinary reprieve and would have wondered what it said about the possibilities for obtaining life after death. He could only have asked about eternal life, and Christ's reply obviously signaled that the law was not as worthless as Marcion thought.[23]

Tertullian's appeals to context appear conservative. He seems to hug the coastline of sacred literature, seldom experimenting with allegory, save for the relatively tame typological readings which permitted him to strike at Marcion's disrespect for the Old Testament. He has been applauded for "realism and restraint," for "a down-to-earth view of the historical character of the Bible."[24] Nonetheless, specimens assembled here suggest that Tertullian liberally seasoned induction with intuition. He cooked up historical context, using the few fresh-picked fragments he retrieved. Earthbound as his expositions were, they were calculated to make interpretations relevant to his times as well as faithful to his texts. The exposition of historical context

---

22. *De fuga in persecutione*, 6.1–2. Tertullian's position in *De fuga* reverses the one articulated in *Scorpiace*, 10.14–17. For the reversal, see Barnes, *Tertullian*, pp. 171–186.
23. *Marc.*, 4.25.14–15.
24. In addition to Hans von Campenhausen, *The Formation of the Christian Bible*, trans. J. A. Baker (Philadelphia, 1972), pp. 276–277 ("down-to-earth") and Hanson, "Notes," p. 275 ("realism and restraint"), see Hanson's "Biblical Exegesis in the Early Church," in *The Cambridge History of the Bible*, ed. Peter Ackroyd and C. F. Evans (Cambridge, 1970); Waszink, "Principles," pp. 27–30; and O'Malley, *Tertullian*, pp. 132–133, 151–152, and 172.

clarified the meaning of revelation; continuities between each passage's original application and its reappropriation in controversies of the second and early third centuries completed revelation, gave it historical rationality, much as application and enforcement gave the criminal law historical rationality.[25]

Tertullian's concern for clarification and completion helps us understand his vindication of Montanist prophecy as a development from his critical practice. That understanding is the profit we may now draw from our investment in the discussion of Tertullian's enduring interests in the historicity and historical rationality of revelation (knowledge of revelation depending on the disclosure of continuities as well as the assessments of historical contexts). The Old Testament could not be fully comprehended without the New and without knowing to whom and on what occasions statements were made. Tertullian also maintained that the meaning of both testaments depended on interpreters' reflective involvements with the past, involvements which fused the contexts or horizons of texts and interpreters. Investigation and paraphrase reconstituted the meanings of the text and the past. However, expositors never simply recapitulated; they selected, sometimes suppressed, usually stressed or subordinated elements of the original. Tertullian would not have termed it tampering and could not have imagined revising revelation, but late in his career he accepted the idea that the best expositors reenvisioned, reappropriated, and completed revelation with the Paraclete's assistance. Excellent evidence for this observation comes from Tertullian's *De monogamia*, a brief on the illegitimacy of second marriage. The *De monogamia* grants that the New Testament gave some confusing counsel on the subjects of marriage and continence. Yet *De monogamia* argues that an awareness of historical contexts should dispose expositors to see that certain concessions had been forced upon the apostle Paul. Tertullian complained that concessions were frequently translated into standards for sexual behavior. He held that stricter requirements for Christian discipline had been fenced in biblical literature, particularly in the Pauline correspondence, awaiting inspired exegetes, able to identify concessions, eager to learn the apostle's true intent, and serious about the text's applicability to their own times.[26]

But Tertullian became increasingly convinced that the church's interpreters were insufficiently serious. Authorities seemed to him to care little for scriptural prohibitions. They pardoned unpardonable sins, incest and adultery, and their clemency played right into the hands of pagan critics of Christianity who exaggerated Christians' immorality.[27] Tertullian asserted that the power to pardon had been misappropriated. In his treatise *De*

---

25. *Apol.*, 4.
26. *Monog.*, 3.8.
27. *Nat.*, 1.7.

pudicitia, he alleged that the Paraclete bestowed the privilege of pardoning sins when it yielded the wisdom to discern scripture's standards for Christian conduct.[28] Discernment, power, and morality were intimately associated. Without discernment, expositors either stupidly or wickedly overstated the apostle's willingness to forgive sins, to absolve sinners of their most terrible crimes. They forgot that Paul had been the church's most severe censor.[29] They claimed power to pardon for priests and bishops who were never meant to have them. Finally, they so lowered standards for morality that Christians who were not too unchaste were considered chaste.[30] Tertullian let out that bad exegesis was as dangerous as bad conduct; practicing the first led to toleration of the second, and toleration of the second produced more of the first.[31]

The Paraclete yields discernment (*intellectus reformatur*), redistributes the power to pardon, and improves Christian discipline (*disciplina dirigitur*). In his comments on veiling virgins, Tertullian referred to this achievement as the completion of revelation, and Paul Monceaux has rightly assumed that, if the completion is realized, its disciplinary or moral implications would have made all Christians ascetics—a transformation much to the liking of Montanist enthusiasts. Exegetical implications of the Paraclete's work, which are of greater consequence for Tertullian's presentation of the rationality of revelation, were adumbrated by his approach to scripture before he identified himself with the spirited Montanist defense of the Paraclete and prophecy.[32]

That observation seems forced on us by the importance of historical context in Tertullian's critical practice. We need only recall how relentlessly he scolded heretics for taking scripture's stories, propositions, and prescriptions from context, and widening or whittling them until they conformed to the truths of some philosophical school or system. In context, according to Tertullian, the same stories, propositions, and prescriptions could be appreciated in light of their authors' intentions. And since God was the ultimate author of those intentions and orchestrated them progressively, that appreciation shed clues to the historical rationality of revelation and was indispensable if revelation were to be usefully reappropriated. The question of context was complicated, though not essentially altered, when the intentions of expositors—as opposed to those of scriptural authors—streamed into Tertullian's later discussions of scriptural interpretation, which specified the optimal conditions for exegesis. Tertullian virtually made Christ's ministry

---

28. *Pud.*, 21.16–17.
29. Ibid., 15–16.
30. Ibid., 1.3.
31. Ibid., 9.22: "Non est levior transgressio in interpretatione quam in conversatione."
32. *Virg.*, 1.4; Monceaux, *Histoire*, pp. 285–286; and Francine Cardman, "Tertullian on Doctrine and the Development of Discipline," *Studia Patristica* 16.2 (1985): 139–141.

and Paul's extrapolations intermediate steps; the final, decisive stage—the completion of revelation—was the refinement of Christian discipline by inspired exegetes. Their obligations and adversaries as well as their ally and abettor, the Paraclete, constituted the context most conducive to the reappropriation and completion of revelation.[33]

Mention of adversaries reintroduces the second of the two questions raised at the start of this article: how did Tertullian relate heresy's persistence to Christianity's progress? It was obvious to him that God could have eliminated heresy and allayed suspicion about the new prophecy—so obvious as to suggest that heresy and skepticism were significant and perhaps necessary parts of the ideal interpretive context. In that context, then, contemporary crisis illumined the meaning of venerable texts, and that meaning illumined the way out of crisis. One might surmise, therefore, that heretics and critics, however implacable, vehement, even volcanic their opposition, existed by virtue of God's desire to bring revelation to completion and discipline to perfection. Unlike Irenaeus, Tertullian disavowed efforts to argue heretics to conversion; they never conceded defeat. Still, he continued to write against them, as if their misguided attempts to establish philosophical rationality were helpful prods, exciting the best expositors to defend the historicity of the resurrection and the historical rationality of revelation.[34]

Heretics almost certainly provoked widespread circulation of those first extensions of revelation, the rules of faith and truth.[35] Tertullian counseled against interpreting a single scriptural passage without determining the whole sense of sacred literature, so to issue rules and require that inquiry or curiosity be kept within their bounds was to presume that the whole sense was somehow contained in those rules.[36] Hence their hermeneutical role was of considerable consequence. The rules must have seemed like scripture's way of restraining exaggerated exegesis. Phrases and formulations varied, but the relative constancy of doctrinal content appeared to furnish, at the very least, a context for further and orderly interpretive advance. And heresy, or perhaps just the memory of heretical misreadings, summoned additional refinements. In the rules themselves, one proposition might acquire emphasis or lose some force. Other texts could become repositories for—or could be composed as—extended counterarguments against heretical exegesis. Tertullian, for instance, took up several of his celebrated causes

---

33. *Virg.*, 1.7; *Pud.*, 11; and Uglione, "Gradualità," pp. 139–140.
34. *Praes.*, 39.7 has already been cited, but also consult *Prax.*, 10.8. All things are possible for God. Monarchians, however, infer the truth of their absurd propositions from their possibility. God, after all, could have made humans with wings yet he did not. God could have obliterated hawks and heresy, but both were necessary; "oportebat enim et milvos esse et haereticos."
35. *Praes.*, 12.4–5.
36. *Carne*, 8.1.

decades after Marcion had died. His *Adversus Marcionem*, finished at about the time he was drawn into the Montanists' camp, boasts his most sustained exposition of scriptural continuities, his longest and most detailed explanation of historical rationality, and the effective exercise of his unswerving conviction that the gospels called believers into a new age but not into the service of a new God. Marcion provided precious provocation indeed![37]

As for the critics of the new prophecy, who saw the Montanists as seditious separatists, they too were valuable parts of the interpretive context in Tertullian's time. It was incumbent upon expositors, he insisted, to get beyond specific statements in the Pauline correspondence, to value the apostle's way of living and thinking. Having experienced difficulties similar to the apostle's, having been opposed, as he was, by wayward, if not wanton, Christians, they could more readily see, even without the Paraclete's prompting, how timely his indignation had been—how timely it still was.[38] Instructed by the Paraclete, expositors could be assured of what Tertullian had learned by writing against Marcion and others; religiously useful cognition was, in significant measure, re-cognition. He long thought the ability to perceive progress and honorably to reappropriate revelation was what distinguished his critical practice from that of his rivals. Christ had improved on Moses; St. Paul, addressing the crises of his time, drew insight from and developed Christ's ministry; apologists' rules of faith and truth refined and reformulated scripture's paramount pronouncements. It was evident that Tertullian placed inspired exegetes on this continuum: "no one making progress," he said, "should be ashamed." What was not evident to many scholars, who limited commerce between Tertullian's pre-Montanist and Montanist phases, and perhaps not evident to Tertullian himself, was that he was making steady progress and that sentiments at the end of his career reflected his enduring exegetical emphases on continuities and contexts.[39]

37. For example see *Marc.*, 5.2.
38. *Monog.*, 3.4–4.1; *Pud.*, 14.27; and Fredouille, *Tertullien*, pp. 165–166.
39. *Pud.*, 1.12: "Nemo proficiens erubiscit."

Augustinian Studies 28-1 (1997) 7-50

The 1996 Saint Augustine Lecture

History and Faith in Augustine's De Trinitate

Basil Studer, O.S.B.

Pontificio Ateneo S. Anselmo
Rome, Italy

Introduction

In an essay published last year, Michel Barnes reviews several trinitarian studies written in French or English.[1] Barnes argues that their authors either rely too much on the famous work of Th. de Régnon, or that they excessively criticize the main thesis of this well-known French Jesuit. Barnes, however, limits his discussion of this contrasting position to the question of essentialism or personalism. He leaves largely unexamined the soteriological aspects of the text. Moreover, it would have been interesting had he considered at least two studies published in German: that of Alfred Schindler, who follows somewhat the line taken by de Régnon,[2] and that of F. Courth, who distances himself both from his master, M. Schmaus, and from de Régnon.[3]

---

1. M. R. Barnes, "De Régnon Reconsidered," *AugStudies* 26 (1995) 51-79. See also A. de Halleux, "Personalisme ou essentialisme trinitaire chez les Pères cappadociens?", *Patrologie et Oecuménisme* (Leuven 1990) 215-268; R. Williams, "Sapientia and the Trinity: reflections on the De Trinitate," B. Bruning et al. (eds.) *Mélanges T.J. Van Bavel* (Leuven 1990) 317-332, and L. Ayres, "The Trinity and Modernity" *AugStudies* 26 (1995) 127-133, who discuss similar questions.
2. A. Schindler, *Wort und Analogie in Augustins Trinitätslehre*, Tübingen 1965.

At almost the same time, I offered a paper on Augustine's trinitarian theology at a Roman conference of patristic scholars.[4] In this paper, I called into question the distinction, introduced by de Régnon, between the trinitarian approach of Eastern theologians and the unitarian approach of Western theologians. I also rejected the approach of Karl Rahner and other theologians, who, by remaining within what I would term a Western essentialist framework, also neglected the soteriological aspects of Augustine's *De Trinitate*.[5] In view of the research published by others such as E. TeSelle,[6] F. Bourassa,[7] J. Verhees,[8] and above all by J. Arnold,[9] I demonstated the importance of soteriology within Augustine's trinitarian doctrine.[10] It would have been possible to add E. Hill to the above mentioned authors.[11]

In addition to the inadequate attention paid to the soteriological focus of *De Trinitate,* a second deficiency in Augustinian research on this work in general concerns the role assigned to history. Forty years ago, my col-

---

3. F. Courth, "Trinität in der Schrift und Patristik" in *HDG* II/1a, (Freiburg 1988) 189-209; see especially 190-193.

4. B. Studer, "La teologia trinitaria in Agostino d'Ippona. Continuità della tradizione occidentale," *Studia Ephemeridis "Augustinianum"* 46 (Roma 1994) 161-177.

5. K. Rahner, "Methode und Struktur des Traktates 'De Deo Trino,'" J. Feiner - M. Löhrer (eds.), *Mysterium salutis* II (Einsiedeln 1967) 318-347. Those who want to criticize Augustine's overly abstract approach to trinitarian thought may consult E. Bromuri, "Le analogie trinitarie di s. Agostino tra psicologia e mistica," *Studia Ephemeridis "Augustinianum"* 25 (Roma 1987) 169-185.

6. E. TeSelle, *Augustine the Theologian,* London 1970.

7. F. Bourassa, "Théologie trinitaire chez saint Augustin," *Gregorianum* 58 (1977) 675-725; 59 (1958) 374-412.

8. J. Verhees, "Heiliger Geist und Inkarnation in der Theologie des Augustinus von Hippo," *REAug* 22 (1976) 234-253. See also other studies of the same author, quoted below (note 177).

9. J. Arnold, "Begriff und heilsökonomische Bedeutung der göttlichen Sendungen in Augustinus' *De trinitate*," *RchAug* 25 (1991) 3-69; especially 58-58 with criticisms of Rahner.

10. See also F. Courth, *Trinität,* 208f.

11. E. Hill, Saint Augustine, *The Trinity* in *The Works of Saint Augustine* I,5 (New York 1991), especially 19f for the difference between Saint Thomas Aquinas and Saint Augustine; and 23; 48f; 56 and 148: the missions of the Son and the Holy Spirit reveal the eternal mystery of Trinity.

league and friend, M. Löhrer, published a paper, titled "Glaube und Heilsgeschichte in *De Trinitate* Augustins."[12] His main interest in that paper, however, was methodological. He analyzed the texts concerning Augustine's concept of faith, but did not apply the results of his certainly fine analysis to Augustine's trinitarian faith. In like manner, Rudolf Lorenz exposed Augustine's scientific method without carrying his conclusions over to Augustine's faith in the Holy Trinity.[13] Similar observations could be made about two studies on Augustine's concept of history, published respectively by J. Amari[14] and C. Müller.[15] Each scholar extracts for his own purposes passages from *De Trinitate,* but neither asks in what sense Augustine's trinitarian thought is founded on historical knowledge.[16] Finally, recent years have witnessed an increase in scholarly interest in Augustine's exegesis. Scholars who endeavor to show the influence of the apostles John and Paul and of other biblical authors on *De Trinitate* ought not to overlook the soteriological orientation of this work; and yet that is the case.[17]

In this paper, I would like to continue the discussion about the historical and soteriological aspects of Augustine's deepest theological work. In the first place, I hope to clarify in what sense his trinitarian thinking was based on what might be termed historical knowledge. It shall become clear that, for Augustine, faith in the Trinity is supported by his-

---

12. M. Löhrer, "Glaube und Heilsgeschichte in De Trinitate Augustins," *FZThPh* 4 (1957) 385-419. See also M. Schmaus, "Die Spannung von Metaphysik und Heilsgeschichte in der Trinitätslehre Augustins," *Studia Patristica* 6 (TU 81) (Berlin 1962) 503-518.

13. R. Lorenz, "Die Wissenschaftslehre Augustins," *ZKG* 67 (1955) 29-60; 213-251. See also J.M. Rist, *Augustine: Ancient thought baptized,* Cambridge 1994.

14. J. Amari, *Il concetto di storia in Agostino,* Roma 1951.

15. C. Müller, "Geschichtsbewusstsein bei Augustinus. Ontologische, anthropologische und universalgeschichtlich/heilsgeschichtliche Elemente einer augustinischen 'Geschichtstheorie'" in *Cassiciacum* 39/2, Würzburg 1993. See especially 100-103; 160-169.

16. Müller even includes in his study a paragraph on the *dispensatio temporalis,* but he does not question how the economy of salvation manifested the eternal Trinity. See C. Müller, *Geschichtsbewusstsein,* 225-229.

17. See B. Studer, "Zur Pneumatologie des Augustinus von Hippo (*De Trinitate* 15,17,27 – 27, 50)," *Augustinianum* 35 (1995) 567-583; B. Studer, "Le lettere paoline nella teologia trinitaria di Agostino," L. Padovesi (ed.), *Atti del IV Simposio di Tarso su s. Paolo Apostolo* (Roma 1996) 159-168 (with other bibliographical indications).

torical procedures or methods, such that even trinitarian faith can be said to constitute a kind of historical knowledge (*cognitio historica*).[18] Secondly, I shall discuss a particular aspect of this historical orientation: the relationship between economy and theology. Working within an Augustinian framework, historical knowledge can be said to lead generally to contemplative wisdom; it is also worth asking in what sense historical knowledge can lead to wisdom when working within a trinitarian context. More concretely, I wish to see, whether, in the view of the bishop of Hippo, the trinitarian economy of salvation reveals the theology of the eternal Trinity. The question of the relation between the history of salvation and the eternal Trinity is without doubt a modern one.[19] Yet, surely we are allowed to ask in what sense Augustine anticipates that question, without which there can be no trinitarian theology! However, before I enter into this two-fold question, something has to be said in as comprehensive a manner as possible about Augustine's general concept of historical knowledge. We can understand how trinitarian faith is a kind of historical knowledge and how the mysteries of salvation manifest the eternal life of the Father, the Son and the Holy Spirit only if we have some idea of Augustine's concept of historical thinking in general.[20]

I. Historical knowledge

In examining the meaning and place of history in Augustine's thought, one naturally turns to the numerous, well-known monographs on his theology (or philosophy) of history.[21] However, this research contributes nothing that is relevant to our particular topic. More illuminating are the published studies concerning Augustine's historical method. H.I.

---

18. It may be useful to point out that I refer to "history" and "historical" in the augustinian sense of this words. See notes 26 and 31.

19. See the rapid resumé in C. Becker, "Trinité II," *DSpir* 15 (1991) 1310-1314.

20. The latin texts are quoted following the edition prepared by W.J. Mountain and F. Glorie for CCL 50 and 50A. English quotations of Augustine's *De Trinitate* are taken over from the English translation, published by E. Hill in "Works of Saint Augustine" 5,1. The abbreviations of Augustine's writings correspond to those used in the *Augustinus-Lexikon* (*AugLex*) edited by C. Mayer an published by Schwabe & Co., Basel 1994ff.

21. See the bibliographical bulletin in C. Müller, *Geschichtsbewusstsein*, 7-11.

Marrou, in his famous book on Augustine and the end of ancient culture, outlines this method[22] and records the influences on Augustine of the grammarians and rhetoricians who explained and embellished their texts with *exempla* borrowed from the fields of mythology and historiography. Marrou also notes the influence of the catalogues of various philosophers which lie behind some texts of *De ciuitate Dei*.[23] Moreover, he stresses how the polemics against the Donatists and Roman pagans motivated the bishop of Hippo to improve his knowledge of history and to give greater importance to historiography even in his theory of exegesis.[24] In this way, Marrou points out that Augustine developed his ideas on history in different contexts.[25] As a result of Marrou's studies, scholars today have to pay greater attention to the various groups which provide the contexts for Augustine's discussions of history.[26] Others scholars, such as Amari,[27] Lorenz,[28] and Müller,[29] have offered greater specificity to Marrou's more general indications on this matter. It is particularly worthy of note that Lorenz, in his famous essay on Augustine's "Wissenschaftslehre" indicates the presence in Augustine's anti-Manichean writings of a certain historical criticism concerning the Bible, while in *De ciuitate Dei*, the same nascent, historical-critical method is applied to the question of miracles.[30] I tried to demonstrate in

---

22. H. I. Marrou, *Saint Augustin et la fin de la culture grecque*, Paris [4]1958.

23. H.I. Marrou, *Augustin*, 131-135.

24. H. I. Marrou, *Augustin*, 404f; 417ff.

25. See for instance *vera rel.* 7,13: history and prophecy; 50,99: faith needed for history and intelligence; *ep.* 143,12 (*ad Marcellinum*): historical value of *litterae saeculares*; *spir.litt.* 31,54-34,60: on faith as a divine gift

26. See B. Studer, "La cognitio historialis di Profirio nel De ciuitate Dei (2)," E. Cavalcanti (ed.) *Il De ciuitate Dei. L'opera, le interpretazioni, l'influsso* (Roma 1996) 51-65, especially 51-54, where the readers' interest in this apology is recorded.

27. J. Amari, *Concetto di storia*, especially 60-73: Augustine's historical interests.

28. R. Lorenz, *Wissenschaftslehre*, 37-45.

29. C. Müller, *Geschichtsbewusstsein*, especially 90: History as science; 100-103.

30. See R. Lorenz, *Wissenschaftslehre*, 216-229: The knowledge of the authority, with *mor.* 1,29,6 and *ciu.* 21,6f. See also 37f, with the observations on history and exegesis in *doct.chr.* 2,28,42-30,47.

my two essays on the *cognitio historialis* of Porphyry that Augustine, in his dialogue with Roman intellectuals, adhered closely to an historical method which is quite similar to that found in the historical investigations of Porphyry.[31] Approaching the question from another point of view, Ulrich Duchrow, in his study on the language of Augustine, touched upon the historical aspects of his thought.[32] Finally, returning again to the essay of M. Löhrer, one notes in his very accurate analysis of the most important texts of *De Trinitate*, the establishment by Augustine of a connection between Christian faith and the history of salvation. However, as I have said, Löhrer does not apply the results of his research to Augustine's trinitarian doctrine itself. Above all, Löhrer does not pay sufficient attention to the concept of history.[33] This lacuna gives me one further reason to deepen the historical background of Augustine's trinitarian theology.

According to Augustine, then, what is the importance of historical knowledge for trinitarian faith? To prepare our answer to this fundamental question, I would like first to look at two highly significant texts of *De Trinitate*.[34]

The first is found in the fourth book.[35] Here, within his discussion of the incarnation as the highest form of theophanies, Augustine includes an exposition on the mediation of Christ. He declares that the Incarnate Word was mediator as far as he received in himself our faith through which he wanted to lead us to the truth.[36] Working within an anti-Por-

---

31. B. Studer, "La cognitio historialis di Porfirio nel De ciuitate Dei di Agostino (1) (*ciu.* 10, 32)," *Studia Ephemeridis "Augustinianum"* 50 (1995) 528-553, B. Studer, *Cognitio historialis (2),* quoted in note 26.

32. U. Duchrow, *Sprachverständnis und biblisches Hören bei Augustin* in *Hermeneutische Untersuchungen zur Theologie* 5, Tübingen 1965.

33. This remark is valid even for E. Hill, who in his notes to Augustine's *De Trinitate* compares the historical view of man as image of God with the historical view of the divine missions (see especially, 23-27 and 263f). In the second case, in fact, we deal with particular historical events, while in the first case it is a question of "the dramatic history of image," that is, of the "common" history of Everyman (see n. 26).

34. It is noteworthy that Augustine develops his ideas about human knowledge principally in *De Trinitate*. On this remarkable fact see J.M. Rist, *Augustine,* 90.

35. *trin.* 4,15,20-17,24. See on *trin.* 4,16,21, J. Amari, *Concetto di storia,* 23, and R. Lorenz, *Wissenschaftslehre* 215.

phyrian context, he goes on to explain in particular the Neoplatonist philosophers' rejection of the notion of human resurrection.[37] He contests their competence in the matter,[38] arguing that they cannot reject the resurrection on philosophical grounds, because the resurrection belongs to the *successio saeculorum*. He suggests that were the Neoplatonists to argue their case in temporal terms, they could at least turn to historical procedures in so doing. In fact, in researching different kinds of animals, their origin and the measure of their growth, the Neoplatonists "have not sought the truth about these matters via the unchanging wisdom, but by studying the history of times and places, and by believing what others have discovered and recorded." Thus, the Neoplatonists have been able to investigate the unfolding of the ages: the beginning, the outward course and the end of the human race, but only by means of historical procedures and methods, and not by recourse to philosophy.[39] "Not even historians have been able to write about the things that lie far in the future and have not been experienced or described by anyone." The resurrection as a future fact is therefore accessible only to prophetic knowledge, and not to historical knowledge as the Neoplatonists and other philsophers understand it. The prophets, inspired by the Holy Spirit, could foretell even the distant future.[40] They gained credence for their predictions either by miracles or by fulfilled prophecies.[41] The Christian faithful have at least one additional reason to accept their predictions: the Son of God came in order to become Son of man and to capture our faith and draw it to himself and to lead us to this truth.[42] Philosophers, on the other hand, do not reason to eternal truths from temporal events;

---

36. *trin.* 4,18,24.

37. For the connection of this soteriological chapters with *ciu.*, books 8 - 10, see E. Hill, *The Trinity*, 149ff.

38. *trin.* 4,15,21.

39. It it remarkable that Augustine presents here the concept of the "history" as *successionis series* which has an *exordium*, an *excursus* and a *debitus terminus*, as he develops it in *De ciuitate Dei*. See B. Studer, "Zum Aufbau von Augustins De ciuitate Dei," B. Bruning u.a. (ed.), *Mélanges T.J. van Bavel, Collectanea Augustiniana* (Leuven 1990) 937-951.

40. *trin.* 4,17,22.

41. *trin.* 4,17,23.

42. *trin.* 4,17,24.

they do not reason by any historical method, but rather by a philosophical method rooted in direct apprehension of eternal ideas. Purified by adaptation to eternal realities by temporal realities, by prophecies and by faith in Jesus Christ, Christians are in a better position to understand eternal truths than the philosophers who are not purified by faith because they are too fixated on the realm of eternal ideas.[43]

The second text concerns the question of the relationship between *scientia* and *sapientia*.[44] To deepen the distinction made before between wisdom as the proper activity of the higher reason, and knowledge as the function of lower reason, Augustine analyses the Prologue of John's Gospel. He notes that the first words of the text signal what is unchangeable and everlasting, and what is thus the object of contemplation. In the following passages eternal realities are discussed in terms of their being mixed with temporal realities. Thus, light is discussed in terms of its relationship to darkness, and we are reminded above all that John was sent to bear witness to the light, that all might believe through him. "This is already something that happened in time and belongs to the knowledge which is contained in awareness of history (*cognitione historica*)," Augustine tells us. But accepting by faith that John was sent by God, we think in *phantasia* about what a man is and even about what God is.[45] Augustine distinguishes in this way between *fides* and *cogitatio,* the two principal elements of the *cognitio historica.* That is not all. He specifies, moreover, in what sense we know the faith which is in our hearts. He explains how the words of the biblical testimonies sound in us and how we can understand them either from things we know, such as men, or through conscious reasoning, as in the proposition, "his own people did not receive him."

In both of these texts, Augustine discusses historical knowledge and its conditions. To understand both expositions, it may help us first to look at the use of the word *historia.* Reading, then, with both texts in

---

43. See *trin.* 4,17,23, and especially *trin.* 4,17,24: "Nunc ergo adhibemus fidem rebus temporaliter gestis propter nos, et per ipsam mundamur." The connection of *historia* and *prophetia* appears again in *vera rel.* 7,13.

44. *trin.* 13,1,1-2,5.

45. *trin.* 13,1,2.

view, we may conclude that Augustine used the term with a two-fold meaning or signification in mind. The first meaning is investigation or research, the second one is narration. Hence, in terms of research, *historia* takes in both the past and the present, and is based upon the experience both of the person conducting the investigation and on the testimonies of other people.[46] Yet, looking at its other context or signification, the word *historia* does not denote a succession of events, but, rather, the narration or exposition of either present or past persons or events. This *narratio rerum* which permits us to enter into contact with the past or present as far as it concerns what is remote from us, is communicated by words, especially by written words.[47] This double sense of the term *historia* was common to Greek and Latin authors alike, a fact demonstrated by the technical lexica of both languages.

The two-fold meaning of *historia* is reflected by the use of the expression *cognitio historica,* an important concept in *De Trinitate.*[48] To demonstrate by biblical texts the difference between wisdom and knowledge, Augustine stresses that knowledge or discipline helps us to avoid evil and seek the good. In view of this practical orientation of *scientia,* he concludes that "whatever we need for the sake of examples to be avoided or imitated, and for the sake of the necessary information about anything useful for us, we gather by means of historical knowledge."[49] Moreover, he explains that the knowledge, due either to our own experience or to the experience of our authorities, is obtained by bodily senses, by the images in our mind and by judgements made according to the eternal ideas.[50] Finally, he appears convinced that historical knowledge

---

46. *trin.* 4,16,21: "... sed per locorum ac temporum historiam quaesierunt, et ab aliis experta atque conscripta crediderunt."

47. *trin.* 4,17,22: "... etiam litteris mandauerunt, quae ipsi experta notauerunt." See also *trin.* 14,8,11: "uel in litteris fide dignis, sicut est omnis grauis et approbandae auctoritatis historia."

48. On the place of the cognitio historica in the whole complex of knowledge see G. Watson, "cognitio," *AugLex* 1 (1994) 1051-1064. Note also *diu.qu.* 48: on the *tria genera credibilium,* especially: "alia sunt quae semper creduntur, et nunquam intelliguntur: sicut est omnis historia, temporalia et humana gesta percurrens."

49. *trin.* 12,14,22: "et quidquid propter exempla vel cauenda vel imitanda et propter quaecumque rerum quae nostris adcommdata sunt usibus necessaria documenta historica cognitione colligimus." See G. Watson, "cognitio," *AugLex* 1 (1994) 1055f.

50. See *trin.* 12,2,2: "Possunt autem et pecora et sentire per corporis sensus extrinsecus cor-

is not only fundamental for a virtuous life,[51] but constitutes the basis of the Christian religion. As is the case with all temporal things, so too everything that Jesus did for our sake pertains to *scientia*, and thus is not accessible without historical knowledge.[52]

The second aspect of the *cognitio historica*, narration, is not as explicit in *De Trinitate*. Augustine uses the terms *historia, historici, narratio* and *narrare* many times in this work, but he does not define *historia* here, as he does in *De Genesi ad Litteram*. There, *historia* is defined as *rerum proprie gestarum narratio*.[53] He often asserts that trinitarian faith is based on the Bible,[54] but he does not call the Holy Scriptures *historia sacra* as he does in *De ciuitate Dei*,[55] nor does he distinguish the *historia sacra* from the *historia gentium*.[56] He does record the "trustworthy documents of God, written by his prophets,"[57] but he does not develop

---

poralia et ea memoriae fixa reminisci... Sed sublimioris rationis est iudicare de istis corporalibus secundum rationes incorporales et sempiternas..."; *trin.* 15,12,21f, especially: "Cum enim duo sint genera rerum quae sciuntur, unum earum quae per sensus corporis percipit animus, alterum earum quae per se ipsum....," and: "Haec igitur omnia, et quae per se ipsum, et quae per sensus sui corporis et quae testimoniis aliorum percepta scit animus humanus, thesauro memoriae condita tenet." - See also *trin.* 9,6,9-11: judgement according to *rationes*; 11,8,14; 14,8,11. On this question see G. Watson, "cogitatio," *AugLex* 1 (1994) 1049f, and also the scheme in E. Hill, *The Trinity*, 261.

51. See *trin.* 12,14,21: "Sine scientia quippe nec uirtutes quibus recte uiuitur possunt haberi, per quas uita misera sic gubernetur, ut ad illam quae uere beata est, perueniatur aeterna." - See also *trin.* 12,12,17: definition of *scientia*: knowledge of changeable and practical things, and even *trin.* 12,14,21.

52. See *trin.* 13,1,2, and also *trin.* 14,15,21: we know our postlapsarian situation only thank "fide dignis litteris dei per eius prophetas conscriptis narrantibus... et historica traditione indicantibus." According to J. Amari, *Concetto di Storia*, 26f, history as *narratio rerum gestarum* refers only to public events. Thus, in the *Confessions*, Augustine uses *recordatio* or *memoria*, not *historia*.

53. *Gn.lit.* VIII 1. See also *Io.eu.tr.* 61,4; *ciu.* 13,21.

54. See *trin.* 12,5,5: "secundum sanctae scripturae fidem satis ostenditur."

55. See B. Studer, "Cognitio historialis" (1), 533: *historia sacra* appears only in *ciu.* 15 and 1, except *ep.* 17, where it is used in pagan sense.

56. See B. Studer, "Cognitio historialis" (1), 545.

57. *trin.* 14,15,21: "Credit autem de illa fide dignis litteris dei sui per eius prophetas conscriptis narrantibus de felicitate paradisi atque illud primum et bonum hominis et malum historica traditione indicantibus."

as much of a demonstration of historical authority as he does even in his anti-pagan apologies.[58] Yet, he leaves no doubt that trinitarian faith is based on the historical narratives of both the prophets and the apostles. In fact, he speaks in terms of *narrare* in a similar manner in both contexts.[59] His manner of quoting biblical texts evidences his overall reliance upon narration, in particular, in terms of the value he assigns narratives related by biblical authors themselves.[60] Finally, he reflects on the relationship between the narrative founded on sense perceptions and then transmitted by the perceived word and the thought (*cogitatio*) of the hearer or reader of that historical tradition.[61]

Behind the two-fold conception of history as 'research' and as 'narrative,' one always finds a certain confidence at work. The historian-investigator manifests this confidence with reference not only to *experta*, things perceived by the senses, but also to *narrata*, things accepted by faith.[62] The historian-narrator believes (has confidence in) what he communicates to other people. Historical knowledge is impossible without faith. Whoever accepts the historical tradition, does so because he is confident in the authority of his witnesses.[63]

To understand this fundamental human reality of confidence more deeply, we need to consider the distinction between *fides historica* and *fides spiritualis*.[64] By means of historical faith, *fides historica*, we have

58. B. Studer, "Cognitio historialis" (1), 541f. See also *ep*. 143,13: authority of pagan historiography.

59. See *trin*. 4,11,14; 4,16,21.

60. See *trin*. 2,10,19: "Sic tamen scriptura illam rem gestam narrare coepit... inde consequenter exponens quomodo ei sit uisus dominus attexit narrationem de tribus uiris..." - See also *trin*. 2,10,17; 3,10,24f; 7,3,4; 15,10,17).

61. See *trin*. 11,8,14, especially: "Quamquam saepissime credamus etiam uera narrantibus quae ipsi sensibus perceperunt. Quae cum in ipso auditu quando narrantur cogitamus, non uidetur ad memoriam retorqueri acies ut fiant uisiones cogitantium; neque enim ea nobis recordantibus sed alio narrante cogitamus."

62. See *trin*. 4,16,21: experta atque conscripta; experta atque narrata.

63. See J.M. Rist, *Augustine*, 74.

64. For that distinction see *uera rel*. 50,90, where Augustine, in order to explain literal and allegorical interpretation of the Bible, distinguishes between "fides quam debemus historiae et fides quam debemus intelligentiae" and "fides historica et temporalis" and "fides spiritu-

access to the past. Hearing the narrative, the events of the past become nearer to us. We can see them in a certain sense through the eyes of faith. However, the facts and especially the words told to us have a particular signification. They symbolise a higher reality. Any non-Christian might agree with what is written in the Scriptures, that is, that Jesus lived in Galilee and Jerusalem. In doing so, this non-Christian person takes for granted that a city existed which he has never seen. Only a Christian, however, believes in Jesus Christ in so far as he presents himself as Son of God, and believes that his words have been confirmed by miraculous deeds. In just this way, Augustine asserts that the Jews beheld the Crucified, but did not believe in his divinity.[65] This latter belief exemplifies what Augustine means by 'spiritual faith' (*fides spiritualis*).

It is, moreover, noteworthy that, for Augustine, there is no spiritual faith without charity. He does not cease to repeat the Pauline expression *"fides quae per dilectionem operatur"* (Gal 5,6).[66] For Augustine, whoever accepts the testimony of a witness not only thinks about, but loves what is said. He discusses the connection between thought and love especially in Book 8 of *De Trinitate*. Trying to answer the question how we can love the Trinity whom we do not see, he explains how it is we believe that Paul was a just man.[67] We accept that fact and we think about it. Perhaps we imagine the face of the Apostle. Above all, we have some ideas of man and of justice. So we understand the biblical witness about this just man. But when we try to live in justice, we love justice, and so we can comprehend what a just man is and thus love the Apostle all the more as a just man.

---

alis et aeterna." See, too, the interesting observations of E. Hill (*De Trinitate,* 182f) on faith. Directly, faith concerns only temporal things; indirectly, however, it goes through symbols even to eternal mysteries. Hill insists too much on the difference between the augustinian and the later concept of faith. The crucial point in Augustine's doctrine of faith is not that faith concerns temporal things, but that we assent by faith to things which are not seen (*quae non uidentur*).

65. *trin.* 1,6,11.

66. See *trin* 13,2,5; 13,10,14; 13,20,26.

67. See *trin.* 8,6,9.

To understand faith more fully as a kind of *cognitio historica*, we have at least to consider the well-known distinction between *credere Deo* or *credere scripturae*, *credere Deum* or *credere Christum*, *credere in Christum* or *credere in Patrem, Filium et Spiritum Sanctum*.[68] The first two kinds of expression coincide with the *fides historica*. Convinced that the Scripture deserves to be accepted, the Christian believes that Christ died and rose for us. *Credere in deum* or *credere in Iesum Christum*, on the contrary, means to adhere to God or to engage to follow Christ. This union with God or with Christ necessarily includes love and hope. It is what later theology will call *fides formata*, and what Augustine himself distinguishes from the faith of demons.[69]

II. Trinitarian faith as a kind of historical knowledge

Augustine differentiates *credere* and *intelligere* again and again, especially in *De Trinitate*, and often specifies the relationship between the two kinds of knowledge implied therein.[70] With respect to this fundamental theme, he is particularly fond of quoting Isaiah 7,9, according to the Septuagint: "Unless you believe, you shall not understand."[71] He also adapts in *De Trinitate* a theme which was dear to him from the beginning: *auctoritas* and *ratio*.[72] To explain the historical impact or sig-

---

68. See C. Mohrmann, "Credere in Deum. Sur l'interprétation théologique d'un fait de langue," *Études sur le latin des chrétiens I* (Roma 1961) 193-203. See also C. Eichenseer, *Das Symbolum Apostolicum beim Heiligen Augustinus* (St. Ottilien 1960) 157ff.

69. See *trin.* 15,18,32, with Jac 2,19.

70. *trin.* 1,1,1; 8,5,8: "primum credere, deinde intelligere"; 9,1,1: "certa enim fides utcumque inchoat cognitionem; cognitio uero certa non perficietur nisi post hanc uitam cum uidebimus facie ad faciem" (with the whole context); 15,1,1; 15,27,48; 15,28,51. Very interesting is *trin.* 14,7,9, where we find the distinction between the assent by faith and the assent by one's own endeavor: "non quas ueras esse credit (lector) ei qui scripsit sicut legitur historia, sed quas ueras esse etiam ipse inuenit siue apud se siue in ipsa mentis duce ueritate." On this question see E. Hill, *De Trinitate*, 238f, who however simplifies perhaps too much the two movements: "the movement from faith to consequent understanding" and "the movement from a kind of antecedent knowledge to faith."

71. *trin.* 7,6,12; 15,2,2. See CCL 50A.626f, and W. Geerlings, "Jesaja 7,9b bei Augustinus," *Wissenschaft und Weisheit* 50 (1987) 5-12; L. Ferrari, "Isaiah and the early Augustine," B. Bruning u.a. (ed), *Mélanges T.J. van Bavel, Collectanea Augustiniana II* (Leuven 1991) 739-756.

nificance of trinitarian faith, I prefer, however, to start from the well-known definition *fides est cum assensione cogitare.*[73]

One finds this definition in *De praedestinatione sanctorum,* one of Augustine's last works. To demonstrate that the faith through which we are Christians is a divine gift, Augustine stresses that thought must precede faith, that this thought, however, according to Saint Paul, comes to us in the same way that every thought comes to us from God.[74] It is evident that in this demonstration, the accent is put on the thought which precedes faith. Insisting on *cogitando credere,* Augustine nevertheless, insinuates that *cum assensione cogitare* as a whole is a mental process.[75] In the same context, he calls special attention to the will. Those who accept the Word of God are willing to believe, and their will is also prepared by God.[76] In any case, even in *De Trinitate,* Augustine presents faith as a kind of thought-with-assent. Thus he uses expressions such as "to believe and to hold firm and unshaken in ours hearts," and adds a little further on: "and yet we firmly believe those things because we think of them in terms of general and specific notions about which we

---

72. See *trin.* 10,1,1; 13,7,10; 13,12,17; 14,3,4-4,6; 15,5,7. For what concerns the early writings, see J.M. Rist, *Augustine,* 56-59.

73. On cogitare see G. Watson, "cogitatio," *AugLex* I (1994) 1046-1051.

74. See *praed.sanct.* 2,3: fidem qua christiani sumus donum dei. 2,5: prius esse cogitare quam credere...cogitauerit esse credendum... credendi uoluntatem quaedam uoluntates anteuolent... "Quamquam et ipsum credere nihil aliud est, quam cum assensione credere. Non enim omnis qui cogitat, credit, cum ideo cogitent plerique, ne credant; sed cogitat omnis qui credit, et credendo cogitat, et cogitando credit. Quod ergo pertinet ad religionem atque pietatem (de qua loquitur Apostolus), si non sumus idonei cogitare aliquuid quasi ex nobismetipsis, sed sufficientia nostra ex Deo est; profecto non sumus idonei credere aliquid quasi ex nobismetipsis, quod sine cogitatione non possumus, sed sufficientia nostra qua credere incipiamus. ex Deo est." See J.M. Rist, *Augustine,* 161, who declares that, although this definition may not be found, the same idea does appear in the earlier texts (*spir. et litt.* 31,54: consentire uerum esse quod dicitur). See too *s.* 162A,11 (a.404).

75. G. Watson, "cogitatio," *AugLex* I (1994) 1046, with *conf.* 10,11,18: "cogitando quasi colligere atque animaduertere curare," and *trin.* 12,2,2. See also *trin.* 15,9,16-10,18, where Augustine discusses the concept of *cogitatio.*

76. *praed.sanct.* 6,11. See also *praed.sanct.* 5,10, and *ench.* 7,20: "Apud nos autem, Iustus ex fide uiuit (Rom 1,17). At si tollatur assensio, fides tollitur, quia sine assensione nihil creditur. Et sunt uera quamuis non uideantur, quae nisi credantur, ad uitam aeternam... non potest perueniri."

are quite certain."[77] He proves that he is thinking here of a mental proc-ess when he affirms that when we think about things we believe in terms of the *species* and *genera* of things which are either connatural to us or which are gathered from our experience; hence, our faith is not fabri-cated (*non ficta*).[78]

As assent or consent, faith includes a voluntary element.[79] This be-comes clear upon examination of Augustine's use of expressions such as: *fide sanissima accipitur;*[80] *credimus uerum esse quod ab aliis accipimus* (10,8,14); *non possumus resistere certissimae fidei et ualidissimae auc-toritati scripturae dicenti,*[81] *adhibere fidem,* and *firmiter tenere.*[82] One need not stress that when Augustine speaks about *credere in Deum* or *credere in Christum* with reference to the Latin Bible and to the various creeds, he supposes that the whole person is engaged in the act of believ-ing with heart and soul.[83]

Moreover, the bishop of Hippo often affirms that those who believe will to believe. In this regard, Augustine is quite explicit at the end of Book 13 where he summarises his ideas on the trinity of faith.[84] There, he tells us that the will calls the attention of the memory (*acies recorda-tionis*) to the sounds, to the signification of the words which are in the memory, and finally to the things one both accepts as true, and loves.[85]

---

77. See *trin.* 8,5,7: "Hoc enim nobis prodest credere et firmum atque inconcussum corde retin-ere, humiliatatem qua natus est Deus... et... perductus ad mortem summum esse medicamen-tum," and "ea firmissime credimus quia secundum specialem generalemque notitiam quae certa nobis est cogitamus." See the whole context of *trin.* 8,4,7-5,8.

78. See *trin.* 8,5,7f.

79. See on this question M. Löhrer, *Der Glaubensbegriff des hl. Augustinus in seinen ersten Schriften bis zu den Confessiones* (Einsiedeln 1955) 111; 117; 122ff; 141f.

80. *trin.* 14,18,24, with Jn 1,14. See *trin* 1,6,9.

81. *trin.* 9,1,1.

82. *trin.* 13,1,3f. See *f. et symb.* 3,4.

83. The same thing can be said with reference to the theme of vocation. See *spir. et litt.* 34,60, and R. Lorenz, *Wissenschaftslehre,* 266.

84. See U. Duchrow, *Sprachverständnis,* 109-118: Wort und Glaube, with the analysis of *ep.* 147,9-11; *trin.* 13,1,1-2, and especially 112, with *trin.* 13,20,26

85. *trin.* 13,20,26: "Huius igitur uerba fidei quisquis in solis uocibus memoriae commen-

This observation holds even in the case of the two texts of *De spiritu et littera* in which Augustine presents the *uoluntas qua credimus* as a gift of God.[86] Contrary to what Christine Mohrmann maintains, Augustine is not affirming here that faith is an act of will, but only that the Christian who believes is willing to believe.[87]

When, in the passages quoted here and in other writings, Augustine stresses the importance of the will for faith, he never asserts in a clear way that the assent itself is constituted by an act of will. Of course for Augustine, the will is engaged in every aspect of human activity. One must will in order to see, to remember, to think, to love and even to believe. But what is determinative for faith is its obscurity. One believes what one cannot see: *credere quod non uidetur.*[88] When one thinks, one assents to what is present; one can see and understand it.[89] On the other hand, in the case of faith, one assents although the things are remote, absent either spatially or temporally, or absent in the sense of transcending human thought: *transcendentia cognitionem humanam.*[90] One reasons to a truth which one cannot see, confident in the reliability of the authority behind the affirmation.[91] Of course, Augustine accepts the con-

---

dauerit... et inde formatur acies recordationis eius, quando de his cogitat; et uoluntas recordantis atque cogitantis utrumque coniungit... Uoluntas ergo illa, quae ibi coniungit ea quae memoria tenebantur, et ea quae inde in acie cogitationis impressa sunt, implet quidem aliquam trinitatem... Cum autem uera esse creduntur, et quae ibi diligenda sunt diliguntur, iam secundum interioris hominis uiuitur."

86. *spir.litt.* 33,57; 34,60.

87. See C. Mohrmann, *Credere in Deum,* 202f; see also 199, with the references to Albert, In III Sent., D. 23, art. 7, and to Thomas Aquinas, STh II/II,2,2.

88. See *f. inuis 7.,* especially *1,1.*

89. Note well that *assentire* and *assensio* are frequent especially in the philosophical dialogues, see for instance *Acad.* 3,5,12: ueritati assentiendum.

90. See R. Lorenz, *Wissenschaftslehre,* 213f. See also the following texts: *trin.* 15,6,10: uidere-credere: trinitas non conspicitur. — *trin.* 13,1,3f: fides praesens, absentia; fides intus, foris; fides uidetur, res non uidentur, with the quotation of Hebr 11,1, and with the distinction of fides qua and fides quae, and *ep.* 147,10.

91. See *util.cred.* 14,31, and also R. Lorenz, "Gnade und Erkenntnis bei Augustinus," *ZKG* 75 (1964) 21-787, especially 29: the faith as conclusion from that which I don't see to that which I see. See also U. Duchrow, *Sprachverständnis,* 73-81: Learn by authority.; and J.M. Rist, *Augustine,* 57: "...we must follow 'authority,' when it is not possible to have first-hand experience. Such will be the case, at least in part, whenever we acquire information about the

cept of vision by means of faith.[92] He even speaks of the 'eyes of faith;' but when he does so, he does so improperly.[93]

Hence, one does not see what one believes. Augustine confirms this fundamental position in numerous texts in which he recalls that believers are purified by the obscurity of faith. Thus, in terms of the mystery of the Incarnation, he declares: "If this is difficult to understand, then you must purify your mind with faith, by abstaining more and more from sin, by doing good, and by praying with the sighs of holy desire that God will help you to make progress in understanding and loving."[94] It is certainly not necessary that the purification of mind occurs by means of faith in the biblical sense. The believer is purified rather by the faith in which he accepts with humility the authority of Christ, of the Scripture, or of the Church.[95]

For Augustine, faith consists not only in assent, it involves thinking: *cogitatio*.[96] But he views this mental process as a complicated one.[97] The

---

past or the future."

92. See *trin.* 15,27,49; *ep.* 147,2,10.

93. *trin.* 2,17,32: per fidem intelligere.

94. *trin* 4,21,31. See also *en.Ps.* 8,5: "Consulitur autem cum illi quoque nondum capaces cognitionis rerum spiritalium atque aeternarum, nutriuntur fide temporalis historiae, quae pro salute nostra post patriarchas et prophetas ab excellentissima Dei uirtute atque sapientia etiam sucepti hominis sacramento administrata est..."

95. See *trin.* 1,1,3; 2,17,28; 4,2,1; 4,15,20; 8,4,6, and also K.H. Lütcke, "auctoritas," *AugLex* 1 (1994) 498-510, and J.M. Rist, *Augustine*, 59.

96. See G. Watson, "cogitatio," *AugLex* 1 (1994) 1046-1051, and even J.M. Rist *Augustine,* 56-63: "Belief and understanding," and 85-90: "Introspection and understanding," especially 87, with the distinction between *cogitare* and *scire* (*intelligere*).

97. See on the process of *cogitatio* in general, G. Watson, "cogitatio," *AugLex* 1 (1994) 1049f, with *trin.* 11,9,16. See also BA 16,606: explication of *cogitare,* with *conf.* 10,11,18, and 11,3,6: "Quae tria cum in unum coguntur ab ipso coactu cogitatio dicitur." Note further *trin.* 8,4,7: "Necesse est autem cum aliqua corporalia lecta uel audita quae non uidimus credimus, fingat sibi animus aliquid in lineamentis formisque corporum sicut occurrerit cogitanti, quod aut uerum non sit aut etiam si uerum est, quod rarissime potest accidere, non hoc tamen fide ut teneamus quidquam prodest, sed ad aliud aliquid utile quod per hoc insinuatur"; *trin.* 14,6,9-7,10, where Augustine explains the difference between *nosse* and *cogitare,* and *trin.* 15,16,25f, where it is a question of the *cogitatio formata* and of the *cogitationes uolubiles.* To understand well the place of the *cogitatio* in the complex of human knowledge, the two

---

believer thinks not only before he makes the assent of faith and after he has accepted the authorised testimonies, he thinks in the act of faith itself. Thus one can distinguish three levels of thought: the *cogitatio* as moving the spirit before, during, and after the assent of faith.

Before giving his assent, the believer has to think in two distinct modes about what is proposed.[98] He gives assent to belief where belief alone is appropriate. He, thus, both testifies to the absence of any evidence to support his assent, and overcomes in advance the errors which might hinder his assent. He excludes for instance any materialist understanding of divinity which would render it impossible to accept that the Trinity is one God.[99] Likewise, he rejects the heretical interpretations of the Scriptures.[100] The second thing the believer has to think about before he assents is the credibility of the evidence and its sources. He thus examines the authority of faith. In doing so, he recognises the reasons which allow him to consent reasonably to what is proposed to belief. Hence, in that *cogitatio praecedens* one discovers the questions *scire cur et cui credendum sit.*[101]

The assent itself does not consist simply in an attitude of faith, in a *fides qua.* We know that we believe.[102] The act itself of believing includes some content, what Augustine calls *ea quae creduntur* or *quod creditur.*[103] One has to know what one believes, *scire quid credendum sit.*[104] In this sense, Augustine, in order to explain the ecclesiastical use

---

schemes given by E. Hill, *The Trinitate,* 261ff, are very helpful. See at least *en.Ps.* 118,18,2, where it is clearly demonstrated, how complex the mental process of faith is.

98. See J.M. Rist, *Augustine,* 61.

99. *trin.* 1,1,1; 8,2,3.

100. See *trin.* 4,21,32.

101. See *praed.sanct.* 2,5; *ep.* 147,2,7: "Credendum ergo illa quae absunt a sensibus nostris, si uidetur idoneum quos eis testimonium perhibetur"; *ep.* 120,1,4.

102. *f. inuis.* 1,1,: "cogitatio qua nos uel credere alquid, uel non credere nouimus."

103. See *trin.* 13,2,5: "aliud sunt ea quae creduntur, aliud fides qua creduntur"; 14,8,11: "Fides enim non est quod creditur, sed qua creditur, et illud creditur, illa conspicitur." See J.M. Rist, *Augustine,* 61, with the distinction between "belief that such and such is the case and belief in an authority."

104. See *trin.* 14,1,3: "Aliud est enim scire tantummodo quid homo credere debeat propter

of the term *persona,* says: "That there are three is declared by the true faith, when it says that the Father is not the Son, and the Holy Spirit which is the gift of God is neither the Father nor the Son."[105] This *cogitatio concomitans* appears still more clearly in the exposition in which Augustine explains how we believe that Paul is a just man. Consenting to this affirmation of the Scripture, we know what a man is and what justice is.[106]

Thus, the mind moves much more on the third level of *cogitatio* than on the first and second levels. In fact, Augustine repeats so often his dictum *credo ut intelligam,* we get the impression that the thinking involved actually occurs at the deepest level of faith. Among the numerous texts in *De Trinitate,* it is sufficient to quote two passages from his conclusion: "And when (the people) have placed their unshakeable trust in the Holy Scriptures as the truest of witnesses, let them pray and seek and live rightly, and in this way take steps to understand, what it is to be able to see with the mind, as far as it can be seen, what they hold on faith."[107] And a little further on: "...let them first be enlightened by God's gift and become believers, and begin to be light in comparison with unbelievers; and after laying this foundation, let them build themselves up to see the things which they now believe in order that one day they may be able to see them."[108] It is probably not necessary to emphasise just how complex the *intellectus fidei* is in these final texts of *De Trinitate.* As is the case in so many other of his texts,[109] here Augustine intimates that the

---

adipiscendam uitam beatam, quae non nisi aeterna est: aliud autem, scire quemadmondum hoc ipsum et piis opituletur et contra impios defendatur, quam proprio appellare uocabulo scientiam uidetur Apostolus," and also *trin.* 15,12,21: "Absit etiam ut scire nos negemus quae testimonio didicimus aliorum."

105. *trin.* 7,4,7: "... quae tria esse fide uera pronuntiat, cum et Patrem non dicit esse Filium, et Spiritum sanctum quod est donum Dei nec Patrem dicit esse nec Filium."

106. *trin.* 8,9,13.

107. *trin.* 15,28,49.

108. *trin.* 15,27,49. See also *trin.* 8,5,7; 9,1,1; 14,1,3; 15,6,9. On this question see BA 16,624f, and J.M. Rist, *Augustine,* 59, with other texts.

109. See especially *trin* 8,9,13, where Augustine explains, how we understand better what we believe: that Paul was a just man.

more we love, the more we know, and that the more we know, the more we love the *Trinitas quae unus est Deus.*[110]

Let us now turn to the most interesting point for our purposes. Historical elements can be detected as present at each of the three levels of thinking previously mentioned. At first, as we saw, one has to be certain that one can reasonably rely upon the testimonies of faith. In order to arrive at Christian belief, this recognition of authority is founded primarily upon the fulfilment of prophecies. In that sense, Augustine speaks about the patriarchs of the Old Testament who learned from the angels to believe in the resurrection. He declares: "They foretold (these things) and gained credence for their predictions either by the signs they performed there and then, or by the things they foretold for the near future coming true; and so they deservedly won an authority which could be trusted even about things they foretold of the far distant future right up to the end of the world."[111] Certainly, in *De Trinitate* Augustine does not develop, as he does in the anti-Manichean writings,[112] or in his magnificent apologetic work *De ciuitate Dei,*[113] the historical demonstration of the authority of Christian faith. Nor does he expose in our text his position that no human community can exist without faith.[114] However, he supposes without any doubt that the experiences of our fathers in the faith, along with our own experiences, allow us to accept the witnesses of the Holy Scriptures and of the Catholic Church.[115]

---

110. F. Courth, *Trinität*, 196, and also A. Schindler, *Wort und Analogie*, 227f.

111. *trin.* 4,17,23. See R. Lorenz, *Wissenschaftslehre*, 216-229.

112. See *f.inuis.* 3,4-7,10. See B. Studer, *Cognitio historialis* (1), 544f. It is especially noteworthy, how Augustine, in order to demonstrate the value of the prophecies, as well as of the Bible, refers to the *codices iudaei* and excludes therefore a falsification of text by the christian. See s. 200,2,3; 374,15: ed. Dolbeau 550.

113. See *ciu.* 17,17, and also *ciu.* 16,2,3; 18,38, with the note in BA 36,759-762.

114. See *util.cred.* 12,26. On this question see M. Löhrer, *Glaubensbegriff*, 161f. and J.M. Rist, *Augustine*, 60.

115. See *trin.* 8,5,7: "Sic et uirtutem miraculorum ipsius et resurrectionis eius, quoniam nouimus quid sit omnipotentia, de omnipotente Deo credimus, et secundum species et genera rerum uel natura insita uel experientia collecta, de factis huiusmodi cogitamus, ut non ficta sit fides nostra," with the whole context. Perhaps the faith is not "fabricated" (ficta) insofar as it followd by a *cogitatio.*

We could say, therefore, that our faith is always a *fides quae*. It contains affirmations of that to which we assent. This content is based upon the Bible, upon the *regula fidei* which is nothing but a summary of the Scriptures, and even upon the decisions of the ecumenical councils.[116] In other words, accepting the terms proposed by biblical and traditional witnesses, we receive both what they "narrate" and the way in which they "narrate" it. With regard to this fundamental question let us examine a relatively unimportant, but a very interesting text. Talking about the lost image of God, Augustine says: "The mind has totally forgotten it and therefore cannot even be reminded of it. But it believes the trustworthy documents of its God about it, written by his prophets, when they tell (*narrantibus*) about the bliss of paradise and make known through a historical tradition (*historica traditione*) man's first good and first evil."[117] I think it not unprofitable to insist on the fact that the events (*res gestae)* related by these witnesses of faith are more important than the expressions by which they are signified.

The impact of history upon the third level of thinking appears, perhaps, less evident. The deeper understanding of faith seems to be exclusively a work of the *ratio*. We evaluate the terms of a proposition of faith by means of the *rationes aeternae*. Although we do not comprehend why,

---

116. See above all *trin.* 1,5,7f, where Augustine presents the *fides catholica* as the basis of his trinitarian doctrine. See further on *trin.* 15,27,49: "cur non de illa summa Trinitate, quae Deus est, credunt potius quod in sacris litteris inuenitur... Et certe cum inconcusse crediderint scripturis sanctis tanquam ueracissimis testibus... regente duntaxat fidei regula"; *trin.* 15,17,27: following the Scriptures the Holy Spirit is the Spirit of the Father and of the Son; *trin.* 15,20,39: "Uideo me de spiritu sancto in isto libro secundum scripturas sanctas hoc disputasse quod fidelibus sufficit..." See also *trin.* 2,10,17: regula fidei as exegetical principal; *trin.* 4,15,20-18,24: We know the resurrection from the scripture; 14,16,24: "secundum Christum immortales nos futuros fide uera et spe certa firmaque teneamus... De corporis quippe resurrectione tunc loquebatur Apostolus, cum haec diceret." Augustine does not explicitly discuss the authority of the synodal decisions. But it is clear that discussing the trinitarian terminology in *trin.* 5-7, he supposes such decisions. See especially *trin.* 5,8,10, where he refers to the trinitarian formulas of the Greeks and the Latins. See on this question B. Studer, *Trinity and Incarnation,* 182-185, and also B. Studer, "Augustin et la foi de Nicée," *RchAug* 19 (1984) 133-154 (*Dominus Salvator,* 369-400).

117. *trin.* 14,14,21: "Non sane reminiscitur beatitudinis suae... Credit autem de illa fide dignis litteris Dei sui, per eius prophetam conscriptis, narrantibus de felicitate paradisi, atque illud primum et bonum hominis et malum historica traditione indicantibus."

73

in a given proposition, the two terms are connected, we do understand rationally what they signify: for instance, what a man is and what justice is, or what God is and what a trinity is.[118] But if we look more closely, we quickly see that the *intellectus fidei* is founded not only upon the *rationes aeternae* but also upon historical experiences. Augustine is quite explicit at this point. In explaining the similarities between the word of the mind and the divine word, he discusses the "knowledge from which our thought is truly formed when we utter what we know." He distinguishes, therefore, two kinds of perceptions: "There are, after all, two kinds of things that can be known: one, what the mind perceives through bodily sensation, the other, what it perceives through itself." He then adds a third kind of knowledge which is, however, similar to the first. He says in fact: "We know also what we have learnt from the testimonies of others." Thus, he is able to conclude: "All these things then that the human consciousness knows by perceiving them through itself or through the senses of its body or through the testimonies of others, it holds onto where they are stacked away in the treasury of memory."[119] Augustine explains well how, in order to understand faith, one moves the mind by means of sense perceptions or historical testimonies. He explains historical faith in terms of our knowledge of cities which we have never seen. Even though we have never been in Alexandria, we believe that it exists and we imagine it through our knowledge of how it could

---

118. See *trin.* 8,5,8-6,9.

119. *trin.* 15,12,22: "Haec igitur omnia, et quae per se ipsum, et quae per sensus sui corporis, et quae testimoniis aliorum percepta sunt, scit animus humanus, thesauro memoria condita tenet..." See also *trin.* 15,12,22, where Augustine distinguishes four kinds of "trinitates": "Num enim sicut certissimas uidemus trinitates, siue quae forinsecus de rebus corporalibus fiunt: siue cum ca ipsa quae forinsecus sensa sunt cogitantur; siue cum illa quae oriuntur in animo, nec pertinent ad corporis sensus, sicut fides, sicut uirtutes quae sunt artes agendae uitae, manifesta ratione cernuntur et scientia continentur; siue cum mens ipsa qua nouims quidquid nosse nos ueraciter dicimus, sibi cognita est, uel se cogitat, siue cum aliquid quod ipsa non est, aeternum atque incommutabile conspicit..." It is noteworthy that Augustine, even in the second book (2 pr.1), underlines two paths of research on the Trinity: *inuentio ueritatis* and *tractatio diuinorum librorum*, that means *per creaturam* and *per scripturam*, two paths on which we meet two difficulties, that is, the difficulty of fixing one's gaze on inaccessible light and the difficulty of understanding the multifarious language of the Holy Scriptures. It is obvious that the second difficulty is an historical one.

be, a knowledge gained by perceptions of our own and of other people.[120]

The following observations may be helpful in better understanding the very complex historical processes allied with *cogitatio* where assent in faith is concerned. As is true of any Christian belief, trinitarian faith is founded on the Bible. One initially believes in the Father, the Son and the Holy Spirit, because Jesus presented himself as the Son of God and promised to send the Paraclete. Jesus thus witnessed to the Trinity through his own *dicta et facta*.[121] One is not surprised that Augustine did not ask the question to what extent the apostolic community accurately and exactly related the words of Jesus and interpreted his actions. For Augustine, Jesus himself is the true Son of God and therefore the highest authority of faith. What he has done and spoken deserves our confidence. At the same time, Augustine did not fail to emphasise that the Word of God became flesh and therefore, though he is eternal, manifested his relationship with the Father and the Holy Spirit in time.[122]

Another interesting question for us today concerns the manner in which the apostles and disciples came to believe in Jesus Christ. Augustine was hardly interested in this question. As I said earlier, he refers to the Jews who saw the crucifixion, but did not believe in the resurrection of Christ.[123] He observes Mary Magdalene who touched the body of the risen Lord and believed in his divinity.[124] But he was not concerned to explain how it happened that believers were able to transcend what they saw, and yet unbelievers were not able to do so. Apart

---

120. See *trin.* 8,6,9: Carthage and Alexandria; *trin.* 13,3,6: Roma and Constantinople, with the expression *credere testibus*. See also *Io.eu.tr.* 23,11, and even *doct.chr.* 2,8,25-9,26: *auctoritas* and *ratio* as *uiae ad eruditionem*.

121. See on that question P. de Luis Vizcaino, *Los hechos de Jesús en la predicación de san Agustn*, Roma 1983; he refers also to *De Trinitate*.

122. *trin.* 15,11,20: "sicut uerbum Dei caro factum est, assumendo eam in qua et ipsum manifestaretur sensibus hominum." See also *trin.* 2,17,28: the vision of the "posteriora Dei."

123. See *trin.* 2,17,29, and also *en.Ps.* 65,5.

124. See *trin.* 4,3,6, and also *ep.* 147,10: "Nam qui uiderunt uiuentem Christum quem uiderant morientem, ipsam tamen resurrectionem cum fieret non uiderunt, sed eam certissime crediderunt, uidendo et tangendo uiuum quem nouerant mortuuum." See also *Io.eu.tr.* 121,2 and 5.

from the fact that he stresses the importance of the assistance provided by divine grace,[125] and that he perhaps speaks in places of a kind of heavenly inspiration,[126] he recalls only the words of Jesus: *"Loquente Domino nostro Iesu Christo apud Iudaeos et tanta miraculorum signa faciente, quidam crediderunt ... quidem uero non crediderunt."*[127] Obviously, Augustine did not distinguish between the historical Jesus and the Christ of post-Easter preaching. Our one teacher admonishes us exteriorly and at the same time illumines us interiorly by his light.[128] The validity of all we have said up to now about the meaning and role of *historia* for Augustine is confirmed by the fact that the apostles understood the meaning of events in the life of Christ, such as his resurrection, only after coming to understand the Scriptures.[129]

In addition to the Scriptures, the ecclesiastical tradition held great importance in Augustine's approach to trinitarian faith. He did not doubt that the true meaning of the Gospel of Jesus Christ was preserved only in the catholic Church.[130] He excludes, therefore, the value of any hereti-

---

125. See *trin.* 15,18,32. See even *trin.* 1,9,18: "Tactus enim tamquam finem facit notionis," and also 229F,1: the one who is predestined can believe.

126. See *s.* 229F,1: "Apostoli sancti cum Domino ambulauerunt, uerbum ueritatis ex ore eius audierunt, mortuos suscitantem uiderunt, et resurrexisse non crediderunt" (afterwards they believed, as is presumed by the context); *en.Ps.* 78,2: Anna and Simeon did not hear Jesus speaking, but they "spiritu cognouerunt."

127. *Io.eu.tr.* 54,1. See also *en.Ps.* 78,2.

128. See *Io.eu.tr.* 96,4: CCL 36,571: "Sed ille magister interior, qui cum adhuc discipulis exterius loqueretur, ait: 'Adhuc multa habeo uobis dicere, sed non potestis portare modo' (John 16,12), si uellet nobis id quod de incorporea Dei natura dixi, intrisecus ita dicere, sicut sanctis angelis dicit, qui semper uident faciem Patris, nondum ea portare possemus." Augustine explains these words of Jesus in *Io.eu.tr.* 96-98; see especially *Io.eu.tr.* 97,1: CCL 36,573, and 98,8: CCL 36,581. See also *Io.eu.tr.* 18,2: CCL 36,181.

129. See *trin.* 2,17,30f, and also *Io.eu.tr.* 120,9. Augustine does not develop the importance of biblical knowledge for faith in Jesus Christ, but he seems to presuppose that the disciples recognized the testimony of Jesus to be the Son of God as well, thanks, at least in part, to their understanding of the Bible.

130. See *trin.* 2,17,28: "Sed dum pregrinamur a Domino, et per fidem ambulamus, non per speciem, posteriora Christi, hoc est carnem, per ipsam fidem uidere debemus, id est in solido fidei fundamento stantes, quod significat petra; et eam de tali tutissima specula intuentes, in catholica scilicet Ecclesia, de qua dictum est: Et super hanc petram aedificabo Ecclesiam meam." See also 1,2,4. On the question of the catholic faith, see F. Courth, *Trinität*, 193, who refers to M. Schmaus, *Die psychologische Trinitätslehre*, 100-110.

76

cal interpretation of the trinitarian texts of the Bible.[131] Above all, he reminds us that he read all the *tractatores catholici* before he set out to compose the books of *De Trinitate*.[132] But in this connection, it is important to note his criticisms of the traditional formulas, such as the Greek *mia ousia, treis hypostaseis,* rendered in Latin by *una essentia, tres substantiae* and by the expression *tres personae*.[133] In other words, both Augustine's faith in the *Trinitas quae est Deus* and his understanding of it are founded on the Bible as far as it was transmitted by a *cognitio historica*.[134]

Finally, we should not forget that one cannot believe in the Father, Son and Holy Spirit and try at the same time to understand better and better this trinitarian belief without charity and without hope.[135] This living faith, however, is impossible without a day by day experience of its importance for us.[136] It is also impossible outside of communion with other believing Christians. Faith, then, is based on *historia* as far as narration of the past is concerned, but it is also based upon *historia* under-

---

131. *trin.* 1,7,14; 4,21,31f. To understand correctly the biblical texts, that is the economy, we have to follow the traditional principles: the *regula canonica,* according to which we distinguish what is said either concernint Christ-God or concerning Christ-Man; the principle of the unique action of the Father, the Son and the Holy Spirit; the principle according to which "some things are even said about the persons singly by name... to make us aware of the trinity," and the rule according to which some ambiguous texts are to be understood of the eternal origin of the Son or of the Spirit. See these hermeneutical rules *trin.* 1,7,14-8,15; 1,9,19; 2,1,2 and 2,3,5.

132. See *trin.* 1,4,7: "omnes quos legere potui qui ante me scripserunt de trinitate quae deus est, diuinorum librorum ueterum et nouorum catholici tractatores,..." Note that *fides catholica* in *trin.* 1,4,7 refers to the faith of Nicea. See too *trin.* 1,6,13; 1,7,14; 2,1,2; 3, pr.1; 6,1,1, and F. Courth, *Trinität.* 193f. Very interesting, too, is *trin.* 15,26,47, where Augustine declares that the Father is called "ingenitus, non quidem in scripturis sed in consuetudine disputantium et de re tanta sermonem qualem ualuerint proferentium." He refers obviously to the polemics against Eunomius. See above in *trin.* 15,20,38, where this theologian is expressly named.

133. *trin.* 5,8,10-10,11; 7,4,7. See F. Courth, *Trinität,* 197f.

134. It is noteworthy that in Augustine's trinitarian doctrine not only the interpretation of the Holy Scriptures, but also the biblical proofs were for the most part traditional. See *trin.* 1,2,4; 1,6,9: Nicene explication of John 1,1-14; 1,7,14: on the *regula canonica.*

135. See *trin.* 4,18,24; 4,20,27; 8,4,6.

136. See *trin.* 13,1,3, where Augustine says that the *fides rerum absentium* is present in us, but occurs *temporaliter* in our hearts.

stood as contact with the present. Christians experience their faith in the Father, the Son and the Holy Spirit together in the liturgy: in the baptismal conversion and above all in the Eucharist, sacrament of unity. But they also experience it in their communion of faith and charity.[137]

III. Economy and theology

A. Principle

For Augustine, faith, considered as a believing attitude, the *fides qua,* can also normally be said to include some content, the *fides quae.*[138] Confident in the authority of the Scriptures which come to life in the Church, the Christian accepts the mysteries of Jesus.[139] These *res gestae narratae* by the *historia sacra,* however, can always be understood in two ways. First, they convey concern for our salvation; they relate what Jesus, the Son of God, has done through the Holy Spirit for our sake. Second, they point to a higher reality, the eternal Trinity.[140] This distinction between economy and theology was present from the beginning of Christianity, but it was further developed during the fourth century as a strategy aimed at refuting Arian objections against the true divinity of Christ.[141] Augustine himself received this fundamental topic. However,

---

137. See for instance the description of christian initiation in s. 227,1, and also the antidonastist texts which insist on the presence of the Holy Spirit in the unique Church, and *Io.eu.tr.* 6,8 (with the note in BA 71,877).

138. See *trin.* 13,2,5: "sed aliud sunt ea quae creduntur, aliud fides qua creduntur."

139. In *De Trinitate* Augustine does not full summarize the *regula fidei.* In several texts, however, he at least recalls the most importants doctrines. See for instance *trin.* 1,5,8, where he presents his "fides catholica," alluding, in part with "symbolic" expressions, to the trinity and the incarnation; *trin.* 4,18,24: "Nunc itaque illuc quodam modo secuta est fides nostra quo ascendit in quem credimus, ortus, mortuus, resuscitatus, assumptus"; *trin.* 8,5,7: faith in the incarnation (*natus de uirgine*), death and resurrection; *trin.* 15,28,51: the *regula fidei* which concerns the mission of the Son and of the Holy Spirit. See on this question E. Hill, *De Trinitate,* 46f, who however does not underline enough the middle way between the Arians and the Sabellians, and seems to me to overestimate the importance of the "economic" theologians for Augustine.

140. On the question of the relationship between theology and economy, see J. Verhees, "Augustins Trinitätsverständnis in den Schriften aus Cassiciacum," *RchAug* 10 (1975) 45-75, especially 46ff, with the status quaestionis; B. Studer, "La teologia trinitaria," Studia *Ephemerides "Augustinianum"* 46 (Roma 1994) 161ff, with the studies published after 1975.

---

one can hardly maintain that he reflected properly on the methodological principles which allow us to reason from the salvific action of the Father, Son and Holy Spirit, to their eternal common life.

B. Initial Approaches

Nevertheless, Augustine has some quite interesting approaches to the question. While discussing the revelation given to Moses on Mount Sinai, Augustine certainly opposes *Deus in se* to *Deus ad nos.*[142] But this distinction is not a trinitarian one. Above all, it concerns the two levels of religious knowledge. That person who is open to a higher level of thinking about God and the world understands that God is true being, the *ipsum esse,* the *Deus substantiae.* However, for those persons endowed with lesser capacities for such thinking, God has revealed himself as the God of the patriarchs, the *Deus misericordiae.*[143]

The question concerning the two kinds of knowledge is also present in a trinitarian context, but it is present in a different way. In the trinitarian context, Augustine opposes *scientia* and *sapientia,* the knowledge of the temporal and the knowledge of the eternal.[144]

---

141. B. Studer, *Trinity and Incarnation,* 113f. For what concerns the New Testament, see especially Mt 11,25-30, quoted by Augustine himself in *trin.* 1,8,16.

142. See B. Studer, "Deus, Pater et Dominus bei Augustinus von Hippo," L.R. Wickham C. Bammel (ed.), *Essays in Tribute to G.C. Stead* (Leiden 1993) 190-212, especially 191, with s. 7,7 and other texts.

143. In *trin.* 15,19,36, Augustine applies nevertheless the distinction *ad se* and *ad nos* in a trinitarian sense to the Holy Spirit. This is *apud se* God because he is coeternal with the Father and the Son; *ad nos* he is the gift of God given to us. He is therefore love of the Father and the Son and divine gift for us.

144. See *trin.* 12 and 13, especially *trin.* 12,14,21; 12,15,25; 13,1,1-1,2: explication of John 1,1-14. On this concern, see G. Madec, *La patrie et la voie. Le Christ dans la vie et la pensée de saint Augustin* (Paris 1989) 217-222. When Augustine, in *trin.* 13,19,22-24, opposes *scientia* and *sapientia,* it is *res per tempus ortae* and *res aeternae,* he does not refer properly to the problematic of economy and theology. But he suggests the sacramentality of the incarnation, when he declares: "*Ipse nobis fidem de rebus temporalibus inserit; ipse de sempiternis exhibet ueritatem.*" So he moves quite near to the modern distinction of economy and theology. In any way her underlines that "*idem ipse unigenitus a patre plenus gratiae et ueritatis.*" Being together *scientia* and *sapientia,* Christ guarantees us the passage from the faith in his historical facts to the vision of his eternal existence. See also *trin.* 7.3.5: "*Nos autem nitentes imitamur manentem et sequimur stantem et in ipso ambulantes tendimus ad ipsum quia factus est nobis uia temporalis per humilitatem quae maniso nobis aeterna est per diuinitatem.*"

In doing so, he seems to posit a large distance between economy and theology.[145] For instance, he insists that we know, both in terms of *scientia* and in terms of *sapientia,* as if in two distinct ways of knowing, that Christ as man leads us to Christ as God.[146] Moreover, he maintains that we 'see' this only through a belief which remains obscure.[147] Faith, then, seems not to be a communication of new knowledge, but a means by which the mind is rendered pure and humble in order to hear the inner voice of the one Teacher.[148]

However, we should not overlook the emphasis which Augustine places upon the unity of Christ. The one and the same Christ is *uia* and *patria.*[149] Further, being at the same time *scientia* and *sapientia,* he cannot fail to lead us from temporal perspectives to eternal ones.[150] Moreover, Christ is both the exterior and the interior teacher. It is true that

---

It is even noteworthy that Augustine in this context speaks of the temporal testimony about eternal things. See *trin.* 13,14, and also 14,1,3. Although there is no question of economy in an objective sense, the testimony includes the knowledge of economy. In fact, Augustine is not so much interested in the historical events of revelation as in the questions of *exercitatio mentis,* it is of religious knowledge. For him what is important, is how we can know eternal reality through temporal symbols, rather than how the *facta* and *dicta* of Jesus, the voice of the Father and the apparitions of the Holy Spirit revealed the *Trinitas quae est unus Deus.*

145. See on this "dualisme," R. Lorenz, *Wissenschaftslehre Augustins,* 235: regarding the distance between the *uerbum* and the *res.*

146. See G. Madec, Christ, 35-50, and also B. Studer, *Gratia Christi - gratia Dei,* 82-87, with *Io.eu.tr.* 13,4, and other texts.

147. See *trin.* 4,18,24; 13,19,24.

148. See G. Madec, "Admonitio," *AugLex* 1 (1984) 95-99.

149. See *trin.* 15,27,49, and B. Studer, *Gratia Christi - gratia Dei,* 87f. [ed. – The English translation of this work will appear in 1997, Liturgical Press.

150. See *trin.* 13, especially *trin.* 13,19,24: "In rebus enim per tempus ortis, illa summa gratia est, quod homo in unitate personae coniunctus est Deo: in rebus uero aeternis summa ueritas recte tribuitur Dei Uerbo. Quod uero idem ipse est Unigenitus a Patre plenus gratiae et ueritatis, id actum est ut idem ipse sit in rebus pro nobis temporaliter gestis, cui per eamdem fidem mundamur, ut eum stabiliter contemplemur in rebus aeternis." On the question see J. Amari, *Il concetto di storia,* 124f, and also G. Madec, "Christus, scientia et sapientia nostra. Le principe de cohérence de la doctrine augustinienne," *RechAug* 10 (1975) 77-85, especially 81, with the scheme. See too E. TeSelle, *Augustine the Theologian,* 334, with *tr.eu.Io.* 26,4-8: on the interior and exterior revelation by the Father through the eternal and incarnated word

Augustine does not develop this latter theme in *De Trinitate* as fully and properly as he does in other writings;[151] however, he certainly alludes to it in our text.[152] This emphasis on Christ's unity is most apparent in Augustine's exposition of the mystery of the incarnation in an anti-Porphyrian context.[153] Here, it must be granted that he not only opposes eternity to that which has had an origin (*ad id quod ortum est*), but that he also opposes truth to faith. Yet, while accepting this Platonic distinction, he affirms that we can not arrive at eternal reality unless we do so through temporal realities. Quoting Jn 17,3 and Ps 84,12, he re-interprets the Platonic distinction, insisting that "the Son of God came in order to become Son of man and to capture our faith and draw it to himself, and by means of it to lead us to his truth."[154] I agree that Augustine in this famous text is mostly concerned with the purifying effect of faith. However, I believe that it is here that he comes closest to affirming the principle that the temporal economy in fact manifests an eternal theology. At any rate, he insists that the one and the same person is both the way and the end. More importantly, Augustine, especially in *De Trinitate*, develops a regimen of signs which he calls the *dispensatio similitudinum*.[155] Hence, he does not simply oppose temporal and eternal realities. Instead, temporal realities are narrated as symbols of eternal realities.[156] The former are *sacramenta* of the latter, because a *similitudo* ex-

---

151. See *c.ep.Man.* 36,41; *en.Ps.* 118,17,3; and also *Io.eu.tr.* 21,1; 22,1f. Other texts are indicated in F. Schnitzler, *Zur Theologie der Verkündigung in den Predigten des hl. Augustinus* (Freiburg 1968) 113-122.

152. See *trin.* 1,13,31; 15,11,20.

153. *trin* 4,18,24.

154. *trin.* 4,18,24: "... ipsa ueritas patri coaeterna de terra orta est cum filius dei sic uenit ut fieret filius hominis et ipse in se exciperet fidem nostram qua nos perduceret ad ueritatem suam..."

155. See *trin.* 1,8,16: in the eternal life the *dispensatio similitudinum* is no longer necessary. See also *ep.* 55,7,12-8,14, especially *ep.* 55,7,13. It is even remarkable that the word *dispensatio* includes also the idea of adaptation or congruence. The signs must be congruent (see *trin.* 2,15,25; 3,11,22: *dispensatio (temporibus) congrua* and correspond to the times and cicrucumstances (*causae*) of the things (*trin.* 2,17,32). In this "economic" sense Augustine had already defended the Old Testament against the manicheens. To note also that he confirms his ideas on the *dispensatio similitudinum* with Phil 2,7: *in similitudinem hominum factus* (see *trin.* 2,11,20).

156. J. Amari; Il concetto di storia, 25, con *trin.* 13,1,2.

ists between them.[158] While discussing the anti-Arian theme of the biblical theophanies in Books 2 to 4, Augustine demonstrates that the appearances related by the Bible refer to eternal realities.[159] It should be admitted that he is quite reserved in respect to the theophanies narrated by the Old Testament. It is not easy, he declares, to establish in any case, which person of the Trinity actually appeared in which theophany.[160] In the New Testament the situation is different. There, it is a question of three different signs: the voice, the man, and the dove; so we can distinguish the Father, the Son and the Holy Spirit, which are one God.[161] Since the three persons act together in the appearance at the Jordan River, Augustine is able to detect in the appearance a symbol of their inseparability.[162] But it is evident that, in this case, Augustine is reasoning from theology to economy, from his monotheistic conviction to a unitarian interpretation of the biblical narrative.[163]

C. Applications

There is no doubt, however, that Augustine went beyond those approaches and practically applied the principle according to which the economy manifests the theology. In arguing the case for the incarnation, Augustine offers us a quite clear picture of his own thinking about the

---

158. See *ep.* 98,9.

159. See B. Studer, "Zur Theophanie-Exegese Augustins. Untersuchungen zu einem Ambrosius-Zitat in der Schrift 'De uidendo Deo' (*ep.*147)" *Studia Anselmiana* 59, Roma 1971. It is noteworthy that according to Augustine the theophanies constitute the most important part of the *dispensatio similitudinis*. See *trin.* 4,1,2: "missa sunt nobis diuinitus uisa congrua peregrinationi nostrae quibus admoneremus non hic esse quod quaerimus sed illuc ab ista esse redeundum unde nisi penderemus hic ea non quaereremus."

160. See especially *trin.* 2,8,14-9,16; 2,17,32; 12,18,35.

161. *trin.* 4,21,30. Augustine demonstrates in a similar way the thesis that "singulorum quoque in Trinitate opera Trinitas operatur," in s. 52 and 71. See especially s. 52,1,1-3,4 and s. 71,15,25-17,28. But in ths sermons he does not speak about *similitudo unitatis*. He proves the *operatio inseparabilis* rather by biblical testimonies (*dicta*) than by the interpretation of an event in which the whole Trinity appeared. See also *ep.* 169,2,5-4,13.

162. *trin.* 4,21,30.

163. It is also interesting that according to Augustine the knowledge of the eternal Trinity and of the mutability of the creatures permits us to understand the historical events related by the symbol of faith. See *uera rel.* 8,14.

relationship between economy and theology, and about the role of *historia* in that relationship. He begins with the affirmation that the Son alone became flesh, united *in unitatem personae* to human nature. Thus, Christ is shown to be the Son of God from eternity. Later theology will assert *unus ex Trinitate passus est*. Even though Augustine clearly did not arrive at this precise terminology, he shared the conviction that our salvation is founded on the incarnation of the unique Son of God. Later, with respect to the mission of the Holy Spirit, Augustine found an even better expression for making his point. Referring to the Easter narrative in which Jesus breathed on the apostles and said: "Receive the Holy Spirit" (Jn 20,22), he explains: "And I cannot see what else he intended to signify when he breathed and said Receive the Holy Spirit. Not that the physical breath that came from his body and was physically felt was the substance of the Holy Spirit; but it was a convenient symbolic demonstration that the Holy Spirit proceeds from the Son as well as from the Father."[164] A similar *dispensatio significationis* is observed in the fact that the Holy Spirit was given twice, before and after the death and the resurrection of Christ.[165] John 7,39: "The Spirit had not yet been given, because Jesus had not yet been glorified," prompted him to search the meaning behind the two types of mission. He responds to this exegetical difficulty by reminding his readers of the miracle of Pentecost. "For then the coming of the Holy Spirit needed to be demonstrated by perceptible signs, to show that the whole world and all nations with their variety of languages were going to believe in Christ by the gift of the Holy Spirit" as it was announced by the Psalmist's prophetic song.[166] The double dispensation does not, therefore, refer directly to the eternal Trinity. It only indicates that in the time of the fulfilment of prophecies, faith in Jesus Christ became possible through the gift of the Holy Spirit. Such reflections ought instead to demonstrate that the appearances of the Son and the Holy Spirit do not put in question their equality of substance, because they each became visible by means of created forms.[167] In other

---

164. *trin.* 4,20,29.

165. *trin.* 4,20,29: "Sed quod bis datus est dispensationis certe significationis fuit... quodmodo intellegatur nisi quia certa illa spiritus sancti datio uel missio post clarificationem futura erat qualis numquam antea fuerat? Neque enim antea nulla erat, sed talis non fuerat."

166. *trin.* 4,20,29.

words, the double dispensation is not to be taken as proof against the true divinity of the Holy Spirit. However, in saying this, it is worthwhile noting that although Augustine is principally concerned, negatively, with excluding any doubt about the *aequalitas personarum* of the *Trinitas quae unus Deus,* he reasons from the appearances of the Son and the Holy Spirit to their real distinction and even to their mutual relationship. Thus, he can conclude Book 4. The facts related by the Scriptures do not indicate the inferiority of the Son or of the Holy Spirit with respect to the Father, but are mentioned instead in order to bring home the fact that the Father is the origin of all (*propter principii commendationem*).[168] *Demonstratio per congruam significationem, dispensatio certe significationis fuit.*[169] How could Augustine express more clearly the idea that the temporal economy of the Trinity symbolises an eternal theology?

Moreover, Augustine continually drew upon the fundamental distinction between economy and theology in *De Trinitate,* as he did in other writings, especially in *Letter* 147, entitled *De uidendo Deo.* In harmony with the oldest tradition, he derives the distinction of the divine persons from the biblical theophanies. The Arian controversy, however, led him to insist more upon their unity and to exclude any possibility for beholding the divine substance of any person of the Trinity.[170]

His discussion of the biblical theophanies gave Augustine the opportunity to explain the appearances as missions. In this context, he stipulated that the Father was never sent[171] and that, consequently, he did not

---

167. *trin.* 4,21,32.

168. *trin.* 4,21 32. Hill translates too freely: "source and origin of the deity." But see *trin.* 4,20,29: "'Quem ego mittam uobis a Patre,' uidelicet ostendens quod totius diuinitatis uel si melius dicitur, deitatis, principium Pater est."

169. Concerning the expression dispensatio, See also *trin.* 2,15,25: where in respect to the theophanies on Mount Sinai it is said: "Ergo creatura seruienti creatori facta sunt illa omnia et humanis sensibus pro dispensatione congrua praesentata"; *trin.* 3,10,22.

170. See above all *trin.* 4,21,30. For this question see B. Studer, *Thephanie Exegese,* with the studies quoted there of G. Aeby, "Les missions divines de saint Justin a Origène," *Paradosis* 12, Fribourg 1958, and J.L. Maier, "Les missions divines selon saint Augustin," *Paradosis* 16, Fribourg 1960.

171. *trin.* 2,5,8; 2,7,12; 2,12,22; 3 pr.3. See A. Schindler, *Wort und Analogie,* 14.

proceed from anyone else.[172] He is therefore *Deus qui a nullo est*.[173] Moreover, Augustine demonstrates that the Son was sent only by the Father, and that he alone proceeds from him; he is *natus* of the Father.[174] According to the Scriptures, the Holy Spirit was sent both from the Father and the Son, and is therefore the Spirit of both.[175] In a word, the fact that the Father was not sent, that the Son was sent only from the Father, and that the Holy Spirit was sent from Father and Son demonstrates their eternal status.[176]

At the same time, it is noteworthy that the relationship between economy and theology appears much more clearly in Augustine's pneumatology than it does in his Christology. Since philosophers had expressed little interest in the Holy Spirit, Augustine felt the need to develop more clearly the scriptural doctrine on the Holy Spirit. In this respect, the biblical orientation of the last chapters of *De Trinitate* is quite characteristic.[177] It is remarkable, however, that Augustine not only reasons from the Holy Spirit's mission from both the Father and the Son, to the notion of the Spirit's procession from both; he also considers the nature of ecclesial communion from its beginning down to his own time, and reasons from the fact that ecclesial communion is possible only through the activity of the Holy Spirit, to the same Spirit's eternal status as *uinculum amoris,* as the bond between the Father and the Son.[178]

---

172. *trin.* 4,20,28: "Sed Pater eum ex tempore a quoquam cognoscitur, non dicitur missus: non enim habet de quo sit, aut ex eo procedat"; *trin.* 4,21,32: Propter principii commendationem. See A. Schindler, *Wort und Analogie,* 146.

173. See *trin.* 4,20,28: "Pater uero, a nullo." See also *trin.* 15,17,29, and even s. 140,2, and *Io.eu.tr.* 19,13.

174. See *trin.* 4,20,27: "Non quia ille maior est, ille minor: sed quia ille Pater, ille Filius; ille genitor, ille genitur; ille a quo est qui mittitur, ille qui est ab eo qui mittit. Filius enim a Patre est, non Pater a Filio"; 4,20,28.

175. See *trin.* 2,3,5 (first approach); 4,20,29; 15,17,29.

176. It is also very interesting to not how Augustine develops the Johannine topic of glorification. See *trin.* 2,4,6, where he demonstrates that glorification does not mean inferiority neither of the Son nor of the Holy Spirit. However we cannot overlook that he does not regard directly the economic events, but rather the biblical texts which speak about the glorification of the Father, the Son and the Holy Spirit.

177. See B. Studer, "Zur Pneumatologie des Augustinus von Hippo (*De Trinitate* 15,17,27 - 27,50)," *Augustinianum* 35 (1995) 567-583.

178. See especially *trin.* 15,19,36f, and also s. 71,12,18. On this question see B. Studer, "Pneu-

D. Less Prominent Applications

Such a reasoned exposition is absent in Augustine's treatment of the Son, since the latter was much more the subject of general philosophical reflection. Augustine received the biblical and traditional notions of the Logos of God, and found confirmation for his thesis within Hellenistic theories of the Logos of the world.[179] For this reason, he was not concerned with the need to argue from the teaching of Jesus to his eternal condition as complete expression of the Father. Yet it is quite remarkable that Augustine, in the opening section of Book 2, derives from John 5,19 the conclusion that the Son's being with the Father consists in nothing else than in his seeing the Father.[180] The date of this text is somewhat disputed by scholars. Some would compare it favorably with Augustine's Treatises 18 and 23 on the Gospel of John, which according to M.F. Berrouard were preached in 414; others date it later, together with Treatises 20 to 22 and with the *Contra sermonem Arianorum,* after 418.[181] It is not necessary to enter into this chronological dispute. However, I would make two observations. Augustine's interest in John 5,19 is connected with his concerns over the Arian controversy, as is clear from the context of his treatments of the text,[182] and especially from a long discussion of the same text by Ambrose.[183] Secondly, and more importantly, we have to take into account the Neoplatonic background of the expression *uidere Patrem, hoc illi esse Filium.*[184] The *uisio,* in fact, presupposes a

matologie," *Augustinianum* 35 (1995) 579f, and particularly J. Verhees, "Heiliger Geist und Gemeinschaft bei Augustin von Hippo," *REAug* 23 (1977) 245-264. This aspect of the ecclesial experience of the Trinity is lacking in the commentary of E. Hill, *The Trinity.*

179. See A. Schindler, *Wort und Analogie,* 75-118, with indications on the origin of the distinction between exterior and interior word.

180. Regarding this augustinian exegesis in *trin.* 2,1,3, see E. TeSelle, *Augustine the Theologian,* 298f, who also quotes *Io.eu.tr.* 18,10: "Ergo et audit Filius, et uidet Filius, et ipsa uisio et auditio Filius, et hoc est illi audire quod esse, et hoc est illi uidere quod esse," and s. 126,11,15.

181. See BA 72,755f.40. E. TeSelle, *Augustine,* 298, admits a later date.

182. It is question of the *aequalitas* of the Father and of the Son, as well as of the *operatio inseparabilis.* See similar discussions in *Io.eu.tr.* 20,3; *operatio inseparabilis; Io.eu.tr.* 23,15, 22,14: distinction of *uisio filii Dei* and the *uisio filii hominis,* and *Io.eu.tr.* 20,8: *generatio aeterna.*

183. See Ambrosius, *De fide,* 4,4,38-7,76.

conuersio. Augustine is quite explicit about this point in Treatise 21 on the Gospel of John, where he discusses the same text.[185] In any event, he clearly is not reasoning either from the continuous obedience of Jesus to his eternal being, seeing and hearing; or from any temporal demonstration of the Son by the Father to an eternal demonstration. Rather, he is much too concerned to emphasise that everything which is said is substantially said about the Son. While, therefore, he does not attend to the fact that, in the Johannine text, *esse de* or *natum esse* are used properly with reference to the Son, he does not consider the connection between the seeing and hearing of Jesus and the eternal *uisio* and *auditio* of the Son. At least the Johannine texts led him to limit also the hearing to the Son of man.[186] However, we ought not overlook the fact that Augustine rests his position on the sayings of Jesus himself, on authentic interpretations of what Jesus accomplished during his earthly life. Although he regards the biblical texts with a Neoplatonic and above all anti-Arian "Vorverständnis," he clearly admits that Jesus fulfilled what he had said. With this advance, Augustine could then interpret the whole attitude of Jesus as a manifestation of his eternal filiation.

In respect to the Son, the Bible suggested to Augustine another possibility for referring the economy to theology. Here, perhaps, he is not as

---

184. *trin.* 2,1,3: "Non enim aliud illi est esse de Patre, id est nasci de Patre, quam uidere Patrem, aut aliud uidere operantem quam pariter operari." See also *Io.eu.tr.* 21,4: "Sic ergo demonstrat Pater rem quam facit Filio ut in Patre uideat omnia Filius et in Patre sit omnia Filius. Uidendo enim natus est et nascendo uidet. Sed non aliquando non erat natus et postea natus est, sicut non aliquando non uidit et postea uidit, sed in eo quod est illi uidere, in eo est illi esse, in eo est illi natum esse, in eo est illi permanere..."

185. *Io.eu.tr.* 21,4: "Sumus tamen uel non uidentes et, ut uideamus, conuertimus nos ad eum quem uideamus et fit in nobis uisio quae non erat quando nos tamen eramus." Obviously, Augustine applies the topic of *conuersio - uisio* to men and not to the Son of God. See BA 72,274[31.] He insists then on the distinction between *esse* and *uidere,* but he does not exclude the *conuersio* from the Son. For the neoplatonic background, see BA 72,756, where Berrouard refers to P. Hadot, *Porphyre et Victorinus I* (Paris 1968) 320f.

186. See *Io.eu.tr.* 23,15; for the contrary *Io.eu.tr.* 22,14: "Audit Christus a Patre. Quomodo illi dicit Pater?... Quomodo Pater Filio dicit quando Filius Uerbum Patri est?... Unus est Deus, unum Uerbum habet, in uno Uerbo omnia continet. Quid est ergo: Sicut audio, ita iudico? Sicut de Patre sum, ita iudico." See also *Io.eu.tr.* 23,11ff. where Augustine on the one hand affirms: "Sic autem demonstratio Patris Filii gignit, quemadmodum Pater Filium gignit," and on the other hand speaks of the temporal demonstration, directed to the Son made man in the time, it is on the demonstration of the resurrection of the bodies.

explicit. But looking at the soteriological expositions in Books 4, 12 and 13 of *De Trinitate*, we discover the important theme of Jesus' justice.[187] For Augustine, in fact, our savior was the only righteous human being in history. He alone fulfilled completely the will of the Father. He was not overcome even by death. In our place and for our sake, he endured a suffering which culminated in the cruellest possible end. But he could do so only "in virtue of his being compounded into one being with the Word of God."[188] Clearly, Augustine did not formulate the later doctrine of the hypostatic union. But he was not far from saying that the total obedience of Jesus demonstrated that he was always the Son of God.[189]

Finally, it should be acknowledged that Augustine made much of the biblical and even of the philosophical idea of mediator. But it is not so easy to derive from this concept the conclusion that the trinitarian economy reveals a trinitarian theology. The idea of mediation, in fact is too abstract. It expresses a higher reflection on the *res gestae* narrated by the Gospel. If one considers, however, the concrete facts of the life of Jesus, that he preached, that he fulfilled the will of the Father, that he communicated the Holy Spirit, one can indeed reason in Augustinian terms from the economy to theology. In any event, the mediation of Christ consisted primarily in the revelation of the love of God[190] and in a freely accepted death.[191] In both cases, Christ appeared as what he is, the eternal Son of God: the Son who alone knows the Father,[192] and the Son who alone perfectly accomplishes the will of God.[193]

---

187. B. Studer, "Le Christ notre justice selon s. Augustin," *RchAug* 15 (1980) 90-143, resumed in B. Studer, *Trinity and Incarnation,* 180ff.

188. *trin.* 4,13,16.

189. See *trin.* 13,14,18, see also *tr.eu.Io.* 82,4, and *correpl.* 11,30.

190. See B., Studer, *Soteriologie,* 162ff.

191. See B., Studer, *Soteriologie,* 168f.

192. See *trin.* 1,8,16: "Sed quia omnes iustos, in quibus nunc regnat ex fide uiuentibus mediator Dei et hominum homo Christus Iesus, perducturus est ad speciem... Sic enim dicti: Omnia mihi tradita sunt a Patre meo: et nemo nouit Filium, nisi Pater; et nemo nouit Patrem nisi Filius, et cui uoluerit Filius reuelare." See further *trin.* 7,3,4.

193. See *trin.* 13,14,18. On this question see B. Studer, *Le Christ, notre justice, selon saint Augustin,* 307-321.

Final Reflections

Theologians today are clearly confronted with questions other than those of the Christian writers of the fourth and fifth centuries. They want to know how the biblical tradition became an ecclesial one. They then ask the question whether the trinitarian doctrine of the Church really corresponds to the message of the Apostles and above all of Jesus himself. They perhaps call into question even the assumption that we can find an immanent Trinity in the Bible. In any case, there are some who discuss the question how the economy manifests the theology. Above all, several authors doubt that a theory on the unique nature of God and the divine persons can be said to be of soteriological interest.[194]

The vast distance between Augustine's theological orientation and our own soteriological and spiritual preoccupations appears clearly in the Christological interpolations in Book 4 and Book 13. Augustine intimates it at the end of Book 14. After quoting passages from the Hortensius in which Cicero recommends contemplative wisdom, he concludes: "But this course, which is set in the love of an inquiry into truth, is not enough for unhappy men, that is for all mortals who have this reason alone without any faith in the mediator. This point I have tried to demonstrate as best I could in the previous books, especially in the fourth and thirteenth."[195] At the conclusion of Book 13 he expresses even more clearly what he intended in his Christological arguments. Concerning faith in Christ, "who rose in the flesh from the dead to die no more," he said, "I have discussed for some time in this (thirteenth) book as best I could, although I had already said much on the subject in the fourth book of this work. But there it was for a different reason than from here: there it was to show why and how Christ was sent in the fullness of time by the Father, because of those people who say that the one who did the sending and the one who was sent cannot be equal in nature; here it has been to distinguish between active knowledge and contemplative wisdom."[196] In

---

194. See on this problematic B. Studer, *Teologia trinitaria,* 171-174.

195. *trin.* 14,19,26.

196. *trin.* 13,20,25.

other words, Augustine's Christological intent in *De Trinitate* was double: an anti-Arian one and an anti-philosophical one. Discussing the resurrection of Christ, the sole mediator between God and men, he wanted to demonstrate that the Son who was sent by the Father is not lesser than the Father, and that one cannot arrive at true contemplative wisdom without faith and hope in the resurrection.[197] Even Augustine's avowed, primary intention in *De Trinitate,* the *exercitatio mentis,* is not identical with our soteriological investigation. We are not engaged in the search for a deeper understanding of our baptismal faith in order to become more similar to God and to arrive, then, at a beatifying vision in eternal life; we intend, rather, to demonstrate that the history of salvation, nay our own existence, is rooted in the communion of the Father, the Son and the Holy Spirit.[198]

Augustine can, nevertheless, help us to penetrate and realise the mystery of the Holy Trinity in itself and for our sake. That means first, that in terms of trinitarian theology, the study of Augustine's long and complicated exposition on the trinitarian faith of the Church could be more profitable in itself than the study of the history of early Christian doctrines in this connection. He enables us to value more exactly the importance of the *regula fidei.* In fact, he presents it as a summary of the Scriptures to which we must adhere in any inquiry about the deeper meaning of our trinitarian faith.[199] He shows, in particular, that faithfulness to the baptismal faith is motivated by the authority of the Bible as far it concerns the living heritage of the Church, an authority behind which stands the authority of Christ.[200] Moreover, it is noteworthy that Augustine criticises openly the formulas of faith. He recognises the need to define with technical terms the distinction between the Father, the Son and the Holy Spirit, but he admits that he is not altogether content with the expression *persona,* which, he believes, does not express their relationship well. He

---

197. See *trin.* 13,9,12-10,13; 13,16,21. See F. Courth, *Trinität,* 195ff, on the theological orientation of *De Trinitate.*

198. See B.J. Hilberath, Der *dreieinige Gott und die Gemeinschaft der Menschen,* Mainz 1990.

199. See *doctr.chr.* 3,2,2: "...consultat regulam fidei, quam de scripturarum planitoribus locis et ecclesiae auctoritate percepit"; *trin.* 15,28,51 and also s. 52,2,2: "... fides catholica.. testimonio lectionis collecta... apostolica ueritate fundata"; s. 51,4,8: biblical witnesses.

200. K.H. Lütcke, "auctoritas" *AugLex* 1 (994) 506ff.

is also sceptical about the Greek formula *mia ousia - treis hypostaseis* and the Latin equivalent *una substantia - tres personae,* because it is not appropriate to think of God in terms of substance. So he intimates that the dogmatic formulas are not sufficient, although we must always respect the tradition which forged them.[201] Above all, Augustine who was so interested in historical research and particularly in the historical impact of religious knowledge, shows us clearly that faith and deeper understanding are both founded on the historical experience, that is on the experience of the pascal mystery, either that of the apostolic community or of christians who were and continue to be faithful to the tradition of the apostles.

Though Augustine advanced trinitarian speculations much more than most other Christian thinkers, his principal contribution to the evolution of theology is to search elsewhere than in trinitarian speculations. His psychological explication of the baptismal faith certainly exerted a dominant influence on the western theology of Trinity.[202] His approach to a deeper understanding of the relationship between economy and theology is, however, a much more important contribution, even if less acknowledged. It is true that he demonstrates a tendency to separate *uerbum* and *res.* We must even acknowledge that he does not reflect much on the fundamental question of their relationship. But the method by which he explains the divine appearances, narrated by sacred history, and especially the biblical texts which indicate that the Holy Spirit was sent both by the Father and by the Son provide sufficient evidence that Augustine believed that the economy manifests in time the eternal existence of the Trinity. In this connection, let us recall, in particular, how, in view of the obedience of Jesus, Augustine circumscribes the generation of the Son as the eternal *uisio* and *auditio* of the Father.

Perhaps it is true that we moderns do not appreciate much the idea of the *purgatio fidei,* so dear to Augustine. However, his model of *exercitatio mentis* is without doubt a vital one for Christian theology. First of all it includes the faith as far as it is a kind of historical knowledge. In order

---

201. See B. Studer, *Trinity and Incarnation,* 243.

202. See F. Courth, *Trinität,* 209-216: on the premedival reception of the augustinian doctrine on Trinity.

to believe what we cannot see, the faithful have to submit themselves with confidence and humility to the divine authority which is present in time. It leads, therefore, to a spirituality which is anchored deeply in faith in Jesus Christ. How important it is for Augustine to nurture the faith in Jesus Christ, unique incarnated Son of God, follows from the long christological developments in books four, twelve and thirteen. In fact, although he supposes with the christian tradition that the whole Bible, even the books of the Old Testament, talks of the Father, the Son and the Holy Spirit, he is convinced that, strictly speaking, the Trinity was not revealed except by the pascal mystery. In any way, according to him, we can not live the faith in the *Trinitas quae unus Deus* without participating in the death and the resurrection of Christ. Whoever does not have any personal relation to Jesus will not be sincerly and deeply open to the eternal mystery of the Holy Trinity.

Moreover abandonment to the God who demonstrates his love in the humility of his Son is impossbile without prayer and a faithful life. Concerning prayer, Augustine wishes to teach us to address it in an authentically Christian manner to the Father, through the Son, in the Spirit. It is certainly true that he glosses the words of St. Paul: *"Regi autem saeculorum immortali soli deo"* (1 Tim 1,17) and *"Quem nemo hominum uidit nec uidere potest"* (1 Tim 6,16), as follows: *"quod de ipsa substantia summa summeque diuina et incommutabili ubi et pater et filius est spiritus sanctus unus et solus deus per sanam fidem intelligitur."*[203] Under the influence of the Nicene tradition, he opens his final prayer in *De Trinitate* with the words: *"Domine deus noster, credimus in te patrem et filium et spiritum sanctum"*[204] and concludes it with the invocation: *"Domine deus une, deus trinitas."*[205] In the *Confessions,* however, Augustine addresses his prayer to the Father. He invokes him as *Domine Deus meus* who acts through his Word and his Spirit.[206] This kind of prayer appears clearly in the liturgy.[207] In harmony with the ancient tradition, the bishop

---

203. *trin.* 2,17,32.

204. *trin.* 15,28,51.

205. *trin.* 15,28,51.

206. See B. Studer, *Gratia Christi - gratia Dei,* 143. Confer however *conf.* 13,12,13.

of Hippo directs the Eucharistic prayer to the Father.[208] In the same way, he often concludes his sermons. "*Conuersi ad Dominum Deum Patrem omnipotentem,*" begin this prayer.[209] Although it can hardly be said that he adheres to these liturgical customs in *De Trinitate,*[210] it is remarkable how, in this text, he reserves the name of God to the Father. He does not explicitly affirm that the Father is properly called God in the same way he explicitly affirms that the Son is properly called *sapientia* and that the Holy Spirit is properly called *amor.* But he does suggest it, saying, in fact, that the Father is *Deus qui a nullo est.*[211]

On the other hand, the act of believing in the Father, Son and Holy Spirit involves the whole of human existence, not least because this belief constitutes the indispensable condition of the *exercitatio mentis.* This is so, not only because the *exercitatio mentis* humbles everyone who searches for God. Since Christian faith comprehends, in the fullest sense of that word, charity and hope, the one who believes in the Holy Trinity is completely engaged in charity and hope. But this does not mean only that whoever loves, knows more deeply.[212] For Augustine, the *fides quae per dilectionem operatur* opens out to the entire ecclesial communion, prepares the faithful for a communal experience of the presence of the Holy Spirit. In like terms, to believe always signifies hope. One who believes in the Father, Son and Holy Spirit hopes to see them face to face in eternity. When Augustine repeats the famous passage of

---

207. See B. Studer, *Gratia Christi - gratia Dei,* 262ff, with the reference to M. Klöckener, "Das eucharistische Hochgebet bei Augustinus," *Festschrift C.P. Mayer* (Würzburg 1989) 461-495.

208. See s. 227.

209. See s. 272; 67,10; 183,15 etc.

210. Therefore one can understand that E. Hill, *De Trinitate,* does not deal with the liturgical aspects of Augustine's trinitarian theology, even if that can be regarded as a serious omission. See 19 and 39.

211. See B. Studer, *Gratia Christi - gratia Dei,* 283f, with *trin.* 5,11,12; B. Studer, *Teologia trinitaria,* 167-171. It also interesting that Augustine, in *trin.* 1,6,13, interprets some pneumatological texts of the Bible in the sense of *latreia* due to the Holy Spiriti and concludes from that to his true divinity. As Basil of Cesarea and other Fathers he applies the principle of *lex orandi - lex credendi* to the pneumatology, it is, strictly addressing the relationship between economy and theology.

212. See the exposition on the love of Paul, the righteous man in *trin.* 8,9,13.

the Letter to the Philippians: "... one thing, though, forgetting what lies behind, stretching out to what lies ahead I press intently to the crown of our upward calling from God in Jesus Christ," he locates perfection in this life in the stretching out intently to what lies ahead.[213] This continuous 'intention' consists, however, not only in the knowledge of God, but in the whole of human existence. It is not for nothing that Augustine insists on the faith in the resurrection.[214] He even refers the passage of the First Letter of John: "We know that when he appears we shall be like him, because we shall see him as he is" (1 Jn 3,2) to the immortality of body. "In this respect too," he says, "we will be like God, but only like the Son, who alone in the triad took a body in which he died and rose again, carrying it up to the heavenly regions."[215]

Surely, we do not find such an explicit linkage as this between the manifestation of the eternal Trinity and the paschal mystery, except, perhaps, when Augustine discusses Christ as the only righteous human being, or when he treats his doctrine on the *Filioque*. Presenting however the death and the resurrection of the incarnate Word as the highest motive for our hope and confidence in the love of God,[216] Augustine shows us a way to love of the Trinity. We do not know the Trinity, but we can nevertheless love it by believeing (*credendo diligere*).[217] "In order that faith might work through love," he says, "the charity of God has been poured into our hearts through the Holy Spirit which has been given to us (Rom 5,5). And he was given to us when Jesus was glorified in his resurrection."[218] It is in the paschal mystery, then, that the communion

---

213. See *trin.* 9,1,1, where this pauline quotation introduces the research on the *trinitas quae deus est*. See further *trin.* 1,5,8.

214. See *trin.* 2,17,29; 14,18,24. It is above all noteworty that Augustine, in *trin.* 4., sees the principal motif of the mission of the Son in his death and his resurrection, *sacramentum et exemplum* of our resurrection. See E. Hill, *The Trinity*, 147f, with *trin.* 4,5 (= 4,19,25.

215. *trin.* 14,18,24.

216. See *trin.* 13,10,13: "Quid enim tam necessarium fuit ad erigendam spem nostram... quam ut demonstraretur nobis quanti nos penderet Deus quantumque diligeret? Quid uero huius rei tanto isto indicio manifestius atque praeclarius, quam ut Dei Filius.... nostrae dignatus inire consortium, prius sine ullo malo suo merito mala nostra perferret...?"

217. See *trin.* 8,5,8.

218. *trin.* 13,10,14.

of love was founded in which we participate in the love of the Father who loves the Son in the Holy Spirit.

Conclusions

Firstly: the *fides qua*. Augustine is greatly interested in religious knowledge. Again and again he returns to the attitude of faith, to the faith we can see in our heart, to faith in a subjective sense, to *fides qua credimus*. Now, the faith by which we believe and assent to things we cannot see, is a kind of historical knowledge. It includes, therefore, historical elements. In fact, before we believe, we think about themes of our faith. We have to be sure about the authority in whom we put our trust. For that reason we remember the prophecies and their fulfillment. We rely on the historical narrations of the Bible and on the testimonies about Jesus and his Church. In the act of faith itself we assent to truths which were formulated by the Holy Scriptures and by the common ecclesiastical tradition. Even in our effort at a deeper understanding of what we believe we proceed historically. We try to prove the value of christian doctrine with standard biblical texts and we follow the *tractatores catholici* who gave a solid interpretation of the Holy Scriptures, perhaps even with the help of philosophical reasonings. Above all the whole complex of the *fides qua* is not only an intellectual phenomenon. It is rather an existential reality. We experience our faith in prayer and in life, together with all the christians of the past and of the present. It is that very experience which allows us eventually to pass from pure historical faith to spiritual faith, from *credere Ecclesiae* to *credere in Trinitatem quae est unus Deus*. We investigate the mysteries of faith and narrate them through a life of faith.

Secondly: the *fides quae*. It is obvious that the attitude of faith is not to be separated from what we have to believe. Confident in the divine authority still present in the Church, Christians accept the mysteries of Jesus. Together with all the faithful, they embrace the *res gestae* narrated by the *historia sacra*. As far as the things they believe concern the Father, the Son and the Holy Spirit, Christians do nothing but say yes to the baptismal creed which constitutes a summary of what the Bible tells us. In more concrete terms: they assert that the Father sent the Son and that the Father and the Son together sent the Holy Spirit. The Christians are also convinced that only the Son became man to be obedient until death and to be glorified by the Father. Finally they believe that the Spirit of the risen Christ is the source of life amid the people of God. But that is not all. According to Augustine the narration of the trinitarian action in time has a deeper sense. The temporal economy of salvation symbolizes the eternal reality of the Holy Trinity. Although he did not reflect much on that fact, he always expresses his conviction that the *dispensatio salutis* is a congruent expression of what the Father, the Son and the Holy Spirit have been since eternity. That is, the Father is the origin; the Son is both expression of the Father and conversion to the Father; the Holy Spirit is the bond of the Father and of the Son. In one word: in the last analysis, the Augustinian doctrine on the Trinity, as well as the faith of all Christians, is based on how the apostolic community and Augustine himself experienced the pascal mystery.

Revue des Études Augustiniennes, 43 (1997), 3-13

Radix catholica

In 1993, I published an article in *Vigiliae Christianae* entitled : "The Significance of the Lists of Roman Bishops in the anti-Donatist Polemic"[1]. In it I argued that the ecclesiological viewpoint of Cyprian was still predominant in the work of Optatus of Milevis and, to a lesser extent, even in Augustine. The continuity of thought among these authors is clear in a variety of ways. In this article, I have chosen to explore in more detail one aspect of vocabulary which is indicative of this unity of thought. *Caput* and *princeps*, for example, may at first sight strike the reader as connoting headship. And a first impression such as this is strengthened when a statement in which these words occur is taken out of context.

So, in Cyprian, *ep.* 59.14, the Christian community of Rome for which certain African dissidents have set sail, is referred to as the "cathedra Petri" and the "ecclesia principalis unde unitas sacerdotalis exorta est"[2]. In the article mentioned above, I suggested that the expression "ecclesia principalis" should be understood in the context of Cyprian's symbolic explanation of the *cathedra Petri*. The adjective "principalis" here pertains to the prestigious, apostolic origins of the Roman church rather than some jurisdictional superiority.

A related example may be found in *ep.* 48 where Cyprian assures Cornelius of Rome of his support. He instructed Carthaginian Christians travelling to Rome to seek out the community led by Cornelius and not that of Novatian, "ut ecclesiae catholicae radicem et matricem agnoscerent ac tenerent"[3]. Many, including Charles Pietri[4], have argued that Cyprian regarded Rome as the

---

1. Robert B. ENO, «The Significance of the Lists of Roman Bishops in the anti-Donatist Polemic», *Vigiliae Christianae*, 47 (1993) 158-169. I also wish to thank Allan Fitzgerald, O.S.A. of Villanova University for supplying me with material from the Augustine data bank.

2. Cyprian, *Ep.* 59.14 BAYARD p. 183. The monograph of U. Wickert comments on this text : *Sacramentum unitatis. Ein Beitrag zum Verstandnis der Kirche bei Cyprian*, Berlin, de Gruyter, 1971.

3. Cyprian, *Ep.* 48.3 (*CCSL* IIIB. 229).

4. Charles PIETRI, *Roma Christiana*, Vol. 1, p. 306 (BEFR 224), Paris, de Boccard, 1976.

"matrix et radix". I maintain that philology and the context of letter 48 show rather that the meaning is the following : that Cornelius and Cornelius alone is the "episcopus ecclesiae catholicae" in Rome and that therefore it is to Cornelius and his community that all Catholics should adhere when in Rome because his community is the Catholic Church in Rome. A study of these significant words will, I believe, contribute to an understanding of the North African ecclesiology. Hence this survey of the use of *caput*, *radix*, and *princeps* in the writings of Tertullian, Cyprian, Optatus and Augustine.

TERTULLIAN

Tertullian is, of course, the first important author of Latin North Africa, indeed of western Christendom in general. His vocabulary is of foundational significance for western theology, although in this instance, one may well claim that Cyprian's usage rather than Tertullian's set the ecclesiological agenda for the future.

One way Tertullian uses these "source words" is in the context of the origins of the human race. Each individual soul is "...velut surculus quidam ex matrice Adam in propaginem deducta...". The one nature which God conferred on Adam has become the "matrix omnium". Eve in turn is the "matrix generis feminini"[5].

Proceeding further in the sacred history, Tertullian calls the patriarchs the "originales personae" and the Jews of the Old Testament outstanding because of the justice and faith of their "originales auctores". Christ was the promise made to the tribe of Judah so that they might know that they should look for and find their "matrix religionis et fons" in Jerusalem[6]. Tertullian also used the word "matrix" in a Trinitarian context. The Spirit has gone forth from the matrix but has not been separated from it. The Father is the "caput" of the Son[7].

"Caput" can be used to indicate the essential elements of anything as in "caput fidei" or "caput legis"[8]. Frequently it indicates the source of a vice as in the *De idololatria*. Idolatry produces injustice and any art which produces idols itself becomes the "caput... idololatriae". Even more common here is the word "radix", as in 1 Tm 6.10 where "cupiditas" is the "radix omnium malorum". Conversely, to stop sinning is the "radix veniae"[9].

---

5. Tertullian, *De anima*, 19.6 (*CCSL* 2. 811) ; *De anima*, 20.6 (*CCSL* 2. 813) ; *De virginibus velandis* (*CCSL* 2. 1215).

6. Tertullian, *De monogamia*, 7.1 (*CCSL* 2. 1237) ; *Apologeticum*, 21.4 (*CCSL* 1. 123) ; *Adversus Marcionem*, IV.35.10 (*CCSL* 1. 641).

7. Tertullian, *Apologeticum*, 21.13 (*CCSL* 1. 125) ; *Adversus Praxean*, 8.7 (*CCSL* 2. 1168) ; 14.10 (*CCSL* 2. 1178).

8. Tertullian, *Adversus Marcionem*, IV.2.2 (*CCSL* 1. 547) ; IV.25.15 (*CCSL* 1. 614).

9. Tertullian, *De idololatria*, 2.5 (*CCSL* 2. 1102) ; 3.2 (*CCSL* 2. 1103), *De pudicitia*, 10.14 (*CCSL* 2. 1301).

"Principalis" is the adjectival form of the word "princeps". It and related forms of "princeps" frequently refer to the temporal or logical priority of some fact or concept. So, for example, idolatry is the "principale crimen" of the human race[10]. Tertullian's great argument against heresy revolved around the temporal priority of truth. And so in the *De praescriptione haereticorum* 31. 1, he contrasted the "principalitas veritatis" with the "posteritas mendacitatis". A little later in the same work, he repeated the point : "posterior nostra res non est, immo omnibus prior est. Hoc erit testimonium veritatis ubique, occupantis principatum"[11].

As with "caput", "princeps" is used by Tertullian to describe Adam, the "princeps et generis et delicti". Satan is also and, more fundamentally, the "princeps transgressionis". God's plan for monogamy derives from the order of creation "determined from the beginning" ("de principali regula"). Ecclesiologically the most important statement of Tertullian using these words is to be found in the *De praescriptione haereticorum* 21. 4 where the apostolic churches are termed the "matrices et originales fidei"[12]. So, even as Tertullian's words are inevitably significant for Latin theology, it is rather to Cyprian that we must turn to look for the usage of these "source-words" that is more important for the theology of the Church.

CYPRIAN

The scope of Cyprian's writings is considerably narrower than that of Tertullian. Tertullian confronted all challengers ; Cyprian was a bishop concerned especially for the unity of the Church. His usage of this vocabulary is accordingly more ecclesiological in aim than Tertullian's. But he has other uses also. He sometimes joins together concepts which convey the same meaning. So, for example, in order to understand jealousy and envy more fully, he says that one must go to their source and origin (*caput atque origo*). He also speaks of the source of virtue or the source of the rival faction of Felicissimus. Abraham by believing was the first to establish the "radix ac fundamentum fidei". In responding to the pagan critic Demetrianus, Cyprian noted that he was

10. Tertullian, *De idolatria*, 1.1 (*CCSL* 2. 1101).

11. Tertullian, *De praescriptione haereticorum*, 31.1 (*CCSL* 1. 212) ; 35.3 (*CCSL* 1. 216). In the 1954 supplemental volume of Pauly-Wissowa, L.Wickert gives some classical examples of the chronological sense of "princeps", col. 2011.

12. Tertullian, *Exhortatio castitatis*, 2.5 (*CCSL* 2. 1017). See also : *De anima*, 20.6 (*CCSL* 2. 813) ; *De paenitentia*, 2.3 (*CCSL* 1. 322) ; *De virginibus velandis*, 11.2 (*CCSL* 2. 1220) where Eve is included. "Princeps transgressionis", *Adversus Marcionem*, V.6.6 (*CCSL* 1. 679) and *Apologeticum*, 22.2 (*CCSL* 1. 128) ; *De monogamia*, 2.4 (*CCSL* 2. 1230) ; *De praescriptione haereticorum*, 21.4 (*CCSL* 1. 202).

also answering those whom Demetrianus was stirring up against the Christians, i.e. "comites... plures radicis atque originis tuae pullulatione fecisti"[13].

For the present context, the ecclesiological use of these words is of more significance. First, there is tradition. Human error is ended when we return to the "caput et origo" of divine tradition. "We must go back to the Lord as our source and to the tradition of the gospels and the apostles". He exhorted his fellow bishops to return to the "fundamental and original doctrine" of the Lord. (*radix atque origo traditionis dominicae*)[14].

In the fifth chapter of the *De unitate ecclesiae,* Cyprian developed some elaborate comparisons to illustrate the one and the many in the Church, with the emphasis on unity. While the rays of the sun are many, the light is one ; while a tree has many branches, it has one strength from its roots. There are many streams but they derive from one spring. So there are many churches but "unitas servatur in origine". Later in the same chapter, he draws out the comparison further. "She spreads her branches in generous growth over all the earth ; she extends her abundant streams ever further; yet one is the head spring (*caput*), one the source (*origo*), one the mother...". In this same sense of origins, then, and taking into account Cyprian's *cathedra Petri* symbolism, Bevenot has translated the words "ecclesia principalis" of *ep.* 59.14 as "the primordial church"[15].

For Cyprian, the Church is itself the root and the mother. Plumpe many years ago explored the *mater ecclesia* motif[16]. The important text of *ep.* 48.3.1 has already been mentioned in the introduction. The Carthaginian dissidents, acting with perverse obstinacy, Cyprian insisted, had rejected the embrace of their mother and had "cut themselves off from their source of life" (*radix et mater*). Catholics, on the contrary, i.e. Cyprian and those loyal to him, had held to the "ecclesiae unius caput et radicem". Finally in the *Ad Fortunatum,* Cyprian found the foreshadowing of the Church in the mother of the Macchabees : "With the seven children is clearly joined the mother also, their origin and root (*origo et radix*) who later bore seven churches, herself the first and only one founded by the Lord's voice upon a rock[17].

13. Cyprian, *De zelo et livore,* 3 (*CCSL* IIIA. 76) ; *De bono patientiae,* 3 (*CCSL* IIIA. 119) ; *Ep.,* 43.2.1 (*CCSL* IIIB. 201) ; *De bono patientiae,* 10 (*CCSL* IIIA. 123) ; *Ad Demetrianum,* 2 (*CCSL* IIIA. 36).

14. Cyprian, *Ep.* 74.10.2-3 BAYARD p. 287 ; *Ep.* 63.1.1 BAYARD p. 200.

15. Cyprian, *De unitate ecclesiae* (*CCSL* III. 253). Bevenot's translation : Cyprian, Oxford Early Christian Texts p. 118 (Oxford : Clarendon Press, 1971).

16. Joseph PLUMPE, *Mater Ecclesia. An Inquiry into the Concept of the Church as Mother in Early Christianity* (Washington : Catholic University of America Press, 1943), pp. 81-108.

17. Cyprian, *Ep.* 45.1.2 (*CCSL* IIIB. 216) ; *Ep.* 73.2.2 BAYARD p. 263 ; *Ad Fortunatum,* 11 (*CCSL* III. 205-206).

OPTATUS OF MILEVIS

It is my contention that the work of Optatus, the only significant Catholic anti-Donatist polemic before Augustine, remains very much in the line of Cyprian. As I have argued elsewhere, the ecclesiological problems faced by Optatus had moved well beyond the scope of schism within the local church against which Cyprian fought[18]. The Donatist schism was a region-wide split. Yet, despite this, Optatus' words still resound with Cyprianic meanings.

Optatus' use of the various forms of "princeps" almost always refer to the Donatist founder, Donatus himself and his immediate associates. "Principes vestri" occurs many times and it can be argued, refers not just to those who were chronologically prior and the historical founders but also those who were the sources of the calamity. Donatus was the "fons malarum causarum[19]". Peter, on the other hand, is "princeps noster", the Catholic source. The term "caput" is much less prominent in Optatus but Peter is referred to as the "omnium apostolorum caput" in a passage which also mentions the "cathedra Petri" in its Cyprianic symbolic sense, "... in qua una cathedra unitas ab omnibus servaretur...[20]"

As with Cyprian *radix* is also a very significant term for Optatus' ecclesiology. His task, he asserts, is to demonstrate from what root and from what source (*fons*) came the branches and the streams of the Donatist error. Speaking of the small Donatist community in Rome, he portrayed it as a "branch of your error", having come forth from a lie, "not from the root of truth". Elsewhere he described the Donatist faith as the tattered rags that hang from the one garment and the divided branches from the one root[21]. This last comparison might bring the reader to ask if these rags or branches were still hanging on to the original by a thread, i.e. that they were not yet totally severed.

In any event, it is clearly the Catholics who remain attached to the root. Optatus' writings will show who it is that have remained "... in radice cum toto orbe". While dissidents have deserted their Catholic mother and have been cut off from the root of mother Church, Catholics have remained in the root and are one with all throughout the world. Catholics who have never left are those who live within[22].

18. Robert B. ENO, «The Work of Optatus as a Turning Point in the African Ecclesiology», *The Thomist*, 37, 1973, pp. 668-685.

19. Optatus, *Contra Parmenianum*, I.10.5 (*SC* 412. 194) ; I.13.3 (*SC* 412. 200) ; I.14.1 (*SC* 412. 202) ; I.15.1 (*SC* 412. 204) ; III.3.1 (*SC* 413. 20) ; VI.3.3 (*SC* 412. 170) ; VII.1.45 (*SC* 412. 216) ; VII.2.1 (*SC* 412. 216) ; "fons" : III.3.25 (*SC* 412. 36).

20. Optatus, II.4.6 (*SC* 412. 250) ; II.2.2 (*SC* 412. 244). Cf. also VII.3 (*SC* 413. 220 ff.).

21. Optatus, I.15.1 (*SC* 412. 204) ; II.4.1 (*SC* 412. 246) ; III.9.2 (*SC* 413. 62).

22. Optatus, I.15.3 (*SC* 412. 206) ; I,11.1 (*SC* 412. 196) ; I.28.3 (*SC* 412. 234) ; III.7.4 (*SC* 413. 52).

AUGUSTINE

The writings of Augustine far outweigh in number those of the three previous North African authors. Yet I believe that his use of the words in question is similar to theirs. First, "princeps" and cognate forms. Such words are sometimes used to indicate beginnings in a general way (e.g. "principia"). For example, Augustine explained in the *Retractationes* that in his attacks against the fundamental letter of Mani, he had discussed only the beginnings of that work. Of his own early writings on the liberal arts, only the beginnings remain. He speaks of the beginnings of Genesis or of the opening lines of the letter to the Romans. For Epicurus, atoms are the "principia rerum". The same word finds some employment in his discussion of the Trinity. There cannot be two independent principia in God. But in some sense the Son is a principium as well as the Father[23].

A more important usage of *Princeps* for Augustine is found when he wishes to speak of some thing or person who is variously the cause, prototype or exemplar of something or someone who comes after. So, Zeno is the "princeps" of the Stoics. Within the Christian realm, Christ himself is our "princeps" in many senses. He is the *princeps martyrum* ; *princeps pastorum* ; *princeps fidei*, the *caput et princeps apostolorum* ; *princeps principum.* Mary is the *virginum princeps*[24].

Satan, on the other hand, is the "princeps peccatorum". He is the "princeps rexque vitiorum" as well as the "princeps omnium fallaciarum et errorum" and the "princeps iniuriarum et iniquitatum omnium". Subordinate in evil but principes in a lesser sense are heretics. Donatus who was "principalis vester" is also the "princeps totius mali". In the Acts of the Conference of Carthage of June, 411, Petilian owned Donatus as his *princeps.* Augustine later accused Julian of Eclanum of having Pelagius and Celestius as his *principes.* As Adam is the "princeps generationis", so Christ is the "princeps regenerationis"[25].

Augustine also made considerable use of *Caput.* Of course, it may mean the head of the physical body. In innumerable instances, especially in the

---

23. Augustine, *Retractationes* II.2 (*CCSL* 57. 91) ; I.6 (*CCSL* 57. 17) ; *Sermo* 1.1 (*CCSL* 41. 3) ; *Ep. ad Rom. inchoata exp.*, 12 (*CSEL* 84. 160) ; *Ep.* 118.4.28 (*CSEL* 34/2. 692) ; *De civitate Dei*, VII.34 (*CCSL* 47. 214 citing Varro) ; *De Trinitate*, V.13 (*CCSL* 50. 220-221) ; *En in Ps.* 109.13 (*CCSL* 40. 1614) ; *Tr. in Jn.*, 39.2 (*CCSL* 36. 345) ; *De fide et symbolo*, 19 (*CSEL* 41. 23).

24. Augustine, *Contra Academicos*, 3.17.38 (*CCSL* 29. 58) ; *Contra ep. Parmeniani* I.14.21 (*BA* 28. 262) ; *S.* 284.2 (*PL* 38. 1289) ; *S.* 309.4 (*PL* 38. 1411) ; *De perfectione iustitiae hominis*, 19.41 (*BA* 21. 210) ; *Tr. in Jn.*, 89.1 (*CCSL* 36. 549) ; *S.* 335B.4 (*PLS* 2. 635) ; *S.* 188.4 (*PL* 38. 1004).

25. Augustine, *Contra Julianum op. imp.*, I.62 (*CSEL* 85/1. 58) ; *De peccatorum meritis et rem*, I.26.39 (*CSEL* 60. 37) ; *De continentia*, 5.13 (*CSEL* 41. 155) ; *Contra Cresconium*, I.11.14 (*BA* 31. 96) ; *Adnotationes in Job*, 35 (*CSEL* 28. 585) ; *S.* 28.5 (*CCSL* 41. 371) ; *Ep.* 43.5 (*CSEL* 34/2. 98) ; *Ps. contra partem Donati*, vs.100 (*BA* 28. 164) ; *Acta conlationis Carth.*, III.32 (*SC* 224. 1004) ; *Contra Jul. op. imp.*, II.187.215 (*CSEL* 85/1. 306 ; 325-326).

Enarrationes on the Psalms, he speaks of Christ as the head of the body, e.g. Christ the Head, the Church the Body. In *Enarr. in Ps.* 71.6, Adam is the "caput mortis nostrae" but Christ is the "caput salutis nostrae"[26].

Capita can also signify the first letters of words. So the first letters of the four winds or of the four corners of the world spell ADAM. In a similar way, he explains the meaning of ichthys. *Caput* can also refer to the beginning of a psalm. After seven days, one returns to the beginning of the week[27].

Caput is also found in Augustine in the meaning of a capital or a leading city. Rome is the "caput gentium" or the "quasi caput Babylonis". The disciples went to Rome so that their teaching could spread more easily to the whole world from the "caput" of the world. Carthage was the caput of Africa and Capernaum the caput of Galilee[28].

Of the use of *caput* in the sense of source, there are many examples. For Augustine, pride (*superbia*) is the root of other vices. It is the *radix* and *caput peccati*, the "caput omnium peccatorum", the "caput et origo omnium malorum", the "initium omnis peccati". The Devil is the "ad haec sacrilegia caput et auctor". As Christ is the "caput iustorum", Judas is the "caput peccatorum". In the polemic against Julian, Augustine said that Pelagius was Julian's "caput" and Julian himself the "caput horum calumniorum". Julian had earlier called Augustine the "caput horum et causa malorum"[29].

In a watery scenario, a fountain is a "caput aquae" and the four rivers of Paradise came forth from such a caput. This image took on ecclesiological ramifications in the closing lines of the letter sent by Augustine and his episcopal colleagues to Pope Innocent in 416 to ask for the condemnation of Pelagius. "We wish to be assured by you that this trickle (*rivulus*) of ours, however scant, flows from the same fountainhead as your abundant stream..." (*ex eodem capite fluentorum*)[30].

The most striking use of "caput" as well as of related terms is to be found in the anti-Donatist writings. Early in the *Contra litteras Petiliani* he cites a basic principle of his opponent : "omnis res enim origine et radice consistit, et si caput non habet aliquid, nihil est". Augustine added his own immediate commentary: "... cumque originem et radicem et caput baptizati hominem a quo baptizatur velit intelligi, quid prodest misero baptizato, quod ignorat quam

---

26. Augustine, *Ep.* 129.2 (*CSEL* 44. 35) ; *En. in Ps.* 71.6 (*CCSL* 39. 975).

27. Augustine, *Tr. in Jn.*, 9.14 (*CCSL* 36. 98) ; *En. in Ps.* 95.15 (*CCSL* 39. 1352) ; *De civitate Dei*, XVIII.23 (*CCSL* 48. 613) ; cf. *En. in Ps.* 30, en., 2, s. 1.11 (*CCSL* 38. 199) ; *En in Ps.* 80.22 (*CCSL* 39. 1135) ; *S.* 350A.3 (*PLS* 2. 451) ; *S.* 83 (*PL* 38. 518).

28. Augustine, *S.* 381 (*PL* 39. 1684) ; *S.* 24.6 (*CCSL* 41. 331) ; *En in Ps.* 86.8 (*CCSL* 39. 1205) ; *Ep.* 194.3.7 (*CSEL* 57. 266) ; *S.* 313C (*PLS* 2. 610) ; *De consensu evang.*, II.25 (*CSEL* 43. 161).

29. Augustine, *En. in Ps.* 35.18 (*CCSL* 38. 335) ; *Tr. in Jn.*, 25.16 (*CCSL* 36. 256) ; *De civitate Dei*, XIV.3 (*CCSL* 48. 417) ; *En. in Ps.* 139.13 (*CCSL* 40. 2020) ; *Contra Faustum*, XXII.93 (*CSEL* 25. 699) ; *De pecc. mer. et rem.*, I.15.19 (*CSEL* 60. 19) ; *Contra Jul. op. imp.*, II.104 (*CSEL* 85/1. 235-236).

30. Augustine, *De Gen. ad lit.*, V.7.21 (*BA* 48. 402) ; *Ep.* 177.19 (*CSEL* 44. 688).

ROBERT B. ENO

malus sit baptizator eius ?" Much of the rest of this work is taken up with discussion of this basic axiom enunciated by Petilian. The discussion is resumed in the *Contra Cresconium*. Cresconius the Donatist grammarian took up the cause of saving the honor of Petilian the Donatist champion when he was attacked by Augustine[31].

Petilian conceded that if, indeed, the apparently virtuous minister of baptism was in reality wicked, then it was Christ who passed on his righteousness to the neophyte. He made use of I Cor 3, 6. But, for Augustine, not even Paul or Apollos could qualify as the source of salvation for those being baptized. Petilian's response to the perennial dilemma posed by Augustine led the latter to quip that since it was preferable to have Christ as one's source and head rather than even the most holy and virtuous minister, then it behooved the baptizand to pray for a wicked minister of baptism so that Christ would be his *origo, radix* and *caput*. Of course, for Augustine, such reasoning was absurd.

For Augustine, Christ is always the sole "origo regeneratorum et caput ecclesiae". The Catholic answer to the Donatist question would always be : "origo mea Christus est ; radix mea Christus est ; caput meum Christus est". Catholics, unlike Donatists, never placed their hope in human beings but always in Christ "tamquam ad originem quae non mutatur, ad radicem quae non evellitur, ad caput, quod non deicitur[32]".

The same theme returns in the *Contra Cresconium*. Augustine cites Cyprian's text from the *De unitate* which we have discussed above concerning the many branches and the many streams but the one root and the one source. Augustine is sceptical of the competence of Cresconius as a Donatist theologian and apologist when the latter agrees with him that "Christus est origo christiani, in Christo radicem christianus infigat, Christus christiani sit caput". Returning to more traditional Donatist fare, Augustine rejects Cresconius' charge that his (Augustine's) "creator" and "caput" were *traditores*. His episcopal predecessors neither created him nor were they his "fons" or "caput"[33].

This Donatist line of argumentation resurfaced at the Conference of Carthage in June 411. On the third day when discussion of what Augustine considered the substantive issues had begun, Petilian asked him whether he was a "son of Caecilian" or not. Petilian had already claimed that Donatus was his "princeps". Augustine retorted with the Gospel exhortation to call no one on earth your father. But Petilian persisted and added that if Augustine had neither "origo" nor "pater", he must be a heretic. Augustine granted that Caecilian was a brother in the faith. Whether he was a good or a bad brother could be answered only by history, since he was also an older brother[34].

---

31. Augustine, *Contra litteras Petiliani*, I.4.5 (*BA* 30. 142).

32. Augustine, *Contra lit. Pet.*, I.5.6 (*BA* 30. 142) ; I.6.7 (*BA* 30. 144) ; I.7.8 (*BA* 30. 146) ; III.52.64 (*BA* 30. 720) ; I Cor. 3.6 : "I planted, Apollos watered but God caused the growth".

33. Augustine, *Contra Cresconium*, III.7.7 (*BA* 31. 280) ; III.37.41 (*BA* 31. 352).

34. *Acta Conl. Carth.*, III.221 (*SC* 224. 1162) ; III.32 (*SC* 224. 1004) ; III.222 (*SC* 224. 1162) ; III.229, 231 (*SC* 224. 1168, 1170) ; III.230, 233 (*SC* 224. 1170, 1172).

104

But Petilian would not give up and insisted : "Non enim potest aliqua res sine generatore suo nasci, aut sine capite incipere aut sine radice sua crescere". Going on, he demanded to know what bishop had ordained Augustine. In his earlier work, Petilian had attacked Augustine personally by reviving stories concerning the primate of Numidia, Megalius, who had hesitated to ordain Augustine to the episcopate on the strength of reports about his Manichaeism. Finally, Augustine claimed that the Donatists taught that children were affected by the sins of their parents. In an ironic reversal, Augustine, the great theologian of original sin, observed that children were affected by their parents' sins only by imitating them !35.

For Augustine, the meaning of root depends on the context and the context is frequently a discussion either of Jn 15, the vine and the branches in an ecclesiological setting, or of Rm 11.16ff, the Gentiles grafted on to the root of the Hebrew patriarchs and prophets. He elaborated on this theme in *Tr. in Jn.* 16.5 among other places.

The proud branches (The Jews of the time of Christ and since) have been broken off but the root of the patriarchs remains. At the root of this vine are Abraham, Isaac and Jacob. In the *Adv. Jud.* he adds the prophets as well. In the *Contra adversarium legis et prophetarum*, he mentions David as well as the root into which the wild olive tree is grafted. Even further back, Adam is the "radix vitiata" of the human race36.

As with *caput*, the use of *radix* in the anti-Donatist works is most significant from an ecclesiological viewpoint. Schism, for Augustine, is a sin against charity whereas heresy is a sin against faith. The Donatists were branches that had been severed from the root. In order to have life restored to them, unity must be re-established. They must return to live in the *radix*. In *ep.* 52.2 he noted in particular that the Donatists had been cut off "ab illa radice orientalium ecclesiarum". The Catholic Church (*radix catholica*) doggedly seeks reunion with the Donatists37.

Another of Augustine's themes was that while the Donatists had many things that Catholics had, they in fact had only the outward appearance, not the inner reality. "You have the form but I seek the root". The essence of the difference is that the Donatists in sinning against unity lack charity. But this is the only foundation of salvation : viz. "habere radicem caritatis". The outward form is useless without the root. Charity in the root means life. These points are made again and again in the anti-Donatist works. So, for example, in the earliest such work, Augustine wrote for his people : "Do you want to know who speaks the

---

35. *Acta Conl. Carth.*, III.236 (*SC* 224. 1174) ; III.243 (*SC* 224. 1180) ; On Megalius, see A. Mandouze ed., *PCBE* Afrique, pp. 741-742. Augustine, *Breviculus Collationis,* III.9.17 (*CCSL* 149A. 284).

36. Augustine, *Tr. in Jn.*, 16.5 (*CCSL* 36. 168) ; *Contra adversarium legis...*, 2 .2.6 (*CCSL* 49. 95) ; *Adversus Judaeos,* 6.7 (*PL* 42. 55) ; *En. in Ps.* 65.5 (*CCSL* 39. 843) ; *De civitate Dei* XIV.26 (*CCSL* 48. 450).

37. Augustine, *Ep.* 53.1 (*CSEL* 34/2. 195) ; *Ep.* 61.2 (*CSEL* 34/2. 224) ; *Ep.* 185.10,44 (*CSEL* 57. 38) ; *Ep.* 52.2 (*CSEL* 34/2. 150) ; *Ep.* 128.4 (*CSEL* 44. 33).

truth ? Those who have remained in the root". And : "Of what use is the outward appearance (*forma*) to them, if they do not live in the root"[38].

Finally, in the *Contra litteras Petiliani*, as we have already seen, *caput* and *radix* are often linked in both Petilian's formula and Augustine's counter-arguments. Donatists must be "restored to the Catholic root" in order to "bear the fruits of charity". If they return, they will not be rebaptized but, having been rejoined to the root of charity and unity, they will be restored to life[39].

CONCLUSION

In this brief survey of North African authors, I have emphasized that their use of words like "caput", "radix" and "princeps" can have a specialized meaning different from the obvious first meaning. In particular, my purpose has been to demonstrate that the words in question have the sense of origin or source as well as the meaning of power, authority or headship.

To this development, Tertullian contributes little. Here Cyprian is the foundational author with Optatus following largely in his footsteps. Did the theme of the root derive primarily from the imagery of the root and the branches in Jn 15 ? The role of Augustine is the most difficult to evaluate. Most of his ecclesiologically significant use of these words comes in the anti-Donatist works. But this is hardly a surprise. He is also the one who puts so much stress on Jn 15. Yet despite this, one also has the feeling that he is reacting to the Donatists, especially to Petilian when he makes use of such imagery and terminology. Perhaps here too the Donatists had captured the heritage of Cyprian to the degree that Augustine and the Catholics were forced into a defensive and reactive stance.

It becomes even more significant with the rise of Donatism and the questions of legitimacy which it inevitably raised. If we have a more adequate understanding and appreciation of their use of such words, we shall also begin to have a deeper knowledge of their thought on the Church.

* Robert B. ENO
Washington, D.C.

38. Augustine, *Tr. in Jn.*, 13.16 (*CCSL* 36. 139) ; *Tr.Ep.Jn.*, 2.9 (*PL* 35. 1994) ; *En. in Ps.* 36, s. 1.3 (*CCSL* 38. 340) ; *Ps. contra partem Don.*, vs.43 (*BA* 28. 156) ; vs. 235 (*BA* 28. 182).

39. Augustine, *Contra lit. Pet.* I.1.1 (*BA* 30. 132) ; *Contra Cresc.* IV.61.75 (*BA* 31. 624, 626) : "reviviscant".

* Robert E. ENO, sulpicien, professeur à "The Catholic University of America", Washington, né le 11 décembre 1936 est décédé subitement le 14 février 1997.

SUMMARY : The question of roots, sources and successions holds an important place in the North African ecclesiology. Certain expressions in Tertullian, Cyprian, Optatus of Milevis and Augustine, especially those involving *caput, radix, princeps* and a few related words should at times be understood as indicating the source out of which something comes rather than as words indicative of power and authority.

RÉSUMÉ : La question des racines, des sources et des successions tient une place importante dans l'ecclésiologie nord-africaine. Certaines expressions de Tertullien, de Cyprien, d'Optat de Milève et d'Augustin, particulièrement celles qui comportent *caput, radix, princeps* et quelques mots apparentés, doivent parfois être entendues comme indiquant la source d'une chose, plutôt que comme des mots signifiant pouvoir et autorité.

ORIGEN'S TWO RESURRECTIONS

THAT Origen maintained two resurrections is as certain as any deduction from his writings. Some would make both resurrections figurative,[1] denying that the body could be for Origen a subject of redemption; Crouzel, to whom we owe the most compendious refutations of this view, finds here the two climactic moments of New Testament theology—the partial resurrection of the soul, which begins in mortal life, and that of the body on the final day.[2] Following Crouzel, Charles Hill opines that before this date the souls of saints exist without bodies in an intermediate realm.[3]

I shall argue here that Origen envisages no end to corporeality, not even an intermission when the soul forsakes the corpse. I shall then set out the evidence that all traditions—Jewish, pagan, Gnostic, and orthodox Christian—would support him in the view that soul and body depart together for a paradisal region. This will both increase the plausibility of attributing such opinions to a third-century theologian and explain how he came to hold them, as the third part of this article will show.

I

Our primary text should be the *De Principiis*, which is not only one of Origen's earliest writings, but his only aspiration to a system. We find in two of its longest subdivisions an itinerary of salvation for the just. After the body's death, the saint remains on earth in a temporary paradise, where the fire of God begins to burn away the marks of sinfulness. As his peccant qualities disappear, he can ascend by gradual stages, first to the air, then to the heavens, then to a place beyond the heavens (ii.11.6), until the final state in which his blessedness is immutable and God is all in all (iii.6.3, 9, etc.). This is a state 'to which nothing can be added', and Origen's critics said that he denied it to the material part of man. Rufinus attributes to him a more subtle exposition:[4]

---

[1] See further my 'Origen no Gnostic, or on the Corporeality of Man', *JTS*, NS, 43 (1992), 23-37.

[2] See especially H. Crouzel, 'La "première" et la "seconde" résurrection des hommes selon Origène', *Didaskalia* 3 (1973), 3-19.

[3] C. Hill, *Regnum Caelorum* (Oxford, 1992), 127-43, emphasizing the absence of a body at p. 135.

[4] On the characteristics of Rufinus' rendering, see now N. Pace, *Richerche sulla traduzione di Rufino del 'De Principiis' di Origene* (Florence, 1989). Pace finds that Rufinus inclines to paraphrase where the philosophy is intricate, and to eliminate distinctions between simpler readers and the more proficient. Rufinus' allegation of corrupt and interpolated passages (*De Princ.* Proem 3) cannot now be verified, but should not be ruled impossible a priori.

© Oxford University Press 1995

[Journal of Theological Studies, NS, Vol. 46, Pt. 2, October 1995]

Regarding the body's condition...we should think that, as it were minis-tering to the spirit, it progresses to the spiritual condition and quality, particularly seeing that, as we have frequently demonstrated, the corporeal nature has been made by the creator such as easily to assume whatever quality he may desire or the case demand. (iii.6.7)

This doctrine is not the creation of Rufinus, although Jerome quotes as Origen's a suggestion that the body will be discarded in the soul's progress to immortality.[5] Neither has erred, since Origen himself, at the conclusion of this chapter, invites us to choose between two hypotheses, of which Rufinus has rendered only one.[6] Jerome's quotation is evidently the other one, which Rufinus, in the light of his stated principles, had more licence to omit than to emend.

The hope of some continuance or revival of the body after death is expressed in works by Origen which need not be read through a Latin mediator. In the *Contra Celsum*, if anywhere, he might have been expected to disguise this Pauline stumbling-block; yet in fact he rather insists that it is faith in a corporeal resurrection that sets apart the Christian from the Greek (v.18–19). Even in the treatise which Methodius quoted as proof of his injustice to the body, he declares that it does not entirely perish, but transfers its form or *eidos* to the soul.[7]

Methodius takes his adversary to mean that the soul retains a mere appearance of the body without its underlying matter. Even if this thesis is coherent, it cannot be that of Origen, who defends the transformation of the body as the effect of God's authority over matter. Among the 'frequent demonstrations' referred to in the previous quotation is the following:

Now it seems right, since the diversity of the world cannot be sustained without bodies, to discuss the principle of corporeal nature. From the very phenomena it is clear that corporeal nature admits of diverse and various transformations... Now by matter we understand that which underlies bodies... This matter, then, is of such a quantity and kind as to be able to suffice for all the bodies in the world whose existence God desires, and obeys and subserves the Creator with respect to whatever forms and kinds he desires in everything. (ii.1.4)

This is good philosophy, and hardly the creation of Rufinus. Matter in Greek metaphysics is the nominal, almost notional, but

[5] *Ep. ad Avitum* 10, quoted in conjunction with *De Princ.* iii.6.9 by Koetschau.

[6] Jerome, *Ad Avitum* 5 reports that Origen left open a choice between three notions: disappearance of all corporeality, union with Christ in the form of aether, elevation of the saints to a sphere beyond the planetary orbits.

[7] Methodius, *De Resurrectione* 25.2 (*apud* Epiphanium, *Panarion* 64), confirmed at *De Princ.* ii.10.2. E. A. Clark, *The Origenist Controversy* (Princeton, 1992), 93–94 remarks that Origen's view could be construed as orthodox.

504   M. J. EDWARDS

all the more indispensable guarantee of continuity when the properties of an object are negated by a change.[8] Because it is unchangeable, it is the necessary substrate of all changes, and to assert a
change is therefore to assert the perpetuity of matter. At *Contra
Celsum* iv.57, Origen writes elliptically, but evidently with reference to the spiritual body, of the laws of change implicit in
the world.

There is no doubt, then, of a posthumous assumption of the
body; the question is at what stage it is assumed, and for how
long. Many remarks in the *De Principiis* show that the body
participates in the glory of the saint. How else could he move
after death from one locality to another, and how could he dwell
in air without a body, when Origen in the proem assigns a body
to those creatures that have air as their perpetual habitation? The
spiritual body itself is said to go from rank to rank of glory; it can
hardly be supposed that this takes place without a corresponding
progress in the soul. If the soul were to reach alone the perfection
'to which nothing can be added', it would be absurd to encumber
it at that point with a costume that was initially defective, and
even in its last and best condition otiose.

But even if the soul requires a body for its ascension, might it
not surrender it gladly when its journey was complete? Might not
a body of ever-increasing subtlety at last become so rare as to
escape the definition of a body altogether? Two of Origen's teachings seem to stand against this inference: first, he says that matter
is required to differentiate God's creatures from himself and one
another;[9] secondly, if the soul regards the body as its 'companion
and beloved friend',[10] it would be natural to conclude (with certain
Platonists) that it cannot fulfil its lot without embodiment. The
second of these points will be discussed at greater length, but first
we must account for Origen's statement, which might seem to

[8] Cf. *De Princ.* ii.10.3 and iii.6.6–7 for the transformative power of God, and
on the Neoplatonic assertion of the necessity of matter, R. Sorabji, *Matter, Space
and Motion* (London, 1988), 115–17. Origen alludes at iv.4.7 to those who deny
that substance consists of anything but properties, and this passage should be
added to the anticipations of Berkeley quoted by R. Sorabji, *Time, Creation and
the Continuum* (London, 1983), 287–96.
[9] See *De Principiis* i.6.4, and on the spiritual vehicle H. Crouzel, 'Le thème
platonicien du "véhicule de l'âme" chez Origène', *Didaskalia* 7 (1977), 225–37;
A. B. Scott, *Origen and the Life of the Stars* (Oxford, 1992); H. Schibli, 'Origen,
Didymus and the Vehicle of the Soul', *Origeniana Quinta* (1992), 381–91.
[10] At *De Principiis* ii.10.2, where no doubt, as for the Platonists, only the lower
soul is intended.

110

close the case against the survival of the body, that the saint in his final purity goes to meet God 'as a mind'.[11]

In Origen's vocabulary, such terms as 'spirit', 'soul', and 'mind' are apt to denote the ethical state of the bearer, rather than his physical constitution.[12] Thus, noting that the word 'soul' is often used in Scripture of those who are acting wickedly or weakly (ii.8.3–4), he infers that 'mind' is the name conferred on soul when it escapes the bonds of sin. There is nothing here to imply that it does not remain a soul. Nor does the appellation 'soul' in itself imply the absence of a body; if the immaterial soul is said at i.7.1 to be man's true nature, that is only the same assertion as we later find in Gregory of Nyssa and Augustine, who could hold that the soul is prior to the body in the definition of man without concluding that it is also prior in physical creation.[13] We ought not to doubt Rufinus as a witness to the nuances of Origen's anthropology, since this Latin intermediary is unlikely to have contrived for himself a doctrine based on Aristotle's dictum that a composite thing is often called by the name of its superior element.[14]

This higher part of soul, the mind, is sometimes spirit, sometimes only the ally and companion of the spirit. Origen is candidly equivocal, but never loses sight of the distinction between the spirit of humanity and the third person of the Godhead.[15] The promise that the saint will be 'one spirit' with the Father, cited repeatedly by Origen,[16] says nothing as to his incorporeality, for Origen could say much the same of any pupil's relation to his teacher,[17] and even the soul of Christ embraced the logos, not through affinity of substance, but because of an incomparable harmony of wills.[18]

If, therefore, the soul, which has acquired the form (εἶδος) of a body, can be called a mind while retaining its identity as a soul,

[11] *De Principiis* ii.11.7: the rational creature is said to advance as a mind already perfect in knowledge without the encumbrance of the flesh.

[12] Cf. *Comm. in Rom.* vi.12 on the difference between the carnal and the spiritual, etc.

[13] On the priority of the universal man to the particular (dyadic) males and females, see Gregory of Nyssa, *De Opificio Hominis* 16; for the soul as the real man see Augustine, *De Moribus Manichaeorum* ii.52. For passages in Origen which refer to Adam see C. P. Bammel, 'Adam in Origen', in R. D. Williams (ed.), *The Making of Orthodoxy* (Cambridge, 1989), 62–93.

[14] See e.g. *Met.* 1049b–1051a on the priority of form and actuality in sensible particulars.

[15] See e.g. *Dialogue with Heraclides* 7–8; *Comm. in Rom.* vii.1–5.

[16] 1 Cor. 6:17 is quoted at *De Princ.* i.8.4, ii.3.7, ii.6.3, ii.10.7, iii.6.6.

[17] See [Gregory Thaumaturgus], *Oratio in Origenem* 6 on 1 Sam. 18:1.

[18] See especially *Contra Celsum* viii.12.

Origen is acquitted both of heresy and of its antidote, ambiguity. The saint remains a composite of body, soul, and spirit but, as body and soul are purified, the whole of him can be subsumed in the name of his highest part. No doubt the elevation of the body entails a purging of its gross materiality, but this does not make it any less a body, just as the soul is none the less a soul when it sheds its sins.

But if such is the destiny of the saint, beginning instantly with its exit from the world, what place can be found for a Second Coming and a final judgement of all men to election or destruction? Many, long before that time, should have reached an indefeasible beatitude, and even those who are on the way can receive no other judgement than the one that is already being passed upon them by the discipline of glory. We can allow, perhaps, the consummation of all things in eternity which will entail the end of the visible and temporal, but each soul must be credited with a private eschatology that depends upon its merits and can thus be completed only in its own time.

This inference is supported almost everywhere in the *De Principiis*, for the one assertion of the Second Coming is a quotation from the Apocalypse,[19] and even Origen's understanding of this is obscured by reticence, or perhaps by the discretion of his translator:

That more illustrious and glorious second advent in the glory of his Father is meant, in which the archetype of Deuteronomy will be fully realised, when all the saints in the kingdom of the heavens live by the laws of that 'eternal gospel'. (iv.3.13)

Origen here looks forward to an epiphany of the Saviour, which translates the saint from temporal to eternal blessedness. This, in the opinion of Crouzel, implies an assumption of new bodies which will coincide 'avec la fin du temps'.[20] But what does Origen say here of the body? If the ones transferred are already saints then there is 'nothing to be added', and the world from which the Saviour will translate them is not the earth. Jerome avers that Origen predicted such epiphanies in other realms than this;[21] so Christ might wait, long after the end of history, for all to be perfected, or even (such is Origen's vagueness here) translate perfected individuals one by one.

Hell, too, need not wait on the dissolution of the present world,

[19] See *Rev.* 14:6.
[20] Crouzel (n. 2 above), 19.
[21] *Ep. ad Avitum* 12, cited by Koetschau on this passage from *De Principiis*. Jerome's comments are of an avowedly speculative cast.

since human beings create it for themselves when they reject the love of God:

The meaning of these words appears to be that every sinner kindles for himself the flames of his own fire, and is not immersed in some fire that was previously kindled by another or before himself. (ii.10.4)

If we can trust Jerome, the darkness is increased for the unbeliever by the assumption of a gross material body;[22] a Byzantine author tells us that this suffering was transitory and a prelude to the gradual preparation of the soul for the life of heaven.[23] This report is certainly compatible with Rufinus' text, and implies that, while the body may change in a future life under the action of grace and chastisement, there is no deferred resurrection, no point when God will clothe all souls with bodies and decree the end of change.

What sense is to be made, on such a thesis, of the double resurrection which is so frequently asserted in the commentaries and homilies of Origen? It is on these statements that Crouzel and others build the theory of a resumption of the body at some future point which supervenes, for the saints at least, on a time spent by the risen soul in an intermediate state. In favour of this construction, it is claimed that it places Origen, who never courted heresy, on the side of his more distinguished predecessors. I argue here, however, that the notion of a double resurrection must be understood in accordance with the views derived above from the *De Principiis*, that this is indeed the only way of reading the texts univocally and is perfectly in keeping with the beliefs of the early Fathers on the translation of the body after death.

The evidence might be thought to show that the notion of first and second resurrections, which derives from the Apocalypse (20:6), has three senses in the extant works of Origen.[24] The first resurrection begins in life, the second after the physical dissolution of the body; or the first is that of the just to life, the second that of the unjust to tribulation; or the first takes place immediately, the second after an age of purgatorial detention, and both for the

[22] *Ep. ad Avitum* 7, with reference to Matt. 8:12, though I am not sure whether this refers to a body of any greater density than the present one. Jerome maintains that Origen here supports the Pythagorean doctrine of transmigration; for other intimations of this see Koetschau's supplements to *De Princ.* i.8.4.

[23] See [Leontius] *De Sectis* 10.6; Justinian, *Ad Mennam* (Mansi ix.517), cited by Koetschau at *De Princ.* ii.10.3.

[24] See Crouzel (n. 2 above) and 'L'Exégèse Origénienne de 1 Cor 3.11–15 et la purification eschatologique', *Epektasis: Mélanges Daniélou* (Paris, 1972), 273–82. I do not think that Crouzel himself makes this tripartite distinction, though he does observe that three kinds of immortality correspond to the three kinds of death in his 'Mort et immortalité selon Origène', *Bulletin de Littérature Ecclésiastique* 79 (1982), 81–96.

just alone. Of these distinctions the third is drawn from a favourite text of Origen's (1 Cor. 3:11–15), but seldom as a comment on the term 'first resurrection' in the Scriptures. The second, which professes to be such a comment, stands alone in its clear discrimination of the wicked from the elect.

Hill contends that the saints enjoy the first resurrection alone and without a body in an intermediate paradise, while the body returns in a second resurrection, which is a universal rising of the dead.[25] This is to ignore those texts that express our first distinction, and treat both resurrections as consecutive epochs in a single life. Crouzel, by contrast, gives priority to the following passage from the exposition of Romans:[26]

Resurrection is understood in a double sense: in one we rise with Christ by thought, intent and faith from earthly things and apprehend heavenly things and eternal rest; the other will be the general resurrection of all in the flesh. (v.9; *PG* 14.1017)

This passage has a bearing on our question, as we shall see, but Hill's omission is justified, since to speak of a double resurrection is not exactly to speak of a first and second. It is not said that the carnal resurrection will occur for all at once or at the end of history; it is merely said that, unlike the regeneration of the saints on earth, it is the certain lot of all. There is no divorce to be made between participants in the first and in the second resurrection, since the carnal one, being universal, is not contrasted with, but must subsume, the glorification of the saints.

In the *De Principiis* the change of the resurrected body from gross to subtlest matter, possible for all, is most secure and expeditious when the soul has been refined on earth by a virtuous career. For those who have already been revived by grace, the body's death continues the inchoate resurrection under easier conditions; for those who have not believed, the same event subjects them to the chastisement of God.

Is this not also a form of resurrection? There is no true resurrection that is not regeneration and, to judge by the *De Principiis*, there is no regeneration of the soul without its body. Jerome records the commentary of Origen on 1 Thess. 4:14–16, which seems to speak of two communities, the living and the dead:[27]

---

[25] Hill (n. 3 above) esp. p. 135. Cf. Crouzel, 'Mort et immortalité' (n. 24 above), 185: 'après la mort et avant la résurrection l'âme, incorporelle par elle-même, reste entourée d'une certaine enveloppe corporelle correspondant au corps epais dont elle s'est separée'. I agree with all but the words 'avant la resurrection'; the spiritual body is the resurrection.
[26] Crouzel (n. 2 above), 4–5.
[27] See ibid. 12–19.

And not they only, but anyone who resembles Paul in his insight and behaviour can say 'We, the living', those whose body is dead through sin, but whose spirit is alive through righteousness ... the dead in Christ are those who, wishing to live in Christ, are none the less dead through sin. (Jerome, Letter 119.9)

Origen cannot deny that the living are Paul and his associates, all of whom had long ago succumbed to the death which the body incurs by sin; but this, by which he no doubt understood the sin of Adam, could have no hold on the spiritual body which is taken into paradise. Those who must submit to death are not the lost, but those who have failed to gain the first resurrection by their obedience in Christ. Since he does not include among the 'living' any of those who wear the first, adamic body, we may surmise that for Origen the first and second resurrections happen simultaneously. In other words this passage makes no use of a belief in Christ's appearance at the end of the present world.

Methodius was therefore right to say that the living in Origen are the spiritually regenerate,[28] but wrong to allege that this precludes the bodily survival of the wicked. If men are not to be saved without a body, there is no cause for them to be damned without a body, and here a body appears to be presupposed for those who are caught up in the air.

A general resurrection of the righteous and the unrighteous is deduced from the Apocalypse:

Even granting that all rise, and each in his order, we must, however, consider this verse of John which he utters in his Apocalypse: 'Blessed is he who has a part in the first resurrection; in him the second death shall have no dominion'. Perhaps every kind of resurrection can be divided between two parties, that is, the just who are to be saved and the sinners who are to be tormented; so that there is one of the good, which is called the first, but that which is of the wretched is called the second. (In *Apologia Pamphili*, from Homily 28 on Isaiah)

Crouzel's omission of the opening sentence is unfortunate,[29] since the claim that each will rise, and in his own order, scarcely savours of a catastrophic judgement or the eternal condemnation of the sinner. Origen, as we have noted, speaks of sinners as the dead with no presumption of an eternity of punishment; and the phrase

[28] See ibid. 17–19.

[29] *Ibid.* 8, paraphrasing rather than translating. Cf. Crouzel, 'Differences entre les ressuscités selon Origène', *Jahrbuch für Antike und Christentum*, Ergänzungsband 9, Münster 1982, 107–16, esp. p. 113. On p. 112 Crouzel notes a distinction between the judgement of the pious and of the impious, each resulting in its own resurrection; but I cannot see that this or any other of the passages which he cites disproves the thesis which I have endeavoured to construct from the longest and plainest of Origen's extant writings.

'each in his order' is derived from Paul's account of a resurrection
which is only for the saved.[30] If that is the implication of this
passage, then the righteous will differ from the wicked in that he
anticipates in his mortal body what will come to the other only
after physical decease. Nevertheless, in both the regeneration of
the soul is indispensable to the redemption of the body, and we
have already seen what follows. In saints the posthumous body
has the form that matches the soul to its redeemed state; the
sinner begins his punishment after death in a grosser body and,
since this is itself a kind of resurrection, he may justly be said to
undergo a second when he is raised to the condition of the saint.

We saw above that a partial resurrection of the faithful is
included in the full and universal resurrection of humanity. Only
the saint can experience a moral renovation without advantage to
the body, since the renewal of his inner man commences while
the former is still in bondage to corruption. This partial resurrection is completed after death, but the beneficiary is not said to
participate in a second resurrection, since this process is continuous with the first.

We now have a consistent definition of the first and second
resurrections consonant with the thought of the *De Principiis*, and
this is of a piece with Origen's numerous expositions of 1 Cor.
3:15:

Those who build above, if they are among the orthodox through their
eternal doctrines, their divine thoughts and their holy actions, build on
the foundation with gold, silver and precious stones. (Fr. 15 on 1
Corinthians)

The baptism of fire effects the latter resurrection, but appears to
be irrelevant to the former. We might expect that all allusions to
it would make it posthumous, and confine it to a portion of
humanity; but, as Crouzel has noted,[31] there are passages where
both assumptions fail. We hear, for example, that each of us must
experience the fire, though he be equal to the first of the Apostles:

If there exists a sinner like myself, he will certainly come to this fire like
Peter and Paul, but he will not pass it like Peter and Paul. (*Hom. in
Psalmum* 36.3.1)

We are also told that the fire, which is identical with God, acts
on the saint in his earthly life:

Happy is he who is baptised in the Holy Spirit and has no need of the
baptism which comes from the fire. Thrice unhappy he who has need of

---

[30] 1 Cor. 15:23, with Christ as the firstfruits.
[31] Crouzel, '1 Cor. 3.11–15' (n. 24 above) esp. pp 275 ff.

baptism in the fire ... And happy he who has part in the first resurrection, he who has preserved the baptism of the Holy Spirit. Who is he who is saved in the other resurrection? He who has need of the baptism which comes from the fire. (*Hom. in Jeremiam* ii.3)

On the one hand, everyone must pass the fiery sword to reach the garden; on the other, the cautery is necessary only for those in whom the Spirit has not yet finished work. This seeming contradiction is explained if we remember that the two resurrections are not so much the rewards of different persons as the application of love to different states. Insofar as a man is already spiritual, he has the first resurrection; insofar as he needs regeneration, he must undergo the second. Other texts imply a geographical location for the trial:[32] since paradise (as we saw in the *De Principiis*) is the first inn on the body's route to heaven, every saint must pass the flaming sword; but if he has already secured those rudimentary benefits which its fire confers, he need not burn again.

Origen here alludes to the two resurrections, but can this bifurcated route to heaven be equated with the double resurrection of the Apocalypse? It might be said that Origen is speaking here of those who have built on Christ, who thus were never among the reprobate and cannot be styled 'unjust'. Universalism, as we have noted, is the charge that was laid against the *De Principiis* by Origen's critics and, though his Latin translators are forced to credit him with a belief in *aeterna poena*, we know that the word αἰώνιος, which they render by *aeternus*, is allowed by him to mean not only 'eternal', but 'enduring for an age'.[33]

In the fiery energy of God consists not only the power of cleansing but his likeness to the saint; the very soul (ψυχή) derives its Greek name from the cooling, the decline in zeal and fervour, that has severed it from bliss (*De Princ.* ii.8.3). If God, then, is 'a consuming fire' (one of Origen's favourite verses), he is so for everyone, and in the *De Principiis* Origen cites this very passage from the Corinthian Epistle as a commentary on the notion of eternal punishment:

Let us see now what is meant by this threat of eternal woe. In the prophet Isaiah each is said to have a personal fire by which he is punished: 'Walk in the light of your own fire' (Isaiah 30.11). Of which fire the matter is our sins, which are called by the Apostle Paul wood and hay and straw.

As Origen proceeds to argue, even eternal punishment is only for a season; our sins are the very matter that will be transmuted

---

[32] Crouzel, art. cit. 279 cites Exh. Mart. 36.
[33] See *Commentary on Romans* vi.5, with H. Crouzel, 'L'Hadèes et la Gehènne selon Origène', *Gregorianum* 59 (1978), 291–331 and esp. pp. 320–21.

512 M. J. EDWARDS

into spiritual glory. The exposition of one verse of Isaiah required a contrast between the first and second resurrections; here another is cited to explain why one resurrection is immediate while the other is delayed. If Origen does not always extend salvation beyond the church, he may not have thought it needful or expedient to do so in his homilies, addressed as they are to a single congregation and advancing texts primarily for their application to the Christian life.

There is little to do with Christians in the treatise *On the Sorceress*, where the souls of Jewish saints are said to have dwelt in a subterranean locality, the Sheol of the Old Testament.[34] This is thus the place from which the sorceress conjured Samuel, perhaps the bosom of Abraham in which the rich man saw the exalted Lazarus; but even if its inhabitants are 'souls', it is most probable that this term includes the body, since no immaterial being could be fixed in an abode beneath the ground. In any case, this tenement is not the paradise that Christ has opened to all believers, and appears to have emptied for all time by his descent.

Nothing so distinguishes the Christian saint from the Jewish one as his permanent retention of the spirit. This gift of God returned at death to its source in Ecclesiastes; and even Christ, in Origen's view, surrendered it in the days between his cross and resurrection.[35] Now, with Hades overcome, the Holy Spirit works in every Christian, and his personal spirit therefore never leaves him or neglects to refine the body in the course of its ascent.

Paul's phrase 'in the twinkling of an eye' (1 Thess. 4:14) implies an instantaneous rapture and transformation of the body, but his commentator cites it less for itself than as an analogue to the wakening of memories in the soul:

For God, wishing to stir up simultaneously in the memory all the good and base deeds of a whole life, will do this with ineffable power and remind each of what he has done, so that, being conscious of our actions, we may apprehend the reasons for our punishment or honour. For the assertion must be ventured that *the event of the foreseen judgment requires no times*, for, just as the resurrection is said to happen 'in an instant, in the twinkling of an eye', so also I think is the judgment. (*Fr. in Lucam* 228)

This will supervene upon the soul's emancipation from its sins, not on the historical event of a Second Coming. There is thus no reason to postulate for Origen an intermediate state in which the soul is disembodied, or a chronological interval between the first

---

[34] See *De Pythonissa* 9 for the equation of this place with Abraham's bosom; the word 'souls' is dictated by such texts as Ps. 16:8. On the location of Hades see Crouzel (n. 33 above), pp. 304–309.

[35] See *Dialogue with Heraclides* 8.

and the second resurrections. We may say that the former sanctifies the righteous and the latter requites the wicked, but the penalties of the second are enjoined in a milder form upon partakers of the first. The fire of God is the sequel to the first resurrection in those who have been prepared for ascent to heaven in their mortal lives, but it is the first means of enlightening the wicked, who thus receive after death with tribulation what the righteous taste before it, and with joy.

II

Much of this speculation is peculiar to Origen, but how far does his notion of an immediate sublimation of the body accord with previous Christian teaching? The answer appears to be that, in his rejection of a terminal catastrophe, he generalized those privileges which were formerly accessible only by martyrdom or by visionary ascent.

Jewish literature abounds in sages who rise bodily to heaven, and receive there for a moment the transformation that its residents enjoy in perpetuity. Enoch, Elijah, and Moses are the most eminent of those who have passed through death without corruption;[36] their luminous robes remind a modern reader of the spiritual body which in Pauline thought is the glorious and imperishable clothing of the saints.[37]

Christ is said to have made the ascent in a body that was already transfigured by his resurrection. He was glorified before his death in the company of Moses and Elijah though, since he bore the kingdom in his person, it was not he who came to them but they to him.[38] Paul describes an ascent to the ineffable, which he will not judge to have been either in the body or out of it;[39] Irenaeus makes the decision for him by equating his third heaven with a paradise, above this world but not without its physical dimensions, into which the translated patriarchs have entered as the first of Christ's elect.[40]

In the Apocalypse there is no ascent by the visionary, and those

[36] On the many apocalyptic writings of this character see now M. Himmelfarb, *Ascent to Heaven in Jewish and Christian Apocalypses* (Oxford, 1993).

[37] Himmelfarb, op. cit. 40.

[38] See M. Thrall, 'Elijah and Moses in Mark's Account of the Transfiguration', *NTS* 16 (1969), 305–17.

[39] 2 Cor. 12:1–12, on the relation of which to apocalyptic and to Paul's vision of Christ see C. R. A. Murray-Jones, 'Paradise Revisited (2Cor 12.1–12)', *HTR* 86 (1993), 265–92. Paul's allusion to a *harpagmos* suggest a relation both with the rapture of 1 Thess. 4:11–14 and with the state of Christ when in the form of God at Phil. 2:5.

[40] See *Adv. Haer.* v.5.1 and v.31–2.

who have been admitted to the altar appear as 'souls'.[41]
Nevertheless, they too wear shining garments, which Tertullian
took as evidence of the soul's corporeality.[42] We may find hints
of a bodily ascent in another author, who resembles the seer of
Patmos in his zeal, as he is close to him in place and period.
Ignatius holds that death in the arena will be a means of 'attaining
Christ' without delay, but he also speaks of rising in his fetters;[43]
the most economic reading is that he looked for instantaneous
resurrection with a physical form at once as new, as real, and as
continuous with the old one as the one that he ascribes to Christ
himself.[44]

Tertullian can combine his expectation of the judgement with
a theory of progressive initiation into the kingdom. After
Armageddon the saints will rule for a millennium, being severally
transferred to earth from a subterranean purgatory as soon as each
has paid his debt of sin.[45] Only for the martyrs, who anticipate
this reckoning in a Roman cell,[46] is access to God immediate; the
wicked know nothing before their condemnation on the last day.
This is almost exactly the opinion that Crouzel ascribes to Origen,
but the latter is no chiliast like his African contemporary.[47] He,
too, holds that every saint is perfected in his own time, but not
that there is a period set aside for this between the end of history
and the judgement of the world.

Origen cannot make the soul a body or allow it to survive

---

[41] See Rev. 6:9. Hill (n. 3 above), pp. 188–92 attempts a 'non-chiliastic exegesis'
of Revelation 20, denying that the immediate admission to the kingdom is reserved
for martyrs. For criticism see my review, forthcoming in Hermathena.

[42] Rev. 6:11, though the commentary of A. Farrer (Oxford 1964) notes ad loc.
that the resurrection body is granted only at 20:4. Tertullian has 6:9–11 in mind
when he argues at *De Anima* 8.5 that the soul has a body which is visible only to
spiritual creatures, and at *De Resurrectione* 25 repudiates the inference that the
spiritual and corporeal resurrections are the same. Augustine, *De Anima* iv. (21).34,
may have this montanistic reasoning in mind when he admonishes his readers that
the depiction of the martyrs is a true vision but not a vision of true bodies.

[43] Eph. 11:2; see Hill (n. 3 above), 76–78, where the translation seems to me
forced. On pp. 73–76, however, Hill assembles cogent evidence that Ignatius hoped
for immediate admission to God's presence. The fetters are said to be spiritual
(*pneumatikoi*) pearls, using Paul's adjective for the resurrection body.

[44] An unknown saying, quoted at *Smyrnaeans* 3, denies that the risen Christ is
a spirit; he is none the less, like his children, spiritual (*Ephesians* 7.2, *Trallians*
12, etc.).

[45] On the intermediate state in Tertullian see *de Anima* 58.8 (on payment of the
last farthing) and 55.3 (apparently extending subterranean detention to all souls
without exception).

[46] See *Ad Martyras* 1 and Hill (n. 3 above), 24–28.

[47] On Origen's opposition to chiliasm see *De Princ.* ii.11.2 and Hill, op cit.
127–32.

without a body; therefore he cannot simply accept Tertullian's purgatory while denying his millennium. Nor can he suppose that the soul will wake and enter heaven with a sudden resuscitation of the body, since salvation is for him not legal righteousness, but a journey to perfection. Nor, finally, can he doubt that certain saints, such as the Apostles, have had time to achieve perfection since their deaths. Nothing, then, is left to him but to postulate an extension of corporeal life in which the body shares the transmutation of the soul.

It is sometimes thought that Origen's debts to secular philosophy would have led him into different views from those ascribed to him here. It is even insinuated that Rufinus is the author of those parts of the De Principiis which deny that the soul can survive without a body; did not Plato, after all, believe that the liberation of soul from body was the goal of all philosophy? In fact, however, the tenor of philosophy in this period would not have encouraged Origen to divorce the two, but rather to insist upon their union. Plato grants long holidays to the soul between corporeal existences, but his readers in late antiquity were troubled by the ability of departed souls to recognize each other,[48] and inferred that there is a certain tenuous envelope, the chariot (ὄχημα) of the Phaedrus,[49] which enables souls to retain the marks of identity for a longer or shorter period after death.

Nowhere does Origen prove a better student of the trends in Platonism than when he states in the De Principiis that the soul has an innate love of the body. All who held the soul to be eternal were obliged, in the light of Aristotle's questioning,[50] to equip it with eternal operations; since its only visible operation was the governance of the body, its presence there could not be understood as a merely temporary and penal servitude. Plotinus found that souls descend to matter in the first instance with a mandate to inform and beautify it;[51] Sallustius remarked that transmigration was an inevitable consequence of the soul's need for an animating function.[52] Alcinous, as the fourth reason for the soul's successive

---

[48] See Proclus, Comm. in Rem Pub. II. 165 Kroll.

[49] See Phaedrus 247b and Timaeus 41e, with Proclus, In Tim. III.234.32 ff.; 236.31 ff.; 298.12 f.; idem. Elementa 207–209; Porphyry, Sententiae 13.8; Ad Gaurum 11.3.

[50] See e.g. R. M. Grant, 'Aristotle and the Conversion of Justin', JTS, NS, 7 (1956), 246–48; and for the sources of Christian polemic against the Platonists J. Waszink, Tertullian: De Anima (Amsterdam, 1947), 41–44.

[51] See e.g. Enneads iv.8, with J. M. Rist, Plotinus: The Road to Reality (Cambridge, 1967), 112–29.

[52] Sallustius, De Diis et Mundo, 20.

visits to the body, alludes, like Origen, to the natural affinity of the body for the soul.[53]

Thus no one trained in the latest schools, as Origen was, would have found it easy to countenance even a temporary secession of the soul from the world of matter. If such a theory could have flourished anywhere it was among the Valentinians, but even here the gravest doubts obtain. According to Peel's translation,[54] the *Epistle to Rheginus*, while it postulates an immediate translation to eternity, insists upon the retention of 'the flesh' to form a spiritual body. It may be that this tenet was a late appropriation;[55] but in that case, the decay of Valentinianism shows us how untenable the division of soul and body was found to be in late antiquity. Even Bentley Layton, who disputes many things with Peel, suspects the *Epistle* of subscribing to the axiom that a soul without a body is deprived of its proper task.[56]

There is no true innovation, then, in the elements of Origen's eschatology. The synthesis is original, but I shall argue that it came almost of itself through his reflection on the logic of inherited traditions—in particular, by reflection on the problems which arise, for both philosophy and the gospels, from the doctrine of an intermediate state.

III

The earliest Christian authors were content with slight allusions to a place where souls await the resurrection;[57] the question of their knowledge or experience is forestalled by the expectation of Christ's imminent return. As the new Jerusalem receded, it was natural to speculate that God employs the interval to cleanse his saints of residual demerits. This hypothesis would have seemed less felicitous had the Christians been encumbered, like the Platonists, with a doctrine that the soul is absolutely incorporeal; but, in fact, Tertullian urges that the soul, being a substance, is

---

[53] See *Didaskalia* 28 and J. M. Dillon, 'The Fall of the Soul in Middle Platonic and Gnostic Theory', in B. Layton (ed.), *The Rediscovery of Gnosticism I* (Leiden, 1980).

[54] In J. M. Robinson (ed.), *The Nag Hammadi Library in English* (Leiden, 1988), 52–57 and with a commentary, *The Epistle to Rheginus* (London, 1969). See further the article cited in the following note.

[55] As I suggest in my 'The Epistle to Rheginus: Valentinianism in the Fourth Century?', forthcoming in *Novum Testamentum*.

[56] B. Layton, *The Gnostic Treatise on the Resurrection from Nag Hammadi* (Missoula, 1977), 80, citing Sallustius, *De Mundo* 20.

[57] See Hill (n. 3 above), pp. 66–111.

a corpus,[58] while Irenaeus, who holds that it acquires shape from the body, must suppose that it partakes of the body's nature in some degree.[59] The identity of the soul is therefore guaranteed by its previous relation to the body. Yet both these pioneers appear indifferent to the insidious corollary: if body and soul are equally responsible for conduct, and therefore equally rewarded, why is the spell in purgatory restricted to the soul?

Origen's Greek education had convinced him that the soul is immaterial, but had also made him wonder how its individual being could be sustained. The concept of the spiritual body as a vehicle for the soul was both a reply to this objection and a solution of the unnoticed difficulty as to the state of the human being in purgatory. Body and soul are purified together, in accordance with their joint pursuit of virtue; Origen is thus still less of a dualist than his Christian predecessors, who maintain that soul must sympathize with body, but do not propose that the body may be affected by the soul.

Though Origen held both tenets,[60] he could not assign the passions of the body to its immaterial partner, and concluded that the fire which burns the soul is not the element, but its spiritual remorse. Having said this, he could hardly fail to argue that the torments of the wicked after death are in part the same as those that the saints endure in life. Only in part could this be said, for the saint will take a body into paradise, while the wicked will be banished to Gehenna, which is a region under Hades.[61] The unconsoled repentance of the soul, as Jerome intimates,[62] is the bitterest estrangement; though felt already in mortal life, it is none the less compatible with the subsequent confinement of the body in this underground bastille.

Neither for the wicked nor for the just will the later body be identical with the matter that we reserve for inhumation. The vehicle or integument which the soul retains is the εἶδος of the body, which is both the substrate of corporeal functions and a superficial form. The best gloss on this concept is the chariot of the *Phaedrus*, the astral body of Neoplatonism, which preserves

---

[58] See the introduction to Waszink (n. 50 above) and J. Daniélou, *The Origins of Latin Christianity* (London, 1977), 214–33.

[59] See esp. *Adv. Haer.* ii.55 on the corporeality of Lazarus.

[60] For the action of body on mind see *De Princ.* i.1.6, and for his assertion of the soul's immateriality i.1.7, etc.

[61] See Crouzel (n. 33 above), 307. Crouzel notes that fire is the concomitant of Gehenna rather than Hades; I do not share his conclusion that this fire is to be sharply distinguished from that of Purgatory (p. 330, etc.).

[62] See *Ad Avitum* 7 and Crouzel, art. cit. 309–31.

518   M. J. EDWARDS

the body's shape, but in a rarer kind of matter.[63] Nevertheless, this borrowing enables the Alexandrian theologian not only to interpret Paul, but to answer the infamous question of those whose bodies have been eaten and have hence become identical with the bodies of other persons.[64] As he does not affirm the preservation of the elemental body, he need not plead, like Augustine and Methodius,[65] that God will reassemble the annihilated body from whatever it has discarded or expelled.

If Origen's eschatology refuses the constraints of church tradition, it is not because he has lost his Christianity to the Greeks. He adopts the tools of secular philosophy to answer questions forced upon the church by its expectation of the kingdom. A profound and constant faith in the resurrection of the body and a belief that grace must act upon the dead so long as it acts upon the living are the pillars of his doctrine; both rest on the axiom that body and soul are equally indispensable to the purposes of God.

M. J. EDWARDS

[63] See E. R. Dodds, *Proclus: Elements of Theology* (Cambridge, 1963), 313–21; H. Schibli, 'Hierocles and the Vehicle of the Soul', *Hermes* 121 (1993), 109–17.
[64] R. M. Grant, 'Athenagoras or Pseudo-Athenagoras?', *HTR* 49 (1956), 121–29 argues persuasively that the rebuttal of this argument in the treatise *De Resurrectione* attributed (by moderns) to Athenagoras is one proof of its later date.
[65] See Methodius, *De Resurrectione* II (*apud* Photium, *Bibliotheca* 4.9), replying to Origen; Augustine, *De Civ. Dei* xxii.12 and ii.20.

Origen of Alexandria: The Fate of the Soul and the Body after Death

This discussion of the fate of the soul and the body after death can easily be divided into two distinct parts: the first part concerns Origen's tripartite division of the immortality of the soul and two demonstrations of the soul's immortality; the second part examines his ideas on the resurrected body, specifically in light of his use of the Middle-Platonic *ochēma,* "the vehicle of the soul."

Before proceeding to part one, however, it is necessary to preface the whole discussion with a few remarks about Origen's theology of death. Death, for Origen, is a human act: first of all in the sense that death entered the realm of human existence by a free will act of our first parents (e.g., *Hom. Ez.* I. 9; *Hom. Jer.* II. 1);[1] and second, and more immediately, in the sense that each human death is good or bad according to each person's choice of a life of virtue or a life of sin (*e.g., Com. Rm.* IX. 39; *Hom. Lv.* V. 3).[2] In his discussions on death, Origen sometimes distinguishes between three separate kinds. The first kind is physical/ common death (an indifferent death); the second is the death because of sin (a bad death); the third is the death to sin (a good death). This tripartite distinction applied to death is apparently drawn from the tripartite distinction which dominates the Stoic understanding of human acts as good, bad, and indifferent. The way this tripartite distinction actually functions in Origen's theology is beyond the scope of this present discussion.[3]

Rev. LAWRENCE R. HENNESSEY teaches at Washington Theological Union, 9001 New Hampshire Ave., Silver Spring, MD 20903

[1]*Hom. Ez.* I. 9: *GCS* VIII, 333, 7; *Hom. Jer.* II. 1: *GCS* III, 16, 18; *SC* 232, 238, 1.

[2]*Com. Rm.* IX. 39: *PG* 15. 1238C-1239A; *Hom. Lv.* V. 3: *GCS* VI, 338, 26; *SC* 286, 216, 42.

[3]H. Crouzel, "Mort et immortalité selon Origène," *Bulletin de littérature ecclésiastique* 79 (1978):20.

However, the fact of the distinction is a presupposition for Origen's approach to immortality.

I
Origen's Tripartite Division of the Immortality of the Soul

In reflecting on the soul's fate after death, Origen posits a tripartite immortality, a distinction which corresponds to the previously mentioned distinction of death. The following text from the *Dialogue with Heraclides* illustrates the idea:

> So then, since there are three deaths, let us see whether the human soul is immortal in respect to the three deaths, or, if not in respect to the three deaths, then whether it is immortal in respect to some of them. In regard to in-between (*meson*) death, which all of us who are human die, we consider it to be a dissolution. No human soul dies this death: if it did die, it would not be punished after death. It is said: *Men seek death, and they do not find it* (Rv. 9, 6). In this sense, every human soul is immortal. But as for the other senses, in regard to one of them, the soul is mortal and it is happy if it dies to sin. Balaam spoke of this death in his prophecy, while praying under divine inspiration: *May my soul die among the souls of the just!* (Nb. 23, 10). About this death, Balaam made his astonishing prophecy; and by God's word, he made this most beautiful prayer in his own behalf: he prayed to die to sin, so he could live for God! And so he said: *May my soul die among the souls of the just, and may my posterity be like their posterity!* (Nb. 23, 10). There is another death in regard to which we are not immortal, but we can protect ourselves from dying (from it). And, perhaps, what is mortal in the soul is not always mortal. For to the extent that the soul takes sin into itself—the kind of sin that makes it *the soul that sins, itself dies* (Ez. 18, 4)—the soul is mortal, subject to real death. But if it becomes grounded in blessedness, so that it cannot receive death, it then possesses eternal life and is no longer mortal, but it has even become, according to this sense, immortal—How is it said by the Apostle, speaking of God, *He alone has immortality?* (1 Tim. 6, 16). Upon investigation, I find that Jesus Christ *died for all except for God* (*choris theou*) (2 Cor. 5, 15, Hb. 2, 9). There you have an explanation how God alone possesses immortality. (*Dial. Herac.* 25–28)[4]

The distinction can be summarized like this:

1. in regard to common, physical death, the human soul enjoys absolute immortality;

2. in regard to the death because of sin (bad death), the human soul has a relative immortality and a relative mortality;

3. in regard to the death to sin (good death), the human soul also

---

[4]*Dial. Herac.* 25-27: *SC* 67, 104, 19. Note the repetition of the example of Balaam. The editor of this text, J. Scherer, conjectures that there were probably at least two recensions of this dialogue: the second, richer and more nuanced, was apparently to replace the first. The double redaction undoubtedly corresponds to two different stenographic reports, which were inadvertently juxtaposed in the final copy.

has a relative immortality and a relative mortality. Each one will be examined in turn.

The Immortality from Common, Physical Death

One of the clearest passages from Origen's writings, in which he defends the soul's absolute immortality from common, physical death, is found in the *Dialogue with Heraclides* 10–27.[5] The context is a dispute with the Thnetopsychites, who held that the human soul was identified with the body's blood; and so the soul died when the body did. Origen's refutation of this position is grounded in both scripture and the common faith of the church.

From Origen's perspective, the Thnetopsychic position eliminates the possibility of *being with Christ* (Phil. 1:23) on the other side of the grave, a possibility which, for Origen, is rooted in the core of Paul's own understanding of faith and hope.[6] This doctrine of the soul's mortality destroys the belief that the just soul from the moment of death is with Christ— enjoying, says Origen, repose in Abraham's bosom in God's Paradise. These last two expressions, "Abraham's bosom" and "Paradise," refer implicitly to the stories of the rich man and Lazarus (Lk. 16:19–31) and the "good thief" (Lk. 23:29–43) respectively. These stories, together with the text from Paul (Phil. 1:23), had already in Origen's time become the classic passages used by the Fathers to ground the doctrine of the soul's survival after death. The same is true of the verb *anapauesthai*—"to be at rest"—which Origen uses in this passage (*Dial. Herac.* 23): by the beginning of the third century, it had become one of the technical terms used to designate the blessed state of the soul just after death. For Origen, these diverse expressions are apparently equivalent. Combined with the biblical argument for the necessity of retribution for the wicked soul, which he also uses, these expressions are all rooted in the church's common faith.[7]

It should be noted in this context that Origen's understanding of these texts as meaning that just souls ascended to heaven and enjoyed a blessed life with Christ immediately after death was by no means universally held. In fact, the more widespread opinion understood "Paradise" and "the bosom of Abraham" to be an intermediate place where souls awaited the final resurrection. However, almost all the Fathers made an exception for the martyrs, who were united with Christ at the moment of their deaths.[8]

[5]Ibid., pp. 10–27: *SC* 67, 76–106.

[6]G. Kretchmar, "Origenes und die Araber," *Zeitschrift für Theologie und Kirche* 50 (1953):272.

[7]F. Refoulé, "Immortalité de l'âme et resurrection de la chair," *Revue de l'histoire des religions* 163 (1963):36–37.

[8]Ibid.

Origen's assertion of the absolute immortality of the soul from physical, common death is also developed more philosophically elsewhere in
his writings. For example, in the *De principiis,* when Origen discusses
the soul's longing to know the designs of God, his argument presupposes
immortality in the absolute sense:

> Therefore, just as in regard to the manual arts, the mind (*sensu*) furnishes the design
> of the work, showing what is to be done, how it is accomplished, and for what
> uses it is made, but the execution of the work requires the use of our hands; so also
> in regard to the works of God, which He accomplished and we can see, we must
> understand, all the same, that their design and meaning remain hidden. And again,
> in regard to things made by an artisan, if our eye lights on one that is quite skillfully
> made, our mind (*animus*) immediately burns with the desire to know what it is,
> and how, or why, or for what uses it was made. How much more, and beyond all
> comparison with such man-made things, does our mind burn with an ineffable desire
> to know the design behind those things we perceive have been done by God! We
> believe that this longing, this love, has been implanted in us by God: just as the
> eye naturally requires light and vision, and our body by its very nature desires food
> and drink, so too our mind (*mens*) carries about a fitting and natural desire to know
> God's truth and to find out the causes in such a way that it ought never be, or can
> never be fulfilled; otherwise, it would seem that God the Creator implanted the love
> of truth (cf. 2 Thess. 2, 10) into our mind for no purpose, if the gratification of
> this longing can never be accomplished. (*De princ.* II. 11. 4)[9]

Because immortality is presupposed here, this passage is an *indirect* argument for absolute immortality. He says that the divine design, which
the human mind desires so strongly to know, is placed in each being by
God. It is not a static essence, but a dynamic principle of development,
such as the seminal design which explains the development of the human
seed from an embryo, to a child, an adult, an old person, and for Origen,
a resurrected person.[10] The desire to know this design cannot be satisfied
this side of death. However, since God has placed it in every person, it
must receive its gratification, which presupposes the immortality of the
human mind, the *mens* or *nous,* which is the highest part of the soul and
the seat of the personality.[11]

This discussion itself presupposes the existence of God; it is rooted in
the principle that since nature is the work of God, its true desires cannot
be frustrated. Much later, in Aquinas, this principle will be expressed in
its classic form, *Desiderium naturae nequit esse inane*: "a desire of nature
cannot be empty."[12] Since of its nature the human soul desires to see the

---

[9]*De princ.* II. 11. 4: *GCS* V, 187, 1; *SC* 252, 400, 103.

[10]H. Crouzel and M. Simonetti, *Origène: Traité des principes* II (*SC* 253; Paris, 1978)
245, n. 19. On the resurrected body, cf. *De princ.* II. 10. 3.

[11]Crouzel, "Mort . . .," p. 85.

[12]Ibid. Cf. Thomas Aquinas, *Summa contra gentiles* III. 51. 57; *Summa theologiae* Ia,
q.12, a.1, c.

design of God, a desire that can only be satisfied after death, an incorporeal and immortal soul is essential to the nature of a human being.

Another discussion, also from the *De principiis*, takes Origen's demonstration of the soul's absolute immortality an important step further:[13] the desire arising from the soul's nature points to the soul's participation in the very life of God. This discussion is a *direct* argument for the soul's absolute immortality. The participation in God's life is of a greater or lesser degree; the degree is determined by the number of *epinoiai*—"virtues or attributes"—the soul acquires.

This demonstration uses two arguments, both rooted in the idea of participation: The first argument demonstrates the soul's immortality from the traditional Platonic principle that only like knows, i.e., recognizes, like; only like things can enter into a relationship with realities of the same nature. Since both human minds and angelic powers participate in intellectual light, they must be of the same nature. The celestial powers, however, are immortal; therefore, the human mind must be so too:

> I think that it will certainly not seem contrary to the plan of this work of ours, if we repeat, as briefly as we can, our position on the immortality of rational natures. Everyone who participates (*participat*) in something is undoubtedly of one substance and of one nature with him who is a participant (*particeps*) in the same thing. For instance, all eyes participate in light: therefore, all eyes sharing in the light are of one nature. But granted that each eye participates in the light, nevertheless, since one eye sees more sharply, while another sees more weakly, not every eye shares equally in the light. Or again, every hearing receives a voice or a sound; and therefore, all hearing is of one nature. But it is also true that each person hears either quickly or slowly in proportion to a clean and healthy hearing faculty. Let us move on then from these examples of the senses to the consideration of intellectual realities.

> Every mind (*mens*) that participates in intellectual light undoubtedly must be of one nature with every mind that shares in intellectual light in the same way. If then, the heavenly powers receive a share (*participium*) in intellectual light, i.e., in the divine nature, because they participate in wisdom and sanctification, and if the human soul receives a share in the same light and wisdom, then these beings will together be of one nature and of one substance. However, the heavenly powers are incorruptible and immortal: and so the substance of the human soul will undoubtedly be incorruptible and immortal. (*De princ*. IV. 4. 9)[14]

Now the intellectual light, in which both the angelic powers and the human minds participate, is the very nature of the Trinity. This is the point of departure for the second argument from participation. Here, the human soul is placed in direct contact with divinity, without passing through the celestial powers as intermediaries. The human soul participates in

---

[13]*De princ*. IV. 4. 9–10; *GCS* V, 361, 14; *SC* 268, 422, 336.

[14]Ibid. Crouzel and Simonetti, *SC* 269, 270, n. 68.

divinity, which is incorruptible; therefore, the human soul is incorruptible
and immortal, and can thus always benefit from the divine favor:

> Not only for this reason, but also, since the nature of the Father and the Son and
> the Holy Spirit, from whose intellectual light alone every creature draws a share,
> is incorruptible and eternal, it follows logically and necessarily that every substance
> which draws a share of this eternal nature, also must itself remain incorruptible and
> eternal forever. This is so in order that the eternity of divine goodness may also be
> understood in this way: those who acquire its blessings are eternal too. But just as
> a diversity was maintained in the examples of light—perception—when the sense
> of sight was described as either weaker or sharper—so too, in regard to participation
> in the Father and the Son and the Holy Spirit, a diversity must be maintained in
> proportion to the soul's (*sensus*) exertion and the mind's capacity.
>
> Otherwise, let us consider if it does not seem impious to say that a mind, which
> has a capacity for God, might undergo a destruction of its substance; as if the very
> fact that it can know and experience God would not be sufficient for it to enjoy
> perpetual existence. This is especially so, since, even if the mind, through its own
> neglect, falls away from the pure and complete reception of God into itself, never-
> theless, it always has within itself some seeds, as it were, of reparation and of recall
> to a better understanding, because *the inner man* (cf. Rm. 7, 22), who is also called
> rational, is recalled to *the image and likeness* (cf. Gn. 1, 26) of God, who created
> him. For this reason, the prophet says: *All the ends of the earth will remember,*
> *and they will turn back to the Lord, and all the families of nations shall worship*
> *in His sight* (Ps. 21 [22], 28). (*De princ.* IV. 4. 9)[15]

Incorruptibility and immortality are, of course, divine *epinoiai* (attributes). Participation in divine *epinoiai* like these also implies a kind of
unity of substance. In other words, the primary ground of the soul's unity
with the Father or with the divine Logos is the real participation in their
divine perfections, the *epinoiai*.[16] This participation of the soul in God
cannot be lost because it results from the soul's creation *kat' eikona* (Gn.
1:26), according to the image and likeness of God:

> However, if someone dares to posit a corruption of substance in one who has been
> made according to *the image and likeness* of God, then, I think that he also directs
> this impious charge against the Son of God Himself; for in the Scripture, He too
> is called *the image of God* (cf. Col. 1, 15; 2 Cor. 4, 4). But one thing is certain:
> the man who wants things this way is indicating the authority of Scripture, which
> says that man was made *in the image* (cf. Gn. 1, 26) of God. It is also clear that
> the signs (*indicia*) of the divine image can be recognized, not in the form (*effigiem*)
> of his corruptible body, but in the prudence of his mind (*animi*), and its justice, its
> moderation, its courage, its wisdom, its discipline, in short, in the whole choir of
> virtues, which exist essentially in God. This is what the Lord indicates in the Gos-
> pel, when He says: *Be compassionate just as your Father is compassionate* (Lk. 6,
> 36). And again, *Be perfect, just as your Father is perfect* (Mt. 5, 48). This clearly
> shows that all these virtues are always in God, and nothing can ever be added to

---

[15]*De princ.* IV. 4. 9: *GCS* V, 362, 11; *SC* 268, 424, 359; ibid. 273, n. 71.

[16]A. Lieske, *Die Theologie der Logosmystik bei Origenes* (Münster, 1938) 54.

them or subtracted from them; whereas in human beings, they are acquired gradually, one at a time. From this fact, it seems that human beings have a certain blood-relationship (*consanguinitatem quandam*) with God. And since God knows everything, and not a single intellectual reality is hidden from Him—for God alone, the Father, His Only-Begotten Son, and the Holy Spirit, has knowledge, not only of the things that He has created, but also of Himself—it is also possible, nevertheless, that a rational mind (*mens*), proceeding from small things to greater, and from *visible things* to *invisible* (cf. Col. 1, 16), can arrive at more perfect understanding. For the mind has been placed in a body, and by necessity it progresses from sensible things, which are corporeal, to those that are not sensible, but incorporeal and intellectual. But lest it seem inappropriate to say, as we have, that intellectual things are not sensible, we will use the example of Solomon's opinion, when he said: *You will also find a divine sense* (Prov. 2, 5). This shows that intellectual things are to be sought out, not by a corporeal sense, but by another sense, which is called divine. (*De princ.* IV. 4. 10)[17]

Origen seems to say several times that because of sin, a human being loses the character which creation "according to the image" has put in that being.[18] Nevertheless, his dominant idea is that this character can be covered over and obscured by sin, but not eliminated.[19] Origen's conviction on the soul's immortality rests above all on this argument. From the time of Plato on, the concept of image—Plato himself only speaks of kinship—does not only indicate a generic and exterior likeness with the model, but a true participation in its reality, even though on an inferior level.[20]

A similar proof for the immortality of the soul is found in the Middle Platonist, Albinus. Both he and Origen use the same starting point: they both ground their demonstrations in the soul's relationship with God and in the shared perception that the soul is *autokinetos*, "self-determined or self-moving." These demonstrations, in turn, are dependent on Plato's *Timaeus* and *Phaedo*.[21] The soul's self-determination is an essential aspect of its life, and this quality provides the link to the other two kinds

---

[17]*De princ.* IV. 4, 10: *GCS* V, 363, 14; *SC* 268, 426, 385. Crouzel and Simonetti, *SC* 269, 273, n. 71.

[18]E.g., *Com. Rm.* I. 17: *PG* 14, 864C; *Hom. Lv.* II. 2: *GCS* VI, 292, 17; *SC* 286, 100, 68.

[19]E.g., *Hom. Gn.* XIII. 4: *GCS* VI, 119, 15; *C. Cels.* II. 11; IV. 25; IV. 83: *GCS* I, 139, 5; *SC* 132, 310: *GCS* I, 294; 19; *SC* 136, 242, 21: *GCS* I, 354, 15; *SC* 136, 392, 43.

[20]Crouzel and Simonetti, *SC* 269, 274, n. 74.

[21]P. Louis, *Albinus: Epitomé* (Paris, 1945), *e.g.*, XIV, pp. 78 ff.; XVII, pp. 92 ff.; XXV, pp. 116 ff. The demonstrations in chapters XIV and XVII are based on Plato's *Timaeus*; the argument in chapter XXV, on the *Phaedo*. H. Koch, *Pronoia und Paideusis, Studien über Origenes und sein Verhältnis zum Platonismus* (Leipzig, 1932; reprint, New York, 1979) 264.

of relative immortality, which the soul can possess for better or worse. For it is the self-determined soul that actively seeks out, or rejects, participation in the *epinoiai* by a free human decision.

Immortality in Relation to the Death Because of Sin (Bad Death) and the Death to Sin (Good Death)

It has already been seen how Origen expresses his understanding of immortality in such a way as to posit a tripartite immortality to correspond to the three kinds of death: to common, physical death corresponds the soul's absolute immortality; to the death because of sin (bad death) corresponds the soul's relative immortality; and to the death to sin (good death) corresponds also the soul's relative immortality. Although the distinction is tripartite, in effect there are only two kinds of immortality, absolute and relative. The relative immortality is subdivided by being combined with relative mortality: the degree of relative mortality in the combination produces an immortality appropriate to either the bad death because of sin or the good death to sin. That is why it can be said that Origen posits a tripartite immortality to correspond to his tripartite distinction of death.

This idea becomes clearer, perhaps, when it is recalled that in his discussion of immortality in the *Dialogue with Heraclides* (25–27), Origen established that the soul can be mortal or immortal in what concerns the death because of sin: the soul is mortal insofar as it is not established in beatitude, and it is immortal when it is so established, i.e., when it is dead to sin. The second kind of immortality, relative immortality, is related to the first kind, absolute immortality, as mystery to image—relative immortality is the mystery, since it involves the grace of redemption; and absolute immortality is the image of it, since it belongs to the soul by its very nature. This, of course, puts relative immortality on a higher level than its image; nevertheless, unlike absolute immortality, it is not a prerogative of human nature received at creation.[22]

Creatures do not possess this relative immortality essentially (*ousiodos*)[23] because they belong to the unstable world of becoming; Christ, on the other hand, is Truth, Justice, Immortality essentially, because he is likewise divinity.[24] It is important, then, to notice that Origen identifies beatitude with the immortality which God alone possesses (*Dial. Herac.* 26–27). This is why relative immortality—which is a share in that beatitude—unlike absolute immortality, does not belong to the nature of a

[22]Grouzel, "Mort . . .," p. 93.

[23]*Com. Jn.* II. 18 (12). 124–125: *GCS* IV, 75, 4; *SC* 120, 288.

[24]C. Blanc, *Origène: Commentaire sur s. Jean* (*SC* 120; Paris, 1966) 288, n. 2.

rational creature, a nature conferred in the divine creative act.[25] The identification of beatitude and God's immortality points to the essentially participatory nature of relative immortality: a soul will obtain it only by participation in Christ, who possesses it from the Father as an *epinoia*
(attribute).

Another fact emerges from the identification of beatitude and God's
immortality: the soul here below cannot be absolutely immortal in regard
to the death because of sin, the bad death. While they live in the world,
all the saints are also sinners:[26]

> Saints are said to be those, who, while they are at the same time sinners, have
> nonetheless consecrated themselves to God, and have separated their lives from
> common dealing in order to serve the Lord. (*Hom. Nb.* X. 1)[27]

This is a very important emphasis in Origen's theology. Every Christian
should be a student of holiness, striving to share more fully in Christ's
epinoiai, for this participation is the measure of the soul's relative immortality, its beatitude. Conversely, because the soul here below is vulnerable to the death because of sin, the bad death, every precaution must
be taken against it. Nevertheless, some souls succumb to it.

For Origen, to suffer death in the soul because of sin is to be unfaithful
to one's baptismal commitment.[28] Since baptism does not produce an
abiding sinlessness, the soul is always vulnerable to death because of sin.
In fact, Origen says every human being is a sinner, "since he/she is
necessarily negligent in many things" (*Hom. Nb.* X. 1).[29] Sin exists and
will always exist in the church, like the weeds in the wheat (Mt. 13:24–
30), or the pagan Jebusites in Jerusalem (Josh. 15:62).[30]

Given the fact of sin in the church and the world, a person living the
Christian life should be aware of the sin in his/her life and what it can
do. Only God is impeccable, for to him alone belongs true holiness in a
substantial way; for everyone else, it is only accidental.[31] In possessing
holiness only in an accidental way, a rational creature is always open to
progression or regression. The reality of sin, especially as it is manifest
in the church and in the life of a Christian, shows the rational creature's
vulnerability to the death of sin. That is why the soul has a relative im-

[25]Crouzel, "Mort . . .," p. 93.

[26]Ibid.

[27]*Hom. Nb.* X. 1: *GCS* VII, 70, 16.

[28]*Hom. Ps. 37.* I. 6: *PG* 12, 1380C.

[29]Crouzel, "Mort . . .," p. 94.

[30]A. Jaubert, *Origène: Homélies sur Josué* (*SC* 71; Paris, 1960) 432, n. 1.

[31]*De princ.* I. 8. 3: *GCS* V, 100, 11; *SC* 252, 226, 92.

mortality in the face of this bad death. In the same way, the life of virtue points to the gradual acquisition of that relative immortality which is identified with beatitude and with God's holiness and immutability, i.e., with God's sinlessness:

> God, then, is immutable, and because of this, He is called "one," since He does not change (cf. Mal. 3, 6). So then, the just imitator of God (cf. 1 Cor. 11, 1)—who was made to His image (cf. Gn. 1, 27)—is also called "one," when he has come to perfection, because he too, when he stands on the pinnacle of virtue, does not change, but stays always one. (*Hom. 1 Rg. /1 Sm.* I. 4)[32]

Perhaps a concrete example can make all of this clearer: Sometimes, in order to emphasize the damage done by the death because of sin, but more especially to underscore the immortality restored by Christ, Origen will contrast the two immortalities, absolute and relative, as he does in his exegesis of the parable of the Good Samaritan (Lk. 10: 30 ff.). Here, he equates the man who fell in with robbers and was beaten, stripped, and robbed with Adam:

> The wounds are his disobedience and his sins. The stripping of the garments is the loss (*gymnosin*: lit. denuding) of incorruptibility and immortality and the deprivation of every virtue. It is clear that the man being left half-dead signifies that death has advanced into half of his nature—for the soul is immortal. (*Frag. Lc.* 168)[33]

In this exegesis, Adam is half-dead; this signifies common, physical death, which only touches half of his nature—the corporeal part—since his soul is immortal in an absolute sense. However, the stripping of the garments is seen as a loss of incorruptibility and immortality and a consequent loss of all virtue. This occurs because of disobedience and sin. The immortality lost here is the relative immortality, which is lost to the death because of sin. Christ, of course, is identified with the Good Samaritan—Christ incarnate from the Virgin Mary. The donkey that carries the wounded man is identified with Christ's human body; the wine he pours on the wounds (i.e., the sins) is his teaching and correcting word; the oil used for the same purpose is the doctrine of love and mercy; and the inn and the innkeeper are the church and her leadership. The two coins are the two Testaments, Old and New, or else love of God and love of neighbor, or, even better, the knowledge of the Father and the Son. Finally, the return of the Samaritan is the second coming of Christ.[34] What Origen presents here, in effect, is a brief summary of salvation history centered on the two immortalities, especially the second one. Salvation history

---

[32]*Hom. 1 Rg. (1 Sm.)* I. 4: *GCS* VIII, 6, 23.
[33]*Frag. Lc.* 168: *GCS* IX², 296, 7; *SC* 87, 520.
[34]Ibid.

could be understood in terms of the loss and restoration of relative immortality.

The exegesis of the parable of the Good Samaritan makes clear that the restoration of relative immortality is a gift of grace. This is a point that Origen insists on over and over again. Ultimately, this gift has its source in the life of the Trinity. Proximately, we share in this gift through Christ. By his incarnation into this world, Christ makes it possible for us to share in his *epinoiai* (attributes), which he, in turn, receives from the Father, who is the ultimate source of immortality.[35]

It should be noted that the *epinoiai* are not only expressions of participation, reflecting their subjective side, but are also the means of participation, reflecting their objective side: it is by participation in the Son of God insofar as he is Wisdom, Life, Truth, etc., that we become, on our level, wise, living, true, etc., and can be called such.[36]

As far as Origen is concerned, the incarnation means the real arrival of the Logos.[37] The excellence of this mission, according to Origen, is revealed by an immediate presence of the Son of God among us, by the totality of salvation, and by the growth of the knowledge of the mystery of the Trinity which the incarnation brings with it.[38] Even if, for Origen, the corporeality of Christ has in some respects the more negative function of a filter—corporeality, in his thinking, necessarily means concealment of the Godhead—and appears to lose much of its positive significance as a medium of revelation in the view of eternity; nevertheless, the whole possibility of this view and the ascent to it through participation in the *epinoiai* depend on the fact of the incarnation.[39] Even for a soul in glory, the Lord's humanity will be an object of contemplation.[40] In the *historicity* of the Lord's incarnation is grounded the possibility of participation by the individual soul in his *epinoiai*. Only by such participation, according to Origen, is salvation possible. This is the way an individual Christian achieves death to sin and the consequent reward of blessed immortality.

---

[35]Cf. *Com. Jn.* II. 12–18. *GCS* IV, 54, 6; *SC* 120, 214, 13.

[36]Blanc, *SC* 120, 217, n. 3.

[37]*Com. Jn.* I. 198–200: *GCS* IV, 36, 14; *SC* 120, 214, 13.

[38]G. Aeby, *Les missions divines de saint Justin à Origène* (Fribourg, 1958) 150; cf. *De princ.* II. 6. 2: *GCS* V, 140, 25; *SC* 252, 310, 51.

[39]A. Grillmeier, *Christ in Christian Tradition* (London, 1975) 144–45; 144, n. 142.

[40]*Com. Jn.* II. 61: *GCS* IV, 62, 19; *SC* 120, 242, 25.

II
Is the Soul Entirely Deprived of a Body after
Common, Physical Death?

The question now arises about the relationship, after common death, of the immortal soul to its body. Specifically, will it possess any kind of body?

Most of Origen's texts present the soul without a body between the time of death and the final resurrection.[41] However, for Origen, both the word "body" and the word "incorporeal" always have a certain ambiguity. The idea of being without a body, i.e., incorporeality, can be understood, for example, in at least two ways: first, it can refer to having no body at all; and second, it can refer to having not an earthly body, but one which is subtle and invisible, and so is commonly called incorporeal.[42]

This second sense of incorporeality—referring not to an earthly body, but to one which is subtle and invisible—occurs at least a few times in Origen. In describing the subtle, invisible body as the *ochēma* "vehicle of the soul," Origen is using an image rooted in classical philosophy. The *ochēma*, "vehicle of the soul," is variously called a "luminous body," an "etheral" or "pneumatic body," or an "astral body," the latter term apparently not used earlier than Proclus (410/12–485 C.E.). The imagery is based on the theory that the mind and body are linked together by a *tertium quid*, an inner envelope of the soul, which is less material than the fleshy body and survives its dissolution, yet it does not have the pure immateriality of the mind.[43]

In the early Christian writers, the question becomes complicated by the Pauline doctrine of the "spiritual body" (cf. 1 Cor. 15:44ff.), which has a different origin from the Greek *ochēma-pneuma* theory, but is often fused with it by Christian Platonists. Origen, for example, uses the "luminous body" to explain apparitions of the dead.[44] Origen also uses the *ochēma* in his exegesis of the creation story in Genesis: the creation from dust (Gen. 2:7) refers to the subtle, luminous body, which from the beginning was furnished to rational creatures.[45] He uses it once more to

[41]Crouzel, "Mort . . .," p. 181. *E.g., Ser. Mt.* 51: *GCS* XI, 113, 31; *Com. Jn.* XXVIII. 6 (5), 44: *GCS* IV, 395, 44; *C. Cels.* II. 43: *GCS* I, 166, 8; *SC* 132, 382, 6.

[42]*E.g., De princ.* I. pref. 8: *GCS* V, 14, 16; *SC* 252, 86, 147.

[43]E. R. Dodds, *Proclus: the Elements of Theology,* 2nd ed. (Oxford, 1963) 313.

[44]Ibid. 315, 314; cf. *C. Cels.* II. 60: *GCS* I, 183, 5; *SC* 132, 424, 10; *Phaedo,* 81d.

[45]For this discussion, cf. M. Simonetti, "Alcune osservazioni sull' interpretazione origeniana di Genesi 2,7 e 3,21," *Aevum* 36 (1962):370–381.

describe the body of the glorified Lord.[46] Then, again, in a text preserved by Methodius, he uses it to describe the soul between death and resurrection:

> Concerning the rich man and Lazarus (cf. Lk. 16, 19 ff.), it is possible to be embarrassed. Simple folk believe that this passage means that both of them receive with their bodies (*meta tōn sōmatōn*) the rewards for what they accomplished in life. Those who are more intelligent do not think that these events take place in the resurrection, since after the resurrection, no one will be left behind in this life.— For the rich man says: *I have five brothers; and lest they come to this place of torment, send Lazarus to tell them what goes on here* (cf. Lk. 16, 28).—On this account, they investigate the tongue, and the finger, and the bosom of Abraham and the reclining position. Perhaps this (i.e., the reclining position) can be taken as the vehicle (*ochēma*) of the soul at the moment of departure, being in the same form (*homoieides*) with the dense, earthly body. Whenever someone who has fallen asleep is reported to have appeared, he is seen to be like the appearance (*schemati*) which he had when in the flesh. But when Samuel appeared (cf. 1 Sm. 28, 3–25), as it is plain, he was visibly standing there clothed with a body, especially if we are constrained to clarify by demonstrations that the substance of the soul is incorporeal (*asōmaton*). But the rich man is being punished and the poor man is resting in the bosom of Abraham before the *parousia* of the Savior and before the consummation of the ages, and because of this, before the resurrection. And the two of them, the one said to be in torment in Hades, and the other to be resting in Abraham's bosom, teach us that the soul, both now and in separation, uses a body. (*De resurrectione*, III. 17)[47]

For our discussion, Origen's use of the Middle Platonic *ochēma* helps to clarify a critical problem in his Christian theology of the resurrection: there must be a real continuity between the earthly and the glorified body. Origen accepted this necessity as arising from the clear teaching of the apostle on this matter, when he discussed the transition from the earthly to the glorified body in terms of a seed developing into a plant (1 Cor. 15:35–44). The mystery of the relationship between the two bodies is one of identity and difference, just as between the seed and the plant there in both continuity and difference.[48]

The importance of this point in Origen's theology becomes clearer when it is realized that he is trying to defend the reality of the resurrection of the dead against unbelievers, heretics, and others who deny it or distort it. The most prominent among the last group are the Millenarians, whom Origen accuses of simply transposing earthly existence into heavenly existence. In other words, the physical body would be no different from the spiritual one. In terms of the relationship between the earthly body and

---

[46]*Com. Mt.* XVI. 19: *GCS* X, 539, 11.

[47]Methodius, *De resurrectione* III. 17: ed. N. Bonwetsch, *GCS* XXVII, 413, 17.

[48]H. Crouzel, "La doctrine origenienne du corps ressuscité," *Bulletin de littérature ecclésiastique* 81 (1980):176.

the glorified one, the Millenarians would keep the identity but suppress the difference—a difference affirmed by the apostle.[49] It is toward and against the Millenarians above all that Origen directs his own theology of the resurrected body.

Here is an example of just one of his theological arguments, one which incorporates the idea of the *ochēma,* "vehicle of the soul." This argument will deal with difference, not identity. As we have just seen, central to the apostle's theology, according to Origen, is not only the identity between the earthly body and the risen one, but also the difference. Jesus' own refutation of the Sadducees' attack on the resurrection (Mt. 22:29–33; Mk. 12:24–27) furnishes four ideas, three of which Origen uses in discussing the *difference* between the earthly body and the glorified one—a difference denied by the Millenarians. The four ideas are:

(1) The Sadducees are in error because they know neither the scripture nor the powers of God.

(2) In the resurrection, men and women will not marry.

(3) The resurrected will be like the angels in heaven.

(4) The resurrected will not be the dead, but the living.

Origen develops most of his ideas around point 3, and secondarily point 1, insofar as it is the scripture he is seeking to explain, with point 2 rounding off his discussion.[50]

One of the major differences between the resurrected body and the earthly body is that the former will be like that of an angel; this is a direct testimony from scripture (Mt. 22:30; Mk. 12:25; Lk. 10:36). Origen makes frequent use of these texts in discussing both spiritual beings (i.e., souls) and the resurrected.[51] He explicitly taught that both angels and demons have bodies, but of a subtle, light texture much more attenuated than our own. The idea of the *ochēma* provides the common thread and the link. The etheral, luminous body called the *ochēma,* the "vehicle of the soul," before it was clothed in the dense, heavy body of flesh and blood, is not only the soul's resurrected body too, but is also equivalent to an angelic body:

[49]Ibid. pp. 176, 178–79.

[50]Ibid. p. 184.

[51]Ibid. p. 185; cf. *Hom. Lv.* IV. 4; IX. 11 for Mt. 22: 30: *GCS* VI, 320, 1; *SC* 286, 172, 32: *GCS* VI, 439, 1; *SC* 287, 122, 3; *Ser. Mt.* 72 for Lk. 20: 36: *GCS* XI, 172, 14; *Com. Rm.* III. 1 for Mt. 22: 30: *PG* 14, 926A; *Com. Ct.* III (IV) for Mt. 22: 30: *GCS* VIII, 228, 14.

> I think, then, because of these things, it becomes clear that not only because there is no marriage or giving in marriage do those judged worthy of the resurrection of the dead become like angels in heaven, but also because their bodies of humiliation (cf. Phil. 3, 21), being transfigured (*metaschematizomena*), became like (*hopoia*) the bodies of angels, ethereal (*aitheria*), a luminous (*aygoeides*) light. (*Com. Mt.* XVII. 30)[52]

The ethereal body of a demon is the same as that of an angel, except that it is not luminous, but murky and dark. Those who rise to damnation have bodies very much like demons, although Origen does not explicitly assimilate them to demons:

> We must also see if, perchance, this expression does not signify what follows: just as the saints will receive back in the resurrection their own bodies, now become luminous and glorious—the bodies in which they lived in a holy and pure manner while in this life—so too the wicked—who in this life loved the darkness of errors and the night of ignorance—will be clothed after the resurrection with murky and black bodies, so that the very darkness of ignorance, which in this world occupied the interior of their mind, might in the future appear outwardly through the garment of the body. (*De princ.* II, 10, 8)[53]

The resurrection of the body thus parallels the relative immortality of the soul: a soul that dies a good death to sin has a bright luminous body; a soul that dies a bad death because of sin has a dark, murky body.

In conclusion, it should be noted that Origen over-emphasized the difference of the resurrected body from the earthly one to the point of putting the identity in real danger. In the second point of his answer to the Sadducees, Jesus said the resurrected person does not marry, nor is given in marriage. Using the postulate that the Creator makes only what is useful, Origen argues that in the world of becoming there is generation and corruption, thus the necessity of sexual relations, procreation, and familial, spousal, and fraternal relationships. However, in the world to come, none of this will be necessary; there will only be a spiritual paternity and fraternity, and the only marriage celebrated will be the eternal marriage of Christ and the church.[54]

What Origen is, in fact, doing here opens up his arguments to a serious weakness: to stress the difference between the resurrected body and the earthly body to the point of suppressing not only the physical organs of becoming, but also the fundamental relationships that have been constitutive of the person in this life is to place in jeopardy the principle of identity between the person here below and the person in the future life.

[52]*Com. Mt.* XVII. 30: *GCS* X, 671, 10.
[53]*De princ.* II. 10. 8: *GCS* V, 182, 3; *SC* 252, 392, 265.
[54]*Com. Mt.* XVII. 29 and 33: *GCS* X, 670, 15 and 688, 22.

In other words, his stress on difference has put identity in real danger, not in relation to the body but in relation to the spiritual personality, i.e., the soul. Origen did not appreciate this danger, but it was one of the points that was most criticized during the Origenist quarrels of subsequent centuries.[55]

[55]Crouzel, "Corps ressuscité . . .," pp. 196–200.

The Catholic Historical Review

VOL. LXXX   APRIL, 1994   No. 2

IMAGES OF THE RESURRECTION BODY IN THE
THEOLOGY OF LATE ANTIQUITY

BY

CAROLINE W. BYNUM[*]

Those of you who are practicing Christians (at least if you are Roman
Catholic or from mainline Protestant denominations) and those of you
who are observant Jews may perhaps know that you are supposed to
affirm the resurrection of the dead. *Resurrectio carnis* or *mortuorum*
is in the Christian creeds; Luther and Calvin asserted it. The resurrection of the dead is one of the three core beliefs of rabbinic Judaism.
The greatest Jewish and Christian theologians of the Middle Ages—
figures such as Maimonides and Thomas Aquinas—wrote about the
doctrine in similar ways.[1]

The idea is, however, implausible to common sense. It may be
difficult to believe that soul or spirit or psyche survives after death,

---

[*]Ms. Bynum is the Morris and Alma Schapiro Professor of History in Columbia University, Dean of General Studies, and Associate Vice-President for Undergraduate Education. She read this paper as her presidential address at a luncheon held in the San
Francisco Hilton Hotel on Saturday, January 8, 1994, during the seventy-fourth annual
meeting of the American Catholic Historical Association.

[1]See A. Michel, "Resurrection des morts," in *Dictionnaire de théologie catholique*,
ed. A. Vacant *et al.* (Paris, 1909–1950), vol. 13, pt. 2, cols. 2501–2571; H. Cornélis, J.
Guillet, Th. Camelot, and M. A. Genevois, *The Resurrection of the Body*, Themes of
Theology (Notre Dame, Indiana, 1964); George W. E. Nickelsburg, Jr., *Resurrection,
Immortality and Eternal Life in Intertestamental Judaism* ("Harvard Theological Stud-
ies," Vol. 26 [Cambridge, Massachusetts, and London, 1972]); Günter Stemberger, *Der
Leib der Auferstehung: Studien zur Anthropologie und Eschatologie des palästinischen
Judentums im neutestamentlichen Zeitalter (ca. 170 v. Chr.–100 n. Chr.)* ("Analecta
Biblica: Investigationes scientificae in res biblicas," Vol. 56 [Rome, 1972]); Joanne E.
McWilliam Dewart, *Death and Resurrection* ("Message of the Fathers of the Church,"
Vol. 22 [Wilmington, Delaware, 1986]); Gisbert Greshake and Jacob Kremer, *Resurrectio
mortuorum: Zum theologischen Verständnis der leiblichen Auferstehung* (Darmstadt,
1986); Shaye J. D. Cohen, *From the Maccabees to the Mishnah* (Philadelphia, 1987),
pp. 23, 89, 91–103, 220–224; H. Crouzel and V. Grossi, "Resurrection of the Dead," in
Encyclopedia of the Early Church, ed. A. Di Berardino, tr. Adrian Walford, 2 vols. (New
York, 1992), vol. 2, pp. 732–733. This lecture is adapted from part of chapter 1 of my
book *The Resurrection of the Body in Western Christianity, 200–1336* (New York:
Columbia University Press, forthcoming).

but it seems to modern western folks to be even more difficult to think that the whole embodied person can come back after hundreds of years. We *see* after all that corpses—even mummified corpses—decay. How can a body come back? Uncomfortable with a kind of survival after death that even medieval Jews and Christians thought to be in some ways miraculous (or contrary to nature), many modern religious people try to interpret resurrection as if it *means* the immortality of the soul.[2] But for hundreds and hundreds of years, resurrection meant return at the end of time of the embodied person or restoration to the surviving soul of its own body exactly (with some exceptions of detail) as it had been on earth. Why did it matter so much to get the body back? Why did theologians and ordinary believers keep on trying to formulate and argue for *bodily* resurrection?

The answer to this question lies in part before the emergence of Christianity, in Jewish ideas of return, restoration, and resurrection. The hope that early Christians placed in the empty tomb was based, as Oscar Cullmann has shown, on Jewish ideas of the resurrection or return from the dead of a psychosomatic entity—a whole person.[3] Second-century Christian martyr accounts echo with great faithfulness the literalism of II Maccabees 7:10–11, where the third son to be put to death for refusing to violate dietary laws says to his tormentor as he holds forth his hands to the sword: "These I had from heaven . . . and from [God] I hope to receive them again."

Nonetheless the earliest Christian texts that promise general resurrection—pre-eminently I Corinthians 15, fundamental to all later theologies of resurrection—are deeply enigmatic, subject to spiritualist as well as literal, materialist interpretation.[4] What does it mean to hold that we, "sown a natural body," shall rise "a spiritual body"

[2]Colleen McDannell and Bernhard Lang, *Heaven: A History* (New Haven, 1988), pp. 307–352; James Bowman, review of Garry Wills, *Under God: Religion and American Politics* (New York, 1990), in *The Times Literary Supplement*, March 29, 1991, p. 11; and Timothy C. Morgan, "The Mother of All Muddles," in *Christianity Today* (April 5, 1993), pp. 62–66.

[3]Oscar Cullmann, "Immortality and Resurrection," in Krister Stendahl (ed.), *Immortality and Resurrection* (New York, 1965), pp. 9–53; idem, "Immortality of the Soul or Resurrection of the Dead? The Witness of the New Testament," in Terence Penelhum (ed.), *Immortality* (Belmont, California, 1973), pp. 53–84.

[4]C. F. D. Moule, "St. Paul and Dualism: The Pauline Conception of Resurrection," *New Testament Studies*, 13 (1965–1966), 106–123; Robert H. Gundry, *Soma in Biblical Theology with Emphasis on Pauline Anthropology* (Cambridge, 1976); and Paul Gooch, *Partial Knowledge: Philosophical Studies in Paul* (Notre Dame, Indiana, 1987), pp. 81–83.

(1 Cor. 15:44)? that the bare seed shall return a sheaf (1 Cor. 15:37–38)? that "flesh and blood cannot inherit the kingdom" (1 Cor. 15:50)? Even without the garbling the verse underwent in translations of the first few centuries, I Corinthians 15:51 ("we shall [not?] all be changed") could be interpreted to indicate many different kinds of survival. Moreover, Jewish Apocalyptic literature of the first centuries before and after the Common Era already made use of a variety of technical philosophical concepts (including the idea of soul) to explain return after death. And Gospel accounts of Jesus's resurrection clearly imply a range of interpretation. They stress the materiality of the body of Jesus, who ate boiled fish and honeycomb and commanded Thomas the Doubter "Handle and see" (Luke 24:39, 41–43). But they also underline the radical transformation of the resurrected Christ, who passed through closed doors and bade his friend Mary Magdalen, "Touch me not!" (Luke 24:16–30, 31, 36, and 51; John 20:14, 19, and 21.4).[5] If in the first six centuries those Christian polemicists who argued for literal bodily resurrection tended to find their positions enshrined in doctrine by creeds and councils, emerging victorious over spiritualizing interpretations that were often more coherent philosophically and more plausible to common sense, the outcome was not predetermined by the Scriptures—either Hebrew or Christian. Something deep in the historical circumstances and the spiritual needs of many in the ancient world led to the victory of theological and exegetical positions in which Jonah, vomited up undigested by the whale, and Daniel, uneaten in the lions' den, were the paradigms of salvation.

Two sets of controversies in the early church were crucial to the establishment of the literalist interpretation of the doctrine of bodily resurrection: the controversy over Gnosticism and Docetism of the years around 200 and the controversy over Origenism in the early fifth century. Both have been exhaustively studied, with methods which vary all the way from the narrowly textual to the broadly contextual. Internalist histories of theological and philosophical ideas have made it clear that highly technical questions about identity, survival, and self were at stake in debates not only over resurrection but also over eucharist, ecclesiology, and asceticism. Durkheimian and feminist interpretations have recently demonstrated that the materialist, orthodox stance did in some ways enforce a hierarchical and gendered social order, although they have been less successful in

---

[5]Peter Carnley, *The Structure of Resurrection Belief* (Oxford, 1987), pp. 16–19.

showing liberating implications in the spiritualist reading of body. Despite the wealth of available interpretation, however, I would like to consider again the early Christian idea of bodily resurrection in order to suggest that those scholars who have focused on doctrine and those who have focused on social context have neglected to study the place in the texts themselves that most successfully links these two approaches. That place is the images—that is, the analogies, metaphors, limiting cases, scriptural quotations, etc.—with which the idea of resurrection is glossed. Without a way of linking ideas to context, historians of doctrine have been left with the dubious argument that ideas win out because they are "better" ideas—an argument that is highly embarrassing if one takes one's stand in, for example, 401, with Jerome against Origen. Without any way other than the *a priori* (for example, Marxist, feminist, new historicist, etc.) of choosing which context is appropriate, social historians have been left with the tautological finding that ideas reflect the context against which one chooses to locate them. I want to suggest that the extensive writings on resurrection from the first six centuries inform us—not so much in their formal theological and philosophical arguments as in their asides, their analogies, the examples they adduce from common experience, their quotations and misquotations—which social context we should refer to in assessing the victory of a materialist theology. I want, that is, to argue that the texts do tell us—if we read enough of them and read them carefully—why it mattered so much to get the body back.[6] Although full analysis requires consideration of both the debates of 200 and those of 400, I will limit myself today to texts from the late second and early third centuries and to the contexts in religious and social practice they suggest for themselves.[7] I begin, as I have argued one should, with images.

Most Christian writers of the second century assumed some sort of resurrection of the dead, at least of the just dead; frequently they connected such resurrection to a millennial age. Their metaphors were

[6]For internalist histories of ideas see the works cited in fn. 1. For recent Durkheimian and/or feminist interpretations see Elaine Pagels, *The Gnostic Gospels* (New York, 1979); *eadem, Adam, Eve and the Serpent* (New York, 1988); John Gager, "Body-Symbols and Social Reality: Resurrection, Incarnation and Asceticism in Early Christianity," *Religion*, 12 (1982), 345–364; Elizabeth A. Clark, "New Perspectives on the Origenist Controversy: Human Embodiment and Ascetic Strategies," *Church History*, 59 (1990), 145–162; and *eadem*, review of Peter Brown, *The Body and Society*, in *Journal of Religion*, 70 (1990), 432–436.

[7]In the book I am writing on bodily resurrection I treat both periods at length: see *The Resurrection of the Body* (forthcoming), chapter 2.

naturalist images of return or repetition: the cycle of the seasons, the flowering of trees and shrubs, the coming of dawn after darkness, the fertility of seeds, the return of the phoenix after five hundred years. The point of the metaphors is to emphasize God's power and the goodness of creation. If the Lord can bring spring after winter or cause the grape to grow from the vine, if he can create Adam from dust and cause the child to emerge from a drop of semen, surely he can bring back men and women who sleep in the grave. In these early texts, resurrection (which is, in some cases, the advent of an earthly paradise) is connected to the most extraordinary fertility. Papias, for example, says:

> A time is coming when vineyards spring up, each having ten thousand vines ... and every grape, when pressed, will yield twenty-five measures of wine. And when anyone of the saints takes hold of one of their clusters, another cluster will cry out: 'I am better. Take me....'[8]

Late first- and early second-century texts thus depend in their resurrection imagery on Pauline metaphors of seeds and first-fruits. But they do not convey the sense of radical change implied by the resurrection verses in I and II Corinthians. Rather they make the world to come a grander and more abundant version of this world. Indeed, they draw such a close analogy between resurrection and natural change that they either make resurrection a process set in motion by the very nature of things or they make *all* growth dependent on divine action.

Like I Corinthians, these texts suggest a kind of continuity but attribute it to no principle. Identity is not yet an explicit issue. As is true in some contemporary Jewish texts, the natural metaphors mean that the whole person returns—changed, perfected, pure, and fertile like a green tree, but the same self. Neither in philosophical argument nor in image is the question yet raised: what would account for the "me-ness" of the "me" that returns? When, for example, the text known as I Clement uses the return of the phoenix as an analogy to resurrection, the author speaks of two birds. A new phoenix, bearing aloft the bones of the old, seems to him an adequate image for return from putrefaction and death.[9]

---

[8]The text, Papias Frag. 1.2–3, is close to II Baruch 29:5, it is quoted in Angelo P. O'Hagan, *Material Re-Creation in the Apostolic Fathers* ("Deutsche Akademie der Wissenschaften zu Berlin, Texte und Untersuchungen zur Geschichte der altchristlichen Literatur," Vol. 100 [Berlin, 1968]), p. 39.

[9]Clement of Rome, *Epître aux Corinthiens*, ed. and tr. A. Jaubert ("Sources chrétiennes," Vol. 167 [Paris, 1971]), cc. 23–26 and 38, pp. 140–145 and 162–165.

By the end of the second century, "resurrection" was no longer simply a minor theme of discussion and apologetics; it became a major element in disputes among Christians and in Christian defenses against pagan attack. Entire treatises were devoted to the topic. Resurrection not of "the dead" or "the body" (*soma* or *corpus*) but of "the flesh" (*sarx* or *caro*) became a key element in the fight against Docetism (which treated Christ's body as in some sense unreal or metaphorical) and Gnosticism (which carried "realized eschatology" so far as to understand resurrection as spiritual advance in this life, and therefore as escape from body). The "creeds" that began to appear around 200 required assent to the doctrine of *resurrectio carnis*.[10]

We can see what was at stake in this first period of intense insistence on bodily resurrection if we look at how metaphors and images from the previous 150 years were used and how they changed. In treatises from around 200, the organic, naturalistic images common since Paul continue, but with three striking differences. First, the metaphor of the seed from I Corinthians 15 sheds, as it had already largely done in writers such as Papias and I Clement, implications of radical change between life and afterlife. What is stressed is the similarity between the sheaf that bears the seed and the new sheaf that flowers from it, not the difference between seed and plant. Second, the technical question of identity emerges into prominence; organic images of repetition and return are now interpreted so as to guarantee material continuity from instance to instance—from, for example, chicken to egg to chicken. Third, mechanical, inorganic analogies become more common as images for resurrection. Return from the dead is seen as the reassemblage of a broken pot or destroyed temple, the survival of a gemstone through fire. Images of growth and change—assimilated increasingly to images of decay—come to represent a threat to (as well as a guarantee of) identity. Survival is spoken of as the persistence of food or flesh despite consumption, digestion, and excretion. I give examples from two proponents of literal, bodily resurrection—Theophilus of Antioch and Athenagoras—who wrote between 180 and 200.

Theophilus and Athenagoras both employed arguments taken from the science of their day to support their interpretation of survival as material continuity. Theophilus explains resurrection in mechanical, inorganic metaphors, as the remolding of a vessel so that flaws are removed. When he deploys the standard set of organic images, found

[10]J. N. D. Kelly, *Early Christian Creeds*, 3rd ed. (New York, 1972), and J. G. Davis, "Factors Leading to the Emergence of Belief in the Resurrection of the Flesh," *Journal of Theological Studies*, N.S. 23 (1972), 448–455.

in I Clement, he changes them so as to convey a sense that a material element persists; in his account, true biological change becomes inexplicable. Resurrection is, he says, like the recovery of an invalid from sickness. The sick man's flesh disappears and we know not where it has gone; he recovers and grows fat, and we cannot tell whence comes the new flesh. We say it comes from meat and drink changed into blood, but how can such change occur? It is really the work of God.[11] The argument is so bizarre that one distinguished modern scholar has simply dismissed it as "confused."[12] But we need to note that it not only protects a constant core as the body which rises; it also protects that core against change via digestion as natural process—that is, against destruction by eating or being eaten.

Theophilus's discussion was a response to pagan critics, who found the idea of resurrection not only ludicrous but also horrifying. Who would want to recover his body? asked the pagan Celsus. Corpses are revolting—worse than dung.[13] Such pagan attacks clearly found an echo in ordinary Christian congregations. Although an early third-century text warned Christians against what it saw as Jewish notions of corpse pollution, two later second-century apologists, Tatian and Aristides, agreed that decaying matter was digusting, even polluting.[14] By the time of Athenagoras's treatise on the resurrection in the closing years of the second century, the very choice of images seems to protect "body" from any suggestion that it might rot, either above or in the earth. Athenagoras distrusts organic process. He struggles to establish, through scientific arguments, that body can be broken and reassembled, exactly because it does *not*, through biological mechanisms, absorb anything else.

[11]Theophilus of Antioch, *Ad Autolycum*, ed. and tr. Robert M. Grant ("Oxford Early Christian Texts" [Oxford, 1970]), bk. 1, cc. 8 and 13, bk. 2, cc. 14–15, 26, and 38, bk. 3, cc. 4–5 and 15, pp. 10–13, 16–19, 48–53, 68–69, 96–99, 102–105, and 118–121.
[12]R. M. Grant, "Theophilus of Antioch to Autolycus," *Harvard Theological Review*, 40 (1947), 227–234.
[13]R. M. Grant, "The Resurrection of the Body," *Journal of Religion*, 28 (1948), 188–199.
[14]See Arthur Voobus (tr.), *The Didascalia Apostolorum in Syriac* ("Corpus Scriptorum Christianorum Orientalium," Vol. 402: "Scriptores Syri," Vol. 176 [4 vols.; Louvain, 1979]), vol. 1, pt. 2, pp. 242–247. (The Syriac text is made from a Greek original of the third, possibly the early third, century.) For Tatian, see *Oratio ad Graecos and Fragments*, ed. and tr. Molly Whittaker (Oxford, 1982), cc. 6, 16–18, 20, 25, pp. 11, 33–39, 41, 47–49. For Aristides, see Apology, cc. 4–5, 12, in R. Harris (ed.), *The Apology of Aristides* ("Haverford College Studies," Vols. 6–7, reprinted from "Texts and Studies: Contributions to Biblical and Patristic Literature" [Cambridge, 1891]), pp. 38–39 and 45–46.

To Athenagoras, the issue of identity is crucial. Chapter 25 of his *De resurrectione* argues that the human being cannot be said to exist when body is scattered and dissolved, even if soul survives. So "man" must be forged anew. But it will not be the same man unless the same body is restored to the same soul: such restoration is resurrection.[15] Resurrection must involve transformation, to be sure. We must rise incorruptible; else we would merely dissolve again. But Athenagoras mentions the growth and decay of seeds and semen only to argue against such processes as paradigms of resurrection. Resurrection is the reassemblage of parts. God "unites and gathers together again" bodies that are "entirely dissolved into their elements." And God can do this because he knows what nature must be reconstituted and he knows where the particles are. Even if the body has been divided up among many animals who have eaten it and "made it part of their members," God can still find the human bits to reassemble.

This is the famous chain consumption argument that became increasingly important in the third century.[16] And Athenagoras understands it in its full complexity. For the problem is not really the attacks of carrion beasts or of worms in the grave: the problem is digestion and cannibalism. If meat and drink do not merely pass through us but become us, there will be too much matter for God to reassemble; on the other hand, if people really eat other people, even God may have trouble sorting out the particles. Athenagoras handles the problem by asserting, in chapters 5–7, that most food and drink pass through our bodies without really becoming them. God has designated certain foods as suitable for each species, and only those can be absorbed. Athenagoras then moves on, in chapter 8, to the astonishing argument that it is impossible for human flesh to absorb human flesh. He even asserts that we can find empirical verification for this in the fact that cannibals lose weight and waste away.[17]

[15]Athenagoras, *De resurrectione*, in *Legatio and De Resurrectione*, ed. and tr. William R. Schödel ("Oxford Early Christian Texts" [Oxford, 1972]), cc. 2–12, 14–15, 17, and 25, pp. 90–119, 120–127, 128–131, and 146–147.

[16]See Grant, "Resurrection of the Body," pp. 20–30 and 188–208; and L. W. Barnard, "Athenagoras: *De Resurrectione*: The Background and Theology of a Second Century Treatise on the Resurrection," *Studia Theologica*, 30 (1976), 1–42.

[17]Athenagoras, *De res.*, tr. Schödel, cc. 5–8, pp. 98–109. On the fear of cannibalism and digestion, and the tendency to assimilate stomach to tomb, see his *Legatio*, tr. Schödel, c. 36, p. 85: "What man who believes in a resurrection would offer himself as a tomb for bodies destined to arise? For it is impossible at one and the same time to believe that our bodies will arise and then eat them as though they will not arise, or to think that the earth will yield up its dead and then suppose that those whom a man had buried within himself will not reclaim their bodies."

Theophilus and Athenagoras thus appear to be driven by more than a need to reject the spiritualizing interpretation that saw resurrection as metaphor for moral reform in this life or for survival of the soul after death. As the analogies they use make clear, they insist first, on the palpable, fleshly quality of the body that will be rewarded or punished at the end of time, and second, on the identity—through material continuity—of that body with the body of here and now.

We find a similar insistence in the three great treatises on resurrection from the years around 200: Irenaeus's *Adversus Haereses*, Tertullian's *De resurrectione carnis*, and Minucius Felix's *Octavius*. Irenaeus, for example, asserts that what falls must rise, and draws analogies to the three children in the fiery furnace and Jonah in the whale.[18] He explains that, in the process of grafting, substance lasts although quality changes, and in healing, the withered and the healthy hand is the same hand. Indeed, he treats resurrection as a special case of bodily restoration and underlines man's materiality by stressing that the missing eye Christ repaired with a paste of dust was created from that dust.[19]

Tertullian also sees resurrection as reassemblage of bits. In fact, Tertullian—following Stoic metaphysics—holds that all reality is corporeal. Even soul is composed of very fine material particles.[20] But only body can rise, for only body is cast down; soul is immortal. Bodies, therefore, do not vanish; bones and teeth last and are "germs" that will "sprout" in resurrection. Jonah was not digested in the whale.[21]

---

[18]Irenaeus, *Adversus haereses*, bk. 5, cc. 5 and 12, Irenaeus of Lyons, *Contre les hérésies*, ed. and tr. Adelin Rousseau, 2 vols. ("Sources chrétiennes," Vols. 152–153 [Paris, 1969]), vol. 2, pp. 60–73 and 140–163. Irenaeus's complete treatise survives only in a rather literal Latin translation; Syriac and Greek fragments survive and an Armenian translation of bks. 4 and 5. And see A. H. C. Van Eijk, " 'Only That Can Rise Which Has Previously Fallen': The History of a Formula," *Journal of Theological Studies*, N.S. 22 (1971), 517–529.

[19]Irenaeus, *Adv. haer.*, bk. 5, cc. 9–12, ed. Rousseau, vol. 2, pp. 106–163. For similar opinions in Minucius Felix, see Minucius Felix, *Octavius*, in *Tertullian and Minucius Felix*, tr. T. R. Glover and G. H. Rendall (Loeb Classical Library [Cambridge, Massachusetts, 1931; reprint, 1977]), especially c. 34, p. 421.

[20]Tertullian, *De resurrectione mortuorum*, ed. J. G. P. Borleffs, c. 17, in *Tertulliani Opera*, pt. 2: *Opera Montanistica* ("Corpus christianorum: series latina" [hereafter CCL] [Turnhout, 1954]), pp. 941–942. Tertullian asserts in his *De anima*, ed. J. H. Waszink, c. 51, *ibid.*, pp. 857–858, that soul is, however, indissoluble; it is not divided into particles at death.

[21]Tertullian, *De res.*, cc. 42, 43, 53, 58, pp. 976–979, 998–1000, 1006–1007. See also his *Apologeticum*, ed. E. Dekkers, c. 48, in *Tertulliani Opera*, pt. 1: *Opera catholica*, CCL (1954), pp. 165–168 (written at least twelve years earlier).

Tertullian even argues that the shoes and clothing of the children of Israel did not wear out, nor did their hair and fingernails grow, while they wandered forty years in the desert.[22] If God can thus suspend natural laws in order to preserve shoe leather and garments, how much more can he preserve flesh or the particles thereof for resurrection? Although Tertullian uses naturalistic images that suggest repetition rather than continuity, he also employs materialistic images of the body as a mended pot, a rebuilt temple, or clothing donned anew.[23] He even understands that the need to affirm identity through radical change is a philosophical challenge so deep as to necessitate a rejection of the standard Aristotelian definition: "a thing that has changed ceases to be what it is and becomes something else." Rather, Tertullian argues, "to be changed is to exist in a different form"; exactly that flesh which sinned must be rewarded.[24]

Sometimes, to Tertullian, identity lodges more in structure than in matter. He argues that, in the resurrection, all of our organs are retained. Defects are healed, mutilations undone. We rise "whole" (*integer*), like a damaged and repaired ship whose parts are restored though some of the planks are new. Indeed, the functions of the risen organs may change or disappear, but no part will be destroyed.[25] Mouths will no longer eat, nor will genitals copulate in heaven; eating and procreation are aspects of the biological change that is part of corruption. But some of these organs will have new uses. Mouths, for example, will sing praise to God. Even the genitals are good, argues Tertullian, because the cleansing of urination and menstruation are good in this life. Such organs will have no function in the resurrection, but they will survive for the sake of beauty.[26] We will not chew in heaven, but we will have teeth, because we would look funny without them. Everything intrinsic to what we are must reappear in the res-

[22]*De res.*, c. 58, pp. 1006–1007. See David Satran, "Fingernails and Hair: Anatomy and Exegesis in Tertullian," *Journal of Theological Studies*, new ser. 40 (1989), 116–120. On Tertullian's use of Jewish exegesis, see also J. Massingberd Ford, "Was Montanism a Jewish-Christian Heresy?" *Journal of Ecclesiastical History*, 17 (1966), 145–158.

[23]*De res.*, cc. 11–12, 32, 40–44, pp. 933–935, 961–963, 973–981.

[24]*De res.*, c. 55, pp. 1001–1003; and see Francine Jo Cardman, *Tertullian on the Resurrection* (Ph.D. dissertation, Yale University, 1974), p. 118.

[25]*De res.*, c. 57, pp. 1004–1005.

[26]*De res.*, cc. 59–62, pp. 1007–1011, esp. c. 61, pp. 1009–1010. This passage makes clear how much more complex Tertullian's ideas are than the charge of misogyny (so often made against him) allows. See F. Forrester Church, "Sex and Salvation in Tertullian," *Harvard Theological Review*, 68 (1975), 83–101.

urrected body, for it is "particulars" that make bodies who they are.[27] Tertullian even argues, in his treatise on women's dress, that if cosmetics and jewels were essential to women they would rise from the dead—an argument echoed by Cyprian fifty years later when he exhorts women not to wear face powder in this life lest God fail to recognize them when they appear without it in the resurrection.[28] In his two works on marriage, Tertullian asserts that—although there will be no marrying in heaven—we will rise male and female, and we will recognize those to whom we have been bound.[29]

Of the three authors I have just mentioned, only Minucius Felix, who draws on standard pagan cosmological notions, sees the resurrected body merely as the reassemblage of bits and parts.[30] Both Irenaeus and Tertullian—with the daring inconsistency of genius—join to an extravagantly materialistic notion of the resurrection body an emphasis on radical change that retains overtones of Paul. Indeed, in contrast to Athenagoras or Minucius Felix, whose metaphors identify body with subsisting particles and suggest that organic change threatens identity, Irenaeus's so-called materialistic view of the body is often expressed in metaphors of fertility and biological transformation. Repeatedly Irenaeus uses the Pauline seed but stresses, as Paul did not, the decomposition it undergoes in the earth.[31] Even the flesh of the saints is torn and devoured by beasts, ground into dust, chewed and

[27]Tertullian, *De anima*, cc. 31 and 56, pp. 828–829 and 863–865; quotation from c. 56, p. 864, 11. 38–41. See also *De res.*, cc. 55–63, pp. 1001–1012.

[28]Tertullian, *De cultu feminarum*, ed. A. Kroymann, bk. 2, c. 7, in *Opera*, pt. 1, p. 361. Tertullian's basic argument is that women as well as men must be prepared for martyrdom; the body in which discipline, suffering, and death happen is the same body that will be lifted to heaven. Cyprian, *De habitu virginum*, c. 17, in Cyprian, *Opera omnia*, ed. William Hartel ("Corpus scriptorum ecclesiasticorum latinorum" [hereafter CSEL], Vol. 3, pts. 1 and 2 [Vienna, 1868]), p. 199.

[29]*Ad uxorem*, ed. A. Kroymann, bk. 1, c. 1, parags. 4–6, in *Opera*, pt. 1, pp. 373–374; *De monogamia*, ed. E. Dekkers, c. 10, parag. 6, in *Opera*, pt. 2, pp. 1243. In *De pallio* (which may be a late work of Tertullian's Montanist period or an early work from just after his conversion),Tertullian connects ostentation with gender confusion and crossdressing; upset because sumptuous dressing can efface the difference between a matron and a brothel keeper here on earth, Tertullian suggests that we need to keep the marks of particularity in heaven in order to maintain there such differences of rank. See *De pallio*, ed. A. Gerlo, cc. 3–4, in *Opera*, pt. 2, pp. 738–746.

[30]See Minucius Felix, *Octavius*, cc. 5 and 11, tr. Rendall, pp. 320–327 and 340–345.

[31]Irenaeus, *Adv. haer.*, bk. 5, c. 2, parags. 2–3; c. 7, parag. 2; c. 10, paragr. 2; c. 28, parag. 4; cc. 33–34; ed. Rousseau, vol. 2, pp. 30–41, 88–93, 126–133, 360–363, 404–437.

digested by the stomach of the earth.[32] The paradigmatic body is the cadaver; flesh *is* that which undergoes fundamental organic change. The sprouting of the resurrected seed into the sheaf of wheat is a victory not so much over sin, or even over death, as over putrefaction. Irenaeus writes:

> ...how can [anyone] affirm that the flesh is incapable of receiving ... life eternal, [when flesh] is nourished from the body and blood of the Lord, and is a member of Him? ... Just as a cutting from the vine planted in the ground fructifies in its season, or as a grain of wheat falling into the earth and becoming decomposed, rises with manifold increase ... and then ... becomes the Eucharist ... ; so also our bodies, being nourished by it, and deposited in the earth, and suffering decomposition there, shall rise at their appointed time, the Word of God granting them resurrection....[33]

Thus, to Irenaeus, the proof of our final incorruption lies in our eating of God. The fact that we become Christ by consuming Christ, but Christ can never be consumed, guarantees that our consumption by beasts or fire or the grave is *not* destruction. Death (rot, decomposition) can be a moment of fertility, which sprouts and flowers and gives birth to incorruption. Because eating God is a transcendent cannibalism that does not consume or destroy, we can be confident that the heretics who would spiritualize the flesh are wrong.[34] Flesh, defined as that which changes, is capable of the change to changelessness.

Tertullian also sees resurrection as radical transformation. The earthly body that eats, procreates, and rots must be glorified, like Stephen who appeared as an angel at his stoning, or Moses and Elias who shone with a foretaste of glory when they appeared with Christ on the mountain.[35] Thus, even before death, those who fast prepare themselves not only for prison and martyrdom but also for the res-

[32]Irenaeus, *Adv. haer.*, bk. 5, cc. 14–16 and 28; ed. Rousseau, vol. 2, pp. 182–221 and 346–363.

[33]Irenaeus, *Adv. haer.*, bk. 5, c. 2, paragr. 3; ed. Rousseau, pp. 34–41; tr. A. Robertson and J. Donaldson, in *Ante-Nicene Fathers*, vol. 1 (1885; reprint, Grand Rapids, Michigan, 1981), p. 528.

[34]At the end of bk. 5, Irenaeus's vision of the coming kingdom is of full material recreation, ablaze with fertility. The dead will rise to an earth of abundant food, in which animals will no longer eat animals. Thus the resurrection will bring a world in which consumption is filling and sustaining, not destructive; the problem of incorporation (how can one take in, or be taken into, without being destroyed?) is finally solved in the "new heaven and new earth."

[35]Tertullian, *De res.*, c. 55, pp. 1001–1003.

urrection. Slenderer flesh will go more easily through the narrow gate of heaven; lighter flesh will rise more quickly; drier flesh will experience less putrefaction in the tomb.[36] Asceticism prepares us for glory by moving our bodies away from mutability and toward the incorruptibility and impassibility of heaven.

Tertullian fulminates against pagan gladiatorial combat as heinous assault on the beauty of bodies created by God; yet he emphasizes that all bodies come eventually to the ugliness and destruction of the grave.[37] Whether laid gently to rest in the tomb, or torn and twisted—eaten by the "maws of beasts," the "crops of birds," and the "stomachs of fishes"—we are all cadavers; we all end up in "time's own great paunch."[38] Thus the final victory must be the eating that does not consume, the decay that does not devour. The fact that we eat God in the eucharist and are truly fed on his flesh and blood is a paradoxical redemption of that most horrible of consumptions: the cannibalism Tertullian thinks pagans practice on the Christian saints.[39]

Tertullian and Irenaeus, like Theophilus, Athenagoras, Minucius Felix and other apologists, wrote to oppose Gnosticism and Docetism, which saw flesh as evil, Christ's body as in some sense unreal, salvation as of the spirit. Yet much about the specificity, passibility, and changeability of body frightened them as well. Whether the subject or object of nutrition, digestion, and decay, body was, by their own accounts, at least as much a threat to as a locus of identity. Why then did they

---

[36]*De ieiunio adversus psychicos*, ed. A. Reifferscheid and G. Wissowa, c. 12 and 17, in *Opera*, pt. 2, pp. 1270–1271 and 1276–1277; *Ad Martyras*, ed. E. Dekkers, cc. 2 and 3, in *Opera*, pt. 1, pp. 3–6. In the *De anima*, Tertullian stresses that what happens in the tomb does not matter; see cc. 51–57, pp. 857–867.

[37]*De spectaculis*, ed. E. Dekkers, cc. 12, 19, 21–23, in *Opera*, pt. 1, pp. 238–239, 244–247; and *De anima*, cc. 51–52, pp. 857–859.

[38]*De res.*, c. 4, pp. 925–926.

[39]*De res.*, c. 8, pp. 931–932. See also Tertullian, *Ad nationes*, ed. J. G. P. Borleffs, bk. 1, c. 2, in *Opera*, pt. 1, pp. 12–13, for charges of cannibalism against pagans; *Apologeticum*, c. 48, pp. 165–168, where Tertullian reports that some pagans abstain from meat because it might be a relative reincarnated; and *De pallio*, c. 5, pp. 746–750, where he tells the story of a pagan who dined indirectly on his slaves by first feeding them to fish, which he then cooked. Minucius Felix, *Octavius*, c. 30, pp. 191–192, makes a similar charge of cannibalism against pagans. Eusebius, *The Ecclesiastical History*, bk. 5, c. 1, tr. Kirsopp Lake, 2 vols. (Loeb Classical Library [London and Cambridge, Massachusetts, 1926; reprint, 1980]), vol. 1, pp. 431–433, reports that one Attalus, while being burned, accused his persecutors of "eating men," something Christians would never do. Aline Rousselle, *Porneia: On Desire and the Body in Antiquity*, tr. Felicia Pheasant (Oxford, 1988), pp. 118–119, uses Tertullian's charges as evidence of (at least indirect) human sacrifice.

choose to privilege Christ eating the honeycomb rather than the *Noli me tangere*? Why did they stress I Corinthians 15:38 ("but God giveth it a body") over I Corinthians 15:50 ("flesh and blood cannot inherit the kingdom")? If we follow, as I have suggested we should, their own images and arguments, Tertullian and Irenaeus suggest that the answer lies in persecution and the arena, in burial practices and funerary meals, and finally, in an understanding of biological process that equates change with corruption. The paradox of transfiguration and continuity that characterizes their images of the risen body seems to originate, in the first instance, in the facts of martyrdom.[40]

Martyred flesh had to be capable of impassibility and transfiguration; suffering and rot could not, to Tertullian, Irenaeus, and Athenagoras, be the final answer. If flesh could put on, even in this life, a foretaste of incorruption, martyrdom might be bearable. Those who watched and feared execution, yet exhorted themselves and others toward it, clung to the belief that (as Tertullian said) "the bites of wild beasts" are "glories to young heroes," because the body, disciplined by asceticism, has already "sent on to heaven" the "succulence of its blood."[41] One of our oldest accounts of a martyrdom asserts that the fire "felt cold" to those who, under torture, fixed their thoughts on Christ.[42] Later martyr stories are filled with examples of saints who do not even notice the most exquisite and extraordinary cruelties. Death for the faith was a necessary and palpable concern in late-second-

[40]Recent scholarship has been inclined to play down the numbers of Christian martyrs and to underline parallels between the expressionism and exhibitionism of pagan games and Christian executions. See G. E. M. de Ste. Croix, "Aspects of the 'Great' Persecution," *Harvard Theological Review*, 47 (1954), 75–113; Charles Saumagne, "Une Persécution de Dèce en Afrique d'après la correspondance de S. Cyprien," *Byzantion*, 32 (1962), 1–29; Aline Rousselle, *op. cit.*, pp. 108–140; W. Rordorf, V. Saxer, N. Duval, and F. Bisconti, "Martyr-Martyrdom," in *Encyclopedia of Early Church*, vol. 1, pp. 531–536; and Carlin Barton, *The Sorrows of the Ancient Romans: The Gladiator and the Monster* (Princeton, 1992). Nonetheless, fear of martyrdom was a real factor in the responses of second-century Christians.

[41]*De Anima*, c. 58, pp. 867–869; *De ieiunio*, c. 12, pp. 1270–1271. The passage in *De anima* also emphasizes a disjunction between body and soul, suggesting that soul can avoid feeling the pain to which body is subjected if it concentrates on heaven. Along similar lines, the letters of Cyprian provide advice to future martyrs about how to avoid terror and pain by imaging torture as a means of uniting with Christ's passion; see Cyprian, Letters 76, c. 2, and 77, c. 3, *Opera*, ed. Hartel, CSEL, vol. 3, pt. 2, pp. 829–830 and 835.

[42]*Martyrdom of Polycarp*, c. 2, in Ignatius of Antioch and Polycarp of Smyrna, *Lettres; Martyre de Polycarpe*, ed. and tr. P. T. Camelot ("Sources chrétiennes," Vol. 10 [3rd ed.; Paris, 1958]), pp. 244–245. Eusebius, *Ecclesiastical History*, bk. 5, c. 1, vol. 1, pp. 433–435, also suggests that God keeps the martyrs from feeling pain.

century writing and behavior; thus it is not surprising that the impassibility of the risen body was stressed as a reward for such sacrifice, or that the terror of execution was allayed by the suggestion that a sort of anesthesia of glory might spill over from the promised resurrection into the ravaged flesh' of the arena, making its experience bearable. Cyprian, who in life exhorted, comforted, and advised future martyrs, supposedly appeared after his death to the martyr Flavian, saying: "It is another flesh that suffers when the soul is in heaven. The body does not feel [the death blow] at all when the mind is entirely absorbed in God."[43]

But the context of martyrdom, within which so much early theological writing emerged, made continuity of body important also. Irenaeus and Tertullian avoided any suggestion that the attainment of impassibility or glory entailed a loss of the particular self that offered up its own death for Christ. Identity was a crucial issue. As Tertullian said, all death (even the gentlest) is violent; all corpses (even the most respectfully buried) rot. Resurrection guarantees that it is *these very corpses* that achieve salvation.[44] The promise that *we* will rise again makes it possible for heroes and ordinary Christians to face, for those they love and revere as well as for themselves, the humiliation of death and the horror of putrefaction.

To place the doctrine of bodily resurrection in the context of martyrdom, as I have just done, is not to make a novel argument. Historians have long recognized that belief in resurrection tends to emerge in response to persecution; and such explanation has been given for the growth of Jewish resurrection belief in the time of the Maccabees as well as for the Christian response to the persecutions of the second century.[45] Yet posed as a rather crude form of compensation theory, the argument does not seem to work especially well for Christian teaching. Much as Tertullian, for example, stresses reward and punishment, he does not mention resurrection in his early exhortations to martyrdom. His basic argument is: if pagans can die for worldly glory, surely Christians can die for God.[46] He never says: God will

[43]*The Passion of Montanus and Lucius*, c. 21, in Herbert Musurillo, *The Acts of the Christian Martyrs* (Oxford, 1972), p. 235.
[44]Tertullian, *De anima*, cc. 51–52, pp. 857–859.
[45]See, for example, G. A. Barton and Kaufmann Kohler, "Resurrection," in *The Jewish Encyclopedia*, ed. Isidore Singer *et al.*, vol. 10 (New York and London, 1905), pp. 382–385; and Frank Bottomley, *Attitudes to the Body in Western Christendom* (London, 1979), p. 52.
[46]See *Ad martyras* (from 197) and *De Corona militis* (from 208 or 211). *Ad martyras*, c. 3, pp. 5–6, does mention attaining an incorruptible crown, and the *Scorpiace* (prob-

reward the martyrs with resurrection and punish their persecutors with hell. When he does treat resurrection as reward, the context is the question of burial. Tertullian is concerned to refute those who think delay in burial injures the soul, or that persons who die violently will wander the earth as ghosts. He devotes much scorn to the pagan idea that souls survive in properly prepared corpses and carefully explains that Christian opposition to cremation has nothing to do with a need to preserve cadavers. Christians prefer to treat corpses gently out of respect, he says, but death is absolute. Resurrection is promised to all bodies, no matter how they died or how they are buried.[47]

Thus it appears that Lionel Rothkrug is right when he gives a more profound version of the compensation argument, suggesting that to Jews of the Maccabean period and to early Christians resurrection was a substitute for the burial owed to the pious.[48] The fourth-century church historian Eusebius, incorporating into his history what we believe to be an authentic account of the martyrdoms at Lyons in 177, reports that the Romans scattered and burned the bodies of the executed in order to dash Christian hopes of resurrection. Christians, however, argued explictly that such repressive measures were useless; divine power renews even pulverized dust. It is resurrection that brings together the scattered bits of the Church's heroes and heroines, providing for them the quiet sepulchre their executioners might prohibit and prevent.[49]

Second- and third-century texts suggest that Christians did worry passionately about the bodies of the saints. Ignatius of Antioch prayed to be totally devoured exactly so that his followers would not be

---

ably 211–212), c. 6, pp. 1079–1081, argues that a special "mansion" in heaven is a reward for martyrdom. But Tertullian's major argument is to compare pagan and Christian self-sacrifice. He even argues that, to pagans, gladiatorial combat is "qualem potest praestare saeculum, de fama aeternitatem, de memoria resurrectionem" (*Scorpiace*, c. 6, pp. 1079–1081, esp. p. 1079, 11. 24–26); how much more therefore should Christians eagerly welcome the true resurrection?

[47] *De anima*, cc. 51–58, pp. 857–869.

[48] Lionel Rothkrug, "German Holiness and Western Sanctity in Medieval and Modern History," *Historical Reflections/Réflexions historiques*, 15 (1988), 215–229.

[49] Eusebius, *Ecclesiastical History*, bk. 5, c. 1, vol. 1, pp. 435–437. Book 8, c. 7, pp. 270–273, makes it clear that denial of burial is an insult. Throughout bk. 5, c. 1, bk. 8, cc. 7–12, and bk. 10, c. 8, Eusebius displays considerable fascination with the details of torture. See also Minucius Felix, *Octavius*, cc. 11, 34, 37–38; pp. 340–345, 416–421 and 426–435; and Arthur Darby Nock, "Cremation and Burial in the Roman Empire," *Harvard Theological Review*, 25 (1932), 334.

endangered by their desire to care for his remains.[50] Cyprian stressed burying the dead, especially the martyrs, as an act of charity.[51] Looking back from the early fourth century, Eusebius reports that the Romans had to post guards to prevent Christians from stealing the ashes or bones of the saints in order to bury them.[52] Although there is no evidence that the Romans regularly denied Christian adherents access to the bodies of the executed, early martyrdom accounts reflect a Christian fear that the authorities want to insult cadavers and prevent burial.[53] The martyrdom of Polycarp, for example, asserts that Romans, Jews, and the devil burnt the body in order to prevent Christians from recovering the sacred flesh which had remained unconsumed on the pyre of execution. But such evil was without success. The body remained unchanged "like bread in the baking, or gold and silver in a furnace."[54] The images are exactly those we find in theological treatises about resurrection; the martyr becomes, while still on earth, the hard and beautiful minerals or undigested bread all our bodies will finally become at the end of time.

There is nothing particularly novel in the suggestion that Christian teaching about resurrection should be located in the context of Jewish and Greco-Roman funerary practice. It is well known that the second and third centuries saw basic changes in Roman burial rites. From about the time of Trajan (d. 117) cremation, fashionable in the first century, began to be replaced by the earlier practice of inhumation.

---

[50]Ignatius, *Epistle to the Romans*, in Ignatius and Polycarp, *Lettres*, ed. Camelot, pp. 130–133.

[51]Victor Saxer, *Morts, Martyrs, Reliques en Afrique chrétienne aux premiers siècles: Les Témoignages de Tertullien, Cyprien et Augustin à la lumière de l'archéologie africaine* ("Théologie historique," Vol. 55 [Paris, 1980]), p. 88.

[52]Eusebius, *Ecclesiastical History*, bk. 5, c. 1, vol. 1, pp. 435–437. The *Acts of Carpus, Papylus and Agathonice*, c. 47, (from the 160's) reports that the Christians secretly took up and guarded the remains; see E. C. E. Owen (tr.), *Some Authentic Acts of the Early Martyrs* (Oxford, 1927), p. 46. For stories of early Christians caring for remains, see Nicole Hermann-Mascard, *Les Reliques des saints: Formation coutumière d'un droit* (Société d'Histoire du Droit: "Collection d'histoire institutionelle et sociale," Vol. 6 [Paris, 1975]), pp. 23–26, and Alfred C. Rush, *Death and Burial in Christian Antiquity* ("Catholic University of America Studies in Christian Antiquity," Vol. 1 [Washington, D.C., 1941]), *passim*, especially pp. 122, 205–206.

[53]See Henri Leclercq, "Martyr," *Dictionnaire d'archéologie chrétienne et de liturgie*, ed. Cabrol and Leclercq, vol. 10 (Paris, 1932), cols. 2425–2540, and Nock, *op. cit.*

[54]*Martyrdom of Polycarp*, cc. 15, 17, and 18, in Ignatius and Polycarp, *Lettres*, ed. Camelot, pp. 262–265, 266–269; quoted passage at p. 264. The prayer put in Polycarp's mouth refers to sharing "the cup" with Christ and to rising in body and soul; *ibid.*, p. 262.

But the older scholarly theory that this change was owing to Christian preference for inhumation has been discredited, and much recent cross-cultural work in both anthropology and history suggests that we can never find a simple, causal relationship between doctrine and burial practice.[55] It is not my contention that Christian doctrine caused a change in funerary practices or that changing burial rites determined Christian teaching. Rather I wish to argue that the images in which polemicists, preachers, and authors of hymns thought of redemption and resurrection reflect what they saw, what they loved and honored, when they prepared bodies for burial and laid them in the grave.[56]

In general it is clear that both cremation and inhumation were efforts to mask and therefore in some ways to deny putrefaction.[57] Cremation was never, in the Roman world, antithetical to inhumation but was in fact a version of it. Ashes were frequently buried in sarcophagi, and a finger (the *os resectum*) was cut off before cremation to be buried with the ashes.[58] The increased popularity of inhumation in the later second and third centuries expressed, as both Nock and Toynbee have pointed out, a growing concern to treat cadavers gently and to minimize images of violence in the afterlife, however conceived.[59] Such

---

[55]Franz Cumont, *After Life in Roman Paganism* (New Haven, 1922); Henri Leclercq, "Incinération," *Dictionnaire d'archéologie chrétienne*, vol. 7, pt. 1 (1926), cols. 502–508; Nock, *op. cit.*; Rush, *op. cit.*; J. M. C. Toynbee, *Death and Burial in the Roman World* (Ithaca, New York, 1971). On the general point, see Paul-Albert Fevrier, "La mort chrétienne," in *Segni e riti nella chiesa altomedievale occidentale*, 2 vols. (Settimane di studio del centro italiano di studi sull'alto medioevo, Vol. 33 [Spoleto, 1987]), vol. 2, pp. 881–942; Frederick S. Paxton, *Christianizing Death: The Creation of a Ritual Process in Early Medieval Europe* (Ithaca, New York, 1990), pp. 3–4; Michel Vovelle, "Les attitudes devant la mort: problèmes de méthode, approches et lectures différentes," *Annales ESC*, 31 (1976), 120–132; and Patricia Ebrey, "Cremation in Sung China," *American Historical Review*, 95 (1990), 406–428.

[56]For pioneering work on the relationship between, on the one hand, the rituals and images used by the living and, on the other, the state of the deceased, see Robert Hertz, "A Contribution to the Study of the Collective Representation of Death," in his *Death and the Right Hand*, tr. R. and C. Needham (Glencoe, Illinois, 1960), pp. 27–86, first published in *Année sociologique*, 10 (1907).

[57]In addition to the works cited in fn. 55 above, see Louis-Vincent Thomas, *Le cadavre: De la biologie à l'anthropologie* (Brussels, 1980).

[58]See Richard Broxton Onians, *The Origins of European Thought About the Body, the Mind, the Soul, the World, Time and Fate: New Interpretations of Greek, Roman, and Kindred Evidence...*, 2nd ed. (Cambridge, 1954), p. 267; Toynbee, *op. cit.*, pp. 48ff.; Rush, *op. cit.*, pp. 241–244; E. Valton, "Crémation," in *Dictionnaire de théologie catholique*, vol. 3, pt. 2 (1938), col. 2316.

[59]As Paxton points out (*op. cit.*, p. 20), funerary rituals both protected the living from the dead and protected the dead from demons.

concern for a peaceful end was expressed in the traditional practice of funerary banquets, celebrated on tombs and understood as feeding and comforting the dead.[60] This desire for a quiet sepulchre was in part a response to the rampant sadism of animal shows and public executions and to the growing moral outrage they generated.[61] Christian images of the resurrected body not only refer, often explicitly, to the martyr's tortured cadaver but also give to it, in metaphor and doctrine, the dignified and pious burial valued in the Mediterranean world. They speak of its survival in language which reflects the characteristic concern of ancient funerary practice for the production of clean, dry bones or ashes. Moreover, they use metaphors of digestion and consumption that echo both a fear of being eaten by wild beasts in the arena and a traditional notion that funerary meals can unite the living and the dead.[62]

Early Christianity, rabbinic Judaism, and the Koran all speak of the body that rises as bones or a seed.[63] Christian exegesis, like rabbinic, came to read the dry bones of Ezekiel 37:1–14 as referring not to the nation of Israel but to individuals. The early rabbis taught that the person would rise when the "nut" of the spinal column was watered or fed by the dew of resurrection, and that the bones of the just would

---

[60]See Nock, op. cit.; Cumont, op. cit., pp. 44–56, and Toynbee, op. cit. On funerary meals, see Saxer, Morts, Martyrs, Reliques, pp. 123–149, and Joan M. Petersen, The Dialogues of Gregory the Great in Their Late Antique Cultural Background ("Studies and Texts," Vol. 69 [Toronto, 1984]), p. 142.

[61]See Barton, op. cit.; Jacques Paul, in L'église et la culture en occident, IXe–XIIe siècles, 2 vols. (Paris, 1986), vol. 2, pp. 674–683; and Michel Rouche, "The Early Middle Ages in the West," in A History of Private Life, vol. 1: From Pagan Rome to Byzantium, ed. Paul Veyne, tr. Arthur Goldhammer (Cambridge, Massachusetts, 1987), pp. 485–517. Lactantius, a polemicist of the late third century who has a strong sense of body/soul dualism, gives a truly horrific description of the brutality of the arena; see Institutes, bk. 6, c. 20, in Lactantius, Opera omnia, ed. Samuel Brandt (CSEL 19 and 27, pt. 2 [Prague-Vienna-Leipzig, 1890; reprint, 1965]), pp. 555–562.

[62]In my different layers of the Old Testament, the grave or the underworld or even Yahweh are spoken of as "eating" the dead; see Nicolas J. Tromp, Primitive Conceptions of Death and the Nether World in the Old Testament ("Biblica et Orientalia," Vol. 21 [Rome, 1969]), pp. 8, 21–32, 107, 172, 191–195, 212. On the prominence of metaphors of consumption in the Greco-Roman world, see Wilfred Parsons, "Lest Men, Like Fishes...," Traditio, 3 (1940), 380–388; Bruce Dickins, "Addendum to 'Lest Men, Like Fishes...,'" Traditio, 6 (1948), 356–357; Saxer, Morts, Martyrs, Reliques, pp. 44–46; and Maggie Kilgour, From Communism to Cannibalism: An Anatomy of Metaphors of Incorporation (Princeton, 1990), pp. 20–62.

[63]Koran, Surah 56:60–61. See Onians, op. cit., pp. 287–289, and Helmer Ringgren, "Resurrection," in The Encyclopedia of Religion, ed. Mircea Eliade (New York, 1987), vol. 12, p. 349.

roll through special underground tunnels to be reassembled in Palestine at the sound of the last trumpet—ideas which clearly reflect the Jewish practice of ossilegium and reburial in the Holy Land.[64] Without a homeland—a clear sense of holy place to focus eschatological dreams—Christians projected into heaven their hope of reassemblage and sprouting. But their basic images retained the notion that the person in some sense survives in hard, material particles, no matter how finely ground or how widely scattered. The grave will not consume us. It cannot be irrelevant to such imagery that the funerary practices of Romans and Jews—both cremation and inhumation—focused on the production of hard remains (ashes and bones), or that both groups found the idea of scattering these abhorrent and increasingly emphasized gentle burial.

Nor can it be irrelevant that both practice and polemic in the Mediterranean world closely connected ideas of eating and ideas of sepulchre. Christians first opposed, then adopted the Roman funerary meal. By the fourth century, the eucharist was celebrated in graveyards, and the practice continued at least until the fifth century, despite some episcopal opposition.[65] The custom of placing the bodies of the martyrs in altars meant that the Mass came to be celebrated over the "blood of the martyrs," even in churches.[66] Moreover, cannibalism—the consumption in which survival of body is most deeply threatened—was a charge pagans leveled against Christians and Christians against pagans. Polemicists for both positions assumed that cannibalism is the ultimate barbarism, the ultimate horror. To eat (if it were really possible) would be to destroy—and to take over—the power of the

[64]Babylonian Talmud (Soncino ed.), Kethuboth, 111a–111b. For the use of Ecclesiastes 12:5 ("the almond shall blossom") to refer to the "nut" of the spinal column growing into the person at the resurrection, see Midrash: Rabbah (Soncino, 3rd ed., New York, 1983). Leviticus Rabbah c. 18.1; Genesis Rabbah 28.3. On some of these passages, see George Foot Moore, *Judaism in the First Centuries of the Christian Era: The Age of Tannaim*, 2 vols. (1927; reprint, Cambridge, Massachusetts, 1966), vol. 2, pp. 377–387. On Jewish ossilegium, see Joseph A. Callaway, "Burials in Ancient Palestine: From the Stone Age to Abraham," *Biblical Archaeologist*, 26 (1963), 74–91; Eric M. Meyers, "Secondary Burials in Palestine," *Biblical Archaeologist*, 33 (1970), 2–29; idem, *Jewish Ossuaries: Reburial and Rebirth* ("Biblica et Orientalia," Vol. 24 [Rome, 1971]); Pau Figueras, *Decorated Jewish Ossuaries* ("Documenta et Monumenta Orientis Antiqui," Vol. 20 [Leiden, 1983]).
[65]Saxer, *Morts, Martyrs, Reliques*, pp. 123–149.
[66]André Grabar, *Martyrium: Recherches sur le culte des reliques et l'art chrétien antique*, 2 vols. (Paris, 1946), vol. 1, p. 35.

consumed.[67] Surely the odd assurances of Theophilus and Athenagoras that this cannot happen suggest their fear that it can. Such fears indeed may provide a deeper link than has previously been noticed between early eucharistic theology and the doctrine of the resurrection. Eucharist, like resurrection, was a victory over the grave. Tertullian and Irenaeus expressed in paradox what Athenagoras expressed in (questionable) science: even if executioners feed our bodies to the beasts and then serve those beasts up on banquet tables, we are not truly eaten. To rise with all our organs and pieces intact is a victory over digestion—not only the digestion threatened by torturers and cannibals but most of all that proffered by the grave itself. Small wonder that the funerary eucharist, at first condemned as a continuation of pagan piety, came to be seen as a palpable assurance that our flesh unites with the unconsumed and unconsumable flesh of Christ in heaven. The eucharist is a guarantee that the risen body we shall all become cannot be consumed.

In the deepest sense then, resurrection belief expressed a need to remove the threat not only of decay but of all natural process as well. Death was horrible not because it was an event that ended consciousness but because it was part of oozing, disgusting, uncontrollable biological change.[68] It was the final permutation in a body that was forever in process (eating, growing, giving birth, sickening, aging).[69]

[67]See fn. 62 above. On cannibalism as a way of taking over the power of the consumed (with the concomitant idea that torturing the one who is finally eaten increases his power), see Peggy Reeves Sanday, *Divine Hunger: Cannibalism as a Cultural System* (Cambridge, 1986), pp. 83–122 and *passim*; and Caroline W. Bynum, *Holy Feast and Holy Fast: The Religious Significance of Food to Medieval Women* (Berkeley, California, 1987), pp. 30, 319 n. 75, and p. 412 n. 77.

[68]See Jean-Marie Mathieu, "Horreur du cadavre et philosophie dans le monde romain: Le cas de la patristique grecque du IVe siècle," in *La Mort, les morts et l'au-delà dans le monde romain* (Caen, 1987), pp. 311–320; and Piero Camporesi, *The Incorruptible Flesh: Bodily Mutation and Mortification in Religion and Folklore*, trans. T. Croft-Murray and H. Elsom (Cambridge, 1988).

[69]The Jewish philosopher Philo said: "The body is wicked and a plotter against the soul, and is always a corpse and a dead thing.... each of us does nothing but carry a corpse about, since the soul lifts up and bears without effort the body which is in itself a corpse." See E. R. Goodenough, "Philo on Immortality," *Harvard Theological Review*, 39 (1946), 97. See also the curious polemic of Arnobius [*Adversus nationes*, ed. A. Reifferscheid, CSEL 4 (Vienna, 1875)], which argues that God must bestow immortality on soul as well as resurrection on body and voices violent rejection of embodiment. Book 2, cc. 39–43, pp. 79–82, questions whether God could have sent souls into bodies to "be buried in the germs of men, spring from the womb, ... keep up the silliest wailings, draw the breasts in sucking, besmear and bedaub themselves with their own filth, ... to lie, to cheat, to deceive....," and details the horrors of the arena as special proof

Indeed the use of both digestion and cannibalism as images of ultimate destruction, found in Theophilus, Athenagoras, and Tertullian as well as later in Augustine and Jerome, seems to reflect a fear that body is not an entity at all but merely a place or moment through which food passes on its way to excrement or rot.[70] As the great third-century theologian Origen said: "River is not a bad name for the body," yet in the topos known since Heraclitus, "you cannot step into the same river twice."[71] How then (asked ancient authors) do we survive the rushing river of death within us? How can we be and remain ourselves? Athenagoras, Minucius Felix, Tertullian, Irenaeus (and later Augustine and Jerome) answered that question by asserting God's power to freeze every moment and sustain every particle of the flux that is "us." Resurrection made decay itself incorruptible.[72]

---

of human depravity. Arnobius says spectators at the animal shows delight in blood and dismemberment, and "grind with their teeth and give to their utterly insatiable maw" pieces of animals which have eaten humans (tr. H. Bryce, in *Ante-Nicene Fathers*, vol. 6 [reprint, Grand Rapids, Michigan, 1978], pp. 449 and 450). In bk. 2, c. 37, Arnobius speaks of the embodiment of souls as a process of going to earthly places ". . .tenebrosis ut corporibus inuolutae inter pituitas et sanguinem degerent, inter stercoris hos utres et saccati obscenissimas serias umoris. . ." (CSEL 4, pp. 77–78).

[70]See above footnotes 17 and 69. Tertullian argues, in *De ieiunio*, c. 3, pp. 1259–1260, that food is poison; eating threatens what we are. Nonetheless, he also uses images of eating for incorporation with God. For example, in the *Scorpiace*, c. 7, pp. 1081–1082, where Tertullian defends God against the charge that he wants human sacrifice because he allows the martyrdoms, the word for "sacrifice" or "destroy" is "eat" or "devour." If God really wants martyrdom, says Tertullian, we must count happy the man whom God has eaten (. . .*et non beatum amplius reputasset quem deus comedisset*), p. 1082, 11. 10–11. The martyrs are not really devoured, of course, because they will rise again. *De res.*, c. 32, pp. 961–962, equates resurrection with regurgitation: "Sed idcirco nominantur bestiae et pisces in redibitionem carnis et sanguinis, quo magis exprimatur resurrectio etiam deuoratorum corporum, cum de ipsis deuoratoribus exactio edicitur" (p. 962, 11. 8–11).

[71]Origen, Fragment on Psalm 1:5, in Methodius, *De resurrectione*, bk. 1, cc. 22–23, in *Methodius*, ed. Nathanael Bonwetsch ("Die griechischen christlichen Schriftsteller der ersten drei Jahrhunderte," Vol. 27 [Leipzig, 1917]), pp. 244–248, and Epiphanius, *Haereses*, bk. 2, tom. 1, haeres. 64, paragrs. 14–15, *Patrologia graeca*, 41 (Paris, 1858), cols. 1089–1092; tr. by Jon F. Dechow, *Dogma and Mysticism in Early Christianity: Epiphanius of Cyprus and the Legacy of Origen* ("Patristic Monograph Series," Vol. 13 [Macon, Georgia, 1988]), pp. 373–374. And see Heraclitus, *On the Universe*, fragment 41, tr. W. H. S. Jones (Loeb Classical Library [Cambridge, Massachusetts, 1979]), p. 483. See also fragment 78: "When is death not within ourselves? . . . Living and dead are the same, and so are awake and asleep, young and old," tr. Jones, p. 495.

[72]By the time of Jerome, transmigration of souls was seen as a kind of chain consumption. See Jerome, letter 124 to Avitus, c. 4, *Patrologia latina*, Vol. 22 (Paris, 1842), cols. 1062–1063.

To end discussion of the materialism of western resurrection belief in the third century is, of course, to end at the beginning. In order to explain the triumph of such materialism in the Latin West by the twelfth century, I would need to consider the new alternatives offered by Syriac and Greek formulations in the third and fourth centuries, Jerome's debate with the Origenists in the early fifth century, Augustine's view of the resurrection body and its connection to relic cult, and many details of hagiography, eucharistic theology, and burial practice in the Carolingian and Ottonian West. Although I hope to tell that story elsewhere, it is too complex to summarize without violating exactly the attention to specific images and texts I have called for here.

What I wish to underline then in closing is the courage implicit in resurrection belief. The doctrine was not, I think, a displaced discussion of power or status, of sensuality, gender or sex, of cultural encounter and otherness.[73] It was a discussion—exactly as its proponents said it was—of death: painful, oozing, slimy death that takes from us our heroes and heroines, our loved ones, and even (or so we fear in our darkest moments) our selves. To ask why people in late antiquity had the stubborn courage to face the putrefaction that joins death to life is to ask for causal explanation at a level no modern theory addresses. But to ask what that courage confronted, it is enough to read the texts, as long as we study not only their arguments but their images as well.

[73]For one of the passages that could be used to argue otherwise, see above fn. 29. I deal with this matter at considerably greater length in chapter 2 of *The Resurrection of the Body*, forthcoming.

Predestination and Divine Foreknowledge in the Sermons of Pope Leo the Great

PHILIP L. BARCLIFT

During the fifth century of our common era the Latin church fathers struggled to explain how we humans are saved and why it seems that not all humans are saved. Most of these attempts pivoted on the writings of Augustine of Hippo. The fathers either borrowed from Augustine's thought, adapted it, or reacted to it. Beginning with the generation of theologians who thrived at the end of Augustine's life and just following his death, there arose a tendency in the western church to moderate his more extreme positions concerning grace and predestination by realigning them with accepted church tradition. This tradition includes those Christian doctrines which were held and promoted most widely by theologians—up to, but not including, Augustine himself—whom the early church accepted as orthodox.

The process of moderating the great bishop's theology began in the monasteries in Gaul that John Cassian had founded, one in Marseilles and the other in Lérins. In reaction to Augustine's more deterministic thesis that human salvation flows entirely from the divine initiative without any reliance on the human's capacity for free choice, the monks in Gaul developed the antithetical *initium fidei* formula in order to preserve the notion that human free will was essential to the economy of human salvation. Scholars call the antithesis put forth by the monks of Marseilles and Lérins "Semi-Pelagianism."[1] Scholars understand it to assert the primacy of the free will in the initial moment of the decision of faith. One should note, however, that this Semi-Pelagian antithesis was not intended as a rejection of all of Augustine's teachings; rather it was meant to correct his more extreme stance on the nature of grace and predestination.

The dominant orthodox position on the matter in the west would be a synthesis of Augustine's doctrine of grace and predestination and the "Semi-Pelagian" assertion of the necessity of human free choice to the economy of salvation, even though orthodox theologians in the west unequivocally rejected the Semi-Pelagian *initium fidei* formula, as Pope Leo does in his first

---

1. On the Semi-Pelagian doctrine of the *initium fidei* see E. Amann, "Semi-pélagiens," *Dictionnaire de théologie catholique* 14 (Paris, 1941 ed.), col. 1810 and J. Chéné, "Que significait ≪ *initium fidei* ≫ et ≪ *affectus creduliatus* ≫ ?" *Recherches de science religieuse* 35 (1948): 566–588.

Mr. Barclift is theologian in residence at First Christian Church of Kent, Washington, and adjunct professor of historical theology in Pacific Lutheran University, Tacoma, Washington.

official correspondence.[2] The trail of this synthesis would be blazed first by Prosper of Aquitaine and Pope Leo the Great, possibly under the tutelage of John Cassian himself. Both Prosper and Leo considered themselves faithful Augustinians, even though neither of them accepted Augustine's thought in every detail. Over a period of time, Prosper came to speak only in terms of divine foreknowledge in order to soften the deterministic elements of Augustine's doctrine of predestination. Pope Leo stepped even farther away from Augustine's doctrine of predestination by rejecting every hint of determinism even from the bishop's theory of divine foreknowledge.

In this paper I attempt to outline the general trend of western theologians to moderate Augustine's doctrine of grace and predestination in keeping with the pre-Augustinian tradition of the church, showing in particular that Pope Leo follows and promotes this trend by pushing aside the deterministic elements of Augustine's doctrine and by insisting on the inviolable necessity of human free will to the completion of the economy of salvation. It is not my purpose to render a detailed exposition of Pope Leo's doctrine of salvation. That task would be much too involved for such limited space. In order to do justice to his soteriology, one must investigate the interrelationship of Leo's christology, his ecclesiology, his broader doctrine of grace as *sacramentum* and *exemplum*, his doctrine of redemption, and his highly developed sacramental theology of the liturgy. For our purposes it is enough to note that the pope does not choose to use Augustine's doctrine of grace and predestination as a means to describe how we are saved.

Augustine developed many of his doctrines in the heat of controversy. For instance, it was in controversy with the Pelagians and the Semi-Pelagians that he pushed the limits of his doctrine of grace. He seems to state the obvious in *De dono perseverantiae* when he tells us that grace is by definition a gratuitous gift of God.[3] In this light, and in view of the realities around him that the majority of the world was perishing in sin, Augustine arrives at his doctrine of the predestination of the saints. The only explanation for the salvation of any humans is the reality of grace, which always lies within the divine initiative.[4] He wishes to avoid any hint of the Pelagian doctrine that humans can in some way merit salvation through an act of saving faith.[5] According to Augustine, the elect are efficaciously called by grace which meets them and enables them to come to saving faith.[6] Thus faith itself is a gift from God, such that from

2. See Leo, epist. 1.3 (J.-P. Migne, *Patrologia, Series Latina* [PL] 54.595 [Paris, 1844-]): "Cumque omnes definitiones suas ad subrependi facilitatem, improbare se simulent atque deponere, noc sibi tota arte fallendi, nisi intellegantur, excipiunt, ut gratia Dei secundum merita dari accipientium sentiatur. Quae utique nisi gratis detur, non est gratia."
3. Augustine, *De dono perseverantiae ad Prosperum et Hilarium* 17.42 (*PL* 45.1019).
4. Augustine, *De correptione et gratia ad Valentinum* 14.43 (PL 44.942).
5. Augustine, *Opus imperfectum contra Iuliam* 2.139 (*PL* 45.1199).
6. Augustine, *De praedestinatione sanctorum ad Prosperum et Hilarium* 8.14 (*PL* 44.971).

beginning to end, our salvation is a work of God in Christ. Indeed, only those who are called efficaciously can persevere to the end in faith and finally reach the beatific vision.[7] But for those who are called efficaciously, this grace is nearly irresistible.[8] Furthermore those who are not called efficaciously have no basis for complaint, since the call of the few is itself a great work of loving grace, without which every human being would perish in eternal damnation.[9]

Along this line Augustine also rejects John Cassian's inchoate Semi-Pelagianism. In Augustine's eyes, Cassian asserts that the initial moment of faith belongs to the human individual, after which God's grace immediately meets the believer in order to draw the believer to salvation. This notion would presuppose the *initium fidei* formula, against which Augustine would explain that even the initial moment of faith is a gift of God, lest we boast that we somehow deserve to be saved because of our act of faith.[10]

Augustine's doctrine of grace pushes him to conclude that some people were predestined to salvation, while others were not, as he observes in *De dono perseverantiae*, a book which he addresses in part to Prosper of Aquitaine.[11] But Prosper, whose Augustinian credentials are impeccable, is not fully persuaded, and he slowly moves away from this element of Augustine's doctrine between the time of Augustine's death and the time Prosper joins Pope Leo's staff in 440 C.E.[12] Aime Solignac summarizes the opinion of scholars that Prosper's movement away from a strict Augustinian interpretation of grace and predestination can be seen in three phases: 1) the period of his strict adherence to the Augustinian interpretation of grace (up to 432 C.E.); 2) the period of his first concessions to the Semi-Pelagians in Gaul (433–435); and 3) the period of his more substantial concessions to them (after 435).[13] Prosper was in Marseilles when the Semi-Pelagian controversy erupted in 426 C.E. Along with Hilary, Prosper took this time to write to Augustine, alerting him to the new threat to his model of grace. In response the great bishop of Hippo wrote *De dono perseverantiae* and *De praedestinatione sanctorum*. In 431, after Augustine's death (28 August 430), Prosper moved to Rome in order to carry on the bishop's struggle against Semi-Pelagianism,

---

7. Ibid. 10.19 (*PL* 44.974); see also *De dono perseverantiae* 17.15, 34, 41 (*PL* 45.1002, 1015, 1018).
8. Augustine, *De correptione* 12.38 (*PL* 44.940); see also *De diversis quaestionibus VII ad Simplicianum* 1.2.13 (*PL* 40.118).
9. Ibid. 15.47 (*PL* 44.945); see also *De praedestinatione* 1–21 (*PL* 44.959–992).
10. See J. Chéné, "*Que significait « initium fidei »?*" pp. 566–588, and compare Augustine, *De praedestinatione* 1–21 (*PL* 44.959–992).
11. *De dono perseverantiae* 17.42 (*PL* 45.1019).
12. See Berthold Altaner, *Patrology*, trans. Hilda C. Graff (Edinburgh, 1960), pp. 535–537.
13. Aime Solignac, "Prosper d'Aquitaine," *Dictionnaire de spiritualité ascétique et mystique* (Beauchesne-Paris, 1990 ed.), col. 2447. See also Adalbert Hamman, "Writers of Gaul," in Angelo di Berardino, ed., *Patrology* (Westminster, 1988), vol. 4, *The Golden Age of Latin Patristic Literature from the Council of Nicaea to the Council of Chalcedon*, p. 556.

pushing Pope Celestine to defend Augustine's authority on the subject of grace against the *initium fidei* of the Semi-Pelagian monks at Marseilles and Lérins in a letter to the bishops of Gaul.[14]

Prosper must have been disillusioned by his experiences in Rome. He had hoped for a clear condemnation of the Semi-Pelagian "heresy" instead of Celestine's passionless defense of Augustine's authority. In addition, he discovered that Rome's influential Archdeacon Leo (the future Pope Leo the Great), who was behind many of the papal policies, had actually commissioned the Semi-Pelagian John Cassian to write a confutation of the Nestorian heresy, which Rome now viewed as a more serious threat to orthodoxy than Semi-Pelagianism. Rome's confidence in Cassian for such a sensitive theological issue must have perplexed Prosper. It clearly indicated to him that Rome did not consider Cassian dangerous to the church. In the absence of a clear condemnation of Semi-Pelagianism from Rome, then, Prosper would later take it on himself to add the *Capitula caelestini* to Celestine's letter after the latter's death in order to bolster the Augustinian position.[15]

Some time after Celestine's death, Prosper moved back to Gaul in order to open dialog with the monks at Marseilles and Lérins. During this time he made his first concessions to them. It is impossible, of course, to discern with certainty what precipitated this shift in Prosper's stance, but one can surmise that it involved a combination of Rome's moderate posture on the Semi-Pelagian issue and of Rome's high confidence in John Cassian, whom Prosper felt to be in error doctrinally. Furthermore, one should not overlook the possibility that Cassian himself had some influence in helping Prosper to moderate his position on the Augustinian understanding of grace and predestination. Whatever precipitated his shift to a more moderate position, Prosper went back to Gaul ready to listen to the monks there.

John Cassian's death (around 435) would have a profound, even liberating effect on Prosper. Perhaps it removed the pressure Prosper felt to preserve the purity of Augustine's teaching from attack, or perhaps it capped a period during which Cassian slowly "converted" Prosper to a more moderate stance. The relationship between the two theologians is unclear. Certainly, after this time Prosper would make some major concessions to Cassian's position, possibly following the lead of Rome itself or possibly by dint of Cassian's own authority. Either way, by the time Prosper joined Pope Leo's staff in 440, the former was already predisposed to accept Cassian's insistence on the universality of the divine call to salvation and on the necessity for the freedom of the will to play a greater role in the economy of human salvation.

Probably in the same year that he joined Leo's staff, Prosper tried to

14. Pope Celestine, epist. 21 (*PL* 50.528–530).
15. For a survey of the evidence that Prosper was behind the addition of the *Capitula caelestini* to Celestine's epistle 21 see D. M. Cappuyn's article, "L'origine des capitula pseudo-célestiniens contre le sémipélagianisme," *Revue bénédictine* 41 (1929): 156–170.

temper the Augustinian doctrine of predestination in a work entitled *De vocatione omnium gentium*. The title itself indicates Prosper's driving concern: the call of every human being to salvation.[16] In this work Prosper does not so much as mention either the doctrine of predestination or Augustine himself. One can only guess what lies behind this obvious omission. Prosper has moderated his position in favor of what John Cassian and Archdeacon Leo considered to be the traditional teaching of the church. Prosper now believes that God's will for all to be saved (see 1 Timothy 2:4) is an essential part of the faith (*pars fidei*) and an essential component of the teaching of the church from earliest times.[17] Nevertheless, he still believes he can explain the apparent disparity between God's universal salvific will and the salvation of a smaller number of humans, called the "elect," by using such Augustinian phrases as *praescientia Dei* and *consilium Dei*.[18] In view of this evolving theory of divine foreknowledge, Prosper speaks in *De vocatione* 1.21–25 of the inscrutable quality of God's justice, which does not conflict with his universal will.[19]

In *De vocatione* 2.25 Prosper distinguishes between God's universal salvific will (*benignitas generalis*) and his special mercy (*misericordia specialis*) by which a large number of humans actually will be saved.[20] This distinction corresponds roughly to Cassian's two levels of grace, except that Prosper places a limiting factor on the second level.[21] All humans are justified by Christ, but not all are saved because God has not prepared the will of everyone to cooperate with the gift of divine grace, by which we are saved.[22] Prosper calls those people who are ultimately saved the "elect," but this group more accurately consists in those whom God knew in advance would not shun or frustrate his gift of salvation in themselves.[23] Thus the mere fact that God has chosen to save only a certain number of humans does not remove the need of

16. See esp. *De vocatione omnium gentium* 1.1 (*PL* 51.649) and 2.2 (*PL* 51.687–688).
17. Prosper, *De vocatione* 2.19 (*PL* 51.703) and 1.25 (*PL* 51.686). Compare Czeslaw Bartnik's analysis of Prosper's *De vocatione*, "L'universalisme du salut dans le De vocatione," *Revue d'histoire ecclésiastique* 68 (1973): 731–758. Bartnik does not address the question of authorship in this article, even though there is little debate concerning its origin.
18. *De vocatione* 1.9 (*PL* 51.659).
19. Ibid. 1.21–25 (*PL* 51.674–686); see also 1.12 (*PL* 51.663–665) and 2.3 (*PL* 51.688–689).
20. Ibid. 2.25 (*PL* 51.711): "Quae licet copiosius nunc quam ante praestetur; causas tamen distributionum suarum Dominus apud scientiam suam tenuit, et intra secretum potentissimae voluntatis occuluit: quae si omnibus uniformiter affluerent, non laterent; et quam nulla est ambiguitas de benignitate generali, tam de speciali misericordia nihil quod stupendum esset exsisteret: ac proinde illa esset gratia, ista non esset." See 2.1 (*PL* 51.685–687).
21. See nn. 58, 59, and 60, below.
22. *De vocatione* 2.26–28 (*PL* 51.711–715).
23. Ibid. 2.34–35 (*PL* 51.719). See Augustine, epist. 225.5 (*PL* 33.1004): "Tales aiunt perdi, talesque salvari quales futuros illos in annis majoribus, si ad activam servarentur aetatem, scientia divina praviderit."

prayer or Christian labor, since these works help us remove obstacles that might frustrate the plan of our salvation and because there is no way to know with certainty in this life if one is saved.[24]

On that basis Prosper retains the Augustinian notions that the number of the elect is predetermined and that only those who were given a special grace would ultimately persevere to salvation; since only those whose wills have been prepared to cooperate with the gift of divine grace unto salvation are actually saved.[25] Prosper attempts to balance this doctrine against his evolving conviction that the identities of those who would be saved is only foreknown, not predestined. But his balancing act amounts only to theological sleight-of-hand.

By contrast, Pope Leo would not even attempt to balance these two doctrines. Instead, he selects only the latter one which emphasizes God's universal salvific will and which presents a theory of divine foreknowledge that downplays the deterministic tone of Augustine's doctrine. Taking Prosper's latter doctrine as his starting point, the pope would go to great lengths to remove all deterministic elements from his own teachings.

An associate of Augustine during the Semi-Pelagian controversy and later an associate of and theological advisor to Pope Leo, Prosper of Aquitaine stands as a direct link between the bishop of Hippo and the pope.[26] And Leo, whose own Augustinian credentials are normally flawless, begins where Prosper left off, tempering the Augustinian doctrine of grace to include God's truly universal salvific will; yet the pope does not settle even for Prosper's version of the doctrine.[27] Unlike Prosper's, Pope Leo's thought shows no evidence of development. From the very beginning of his pontificate onwards, Leo is convinced of both the universality of God's salvific will and the necessity of the freedom of the human will, and he repeatedly stresses their importance by softening Augustine's doctrine of grace in order to remove every hint of determinism and by denying that we humans are left in uncertainty concerning our salvation.[28]

---

24. Ibid. 2.35–37 (*PL* 51.719–722).
25. Ibid. 2.26–28 (*PL* 51.711–715).
26. See Altaner, *Patrology*, pp. 535–536.
27. See Henri Rondet, who considers Pope Leo to be one of the purist Augustinians, *The Grace of Christ: a Brief History of the Theology of Grace*, trans. Tad Guzie (Amsterdam, 1967), pp. 171–172.
28. See for example sermons 58.4; 59.2, 5; 61.5; 62.4; 63.5–6; 67.2; 74.5. All texts of Pope Leo's sermons are derived from the critical edition by Antoine Chavasse, *Sancti Leonis Magni. Romani Pontificis tractatus septem et nonaginta (CCL* 138; Turnholti Prepol Editores Pontificii, 1973). Because of the relative brevity of each sermon, no additional notation is necessary. Also see serm. 71.4: "ex quo, inquit, initium nobis factum est resurrectionis in Christo, ex quo in eo qui pro omnibus mortuus est, totius spei nostrae forma praecessit. Non haesitamus diffidentia, nec incerta expectatione suspendimur, sed accepto promissionis exordio, fidei oculis quae sunt futura iam cernimus, et naturae prouectione gaudentes, quod credimus iam tenemus."

1.

Following Prosper's lead, Pope Leo avoids the term *praedestinare*. In fact, he uses it only once. In sermon 22.1 the pope invites his congregation to celebrate the new day of redemption that has dawned but was prepared long ago.[29] He continues, "The revolution of the year makes the sacrament of salvation continuously at hand, as promised from the beginning and completed in the end. Consequently, our hearts are lifted upwards to adore the dignity of the divine mystery in order that whatever is accomplished by God's grand gift may be celebrated in the great joy of the church. For as soon as the malice of the devil murdered us with the venom of his hatred, the omnipotent and merciful God, whose nature is goodness, whose will is power, and whose work is mercy, presignified the remedy of his love which was predestined at the very beginning of the world for the renewal of us mortals."[30] The remedy of God's love, not the number of the elect, was predestined, according to Leo. In the same way, the pope's observation that the remedy was predestined at the dawn of time merely shows the fundamental continuity of God's will: God has always intended to bring us this remedy. Leo explains in the same paragraph that the predestined remedy for the human condition is present to those who celebrate it in the liturgical cycle.

Later in sermon 22 Pope Leo notes that the Son of God appointed beforehand (*praestituere*) the time when Christ would come to redeem humanity by means of his unique birth.[31] Again, Leo does not speak of a preappointed "elect." Only the moment of Christ's redemptive birth was predetermined. Leo wishes to show that God has always meant to redeem humanity and that the dispensation of redemption is now a reality.

In Pope Leo's sermons there are numerous other terms that theologians tend to associate with the doctrine of predestination. For example, the pope uses derivatives of *praeordinare* twice. In sermon 29.2 he uses one of them to signify that the Son's incarnation was preordained, and in sermon 82.5 he uses the other to explain how it is preordained that honor and glory await those who draw near to the cross of Christ.[32] In the first instance, an element

29. Serm. 22.1: "inluxit dies redemptionis nouae, praeparationis antiquae."
30. Ibid.: "Reparatur enim nobis salutis nostrae annua reuolutione sacramentum, ab initio promissum, in fine redditum, sine fine mansurum. In quo dignum est nos sursum erectis cordibus diuinum adorare mysterium, ut quod magno Dei munere agitur, magnis Ecclesiae gaudiis celebretur. Deus enim omnipotens et clemens, cuius natura bonitas, cuius uoluntas potentia, cuius opus misericordia est, statim ut nos diabolica malignitas ueneno suae mortificauit inuidiae, praedestinata renouandis mortalibus pietatis suae remedia inter ipsa mundi primordia praesignauit."
31. Ibid. 22.2: "Aduenientibus ergo temporibus, dilectissimi, quae redemptioni hominum fuerant praestituta . . . noua natiuitate generatus."
32. Serm. 29.2: "Natalem igitur, dilectissimi, diem Domini celebrantes, qui ex omnibus praeteritorum temporum diebus electus est, licet dispensatio actionum corporalium, sicut aeterno consilio fuerat praeordinata." Serm. 82.5: "tropeum crucis Christi Roma-

of Christ's life, not ours, was predetermined. In the second case, the effects of a saving lifestyle are predetermined for those who imitate Christ's cross. Leo does not introduce the notion of the salvation of human individuals into this equation.

Leo's use of other terms also supports this kind of distinction. He uses the term *praesignare* twice: in sermon 22.1, to express that the remedy for the human condition was signified in advance and in sermon 59.5, to indicate that the faith of the Gentiles was prefigured by Simon of Cyrene carrying Jesus' cross.[33] We may not infer on the basis of this sermon that the salvation of a certain number of human individuals was predetermined; rather Pope Leo wishes to show that the scope of the plan of salvation would expand to include Gentiles, as presignified by Simon of Cyrene. The pope uses *praestituere* the same way. In the seven times he uses that term, Leo never employs it to indicate that the destiny of human individuals was predetermined. He speaks on four occasions of time periods being determined in advance (sermons 22.2, 47.2, 74.2, 88.3); and he mentions twice that certain fast and feast days were predetermined (sermons 14.1, 15.1). And in sermon 67.5 he explains that Jesus' crucifixion was set in advance.[34] The pope never uses *praestituere* to designate the number or the identities of those humans who would be saved in the end.

Pope Leo applies the terms *praefinire* and *praeformare* in the same manner. He uses *praefinire* once to indicate that the days of fasting were set in advance (sermon 87.1), once to signify that the time period marked by Christ's love was predetermined (66.1), and twice to express his conviction that the economy of the salvation of the human race was determined in advance (33.1, 58.4). Likewise, Leo employs the term *praeformare* once to designate the predetermined times of fasting in preparation for Easter (47.1) and once to note that both the sign of the cross and the passion were set in advance (33.4).

The pope never speaks in terms of a predetermined number of the elect. The idea that the ultimate destiny of human individuals was set in advance is completely foreign to him. Leo speaks only in terms of a predestined economy of salvation and of predetermined times or periods of time. He does not address his understanding of predestination to the fate of human individuals. Clearly, then, the pope's understanding of predestination does

---

nis arcibus inferebas, quo te diuinis praeordinationibus anteibant et honor potestatis et gloria passionis."
33. On serm. 22.1, see n. 30, above. Serm. 59.5: "Simon quidam Cyrenaeus inuentus est, in quem lignum supplicii transferretur a Domino, ut etiam tali facto praesignaretur gentium fides."
34. Serm. 67.5: "Quod igitur in tempore praestituto, secundum propositum uoluntatis suae Iesus Christus crucifixus est et mortuus ac sepultus."

not answer the question why some but not others are saved. It merely postpones it.

2.

Pope Leo's understanding of divine foreknowledge brings us no closer to an answer. Taking Prosper of Aquitaine's adaptation of Augustine's doctrine of divine foreknowledge as his point of departure, Leo distances himself entirely from the deterministic properties of divine foreknowledge, as indicated in sermon 67.2. "Therefore, everything that Jewish impiety committed against the Lord of majesty was predicted beforehand. Now the context of the prophetic word is not as much future as it is past. What else is disclosed to us except the immutable order of God's eternal disposition, with whom whatever is to be discerned is already distinguished, and future events are already present. Since divine knowledge anticipates the character of our actions and the fulfillment of our desires, how much more does God take note of his own works! And he is justly pleased as if he were recalling past actions that nothing can keep from being accomplished."[35] Pope Leo's main concern in this passage is to show once again that God has always intended to redeem us. The pope wishes to show that God's knowledge of his own actions is certain, and he is pleased by them, as if they were already past events, whose accomplishment nothing could inhibit; whereas divine foreknowledge of human actions has more the character of prediction than of knowledge per se. God knows us humans so intimately that he can anticipate all of our choices and actions, based on our character and our desires. But Leo wants us to make no mistake: the fact that God anticipates the choices we will make does not mean that he chooses our path for us.

In the same paragraph of sermon 67.2 Leo uses the example of the Jews who had Jesus put to death to illustrate this point. "Did the iniquity of Christ's persecutors thereby originate in God's plan? And was this deed which is greater than all other crimes implemented by the hand of divine preparation? Such a suggestion is unthinkable of the highest justice! That which was foreknown concerning the malignity of the Jews is very different than and quite opposite to what was arranged concerning the passion of Christ. Their will to murder him did not proceed from the same source as his [will] to die; nor did their wicked atrocities come into being from the same Spirit as [Christ's] redemptive endurance. The Lord did not incite but allow

35. Serm. 67.2: "Cum ergo omnia quae in Dominum maiestatis iudaica admisit impietas, tanto ante praedicta sint, et non tam de futuris quam de praeteritis propheticus sit sermo contextus, quid aliud nobis quam sempiternarum dispositionum Dei incommutabilis ordo reseratur, apud quem et discernenda iam diiudicata, et futura iam facta sunt? Cum enim et qualitates actionum nostrarum et effectus omnium uoluntatum scientia diuina praeueniat, quanto magis nota sunt Deo opera sua! Et recte placuit quasi facta recoli, quae non poterant omnino non fieri."

the impious hands of those lunatics; nor by knowing in advance what would happen did he compel it to happen. Yet it was because it would happen that he assumed flesh."[36] God did not cause what Leo identifies as the wickedness of the Jews by knowing in advance that they would commit it; nor was their violence against Jesus in God's divine plan for the universe. Pope Leo views this murder as the Jews' own freely chosen misdeed. The plan of God pertains only to the redemption of humankind wrought by Christ, not to the acts of human individuals. Accordingly, Leo argues that the Holy Spirit did not incite the Jews to execute Jesus, but he did allow it. And the pope contends that, because God knew those Jews intimately enough to anticipate their murder of Jesus, he devised a means by which Christ's death would serve as our redemption.

The terms used here in sermon 67.2 to denote this quality of divine foreknowledge are *praecognoscere* and *praescire*, both of which mean basically "to know in advance." The pope uses the term *praecognoscere* only this one time in his sermons, and he uses *praescire* only one other time in them, in sermon 58.3. Yet this second time the term does not have God as its subject. It now pertains to Judas Iscariot, who knew in advance (*praescire*) the kind of injustice he would commit against Jesus. Obviously, this latter use cannot add anything to our understanding of the pope's doctrine of divine foreknowledge. Indeed, the only time he employs these critical terms with God as their subject (sermon 67.2), Leo carefully qualifies his statement in order to remove every hint of determinism from his doctrine of divine foreknowledge. God perfectly knows his own future actions, but he simply predicts ours on the basis of his intimate knowledge of our individual character and desires. This knowledge, then, is contingent on our disposition. And Leo explains unambiguously that God's contingent knowledge of our future actions does not cause or determine the course of those actions. God allows us to follow the course of our free will, and he knows us so well that he can anticipate what those choices will be.

There are other terms, in addition, that the fathers sometimes used as near synonyms of *praecognoscere* and *praescire*, such as *praevidere, praenuntire*, and *praenotare*. In sermon 54.5 Leo speaks of Jesus seeing in advance (*praevidere*) that Peter would be dumbfounded by Jesus' passion.[37] The former's fore-

---

36. Ibid.: "Numquid iniquitas persequentium Christum ex Dei est orta consilio, et illud facinus quod omni maius est crimine manus diuinae praeparationis armauit? Non hoc plane de summa iustitia sentiendum est, quia multum diuersum multumque contrarium est id quod in Iudaeorum malignitate praecognitum, et quod in Christi est passione dispositum. Non inde processit uoluntas interficiendi, unde moriendi, nec de uno extitit spiritu atrocitas sceleris et tolerantia Redemptoris. Impias furentium manus non inmisit in se Dominus, sed admisit, nec praesciendo quod faciendum esset, coegit ut fieret, cum tamen ad hoc carnem suscepisset ut fieret."
37. Serm. 54.5: "Respexit igitur Dominus Petrum . . . illis turbatum discipulum conuenit oculis, quibus eum praeuiderat esse turbandum."

knowledge of the latter's dismay did not produce it in him. Nor did Jesus'
knowledge of the latter's distress cause either his salvation or the salvation of
a single person. Indeed, this knowledge is unrelated to the economy of
salvation. Jesus simply knew Peter well enough that he could foresee how
shaken Peter would be by Jesus' crucifixion.

Pope Leo uses *praevidere* again in sermon 58.3 in order to indicate that
Jesus knew in advance that Judas would betray him.[38] Leo does not hint
either at how Jesus knew this fact or what implications it might have for his
doctrine of divine foreknowledge. Later in this context, however, the pope
stresses a point that militates against a deterministic interpretation of this
kind of foreknowledge. Judas, Leo contends, was in every way the source and
cause of his own malevolent act against Jesus. Judas "decided in advance of
his own free will on his betrayal [of Jesus]. He was the source of his own
destruction, the cause of his own wickedness, for he followed the guidance of
the devil and refused to have Christ as his leader.[39] In this same paragraph
Leo stresses that the opportunity was always open for Judas to change his
mind and to avert the course of his wickedness.[40] As Leo sees it, Jesus'
advance knowledge of Judas' perfidy did not determine the latter's behavior
in any way. It merely notes what would take place. The option was always
available for Judas to choose a different course of action.

Pope Leo exploits the term *praevidere* a third and final time in order to note
that Isaiah foresaw Jesus' birth and passion.[41] Any hint of a deterministic
character to this foreknowledge would have been unthinkable to the pope.
The prophet does not cause future events by foretelling them. The prophet is
merely a spectator to those events.

Moreover, Leo applies the term *praenuntire*, "to foretell," in essentially the
same way. Of the ten occasions he uses this term, he applies it nine times to
Old Testament prophecies or figures that proclaimed in advance some aspect
of Christ's salvific life or passion, by which was accomplished the economy
through which we can be saved.[42] In the tenth instance of this term in Leo's
sermons, the pope uses it to express his belief that every celebration in the
liturgical cycle anticipates the *magnum sacramentum* of the Easter festival.[43]
There is no tinge of determinism in Leo's use of this term or in the doctrine it
expresses.

As it turns out, neither Pope Leo's doctrine of predestination nor his

---

38. Serm. 58.3.
39. Ibid.: "qui [Judas] in uoluntaria erat impietate praescitus. Ipse enim sibi fuit materia
    ruinae et causa perfidiae, sequens diabolum ducem, et nolens Christum habere
    rectorem."
40. Ibid.: "Redi in integrum, et deposito furore resipisce. Clementia inuitat, salus pulsat,
    uita te reuocat."
41. See serm. 59.4.
42. See sermons 12.1, 34.2, 51.7, 54.1, 55.2, 55.3, 60.3, 65.3, 75.1.
43. See serm. 32.2.

doctrine of divine foreknowledge can explain why some but not all are saved. Leo's doctrine of predestination pertains only to the remedy for the human condition, and his doctrine of divine foreknowledge is completely nondeterministic; thus it could not be used to answer any questions that his doctrine of predestination did not answer. In point of fact the pope prescinds from every sense of determinism in his writings. He denies that God's foresight could in any way influence the course or destination of our lives. Rather God allows us to follow the inclinations of the free will he restored in the general redemption, and he knows us so well that he can anticipate what we will choose.

3.

If no answer lies in either the doctrine of the predestination of the saints or of divine foreknowledge, does one perhaps lie in the divine call itself that would explain why some but not all are saved? Probably not. Pope Leo explicitly refers to the universal call of the entire human race in sermon 4.2.[44] Moreover, he explains repeatedly in his Epiphany sermons that the call to the Magi is a type of the universal call to all humankind.[45] In sermon 35.1, for example, Leo narrates the story of the three wisemen who came from afar to adore the new king. The pope explains how this salvation-bearing mystery (*salutiferum mysterium*) is present to the celebrants in the liturgical celebration, during which that mystery is imprinted on the minds of those who perceive it in faith. At the same time, the star that called to the Magi was itself an act of grace which initiated the call of the gospel of Christ throughout the world.[46] Leo adds in 35.2 that the character of those mystical events persists and now appears clearly: that which began in figures is now complete in truth.[47] Today the star calls the entire world of sinners to salvation. Therefore, Pope Leo explains in 35.3, in view of that call "let us cooperate with the grace of God which operates in us."[48]

This cooperation takes place within the Augustinian *sacramentum-exemplum* framework, as Leo indicates here in 35.3: "The way for us has been run, which the Lord attested of himself (John 14:6); whereas no meritorious work could be adduced in our defense, [the Lord] counseled us with both a *sacrament* and an *example*. Through the former he provided a call in adoption to salvation, and through the latter he provoked us to labor."[49] By qualifying this "call" with the phrase *in adoptionem* Leo specifies the means, not the

44. Serm. 4.2: "uniuersarum gentium uocationi."
45. For example, see sermons 32.4; 33.5; 35.1–4; 36.2; 38.1, 7.
46. Serm. 35.1
47. Ibid. 35.2: "Permanet igitur . . . sicut euidenter apparet, mysticorum forma gestorum, et quod imagine inchoabatur, ueritate completur."
48. Ibid. 35.3: "Considerantes itaque, dilectissimi, ineffabilem erga nos diuinorum munerum largitatem, cooperatores simus gratiae Dei operantis in nobis."
49. Ibid.: "qui nobis nullis operum meritis suffragantibus, et sacramento consuluit et exemplo, ut in adoptionem uocatos per illud proueheret ad salutem, per hoc imbueret ad laborem" (emphasis added).

number, of those who are called. He is not limiting the amount of people who are called to a quantity that is smaller than the total number of humans by adding this phrase. He has already said several times in this sermon that absolutely all humans are called to adoption, and he reiterates this conviction once again in 35.4: "God's goodness remains extended to everyone. He does not refuse his mercy to anyone, distributing his generosity to all without discrimination. Those who have earned punishment, he prefers to invite to his benefits."[50] In 35.3, then, the pope simply specifies how or perhaps when that call occurs: it takes place in the general adoption of the human race. At the same time Leo gives content to this call: it is a *sacrament* and an *example* that will enable us to cooperate with the grace of God in the completion of our salvation.

Pope Leo not only prescinds from all forms of determinism, but he also pushes aside the dogma that the number of the elect was somehow limited to an amount of persons that is smaller than the total number of all human beings. Neither of these notions could stand in his theology. Whereas Prosper of Aquitaine theorizes that a smaller group than the total number of all humans would receive the level of grace that leads to ultimate salvation because God only prepared the will of a certain, smaller group of people to cooperate with his gift of divine grace, Leo contends that God did not limit the universal availability of salvation even on that level.[51] In the call to all humans, God also gave everyone the means to respond affirmatively to that call. Not only redemption but also the means to cooperate with the salvation-bearing grace of God is available to every man, woman, and child. This notion would become Pope Leo's version of the doctrine of "prevenient grace."[52] Grace precedes every act of the will, since grace was infused in the restored will by means of the redemption. Leo postulates a "general redemption" of all humanity which has created the possibility for everyone to attain salvation.[53] He explains that Christ restored human nature to its original dignity and flooded it with his grace, in such a way that the freedom of the will was also restored.[54] In the aftermath of this marvelous act by the Son of God, every human being now has the freedom and the ability to respond in faith to Christ. Now the onus falls on the human individual to cooperate willingly with God's grace in order to complete that salvation. "The Savior's grace restores us daily to this character, since whatever fell in

50. Ibid. 35.4: "Inter haec autem permanet super omnes benignitas Dei, et nulli misericordiam suam denegat, cum indiscrete uniuersis bona multa largiatur, eosque quos merito subderet poenis, mauult inuitate beneficiis."
51. See Prosper, *De vocatione* 2.26–28 (*PL* 51.711–717).
52. See Pope Leo's serm. 30.4.
53. On Leo's doctrine of the general redemption, see serm. 62.4: "quam sacramentum Christus *generalis redemptionis* impleret. Nam mortuo pro omnibus impiis Domino, potuisset etiam forte hic consequi remedium, si non festinasset ad laqueum" (emphasis added). See also sermons 20.3, 22.2, 27.6, 28.3, 33.1–2, for example.
54. See serm. 53.3. Compare C. Fernandez's lengthy analysis of this aspect of Pope Leo's doctrine of grace in *La Grâcia según San León el Grande* (Mexico City, 1951), pp. 90–97.

the first Adam is raised again in the second. Now the cause of our restoration is nothing other than the mercy of God, whom we would not have loved, if he had not first loved us. . . . So it is that God, by loving us, restores us to his image; and in order that he may discern in us the character of his goodness he also gives us the means to do the work that he does, lighting the lamps of our minds and inflaming us with the fire of his love, that we should not only love him, but also whatever he loves. . . . For we shall not otherwise attain the dignity of the divine majesty, unless we imitate his will."[55] We cannot attain the image of God until we complete it in ourselves by imitating Christ, who enabled humanity to follow his example by renewing the free capacity of the will and by inspiring the will with the love toward God which inclines us to do what he wills. Now Christ requires us to do of our own free will what he has enabled us to do through grace.[56]

Pope Leo's theory of grace permits him to make the critical distinction that all are redeemed, but not all are saved; yet the persistent reality that not all are saved does not derive from a necessary attribute of God's will concerning the salvation of humankind. In accordance with his will, all humans have been redeemed; the freedom of the will has been universally restored; grace inspires everyone to do what God wills; and grace helps them finish what they have freely chosen to do. The reality that not all humans are saved, then, merely reflects God's fundamental intention for us humans to participate in the consummation of our own salvation. The completion of the salvation process of distinct human individuals requires an act of faith which proceeds from the free movement of the restored human will.[57]

Pope Leo's understanding of grace shows the influence of John Cassian on his theology. In *Collationes* 13.7 Cassian also taught the universal call and dispersal of grace to all humans, without exception, by which God's will that all be saved could be fulfilled.[58] Grace is always with us. In fact, it both accompanies and even precedes our actions.[59] With this quality of grace presupposed, then, Cassian goes on to explain in 13.8 that God's grace meets us, enlightening and strengthening us, when he sees the beginning of a good

55. Serm. 12.1: "Ad quam utique nos cotidie reparat gratia Saluatoris, dum quod cecidit in Adam primo, erigitur in secundo. Causa autem reparationis nostrae non est nisi misericordia Dei, quem non diligeremus, nisi 'nos prior ipse diligeret' (1 John 4:10). . . . Diligendo itaque nos Deus ad imaginem suam reparat, et ut in nobis formam suae bonitatis inueniat, dat unde ipsi quoque quod operatur operemur, accendens scilicet mentium nostrarum lucernas et igne nos suae caritatis inflammans, ut non solum ipsum, sed etiam quidquid diligit diligamus, . . . quia non aliter in nobis erit dignitas diuinae maiestatis, nisi imitatio fuerit uoluntatis."
56. See also serm. 53.3.
57. See for example serm. 43.1: "Gratiae igitur Dei oboedientia se humana non subtrahat, nec ab illo bono sine quo non potest bona esse, deficiat."
58. John Cassian, *Collationes* 13.7 (*PL* 49.909): "Praesto est quotidie Christi gratia, quae dum vult omnes homines salvos fieri cunctos absque ulla exceptione convocat."
59. Ibid. 13.8 (*PL* 49.912): "Tanta est erga creaturam suam pietas Creatoris ut non solum comitetur sed etiam praecedat jugi providentia."

deed in us so that he can use it to produce our salvation by nurturing what he himself planted in us.[60] Scholars see the *initium fidei* formula in this statement, but one wonders if it is really there, seeing that Cassian premises this statement with his supposition that grace both accompanies and precedes our actions. Could it not be just as likely that Cassian actually postulates two separate levels of grace, one very general level of grace that precedes our acts and another that enables us to complete the acts that we begin of our own free will? That is certainly Pope Leo's understanding of grace. It makes one wonder how many "heresies" or "semi-heresies" are more accurately simple "imprecisions of expression." Cassian himself flatly rejects Pelagianism, and he expresses his belief in *Collationes* 13.3 that all human endeavors are impossible without God's help, since he gives us both the inspiration to pursue those endeavors and the means to complete them.[61] Cassian does not espouse the Semi-Pelagian *initium fidei* formula, even though his disciples in the monasteries did. He simply distinguishes two levels of grace, as he sees them. The first level restores the freedom of the will and inspires us to perform good works, and the second helps us complete that which God's grace inspired in us and which we can freely choose to do.

Pope Leo likewise distinguishes levels of grace in his attempt to balance the necessity of grace with the traditional doctrines of God's universal salvific intent and of the freedom of the will. Yet Leo's description of these levels shows that he finds a sharper distinction between them than Cassian had described. Rather than two, the pope finds three levels of grace. In sermon 72.1 he explains that the first level of grace was distributed to all humans during the general redemption of humankind, enabling them to initiate good works of their own free will; the second inspires us humans to produce good works; and the third enables us to complete those works.[62] Once the redemption was accomplished, Leo adds in sermon 39.3, the way was paved for all humans to participate freely in the salvation-bearing process that the Son established and to which his example leads us.[63] The grace that was distributed to all humans in the redemption renders God's commands possible for us to do, as Leo explains in sermon 51.4.[64] Consequently, he

---

60. Ibid.: "qui cum in nobis ortum quemdam bonae voluntatis inspexerit, illuminant eam confestim atque confortat et incitat ad salutem, incrementum tribuens ei quem vel ipse plantavit, vel nostro conatu viderit emersisse."
61. Ibid. 13.3 (*PL* 49.899–901). See also 13.15–17.
62. Pope Leo, serm. 72.1: "Crux enim Christi, quae saluandis est impensa mortalibus, et sacramentum est et exemplu; sacramentum, quo uirtus impletur diuina; exemplum, quo deuotio incitatur humana, quoniam captiuitatis iugo erutis, etiam noc praestat redemptio, ut eam sequi possit imitatio."
63. Serm. 39.3: "quia ob hoc se Dominus temptari a temptatore permisit, ut cuius munimur auxilio, eius erudiremur exemplo. . . . Pugnauit ergo ille tunc, ut et nos postea pugnaremus, uicit ille, ut et nos similiter uinceremus . . . si uolumus superare, pugnandum est."
64. Serm. 51.4: "possibilia facit mandata per gratiam."

argues, because of the universal reality of grace in redeemed humanity, God justly requires us humans to cooperate of our own free will with his grace in order mysteriously to merit salvation.[65] In fact, the pope warns in sermon 43.1 that without the free use of the human will in obedience to God, grace no longer works efficaciously for our salvation.[66] As Leo adds in sermon 32.4, God is within his rights to enjoin us to cooperate with his grace so that we might complete our own salvation.[67] Grace without the free choice of the human will is impotent to Leo.

In his old age Augustine wrote in *Retractationes* 2.1 that he struggled to preserve the free choice of the human will, but that the grace of God defeated him.[68] To Pope Leo such a statement would be ludicrous. In his eyes, both grace and the human capacity of free choice are essential to the economy of salvation. And he devised a doctrine of grace that brings their interrelationship into focus. On this particular issue, Leo had to set aside the teaching of his mentor Augustine in order to preserve what he considered the clear tradition of the church that salvation requires a free act of the human will. Nevertheless, neither Leo nor his friend Prosper rejected everything Augustine taught. Both theologians relied heavily on Augustine's doctrines for their theological constructions, even though they felt it necessary to put aside his doctrine of grace and predestination. So it would be inaccurate, at best, to infer from this paper that they prescinded from their Augustinian heritage in every detail. Nor is it the intention of this paper to correct what I believe to be the misconception that John Cassian is a "Semi-Pelagian." It is not even central to my paper that John Cassian influenced either Prosper or Leo to abandon Augustine's teachings on grace and predestination; although Cassian's influence should not be overlooked in the development of their respective theologies.[69] My single purpose for writing this paper has been to demonstrate that, whatever the source of their concern, we may be certain that Pope Leo, along with Prosper of Aquitaine, recoiled from the deterministic elements that Augustine had located in his doctrine of grace and predestination. In fact, Leo pushed Prosper's argument in *De vocatione* to its logical extreme by excluding every hint of determinism also from his doctrine of divine foreknowledge.

65. See serm. 53.3: "ad eius imaginem, qui deformitati nostrae conformis factus est, formemur; et ut resurrectionis eius mereamur esse consortes, humilitati et patientiae ipsius per omnia congruamus."
66. Serm. 43.1: "Gratiae igitur Dei oboedientia se humana non subtrahat, nec ab illo bono sine quo non potest bona esse, deficiat." See also sermons 35.4 and 39.1.
67. Serm. 32.4: "Quamuis enim omnium bonorum sit ipse largitor, etiam nostrae tamen fructum quaerit industriae. Non enim dormientibus prouenit regnum caelorum, sed in mandatis Dei laborantibus atque uigilantibus."
68. Augustine, *Retractationes* 2.1 (*PL* 32.629).
69. Indeed, I suspect even Cassian considered himself a faithful Augustinian, though he was intent on saving Augustine from what Cassian considered Augustine's overstatements on grace and predestination. Cassian continued to cite Augustine's authority in other matters even after the latter's death, as he did in *De incarnatione Christi* 7.27.

In Prosper of Aquitaine and, particularly, Pope Leo the Great we see two of the most influential Latin theologians of the generation that rose up toward the end of Augustine's life and just following his death. Through their efforts the western church was able to nuance the great bishop's teaching in order to bring it more in line with the tradition of the church that was held in both the east and the west. In so doing these Latin fathers prevented Augustine's influence from being lost or ignored by later generations as phenomena of fifth-century dialectics. Because of their moderating influence, Augustinian theology was made acceptable to the western church at large; it was canonized at the Council of Orange in 529 C.E.; and its influence continued throughout the Middle Ages and still persists to our present day.

Theology and Language in Irenaeus of Lyon

RICHARD A. NORRIS. JR.*

It is safe to say that issues about the nature of theological discourse, and, by implication, about the procedures or methods that are appropriate for handling theological questions, rank very high on the agenda of contemporary theology. The popularity of the Greek preposition *meta*—regularly compounded with such abstract substantives as "language," and even "theology"—is perhaps a fair measure of the prominent role that is currently played by this interest. One might, of course, argue that this is not entirely a new thing. That preposition also had a place in the vocabulary of ancient exegesis, which, perhaps not so oddly, employed it occasionally, though in a somewhat different sense, for a purpose analogous to that for which we use it: namely, to mark a shift in the level of one's discourse. Our forebears, of course, when they spoke in this manner, were identifying themselves as engaged in anagogy or allegory: they were "transposing" language from one key into another—"elevating" it, as Paul was alleged to have done in Galatians.[1] We, on the other hand, should be loath to describe our *meta*-operations as allegory, "saying something else". Rather, we see ourselves to be looking back (or down, or over the shoulder) on a common and traditional way of speaking to see what it does and how it works and in what manner it can legitimately be used. In both cases, however, language is seen to operate at two levels, and its operation at one of them seems either to determine or to describe its true "sense" at the other.

I allude to this set of issues not because I intend to pursue it in high systematic fashion, but because I have observed that it figured as a principal ingredient in the second-century debate between Irenaeus of Lyon and his Valentinian or Ptolemaean "gnostics"—a debate whose issue determined to a remarkable extent the shape of later Christian tradition. In what follows, I want to show simply *that* it figured, and then *how* it figured, and finally what Irenaeus's resolution of it implied.

---

* Richard A. Norris, Jr., a priest of the Episcopal Church, is Professor of Church History at the Union Theological Seminary in New York City. The author of several major patristic studies, he was also a member of the Inter-Anglican Theological and Doctrinal Commission. This article was presented at the Oxford Patristics Conference in 1991.
[1] See Gregory of Nyssa, *Homilies on the Song of Songs*, Preface (in W. Jaeger, ed., *Gregorii Nysseni Opera*, Vol. VI, p. 5).

I.

No one who undertakes a reading of Irenaeus's lengthy treatise *Adversus haereses* can fail to notice one of his most consistent charges against his Valentinian opponents. He phrases it in the very preface to his first book: these disciples of Ptolemy "say things that are like [what we say], but they think something different." The same accusation is brought in stronger form in another passage: his adversaries are "sheep on the outside, because by their outward speech they are similar to us, and speak the same things; but inwardly they are wolves. For what they *think* [*sententia . . . eorum*] is death-dealing."[2] The basic contrast with which Irenaeus is working, then, is between what is said and what is thought, and it is his firm conviction that in the case of the "disciples of Ptolemy" these two are not merely different but indeed inconsistent.[3] He can even allege that it is embarrassment in the face of this inconsistency which leads them to conceal their true teachings from public view. In this way, the contrast between speech and thought becomes equivalent in his mind to one between what the Valentinians teach in public and what they teach privately.[4] This "thought" of theirs turns out in fact to be, in Irenaeus's mind, another way of talking.

Needless to say, the Valentinians themselves would have given a different account of the matter. Even Irenaeus notes that they claim to "think as we do" and indeed to "have the same teaching"[5]; and their sincerity in this contention is attested by the fact that, as Irenaeus again reports, they expressed surprise and annoyance that the church at Lyon refused to take them into its communion.[6] Furthermore this testimony from Irenaeus is liberally confirmed by other sources. There can be no doubt that the Valentinians regarded themselves as Christians, even if not as Christians of an ordinary sort, or that their distinctive teaching, whatever its ultimate sources, was developed and presented as an interpretation of the message conveyed by the church's books and by its ordinary public teaching. We may take it that they thought of this teaching of theirs simply as the enlightened version of that message. And if they reserved communication of this teaching for special and more or less private occasions, as Irenaeus suggests, this need not have implied any hypocrisy on their part: only that the language of their special teaching conveyed mysteries that were too deep and difficult for unregulated popular consumption. There is little reason to suppose, then, that they thought themselves to be dispensing beliefs inconsistent with the church's message, even if they did have their own special way of talking;

---

2   *AH* 3.16.8.
3   "Non solum dissimilia . . . , sed et contraria:" *AH* 3.17.4.
4   The Ptolemaeans teach "alia quidem in abscondito, alia vero in manifesto:" *AH* 3.15.1.
5   *AH* 3.15.2.
6   *Ibid.*

and Irenaeus himself concedes that the sort of thing the Valentinians said was "similar to the truth" and even—a grudging concession—"persuasive".[7]

But then why the charge of inconsistency between speech and thought, or between public and private teaching? Again it is Irenaeus himself who intimates an answer to our question. In the course of his career—as the perceptive reader of *Adversus haereses* can hardly fail to notice—he had made the acquaintance of writings directed by earlier Christian authors against Valentinian teachings—or at any rate against teachings with a strong family resemblance to those of his Valentinians. Furthermore, his ears had been filled with denunciations of these same heretics, denunciations he is never loath to reproduce. He tells us, however, that taken simply as attempted refutations, none of them was very effective. Their authors, though persons of greater stature than Irenaeus himself would claim to be, "were not sufficiently capable," he says, "of controverting" the heretics.[8]

Now this remark is interesting. Irenaeus's leniency in the face of his predecessors' apparent ineptitude can only have proceeded from a profound sympathy with the difficulties they had faced in their enterprise; and such sympathy, in turn, is only comprehensible if Irenaeus himself had experienced some of the same difficulties. It looks, in fact, as if the bishop of Lyon had found it hard to get a handle on his Valentinian fellow-travelers and infiltrators—hard to see what it was that made them seem, to him and others like him, not merely dangerous but out of place. And this guess is confirmed not only by his frequent admission that their line was "persuasive", but— even more important—by the reason he gives for thinking that his treatise represents a distinct improvement over the efforts of his predecessors. The fact is, he says, that he has contrived, as his teachers had not, to acquaint himself with the *hupothesis* of his opponents[9]—with what his Latin translator calls their "rule" (*regula*) or their "theme" (*argumentum*). What this meant concretely we gather from another passage where Irenaeus explains first that he had read his adversaries' "treatises" (*hupomnêmata*[10]) and then that, through conversation with some of them, he has come to understand their "mind" or "thought" (*sententia, gnômê*).[11] In short, Irenaeus thinks that he has uncovered the key to the discourse of his opponents: that which explained, as we might say, where they were coming from and thus made manifest the real logic of their position—a logic hitherto half concealed in the camouflage of their "persuasive" speech.

What this "key" amounts to is plain from the first eleven chapters of

---

[7] *Ibid.*

[8] See *AH* 4. pr.2.

[9] *Ibid.*

[10] "Treatises" is almost certainly an inadequate translation of this word, but there is probably no exact English equivalent. See the discussion of A. Méhat, *Étude sur les 'Stromates' de Clement d'Alexandrie* (Paris, 1966), pp. 117f.

[11] See *AH* 1.pr.2.

Book 1 of Irenaeus's treatise. It is, in fact, the great, quasi-philosophical myth of creation, fall, and restoration that Irenaeus's Valentinians apparently told to explain who they were, where they came from, and what their destiny was to be. Our business, however, is not to rehearse this myth (which is almost infinitely fascinating in itself), but to grasp what it signified to Irenaeus. For him, it served to define what his adversaries really thought. Consequently, it explained why their ordinary discourse—which, we may presume, did not explicitly or fully convey this myth—seemed at once persuasive and evasive. That discourse, even though it employed, in its own way, the language and symbols of the church's catechesis, had a presupposition, or a set of presuppositions, which it subserved and hinted at but did not plainly reveal. It was this fact that had made it difficult for Irenaeus and his predecessors to get a handle on the logic of the Valentinian position; and it was this discovery, we may suspect, that induced Irenaeus systematically to contrast the "thought" of his opponents with their "speech". For now he knew what their "thought" was. It was in fact another way of talking, a second discourse, that they wanted somehow to connect up with his own.

II.

This very contrast, however, though it served Irenaeus's polemical purposes nicely, got him into a curious form of trouble, which we must now try to explicate in a series of cautious steps. The fact is that he had—precisely in his apparently useful distinction between thought and speech—noticed and tacitly admitted the possibility of different levels of religious or theological discourse; and this possibility, once discerned, not only disturbed him, but led him into some ventures of his own.

His agitation manifests itself as early on as the first book of the treatise *Adversus haereses*. There he is in the business of revealing what he has found out about the *hupothesis* that governed the discourse of his Valentinians—about its content first, and then about what he takes to be its dubious pedigree and dangerous associations. In the first phase of this exposition, he intermittently takes time out to provide illustrations of the way in which his adversaries use this "hypothesis" of theirs to explicate the meaning of certain passages in the church's books—the opening verses of the Fourth Gospel, for example, and various remarks of the Apostle Paul. In the end, however, he feels impelled to desert a policy of mere illustration and to address the problem of their curious exegetical habits directly.

To this end, Irenaeus employs a pair of well-known analogies. He first calls upon his readers to imagine a person who comes upon a mosaic in which some able artist has arranged the stones to form the portrait of a king, but who then proceeds to extract the individual stones and rearrange them to produce the likeness "of a dog or a fox". In just such a fashion, Irenaeus argues, do the Valentinians treat the Scriptures. They make use of non-scriptural sources, and then "adapt" the parables of the Lord, the pronouncements of the prophets, and the words of the apostles to their own notions, thus, presumably, making them portray not a king but a fox.[12] So taken is Irenaeus by this idea that he works it up in improved form just a chapter later. Now he asks us to imagine someone who performs the rhetorical exercise of taking a series of lines from here and there in the poems of Homer and arranging them to tell a story that Homer never wrote.[13] The question then becomes, Is this Homer? Irenaeus's answer, of course, is that it is not; and his reason, significantly enough, is that the *hupothesis* is different. An Homeric poem has its own *hupothesis,* and the individual lines have to be understood in their own relation to it. To take the lines and arrange them according to another *hupothesis* is to falsify their sense: i.e., to produce a non-Homeric effect—a fox, if you like, and not a king.

I am inclined to think that this passage from Book 1 provides the clearest indication of the sort of thing Irenaeus had in mind when he used the word *hupothesis.* The doubtfulness on this score of his Latin translator—who alternates, as we have noticed, between "rule" and "theme"—is indicative of the problem. More recent translators have favored—at least in this passage—something like "subject-matter".[14] In the case of the Homeric poems, however, what underlies and governs their meaning—their subject-matter, in short—is what we would call a "plot", a coherent story-structure of some sort that involves and identifies a particular set of characters. And what Irenaeus seems to be arguing is precisely that the Valentinian *hupothesis,* which he has just recited with great diligence and at great length, does not in fact represent or reproduce the "plot" of the Scriptures: that in fact it is a different plot altogether, and indeed involves, at least in part, a different set of characters.

It is worth pointing out, in support of this suggestion, that Sextus Empiricus[15], in one of his critical treatises, identifies three meanings of the word *hupothesis* as it was used in learned circles in his day. It could, of course, mean "an inquiry into particular circumstances"[16], and it could further mean a presupposition or assumption. But it could also mean "the

---

[12]   See *AH* 1.8.1.
[13]   *AH* 1.9.4.
[14]   There is on this score a surprising agreement between the 1868 version of Roberts and Rambaut, and that of A. Rousseau in *Sources Chrétiennes* 264. Hefner's suggestion (*Journal of Religion* 44 (1964), p. 296) that "hypothesis" denotes "that which inheres in an entity so as to give it form, existence, substance, unity, and meaning" will work only if the "hypothesis" in question is the correct one.
[15]   *Adversus Mathematicos* 3.3–4.
[16]   *Ibid.,* 3.4: *hē tōn epi merous zētēsis.*

development of events in a drama"[17]—the plot, in short, or argument of a play. Furthermore, it seems apparent that Irenaeus understands the term in this way. When he compares the Valentinian myth to the *Theogony* of one "Antiphanes", what he claims is that his adversaries take over the very same story-line (*hupothesis*) that this work employs, but disguise the fact by changing the names of the characters. This is, of course, as Irenaeus sees it, the converse of the policy they follow in the case of the opening verses of John's Gospel. In that instance, they retain the names of the characters, but misapply them "and refer them instead to their own 'hypothesis'": which means, I take it, that they change the story.

Having made this point many times over, Irenaeus is bound to identify the real "plot" of the Scriptures; and indeed he proceeds in Book 1 to do so almost immediately. It is to be found, he says, in the "rule of truth"—and here the word "rule" correctly renders the Greek *kanôn*—which one "receives by way of baptism"[18], and which Irenaeus also allows himself to describe, in the same place, as "the body (*sômation*) of the truth", by this phrase emphasizing, I take it, the character of this rule as an organic whole.[19]

I need hardly point out that the question what Irenaeus meant by this phraseology has been the subject of a lengthy, learned, and continuing debate. Nineteenth-century German scholarship, as represented for example by Harnack, tended to identify the "rule of truth" as an early form of declaratory creed, which, in his varying formulations of it, Irenaeus paraphrases, expands, or abbreviates according to his purpose of the moment. Since, moreover, one of Irenaeus's equivalents for the phrase "rule of truth" is the term "tradition", much ink has been expended in an attempt to determine his views on the sixteenth-century issue of the relative authority of "scripture" and "tradition". Once one realizes, however, that Irenaeus had never seen a declaratory creed, and that his "rule of truth", considered materially if not formally, represents for him the "theme" or "plot", the *argumentum* of the Scriptures, one is set free from any temptation to think that he opposed "tradition" as creed to "Scripture"—or for that matter that he was concerned to rank them in some fashion. Such issues were simply not on his mind. His question is: Given the *hupothesis* of the Valentinians, to which, as to a Procrustean bed, they "adapt" the Scriptural text and the message of the church, where does one go to find the correct *hupothesis*? And what he wants to answer is that the true *hupothesis* can be discerned easily enough by simply reading the Scriptures, as long as you let the straightforward and explicit bits guide you; like the Homeric poems, the

---

[17]   *Ibid.* 3.3: *hê dramatikê peripeteia.*
[18]   *AH* 1.9.4.
[19]   Cf. *AH* 2.27.1, where Irenaeus speaks of "the body [*sôma*] of the truth" and its "members": the allusion to Paul's metaphor for the church is apparent.

Scriptures tell their own story. But if a person is confused, or, being a barbarian, cannot read Greek, or is engaged in some controversy about the interpretation of obscure scriptural passages, this is no reason for despair; for the same story-line governs, and indeed is laid out in, the teaching which everywhere accompanies baptism and which identifies the characters that figure most prominently in the baptismal confession: God, God's Word, and God's Spirit.[20]

Irenaeus, then, wants to say two things. First, he wants to insist that if the Valentinians have an *hupothesis*—a "plot" that is taken to articulate the correct sense of the Christian message—ordinary Christians have one too; and the easiest, if not the only, way of discovering it is to consult the very shape and logic of the standard baptismal catechesis. Second, however, he wants to insist that what marks this *hupothesis* out as the truthful one—as "the rule of truth"—is the fact that it is not independently derived. It is conveyed, as we might say, in, with, and under the church's books and the church's catechesis, both of which must be taken with infinite seriousness (he thinks) because both can be shown to have apostolic credentials. One can, to be sure, summarize this narrative, for one or another purpose, by mentioning its principal characters—the one Creator God, God's Word, and God's Spirit—and by alluding to the high-points of their purposeful activity: creation, for example, and incarnation. Such summaries, however, do not stand on their own: they are merely disengagements of central elements in the divine "plot", comparable, perhaps, to an unusually terse study-guide to the *Iliad*.

Precisely here, though, Irenaeus's problem emerges. He wants, like most of us, to have his cake and to eat it. He wants, in effect, to say both that there *is* a correct *hupothesis* and that no one really needs it. To phrase the point more carefully: Irenaeus is induced by his Valentinian opponents both to perceive the usefulness—and indeed, in some circumstances, the necessity—of study-guides, and at the same time to distrust such devices profoundly. Hence on the one hand he will—in forms that vary according to the issue at hand—set out straightforward formulations of his "rule of truth" and insist that instruction and exegesis be guided by it; whilst on the other hand he can, from time to time, simply dissolve his "rule" into its sources and thus intimate that it has no independent status. He cannot decide—because he does not want to decide—whether the church's "rule" as he understands it is a true functional equivalent of the Valentinian myth; for the latter after all, in his eyes, is a tool for disassembling—and then, to be sure, for re-assembling—both Scriptures and catechesis. He is secretly afraid, I suspect, that he too might find himself in a situation where his thought and

---

[20]   See R.P.C. Hanson, *Tradition in the Early Church* (London, 1962), p. 93: the "rule of truth" is "an account . . . of the content of the preaching and teaching of the church," which "looks like material used . . . for catechetical teaching before baptism."

his speech were dissociated—where he was telling two stories and thus talking two languages.

III.

Let us say, then—to speak in a more constructive and sympathetic vein—that Irenaeus's ambiguities about his own *hupothesis* stem from the fact that he wants to assign it a distinctive and different function: that of keeping thought and speech together. He desiderates, in effect, a certain wholesome circularity in the discourse of people who are in the business of saying, with regard to the message that the church conveys, "what it all means". Their "rule" must somehow be derived out of the materials whose interpretation it governs, even as those materials are understood through the "rule". Or, to use his original, rather unhandy contrast: the thought must be a distillation of the logic of the speech, even as the speech is interpreted and disposed according to the logic of the thought.

In support of this suggestion, I want to adduce two considerations. The first concerns Irenaeus's perception of his opponents' stance—its basis and its implications. The second concerns his notion of a proper alternative to that stance. It is in this way, I think, that we can get an appreciation of how he wants his rule or "argument" to function.

The first consideration, then, is drawn from Irenaeus's portrayal—or better, as I have said, his perception—of his opponents' stance and of what is involved in it. Needless to say, Irenaeus has more than one general charge to bring against the system of the opponents he calls "gnostics". One—which I take to be the polemical working out of a rhetorical common-place—is that they are always coming up with new and inconsistent versions of their basic "plot"; another is that their ideas are ultimately foreign to the Christian movement—a perception which he tries to support by insisting that their teaching stems, not from the apostles, but from Simon Magus (or from "philosophy"). Here, however, my interest is in the perception expressed[21] by one particular verb which Irenaeus uses with an odd frequency[21]: *huperbainein* or, in the Latin version, *supergredi*. The Greek word can probably best be translated for our purposes as "going over" or "going beyond," but it also carries suggestions of outdoing and (of course) transgressing. Perhaps Irenaeus secretly thought of his Valentinian friends as compulsive over-achievers who were in the business of competing with everyone, including God.[22] What is certain is that he pictured them as

---

[21]   He employs it at least 14 times: see B. Reynders, *Lexique comparée . . . de l' "Adversus Haereses" de saint Irénée* (CSCO 141, Louvain, 1954), s.v. "supergredior".

[22]   See *AH* 2.26.1: Paul knew, says Irenaeus, that some people would "opinari seipsos perfectos, imperfectum autem Demiurgum introducentes. . . ."

people who (falsely) claimed to get "entirely beyond God in their thought"[23] and thus believed that on death they would "mount beyond" the heavens and the Creator to another realm. Hence they think, he says, that they know "the mysteries that are beyond God"[24] and have uncovered "something more than the truth"[25] (by which, of course, Irenaeus means more than the content of his own *hupothesis*). It is unfair of him to say that his opponents are "always seeking and never finding truth"[26], for he knows, having expounded their grand myth, what truth it is that they have found. It is, as he himself puts it with heavy sarcasm, "the great God . . . whom no-one can know"[27], or, as we might say, following Professor Tillich, the "God beyond God". What this meant in practice, though, was simply that they had discovered themselves to be natives of another, different, higher order of things.

In that case, however, it was only natural, as he sees, that the Valentinians should experience difficulty in getting their thought, which went "entirely beyond" the Creator God, and their speech, which they shared with that God's subjects, together. The two could scarcely be of a piece; if they were, there would be no point in "going beyond". By the same token, their *hupothesis,* which embodied that thought, could scarcely conform, as to "plot" and characters, with that implicit in the church's elementary catechesis; for the latter reflected, presumably, not the realm beyond, but what Theodotus had called "this system of things". The dissonance that Irenaeus identified between his adversaries' "thought" and their "speech", then, corresponded to the structure of the Valentinian world—was indeed reproduced in it. And if at the same time the good bishop was compelled to admit that the dissonance was not complete, that the Valentinians' thoughts could seem *verisimiles,* "like" the truth embodied in the church's language, this circumstance too had its explanation. Did they not maintain that there was a kind of image-relation between the world beyond and this visible order of things? Nevertheless, it turned out to be, in their case, an odd sort of imaging, in which the two terms of the relation somehow remained latently hostile even in their likeness. Many years later Plotinus, who knew an image-relation when he saw one, brought this curious ambiguity to light. He openly wondered why it was that the gnostics would want to dwell in the archetypical original of a world they despised.[28] In Plotinus's thought, the image is to be "cashed into" the original; but at least as Irenaeus perceived it, this was not really possible in the world of his Valentinians, and the proof

---

[23]   *AH* 5.31.1. Cf. 4.19.1: "Supra enim Deum factae sunt cogitationes ipsorum."

[24]   *AH* 3.7.1.

[25]   *AH* 5.20.2.

[26]   *Ibid.* What Irenaeus means by this is indicated in 4.19.1. He thinks there is an infinite regress involved in their unending search for "types of types and images of images".

[27]   *AH* 3.24.2.

[28]   See the argument in *Enneads* 2.9.17–18.

of this fact was that the scriptural language of the church's catechesis could not in the end—despite all "verisimilitude"—be cashed into the language of the Valentinian myth. It was just this circumstance that Irenaeus so profoundly, and polemically, regretted.

Perhaps this explains—and here we come to our second consideration—why it is that Irenaeus lays it down that human beings have no business trying to "go beyond" God or to "look into what there might be beyond the Creator".[29] It is important, however, to notice the reason he gives for this prohibition. It is not that the Creator marks a definable "quantity" that sets a limit to what one may ask; rather it is that the Creator constitutes as *such* the "beyond" that no human creature has measured or explored. If one sets out to indulge in *huperbainein*, in "transcending," as it were, the "transcendent" what one arrives at is the Creator. And Irenaeus's point in saying this is plain. He wants to insist that the mystery of things is not the mystery of *another* world—and therefore of another God—beyond this: the mystery is that which grounds *this* realm of human experience. At the same time, of course, Irenaeus is convinced that this mystery is not instantly accessible. At present human beings are incomplete and imperfect, and hence scarcely capable even of dabbling their feet in the infinite sea that is the divine. The claim to "go beyond" God, therefore, in speculation is, as he sees it, doubly absurd. It misunderstands the very meaning of the word "Creator", and it overestimates the capacity of the creature.

Now it has been pointed out[30] that Irenaeus in fact adopts, in arguing this position, the language and attitude of the "Empirical School" of physicians and of the sceptical tradition in Greek philosophy. Knowledge, he thinks, must rest on what is plain and given, not on speculation that takes off from admitted obscurities. "To do otherwise (as the Gnostics do) is to subvert 'the very art of discovery'."[31] The way of knowledge, then, is from the relatively clear to the relatively obscure, and not *vice versa*. To Irenaeus, however, what all this adds up to is an exegetical—and hence theological—principle. There is no doubt, he says, that "we hope always to be receiving and learning more from [God], because [God] is good and possesses unbounded riches and a kingdom without end and knowledge without limit."[32] Such learning, however, can only start with what is *clear*—the "witness concerning God that is out in the open"[33], which Irenaeus identifies as the "rule" that tells the truth and as "solid" (*firmam*) knowledge of God. There can, it seems, be no "going beyond" this *hupothesis*, but only "inquiry into

---

[29] *AH* 2.25.4: "ne . . . supertranscendas ipsum Deum, neque super Demiurgum requiras quid sit, non enim invenies."
[30] By W. R. Schoedel in an admirable article titled "Theological Method in Irenaeus" (JTS 1985, pp. 31ff.).
[31] *Ibid.*, p. 36. The reference is to *AH* 2.27.1: "ipsam inventionis . . . disciplinam".
[32] *AH* 2.28.3.
[33] "In aperto positum de Deo testimonium": *AH* 2.28.1.

the mystery and into the economy of the God that is."[34] The plain data of the writings and of the catechesis, then, define the area of investigation—of progress in knowledge; one cannot get "beyond" it because one cannot get beyond the God who is responsible for the story—and hence the world—whose "plot" it specifies. The Creator God *is* the mystery; but more, the Creator God is—to repeat—the mystery of this realm, not of some other; and here is where we start.

IV.

At every point, then, it seems that the argument between Irenaeus and his opponents turns on two correlative sets of issues. The position that each takes can be—and in fact is—characterized at once in terms of the relation between two languages—the languages that, in the case of his Valentinians, Irenaeus refers to as their "thought" and their "speech"—and in terms of the relation between two ontological realms. Irenaeus agrees with his adversaries that the language whose "plot" constitutes his *hupothesis* is somehow elementary. What he denies is that an alternative to it is available. The mystery that lies "beyond" this language is simply its own ramified depth of meaning, given formally and preliminarily in the language itself as "rule of truth". Correspondingly, Irenaeus presents the ultimate mystery as the Creator God who founds this world and whose enterprise within it gives rise to the language of the church's catechetical narrative. By contrast, his opponents' myth is perceived as constituted by an alternative language, which characterizes, and hence posits, what amount to an alternative God and an alternative world, and is based not in plain givens, but in flights of speculation. The difference of languages—the contrast between "thought" and "speech"—is in their case an intimation of different worlds. That, I take it, is why Irenaeus wants, by contrast, to locate his *hupothesis* or "rule" *on a level* with what it immediately interprets: i.e., he wants a reliable study-guide, and not a discourse which explains the catechesis in other terms. In a word, he distrusts meta-languages, whether in the ancient or in the modern mode. This distaste leaves him, however, in the uncomfortable position of admitting that his *hupothesis,* while it may indeed be the *rule* of truth, cannot claim, like the Valentinian *hupothesis,* to be the *fulness* of truth. When, therefore, he takes up the issue of the nature and limits of theological inquiry[35], he casts his remarks in the form of a meditation on the text *We know in part;* for the beginning, as he once or twice observes, comes only at the end.

---

[34] *Ibid.*
[35] See *AH* 2.25–28.

Revue des Études Augustiniennes, 40 (1994), 45-78

Augustine on Language[1]

I. – INTRODUCTION : AUGUSTINIAN DIFFIDENCE

Although Augustine wrote quite frequently on language, scholars have tended to use his writings on the subject as the means to reconstuct no-longer-extant Stoic theories of grammar[2]. I do not wish to take issue with that endeavor ; rather, I will highlight the extent to which Augustine integrated his theory of language with his epistemological and ontological thought. Augustine considered words, the basic components of human language, to be objects of sense-perception, and as such they have a specific place in Augustinian metaphysics, and it is a lowly one. By following this simple suggestion to its conclusion--and a brief map to my argument follows--we can see that Augustine's frequent expressions of authorial diffidence are not merely rhetorical tropes but also statements of philosophical principle, and that when he urges that he has said nothing meaningful in words about God, he means it.

In his early treatise on language, the *de magistro*, Augustine set forth a theory of language based on signs, and he criticized language as a means for teaching on the basis of its ambiguity. The linguistics adopted in that dialogue are directly relevant to the methods of reading used in the *de civitate dei*. My conviction on this issue arises from a series of interconnected observations. Augustine did not develop a critical theory in the modern sense; rather, his

---

1. I would like to thank Prof. Sabine MacCormack of the University of Michigan for reading several drafts of this paper. Prof. Ann Hanson, also of the University of Michigan, read a final draft on short notice and saved me from several errors. Prof. James O'Donnell's new commentary on the *Confessions* (Oxford, 1992) arrived after this paper had been completed, and I was able to consult it only briefly in making revisions. He does not comment extensively on the issues raised in this essay.

2. See B. DARRELL JACKSON, «The theory of signs in St. Augustine's *de doctrina Christiana*», *RÉAug* 15 (1969) 9-49, and R. MARKUS, «St. Augustine on Signs», *Phronesis* 2 (1957) 60-83.

comments on reading in the *de civitate dei* concentrate on language as a carrier of meaning, as a system of signification, very much in harmony with the thought of the early dialogue. According to Augustine's theory, a text is simply the written representation of speech, and a word, whether written or spoken, merely signifies something else, something real. Furthermore, the reality which lies behind the signs, whether the object of sense-perception or intellection, is alone the proper subject of true knowledge[3].

To understand a text, therefore, one had to know the objects of which the words within the text were the signs ; when an author writes about his own thoughts, it is necessary to know the intent of the author[4]. Augustine does allow for authors who deliberately introduce complexity into their writing[5] ; primarily, however, texts become difficult to interpret when their subject matter brings out the inherent weaknesses of discursive speech. Since the qualities of language as a system of signification directly affect the ability of an author to express, and the reader to grasp, any particular idea, Augustine had to address two different issues in his work on language. He could largely abandon such time-worn issues as the relationship between name and object-- whether names exist by nature or convention, although he does comment on it[6]. Instead, he needed to explain the particular qualities of speech which made it such an imperfect tool for describing abstract ideas and the divine. This effort led Augustine to consider the mechanics whereby man transforms ideas in the mind into perceptible utterances, and whereby that utterance is received by another's senses, yet impacts his mind. By his way of thinking, then, in order to explain the use of signs he needed to outline the relationship between the senses and the mind.

---

3. On Augustine's theory of signs, see C. MAYER, «Prinzipien der Hermeneutik Augustins und daraus sich ergebende Probleme», *Forum Katholische Theologie* 1 (1985) 197-211 and C. KIRWAN, *Augustine*, (London: Routledge, 1989), esp. chapter III.

4. On authorial intent, see *de doctrina christiana* 2.5.6 : *Quam [scripturam divinam] legentes nihil aliud appetunt quam cogitationes voluntatemque illorum a quibus conscripta est invenire et per illas voluntatem dei, secundum quam tales homines locutos credimus.* See also *de utilitate credendi* v.11, *Conf.* 12.18.27 and 12.23.32 ; *de doctrina christiana* 1.36.41-37.41. Augustine uses a variety of words to describe intent : *cogitatio, intentio, voluntas, sentire.* The terminology used in somewhat imprecise. The semantic field covered by these Latin words does not map neatly onto that of the English 'intent'. Of course, similar difficulties in translation were a matter of great concern to Augustine. See *de civ. dei* 5.19 (on *tyrannus*), 10.1 (on *latreia, religio, cultus, eusebeia,* and *pietas*), 14.9 (on *apatheia* and *impassabilitas*) ; *de doctrina christiana* 2.11.16 (on *raca* and *hosanna*), 2.12.18-13.19 ; *de trin.* 15.8.14-9.15.

5. See esp. *Conf.* 12.31.42 : *per quem (Moses) deus unus sacras litteras vera et diversa visuris multorum sensibus temperavit. ego certe, quod intrepidus de meo corde pronuntio, si ad culmen auctoritatis aliquid scriberem, sic mallem scribere, ut, quod veri quisque de his rebus capere posset, mea verba resonarent, quam ut unam veram sententiam ad hoc apertius ponerem, ut excluderem ceteras, quarum falsitas me non posset offendere.*

6. See *de doctrina christiana* 2.24.37, 2.25.38-39, 2.40.60, 3.14.22, *Conf.* 1.8.13, *de trin.* 13.1.4.

The *de magistro* ultimately does not affirm the power of language. Instead, the long discussion of signs is simply part of a demonstration of the incapacity of language to serve as a tool for teaching, where teaching, as Augustine construes it, encompasses practically all communication (*de magistro* 1.1 ; *de doctrina christiana* 1.2.2). If language cannot teach, its importance must be secondary to that which can. Thus, the *de magistro* ultimately closes with a description of the presence to the mind of Christ, the one true teacher[7]. Such a reading of the dialogue is confirmed by the very brief report given to it in the *Retractationes*[8].

He thus creates a philosophy of language which explains, rather than asserts, the privileged status of Christian scripture. Since the ontological gap between divine matters--the highest form of reality--and human speech is so great, any human utterance on so elevated a subject must be inscrutable : the more comprehensible the text, the greater its misrepresentation of divine reality must be. Texts about the true divinity alone have justification for their obscurity, and they alone warrant, and indeed require, the application of a scriptural hermeneutics.

For Augustine, therefore, we can see that the existence of signs, and especially their arbitrary nature, are not nearly as important as the cause for their existence[9]. In following this chain of causation, Augustine connected two important problems : the inability of human language adequately to express thoughts on complex, abstract issues, and the parallel inability of the human mind to think clearly about God. In other words, human thoughts are tied up in fleshy things : *hoc modo ex familiaritate carnis opinantur* (*Conf.* 12.27.37). It would be intolerable for these same inabilities to affect Adam before the Fall, the angels, or the blessed after the resurrection. These impediments to human understanding, and therefore the existence of discursive language, thus relate directly to sin, and to the condition and structure of the human soul.

Augustine had therefore linked the process by which we find meaning in a text to his own theories about the workings of the senses, the memory, and the intellect. Augustine's textbook on the reading of scripture concentrates on the interpretation of signs ; his work on the Trinity, too, discusses signs, but in the context of epistemology; and his treatise on language, the *de dialectica*,

---

7. *de magistro* 11.38 ; see also *de doctrina christiana* 2.12.17. Within his 'sight of the mind' metaphor, Augustine describes this presence of God to the mind as the light which allows the mind to see ; see, for example, *Solil.* 1.6.12, *Conf.* 12.18.27, *de Genesi ad litteram* 12.31.59. This metaphor is creatively explored by G. O'DALY, *Augustine's Philosophy of Mind*, (London: Duckworth, 1987) 204-207.

8. *Retr.* 1.xi : *Per idem tempus scripsi librum, cuius est titulus de magistro. In quo disputatur et quaeritur et invenitur magistrum non esse, qui docet hominem scientiam, nisi deum, secundum illud etiam quod in evangelio scriptum est:* unus est magister vester Christus. See also *de doctrina christiana* 2.12.17. On the *de magistro*, see G. MADEC, «Analyse du *de magistro*», *RÉAug* 21 (1975) 63-71.

9. A rule stressed by Augustine. See *de magistro* 9.26 : *non tamen falsum est omne, quod propter aliud est, vilius esse quam id, propter quod est.*

describes the relationship between mind and body[10]. Yet one cannot analyze Augustine's thought on knowledge and the human mind without also understanding his writings on God ; after all, his own efforts to understand memory and the intellect in the *Confessions* led him to tackle God and time, and his efforts to understand the trinity led him back to the human soul.

Obviously, all of these concerns must intersect when one confronts the text of *Genesis*: Was there time before God created heaven and earth ? What is this Word that John speaks of ? What does it mean that God created man in his image ? How did Adam communicate with God, and how did this means of communication change after the Fall ? Augustine's thoughts on all these disparate issues--history, time, creation, knowledge, sense-perception, signs, language, and God--are connected, and the terminology and concepts which he uses in discussing them are the same (see note 43). Augustine thought that we use language because our souls cannot communicate with each other directly, because they are trapped in physical bodies. Language, like our bodies, is trapped and operates in time, and is thus largely subject to the limitations of the physical world. At the same time, language consists of signs which can cause the mind to think about things other than the sign itself ; hence they are also the means by which we can begin to transcend those same limitations[11].

The essay presented here, therefore, makes its case by tracing connections. Augustine, one might say, had a philosophy of everything ; it is largely coherent, though not always persuasive, and it is comprehensive. Augustine did not shy away from its consequences. He certainly recognized the power of language as a persuasive force, yet his preoccupations with its inadequacies gave him grave doubts about his own philosophical projects, both literary and personal.

Justification for this present enquiry, which gives primacy to his thought on language, is provided by his own writings. Obviously, if Augustine felt that his own literary projects were in danger of misinterpretation because, despite his best efforts to the contrary, his words could not help but fundamentally misrepresent his thoughts, then an understanding of the theoretical basis for this fear becomes a necessary prolegomena to a proper appreciation of his philosophy. Augustine himself provides ample evidence for just such a concern :

> *de utilitate credendi* x.23 : You will say in good conscience that you have not lied, and you will assert this with all the words at your command, but they are only words. For you, being a man, cannot so reveal the hidden places of your mind to another man, that you may be known to the depths of your soul.

> *de trin.* 15.7.13 : That these things are done in our mind, or by it, we know, and we are very certain of it. However, the more that we desire to find out how these things are done, the more our speech fails us, and our intention itself does not

10. On this work, see H.-I. MARROU, *St. Augustin et la fin de la culture antique*, (*BEFAR* 145) Paris, 1938, p. 576-578. The text is cited from the edition of J. Pinborg (Dordrecht and Boston: D. Reidel, 1975).

11. Perceptively noted also by P. RICOEUR, *Time and Narrative*, (trans. K. McLaughlin and D. Pellauer ; The University of Chicago Press, 1984) vol. 1, page 7.

endure, with the result that our understanding, to say nothing of our tongue, fails to reach some level of clarity[12].

Of course, previous writers had expressed concern that their writings could be misinterpreted, and previous readers had suggested that the impossibility of questioning an author dramatically reduced the value of any written text[13]. Augustine, however, thought the gap between saying and meaning inherent in the structure of discursive language, and therefore insurmountable. To be sure, Augustine had theological reasons for denying any human capacity to know God. Yet these theological issues should not, and indeed can not, be considered independently of his critique of human language. Indeed, Augustine rigorously considered the implications of his theological presumptions for his own epistemological and linguistic thought ; while this essay concerns itself most directly with the latter, a very basic examination of some broader issues will be necessary to set the stage. In the end, Augustine himself confesses that he has allowed one of his favorite metaphors to determine, and ultimately to undermine, his pursuit of the truth[14].

Before I begin, two methodological points. Scholarly debates thrive on jargon[15]. Augustine was deeply aware of the inadequacies of the Latin language--and the superiority of the Greek--in its possession of the proper terminology to discuss issues of worship and philosophy[16]. Given his

---

12. With *de utilitate credendi* x.23 compare *de magistro* 13.42-43 ; *de utilitate credendi* v.11 ; *Conf.* 10.3.3, 12.5.5, 12.23.32 ; *de doctrina christiana* 2.13.19, 2.38.56, 3.2.2, 3.2.5, 3.3.6-7, 4.10.24 ; *Enarrationes in Psalmos* 118.18.3 ; *de civ. dei* 19.7 ; *de trin.* 15.25.45. With *de trin.* 15.7.13 compare *de doctrina christiana* 1.6.6 (*Quod autem a me dictum est, si ineffabile esset, dictum non esset.*) ; *Conf.* 11.8.10 (*utcumque video, sed quomodo id eloquar nescio*), 11.14.17 (a similar contrast between the weakness of human intelligence, and the greater weakness of human speech), 13.11.12 ; *de civ. dei* 22.29 ; *de trin.* 1.1.2-3, 15.5.8, 15.27.50.

13. In its most famous expression, see Plato *Protagoras* 347e, where he adopts a model of reading in which the meaning of a text is indentified and coextensive with the author's intent. On Augustine and authorial intent, see note 4. According to him, the very nature of the production of Scripture makes it impossible to know, or even to understand, the intent of its "author". That many interpretations were therefore possible only confirmed its privileged status. See *Conf.* 12, 10.10, 12.18.27, and 12.31.42 (quoted in note 5) ; *de civ. dei* 11.19, 18.42-44, 20.17, 20.21, 20.29 ; *de doctrina christiana* 2.5.6, 2.6.7-8, 3.27.38, 4.6.9 ; *Ep.* 55.xi.21; and *de trin.* 15.25.45.

14. *de trin.* 14.6.8 (discussed in Section VIII). See also *Conf.* 12.5.5, *de trin.* 15.10.18, and *de Genesi ad litteram* 12.4.15, 12.11.22.

15. See the caution offered by R. Markus in his chapters on Augustine (21 through 27) in *The Cambridge History of Later Greek and Early Medieval Philosophy* (Cambridge: Cambridge University Press, 1967) 366.

16. On the superiority of the Greek term *latreia*, see *de civ. dei* 10.1 ; in addition to the texts on translation cited in note 4, see *de utilitate credendi* iii.5. For the invention of new terms to facilitate discussion, see *de magistro* 4.8 : *placetne appellemus significabilia ea, quae signis significari possunt et signa non sunt, sicut ea, quae videri possunt, visibilia nominamus, ut de his deinceps commodius disseramus.* See also *de Genesi ad litteram* 12.7.16 : *Tertium [genus visionum] vero intellectuale, ab intellectu; quia mentale, a mente,*

preoccupation with the precision of his own definitions[17], we should be careful about imposing our own[18]. A professional orator in antiquity understood the difference between words used in their everyday meaning and in their technical application, but he could be sloppy, and he had a precedent in Scripture.

> *Retr.* I.xiii.5 : When I said, "There is a great difference between knowledge maintained by the trustworthy reasoning of the mind, which we say we know, and belief in what has been usefully handed down to posterity either by report or in writing" (*de utilitate credendi* xi.25), and a little later, "Our knowledge we owe to reason, our beliefs to authority" (*ibid*), I should not be taken to mean that we shrink from saying that we know what we believe on the testimony of suitable witnesses. When we speak properly (*proprie*), we say that we know only that thing which we grasp with the steadfast reasoning of our minds. But when we are using words as they are used in ordinary speech (*verbis consuetudini aptioribus*), as indeed divine Scripture uses them, we do not hesitate to say that we 'know' what we perceive with the bodily senses, or believe on the testimony of witnesses worthy of trust ; and at the same time we also understand the difference between the two[19].

Augustine will vigorously maintain this distinction between knowledge and belief throughout his career[20]. In fact, in the passage in the *Retractationes* cited above, Augustine distinguishes between knowing (*scire*) and believing (*credere*) ; in the original passage in the *de utilitate credendi*, the contrast is between believing and understanding (*intellegere*). In the absence of a word for the act of intellection, Augustine here adopts *firma ratio mentis*[21].

Second, for the purposes of this essay I quote from Augustine's works largely without regard for chronology. Augustine had at times considered the nature of language in Heaven (see at note 53), whether it had a capacity to signify that was greater or utterly different in kind. As his thought on these

---

ipsa vocabuli novitate nimis absurdum est, ut dicamus.

17. *de dialectica* V.12-16 : *haec autem omnia quae definita sunt, utrum recte definita sint, et utrum hactenus verba definitionis aliis definitionibus prosequenda fuerint, ille indicabit locus in quo definiendi disciplina tractatur.*

18. On the other hand, one should keep in mind Augustine's own declaration about his writings at *Conf.* 12.31.42, quoted in note 5.

19. On the *consuetudo locutionis humanae*, see, in the *de civ. dei* alone, 9.5, 10.15, 11.8, 15.6, 15.25, 16.5-6, 16.29, 17.5-7, and 22.2. Elsewhere, see *Conf.* 12.27.37.

20. See *de utilitate credendi* ix.22 and xi.25 ; *de civ. dei* 11.3, 11.7-8, 15.25, 16.5, 22.29 ; *de magistro* xi.37 ; *Solil.* 1.3.8 ; *de quantitate animae* 29.57 ; *enarrationes in Psalmos* 118.18.3 ; *de trin.* 1.1.3, 11.8.14, and 14.6.8. As usual, he can be sloppy : see *de civ. dei* 21.7. He also frequently insists that he wants to avoid the appearance of arguing about words ; see, for example, *de quantitate animae* 6.10 (*voca quidquid vis : non enim mihi de nominibus laborandum est, cum res aperta sit.*) ; *de trin.* 15.15.25 (*ne de controversia vocabuli laborare videamur*) ; *de civ. dei* 9.19 (*ne de verbis etiam non certare videamur*) and *de civ. dei* 9.4.

21. On the above passage, see the article by M. BURNYEAT, «Wittgenstein and Augustine's *de magistro*», *Proceedings of the Aristotelian Society*, Supplementary volume LXI (1987) 1-24. On *scire* and *intellegere*, see *Conf.* 1.1, on the interpretation of which I am inclined to agree with O'Donnell ad loc.

issues developed, the Fall began to take on a greater significance in his conception of the origins of human speech (Section V)[22] ; for related reasons he began to have serious misgivings about his previous stance on the origin and pre-existence of the soul[23]. Despite these changes in Augustine's thought, the basic framework of his understanding and, most importantly, the terminology with which he describes it, remain largely the same throughout his life[24]. In this essay, for the sake of efficiency, I hold myself carefully within the limits of the present enquiry, but the cognitive difficulties which I highlight and which Augustine acknowledged early and late in life (Sections VII and VIII) are signs both of the continuity of his doubt about the possibility of secure knowledge concerning the soul, and of the honesty with which he owned up to that doubt.

I begin by describing the hierarchy of matter outlined by Augustine in a variety of his works, and the consequences of this ontology for, and its relationship with, human understanding. This leads to a more direct consideration of the handicaps to human understanding and their origins. The epistemological thought which lies behind these writings is brought into sharp relief by contrasting it with Augustine's comments on God's knowledge, vision, and language. Having thus created a context for considering Augustine's criticisms of language, I will show in greater detail how his linguistic theory and his philosophy are related.

II. – AUGUSTINE'S ONTOLOGY, AND THE PLACE OF LANGUAGE WITHIN IT

The ancient world never escaped the shadow of Platonic epistemology ; Augustine himself, apparently feeling little pressure from his religion to shun this pagan heritage[25], adopts and adapts wholeheartedly many of the basic structures of this system.

> *Conf.* 12.13.16 : My provisional interpretation of that is that 'heaven' means 'heaven of heaven', the intellectual, non-physical heaven where the intelligence's knowing is a matter of simultaneity--not in part, not through an enigma, not through a mirror, but complete, in total openness, face to face. This knowing is not of one thing at one time and of another thing at another moment (*non modo hoc,*

---

22. On the chronology of this process, I am somewhat reluctant to endorse the precision which O'Connell espouses, while applauding the high level of scholarship which his work has aroused. See O'CONNELL in *Augustinian Studies* 4 (1973) 1-32, *RÉAug* 28 (1982) 239-252 and *RÉAug* 30 (1984) 84-99, with G. Madec's edition of the *de liberio arbitrio* and his comments in *RÉAug* 21 (1975) 394 and O'Daly (op. cit note 7) 15-20.

23. E. CLARK's *The Origenist Controversy* (Princeton, 1992) 227-243 seems to me rightly and creatively to highlight Augustine's doubt on these issues.

24. A defense of this position probably ought to have preceded the present study, but is in any event in preparation and will appear separately.

25. See *contra Academicos* 3.17.37 and *de doctrina christiana* 2.40.60.

modo illud), but is concurrent without any temporal successiveness (*sine ulla vicissitudine temporum*)[26].

Only at the end of his life does Augustine explicitly criticize his union of the Gospels with Platonic teachings, but his criticism falls mainly on his acceptance of Platonic *anamnesis*, and even here his criticism must be taken with a grain of salt. In fact, separating the strands of Platonic *anamnesis* from the genuinely Augustinian concepts in his writings on *memoria* would be impossible, and probably pointless[27].

At its most basic level, Augustine's inheritance consists of adapting Plato's theory of forms into a world of abstract truths; these are, needless to say, incorporeal and eternal, and can be contrasted with the physical world which we perceive through our senses : *intellegibilia* vs. *sensibilia*.

> *de magistro* 12.39 : But if, on the one hand, we use the light and our senses in order to perceive colors and the other things which we sense through our bodies, namely both the elements of this world and these same bodies with which we perceive--for the senses are the interpreters which the mind uses to recognize such things; and, on the other hand, we consult with our reason the interior truth in order to perceive those things which are understood ; what answer can be given to the question 'What does anyone teach us with words, beyond the sound which strikes our ears ?' For everything which we perceive, we perceive either through the senses of our body or with our mind ; the former we call *sensibilia*, the latter *intellegibilia*, or, to speak according to the habit of our Christian authors, the former we call *carnalia*, the latter *spiritualia*[28].

Augustine maps this hierarchy onto a parallel hierarchy of knowledge and perception. These two systems operate in tandem to define each other ; and the

---

26. See also *de trin.* 15.25.45, *de civ. dei* 8.5, 22.29 and *Retract.* 1.3.2. For translations from the *Confessiones* I have at times adapted the excellent new version by H. Chadwick (Oxford: Oxford University Press, 1991).

27. I am not persuaded that Augustine ever abandoned his former allegiance to *anamnesis*. I don't think he could. See *de trin.* 15.21.40 : *Cogitando enim quod verum invenerimus, hoc maxime intellegere dicimur et hoc quidem in memoria rursus relinquimus. Sed illa est abstrusior profunditas nostrae memoriae ubi hoc etiam primum cum cogitaremus invenimus et gignitur intimum verbum quod nullius linguae sit tamquam scientia de scientia et visio de visione et intellegentia quae apparet in cogitatione de intellegentia quae in memoria iam fuerat sed latebat, quamquam et ipsa cogitatio quandam suam memoriam nisi haberet, non reverteretur ad ea quae in memoria reliquerat cum alia cogitaret.* See in addition those texts where Augustine describes how we make comparative judgments : we do so, he writes, because the 'idea' of beauty exists in our mind in a more perfect form (*de civ. dei* 8.5-6), or because some conception of sanctity or wisdom was already impressed in our mind (*de liberio arbitrio* 2.9.26). For the use of similar terminology, see *Conf.* 10.6.9, 11.3.5 ; *de civ. dei* 11.27 ; *de Genesi ad litteram* 12.24.51 ; *de trin.* 8.3.4, 10.5.7, 11.3.6, 14.15.21, and 15.27.49. On the other hand, even in his early works one can identify passages where the existence of such *notiones impressae* is not assumed ; see *de utilitate credendi* xiii.28 : How can fools, who have no conception of wisdom, identify a wise man to teach them?

28. For further definitions of these terms, see also *de dialectica* V.1-12, *de doctrina christiana* 1.2.2, and *de civ. dei* 8.6 : *Sensibilia dicamus, quae visu tactuque corporis sentiri queunt; intellegibilia, quae conspectu mentis intellegi.*

entire theory obviously has its crux in the human being, which alone shares in both worlds.

Augustine has therefore set himself two problems : first, to understand the difference between intellection and sense-perception. Since the issues and presumptions surrounding the nature of the divine form the top of his ontological pyramid, he must establish the priority of the intelligible world in a way which situates it between the divine and the carnal. The most important quality separating divine from human, and intelligence from sense-perception, is the relation of each to the two most basic measures of the physical word : space and time. Simply put, God operates independent of space and time, while all physical things, which includes all signs, exist and are defined by their place in space and time.

> *de quantitate animae* 32.68 : Everything that the senses perceive is contained in space and time, or, rather, the senses perceive what time and space contain ; that which we perceive with our eyes is divided by space; that which we perceive with our ears is divided by time[29].

Human beings exist largely as physical entities ; while they can conceive thoughts from immortal truths, the thoughts themselves are fleeting.

These issues come to the fore in a crucial passage from Book 12 of the *de Trinitate*, in which the oppositions discussed above (*intellegibilia* vs. *sensibilia, knowing* vs. *perceiving, eternity* vs. *space/time*) all play a role. Augustine distinguishes between an utterance of knowledge (*scientia*) and an utterance of wisdom (*sapientia*), and to the latter category belong eternal things. Their eternity, furthermore, is such that they are neither created nor destroyed, without any changibleness of times (*sine ulla mutabilitate temporum*) ; they are *intellegibilia* and present only to the gaze of the mind, and as such they are not bodies fixed in space (*non tamquam in spatiis locurum fixa*). Visible and tangible things (*visibilia vel contectabilia* [=*sensibilia*]), on the other hand, are present to the senses of the body. Apart from the *sensibilia* which are fixed in space there exist intelligible and incorporeal reasons (*rationes*), and these are independent of the passage of time (*sine temporali transitu*)--they are *intellegibiles, non sensibiles.* "Only a few succeed in arriving at these things with the gaze of their mind, and when their gaze does arrive--insofar as it is even possible to do so, the one who arrives does not abide among these eternal things ; on the contrary, it is repulsed by the rebounding, as it were, of the gaze itself, and thus a transitory thought is formed of a thing that is not transitory (*fit rei non transitoriae transitoria cogitatio*)[30]".

The second problem arising from Augustine's parallel hierarchies of *intellegibilia* and *sensibilia*, knowledge and perception, was to formulate his results in human language. Since he has begun with the premise that the

---

29. *de quantitate animae* 32.68 : *Cum autem locus et tempus sit, quibus omnia quae sentiuntur occupantur, vel potius quae occupant, quod oculis sentimus per locum, quod auribus per tempus dividitur.*

30. *de trin.* 12.14.23. For translations from the *de trinitate*, I have occasionally adapted the version of S. MacKenna in the *Fathers of the Church* series (Washington, D.C.: Catholic University of America Press).

sensible world is in some way inferior to the intelligible, as human understanding is vastly inferior to the divine, and since words in any form are objects of sense-perception, words must be not only mere signs of *intellegibilia*, but inadequate signs ; they are not simply different from their antecedents, they are inferior to them. As Augustine argues, if an image (*imago*) matches perfectly that of which it is an image, then it is made equal to it (*coaequatur*) and is not the object of its own image. Such a perfect image possesses great beauty on account of its harmony (*congruentia*), equality (*aequalitas*), and because of the lack of difference, disproportion, and dissimilarity (*nulla in re dissidens et nullo modo inaequalis et nulla ex parte dissimilis*) ; such an image is not to be called an image (*imago*), but a 'form' (*species*) (see *de Trin.* 6.10.11 and 15.22.43). *Species*, 'form' is also the name he gives to the Platonic 'idea' of beauty which must exist in the mind in order for the mind to make value judgments on beauty in the physical world :

> *de civ. dei* 8.6 : For there is no kind of physical beauty, either in a stationary object-
> -for instance, a shape--or in a moving one--like a melody--over which the mind
> does not exercise judgment. This could not be the case, if there were not in the
> mind this more perfect image of beauty, without the burden of mass, without the
> sound of a voice, without extent in space or time[31].

His conception of the nature of this *species* matches identically the qualities which he attributes to 'utterances of wisdom' in *de trin.* 12.14.23 ; they are distinguished by their independence from the physical world, from the perception of the senses. As we will see in the closing section, signs operate completely differently[32].

For the purpose of this paper, it is not necessary to explore the intricacies of Augustine's hierarchies of matter and knowledge to any great extent; a simple set of examples from his writings will suffice. To begin with, Augustine notes that man shares sense-perception with the beasts, while God has endowed man alone with a rational soul[33].

This premise imposes a hierarchy on knowledge : animals do not have knowledge ; they seek their food and pleasure through force of habit (*vis consuetudinis*). Knowledge must be the result of intellection, which power God gave to the rational soul, that is, to man alone (*de quantitate animae* 29.56-57 ; 30.58).

Augustine's strict insistence on knowledge as the result of reasoning matches his strict separation of knowledge and belief, though, as noted, he will sometimes use the terminology catachrestically; this insistence is further

---

31. *de civ. dei* 8.6 : *Nulla est enim pulchritudo corporalis sive in statu corporis, sicut est figura, sive in motu, sicut est cantilena, de qua non animus iudicet. Quod profecto non posset, nisi melior in illo esset haec species [sc. pulchritudinis], sine tumore molis, sine strepitu vocis, sine spatio vel loci vel temporis.*

32. On the contrast between principles in the mind and their representation in human language, see *Conf.* 10.12.19.

33. *de quantitate animae* 28.54 ; cf. *de civ. dei* 22.1. Of course, exhortations to the life of the mind by means of comparisons with the beasts were as old as philosophy : Plato *Rep.* 586A. Augustine had no doubt read Sallust on the subject, *Cat.* 1.

reinforced by his distrust of sense-perception as a means of gathering information.

> *de civ. dei* 11.26 : For we exist, we know that we exist, and we are glad of this existence and of this knowledge. In those three things there is no falsehood to trouble us with its similarity to the truth. For we do not apprehend those truths as we do the things which are outside of us, by some sense of the body--as, for example, we perceive colour by sight, sound by hearing, odor by the sense of smell, flavors by the taste, and hardness and softness by the touch. We even turn over in our thoughts images of these *sensibilia*, very much like them and yet incorporeal ; we hold these images in our memory ; and through those images we are aroused to desire those things they represent. But it is entirely certain that I exist, that I know it, and that I am glad of it, without any imaginary and deceptive fantasies[34].

This distrust of the senses has obvious consequences for all forms of human communication, though full exploration of this issue will be postponed for now[35].

Before considering the capabilities of human understanding and its limitations, I quote a number of passages in which Augustine discusses the characteristics of *sensibilia* and *intellegibilia*, because, as we have seen, these terms not only describe categories of object but also boundaries of knowledge.

> *de civ. dei* 10.15 : The person of God himself became visible, not, however, through his own substance, which always remains invisible to corruptible eyes, but through some created thing in subjection to the Creator; in this way he also spoke in syllables, in the passing moments of time, in the words of human language. However, God in his own nature neither begins nor ceases to speak ; he speaks not temporally but eternally ; not corporally but spiritually; not to the senses, but to the understanding.

> *de utilitate credendi* 1.1 : Truth (reality) is far removed from the minds of vain men who, having progressed and fallen too far among physical concerns, think there is nothing beyond what they perceive by the senses, these five well known messengers of the body[36].

The characteristics of the set of *sensibilia* hardly require explanation beyond that which has already been given. However, since our ultimate goal is a better understanding of Augustine's theory of language, it behooves us to demonstrate conclusively that words are *sensibilia*. Here I am concerned only with words as signifiers, and not with broader issues such as tense systems, *etc.*; these will be discussed later. Note that in the second passage Augustine stresses not only that signs belong to the physical world, but that they are somehow inferior to the things which they represent.

> *de magistro* 4.8, 9.26 : Aug : What about written words ? Are they words, or are they not better understood as signs of words, as a word is something which is brought forth by an articulate sound with some significance ? Moreover, a sound

---

34. Cf. *de trin.* 15.21. On these passages see O'DALY (*op. cit.* note 7) p. 169-171. In addition to the passages cited by O'Daly, see *de Genesi ad litteram* 12.4.15, 12.7.16.

35. *de utilitate credendi* v.11 and x.23 ; *de magistro* 13.42-43.

36. See also *Conf.* 10.6.9, 10.10.17, 10.12.19, and *de trin.* 15.12.21.

can be perceived by no other sense than hearing. When a word is written, a sign is given to the eyes whereby something that properly belongs to the ears is brought to mind.... Aug : If these things are true--and you know them to be so--then you can see how much less words are to valued than the things on account of which we use words.

de trin. 15.11.20 : Hence the word which sounds without is a sign of the word that shines within, to which the name of word more properly belongs. For that which is produced by the mouth of the flesh is the sound of the word, and is itself also called the word, because that inner word assumed it in order that it might appear outwardly[37]. (Trans. MacKenna)

Ultimately, some of the factors which render sense-perception inferior to intellection are similar in kind to those which incapacitate human intellection to start with. In other words, the proliferation of signs has its origin in the same event which bound us to this world of flesh. Our familiarity with fleshy things makes metaphors which use the physical world as their source of imagery particularly good pedagogical tools; but the inferiority of fleshy things also renders these same metaphors inherently insufficient for their task. Thus Augustine writes about the mind as if it functioned in a parallel fashion to the body, with its own senses of vision, hearing, and so on. For instance, at *de trin.* 12.14.23 (see at note 30; see also Section VIII), Augustine must describe the present of *intellegibilia* to the sight of the mind on analogy with corporeal sight (*sic intellegibilia ... ista ... visibilia*). This proves remarkably useful within the context of his treatment of time : true knowledge becomes the result of an instantaneous act of 'sight' on the part of the understanding (*Conf* 12.13.16 : *caelum intellectuale, ubi est intellectus nosse simul*, see also *de trin.* 15.7.13). On the other hand, the metaphor collapses when Augustine considers the workings of his own investigation : if the mind 'sees' as an eye sees, how can a mind see itself ? It is a question for which Augustine has no answer.

III. – THE CONNECTION BETWEEN METAPHYSICS AND PEDAGOGY

The preceding section has shown that Augustine thought there to exist a fundamental distinction between the words of men and the realities which they were intended to represent; the existence of this gap urges us to examine Augustine's view of man's ability to understand these realities. In doing so, the fundamental problems which cripple human language will also surface, for, as is obvious, our words, as signs of the thoughts in the mind, share the handicaps

---

37. *de trin.* 15.11.20 : *Proinde verbum quod foris sonat signum est verbi quod intus lucet cui magis verbi competit nomen. Nam illud quod profertur carnis ore vox verbi est, verbumque et ipsum dicitur propter illud a quo ut foris appareret assumptum est.* See also *de trin.* 10.1.2, *de dialectica* V and *de doctrina christiana* 2.3.4 : *Sed innumerabilis multitudo signorum quibus suas cogitationes homines exserunt, in verbis constituta est. Nam illa signa omnia quorum genera breviter attigi, potui verbis enuntiare, verba vero illis signis nullo modo possem.*

of our intellection. At this point, I intend merely to confront these problems in so far as they affect our minds, with brief looks ahead ; the complexities await further treatment at the end of this paper. I begin by focusing on Augustine's recognition that man is tied to his fleshly existence ; second, I examine Augustine's exploitation of this recognition to simplify the process of learning about the trinity ; and third, I trace the connections between his justification of this exploitation and the issues raised in Section II.

First of all, man, as Augustine knew and insisted, is a creature of flesh. The senses of the body, used to perceive physical things, bound us with the other animals of this world ; like them, man used his senses--as much from force of habit as reason--to seek after food and pleasure (*de quantitate animae* 28.54). The processes of intellection are superior, and for that reason much more complicated. In seeking to understand the Trinity, Augustine urges us to examine the trinities within ourselves. The task is not a simple one :

> *de trin.* 1.1.3 : Accordingly, it is difficult to look upon and to comprehend fully the substance of God, which makes changeable things without any change in itself, and creates temporal things without any temporal movement of its own. Therefore the purification of our soul is necessary, as a result of which it may be able to see that ineffable thing in an ineffable manner. Since we do not as yet enjoy this capability, we are strengthened by faith and are led along more accessible roads, in order that we may gain the proficiency and skill to grasp that truth.

Augustine initially decides not to consider evidence procured by the senses, and excludes as well the trinity of our senses in favor of the trinities within the mind itself.

> *de trin.* 10.10.14 : But since we are investigating the nature of the mind, let us not take into consideration any knowledge that is obtained from without through the senses of the body, and consider more attentively the principle which we have laid down : that every mind knows and is certain concerning itself[38].

After further consideration, Augustine decides for pedagogical reasons to proceed slowly, from the things which men are more familiar with.

> *de trin.* 10.12.19 : Should we now, therefore, exert ourselves to the utmost of our mental powers, and ascend to the supreme and highest essence of which the human mind is an imperfect image, but yet an image ? Or should these same three things be manifested still more clearly in the soul, through those things which we comprehend outwardly through the senses of the body, wherein the knowledge of corporeal things is impressed in time ? ... (*de trin.* 11.1.1) Let us, therefore, seek for some image of the Trinity in that which is decaying, insofar as we can, and even if this is not a more precise image, it may perhaps be easier to discern ; for it would in vain be called man if it did not bear at least some resemblance to the inner man. And by the very order of our condition, whereby we are made mortal and carnal, we apply ourselves more easily and, so to speak, more familiarly with visible than with intelligible things, because the former are external and the latter internal, and because we perceive the former through the senses of the body, and the latter through the mind[39].

---

38. See also *Conf.* 13.11.12.

39. *de trin.* 10.12.19 : *Iamne igitur ascendendum est qualibuscumque intentionis viribus ad illam summum et altissimam essentiam cuius impar imago est humana mens sed tamen*

Augustine decides that his readers may apply themselves more readily to that image of the trinity which exists in man's sense-perception. This is an inferior image, but man, he concludes, understands corporeal things more easily. The primary advantage attributed to the trinity of sense-perception is that the senses operate in time (*de quantitate animae* 32.68), and man has difficulty conceptualizing time, let alone those things which operate outside it. Augustine also links this inability to conceptualize immortality directly to the condition of man's soul, "whereby we are made mortal and carnal".

> *Conf.* 11.14.17 : What is time ? Who can explain this easily and briefly ? Who can comprehend this so as to articulate it in words, or even in thought[40] ?

After Augustine has explained the operation of the trinity in our sense perception (*de trin.* 11.2.2), he then describes the process whereby the sight of an external object causes an image to arise in our mind, and to be stored in our memory (*de trin.* 11.2.3-3.6). In doing so, he discusses the origin of the gaze-- that it proceeds from our body at the behest of our mind (*de trin.* 11.2.2), but he also decides that, properly speaking, the image formed in the memory is begat by the object (*de trin.* 11.2.3). He then treats the trinity which is formed in our mind when we think about something we had previously seen ; that is to say, when we look upon an image in our memory with the gaze of our mind.

> *de trin.* 11.7.11 : For the gaze of the mind, which is formed from the memory when we think of something in the process of remembering, does not proceed from that *species* which we have seen and remembered, since we could not have remembered those things unless we had seen them. But the gaze of the mind, which is informed by recollection, existed also before we had seen the body which we remember--how much more so before we had committed it to memory ? Hence, although the form, which arises in the gaze of one remembering, arises from that which is in the memory, yet the gaze itself does not arise from thence, but existed before it. But it follows from this, that if the one is not a true parent, then the other is not a true offspring. Nevertheless, both that quasi-parent as well as that quasi-offspring suggest something from which we gain greater skill and certainty in the study of inner and truer things[41]. (Trans. MacKenna)

---

imago? An adhuc eadem tria distinctius declaranda sunt in anima per illa quae extrinsecus sensu corporis capimus ubi temporaliter imprimitur rerum corporearum notitia? ... (*de trin.* 11.1.1) *In hoc ergo qui corrumpitur quaeramus quemadmodum possumus quandam trinitatis effigiem, et si non expressiorem tamen fortassis ad dinoscendum faciliorem. Neque enim frustra et iste homo dicitur nisi quia inest ei nonnulla interioris similitudo, et illo ipso ordine conditionis nostrae quo mortales atque carnales effecti sumus facilius et quasi familiarius visibilia quam intellegibilia pertractamus cum ista sint exterius, ill interius, et ista sensu corporis sentiamus, illa mente intellegamus...* See also *Conf.* 10.6.9 and *Ep.* 55.11.21.

40. See also *Conf.* 11.8.10.

41. *de trin.* 11.7.11 : *Acies quippe animi quae formatur ex memoria cum recordando aliquid cogitamus non ex ea specie procedit quam meminimus visam quandoquidem eorum miminisse non possemus nisi vidissemus; acies autem animi quae reminiscendo formatur erat etiam priusquam corpus quod meminimus videremus. Quanto magis priusquam id memoriae mandaremus. Quamquam itaque forma quae fit in acie recordantis ex ea fiat quae inest memoria, ipsa tamen acies non inde exstitit, sed erat ante ista. Consequens est autem ut si non est illa vera parens, nec ista vera sit proles. Sed et illa quasi parens et ista quasi proles aliquid insinuant unde interiora atque veriora exercitatius certiusque videantur.*

The trinity which is formed from the gaze of the mind upon the memory is truer, because it lies more inward (*Conf.* 10.6.9). One of the reasons it is superior relates directly to time ; in the trinity of the mind, Augustine argues, the temporal relationships are no longer as simple to discern as they were in the original act of sight. This concern with time is manifested in the issue of procession, that is, in the relationship between parent and offspring, with respect to which the hierarchy within the highest Trinity will only become clear to man after the Resurrection (*de trin.* 15.25.45 ; cf. *Conf.* 12.13.16 at note 26). While Augustine argues that the examination of interior things (ie. things not related to senses) yields a better image with respect to time, already in this second stage the ability of Augustine's language to express the concepts has begun to break down (*quasi parens, quasi proles*). Just as men are bound to their senses, and thus to time and space, their language is similarly tied up in the flesh of this world.

Ultimately, Augustine decides that none of these images will suffice because the constituent elements of these trinities exist as entities trapped in time ; a better image can be found in the trinity formed by the contemplation of *intellegibilia*.

> *de trin.* 14.3.6 : Therefore, neither will the latter trinity, which is not now, be the image of God, nor is the former trinity the image of God, which then will not be ; but that image of the Creator, that has been implanted immortally in its own immortality, must be found in the soul of man, that is, in the reasonable or intellectual soul[42].

Augustine then proceeds to consider the trinity formed in our mind when we think about eternal truths, when we create "utterances of wisdom". Once again, he imagines the process as directly parallel to the one in our senses. However, our gaze does not abide amongst these things, but bounces off ; our thought is thus transitory. Our attention thus cannot be focused eternally on any single object--our minds cannot overcome time (*de trin.* 12.14.23 ; see note 30) ; similarly, we cannot focus the gaze of our mind on more than one object at once--our minds cannot overcome space.

> *de trin.* 11.8.12 : But since the eye of the mind cannot behold everything together which the memory retains with a single glance, the trinities of thought are constantly changing ; while some are coming, others are going, and so that trinity becomes innumerably more numerous ; yet it is not infinite if it does not go beyond the number of things hidden in the memory.

When Augustine has described the trinity formed by the contemplation of true knowledge, he then reminds us that even this word is a poor image : "Such then, is our word in which we indeed find a likeness, be it what it may, but, insofar as we are able, we shall point out how great an unlikeness there also is, and let us not be sluggish in perceiving this" (*de trin.* 15.14.24).

In fact, when he engages in a lengthy criticism of this last trinity, he concentrates most heavily on the transitory nature of human thought. Although

---

42. *de trin.* 14.3.6 : *Nec illa igitur trinitas quae nunc non est imago dei erit, nec ista imago dei est quae tunc non erit, sed ea est invenienda in anima hominis, id est rationali sive intellectuali, imago creatoris quae immortaliter immortalitati eius est insita.*

our minds know that they live and will always possess that knowledge, we as humans are incapable of thinking about that knowledge eternally, and therefore the trinity formed by the contemplation of that knowledge is itself transitory. In the rhetorical climax of the passage, Augustine refers to the Vergilian motion of our minds (*volubili motione*), yet acknowledges the difference between the *verbum* which results from the contemplation of *intellebilia* and the *verba* of speech : *Et tunc fit verum verbum quando illud quod nos dixi volubili motione iactare ad id quod scimus pervenit atque inde formatur eius omnimodam similitudinem capiens ut quomodo res quaeque scitur sic etiam cogitetur, id est sine voce, sine cogitatione vocis quae profecto alicuius linguae est sic in corde dicatur* (*de trin.* 15.15.25).

It is precisely in our relationship to time that we separate from God, and that our understanding fails us. It is possible, Augustine argues, for man to know certain eternal truths ; alas, man cannot think about all these truths at the same time and forever. He describes the act of "knowing" (*scire*) on analogy with speaking ; thus to think about some piece of knowledge (*cogitare scientiam*) produces a *verbum*[43]. Augustine also discusses the possiblility of talking in human language about these eternal truths; the difficulties which confront that endeavor will be taken up later on (see *Conf.* 12.27.37 below and *de trin.* 15.16.25 at note 48). It is sufficient at this point to note that human language also fails when confronted by time : it is hard enough to understand unchanging eternity ; it is harder still to write about it.

> *de trin.* 15.7.13 : What man, therefore, can comprehend that wisdom by which God knows all things, and in such a way that what are called past things are not past for Him, nor does He await the coming of what are called future things as though they were absent, but both past and future things are all present together with present things ? He does not think of things individually and pass in thinking from one item to another, but everything is present to His gaze at the same time : what man, I say, comprehends that wisdom and the like prudence and the like knowledge, since we do not understand even our own wisdom ? For we can perceive in some way or other those things which are present either to our senses or to our understanding, but we know those which are absent and yet had been present through our memory, insofar as we have not forgotten them. We do not conjecture the past from the future, but the future from the past, yet not with a sure knowledge (*non tamen firma cognitione*).
>
> *Conf.* 11.8.10 : I see to some extent (an understanding of God's unchanging eternity), but I do not know how to express it.

As Augustine had precedent in Scripture for his catachrestic use of *scire* (*Retr.* I.xiii.5), so Scripture also provided a model for him when he wrote about the human mind, especially in its role as an image of the Trinity. He

---

43. The vocabulary used in *de trin.* 15.15.25 to the describe the 'formable' word is the same as that used to describe the formable, yet formless mass out of which God created the world at *Conf.* 12.3.3. Augustine envisions God's speech as operating in a parallel fashion to human thought--thus the act of creation becomes a grand act of *cogitatio*, and all of creation and history an utterance of God. See *de trin.* 6.10.12 ; *de spiritu et littera* 12.19, and especially *Conf.* 11.7.9. I intend to pursue this line of thought in an as-yet unwritten paper.

located his model primarily in those passages which describe 'actions' of God in terms borrowed from everyday speech.

> *de trin.* 1.1.2 : Consequently, in order that the human mind may be cleansed from errors of this kind, Sacred Scripture, adapting itself to the little ones, has employed words from every class of objects in order that our intellect, as though strengthened by them, might rise as it were gradually to divine and sublime things. For when it spoke of God, it made use even of words taken from material objects (*verbis ex rebus corporalibus sumptis*), as when it said, "Protect me under the shadow of thy wings" (Ps. 16.8).... Indeed, divine Scripture rarely mentions the things that are properly ascribed to God and which are not found in any creature...

Not everyone understood the meaning of Scripture as well as Augustine did. He himself knew well that the use of such language could backfire : this use of ordinary vocabulary could lead people to believe that God operates in time as people do.

> *Conf.* 12.27.37 : When they read or hear these texts, some people think of God as if he were a human being or a power immanent in a vast mass which, by some new and sudden decision external to itself, as if located in remote places, made heaven and earth, two huge bodies, one high, the other low, containing everything. When they hear 'God said, let there be that, and that is made', they think of words with beginnings and endings (*verba coepta et finita*), making a sound in time and passing away. They suppose that after the words have ceased, at once there exists that which was commanded to exist, and have other similar notions which they hold because of their familiarity with the fleshly order of things. In such people who are still infants without higher insight, faith is built up in a healthy way, while in their state of weakness they are carried along as if at their mother's breast by an utterly simple kind of language. (Trans. Chadwick)

IV. – GOD'S IMMORTALITY, AND ITS CONSEQUENCES FOR AUGUSTINE'S PHILOSOPHY[44]

Augustine fully understood that the verb system of ordinary speech presumes that the subject is acting in some way upon the object, but he was convinced that such language, and the understanding of time which it assumed, were entirely inappropriate to God's true nature[45]. He also realized that an action, a change, is taking place within some object whenever God is described as taking an action. He therefore urged the interpretation that actions of God described in Scripture are merely an attempt to show that such action is taking place, and that these descriptions were not intended to imply that any change or movement was taking place in His divine substance. For Augustine, God's immortality implies complete and utter stability, without any change or action

44. The standard modern work is E.P. MEIJERING, *Augustin über Schöpfung, Ewigkeit, und Zeit. Das elfte Buch des Bekenntnisse* (Leiden: E.J. Brill, 1979). Still very interesting is J. Guitton, *Le Temps et l'éternité chez Plotin et Saint-Augustin* (Paris: 3rd. ed. 1959).

45. Augustine also had fundamental doubts about the ability of our verb system, as he understood it, to represent time even with respect to human actions. More on this below.

or variation of any kind. But the difficulty was that any scripture which wrote
on that basis would have been without drama--it would not have terrified the
proud, or nourished the intelligent (*de civ. dei* 15.25)[46]. His ideas regarding
what God's immortality is had consequences for his portrayal of the language
and thought of God, and for the capacities of man before the Fall. A brief
consideration of his writings on the subject helps to explicate his thoughts on
the intellectual capacity of man and the origins of language.

Augustine thought long and hard about the theoretical qualities of God's
immortality ; he began with the story of creation in *Genesis*, and came to the
conclusion that true immortality must also imply eternal permanence in all
things, for that which changes must, in part, come to an end. In addition, it
would be intolerable for God to be trapped in time, to operate in time, as man
does. Augustine therefore contrasts God with man largely in His independence
from the strictures of time and space (*de civ. dei* 10.15 and 11.21) ; man's
failure in treating of this subject is simultaneously cognitive and linguistic
(*Conf.* 11.14.17 ; *de trin.* 1.1.3 and 15.7.13).

> *Conf.* 11.7.9 : You call us, therefore, to understand the Word, God who is with
> you God. That word is spoken eternally, and by it all things are uttered eternally
> (*quod sempiterne dicitur et eo sempiterne dicuntur omnia*). It is not the case that
> what was being said comes to an end, and something else is then said, so that
> everything is uttered in a succession with a conclusion, but everything is said in the
> simultaneity of eternity. Otherwise time and change would already exist, and there
> would not be a true eternity and true immortality (*alioquin iam tempus et mutatio et
> non vera aeternitas nec vera immortalitas*).

> *Conf.* 11.8.10 : Why, I ask, Lord my God ? In some degree I see it, but how to
> express it I do not know, unless to say that everything which begins to be and
> ceases to be begins and ends its existence at that very moment when, in the eternal
> reason where nothing begins or ends, it is known that it is right for it to begin and
> end. This reason is your Word, which is also the Beginning in that it also speaks to
> us[47].

Similarly, God's knowledge and will must never change, because of his
eternal permanence, and because Augustine would not have God's
foreknowledge be anything less than perfect.

The nature of God's permanence presents problems for the human author,
much as the description of the trinity within the mind did (*de trin.* 11.7.11).
For instance, Augustine thinks that the tenses used in prophetic language are a
consequence of God's perfect prescience :

> *de civ. dei* 17.18 : There, in the usual manner, prophecies of the future are put into
> the mouth of the Mediator himself, in the form of a narrative of past events, because

---

46. See the texts listed in note 19. On the later history of accomodation, see A.
FUNKENSTEIN, *Theology and the Scientific Imagination* (Princeton, 1986), esp. pp. 10-12
and 256-261.

47. *Conf.* 11.8.10 : *Cur, quaso, domine deus meus ? utcumque video, sed quomodo id
eloquar nescio, nisi quia omne, quod esse incipit et esse desinit, tunc esse incipit et tunc
desinit, quando debuisse incipere vel desinere in aeterna ratione cognoscitur, ubi nec incipit
aliquid nec desinit. ipsum est verbum tuum, quod et principium est, quia et loquitur nobis.*
See also *Conf.* 11.13.16, 12.15.18, *enarrationes in Psalmos* 101.2.10.

coming events had already, in a sense, happened, in the predestination and foreknowledge of God.

As so often (eg. *utcumque* in *Conf.* 11.8.10 at note 47), Augustine expresses some concern that the language he uses does not adequately represent the following aspect of the relationship between historical events and his own conception of divinity--that even those events which have not yet taken place have already happened in the foreknowledge of God. The language available to Augustine constrains him to describe God's knowledge as 'fore'knowledge, but the prefix takes its meaning from an understanding of time which is foreign to God ; Augustine may well have sensed that some would find an inconsistency between this doctrine and his own insistence on free will. Augustine no doubt felt that this seeming inconsistency could be explained by properly describing the perfect knowledge of God, which exists always in a present of eternal simultaneity. It is with respect to the unchanging nature of this knowledge that the metaphor invented by Virgil to describe human thought--that of 'turning something over in one's mind--suffices for human thought, and Augustine uses it himself (*de civ. dei* 11.26), but it will not suffice for God, unless, that is, we speak catachrestically, as Scripture does.

> *de trin.* 15.16.25 : Wherefore He is so called the Word of God as not to be called the thought of God, lest it be believed that there is, as it were, something revolving in God that now receives and now recovers a form in order to be a word, and that it can lose this form, and in some manner revolve formlessly. That distinguished master of speech knew both the meaning of words and the power of thought, who said in a poem, "He revolves within himself the changing fortunes of war" (*Aen.* 10.159-160), that is, he thinks. This Son of God, therefore, is not called the thought of God, but the Word of God. For when our thought arrives at that which we know and is formed therefrom, it is our true word. And, hence, the Word of God ought to be understood without any thought on the part of God, in order that it may be understood to be a simple form, having nothing formable that can also be unformed. The Sacred Scriptures, it is true, also speak about the thoughts of God, but do so according to that manner of speech in which they also speak about the forgetfulness of God, and certainly such expressions do not apply in the strict sense to God[48].

Virgil, Augustine argues, understood well the nature of thought--that it involves some motion within the mind, and thus his metaphor applies to human thought very well[49]. God's thought, on the other hand, involves no motion,

---

48. *de trin.* 15.16.25 : *Quapropter ita dicitur illud dei verbum ut dei cogitatio non dicatur ne aliquid esse quasi volubile credatur in deo, quod nunc accipiat, nunc recipiat formam ut verbum sit eamque possit amittere atque informiter quodam modo volutari. Bene quippe noverat verba et vim cogitationis inspexerat locutor egregius qui dixit in carmine: secumque volutat // eventus belli varios; id est, cogitat. Non ergo ille dei filius cogitatio dei sed verbum dei dicitur. Cogitatio quippe nostra perveniens ad id quod scimus atque inde formata verbum nostrum verum est. Et ideo verbum dei sine cogitatione dei debet intellegi ut forma ipsa simplex intellegatur, non aliquid habens formabile quod esse etiam possit informe. Dicuntur quidem etiam in scripturis sanctis cogitationes dei sed eo locutionis modo quo ibi et oblivio dei dicitur, quae utique ad proprietatem in deo nulla est.*

49. On the "motion" of the mind and the measurement of time, see RICOEUR (*op. cit.* note 11) pages 13-16 and chapter 6 in O'DALY (*op. cit.* note 7). Both draw extensively on the

because he knows and he wills everything at once and forever, and therefore his Son is not a thought, created by mental motion, but a word, created by his eternal, unchanging thought and thus coaeternal with himself (*de trin.* 15.15.25 and 15.21.40).

> *de trin.* 15.14.24 : But that word of ours, which has neither sound nor thought of sound, is the word of that thing which we inwardly speak by seeing it, and, therefore, it belongs to no language; hence, in this enigma there is a likeness, be it what it may, to that Word of God which is also God, since it is also so born from our knowledge as that Word was also born from the knowledge of the Father[50].

V. – GOD'S COMMUNICATION WITH MAN ; ORIGINAL SIN AND ITS CONSEQUENCES FOR THE SOUL AND FOR LANGUAGE

Augustine understood that this conception of God's immortal nature affected His means of communication. Signs, as *sensibilia*, operate in time and space, and God does not. Nevertheless, in Scripture God communicates with men and with angels, and Scripture, of necessity, presents him doing so in human terms. Needless to say, God appears to these two groups in entirely different ways. Once again, we can begin at the beginning, with *Genesis*:

> *de civ. dei* 11.8 : When 'God rested on the seventh day from all his works and sanctified that day', this is not to be understood in some childish way (*pueriliter*), as if God had toiled at his work, seeing that 'he spoke and they were made' by a word which was intelligible and eternal, not vocal and temporal (*intellegibili et sempiterno, non sonabili et temporali*).

God's speech in the act of creation thus in no way resembes human speech. In fact, God has no need of human speech to understand what we will, because he can read our thoughts.

> *Epistulae* 130.10.20, 11.21 : In general, this business (prayer) is transacted more by sighs than by speech, more by tears than by utterance. For He sets our tears in His sight and our groaning is not hid from Him who created all things by His word and who does not look for human words... Words, then, are necessary for us so that we may be roused and take note of what we are asking, but we are not to believe that the Lord has need of them, either to be informed or to be influenced[51].

Moreover, the words which we use when we pray, including the formulas taught to us by Christ, are merely signs to remind us, not God, of the realities of our relationship with him.

---

commentary of E.P. MEIJERING (*op. cit.* note 44).

50. *de trin.* 15.14.24 : *Verbum autem nostrum, illud quod non habet sonum neque cogitationem soni, sed eius rei quam videndo intus dicimus, et ideo nullius linguae est atque inde utcumque simile est in hoc aenigmate illi verbo dei quod etiam deus est quoniam sic et hoc de nostra nascitur quemadmodum et illud de scientia patris natum est.*

51. See also *de trin.* 15.10.18.

de civ. dei 10.19 : But they do not realize that these visible sacrifices are the signs of those invisible, greater and better sacrifices, just as spoken words are the signs of things. Therefore, when we pray and praise him, we direct significant utterances (*significantes voces*) to him, to whom we offer in our hearts the realities which we signify with our words (*cui res ipsas in corde quas significamus offerimus*) : thus we should realize that, in sacrificing, we should not offer visible sacrifices to anyone else other than to Him, whose invisible sacrifice we ought to be in our hearts[52].

It is, of course, possible for God or angels to communicate directly with men, and even for them to appear to mortal sight, but they must do so through "something subordinate".

de civ. dei 16.6 : God does not speak to the angels in the same way as we speak to one another, or to God, or to the angels, or as the angels speak to us or as God speaks to us through the angels, but in his own ineffable manner. But his speech is explained to us in our fashion. God's speech, to be sure, is on a higher plane ; it precedes his action as the changeless reason of the action itself; and his speaking has no sound, no transitory noise ; it has a power that persists for eternity and operates in time. It is with this speech that he addresses the holy angels, whereas he speaks to us, who are situated far off, in a different way. And yet, when we also grasp something of this kind of speech with our inward ears, we come close to the angels.

de civ. dei 16.29 : God appeared to Abraham by the Oak of Mamre in the shape of three men who, without doubt, were angels ... It is, of course, within the capacity of divine and invisible power, of incorporeal and immutable nature, to appear even to mortal sight, without any change in itself, not appearing in its own being, but by means of something subordinate to itself ; and what is not subordinate to it[53] ?

If God is to appear in a form which is perceptible to our bodily senses, then it must be through something inferior, as *sensibilia* are inferior to *intellegibilia*. In the same way, there is the slightest chance that we might hear something of that elevated speech (*aliquid talis locutionis*) with our inward ears (*interioribus auribus*), in other words, with our intelligence[54]. Of course, it is not necessary for God to speak to us with *sonantia verba*.

de musica 6.13.41 : But the proud soul desires to operate on (other rational souls) ; and insofar as every soul is better than every body, so far does the action on them seem more excellent than that on bodies. But God alone can operate on rational souls, not through a body, but through Himself. But such is that state of sin that souls are allowed to act upon souls, moving them by signifying through one or the

52. See also *de doctrina christiana* 3.5.9, 3.8.12-9.13 ; *de magistro* 1.2 ; *Conf.* 13.23.34 and 13.24.36.

53. *de civ. dei* 16.29 : *Item Deus apparuit Abrahae ad quercum Mambre in tribus viris, quos dubitandum non est angelos fuisse ; ... Est quidem divinae potestatis et invisibilis, incorporalis inmutabilisque naturae, sine ulla sui mutatione etiam mortalibus aspectibus apparere, non per id quod est, sed per aliquid quod sibi subditum est; quid autem illi subditum non est?*

54. For instance, the "truth" speaks to Augustine's "inward ear" at *Conf.* 12.15.18.

other body, or by natural signs such as a look or nod, or by conventional signs such as words[55].

Augustine represents God's communication with angels using entirely different imagery. For them, God resembles a book, where the words exist forever, a book which is never shut, so that all its words are visible at once. Since Augustine also imagines sight to be instantaneous, he can contrast the 'reading' of God's will with 'syllables' of time.

> *Conf.* 13.15.18 : They ever 'see your face' and there, without syllables requiring time to pronounce, they read what you eternal will intends. They read, they choose, they love. They ever read, and what they read never passes away. By choosing and loving, they read the immutability of your design. Their codex is never closed, nor is their book ever folded shut. For you yourself are a book to them and you are 'for eternity'[56].

It should be noted that man once was, and will again be, able to see God as openly as the angels do; hence the use of *videre* and *contemplare* in *de trin.* 15.25.45 and *de civ. dei* 22.1.

> *de civ. dei* 22.29 : For such reasons it is possible, indeed, it is most probable, that we shall then see the physical bodies of the new heaven and the new earth in such a fashion that as to observe God in utter clarity and distinctness, seeing him present everywhere and governing the whole material scheme of things by means of the bodies we shall then inhabit and the bodies we shall see wherever we turn our eyes. It will not be as it is now, when the invisible realities of God are apprehended and observed through the material things of his creation, and are partially apprehended by means of a puzzling reflection in a mirror... [57]

Augustine therefore extrapolates the pre-existing connection between sin and our fleshly existence to explain our inability to understand God ; he has also connected the condition of our soul with the nature of our communiciations-- all communication between human souls must exist through the mediation of physical objects. Only God can bypass this hurdle and speak directly to our minds.

The connection beween sin and the existence and complexity of human language can be taken still further. That sin is responsible for the condition of our souls, whereby the image of the Trinity in human souls is not perfect, is made explicit in the *de Trinitate*.

> *de trin.* 14.16.22 : But by committing sin the soul has lost justice and the holiness of truth, and thus this image has become disfigured and discolored; but it receives what it had once had when it is reformed and renewed.

---

55. See also *de civ. dei* 19.15.

56. *Conf.* 13.15.18 : *Vident enim faciem tuam semper et ibi legunt sine syllabis temporum, quid velit aeterna voluntas tua. legunt, eligunt et diligunt ; semper legunt et numquam praeterit quod legunt. eligendo enim et diligendo legunt ipsam incommutabilitatem consilii tui. non clauditur codex eorum nec plicatur liber eorum. quia tu ipse illis hoc es et es in aeternum.*

57. See also *de trin.* 14.19.25 : *Imago vero quae renovatur in spiritu mentis in agnitione dei non exterius sed interius de die in diem, ipsa perficietur visione quae tunc erit post iudicium facie ad faciem, nunc autem proficit per speculum in aenigmate.*

Similarly, God begat his Word precisely because, at this time, we are not intended to see him face to face, but rather "through a mirror in an enigma".

> *de trin.* 15.21.40 : I have indeed exerted myself as much as I could to make God the Father and God the Son known to us, that is, God the Begetter, who in some way has uttered everything that He has in His substance in His Word, co-eternal with Himself, and his Word, God Himself, who likewise has nothing more nor less in His substance than what was in Him, who did not beget the Word falsely but truly, not for the purpose now of seeing them face to face, but rather of seeing them through this likeness in an enigma, in the memory and understanding of our own mind, by means of conjectures, however tenuous they might be, attributing to the memory everything that we know, even if we do not think of it, and to the understanding the formation of thought by its own special type of thinking[58].

Furthermore, just as we lost our former ability to look upon God and understand him through that act of sight, our ability to perceive and understand each other has been blocked by the same sin which bound us to this life of flesh. Hence arose the necessity to communicate through signs:

> *Conf.* 13.23.34 : These signs come from the mouth and sound forth so that people may respond 'Amen'. The reason why all these utterances have to be physically spoken is the abyss of the world and the blindness of the flesh which cannot discern thoughts, so that it is necessary to make audible sounds[59].

Man himself increased the inadequacy of such signs by the behavior which led up to the confusion of languages that followed the construction of the tower of Babel (*Genesis* 11). There exist now a multiplicity of such signs, and many languages, increasing still further the chance that men will not be able to communicate with each other.

> *Conf.* 13.20.27 : There are things of which the knowledge is fixed and determined without evolving with the generations, such as the lights of wisdom and knowledge. But while the truths of these things remain the same, their embodiments in the physical realm are both many and varied. These physical things have been produced to meet the needs of people estranged from your eternal truth, but only in your gospel ; for they were the product of the very waters whose morbid bitterness was the reason why, through your word, those signs emerged[60].

---

58. *de trin.* 15.21.40 : *Sane deum patrem et deum filium, id est deum genitorem qui omnia quae substantialiter habet in coaeterno sibi verbo suo dixit quodam modo, et ipsum verbum eius deum qui nec plus nec minus aliquid habet etiam ipse substantialiter quam quod est in illo qui verbum non medaciter sed veraciter genuit, quemadmodum potui, non ut illud iam facie ad faciem, sed per hance similitudinem in aenigmate quantulumcumque coniciendo videretur in memoria et intellegentia mentis nostrae significare curavi, memoriae tribuens omne quod scimus etiamsi non inde cogitemus, intellegentiae vero proprio modo quandam cogitationis informationem.* See also *de civ. dei* 12.16.

59. See also *de musica* 6.13.41. P. BROWN, *Augustine of Hippo*, (Berkeley: University of California Press, 1967) 261 and Darrell Jackson (note 2) both cite the *de Genesi contra Manichaeos* (though different passages) for confirmation that the Fall led to the development of human language. See also J. FYLER, «St. Augustine, Genesis, and the origin of language», pp. 69-78 in *Saint Augustine and his influence in the Middle Ages* (Sewanee: The Press of the University of the South, 1988).

60. *Conf.* 13.20.27 : *quarum enim rerum notitiae sunt solidae et terminatae sine*

We should also recall that this inability to discern and communicate thoughts makes it impossible, according to Augustine, for men to know each other truly or to teach each other anything important.

> *de utilitate credendi* x.23 : You will say in good conscience that you have not lied, and you will assert this with all the words at your command, but they are only words. For you, being a man, cannot so reveal the hidden places of your mind to another man, that you may be known to the depths of your soul[61].

VI. – Words as "something subordinate"

At this point, we can turn back to language, and to the gap between saying and meaning with which we began. As we have seen (see note 32), Augustine believes that ideas, abstract concepts, have an existence as *res* independent of their instantiation through signs (eg. *de quantitate animae* 6.10 ; *Conf.* 10.12.19, 11.3.5, 13.10.27; *de trin.* 12.14.23). Naturally, not all of these *intellegibilia* present equal challenges to the human author. Augustine would no doubt himself assert that he has captured the essence of the three types of questions in his verbal formulation (*Conf.* 10.10.17), but that he certainly has not expressed or described the form of 'Beauty' when he speaks the words *species pulchritudinis* (*de civ. dei* 8.6) ; similarly, the word *Deus* captures none of His essence, but causes us to reflect upon His immortal nature (*de doctrina christiana* 1.6.6). It remains to describe this gap in terms drawn from Augustine's writings on language.

In the *de dialectica*, Augustine develops a vocabulary to describe the process by which ideas in the mind are manifested through signs.

> *de dialectica* v.50-58 : Whatever the mind, rather than the ear, realizes from a spoken word, which is then held within the mind itself, is called a *dicibile*. When a word is spoken, not for its own sake but for the sake of the thing which it signifies, it is called a *dictio*. Moreover, the thing itself, which is not yet a word nor yet realized as a word in the mind, whether or not it has a word by which it can be signified, can be called nothing other than a *res*, at least in proper speech. Therefore these things are subject to these four categories : word (*verbum*), idea (*dicibile*), meaningful utterance (*dictio*), thing (*res*).
>
> What I call a word, both is a word and signifies a word. What I have called an idea (*dicibile*), is a word; however, it does not signify a word, but that which is understood from the word and contained in the mind. What I have called a meaningful utterance (*dictio*) is a word, but of the sort by which two things are signified simultaneously : the word itself, and that which comes to be in the mind

---

incrementis generationum tamquam lumina sapientiae et scientiae, earundem rerum sunt operationes corporales multae ac variae... necessitates alienatorum ab aeternitate veritatis tuae populorum produxerunt haec, sed in evangelio tuo, quoniam ipsae aquae ista eiecerunt, quarum amarus languor fuit causa, ut in tuo verbo ista procederent. See also *de civ. dei* 19.7, *Conf.* 10.12.19 and 13.24.36.

61. See also *de magistro* 10.33, 11.36, and *Conf.* 11.3.5.

because of the word. That which I have called a thing (*res*) is a word which, with
the exception of these other three (which are spoken), signifies whatever remains.

In the context of the *de Trinitate*, he simply uses the word *verbum*, but he
applies this label to concepts which in the earlier treatise he would have called
verba, *dicibiles*, *dictiones*, and *res* (eg. *de trin.* 15.11.20). It is therefore
important to understand in reading Book 15 of the *de trinitate* that in both
works he envisions the utterance of an idea as a process of many stages, in
which the idea itself undergoes a series of changes ; these instantiations differ
from each other sufficiently to warrant a separate label for each stage.

This much is also clear from the text of the *de trinitate* itself. The act of
thinking about "what we know" results in a "word", and the production of this
verbum parallels the production of a spoken utterance :

> *de trin.* 15.27.50 : Yet this very light reveals to you those three things in you, and
> in them you recognize the image of that highest Trinity itself, which you are as yet
> unable to contemplate with your eyes fixed steadily upon it. It also reveals to you
> that there is a true word in you when it is begotten from your knowledge, that is,
> when we say what we know; that, although we do not utter or even think of this
> word as a sound that is significant in the language of any people (*etsi nullius gentis
> lingua significantem vocem vel proferamus vel cogitemus*), yet our thought is
> formed from that which we know; and that there is in the gaze of the thinker an
> image of the thought very similar to that which the memory contained (*sitque in acie
> cogitantis imago simillima cognitionis eius quam memoria continebat*), namely, by
> the will or love as a third joining these two together, as it were, the parent and the
> offspring (*velut parentem ac prolem*).

The act of thinking about something, in this case, the most elevated and pure
sort of knowledge, results in a *verbum*. This word is clearly not the same thing
as the knowledge itself ; Augustine uses the terms 'parent' and 'offspring' once
again. Nevertheless, this *verbum* born of true knowledge resembles most
closely the *res* of the *de dialectica*, insofar as it is not yet conceived of in
human language, even in one's thoughts.

Augustine does not forget in this last book that he must maintain his
hierarchy of matter, and therefore also his hierarchy of knowledge:

> *de trin.* 15.12.22 : The human mind, therefore, knows all these things which it has
> acquired through itself, through the senses of its body, and through the testimonies
> of others, and keeps them in the storehouse of its memory ; and from them a true
> word is begotten when we say what we know, but a word which is anterior to
> every sound and to every thought of sound. For then the word is most like the thing
> that is known, and from which its image is also begotten, since the sight of thought
> arises from the sight of knowledge. This is the word that belongs to no language,
> the true word about a true thing, having nothing from itself, but everything from
> that knowledge from which it was born[62].

Furthermore, when this knowledge is of the most elevated and permanent
sort, the trinity formed in the act of intellection, whose result is this *res-*

---

62. *de trin.* 15.12.22 : ...*Tunc enim est verbum simillimum rei notae, de qua gignitur et
imago eius quoniam de visione scientiae visio cogitationis exoritur, quod est verbum linguae
nillius, verbum verum de re vera, nihil de suo habens sed totum de illa scientia de qua
nascitur.*

verbum, resembles the true Trinity best, when compared to all the other trinities in the human mind.

> *de trin.* 15.23.43 : For although the memory of man, and particularly that which beasts do not have, namely, that in which intelligible things are so contained that they do not come into it through the senses of the body, has, in proportion to its own small measure in this image of the Trinity, a likeness, incomparably unequal, of course, but yet a likeness of whatever kind it may be to the Father ; and similarly, although the understanding of man, which is formed from the memory by the attention of thought, when that which is known is spoken--it is a word of the heart and belongs to no language--has in its great unlikeness some likeness to the Son; and although the love of man which proceeds from knowledge and combines the memory and the understanding, as though common to the parent and the offspring--whence it is understood to be neither the parent nor the offspring--has in this image some likeness, although very unequal, to the Holy Spirit, yet we do not find that, as in this image of the Trinity, these three are not the one man, but belong to the one man, so in the highest Trinity itself, whose image this is, are those three of one God, but they are the one God, and there are three Persons, not one.

As noted above, the trinities within the mind come to resemble the highest Trinity more and more, especially as the 'processional' relationships become harder and harder to distinguish (*de trin.* 11.7.11 and 15.25.45). It is precisely this word which cannot be expressed in any language.

> *de trin.* 15.11.20 : We must, therefore, come to that word of man, to the word of a living being endowed with reason, to the word of the image of God, not born of God but made by God ; this word cannot be uttered in sound nor thought in the likeness of sound (*quod neque prolativum est in sono neque cogitativum in similitudine soni*), such as must be done with the word of any language; it precedes all the signs by which it is signified, and is begotten by the knowledge which remains in the mind when this same knowledge is spoken inwardly, just as it is. For the sight of thought is very similar to the sight of knowledge (*Simillima est enim visio cogiationis visioni scientiae*). For, when it is spoken through a sound or through some bodily sign, it is spoken not just as it is, but as it can be seen or heard through the body. When, therefore, that which is in the knowledge is in the word, then it is a true word, and the truth which is expected from man, so that what is in the knowledge is also in the word.

Augustine does not assert that even this word is identical to the knowledge from which it is born, though at this stage it is "most similar to the thing known" (*simillimum rei notae*). The process of thinking about something introduces a difference, and the images formed from these truths are not equal to the truths themselves (see *de trin.* 6.10.11 and 15.22.43).

> *de trin.* 15.27.50 : He, who is able, sees and discerns that the will indeed proceeds from thought (for no one wills anything of which he is wholly ignorant as to what it is, or of what kind it is), but that it is also not an image of thought ; and that, accordingly, a certain difference is insinuated in this intelligible thing between the birth and the procession, since to see something in thought is not the same as to desire it, or even to enjoy it with the will[63].

---

63. *de trin.* 15.27.50 : *Quam quidem voluntatem de cognitione procedere (nemo enim vult quod omnino quid vel quale sit nescit), non tamen esse cognitionis imaginem, et ideo quandam in hac re intelligibili nativitatis et processionis insinuari distantiam quoniam non*

How much greater, then, must be the difference between the image of this truth in our thought, and the expression of that image in a word ! Here we may borrow the terms Augustine uses to describe God's speech to men : as God shows himself to the corporeal sight of men 'through something subordinate' (*de civ. dei* 16.29), which was not of the same essence as himself, so the process of thinking about true knowledge and producing an utterence-- even one anterior to every sound and all thought of sound--results in something both dissimilar and subordinate.

> *de civ. dei* 10.13 : Just as the uttered sound, which makes audible the thought that has its existence in the silence of understanding, is not the same as that thought, so the visible form in which God, who exists in his invisible substance, became visible was not identical with God himself[64].

VII. – OUR COGNITIVE AND LINGUISTIC FAILURE WHEN CONFRONTED BY DEATH

I have already considered Augustine's concern for time in a variety of contexts ; I have also noted Augustine's concern for terminology, especially in the use of Greek terms in worship where no Latin word is available (see notes 4 and 16). Having now described the reasoning which underlies his fear of the inadequacy of language, especially with regard to theological issues, I turn next to three passages in which Augustine confronts particular problems in the grammar and vocabulary of his own language.

In the same book of the *Confessions* in which he confronts the nature of God's immortality, Augustine tries to understand the tense system of Latin and the understanding of time which lies behind it. He draws his conclusions while desiring to think from a human perspective, as one thinking about his past and predicting the future through expectations based on knowledge of past events (*Conf.* 10.8.14). Because humans operate and think in time, and because time marches ever forward, the past cannot be recovered, cannot be seen or touched through sense perception : we cannot know history ; we can only believe it (*de civ. dei* 11.3 ; *de utilitate credendi* xi.25).

> *Conf.* 11.20.26 : What is by now evident and clear is that neither future nor past exists, and it is inexact language to speak of three times--past, present, and future. Perhaps it would be exact to say : there are three times, a present of things past, a present of things present, and a present of things to come. In the soul there are these three aspects of time, and I do not see them anywhere else : a present memory of past events, a present awareness of present things, and a present exspectation of things to come.

---

hoc est cogitatione conspicere quod appetere vel etiam perfrui voluntate, cernit discernitque qui potest.

64. *de civ. dei* 10.13 : *Sicut enim sonus, quo auditur sententia in silentio intellegentiae constituta, non est hoc quod ipsa; ita et species, qua visus est Deus, in natura invisibili constitutus, non erat quod ipse.*

His thought on the subject is quite sophisticated and flexible. For men, yesterday no longer exists except as a memory, and that memory has its existence solely in the present. Similarly, he argues that the word 'future' is misleading because it presumes a future exists for man to know, which he cannot; man has expectations in the present about future events, expectations based on data from the past[65]. He even recognizes the difference between predicting events based on conjectures and acting out a sequence of repeated actions. This latter type of 'future event' we can see 'more clearly and more certainly' (*de trin.* 15.7.13); examples are the rising of the sun (*Conf.* 11.18.24) and the singing of a song :

> *Conf.* 11.31.41 : A person singing or hearing a song he knows well suffers a distension or stretching in feeling and in sense-perception from the exspectation of future sounds and the memory of past sound.

Augustine later returns to discuss this same failure of language with a specific example. Just as humans inaccurately think about past, present, and future, while in reality the present is but a fleeting moment which nevertheless defines its own past and future (see *Conf.* 11.13.16), so humans speak of dying, when in reality death is instantaneous, and it is really proper only to speak of 'before death' and 'after death' (*de civ. dei* 13.11). This failure to understand death is simultaneously cognitive and linguistic.

> *de civ. dei* 13.11 : Hence I find it significant and appropriate, even if it did not happen through human industry but, perchance, through divine decision, that the grammarians have not been able to decline the Latin verb *moritur* by the same rule as other verbs of this type. For from *oritur* comes the past tense *ortus est*, and all similar verbs are declined in the perfect with the perfect participle. But if we ask the perfect of *moritur*, the invariable answer is *mortuus est*, [which is an adjective]... The adjective *mortuus* is used instead of a perfect participle so as to give a declension to something which cannot be declined.

(I used 'decline' to translate *declinare*, where 'conjugate' would more correct, because Augustine makes a variety of puns on the Latin verb, which can mean both 'conjugate' as well as 'decline', as in 'avoid'). Augustine recognizes that one can say, in Latin, "he is dying" but not "he has died" ; one can only say "he is dead". In any event, Augustine argues that death is no more easily understood than avoided, or described.

> *de civ. dei* 13.11 : Would that we had ensured, by acting rightly in paradise, that there was really no death ! But as it is, death is not only a reality, but so troublesome a reality that it cannot be explained by any verbal formula, nor escaped by any scheme[66].

Finally, we have already examined passages in which Augustine acknowledges that the vocabulary of his language does not describe divine

---

65. *de trin.* 15.7.13 : *Non ex futuris praeterita sed futura ex praeteritis non tamen firma cognitione conicimus.*

66. *de civ. dei* 13.11 : *Atque utinam in paradiso bene vivendo egissemus, ut re vera nulla mors esset. Nunc autem non solum est, verum etiam tam molesta est, ut nec ulla explicari locutione possit nec ulla ratione vitari.*

matters very well, but at least once he does so by criticizing the labels with which we normally classify words, and even the categories themselves.

> *de trin.* 15.5.8 : Hence, if we say : "He is eternal, immortal, incorruptible, unchangeable, living, wise, powerful, beautiful, just, good, blessed, and spirit", only the last of these designations seems to signify substance, but the rest to signify qualities of this substance; but it is not so in that ineffable and simple nature. For whatever seems to be said there according to qualities must be understood according to substance or essence[67].

Augustine refers to 'substance' and 'qualities', that is, to nouns and adjectives. In fact, he argues, all of these modifiers--adjectives--must be understood as substantives, ie. nouns ; all of these qualities must be understood (*intellegendum est*) as substances[68].

VIII. – THE FAILURE OF THE INNER/OUTER BODY METAPHOR

Augustine, as we have seen, divided the realm of his experience between a world of *sensibilia* and a world of *intellegibilia*, and he discussed the qualities of those two categories in some detail. In explicating Augustine on the Trinity, I tried to highlight his pedagogical reasons for moving from "material signs to the spiritual realities which they represent". It is obvious from the characteristics which he attributes to these categories that there can be no item simultaneously in both worlds, and therefore that the adoption of these definitions created a gap between the realm of the mind and the physical world. The mind affects the outside world through its control of the physical body, and it gathers information from that world through the senses, "those five well-known messengers of the body[69]".

It was relatively easy for Augustine to describe and discuss the operation of the senses. If, as previously, we follow Augustine from the world of the senses to the intellect as it reviews the information gathered by the senses, we can see that he needs to create, or adopt, a vocabulary which would allow him to

---

67. *de trin.* 15.5.8 : *Proinde si dicamus:* '*aeternus, immortalis, incorruptibilis, immutabilis, vivus, sapiens, potens, speciosus, iustus, bonus, beatus, spiritus,*' *horum omnium novissumum quod posui quasi tantummodo videtur significare substantiam, cetera vero huius substantiae qualitates ; sed non ita est in illa ineffabili simplicique natura. Quidquid enim secundum qualitates illic dici videtur secundum substantiam vel essentiam est intellegendum.*

68. *Intellegere* is the all-purpose word of choice for Augustine when he talks about the interpretation of Scripture. See, for instance, *de civ. dei* 15.2 : *Haec forma intellegendi de apostolica auctoritate descendens locum nobis aperit, quem ad modum scripturas duorum testamentorum, veteris et novi, accipere debeamus.*

69. *de utilitate credendi* 1.1 ; see also *de trin.* 15.27.49 : *[Mens] cui tamquam in loco superiore et interiore honorabiliter praesidenti iudicanda omnia nuntiant etiam corporis sensus...*

discuss the operations of the mind within a non-physical world. At this secondary stage, the task was simple enough; for Augustine found within his own memory 'images' of things previously perceived through sense-perception, and he found that he could experience again, within the confines of his memory, all those sensations which he had initially felt through his body.

> *Conf.* 10.8.12-13 : I come to the fields and vast palaces of memory, where are the storehouses of innumerable images of all kinds of objects brought in by sense-perception... The objects themselves do not enter, but the images of the perceived objects are available to the thought recalling them. But who can say how images are created, even though it may be clear by which senses they are grasped and stored within. For even when I am in darkness and silence, in my memory I can produce colors at will, and distinguish between white and black and between whatever other colors I wish...

The precision with which he was able to recreate past experiences led him to believe that the mind functioned exactly as the body did, with its own complete set of senses. For instance, after the passage just quoted, he goes on to list images drawn from the five senses which he finds in his memory.

> *Conf.* 10.6.8 : Yet there is a light I love ... and a food, and a kind of embrace when I love my God--a light, voice, odor, food, embrace of my inner man, where my soul is floodlit by light which space cannot contain, where there is sound that time cannot seize, where there is a perfume which no breeze disperses, where there is a taste for food which no amount of eating can lessen, and where there is a bond of union that no satiety can part. That is what I love when I love my God.

In the *de Trinitate*, he explains this process more clearly, and he develops more fully the metaphor of "inner vision" which I have mentioned before.

> *de trin.* 11.3.6 : For even when the image (*species*) of the body which was perceived corporally has been taken away, yet a likeness (*similitudo*) of it remains in the memory, to which the will may again turn its gaze (*acies*) in order to be formed by it from within (*intrinsecus*), as the sense was formed by the sensible body that was presented to it from without (*extrinsecus*). And so that trinity arises from the memory, the inner vision (*interna visione*), and the will which unites both. And when these three are drawn together (*coguntur*) into unity, then from that act of combining itself (*ab ipso coactu*), they are called thought (*cogitatio*).

> But the place of that bodily image, which was perceived from without (*extrinsecus*), is taken by the memory, retaining the image which the soul absorbs into itself through the bodily sense ; and the vision, which was without (*quae foris erat*) when the sense was formed by a sensible body (*ex corpore sensibili*), is succeeded by a similar vision within (*succedit intus similis visio*), when the gaze of the mind (*acies animi*) is formed from that which the memory retains and absent bodies are conceived ; and the will itself, as it moved the sense to be formed to the body that was presented to it from without (*foris*), and combined both of them when it had been formed, so in the act of remembering it causes the eye of the mind to turn back to the memory, in order that it may be formed by that which the memory retains, and that there may be a similar vision in thought (*fit in cogitatione similis visio*)[70].

---

70. The issues raised in this passage are also discussed by Augustine in *de Genesi ad litteram* XII ; on that book (with considerable references to the *de trin.*) see J. PÉPIN, *Revue d'histoire et de philosophie religieuses* 34 (1954) 373-400. I have already eschewed

Obviously, having once adopted the metaphor, Augustine pushes it to the furthest level of detail, weaving his argument back and forth from sense-perception to intellection (*intrinsecus, extrinsecus; intus, foris*). Very early in his career he selects sight as the sense most closely related to the processes of the mind : "reason is the mind's sight, with which it looks upon the truth by itself, without the interference of the body[71]". This allows him to create an enormous apparatus of metaphorical language with which to discuss the workings of the mind. For instance, having concluded that God must be present to the mind for man to learn anything (*de magistro* 11.38), he later refers with great frequency to God as the 'light' of the mind, which illumines those things which he allows us to know and to understand :

> *de trin.* 12.15.24 : But we ought rather to believe that the nature of the intellectual mind is so formed as to see those things which, according to the disposition of the Creator, are subjoined to intelligible things in the natural order, in a sort of incorporeal light of its own kind, as the eye of the flesh sees the things that lie about it in this corporeal light, of which light it is made to be receptive and to which it is adapted[72].

In fact, he envisions the operations of the two to be parallel to such an extent that he frequently refers to the existence of an inner and an outer man (eg. *Conf.* 10.6.9).

As I suggested previously (see end of Section II), this metaphor and its vocabulary hold certain advantages for Augustine with respect to time, for sight is instantaneous and non-sequential in a way that thought can never be (*de trin.* 15.25.45 ; *de civ. dei* 22.1 and 22.29). The consequences of both these assumptions about time, and the use of this metaphor, are on dramatic display in his discussion of the three types of sight in his major commentary on *Genesis.*

> *de Genesi ad litteram* 12.11.22 : When, therefore, one reads the sentence "Love your neighbor as yourself", he sees (*videre*) the letters physically, he thinks (*cogitare*) about his neighbor spiritually, but he looks (*conspicere*) upon this love intellectually. Furthermore, absent letters can be seen with spiritual sight, and one's neighbor, when present, can be seen with bodily vision. However, love cannot be seen as a physical substance with the eyes of the body, nor can an image of love's body be contemplated by spiritual sight; it can be seen and grasped by the mind alone, that is, by the intellect.

---

comment on the questions Pépin raises concerning the Plotinian antecedents for these passages.

71. *de immortalitate animae* 6.10 : *ratio est aspectus animi, quo per seipsum, non per corpus, verum intuetur.* See also *de ordine* 2.3.10 : *quam ob rem si menti hoç est intellegere, quod sensui videre...* and *de quantitate animae* 14.23-24 : *Incorporalia* can be seen by the *interiore quidam oculo, id est intellegentia.*

72. *de trin.* 12.15.24 : *Sed potius credendum est mentis intellectualis ita conditam esse naturam ut rebus intellegibilibus naturali ordine disponente conditore subiuncta sic ista videat in quadam luce sui generis incorporea quemadmodum oculus carnis videt quae in hac corporea luce circumadiacent, cuius lucis capax eique congruens est creatus.*

See also *de Genesi ad litteram* 12.31.59 : God is the light for the soul, for intellectual vision. See also the texts listed in note 7.

The same words are used each time he offers definitions of the three types of sight : corporeal, spiritual, and intellectual (*de Genesi ad litteram* 12.4.15, 12.7.16.) Each type of sight has its own province : *corporalia, corporales imagines* (or *similitudines corporum*), and *intellegibilia*; and each is superior to the former : *habent utique ordinem suum, et est aliud alio praecellentius* (*de Genesi ad litteram* 12.24.51). As above (*de trin.* 11.7.11) he suggested that the trinity formed by the thought of remembered *sensibilia* was inferior because it retained, in part, its relationship to time, so here the language used to differentiate the types of sight suggests a temporal hierarchy : remembered objects are cogitated, while ideas are seen. The former is equated with rumination, the latter is instantaneous.

I discussed above a number problems involved in thinking about God and the Trinity, and the advantages of proceeding from *corporalia* to *intellegibilia* to 'the word which is anterior to every sound and every thought of sound' (Section III) ; I also discussed Augustine's belief that God must appear to our corporeal senses through 'something subordinate' (Section IV). We have also seen that Scripture's use of terms appropriate to human beings to discuss God can backfire (*Conf.* 12.27.37). In adopting this metaphor of mental vision, Augustine exposed himself to the same hazards as Scripture : he used language and concepts appropriate to something subordinate to describe, first, man's soul, and then God himself. In reality, Augustine proved remarkably adept at working through the consequences of his methodology, and he got into trouble only very rarely. I offer two examples.

To begin with, Augustine acknowledged that other metaphors for thought are possible, and indeed sometimes necessary. How can one describe the thoughts of another in a text other than through words ? It evidently sounded as silly to Augustine as it sounds to us to describe someone reading or writing his own thoughts. He therefore accepted that the Biblical phrase 'they said, thinking' as equivalent to 'they thought, saying' : "[in both places] it is indicated that they speak within themselves and in their hearts" (*de trin.* 15.10.17). He himself described the mind speaking to itself (*Conf.* 12.5.5).

> *de trin.* 15.10.18 : Some thoughts, then, are speeches of the heart... Yet because we speak of thoughts as speeches of the heart, we do not, therefore, mean that they are not at the same time acts of sight, which arise from the sights of knowledge when they are true. For when these take place outwardly through the body, the speech is one thing and sight another thing; but when we think inwardly, then both are one. Thus hearing and sight are two things, differing from each other, in the senses of the body, but in the mind it is not one thing to see and another thing to hear[73].

---

73. *de trin.* 15.10.18 : *Quaedam ergo cogitationes locutiones sunt cordis... Nec tamen quia dicimus locutiones cordis esse cogitationes ideo non sunt etiam visiones exortae de notitiae visionibus quando verae sunt. Foris enim cum per corpus haec fiunt aliud est locutio, aliud visio; intus autem cum cogitamus utrumque unum est. Sicut auditio et visio duo quaedam sunt inter se distantia in sensibus corporis, in animo autem non est aliud atque aliud videre et audire.*

Augustine had begun to discuss the production of the *verbum* which arises from the sight of things which we know, and in that context it was necessary for the reader to understand that this act of mental sight is instantaneous, even though in the previous paragraph, as elsewhere, he had described (and indeed, had to describe) the thoughts themselves as speeches in discursive language within the mind. Here the metaphor of the interior man fails : the act of seeing must, he acknowledges, encompass that of hearing. Furthermore, human language, of any and all nations, because it exists in time, cannot by its very nature represent the concept he wishes us to see.

He had already, in fact, acknowledged another failing in his metaphor. At the beginning of book 14 he tries to understand how the mind can think about itself.

> *de trin.* 14.6.8 : The power of thought (*cogitatio*) is so great that the mind (*mens*) can only place itself in its own sight (*conspectus*) when it thinks about (*cogitare*) itself ; and in this way nothing is in the sight of the mind except when it is thought about, with the result that the mind itself, in which everything which is thought is thought, can only be in its own sight by thinking about itself[74].

He does so, initially, by using his 'sight of the mind' metaphor, and discovers a problem. If the mind 'thinks' by seeing, then in order to think about itself, it must see itself. Since, as his metaphor assumes, the body and the mind operate in parallel, he feels that he ought to be able to construct an explanation using a description of corporal sight and physical objects. It doesn't work.

> *de trin.* 14.6.8 : Moreover, I cannot discover how the mind is not in its sight when it is not thinking about itself, since it can never be without itself --as if it were one thing and its sight another. Yet it would not be silly to say the same thing about the eye of the body (*oculus corporis*). For the eye is fixed in its own position in the body, but its sight (*aspectus*) is aimed at things which are external to it, and extends even to the stars. Nor is an eye ever in its own sight, insofar as it does not see itself except in a mirror, as I said earlier (10.3.5) ; which is no parallel for the way in which the mind places itself in its own sight by thinking about itself. Certainly, therefore, the mind does not see part of itself by means of another part of itself, when it sees itself by thinking about itself, as we see with some parts of our body, namely the eyes, those other parts which can be within our sight. What could be more absurd to say, or even to think ?

Augustine has to admit that, in fact, his metaphor fails, and it does so because it draws its imagery from the world of the senses, from things subordinate.

> *de trin.* 14.6.8 : When the truth is consulted, it gives none of these answers, since when we think in this way, we but think with the imagined images of physical objects; and it is absolutely certain that the mind is not such to those few minds which can be consulted regarding the truth in this matter.

---

74. *de trin.* 14.6.8 : *Tanta est tamen cogitationis vis ut nec ipsa mens quodam modo se in conspectu suo ponat nisi quando se cogitat, ac per hoc ita nihil in conspectu mentis est nisi unde cogitatur ut nec ipsa mens qua cogitatur quidquid cogitatur aliter possit esse in conspectu suo nisi se ipsam cogitando.*

227

When Augustine, towards the end of the work, begins to speak of the most profound regions of memory, in which there exists, "as it were, knowledge of knowledge, vision of vision, and understanding of understanding" (de trin. 15.21.40), one might think that he has gotten carried away in a rhetorical flight of fancy and has forgotten his earlier discovery that even vision will not suffice as a metaphor to describe the processes of the mind. Perhaps so. But he does not forget for long. Augustine closes his work, sadly admitting that he has, in fact, said "nothing worthy of the ineffability of that highest Trinity" (de trin. 15.27.50). Those who can, he writes, see that a difference is insinuated between knowledge and the thought of knowledge (de trin. 15.25.50). To the reader he makes one last address :

> de trin. 15.27.50 : You could have seen this, too, although you were unable then, as you are unable now, to unfold with adequate speech what you scarcely saw amid the clouds of corporeal likenesses that do not cease to appear in our human thoughts[75].

Clifford ANDO
Department of Classical Studies
University of Michigan 20 16 Angell Hall
Ann Arbor, MI 481099-1003 U.S.A.

SUMMARY : Augustine's linguistics are considered in relation to his epistemological and ontological thought. According to Augustine, human soul communicate using words which, as *sensibilia*, like our bodies, operate in time and space. Our language thus finds its origin in the sin which bound our souls to our bodies ; and thus also our present means of communication stand in direct contrast to those employed by God. Similarly, the nature of human understanding makes metaphors which draw on physical imagery particularly useful pedagogical tools, but as the same time renders texts which use those metaphors inherently inadequate for discussing complex issues. In the final books of the *de Trinitate* Augustine himself recognizes the consequences of this line of thought and acknowledges that he has said "nothing worthy of the ineffability of the highest Trinity" (*de Trin.* 15.27.50).

---

75. de trin. 15.27.50 : *Potuisti et tu quamvis non potueris neque possis explicare sufficienti eloquio quod inter nubila similitudinum corporalium quae cogitationibus humanis occursare non desinunt vix vidisti.*

The Shifting Tones of Pope Leo the Great's Christological Vocabulary

PHILIP L. BARCLIFT

Over the past several decades Leonine studies have focused attention on Pope Leo the Great's Christology, noting the influence his *Tomus ad Flavianum* had at the Council of Chalcedon. In fact, because of this strong influence twentieth-century scholars have studied the *Tome* nearly exclusively in order to identify the heart of Leo's Christology. There can be no question, of course, that the *Tome* should be consulted in order to understand Leo's Christology, but it marks only one phase in the ongoing development of the ways he chose to express his christological insights. In part the *Tome* itself precipitated this development insofar as it opened up his Christology to scrutiny in the East. The tone of Leo's insights and the language he used to express them shifted and acquired greater precision over time in his letters and sermons in direct response to the dynamics of the christological controversy in the East, of which Leo's *Tome* made him a part. This development is most evident in three areas: his avoidance of the "Mother of God" title for the Virgin Mary after initially using it early in his pontificate; his use of the terms *homo* and *humanus*, which Leo learned to distinguish later in his pontificate; and his adoption of the Antiochene *homo assumptus* formula late in his pontificate to emphasize the fullness of Christ's human nature. These phenomena reflect the pope's careful attempt to distance himself from the rising tide of the Monophysite movement in the East, as he began to channel his traditional, Western Christology more through formulae used by Antiochene theologians. These phenomena can only be observed through careful, chronological analysis of the broader corpus of Pope Leo's works.[1]

There are several reasons to question whether Pope Leo's *Tome* should be considered the summation of his Christology. As J. Gaidioz shows, Leo's *Tome* was almost certainly edited for him by his theological advisor, Prosper of Aquitaine. Moreover, as Herbert Arens and C. Silva-Tarouca demonstrate, the vast majority of the *Tome* is compiled and heavily edited from the pope's own early sermons, combined with citations on the Incarnation from Western theologians. The near certainty that Prosper of Aquitaine compiled the *Tome* for

---

1. All citations from Pope Leo's *Tome* are based on the critical edition of C. Silva-Tarouca, ed., *S. Leonis Magni: Tomus ad Flavianum Episc. Constantinopolitanum* in *Textus et Documenta* (*TD*), Series Theologica, tome 9 (Rome, 1932). See esp. Silva-Tarouca's notes on pp. 24–32 for a careful analysis of the contents of the *Tome*.

Mr. Barclift is visiting professor of theology at Seattle University, Seattle, Washington.

Leo begs the question whether the pope had *any* substantive part in selecting citations either from his theological predecessors or even from his own sermons. The fact that Prosper cited and carefully edited selections only from Pope Leo's earliest sermons merely deepens the problem of whether the *Tome* should be used as Leo's final word on the doctrine of Christ, especially regarding the language he uses to express it.[2]

That Pope Leo sanctioned and signed the *Tome* before publication in 449 suggests, of course, that he had no theological reservations with it at the time, and the fact that he fought for its continued acceptance late in his pontificate indicates that Leo never rejected the *Tome* in its substance. It represents the heart and soul of the Western christological tradition of which Leo is a part. Summarizing Pope Leo's *Tome*, Leo Davis shows that on the one hand, in keeping with the Western tradition, Leo maintains that the incarnate Jesus is continuous with and identical to the divine Word. In fact, according to Leo, the unity of Jesus' person is so close that it is permissible to interchange the predicates used for Christ's two natures. This is the Western *communicatio idiomatum* formula, which Western theologians held in common with the Eastern theologians affiliated with Alexandria.[3] On the other hand, as W. H. C. Frend observes, Pope Leo maintains the Western tradition's insistence that Christ's two natures are distinct, devoid of blending or confusion: Christ is both truly divine and truly human, composed of the divine Word, a human body, and a human soul. This latter emphasis of the Western tradition is shared by the theologians affiliated with Antioch. Therefore, as Frend comments, Leo in this fashion satisfies both the Antiochene emphasis on the reality and independence of Christ's two natures and the Alexandrine contention that "the person of the Incarnate is identical with that of the divine Word."[4]

When Pope Leo commissioned Prosper to edit his *Tome* in 449, the pope intended this discourse to mediate the Eastern christological crisis that was coming to a head at the Second Council of Ephesus. Leo consistently viewed this crisis as a conflict between two extreme factions, the followers of Nestorius and the followers of Eutyches. As Leo saw it, one side overemphasized the distinction between Christ's natures to the point of denying the unity of his person and of doubling the persons in Christ. The other side overemphasized the unity of Christ's natures to the point of blending them and of denying

2. J. Gaidioz, "Saint Prosper d'Aquitaine et le Tome à Flavien," *Revue de sciences religieuses* 23 (1949): 270–301. For additional commentary on the relationship between Pope Leo and Prosper of Aquitaine, see N. W. James, "Leo the Great and Prosper of Aquitaine: A Fifth Century Pope and His Adviser," *Journal of Theological Studies* 44 (1993): 554–584; Herbert Arens, *Die christologische Sprache Leos des Großen: Analyse des Tomus an den Bishopen Flavian* (Freiburg, Germany, 1982), p. 110; and N. Ertl, "Diktatoren frühmittelaltlicher Papstbriefe," *Archiv für Urkundenforschung* 15 (1938): 56–61.
3. Leo Donald Davis, *The First Seven Ecumenical Councils (325–787): The History and Theology* (Wilmington, Del., 1987), p. 176.
4. W. H. C. Frend, *Rise of the Monophysite Movement*, 2d ed. (New York, 1979), p. 131.

Christ's authentic humanity, asserting instead the possibility that the impassible God could suffer.[5] Leo expected his *Tome* to be read at the council in defense of Flavian, the bishop of Constantinople whom Leo believed to be wrongfully accused of heresy. But Dioscorus, then bishop of Alexandria who presided over the council, had Leo's *Tome* suppressed throughout the session. As Frend observes, however, it was probably fortunate that Leo's *Tome* was not read at that time, since within the climate of this council Leo "and his representatives would have been excommunicated then and there."[6] Two years later, when Pope Leo and Empress Pulcheria agreed to call a new council at Chalcedon, his *Tome* was read in a very different climate and became one of the foundation stones of the council's Definition of Faith.

The christological controversy in the East interested Leo long before his pontificate (440–461). Around 430, during Celestine's pontificate, then Archdeacon Leo commissioned the theologian John Cassian to compile a *florilegium* against Nestorius on the Incarnation.[7] In accordance with Leo's wishes, Cassian added his own condemnation of Nestorius's teachings in this work entitled *De incarnatione Domini contra Nestorium.* Throughout Cassian passionately defended the title "Mother of God" (*Theotokos*) for the Virgin Mary in order to emphasize the unity of Christ's person, since Nestorius, once bishop of Constantinople, had objected to that term and argued instead that Jesus' mother should be called "Mother of Christ" (*Christotokos*). Notwithstanding his misunderstanding of Nestorius, Cassian wished to emphasize a traditional tenet: that when God the Son assumed human nature into the unity of his person, somehow God himself was born of the Virgin Mary, since the child she bore was both true God and true man. According to Cassian, it is incorrect to say that only the human Christ (and not God) was born of Mary, since both Scripture and tradition speak unequivocally of Christ as God. If we can say that Christ was born of the Virgin, then we must also say that God was born of her.[8]

In his defense of the *Theotokos* title, Cassian borrowed his terminology from the Eastern fathers, most notably from Gregory of Nazianzus and Athanasius.

---

5. See Leo's sermon 28.5 for his description of both extremes. All citations of Pope Leo's sermons are from the critical edition *Sancti Leonis Magni. Romani Pontificis Tractatus Septum et Nonaginta*, Corpus Christianorum series Latina 138, ed. Antonius Chavasse (Turnhout, Belgium, 1973). Because of the relative brevity of each sermon, I cite them only by sermon and chapter number.

6. W. H. C. Frend, *The Rise of Christianity* (Philadelphia, Pa., 1985), p. 768.

7. "Praefatio," *De incarnatione Domini contra Nestorium* in J. P. Migne, *Patrologia Latina* (hereafter *PL*) (Paris, 1844–), 50.11.

8. Ibid., 2.3 (*PL* 50.39). Cassian mistakenly interpreted Nestorius's statement as a denial that Christ was a divine-human unity, that he was merely human, as the Arians had claimed (2.2; *PL* 50.31-32). Cassian also charged that Nestorius's doctrines smack of Pelagianism insofar as they seem to suggest that Christ as a mere human lived a perfect life, of which other humans are capable (1.3; *PL* 50.20). Indeed, these links to Arianism and Pelagianism form the chief basis of Cassian's entire attack against Nestorius and his *Christotokos* formula.

The title was not yet in use in the West when Cassian compiled his *florilegium* of Western theologians in support of his position, even though the concept was already firmly established. Augustine had affirmed on several occasions the notion that God could be born of a woman; however, Augustine never used the title "Mother of God" for Mary. Up to the time Cassian compiled his *florilegium* for use in *De incarnatione Domini*, *Theotokos* was used almost exclusively in the East. In a sense Cassian introduced the Greek term *Theotokos* to the Latin West, where Pope Leo initially welcomed use of its Latin equivalent, *Dei genetrix.*[9]

One wonders how much impact a commissioned work such as this one might have had on the person who commissioned it. Since he was at this time inclined toward Alexandria for other reasons, to some extent Leo was already predisposed to accept a more Alexandrine slant on Christology. For instance, in 431, while Leo was archdeacon in Rome, Bishop Cyril of Alexandria presided over the Council of Ephesus, for which Cassian's *De incarnatione Domini* was hastily prepared at Leo's request. That same year Cyril appealed to Archdeacon Leo to help him resolve a jurisdictional dispute with Juvenal, bishop of Jerusalem, and Leo never hesitated in siding with Cyril against the ambitious Juvenal. During this time Leo acquired a good deal of respect for Cyril, enough so that when Leo, early in his pontificate, needed to settle the recurring dispute over the correct date of Easter, he consulted Cyril. Leo and Cyril completely agreed on the matter. So it is not surprising to us that in his first Christmas sermon (440) Pope Leo would adopt the title "Mother of God" (*Dei genetrix*) for Mary—the title for which Cassian pleaded in *De incarnatione Domini* and which was a central issue in the debate between Cyril and Nestorius. This sermon (21.1) marks Leo's first good opportunity to offer his own exposition on the Incarnation.

For Leo, this traditional title for Mary underscored a fundamental doctrine which the pope would hold throughout his pontificate: the two natures of Christ are so indissolubly united in his single person that they share a *communicatio idiomatum*, or interchange of predicates. Andrea Valeriani succinctly summarizes Leo's understanding of this formula: "in Christ the humanity and the divinity each operate distinctly, yet in communion with the other. Because of the unity of the person [of Christ] the acts of one [nature] become attributed also to the other nature."[10] This formula enabled Leo to reconcile paradoxical

9. Cassian cites Augustine's lectures on John, *In Joannis Evangelium* 2.15, in his *florilegium*; see *De incarnatione Domini* 77.27 (*PL* 50.260–262). For additional examples of Augustine's doctrine that God was born of a woman, see *De trinitate* 8.5.7 (*PL* 42.952); and *De Genesi ad litteram liber imperfectus* 1.4 (*PL* 34.221). Based on these texts, there can be little doubt that Augustine would have welcomed the *Dei genetrix* title as a theological postulate of his own Christology.

10. Andrea Valeriani, *Il Mistero del Natale* (Madrid, 1984), p. 31: "in Cristo operano l'umanita e la divinita ciascuna con operazione bensi distinta, ma con communione dall' altra 'cum alterius comunione'. A motiva dell' unita di persona le azioni dell' una vengono attribuite anche all' altra natura."

statements in Scripture, such as the Johannine passages in which Jesus is reported to have said on one occasion that he and the Father are one (John 14:28) and on another occasion that the Father is greater than he (John 10:30), as Leo does in a sermon, delivered in 442.[11] In fact, early in his pontificate, the pope used enough hyperbole to express the *communicatio idiomatum* between Christ's two natures that he nearly confused them. For example, Leo stated in a sermon delivered during the third year of his pontificate that the Son of God allowed his divine impassibility to be affected by all the miseries of human existence: "He assumed [into himself] not only the substance but also the conditions of our sinful nature, to such an extent that he permits his impassible divinity to experience all the miseries that pertain to mortal humans."[12] This statement resembles some of Cassian's hasty statements in *De incarnatione Domini.*[13]

In 444 Leo guarded his hyperbole somewhat in sermon 72.5, but he still explained that the unity of Christ's two natures is so close that in Christ "the invisible rendered its substance visible, the nontemporal temporal, and the impassible passible, not that power might sink into weakness, but that weakness might pass into indestructible power!"[14] Again Leo's use of hyperbole creates the mistaken impression that he believes the impassible God was caused to suffer by his assumption of human nature. In Pope Leo's early inclination toward Alexandria and Alexandrine Christology, he emphasizes the unity of Christ's person so much that he relaxes the line between the transference of predicates and the blending of properties. Jose Martorell captures Leo's early intent, then, when he interprets the pope to say in this context that the Son of God therefore suffered on the cross just as much as his flesh suffered.[15] During this period the pope does not hesitate to speak of Mary as *Dei genetrix,* since that title expresses so powerfully the unity of Christ's person and the interchange of predicates in his selfsame person.

As important as the *Dei genetrix* title is to the exposition of the *communicatio idiomatum* doctrine, however, it is interesting to note that only once does Leo use the title "Mother of God" for Mary in any of his letters or sermons after the Council of Chalcedon convened in 451. In a *florilegium* he had compiled in 458

---

11. Serm. 23.2 (delivered in 442): "quam idem Filius Dei ut ostendat in se non discretae neque alterius esse personae, sic cum eadem dicit: 'Pater maior me est' [John 14:28], quemadmodum cum eadem dicit: 'Ego et Pater unum sumus' [John 10:30]."
12. Serm. 71.2: "ut non solum substantiam, sed etiam conditionem naturae peccatricis adsumeret, et ea sibi pateretur inferri diuina inpassibilitas, quae miserrime experitur humana mortalitas."
13. See, for example, *De incarnatione Domini* 3.3 (*PL* 50.19).
14. Serm. 72.5: "inuisibilis uisibilem, intemporalis temporalem, inpassibilis passibilem substantiam suam fecit, non ut uirtus deficeret in infirmitate sed ut infirmitas in incorruptibilem posset transire uirtutem!"
15. Jose Martorell, *Mysterium Christi (Leon Magno),* (Valencia, Spain, 1983), p. 39.

for Emperor Leo in defense of the Definition of Chalcedon, Leo used the title only to explain the basis of Nestorius's condemnation.[16] Besides this one instance, however, the pope did not use *Theotokos* again after Chalcedon, even though he spoke frequently, within the context of the interchange of predicates, of the Son of God assuming human nature from the virgin who bore him.[17] As Augustine had done before him, Leo provided the content of the doctrine but not the title. Augustine seemed unaware of any use of the *Dei genetrix* title in theological discussion; Leo knew the title and its proper use, yet for some reason he avoided using it.

Many scholars might wish to look to Prosper of Aquitaine's influence for Pope Leo's shift away from the *Dei genetrix* title. Given that Prosper certainly edited the *Tome* for Leo, at least the title's absence from that document could be explained this way. However, N. W. James believes that Prosper also had a hand in the composition of the pope's earliest Christmas sermons, which constituted the primary platform for the pope's annunciation of the *Dei genetrix* title.[18] But why, then, would Prosper and Leo together include this title in his first Christmas sermons and edit it out of their citations of these sermons in the *Tome*? James's observation does not greatly alter the question before us. To be sure, it is quite possible that what is said for Leo must also be said for Prosper, but the problem remains. Why did Pope Leo, even under Prosper's influence, surrender the *Dei genetrix* title for Mary in his later sermons and letters?

This much is clear: with Prosper's help on the *Tome*, Pope Leo avoided most of the hazards that the language of his earliest sermons might have caused if Prosper had quoted them all verbatim. The *Dei genetrix* title is edited out, as are numerous other expressions which use hyperbole to make a point. Word-for-word quotations of these sermons with all their hyperbole could have been disastrous for Leo at the Council of Chalcedon. Both factions in the East could have found reason enough in his sermons to suspect his orthodoxy. In the *Tome*, however, there is no question either of division in Christ's person or of the blending of his two natures:

> Therefore, because of this unity of the person whom we understand to be in both natures, we read about the son of man descending from heaven, when the Son of God assumed human nature from the virgin who bore him. Likewise, the Son of God is said to have been crucified and buried, even though it was not really in his deity, in which the only-begotten is coeternal and consubstantial with the Father; rather he suffered these things in his weak human nature. Still, we all confess in the Symbol that the only-begotten Son of God was crucified and buried.[19]

---

16. See Epist. 165.2 (*PL* 54.1157).
17. See for example, serm. 28.2.
18. See note 2.
19. Epist. 28.5. (*TD* 9.28.126–131): "Propter hanc ergo unitatem personae in utraque natura intellegendam, et filius hominis legitur descendisse de caelo cum filius Dei carnem de ea uirgine de qua est natus adsumpserit. Et rursum filius Dei crucifixus dicitur ac sepultus,

Leo skillfully balanced the *communicatio idiomatum* with a declaration that Christ's two natures remain distinct and unaffected by each other.

The theologians in the Eastern church, however, were not all interested in balance. After the Council of Chalcedon closed, Pope Leo's own theology fell under scrutiny in the East, precisely due to the weight he gives to the distinction of Christ's natures in the *Tome*. In 452, the year just following the Council of Chalcedon, a controversy was brewing among the Palestinian monks who believed they saw Nestorian tendencies in Pope Leo's *Tome*. On 13 June 453 Leo responded to their concerns, expressing his frustration over the language barrier between the Latin West and the Greek East and suggesting that the problems the monks have with his *Tome* result from faulty Greek translations rather than actual problems with his orthodoxy.[20] But Leo took great care just the same to ensure that his own Latin vocabulary was as precise as possible.[21]

With his wary eye on the growing Monophysite movement in Egypt and Palestine, Pope Leo expounded in a sermon delivered in 453 that "the virgin Mary, who was fecundated by the Holy Spirit, brought forth at one and the same time, without corruption, both her biological child and the Creator of her race, indissolubly united together in his single person; even though, in fact, Jesus' divinity has no mother, and his humanity has no biological father."[22] Here again Leo described the *Dei genetrix* doctrine without the title, and he qualified his statement as soon as he delivered it. Mary is the "Mother of God" insofar as she is the biological mother of Jesus, who is both divine and human; however, Jesus' divinity has no real mother. Nestorius could have agreed with this statement! By this time the Monophysite monks of Egypt and Palestine were already using the "Mother of God" title as their slogan. Leo sought to take this slogan away from them by reminding them that Mary is not technically the mother of Jesus' divine nature.

That same year Pope Leo explained that Christ's humility is complete in his majesty, and his majesty is complete in his humility. The pope wished to

---

cum haec non in diuinitate ipsa qua unigenitus consempiternus et consubstantialis est Patri, sed in naturae humanae sit infirmitate perpessus. Unde unigenitus filium Dei crucifixum et sepultum omnes etiam in symbolo confitemur."

20. Epist. 124.1 (*PL* 54.1062): "Sollicitudini meae, quam universali Ecclesiae omnibusque ejus filiis debeo, multorum relatione patefactum est dilectionis vestrae animis quiddam offensionis illatum, dum aut imperiti, ut apparet, interpretes, aut maligni, quaedam vos aliter intelligere, quam a me sunt praedicata, fecerunt, non valentes in Graecum eloquium apte et proprie Latina transferre, cum in rebus subtilibus et difficilibus explicandis, vix sibi etiam in sua lingua disputator quisque sufficiat."

21. For an analysis of Pope Leo's use of *substantia* rather than the term *natura* in this letter, which the Palestinian monks found particularly objectionable since it gives the impression that Christ was composed of "two persons," see R. V. Sellers, *The Council of Chalcedon* (London, 1953), pp. 110–111.

22. Serm. 28.2: "ut in uno Dei atque hominis filio, et sine matre deitas, et sine patre esset humanitas. Simul enim per Spiritum fecundata uirginitas sine corruptionis uestigio edidit et sui generis sobolem et suae stirpis auctorem."

establish his orthodoxy with the monks in Palestine at the same time as he maintained his orthodoxy at home and in Antioch. Thus Leo built on the traditional *communicatio idiomatum* formula to express the mystery that Christ is a unity of two natures, yet the pope immediately qualified this statement with his reminder that Christ's two natures remain distinct: "One nature is truly passible, while the other is impassible; but both the humility and the glory belong to the same person who is simultaneously weak and powerful, subject to death and victor over death. The Son of God received a complete human nature and so united the two natures in himself that each nature was present in the other, even though neither nature transferred its essential properties into the other."[23] To be sure, Leo wanted to establish his orthodoxy with the monks in Palestine and Egypt, but he would only bend so far to do it.

In the first Christmas sermon Pope Leo delivered after hearing about the problems in Palestine, he attempted to establish his orthodox position against Nestorius by stating unambiguously that Nestorius should be condemned for suggesting that the Blessed Virgin Mary was only the mother of Christ the man, as if his humanity were not united to his divine nature in the Incarnation. To the contrary, Leo argued, "there is no hope of salvation for the human race if the son of the Virgin were not also the Creator of his mother."[24] Here again we find the *Dei genetrix* formula without the title. Why does Leo not use the *Dei genetrix* title in such a strong statement of the Son's unity when he assumed human nature from his mother? Back in the second chapter of this same sermon Leo had already prepared his audience to distance itself from the more extreme implications one might draw from statements pertaining to the role of the Virgin. In that section he reminded his audience that "Jesus' divinity has no mother, and his humanity has no biological father."[25]

Once Pope Leo established his opposition to Nestorius, he turned his attack on Eutyches and his Monophysite followers. Leo was fully aware by this time that the "Mother of God" title for Mary had become a slogan for the followers of Eutyches, emphasizing their conviction that one can speak only of Christ's two natures *before* the union, whereas *after* the union only one incarnate nature,

23. Serm. 54.1: "Tota est in maiestate humilitas, tota in humilitate maiestas . . . nec infert unitas confusionem, dirimit proprietas unitatem. . . . Aliud est passibile, aliud inuiolabile, et eiusdem est contumelia, cuius et gloria. Ipse est in infirmitate qui et in uirtute, idem mortis capax, et idem uictor est mortis. Suscepit ergo totum hominem Deus, et ita se illi, atque illum sibi misericordiae et potestatis ratione conseruit, ut utraque alteri natura inesset, et neutra in alteram a sua proprietate transiret."
24. Serm. 28.5: "Nam ille beatam Mariam uirginem hominis tantummodo ausus est praedicare genetricem, ut in conceptu eius et partu nulla Verbi et carnis facta unitio crederetur, quia Dei Filius non ipse factus sit hominis filius, sed creato homini sola se dignatione sociauerit. Quod catholicae aures nequaquam tolerare potuerunt, quae sic euangelio ueritatis inbutae sunt, ut firmissime nouerint nullam esse humano generi spem salutis, nisi ipse esset filius Virginis, qui Creator est matris."
25. Serm. 28.2: "ut in uno Dei atque hominis filio, et sine matre deitas."

whose sole operating principle was the divine Word, remained.[26] God the incarnate and God alone was born of the Virgin Mary. Leo now had to combat this notion with as much or even greater vigilance than he used to establish his argument against Nestorius. Therefore, in the same place in this sermon, Leo turned immediately to condemn Eutyches for teaching that only Christ's divine nature remained intact after the union: "If the Incarnation of the Word is the unity of the divine and the human natures, yet through this concurrence the two distinct [natures] became only one, his divinity alone was born of the Virgin's womb; and [Christ's] subjection to being nourished and to bodily growth amounts only to play-acting. Moreover, besides all the other changes of his human condition, only his divinity was crucified; only his divinity died; and only his divinity was buried." In this sermon Leo identified the heart of the danger he found in Eutyches's Monophysite Christology: if Christ was not fully human, his life on earth was merely a charade, and the force of God's plan of salvation is ultimately lost. If Eutyches is correct, Leo explained, all hope for the resurrection is lost, "since [the Son] had no need to be raised, if he were not capable of dying."[27]

A new theological climate had emerged in the mid-fifth century, in which it was no longer safe for theologians to use the long-held, traditional *Dei genetrix* title for Mary without fear of trumpeting the Monophysite call to arms. Consequently, Pope Leo found himself forced to give up the title with which he crowned his first Christmas sermon on the Incarnation. In this new theological climate, brought about by the rising tide of the Monophysite movement in the East, continued use of this title would have only fanned the flames of the Monophysite heresy. Thereafter Leo described the Son's birth from Mary only in such a way as to explain pragmatically the source of the Son's authentic human nature in the unified person of Christ. As important as Leo found the continuity of the Son's existence in Christ, and as critical as the pope found the unity of Christ's person, Leo now found himself forced to protect the doctrine of Christ's real humanity.

26. See Eutyches' declaration in *Acta Conciliorum Oecumenicorum: Concilium Universale Chalcedonense* (hereafter *ACO*), vol. 2, part 4, ed. Edward Schwartz (Berlin, 1932), 1.2.143: "homologō ek duo phuseōn gegenēsthai ton kurion hēmōn *pro* pēs enōseōs, *meta* de tēn mian enōsin phusin homologō" (emphasis mine). For additional comments on Eutyches's declaration, see Grillmeier, *Christ in Christian Tradition*, p. 524; and Czeslaw Bartnik, "Wcielenie Jako Podstawa Teologii Historii u Leona Wielkiego," *Roczniki Teoligiczno-Kanoniczne* (Lublin, Poland, 1960), pp. 33–34.
27. Serm. 28.5: "Si enim Verbi incarnatio unitio est diuinae humanaeque naturae, sed hic ipso concursu quod erat geminum factum est singulare, sola diuinitas utero Virginis nata est, et per ludificatoriam speciem sola subiit nutrimenta et incrementa corporea, utque omnes mutabilitates humanae conditionis omittam, sola diuinitas crucifixa, sola diuinitas mortua, sola diuinitas est sepulta, ut iam secundum talia sentientes sperandae resurrectionis nulla sit ratio, nec sit *primogenitus ex mortuis* Christus, quia non fuit qui deberet reuscitari, si non fuit qui posset occidi."

As a further indication of his movement away from the Alexandrine emphases which colored his earlier christological descriptions, Pope Leo began to
clarify his position in chapter six of the same sermon by using the *homo
assumptus* formula, which the Antiochenes (and Nestorius) also used to speak of
the Son of God assuming a human being, body and soul:

> The man, therefore, who *was assumed* into the Son of God, was received into the
> unity of the person of Christ at the very moment his body came into being, such that
> neither was he conceived without his deity, nor was he born without his deity, nor
> was he nurtured without his deity. The same person in the miracles is the one who
> suffered scorn. He was crucified, dead and buried through his *humanity*; he was
> raised on the third day, ascended to the heavens, and sat down at the right hand of
> the Father through his divine power; and he received in his *human* nature from the
> Father what he himself gave in his divine nature.[28]

Up to this time Pope Leo had used *homo* and *humanus* interchangeably to
designate "humanity" or "human nature." Because of Leo's consistent confusion of the terms, Herbert Arens and M.-J. Nicolas argue that Leo intended to
use the term *homo* abstractly of humanity, humankind, or human nature in this
sermon as well.[29] They contend that Pope Leo is not a speculative thinker with a
mature metaphysical vocabulary; rather, he is a pastor and a preacher whose
theology has always been credited more for the force of its simplicity than for its
subtle nuances. In contrast, Czeslaw Bartnik suggests that Leo used the term
homo here in order to stress the moral and psychic autonomy of Christ's
humanity, by which he asserted that the Son assumed a complete man, body
and soul, as Augustine had done before him.[30] In *Confessions* 7.19, for example,
Augustine carefully distinguished between the terms *homo* and *humanus*. In this
text Augustine consistently used *humanus* generally to designate attributes that
all humans hold in common, and he used *homo* whenever he wished to indicate
the man Jesus in his concrete reality as a human individual, consisting of body,
soul, and mind.[31] For Augustine this kind of precision is second nature, but

---

28. Serm. 28.6: "*Adsumptus* igitur *homo* in Filium Dei, sic in unitatem personae Christi ab ipsis
corporalibus est receptus exordiis, ut nec sine deitate conceptus sit, nec sine deitate editus,
nec sine deitate nutritus. Idem erat in miraculis, idem ub contumeliis; per *humanam*
infirmitatem crucifixus, mortuus et sepultus, per diuinam uirtutem die tertia resuscitatus,
ascendit ad caelos, consedit ad dexteram Patris, et *in natura hominis* a Patre accepit quod in
natura Deitatis etiam ipse donauit" (emphasis mine).
29. Arens, *Christologische Sprache Leos*, pp. 453–475; and Nicolas, "La doctrine christologique,"
pp. 640–641.
30. Bartnik, "Wcielenie Jako Podstawa Teologii Historii u Leona Wielkiego," pp. 32, 37–38. I
wish to express my gratitude to James Wojtkowski for his invaluable assistance in the
translation of this important article.
31. Augustine, *Confessions* 7.19 (*PL* 32.745): "His flesh did not join to your Word without a
human soul and mind (*anima et mente humana*). All who know the immutability of your
Word know this fact, which I myself have come to know, as best I could, but without the
slightest doubt about it. Indeed, in order for him to move parts of his body by his will or at
other times to refrain from moving them, to be aroused with affection at certain times or
not to be aroused at others, to proclaim wise judgments sometimes or to remain silent at
others, these are all manifestations of a mutable soul and mind. . . . Consequently, I

throughout the first decade of his pontificate, Pope Leo was either uncon-
cerned with or unaware of the precise ways Augustine used these two terms. Leo
simply used them as synonyms all this time. In sermon 22.2, for example, Leo
used *homo* when describing Christ's *communicatio idiomatum* to express that the
impassible God did not consider it unworthy of himself to become a passible
human (*homo*).[32] And throughout the third and fourth chapters of this sermon
Leo used *humanum genus* interchangeably with *homines omnes* in speaking of the
human race. Moreover, throughout sermon 23 the pope interchanged *hominis
natura*, *humana natura*, and *humanae substantiae natura*, among others, to
designate human nature, to which the pope adds *homo carnis substantia* in
sermon 24.2. At 24.5 Leo interchanged the phrases *uerum . . . nostrae substantiae
hominem* and *ueram humanae carnis . . . naturam* with reference to Christ's
authentic human nature. In sermon 27.1 Pope Leo claimed that the Son
"renewed humanity in his human nature (*in homine hominem renouans*), even
though he remained unchanged in himself"; whereas in 27.2 Leo explained
that "when God descended into human nature (*ad humana*) he elevated
humanity (*homines*) to his divine station."[33]

Further examples of this kind of interchangeability between the terms *homo*
and *humanus* are too numerous to list here. The point is this: in his early
sermons Pope Leo consistently used these terms as synonyms to designate the
abstract concepts of "human" or "humanity," as Arens and Nicolas have noted.
Therefore, if Pope Leo used *homo* in sermon 28.6 (composed in 452) to
designate a concrete human individual, this use would reflect a remarkable
shift in the pope's christological vocabulary. Of course in view of the growing
Monophysite movement in the East, Leo really had no choice but to alter his
language in order to avoid being identified with that movement.

When Leo finally responded directly to the Palestinian monks in letter 124,
edited from his sermons 64 and 65 delivered in spring of 453 and published in
June of that same year, he addressed their concerns in such a way that
safeguarded the balance achieved in the *Tome*; at the same time, he strengthened his position regarding Christ's complete humanity. In 124.4 he spoke only
of the reality of the Savior's "human" substance (*humanae substantiae*).[34] In

acknowledged in Christ a complete man (*totum hominem*), not merely the body of a man
(*hominis*), or even one with a sensitive soul which is not also rational, but a real man (*ipsum
hominem*), whom I have deemed worthy to be esteemed above all others, not because he is a
person of truth, but because of the great and excellent human nature (*naturae humanae*)
that was perfected in him" (my translation).
32. Serm. 22.2: "inpassibilis Deus non dedignatus est homo esse passibilis."
33. Serm. 27.1: "in homine hominem renouans, in se incommutabilis perseuerans. . . . ut Dei
ad humana descensio fieret hominis ad diuina prouectio."
34. Epist. 124.4 (*PL* 54.1064): "Quam itaque sibi in hujus sacramenti praesidio spem relin-
quunt qui in Salvatoris nostri corpore negant humanae substantiae veritatem?" Compare
sermon 64, which is a particularly significant source for this chapter of Leo's letter: "neque
ullum nostrae religionis officium est quo non tam mundi reconciliatio quam humanae in

124.6 he stated on the one hand that there is "no division between Christ's divine and human substance (*divinam humanamque substantiam*)," while he argued on the other hand that Christ's divine actions do not affect those of his humanity (*humanitas*). Nor do his human (*humanus*) acts affect those of his deity. Instead, both natures co-inhere in the same person. Neither are his twofold attributes absorbed by one another, nor is his individuality doubled.[35] And in 124.7 Leo explained that the Lord Jesus Christ is one, and in him true deity and true "humanity" (*humanitas*) form one and the same person, in whom there is no division at all.[36]

When Leo uses *homo* later in the same chapter of this letter he contextualizes it with a threefold use of *humanus* or its derivatives in order to show that he is attempting to distinguish his terms: "The impassible God's condescension into the form of a slave [see Phil. 2:1 6–11], through which he fulfilled his great sacrament of love, elevated human (*humanus*) weakness into the glory of divine power, since Christ's deity and humanity (*humanitas*) were united so completely in the virgin's conception that Christ performed neither any of his divine acts apart from the man (*homo*) nor any of his human (*humanus*) acts apart from God."[37] Is Leo using *homo* to designate more than simply "human" here? Although he still used the terms more fluidly in other contexts, it is interesting that in this letter and in the two sermons on which it is based, Leo finally used *humanus* or one of its derivatives when he wished to emphasize elements that all humans have in common with Christ in his humanity, such as "human weakness," "humanity," and "human acts," and he now uses *homo* when addressing the actual human person of Christ.

In order to emphasize the distinction Pope Leo was trying to make between these two terms, he takes the step—unusual in the West—of phrasing the term *homo* together with the term *assumptus*, a combination the pope had previously avoided. In the East Antiochene theologians were using the *homo assumptus*

Christo naturae adsumptio celebretur" (64.1); "Solus enim beatae Virginis natus est filius absque delicto, non extraneus ab hominum genere, sed alienus crimine" (64.2); and "Cum ergo in uno Domino Iesu Christo uero Dei atque hominis Filio, diuinam confitemur de Patre naturam, humanam de matre substantiam" (64.3).
35. Epist. 124.6 (*PL* 54.1065): "Quamvis ergo ab illo initio, quo in utero virginis 'Verbum caro factum est' [John 1:14], nihil umquam inter divinam humanamque substantiam divisionis exstiterit, et per omnia incrementa corporea, unis personae fuerint totius temporis actiones; ea ipsa tamen, quae inseparabiliter facta sunt, nulla permixtione confundimus; sed quid cujus formae sit, ex operum qualitate sentimus. Nec divina enim humanis praejudicant, nec humana divinis, cum ita in idipsum utraque concurrant, ut in eis nec proprietas absumatur, nec persona geminetur."
36. Epist. 124.7 (*PL* 54.1066): "Quamvis ergo unus sit Dominus Jesus Christus, et verae Deitatis veraeque humanitatis in ipso una prorsus eademque persona, neque hujus unitioni soliditas ulla possit divisione sejungi."
37. Epist. 124.7 (*PL* 54.1066): "Forma autem servi, per quam impassibilis Deitas sacramentum magnae pietatis implevit, humana humilitas est, quae in gloriam divinae potestatis evecta est, in tantam unitatem ab ipso conceptu Virginis Deitate et humanitate connexu, ut nec sine homine divina, nec sine Deo agerentur humanua."

formula to emphasize the reality and distinction of Christ's two natures in his single person. In order to stress this point they spoke of the Son of God assuming "a man"—a concrete human individual, with a body and a soul—into the unity of his being. Prior to the year 452, however, Pope Leo himself only spoke of the Son of God assuming human nature—and even all humankind—into the unity of his person, and with one exception he abstained completely from using *homo* in conjunction with the term *assumptus* prior to this time. For example, in sermon 21.1, delivered in the first year of his pontificate, Leo spoke of the Son assuming "the nature of the human race into himself" and a little more ambiguously of the Son assuming "what he was not, the actual form of a slave." In his Christmas sermon 22.3 delivered the following year, Leo explained that the Son assumed "the nature of the Lord's mother, without the fault." Two years later Pope Leo stated in another Christmas sermon (24.1) that "the Word who is coeternal and equal with the Creator assumed our humble nature into the unity of his deity." Then in 444, the pope explained in his Christmas sermon that God elevated "our nature" when he assumed it into himself.[38]

The only occasion when the pope used *homo* in conjunction with *assumptus* prior to this time was in his sermon 72.6 on the Passion, delivered in 444, and in this case *homo* seems to represent either "humanity" or "humankind":

> Because the Word and the flesh constitute one person, the received nature is not divided from the receiving nature; and the honor of the elevated nature is spoken of as an augmentation of the one that promoted it. . . . 'Therefore, God exalted him and gave him a name which is above every name' [Phil. 2:9], which refers to the exaltation of his assumed humanity (*homo*) such that the one who remains indivisible from God in his sufferings is nonetheless coeternal in God's glory.

That Leo intended to use *homo* to represent "humanity" rather than a concrete human individual is clear from a warning with which he caps this statement: "No one who denies that human nature (*humanam . . . naturam*) remains in the Son of God, who is true God, can share in this union."[39] Pope Leo is convinced that the *communicatio idiomatum* of Christ's two natures also passes through Christ to all humans who believe, precisely because all humans share a solidarity

---

38. Serm. 21.1: "auctori suo naturam generis adsumpsit humani"; 21.2: "ut manens quod erat adsumensque quod non erat, ueram serui formam"; 23.3: "Adsumpta est de matre Domini natura, non culpa"; 24.1: "ut Verbum illud coaeternum et aequale genitori in unitatem deitatis suae naturam nostrae humilitatis adsumeret"; and 25.3: "In adsumtione enim naturae nostrae nobis factus est gradus quo ad ipsum per ipsum possimus ascendere."

39. Serm. 72:6–7: "Sed quia Verbum et caro una persona est, non diuiditur a susceptus, et honor prouehendi prouehentis nominatur augmentum, dicente Apostolo quod iam commemorauimus: *Propter quod et Deus illum exaltauit et donauit illi nomen quod est super omne nomen.* In quo utique adsumpti hominis exaltatio commendatur, ut in cuius passionibus indiuisibilis manet Deitas, idem coaeternus sit in gloria Deitatis. . . . Cuius unitatis nullum poterunt habere consortium, qui in Dei Filio Deo uero humanam negant manere naturam."

with Christ's human nature. Because Christ was exalted in his human nature, then, all who believe can share in his exaltation. The sense of this argument is lost if *homo* is rendered concretely as a human individual rather than as human nature in which all humans share. In fact, prior to the year 452, every time Pope Leo used a derivative of *assumptus* with reference to the Son's Incarnation, the pope spoke of the Son assuming human nature or humanity as a whole into the unity of his person. And prior to that time Leo purposely refrained from using *homo* in conjunction with *assumptus*, probably to avoid any affinity with the language of Nestorian Christology.

The fact that Pope Leo used *homo* at all in conjunction with *assumptus* in sermon 28.6, then, should alert us to the possibility of something different there. Taken in the context of sermon 28 as a whole and in the immediate context of 28.6 in particular, all doubt fades concerning Leo's intent to employ *homo* in terms of a concrete human individual. As noted above, in 28.2 he reminded his audience that Jesus' divine nature had no mother and his human nature no father in order to take away the common Monophysite weapon—the traditional "Mother of God" title underscored their contention that only one, divine nature existed in the incarnate Son. Once the pope established the unity of Christ's person in 28.5 he then moved immediately to condemn those who contend that in Christ only the divine nature remained, showing them that if Christ did not have an authentic human nature, all of his human acts were merely play-acting. Leo is now ready in this sermon to establish the full reality of Christ's humanity by declaring that the Son of God assumed a complete man into the unity of his person.

Confronting the Monophysite monks in the East, Pope Leo began to develop the precision in his christological terminology that Augustine had used. But more than that, Leo did not settle with Augustine's vocabulary. As Leo's contact with the Monophysite monks in Palestine and Egypt increased both in frequency and tension, the heat of controversy pushed him to embrace language that is more noticeably in line with Antiochene modes of expressing the Incarnation. He now welcomes the Antiochene *homo assumptus* formula, which he and Cassian earlier feared would lead to the doubling of Sons in Christ, the one who assumed and the one who was assumed.[40]

Pope Leo would eventually discover that the language of his *Tome* had been purposely altered by some of the Egyptian monks in order to emphasize what they considered its Nestorian tendencies.[41] In 457 when these monks murdered the orthodox bishop of Alexandria, Proterius, and filled his seat with the usurper Timothy the Cat, the angry pope responded with his bitter Christmas

40. See Pope Leo's *Epist.* 59.5 (*PL* 54.872); and Cassian's *De incarnatione Domini* 6.15.
41. See G. L. Prestige, "The Greek Translation of the Tome of St. Leo," *Journal of Theological Studies* 31 (1930): 183–184.

sermon against the "Eutychians."[42] There can be no question by this time that Leo had acquired the more precise sense of *homo* as a fully viable human being when he accused the Egyptian monks of denying the full reality of Christ's "human flesh" (*carnis humanae*) and of making him instead a "fake man" (*falsum hominem*) and a passible God.[43]

In the same sermon Pope Leo condemned the Egyptians "who nullify the sacrament of the Lord's Incarnation." He contended that the entire gospel teaches that

> the human race (*humanum genus*) is saved by means of this one sacrament of divine mercy toward those who believe that in the only-begotten Son of God, being equal in everything with the Father and remaining what he was in the assumption of our substance, true God deigned to be what he was not, undeniably a real man (*uerus scilicet homo*), except for the stain of sin. He truly united into himself the reality of our whole and complete nature, consisting in both flesh and soul, when he was conceived in the womb of the Blessed Virgin Mother by means of the Holy Spirit's power.[44]

Pope Leo added unequivocally in the same place that Jesus' humanity governs all the actions that pertain to the properties of his human body, such as sensing hunger, sleeping, weeping, being crucified, dying, and being buried. Likewise, his deity governs all the actions that pertain to the properties of his divine nature, such as performing miracles, rising from the dead, and ascending in his flesh into the heavens. On this basis, the pope contended, it is possible to distinguish Jesus' two natures. Moreover, Leo argued, it is possible to distinguish the operations and the wills of two natures in the single person of Christ; thus the pope answered in advance the Monothelite question of whether Christ has only one will or two. Important to this notion of Christ's two wills is Leo's contention that Jesus' moral decisions pertain to his human will. This moral dimension of the human soul, expressed in Jesus' human will, is now fully integrated into Leo's understanding of the concrete human being that the Son assumed into the unity of his person.[45] At this point Bartnik seems correct that Leo used *homo* to designate the moral and psychic autonomy of Christ's humanity.[46] Here the pope's christological language reached its maturity. When

---

42. It should be noted that the Egyptians did not identify themselves with Eutyches but with Cyril of Alexandria. The title "Eutychians" is Leo's own caricature of them.
43. Serm. 96.1: "asserentes solam deitatis in Christo fuisse naturam, nec carnis humanae, quam sumpsit ex beata Maria uirgine, habuisse penitus ueritatem, quae impietas at falsum hominem et Deut dicit esse passibilem."
44. Serm. 96.2: "qui incarnationis dominicae denegant sacramentum: quod unigenitus Dei Filius, aequalis per omnia Patri, nostrae adsumptione substantiae, manens quod erat, dignatus esse quod non erat, uerus scilicet homo, uerus Deus, qui absque cuiusquam sorde peccati, integram sibi nostram perfectamque naturam ueritate et animae at carnis uniuit, et intra uterum beatae uirginis matris Spiritus sancti uirtute conceptus, nec editionem partus, nec primordia fastidiuit infantiae."
45. Ibid.
46. Bartnik, "Teologii Historii u Leona Wielkiego," pp. 37–38.

discussing the Incarnation, Leo now consistently uses *humanus* or one of its derivatives when he wishes to emphasize elements that pertain to human nature generally, and he uses *homo* when addressing the person of Christ in his concrete human situation.

In an attempt to guard his language from the charge of Nestorianism, Pope Leo assured his congregation in the same place that there is no reason to wonder what actions to ascribe to Christ's humanity or what we ought to assign to his deity, "because Christ is one and the same person who did not lose the power of his deity when he assumed the reality of a complete human being (*perfectus homo*) at his birth."[47] Notice the clear use of *homo* to indicate a complete human being in this expression of the unity of Christ's person. Leo used *perfectus* to intensify the fullness of Christ's authentic humanity. Leo insisted on the presence of Christ's two natures in his self-same person, at the same time as he stressed forcefully the absolute completeness of Christ's human nature.

When Leo began his pontificate in the year 440, the christological controversy in the East was in a period of relative calm. Nestorius had been condemned nine years earlier by the Council of Ephesus, at which John Cassian's *De incarnatione Domini*, commissioned by then Archdeacon Leo, was read and received. Rome was indebted to the Alexandrine theologians for their carefully chosen language regarding the unity of Christ's person, for integrating the devotional "Mother of God" title into proper theological usage, and for revealing the dangers inherent in the Antiochene *homo assumptus* formula. It apparently seemed that the Alexandrine theologians provided the terminology with which to frame Western Christology in the East, and their descriptions of the unity of Christ's person seemed unrivaled in Christendom. Sensing the value of Cyril's contribution to Christology, Pope Leo adopted it all into his own vocabulary. He instinctively used the Eastern *Theotokos* title in his own letters and sermons as a means of expressing his own understanding of the indissoluble unity of Christ's person, and he avoided the Antiochene *homo assumptus* formula because of its inherent emphasis on the distinction of Christ's two natures, for which Nestorius was accused of teaching two Sons.

Pope Leo's Western thought patterns could not be fully contained in Cyril's language, however, as Leo slowly came to realize. Following the pattern set for him by Tertullian and Augustine, he also felt it necessary to distinguish Christ's natures and to plead for recognition of the full authenticity of Christ's humanity. Tertullian stated it clearly in *Adversus Praxeas*: "We see the twofold constitution (*statum*), which is not confused, but conjoined in one person, Jesus, God and human. . . . Now the properties of each substance are fully preserved, such

---

47. Ibid.: "ut qui haec credunt, dubitare non possint quid humanitati adscribere, quid debeant adsignare deitati, quia in utroque unus est Christ, qui et Deitatis suae potentiam non amisit, et ueritatem perfecti hominis nascendo suscepit."

that the Spirit [that is, the divine substance] executed everything in Jesus that corresponds to [his deity], such as miracles and works and signs, whereas the flesh governed his passions: sensing hunger under the devil's [temptation], being thirsty with the Samaritan woman, weeping over Lazarus, being anxious about his own death, and finally dying."[48] Tertullian's bitter struggle with Gnosticism brought him to emphasize the distinction between Christ's two natures in order to underscore the reality of Jesus' true humanity, but he did not consider Christ's distinct natures separable; so also the African theologian rejected the notion that there are "two Christs."[49] In fact, he argued that the unity of Christ's natures is so intimate that we may use the *communicatio idiomatum* to describe it; as a result, Tertullian attributed the crucifixion and death of Christ to the Son of God himself.[50]

Bishop Augustine of Hippo closely followed the course set by Tertullian. According to Augustine—in a passage Pope Leo cited in a *florilegium* he collected for Emperor Leo the Great—we ought to

> recognize the twofold substance of Christ: the divine, through which he is equal to God; and the human, to which the Father is superior. Yet together they are not two, but one Christ, lest God become fourfold rather than threefold. Just as the rational soul and the flesh constitute one human, so there is one Christ, God and human. On this basis, Christ is God, rational soul and [human] flesh. We confess Christ in this totality and in each constitutive part (*in singulis*). Who is the one, therefore, through whom the world was made? Christ Jesus, but in the form of God. Who was crucified under Pontius Pilate? Christ Jesus, but in the form of a servant. In the same way, who, being of the same constitutive parts of which a human consists, was left in hell (*in inferno*)? Christ Jesus, but only in his soul. Who was resurrected after lying in the tomb for three days? Christ Jesus, but only in his flesh. Thus he is called Christ in each of his constitutive parts. Yet the totality of these parts is not two or three, but one Christ.[51]

Herein Augustine carefully balanced the recognition of Christ's two natures

---

48. Tertullian, *Adversus Praxeas* 27.6 (*Corpus Christianorum*, series Latina [hereafter *CCL*] [Turnhout, Belgium, 1953–]2.1199–2000): "Videmus duplicem statum, non confusum sed coniunctum in una persona, Deum et hominem Iesum . . . et adeo salua est utriusque proprietas substantiae, ut et Spiritus res suas egerit in illo, id est virtutes et opera et signa, et carro passiones suas functa sit, esuriens sub diabolo, sitiens sub Samaritide, flens Lazarum, anixa ad mortem, denique et mortua est."
49. Tertullian, *De carne Christi* 24.1–4 (*CCL* 2.915–916).
50. Ibid., 5.1–4 (*CCL* 2.880–881).
51. Augustine, *Tractatus 78: Comm. in Joann.* 14.27.28: "Agnoscamus geminam substantiam Christi, divinam scilicet qua aequalis est Patri; humanam, qua maior est Pater. Utrumque autem simul non duo, sed unus est Christus: ne sit quaternitas non Trinitas Deus. Sicut enim unus est homo anima rationalis et caro, sic unus est Christo, Deus et homo: ac per hoc Christus est, Deus, anima rationalis et caro. Christum in his omnibus, Christum in singulis confitemur. Quis est ergo per quem factus est mundus? Christus Jesus, sed in forma Dei. Quis est sub Pontius Pilato crucifixus? Christus Jesus, sed in forma servi. Item de singulis quibus homo constat. Quis non est derelictus in inferno? Christus Jesus, sed in anima sola. Quis resurrecturus triduo iacuit in sepulchro? Christus Jesus, sed in carne sola. Dicitur ergo in his singulis Christus. Verum haec omnia non duo vel tres sed unus est Christus." Compare Pope Leo's citation of this passage in Epist. 165 (*PL* 54.1181).

238 CHURCH HISTORY

and the intimate unity these natures share in his single person. Christ's natures are united and woven together from both his humanity and his deity into the same person, Jesus Christ.[52] As Tertullian had done before him, Augustine explained this unity by way of the *communicatio idiomatum* formula. The unity of Christ's person consists in each nature, the divine and the human, such that each of them shares its predicates with the other.[53]

Pope Leo followed this tradition and intensified it by using the Alexandrine "Mother of God" title to express it. Through his theological advisor, Prosper of Aquitaine, Pope Leo should have had access to Augustine's precise christological vocabulary. Prosper is famous for his defense of Augustine's doctrine of grace and for his friendship with the great bishop of Hippo. By dint of his relationship with Augustine, Prosper was able to compel the aging bishop to write two works against the Semi-Pelagians in Gaul.[54] In the first of these two works, written for Prosper and for his friend Hilary, Augustine outlined the sum of his christological vocabulary as his Christology impinges on his notion of grace.[55] It is surprising, then, that it took Prosper and Leo so long to develop the kind of precision found throughout Augustine's works, since the two could have had this precision all along by referring more closely to documents they had at their disposal, one of which was written directly to Prosper by Augustine. If the chorus of scholars who suggest that Prosper took an active role in helping Leo write many of his letters and sermons is correct, one would expect to see greater evidence of Augustine's precision of thought and expression in these documents; but there is no such evidence until very late in Leo's pontificate. Perhaps Prosper and Leo were unaware that Augustine's christological language was as finely tuned as was his language on grace, although it seems just as likely that both Prosper and Leo were satisfied with the more devotional terminology the pope was using in the pulpit and in his letters. Either way, it is clear that Leo made no progress toward greater precision until he was dragged into the christological controversy in the East after his *Tome* was published. Eventually Leo and Prosper discovered that his devotional language was insufficient in those mean times and that greater christological precision was needed.

After Pope Leo's orthodoxy came into question in the East among the monks and theologians affiliated with Alexandria, the pope—probably with Prosper's help—began to fine-tune his vocabulary in order to prove his orthodoxy while simultaneously seeking to preserve his position as a mediating influence between the theologians of Alexandria and Antioch. Early in his pontificate,

52. Augustine, *Enchiridion* 10.35 (*PL* 40.250): "idemque ipse utrumque ex utroque unus Christus."
53. Augustine, *Contra sermonem quemdam Arianorum* 8.6 (*PL* 42.688).
54. Augustine, *De praedestinatione sanctorum* (*PL* 44.959–992); *De dono perseverantiae* (*PL* 45.993–1034). Prosper's request to Augustine is in Prosper of Aquitaine, *Ep. ad Augustinum de reliquiis Pelagianae* (*PL* 44.947–954).
55. Augustine, *De praedestinatione sanctorum* 30.15 (*PL* 44.981–982).

246

due in part to the position taken by John Cassian in favor of Alexandrine Christology and against Nestorianism and in part to Leo's respect for Cyril of Alexandria, the pope had distanced himself from the Antiochene *homo assumptus* formula. He relied instead on devotional language, such as the traditional *Theotokos* title, to emphasize—sometimes with great hyperbole—the indissoluble unity of Christ's person, as Leo thought the Alexandrine theologians were doing. After Cyril died, however, his banner was picked up by less capable Alexandrine theologians like Eutyches and Dioscorus, who both taught that in the incarnate Christ there was only a single, incarnate nature, in which the sole operating principle was the divine Word.

The powerful Monophysite movement, which grew out of this mutation of Cyril's Christology in the East, showed Pope Leo the limitations of Cyril's vocabulary to express the fullness of the doctrine of Christ Leo inherited from the Western fathers. In response to the Monophysite movement and the political intrigue of the Monophysite monks in Palestine and Egypt, the pope began to distance himself from the Alexandrine theologians. As Eutyches and the Monophysite theologians who followed him took up the "Mother of God" title as their slogan and battle cry, Leo himself prescinded completely from using it. Nevertheless, Leo continued to iterate the *communicatio idiomatum* formula which was paramount in the Western emphasis on the unity of Christ's person, at the same time as he maintained the Western distinction of Christ's two natures. However, balancing these two emphases severely strained the language Leo used to express his doctrine of Christ. In order to ease this strain on his vocabulary, then, Leo began to distinguish the terms *homo* and *humanus.* This distinction made possible the use of the term *homo* to indicate a concrete human individual, whereas he had consistently used the term previously in christological discussion as a synonym of *humanus* to express the general qualities Jesus shares with all humans. Moreover, in Leo's attempt to underscore his more precise usage of the term *homo* and possibly to set in relief his opposition to the Monophysite movement, Leo began to use the same Antiochene *homo assumptus* formula he had purposely avoided during his early pontificate. With this formula the pope could make clear his expressions of Christ's authentic humanity by declaring that the Son of God assumed into the unity of his person a complete "man," consisting of body, soul, mind, and will. Used in conjunction with the Western *communicatio idiomatum,* which the West holds in common with Alexandrine Christology, the Antiochene *homo assumptus* formula provided Leo with the necessary framework to reestablish and to protect the mediating force of the Western christological tradition in the East.

Journal of Ecclesiastical History, Vol. 43, No. 1, January 1992

'Frequenter Legere'
The Propagation of Literacy,
Education, and Divine Wisdom in
Caesarius of Arles

by ALBERTO FERREIRO

Of the literary bequest from the Middle Ages, homilies provide one of the more useful tools in helping us to understand the medieval mind, at least from the perspective of the Church. Homilies provide us with insight on a number of levels, extending well beyond the personal viewpoint of those who wrote and preached them. They also clearly reflect the values, aspirations, and concerns of an era. Homilies are particularly valuable, especially if one has them in large numbers, because they are generally addressed to people of both genders, of all ages, and from every stratum of society. This is especially true of the large corpus of homilies attributed to Bishop Caesarius of Arles who directed his attention to both laity and clergy of all ranks with the aim of encouraging reading in order to promote literacy and divine wisdom. The Caesarian homiliary that survives from the early Middle Ages, is an enviable collection of documents.[1]: one need only consider the scarcity of this type of source for contemporary Visigothic Spain. Homilies did exist in that period in Spain, but the ravages of time and man have caused so much to disappear.

A few preliminary observations on the Caesarian homilies need to be made. The bishop of Arles did not personally write all the homilies. In

I am grateful to Professor Jeffrey B. Russell for his useful suggestions and comments on this article. However, I alone bear the responsibility for its content. A version of this paper was read at the international conference on monastic studies, *Espacios y Tiempo en el Monacato*, 5–10 December 1988 in León. I wish to thank Seattle Pacific University for subsidising the trip.

[1] See J. N. Hillgarth's remarks on 'Saints' Lives', which I believe have equal relevance for the homiletical sources: 'Modes of evangelization of Western Europe in the seventh century', in Próinséas Ni Chatháin and Michael Richter (eds), *Ireland and Christendom: the Bible and the missions*, Stuttgart 1987, 315–17.

some cases he used the sermons of others, especially of St Augustine, which he then adapted, frequently adding his own introductions or conclusions.[2] Those sermons which he wrote *in toto* fall into a number of categories, but both, amended or original, were often meant to be 'models' for use well beyond Caesarius' own diocese. Others reflect very specific local concerns, but even these could serve as model sermons. The bishop certainly intended his homilies to be distributed as widely as possible. The *Vita Caesarii* informs us that he ordered that the sermons should be copied and distributed in 'Francia, Germania, Italia et Hispania'.[3] Further, in *Sermo 2* he urges that his sermons be read frequently, that others be carefully taught from them and that they should then be passed on for further reading and transcription.[4] In the same sermon he continues: 'If these [books] are not displeasing you can and should copy them in careful handwriting and on parchment of as high quality as your means allow. Give them to other parishes too to be copied. For this you will be doubly rewarded in the [spiritual] progress of others as well as in your own.'[5] The proliferation of Caesarius' sermons in medieval Europe confirms that his admonition was faithfully carried out in his own day and beyond, but scholars have yet to ascertain the impact of these homilies on the thought and life of medieval society.

One aspect of Caesarius' thought that is intimately related to the homilies is the subject of *lectio*. The purpose of reading in Caesarius has not gone unexplored, as for example in the work of Adalbert de Vogüé and of Pierre Riché in his masterly *Education and Culture*, yet neither deals with the topic *in extenso*.[6] If we are to reach a deeper understanding of Caesarius' pedagogy, the *lectio* must be considered. There are additional questions: to whom did the bishop direct the sermons; what type of reading did he recommend; what did he hope would result from *lectio*? It

[2] See Mary Magdeleine Mueller on Dom Germain Morin's edition of the Caesarian homiliary in *Caesarius of Arles, Sermons 1–238*, Fathers of the Church Series xxxi, xlvii, lxvi, pp. xix, xxiii–xxv.　　[3] *Vita S. Caesarii episcopi*, PL 67. 1021.

[4] 'In cuiuscumque manibus libellus iste venerit, rogo et cum grandi humilitate supplico, ut eum et ipse frequentius legat, et aliis ad legendum et ad transscribendum non solum tradat': *Sancti Caesarii Arelatensis, Sermones*, ed. G. Morin, CCSL ciii–civ (hereafter cited as *Sermo*): *Sermo* 2.1, ciii. 18. The Caesarian corpus in its entirety can be found in *Sancti Caesarii episcopi Arelatensis Opera omnia nunc primum in unum collecta*, ed. G. Morin, 2 vols, Maredsous 1937–42. The most complete bibliography on Caesarius up to 1984 is Alberto Ferreiro. *The Visigoths in Gaul and Spain, A.D. 418–711: a bibliography*, Leiden, 1988, 615–632.

[5] 'Vobis vero si non displicuerint et potestis et debetis et meliori littera et in pergamenis pro vestra mercede transscribere, et in aliis parrochiis ad transcribendum dare, ut non solum de vestro sed etiam de aliorum profectu duplicem mercedem habere possitis': *Sermo* 2.1, ciii. 19.

[6] *Education and Culture in the Barbarian West*, trans. John J. Contreni, Columbia, S. Carolina 1976, 79–99. The title of Adalbert de Vogüé's article, 'Lectiones sanctas libenter audire: silence, reading, and prayer in St. Benedict', *Word and Spirit: a monastic review* vii (1985), 87–107, originally published in *Benedictina* xxvii (1980), 11–26, is misleading since it concerns itself much more with Caesarius than Benedict. Nevertheless, it is very useful on *lectio* in Caesarius.

is fortunate that Caesarius discusses all these questions in several of his homilies on *lectio* as well as in numerous scattered references in the homiliary.

Caesarius did not believe that *lectio* should be restricted to the clergy. The laity were expected to read the divine lessons for themselves, and if they were illiterate these lessons should be read to them. The individuals to whom the homilies were addressed came from various levels of society; that is, not all of them were exclusively from the upper echelons. When Caesarius preached to the clergy he addressed both literate and near-illiterate bishops, abbots, parish priests, and monks. The laity to whom he preached was just as diverse in social standing: literate and illiterate estate owners, merchants, hired labourers, entire families.

In *Sermo 2* the bishop indicates the numerous pedagogical roles the clergy were expected to fulfil as *pastores*.[7] Although his admonitions in regard to *lectio* were initially intended for the clergy in his own diocese, the exhortations were in the form of a 'model', applicable to any parish. Caesarius encouraged deacons to read the sermons to their flock, presbyters especially during the major feast days.[8] The clergy should not just read the sermons to others, they were also to read frequently themselves.[9] If the clergy were to preach or teach effectively, they must make *lectio* a necessary part of their daily life. Caesarius was intent on stemming the tide of clerical ignorance which resulted from not reading the Scriptures and divine lessons. He even suggested that the clergy should review the content of his sermons in order to refresh themselves in proper orthodoxy.[10] If the clergy failed to read or preach the homilies, this

---

[7] *Sermo* 2.1, ciii. 18–19.

[8] 'Pro intuitu paternae pietatis et qualiscumque pastoris sollicitudine admonitiones simplices parochiis necessarias in hoc libello conscripsimus, quas in festivitatibus maioribus sancti presbyteri vel diacones debeant commissis sibi populis recitare': ibid. 18.

[9] Ibid. 19. There are other places where Caesarius stressed the frequency of reading the scriptures and divine lessons. For example: 'quotidianae lectionis': *Sermo* 1.2, ibid. 2 and in the same sermon 'iugiter lectioni' 4, 3; 'si pro amore doctrinae iugiter lectioni et orationi: insistant' 8, 6; 'ubi sine dubio deo vacare, et lectioni vel doctrinae insistere, si volumus studiose attendere, abundantissime possimus reperire', 18, 14. Also in another sermon, 'ita sacerdotes de diversis sanctarum scripturarum montibus assidue legendo verbum dei debent flores decerpere,' and in the same chapter Caesarius concludes, 'Credimus tamen de dei misericordia, quod ita et nobis studium legendi vel praedicandi, et vobis desiderium praestare dignabitur audiendi', *Sermo* 4.4, ibid. 25. See also the references to frequent reading in *Sermo* 6.8, ibid. 36; *Sermo* 8.3, ibid. 44; and in the same sermon 5, 45; *Sermo* 198.3, civ. 800; and in the same sermon 5, 801; *Sermo* 230.4, ibid. 912, 5, 913, and 6, 914; *Sermo* 234.3, 934. Caesarius suggests in one place that the Psalms are to be consulted with frequency, 'Fratres, si frequentius psalmos nostros recurrimus, cogitationibus mundanis aditum claudimus: dominatur psalmus spiritalis, fugit cogitatio carnalis': *Sermo* 238.2, ibid. 950.

[10] 'Et ideo libellum istum annis singulis cum omni diligentia recensete, ut apud deum et apud homines vos possitis absolvere.' More to the point, he adds, 'Et quia necesse est, et satis oportet, ut fidem catholicam omnes non solum clerici sed etiam laici notam habeant, ideo in libellis istis secundum quod sancti patres ipsam fidem catholicam definierunt': *Sermo* 2.1, ciii. 19.

constituted a serious failure of their calling as pastors of Christ. In almost formulaic fashion, the bishop often refers to impressing upon others the lessons that have been learned.[11] To read without any intent to teach would obviously be a selfish accumulation of divine knowledge, a clear contradiction of the ideals of the pastor. We should recall that sharing the divine word could be done both in written and oral form and Caesarius set both clergy and laity an exemplary model by incessantly writing and preaching to his flock.

However, the laity were expected to do much more than just 'listen' to the lessons read to them by the clergy. In *Sermo 6* the bishop of Arles reveals his hopes for the laity both the literate and illiterate.[12] The illiterate were certainly not excused from assimilating divine knowledge, since, according to Caesarius, 'First of all, if an individual is not able to read the divine lessons because he does not know his letters, he can willingly listen to others read them'.[13] Caesarius is not referring here to the 'listening' that would normally take place in church. He encouraged the illiterate laity to hire others to read to them after church. Such arrangements seem to have been quite frequent, for Caesarius does not leave us with the impression that they would cause any difficulty. To drive his point home he mentions a similar practice amongst illiterate merchants who hired literate employees (*mercennarios litteratos*) to help them in their commercial transactions.[14] If merchants could do this for worldly gain, how much more should they do it for spiritual rewards. In *Sermo 6* Caesarius refers to a very familiar image, that of the farmer who may say, 'I am a farmer occupied with earthly work, and am not able to listen nor read the divine lessons'.[15] Here the bishop succinctly targets the literate

---

[11] See n. 33 below.

[12] 'Et ideo, fratres carissimi, vel sic discamus plus animam amare quam carnem, aeterna potius diligere quam caduca. Quicquid enim pro carne laboramus, totum periet: hoc solum perire non poterit, quod unusquisque pro salute animae suae in caelo reposuit. Nemo se ergo excuset, et dicat litteras non scire; ideo non posse dei praecepta conplere': *Sermo* 6.6, ciii. 34.

[13] 'Primum est, quod lectionem divinam etiamsi aliquis nesciens litteras non potest legere, potest tamen legentem libenter audire'. Ibid. 1, 31.

[14] 'Adtendite, rogo vos, fratres, hoc dico quod non ignoratis. Novimus enim aliquos negotiatores, qui cum litteras non noverint, requirunt sibi mercennarios litteratos': ibid. 1, 31. In other sermons, Caesarius refers to the hiring of these literate mercenaries, 'non possit aut ipse legere, aut alios legentes audire?': *Sermo* 6.2, ibid. 31; in the same sermon 8, 36; 'quia et qui litteras non noverunt, si in veritate deum diligunt, requirunt sibi aliquos litteratos qui eis scripturas divinas legere possunt; quam [rem] etiam negotiatores sine litteris frequentius exercere cognovimus, qui sibi mercenarios litteratos conducunt, et illis legentibus vel scribentibus ingentia lucra conquirunt': *Sermo* 8.1, ibid. 41; in the same sermon 5, 45; and finally, 'Nec solum vobis sufficiat quod in ecclesia divinas lectiones auditis: sed etiam in domibus vestris aut ipsi legite, aut alios legentes requirite et libenter audite.': *Sermo* 196.2, civ. 792.

[15] 'Sed dicit aliquis: Ego homo rusticus sum, et terrenis operibus iugiter occupatus sum; lectionem divinam nec audire possum nec legere': *Sermo* 6.3, ciii. 32. In other places the bishop of Arles refers to the frequent excuses parishioners make for not reading,

and illiterate who do not make time to read or be taught. Lay-people, like the clergy, must make time for divine lessons in their daily lives. If we suppose for a moment that someone did indeed heed the bishop's advice, where was this 'extra' reading or listening outside the context of the church to take place?

Caesarius encouraged the laity to read at home with their families or to have someone read the divine lessons to them. He believed that one of the best times to study at home was in the evening, especially during the long winter months; 'when the nights are longer no-one needs so much sleep that he cannot allow at least three hours for reading himself or listening to others read the divine lessons'?[16] It is reasonable to suggest that the literate who were to be responsible for this home study were not necessarily of the clergy; they could just as well have been members of the family. In *Sermo 7* the bishop continued to direct his attention to these matters. As well as reminding his audience to set aside worldly occupations to make room for reading, he adds a further injunction: the laity are to re-read the lessons they have heard at church either that same day or presumably soon after. Caesarius rebukes those in his flock who after going to church forget all that they have heard and return to their homes without any spiritual fruit or profit.[17] Those who attended church, stayed awake and listened attentively still need to have the message reinforced.[18] And what better way to do this than at home amongst friends or family. Caesarius offered some very good sound pedagogical advice that would permit parishioners to clarify, expound, and recall the lessons of that day. This type of instruction was not possible in the somewhat formal setting

---

particularly the lure of worldly pursuits. Caesarius admits that possessions are necessary, but we should not be too involved in acquisition. 'Nos vero, qui absque possessionibus esse non possumus, vel in illis taliter [non] implicemur, ut verbo dei vacare non valeamus': *Sermo* 1.7, ibid. 5; Caesarius comments further on worldly distractions in the same sermon 19, 15; see also *Sermo* 6.1, ibid. 30–1; *Sermo* 7. ibid. 37, and 4, 40; *Sermo* 8.2, ibid. 42 is very instructive: 'Quando enim aliquos ad lectionis studium provocamus, non nulli se excusare conantur dicentes, quod aut propter militiam, aut propter domus suae ordinationem non illis possit vacare divinis lectionibus insistere'. See also *Sermo* 196.1, civ. 792, 2 on the same page, and 5, 794; *Sermo* 198.2, ibid. 799, 3, 800, and 5, 801. In his sermon *In ordinatione episcopi*, Caesarius warns bishops of the dangers of worldly pursuits: 'Observa et vide, ne te mundialis negocii inplicatio ita teneat occupatum, ut verbo dei vacare non possis': *Sermo* 230.5, ibid. 912–13.

[16] 'Quando noctes longiores sunt, quis erit qui tantum possit dormire, ut lectionem divinam vel tribus horis non possit aut ipse legere, aut alios legentes audire?': *Sermo* 6.2, ciii. 31; see also his other references to 'home study' in the same sermon 8, 36; *Sermo* 7.1, 38; *Sermo* 196.2, civ. 792; *Sermo* 198.5, ibid. 801.

[17] 'Nam si statim ubi de ecclesia decesseris, totum quod ab episcopo audisti oblitus fueris, sine fructu venisti ad ecclesiam, sine fructu inanis redis ad domum tuam': *Sermo* 6.8, ciii. 36.

[18] Ibid; *Sermo* 2.1, ibid. 19; *Sermo* 196.2, civ. 792; and especially, 'Lectiones divinas et in ecclesia, sicut consuistis, libenter laudite, et in domibus vestris relegite. Si aliquis ita fuerit occupatus ut ante refectionem scripturae divinae non possit insistere, non eum pigeat in conviviolo suo aliquid de divinis scripturis relegere': *Sermo* 198.5, ibid. 801.

of the church service. In *Sermo 7*, Caesarius reminds his flock that they stand to gain more spiritually if they listen to the divine lessons both at church and in their homes for several hours at night when the daylight hours are short.[19] This advice is found within the context of remarks made to merchants and farmers – an emphatic indication that the laity is foremost in his mind.[20] Since the divine lessons to be re-read at home are not the 'copies' that Caesarius encouraged his monks to distribute, what did the laity take home to read, aside from the Scriptures? Caesarius does not actually say that entire copies of the sermon were available, or that summaries were produced for those who desired them, but it is clear that copies did exist which reiterated what had been taught at church.[21] Caesarius does not explain who did the actual copying of these sermons. Did lay-people hire their own copyists to do this task, or did monks offer such services? These and other questions are left open to speculation, but we are told that such individuals were easily available for hire. Again, just as illiterate merchants pay literate employees, Christians should likewise seek out and pay if need be those who are able to read the Scriptures.[22] What we are not told is whether these literate mercenaries followed this trade on a full-time basis, or whether they worked *ad hoc*.

Before examining the benefits that Caesarius believed *lectio* would provide, it is necessary to consider the problems of *lectio pagana*, a topic that concerned him deeply and one which he referred to in his comments on *lectio*. Modern research has of course given this matter some consideration, again notably that of Riché.[23] Caesarius himself usually addresses the issue within the broader context of pagan rituals and heresy but if we wish to focus more directly upon his commentary on *lectio pagana*, to which there are numerous references in the homiliary, his *Sermo 99*, entitled *On the Ten Plagues*, provides the clearest exposition of his views.[24]

---

[19] 'Quanto magis in spiritalibus lucris non vobis debet sufficere, quod in ecclesia lectiones divinas auditis, sed in domibus et in conviviis vestris et, quando dies breves sunt, etiam aliquibus horis in noctibus lectioni divinae debetis insistere': *Sermo* 7.1, ciii. 38.

[20] The most direct of the references to the laity is that found in *Sermo* 8.2, ibid. 42; see note 15 above.

[21] Especially note where Caesarius says, 'quod in ecclesia lectiones divinas auditis, sed in domibus et in conviviis vestris': *Sermo* 7.1, ibid. 38; another similar reference, 'Nec solum vobis sufficiat quod in ecclesia divinas lectionis auditis: sed etiam in domibus vestris aut ipsi legite': *Sermo* 196.2, civ. 792.

[22] 'Christiani debent sibi requirere et rogare, et si necesse est, etiam et mercedem dare, ut illis aliquis debeat scripturam divinam relegere': *Sermo* 6.8, ciii. 36.

[23] *Education and Culture*, 79–99, but esp. pp. 86–95 on Caesarius.

[24] *Sermo* 99.1–3, ciii. 403–6; see also Alberto Ferreiro, 'Early medieval missionary tactics: the example of Martin of Braga and Caesarius of Arles', *Studia Historica. Historia antiqua* vi (1988), 225–38. Other useful studies related to Caesarius and general contemporary attitudes are those of E. Mâle, *La Fin du paganisme en Gaule et les plus anciennes basiliques chrétiennes*, Paris 1950; P. Audin, 'Césaire d'Arles et le maintien de pratiques païennes dans la Provence du VIe siècle', *La Patrie Gauloise d'Agrippa au VIème siècle*, Actes

The sermon is an allegorical interpretation of the *Ten Plagues* as found in Exodus. Caesarius refers to Moses and the Egyptian priests as representatives of the two forms of wisdom that are present in the world; Moses is symbolic of the heavenly wisdom that is God-sent while the Egyptian priests symbolise earthly, diabolical wisdom.[25]

Thus when Moses confronted the Egyptian priests, the conflict was not simply mortal; rather, it was a duel between the powers of darkness and light, of God and Satan. In one such confrontation, Moses and the priests engaged one another with their staffs in an attempt to prove the respective superiority of their God[s]. The staff of Moses represents the wisdom of Christ, the new wisdom, while the staffs of the Egyptians are those of Satan and his demonic hordes.[26] When Moses cast down his staff it is miraculously transformed into a serpent. The Egyptians, unafraid, were able to simulate the miracle. Then, the staff of Moses, now a serpent, seized upon the serpents of the Egyptians and devoured them all. This is the crucial moment for Caesarius, and he is ready to point out that the serpent of Moses symbolised a wisdom so great that it devoured all the wisdom of the Egyptians and the world.[27] Caesarius believed that the legacy of antiquity was, without exception, completely useless. As I have pointed out in a previous study, the bishop draws no distinction between the 'safe' and 'unsafe' classics.[28] The Christian has only one option in this matter: complete rejection of pagan learning in all its forms, for it is the fruit of the fallen nature of humanity, spiritual darkness, and a dead wisdom which vainly gropes in utter darkness for the truth. Moreover, 'All authors of heresy and inventors of false religion in this world have together been extinguished by the truth of Christ.'[29] In the coming of

du Colloque, Lyon 1981, Lyon 1983, 327–40; E. Griffe, 'A travers les paroisses rurales de la Gaule au VIe siècle', *Bulletin de littérature ecclésiastique*, lxxvi (1975), 3–26; and, more fundamental still, H. G. J. Beck, *The Pastoral Care of Souls in Southeast France in the Sixth Century*, Rome 1950.

[25] 'Virga vero, per quam Aegyptus subicitur et Pharao superatur, crucis Christi imaginem praeferebat, per quam mundus hic vincitur, et princeps huius mundi cum principatibus et potestatibus triumphatur': *Sermo* 99.1, ciii. 403. Although the staff belonged to Moses, it was Aaron who actually carried out the 'duel', working as Moses's spokesman, which explains why Scripture refers to Aaron's staff (or rod): Ex. vii. 6–13. I touched upon the staff and the encounter with the Egyptian priests in 'Job in the Sermons of Caesarius of Arles', *Recherches de théologie ancienne et médiévale*, liv (1987), 15 n. 8; *Sermo* 95.8, ciii. 392.

[26] 'idcirco virga Moysi, id est, crux Christi postea quam ad terras descendit, id est, postea quam ad credulitatem et fidem hominum venit, conversa est in sapientiam': *Sermo* 99.1, ibid. 403.

[27] 'et tantam sapientiam, quae omnem Aegyptiorum, id est, huius mundi sapientiam devoraret': ibid.　　[28] 'Early medieval missionary tactics', 234–7.

[29] 'Omnes hereticorum auctores et inventores falsarum quae in hoc mundo fuerunt religionum, quas Christi veritas cum suis extinguit auctoribus': *Sermo* 99.2 ciii. 405; in the same sermon we read, 'Ad ultimum primogenitorum infertur interitus. Primogenita Aegyptiorum non incongrue principatus et potestates mundi huius, id est, diabolus et angeli eius intelleguntur, quos in adventu suo Christus traduxisse dicitur, id est, captivos duxisse et triumphasse in ligno crucis suae': 2, 405.

Christ, in the cross and baptism, all forms of worldly wisdom have been destroyed.[30] Caesarius' plenary condemnation is completed by identifying each of the 'Ten Plagues' with the various forms of worldly wisdom: for example the plague of frogs represents the 'poets' whose so-called eloquence is nothing more than meaningless croaking; the plague of 'sciniphs' refers to philosophical skills, as used by heretics whose smooth-talking eloquence masks dead wisdom; the plague of dog-flies represents the Stoics.[31] Since the high purpose of *lectio* is to feed the spirit, what place could classical letters possibly occupy in the life of the believer? In Caesarius' list of suggested readings there is only the Scriptures, the Fathers, church-related writings (such as homilies), and the like. If the laity and clergy did not heed his advice on reading, the consequences would be serious.

Caesarius did not intend *lectio* simply to be a way of self-fulfilment; he had much loftier goals and perceived *lectio* to be of utmost importance in the life of the believer, lay or cleric. In *Sermo 1*, he indicates that *lectio* for one's spiritual fulfilment is but one step in the growth of the individual. If the believer does not share what he has learned, then he is not achieving what God had intended. A frequent commentator on almsgiving,[32] he goes so far as to state that sharing divine wisdom is an alm of sorts. He says that there are two types of almsgiving: one is to extend food to the hungry, the other is to provide instruction to the ignorant.[33] Keeping what one has

[30] 'Decima plaga primogenita percutiuntur: in quibus aut spiritales nequitiae aut originalia peccata intellegi possunt, quae veniente Christo per mysterium crucis et gratiam baptismi deleri vel extingui manifestissime conprobantur': ibid. 3, 406.

[31] 'Secunda vero plaga, in qua inducuntur ranae, indicari figuraliter arbitror carmina poetarum, qui inani quadam et inflata modulatione velut ranarum sonis et cantibus mundo huic deceptionis fabulas intulerunt: ad nihil enim animal illud utile est, nisi quod sonum vocis inprobis et inportunis clamoribus reddit. Post hoc scynifes producuntur … Hoc ergo animalis genus dignissime arti philosophiae vel haereticorum calliditati poterit comparari … Quarto quoque in loco cynomia, id est, musca canina invenitur, quae cynicorum sectae merito comparatur, qui ad reliquas deceptionis suae inprobitates etiam voluptatem et libidinem summum praedicant bonum': ibid. 2, 404; Caesarius also used two Augustinian sermons on the Ten Plagues. These are found in this edition immediately after Sermon 99 and are numbered 100 and 100a.

[32] On almsgiving in Caesarius see Anne-Marie Abel, 'La pauvreté dans la ensée et la pastorale de Saint Césaire d'Arles', in Michel Mollat (ed.) *Études sur l'histoire de la pauvreté jusqu'au XVIe s*, Paris 1974. 111–121; also my 'Job in the Sermons of Caesarius of Arles', wherein Job was portrayed by Caesarius as the exemplar of almsgiving, 13 26; see also, p. 20 n. 29 for a partial listing of Caesarius' references to almsgiving; for the conciliar legislation, including modern research on the topic, see pp. 21–2 n. 32.

[33] 'Non possumus, inquit, largiores eleemosynas facere. Pietatem vestram rogo, ut diligenter consideretis quod suggero. Sicut enim optime nosti, duo sunt eleemosynarum genera: unum est, ut esurienti porrigatur buccella; aliud, quod ignoranti subministretur doctrina': *Sermo* 1.8, ciii. 6. Equally instructive is, 'Fortasse panem ut indigenti elimosinam porrigat non habet, sed maius est quod tribuere valet qui linguam habet: plus est enim verbi pabulo vivituram in perpetuum mentem reficere, quam ventrem moriturae carnis terreno pane satiare. Nolite ergo, fratres proximis vestris elimosinam verbi subtrahere': *Sermo* 8.5, ibid. 45.

learned to oneself can put the soul in peril. Priests are warned about not sharing the divine lessons and thereby through negligence creating a famine of the Word of God. At the Day of Judgement, Caesarius warns, the souls of those who perished may be required of them.[34] The role of the priest, as pastor, is to care for the flock as a shepherd guards his sheep. He eloquently reminds the clergy, 'If we are in truth shepherds, we ought to provide spiritual pastures for the Lord's flock.'[35]

Caesarius stresses that *lectio* is crucial to the soul and to one's standing before God. Using the farmer as example, the bishop effectively communicates his point. He asks why the believer is not as concerned for the soul as he is concerned for the well-being of an estate. He states that all believers should 'plough and plant' the Word of God in their hearts;[36] they have in fact no choice in this matter for it is a divine mandate that all are expected to fulfil. The relationship between God and the believer, according to Caesarius, is not as contractual as it seems. The spiritual cultivation of the soul is to be undertaken in co-operation with God. In *Sermo 6* Caesarius tells us, 'I beg you brothers to pay attention. There are two kinds of fields: one field belongs to God, the other to man; you have your own farm, God has His. Your farm is your land, God's farm is your soul.'[37]

The believer thus carries an enormous responsibility. To neglect *lectio* is to deny God access to what ultimately belongs to Him, the soul. The actual spiritual planting lies in the hands of the believer; to heed Caesarius' advice means the reward of divine wisdom and eternal life. The bishop encourages believers to pursue their goals with earnest conviction,

---

[34] 'Metuendum est enim, ne, quanticumque per neglegentiam passi famem verbi dei perierint, omnium illorum animae de nostris animabus in die iudicii requirantur': *Sermo* 1.15, ibid. 12; also in the same sermon, priests are reminded that as Christ told Peter, they are to 'feed my sheep': 11, 7; and Caesarius reminds the clergy of the peril the soul is put under on account of holding back the Word.' 'Hoc enim ideo timens dico, quia certus sum sic mori animam sine verbo dei, quomodo caro moritur sine cibo terreno': 17, 14. Other references that point to similar concerns are: 'Quomodo enim caro reficitur cibo isto terreno, sic et anima pascitur dei verbo': *Sermo* 4.3, ibid. 24; in the same sermon he tells priests to feed the people the Old and New Testaments: 4, 24, and towards the end of that section on p. 25 is an admonition to feed the soul. The bishop likens a deprived soul to a tortured slave. 'tamquam vile mancipium sine pabulo verbi dei fame et siti cruciare cognosticur': *Sermo* 7.4, ibid. 40; *Sermo* 8.1, ibid. 42. Finally, bishops are reminded of their roles as shepherds: *Sermo* 230.5, civ. 913.

[35] 'Si in veritate pastores sumus, gregi dominico spiritalia pascua providere debemus': *Sermo* 1.19, ciii. 15.

[36] This metaphor is eloquently expounded upon by Caesarius in *Sermo* 6.4–5, ciii. 32–3. He is also quick to note that clergy, especially bishops, can become distracted by the tasks of managing large estates and farms. The primary duty of the bishop is to cultivate souls, not fields: 'Neque enim te Christus hodie cultorem agrorum, sed pastorem constituit animarum': *Sermo* 230.5, civ. 913.

[37] 'Adtendite, rogo vos, fratres, duo genera agrorum sunt: unus ager est dei, alter est hominis. Habes tu villam tuam, habet et deus suam; villa tua est terra tua, villa dei est anima tua': *Sermo* 6.5, ciii. 33.

for God has entrusted our souls to us in order that we should zealously cultivate them, and the main way to do this is through *lectio*.[38] What one does now, or neglects to do, will be reckoned by God in the final days. Caesarius sombrely, but with some optimism, states that believers should labour with God's help to cultivate the field, which is the soul, so that He may find a fine harvest; not one overtaken by thorns, vinegar, and darnel, but one of wine and wheat.[39] If the Christian is to fulfil God's precepts, the *lectio* is the primary way to achieve this goal.

Although the fear of judgement is used by Caesarius to motivate his audience to read, he balances this by describing what he believes is God's attitude towards His creatures. He refers to the Scriptures, as well as to divine lessons, as personal attempts by a loving heavenly Father who wishes to speak to his children. Reading is much more than an encounter with the words of ancient wisdom or the teachings of venerable wise men; rather, it is an opportunity to speak with God. In *Sermo 8* we are told by Caesarius, 'diligently observe that he who reads frequently and listens to the divine Scripture, speaks with God'.[40] So, if one does not read the Scriptures or listen to them, then one is refusing to speak with God – an unthinkable act for one who claims to be a believer. No wonder the bishop of Arles repeatedly spoke out against slothfulness in reading, falling asleep in church, or preoccupation with worldly pursuits at the expense of the soul. In the same sermon Caesarius warns those who are spiritually lazy that they are audacious in believing or expecting God to grant them their eternal reward, when in this life they have refused to speak with Him through divine reading.[41]

Caesarius' attitude towards Scripture explains his impassioned pleas to his flock to read, to undertake the amazing privilege of conversing with God. In what is probably one of his most touching pastoral messages, one that emphasises the closeness that God feels with his people, Caesarius refers to God's Word as a letter from heaven to the soul, whose true home is in heavenly places. He adds, 'beloved brothers listen to me carefully and understand that the divine Scriptures are sent to use like letters from our [heavenly] country'.[42] The concept of the Scriptures as 'letters' carries

[38] 'animam nostram quasi villam suam nobis dignatus est committere deus, ut illam omni studio debeamus excolere': ibid.

[39] 'Totis ergo viribus cum dei adiutorio laboremus, ut cum deus ad agrum suum, hoc est, ad animam nostram venire voluerit, totum cultum, totum conpositum, totum ordinatum inveniat: messem inveniat, non spinas: vinum inveniat, non acetum: triticum magis quam lolium': ibid.

[40] 'diligenter adtendite, quia ille a quo scriptura divina frequenter aut legitur aut auditur, cum deo loquitur': *Sermo* 8.3, ibid. 44.

[41] 'Ille vero qui hoc implere neglegit, qua fronte aut qua conscientia credit quod deus ei aeternum praemium tribuat, cum quo in hoc saeculo per lectionem divinam loqui dissimulat': ibid.

[42] 'fratres carissimi, diligenter adtendite, quia scripturae divinae quae litterae sunt de patria nostra nobis transmissae': *Sermo* 7.2, ibid. 38. He adds in the same section, 'Patria enim nostra paradisus est: parentes nostri sunt patriarchae et prophetae et apostoli et

with it the idea of intimate immediacy, an attempt by God to invite the believer to speak to Him. Not to do so, apart from the harmful consequences, is to snub God's friendship, to cast away a letter from a friend who longs for an answer.[43]

An examination of *lectio* in Caesarius of Arles helps us to understand the bishop's purpose in his homilies. Reading was not an activity restricted to clerics; as we have seen, the laity were just as obliged to read and share the divine lessons. The illiterate were likewise expected to learn, even if it meant hiring what Caesarius refers to as literate employees. The assimilation of divine wisdom had a two-fold purpose: firstly the personal development of the Christian, the deepening of his relationship with God; secondly the imparting of this wisdom to others. Neither aspect should be neglected by believers. The wisdom of classical antiquity, on the one hand, rendered useless by the wisdom of Christ, should be shunned altogether since the soul would profit nothing from pagan learning.

Through the widespread diffusion of his homilies Caesarius of Arles, like others of his time, fostered the sanctification of *lectio* and study, even though he restricted it to the Scriptures and to the divine. Thus he contributed to that sanctification of reading which, in the long term, and as found in the monasteries, was to institutionalise the idea that learning, particularly when expanded beyond the scriptural, was an activity God expected of his followers.

martyres: cives enim angeli, rex noster Christus est... scripturas divinas velut invitatorias ad nos per patriarchas et prophetas dignatus est mittere, quibus nos ad aeternam et principalem patriam invitaret.'

[43] 'Cum haec ita sint, fratres carissimi, quid de se cogitant servi qui ita praesumunt domini sui praecepta contemnere, ut nec ipsa invitatorias litteras quibus ad regni beatitudinem eos invitat dignentur relegere?': *Sermo* 7.3, ibid. 39.

THE LANGUAGE OF IMAGES:
THE RISE OF ICONS AND CHRISTIAN
REPRESENTATION*

by AVERIL CAMERON

INTRODUCTION

ONE has to be brave to return to the subject of Byzantine Iconoclasm, a subject which, we may feel, has been done to death.[1]
But the division in Byzantine society which lasted off and on for
over a century, from 726 to the 'restoration of orthodoxy' in 843, was so
profound that any Byzantine historian must at some time try to grapple
with it. This is especially so if one is trying to understand the immediately
preceding period, from the Persian invasions of the early seventh century
to the great sieges of Constantinople by the Arabs in 674–8 and 717. It is
well recognized by historians that this was a time of fundamental social,
economic, and administrative change, which coincided with, but was by
no means wholly caused by, the loss of so much Byzantine territory to the
Arabs.[2] However, the connection, if any, of this process of change with
the social and religious upheaval known as Iconoclasm still leaves much to
be said; indeed, no simple connection is likely in itself to provide an
adequate explanation. In this paper I want to explore further some of the
background to the crisis, without attempting here to provide a general

---

* Earlier versions of the present paper were given at the Institute of Classical Studies, London,
the Collège de France, and at the Symposium on 'The Holy Image', organized by Professors
H. Belting and H. Kessler at Dumbarton Oaks, 27–9 April 1990.
[1] See, for instance, Anthony Bryer and Judith Herrin, eds, *Iconoclasm* (Birmingham, 1977);
D. Stein, *Der Beginn des byzantinischen Bilderstreites und seine Entwicklung in die 40er Jahre des 8
Jahrhunderts* (Munich, 1980); S. Gero, *Byzantine Iconoclasm during the Reign of Leo III* (Louvain,
1973) and *Byzantine Iconoclasm during the Reign of Constantine V* (Louvain, 1978); A. Grabar,
L'Iconoclasme byzantin (Paris, 1957); Robin Cormack, *Writing in Gold* (London, 1985).
[2] See now John Haldon, *Byzantium in the Seventh Century. The Transformation of a Culture* (Cambridge, 1990), with his earlier articles 'Some remarks on the background to the Iconoclast
Controversy', *Byzantine Studies*, 38 (1977), pp. 161–84, and especially 'Ideology and social
change in the seventh century: military discontent as a barometer', *Klio*, 68 (1986), pp. 139–
90; Alan Harvey, *Economic Expansion in the Byzantine Empire 900–1200* (Cambridge, 1989),
pp. 15–34. The contrasting view (emphasizing continuity) put forward by W. E. Kaegi, Jr.,
'Visible Rates of Seventh-century Change', in F. M. Clover and R. S. Humphreys, eds, *Tradition and Innovation in Late Antiquity* (Madison, Wisc., 1989), pp. 191–208, depends mainly on
institutional and military evidence from the reign of Heraclius itself and does not conflict
with the perception of profound change over a longer period (see further below).

261

explanation for Iconoclasm itself. I shall not venture beyond the first phase of Iconoclasm, which ended with the Second Council of Nicaea in 787, and after which the argument is somewhat different. Indeed, I shall be focusing here not even on the period known as 'first Iconoclasm', but mainly on the preceding period, when the issues inherent in the controversy were already, and increasingly, making themselves felt. Though we shall inevitably be concerned with some of the arguments brought against icons by their opponents, it is the place of images themselves in the context of the pre-Iconoclastic period which will be the main issue. Finally, while I want to offer a different way of reading the rise of icons, I do not pretend that it is the only one, or even possibly the most important. I do suggest, though, that it can help us to make sense of some of the issues that were involved.

It is clear that the suspicion of religious images which took such an extreme form in Byzantine Iconoclasm followed a period of intense questioning about the legitimacy of Christian representation.[3] In 691, for example, the well-known canon 82 of the Council in Trullo forbade the representation of Christ as a lamb or otherwise in symbolic form; he was to be depicted only in human form, so that 'we may recall to memory his conversation in the flesh, his passion and salutary death and his redemption which was wrought for the whole world.' Here I should like to broaden the enquiry beyond the immediate iconographical issue. The first part of the paper will argue that in the period of the 'rise of icons', from the later sixth to the eighth centuries, religious images, which were held by iconophiles to represent objective truth, came to be seen as one of the guarantors of knowledge, and were thus an important component in the evolving belief system of Byzantine society at the time.

One of the functions of religion as a cultural system is to provide a way of making sense of the disasters, injustices, and problems with which people are faced in the world. At this time there were indeed many reasons for uncertainty. First, the period from, say, the late sixth century to the beginnings of Iconoclasm (conventionally set in 726) was precisely the time during which Classical Antiquity finally did become Byzantium. The Greek cities, which until the sixth century had still been the centres of culture and education, were either devastated by invasion or else turned into medieval towns. With them went much of the old educational system, and, with it, access to classical books. By the eighth century it was

[3] See on this Charles Barber, 'The Koimesis Church, Nicaea. The limits of representation on the eve of Iconoclasm', *Jahrbuch der österreichischen Byzantinistik* 41 (1991), pp. 43–60.

a difficult thing to get hold of a classical text even in Constantinople itself, let alone the provinces, and in any case, attention was directed to more immediate concerns elsewhere. Of course, one can exaggerate. But it seems that even educated people now had little idea of their past history beyond legend and fantasy. As for the classical statues which still survived in large numbers even in the shrunken city of eighth-century Constantinople, they were often misidentified, misunderstood, and more often feared as potentially dangerous.[4] During this Byzantine Dark Age, Classical Antiquity was no longer part of the average consciousness.

The reign of the Emperor Heraclius (610–41) probably saw the last manifestation of traditional learning for many years to come. During that period scholarly history was still possible, as were classicizing art, epic poetry, and philosophy; by contrast, the next period is so ill-documented that it was hardly known to the chronicler Theophanes or the Patriarch Nicephorus, to whom we owe the basic Byzantine historical accounts.[5] Classicizing literary forms are not to be found again for nearly three centuries, not until after the end of Iconoclasm and the establishment of a new dynasty in Constantinople. Heraclius's reign also saw tremendous reversals: difficult but successful wars against Persia, followed closely by the loss of most of the eastern provinces of the Empire to the Arabs. In the course of these events the holy city of Jerusalem, the location of the True Cross, was lost, regained, and lost again within the space of twenty-five years. The reign ended in a confusion of religious division. The mental dislocation caused by all this can hardly be exaggerated.[6]

Heraclius's campaigns against the Persians were accompanied by a marked amount of eschatological propaganda; affecting as they did the eastern provinces which were to be the focus and crucible for religious change on a scale as yet undreamt of by the unfortunate Byzantines, they stimulated deep soul-searching, expectation, and then disappointment among the local populations.[7] I shall argue here that as well as representing

---

[4] For a fascinating range of examples, see Cyril Mango, 'Antique statuary and the Byzantine beholder', *DOP*, 17 (1963), pp. 53–75.

[5] See the discussion in Cyril Mango, ed., *Patriarch Nikephoros of Constantinople. Short History* (Washington, DC, 1990), pp. 12–18.

[6] See also Averil Cameron, *Christianity and the Rhetoric of Empire* (Berkeley and Los Angeles, 1991), ch. 6, and 'New Themes and Styles in Greek Literature, 7th–8th Centuries', in Averil Cameron and Lawrence I. Conrad, eds, *The Byzantine and Early Islamic Near East I: Problems in the Literary Source Material = Studies in Late Antiquity and Early Islam*, 1 (Princeton, 1991), pp. 81–105.

[7] See Michael Whitby, 'Greek Historical Writing after Procopius: Variety and Vitality', in Cameron and Conrad, *Problems in the Literary Source Material*, pp. 25–80, with the papers by G. J. Reinink and Han Drijvers in the same volume.

a revival of the Church's own longstanding hesitation about religious images, Iconoclasm was a manifestation of an uncertainty which people felt about their own thought-world. As for the extreme proliferation of religious images itself, together with the massive amount of attention which is given to them in the literature of the seventh century onwards, this can be read in its Byzantine context as part of the replacement for the lost horizons of Classical Antiquity, and indeed as part of an urge to assert a new authority.[8] Images form part of the intellectual framework round which we can see Byzantium reorientating itself. They are an important element in a sign-system through which knowledge, no longer accessible in the old way, could still be reliably assessed. Yet the implications of such a realignment were not to be fully realized or accepted without a profound struggle, of which the seventh century reveals many indications; to be aware of its extent, we have only to look at the anxious canons of the Quinisext Council of 691–2, or at some of the question-and-answer literature from the seventh century, which may be taken to reflect contemporary concerns. When official Iconoclasm began, even though it seems to have been mainly imposed from the top and to have lacked real popular support, the religious divisions which it opened up were often bitter and hard to resolve. Moreover, they happened against a background of equally profound administrative, social, and economic change, in the course of which Byzantium shed the structures still remaining from Classical Antiquity and adopted the medieval appearance of the Middle Byzantine State.[9] But having passed through this painful phase, of which Iconoclasm was the culmination, Byzantium can clearly be seen from the ninth century onwards to be entering a phase of renewed confidence and to have found a level of integration which was to permit advances in new directions.

It is mainly during the late sixth and seventh centuries that the veneration of icons seems to have taken off in Byzantium. Few pre-Iconoclastic icons have survived the efforts of the Iconoclasts (the most famous and striking examples come from the monastery on Mount Sinai); nevertheless, the visual evidence that we do have is sufficiently scattered geo-

[8] For this emphasis (against 'decline'), see Robin Cormack, 'Byzantine Aphrodisias. Changing the symbolic map of a city', *Proceedings of the Cambridge Philological Association*, 216, ns 36 (1990), pp. 26–41.
[9] This is particularly stressed by Haldon: see n. 2 above, and for signs of ideological dislocation, see also G. Dagron, 'Le Saint, le savant, l'astrologue. Étude de thèmes hagiographiques à travers quelques recueils de "Questions et réponses des Ve–VIIe siècles"', in *Hagiographie, cultures et sociétés (IVe–VIIe s.)* (Paris, 1981), pp. 143–55; for administrative change see F. Winkelmann, *Byzantinische Rang- und Ämterstruktur im 8. und 9. Jahrhundert = Berliner byzantinische Arbeiten*, 54 (Berlin, 1985); the origins of the highly contentious 'theme-system' also belong to this period.

The Language of Images

graphically, and we have enough references in other sources to the use of icons in public and private contexts to make it clear that this was a widespread contemporary development.[10] While we tend to think of icons typically as portable images painted on wood, it is important to realize that it was neither the material nor its portability that made a picture into an icon; the Greek word *eikon* in itself simply means 'image'. Nor, for this early period, should we think in terms of the arrangement and use of icons familiar from later Byzantine churches or indeed from Orthodox churches today; whereas in later Byzantine times, a set of protocols developed for their subject-matter and types, together with their position in the church and their liturgical use, this had not yet happened in our period, and some churches, including Hagia Sophia in Constantinople, seem to have had no figural decoration among their furnishings.[11] It would, however, appear that in some cases at least portable icons were indeed displayed in churches. We learn, for example, in the seventh-century *Miracles of Artemius*, a collection of miracle stories associated with the Constantinopolitan church of St John the Baptist at Oxeia, of an icon hanging in the left nave of the church, and of the clergy lending an icon to a great lady, who was so devoted to it that she was reluctant to leave the church.[12] But while there seem to have been several icons in this church, they would not yet have been hung on the familiar closed iconostasis, which is also a later development.[13] Several of the images which attracted the hostility of the Iconoclasts in fact took the form of fixed decoration in churches, in mosaic or fresco; it is rather the subject and treatment of the picture that qualifies it for the term 'icon'—surviving early examples include ivories and textiles as well as wall and ceiling decorations and the portable images painted on wood with which we usually associate the term.[14] This fluidity of Greek terms used for visual art means that where the evidence is literary and the object itself has been lost, as is often the

---

[10] See, in particular, E. Kitzinger, 'The cult of images in the period before Iconoclasm', *DOP*, 8 (1950), pp. 85–150; K. Weitzmann, *The Icon. Holy Images—Sixth to Fourteenth Century* (New York, 1978), pp. 7–23. Marlia Mundell, 'Monophysite Church Decoration', in Bryer and Herrin, *Iconoclasm*, pp. 59–74, collects examples of iconic and aniconic decoration in contemporary churches.

[11] On this question see Mundell, 'Monophysite Church Decoration', at p. 70.

[12] *Miracula Artemii* [hereafter *Mir. Art.*] ed. A. Papadopoulos-Kerameus, *Varia graeca sacra* (St Petersburg, 1909), chs 6, 31. For discussion see V. Déroche, 'L'Authenticité de l'"Apologie contre les Juifs" de Léontios de Néapolis', *Bulletin de Correspondance Hellénique*, 110 (1986), pp. 655–69, at pp. 658–9.

[13] See T. F. Mathews, *The Early Churches of Constantinople: Architecture and Liturgy* (University Park, Pennsylvania, 1971), pp. 168ff.

[14] See also Weitzmann, *The Icon*.

Plate 1   Ivory showing the Nativity and the Adoration of the Magi, Syria or
Egypt, sixth century (Medieval and Later Antiquities 1904, 7–2, 1, by courtesy of
the Trustees of the British Museum).

Plate 2   Ivory Diptych of Christ between Saints Peter and Paul and the Virgin Enthroned with Angels, sixth century (Berlin, Staatliche Museen).

case, it can often be difficult to know exactly what medium is being referred to.[15]

What, then, made a Christian work of art into an icon? By the seventh and eighth centuries the argument over *eikones* was understood to refer to holy images which received special veneration, and particularly to images depicting Christ, the Virgin, or the saints, usually in non-narrative

---

[15] For the ambiguity see Averil Cameron, Judith Herrin, *et al.*, eds, *Constantinople in the Eighth Century: the* Parastaseis Syntomoi Chronikai (Leiden, 1984), pp. 31 (as applied to statues), 48–52 (often mentioning different materials used, but still in the same general vocabulary).

Plate 3   Tapestry Panel of the Virgin Enthroned, wool, sixth century (The Cleveland Museum of Art, Leonard C. Hanna, Jr, Fund 67.144).

representations, that is, in the familiar frontal poses adopted in the great Sinai icons of this period representing the Virgin and Child with arch-angels and saints, Christ, and St Peter (colour plate 1 and plates 4 and 5). Similar images, as we have seen, might also appear in fixed form on the walls of churches, whether in mosaic or fresco; famous surviving examples include the mosaic of the Virgin and Child from Kiti in Cyprus, usually dated to the sixth century (plate 6), the seventh-century mosaics from the church of St Demetrius in Thessaloniki (plate 7), and the frescos in the seventh-century Roman church of S. Maria Antiqua. An encaustic icon of the Virgin also survives from the church of S. Maria in Trastavere, in Rome (plate 8). In addition, there is plentiful evidence for small images owned by private individuals, either fixed in their houses or capable of being carried around.[16] The kind of veneration offered to such images is shown in later illustrations; it consisted of *proskynesis* (bowing, kneeling) and *aspasmos* (kissing the image, as today). These practices, too, become more formalized (though still leaving a good deal to individual habit)[17] only after the final defeat of Iconoclasm. That they were already in use in our period is, however, clear from the fact that they are explicitly dis-cussed by Leontius of Neapolis and others in the seventh century, who defended the practice in terms which were later taken up by John of Damascus and by the Second Council of Nicaea.[18] It is interesting to see that the practice of kissing and bowing down before images is associated in these texts with venerating the Cross, a practice which was also becom-ing more important in this period, with the acquisition by Justin II of the fragment of the True Cross from Apamea, and still more with the recovery by Heraclius of the True Cross from Jerusalem after its capture by the Persians, and its subsequent transfer to Constantinople.[19] Again, it

[16] Cyril Mango, *The Art of the Byzantine Empire, AD 312 to 1453* (Englewood Cliffs, 1972), pp. 113ff., 133–41, gives an excellent introduction to the literary evidence.

[17] See Bishop Kallistos of Diokleia, 'The Meaning of the Divine Liturgy for the Byzantine Worshipper', in R. Morris, ed., *Church and People in Byzantium* (Birmingham, 1990), p. 13.

[18] Mansi, 13, 284A–B; cf. 377E; see N. Baynes, 'The Icons before Iconoclasm', *HThR*, 45 (1951), pp. 93–106, repr. in his *Byzantine Studies and Other Essays* (London, 1955), pp. 226–39, at pp. 232–4. For John of Damascus, veneration of icons, veneration of the Cross, and praying towards the East are main issues. With the increasing awareness of Islam among Christian writers the justification of *proskynesis* becomes even more of an urgent theme.

[19] Justin II: Michael the Syrian, *Chronicle*, ed. J. B. Chabot, 4 vols (Paris, 1899–1910), 2, p. 285 for Jerusalem, see further below. *Mir. Art.*, ch. 33, refers to the adoration of the Cross as a regular rite, and the Feast of the Exaltation of the Cross seems to have received a special impetus with its restoration by Heraclius. See, in general, A. Frolow, *La Relique de la vraie croix. Recherches sur le développement d'un culte* (Paris, 1961), and see Averil Cameron, 'Byzantium in the Seventh Century. The Search for Redefinition', in J. Fontaine and J. Hillgarth, eds, *The Seventh Century: Change and Continuity* (London, forthcoming).

Plate 4   Encaustic Icon of the Virgin Enthroned between St Theodore and St George, Monastery of St Catherine, Mount Sinai (by permission of Princeton University Press).

Plate 5   St Peter, Monastery of St Catherine, Mount Sinai (by permission of Princeton University Press).

Plate 6   Apse Mosaic, Virgin and Child, Kiti, Cyprus.

Plate 7   Mosaic of St Demetrius between a Bishop and a Dignitary, Church of
St Demetrius, Thessaloniki.

Plate 8   Encaustic Icon of Madonna and Child with Archangels (Rome, Santa Maria in Trastevere).

274

is clear that it was not only the liturgy as such that was in the process of evolution during these years, but also the actual practices of individual Christians in churches. Not all the argument over images was on the level of high theory; it was also directed at these and other practical manifestations in Christian piety, especially, as we shall see, the customs to be followed when taking the Eucharist.[20] At one level the questioning of images was part of the response to a period of unusual innovation and development in church practice.

If we wish to discover what it was that made these particular images 'holy' in a sense which set them apart, even, perhaps, at this period, from other sorts of religious art, we must, I think, consider both their subject and the sense of divine presence; the images in question were taken to be not 'works of art' in the modern sense, but depictions of objective reality, and, as such, were held to bring the very presence of the divine to the worshipper.[21] Images 'recalled' the Gospel narrative or the saint who was depicted,[22] but they were also regarded as having all the power of the personage represented. Looking at the great Sinai icons, with their intense gaze, it is easy to see how this could be so.

SCHOLASTICISM AND THE SEARCH FOR AUTHORITY

But if icons claimed to represent the truth, it was indeed precisely the issue of knowledge, that is, of access to the truth, that was now in question. The period before Iconoclasm, that of the 'rise of icons', saw a drastic revision of what now counted as 'knowledge', and coincided with some fundamental developments: the evolution of fanciful *patria* in the place of history, the relegation of Constantine the Great to legend and sainthood, the end of the flourishing Neoplatonism of Late Antiquity,[23] the mushrooming of collections of miracle stories testifying to divine

[20] See n. 119 below.
[21] For the former distinction, see H. Belting, *Bild und Kunst. Eine Geschichte des Bildes vor dem Zeitalter der Kunst* (Munich, 1990); for the idea of presence, cf. Bishop Kallistos, 'The Meaning of the Divine Liturgy', pp. 8–11, citing the *Life of S. Stephen the Younger*: 'the icon may be termed a door' to the heavenly realm (*PG* 100, col. 1113A).
[22] Mansi 13, 288C.
[23] Whatever actually happened to the Athenian philosophers who left the Academy of Athens in 529, Byzantium in the seventh century no longer had the great philosophical schools of Late Antiquity where Christians and pagans could learn side by side; for a brief and lively description of the latter see P. Chuvin, *A Chronicle of the Last Pagans* (Cambridge, Mass., 1990), pp. 91–118, 131–50, and on the Athenian philosophers, especially Simplicius, see I. Hadot, 'The Life and Work of Simplicius in Greek and Arabic Sources', in R. Sorabji, ed., *Aristotle Transformed. The Ancient Commentators and their Influence* (London, 1990), pp. 275–303.

intervention, a sharp decrease in the availability of traditional secular learning, with the establishment of the Byzantine chronicle tradition, the avid collection of proof-texts for dogmatic use—handlists of useful arguments and quotations from the Scriptures and the Fathers, and the growth of a literature of question and answer providing a vade-mecum for seventh- and eighth-century Byzantines.[24] Attention has been drawn by others to this period as marking an incipient Byzantine scholasticism and the formulation of a conception of authority as resting in a fixed canon of the Fathers.[25] The concern for codification intensified in inverse proportion as access to the old knowledge receded, and is vividly illustrated in the lengthy strings of authorities cited by both sides in the proceedings of the Sixth and Seventh Ecumenical Councils. Such a technologizing of religious authority inevitably gave rise to fakes and bogus citations, and laborious measures were taken at the Sixth Council in 680–1 to check authenticity—an interesting reflection on the morality of seventh-century churchmen.[26] The concern for textual evidence and the manufacture of authoritative documents is shown in a story told by Anastasius of Sinai of how a Monophysite *praefectus augustalis* of Egypt employed fourteen scribes to make multiple copies of patristic texts, especially the works of Cyril of Alexandria, rewritten in order to make them into Monophysite propaganda.[27] The same Anastasius argues elsewhere that material signs are superior to written texts, just because texts are so likely to be falsified.[28] It was not easy to get hold even of important texts, and even those who, one might have thought, were well placed to have access to them did not always know the works which are central to our own discussion. Thus Patriarch Germanos in Constantinople did not have access to the *Apology* of Leontius of Neapolis, although it was known to John of

---

[24] See for the *patria* and the question and answer literature respectively, G. Dagron, *Constantinople imaginaire* (Paris, 1984) and 'Le Saint, le savant, l'astrologue'. Constantine the Great: see n. 115 below.

[25] See Patrick Gray, 'The "Select Fathers": canonizing the patristic past', *Studia Patristica*, 23 (1989), pp. 21–36, and 'Neochalcedonianism and the tradition: from patristic to Byzantine theology', *Byzantinische Forschungen*, 8 (1982), pp. 61–70; Averil Cameron, 'Models of the Past in the Late Sixth Century: the Life of the Patriarch Eutychius', in G. Clarke, ed., *Reading the Past in Late Antiquity* (Canberra: 1990), pp. 205–23.

[26] See Judith Herrin, *The Formation of Christendom* (Oxford, 1987), p. 278; examples: Mansi, 11, 225B–9A; 332D; 336D; 381–449; see also G. Bardy, 'Faux et fraudes littéraires dans l'antiquité chrétienne', *RHE*, 32 (1936), pp. 290–2, and esp. P. Van den Ven, 'La patristique et l'hagiographie au concile de Nicée en 787', *Byzantion*, 25–7 (1955–7), pp. 325–62.

[27] *Hodegos*, X.2.7, ed. K.-H. Uthemann, *Anastasii Opera. Viae Dux*, CChr.SG, 8 (1981); PG 89, cols 184–5.

[28] *Hod.*, XII.3, PG 89, col. 198; see the very interesting discussion by A. Kartsonis, *Anastasis* (Princeton, 1986), pp. 40–63.

Damascus in Jerusalem; it is some measure of the general difficulty of access to books that it was brought to the notice of the Second Council of Nicaea by legates from Rome.[29] The Second Council of Nicaea cited the *Miracles of Cosmas and Damian*, but not those of Artemius, and despite the prominence it gave to John of Damascus as a defender of images, did not cite directly from his works. Ironically, we may feel, a new sort of textual criticism evolved in response to this situation, and, in particular, to the attempts to bend the record, which were evidently a serious problem: in order to check authenticity, extraordinary measures were taken to seek out complete texts of works commonly cited only in second-hand extracts, a particularly elaborate procedure of citation, proof-texts, and checking being employed at the Second Council of Nicaea in 787,which ended the first phase of Byzantine Iconoclasm. The florilegia of scriptural and patristic citations, which are so prominent a feature of this period, are yet another indicator of this desire to claim authority for approved texts, and thus to guarantee access to genuine knowledge.[30] Very naturally in such circumstances, iconophiles, attacked by Iconoclasts as innovators, made particular use of the appeal to tradition and authority, though it is also true that in so doing they were selective about the precise elements in the past history of the Church which were to be accepted.[31] Indeed, the appeal to unwritten as well as written tradition is a basic argument used in John of Damascus's apologies in defence of images.

Amongst their other properties, then, icons—religious images—functioned as a component in the system of knowledge which evolved as Byzantine society shed its classical past.[32] Of course, that is far from being the whole story. But let us see what it might add to the existing explanations for Byzantine Iconoclasm.

[29] See Déroche, 'L'Authenticité de l'"Apologie contre les Juifs"', pp. 667–8.
[30] See Cyril Mango, 'The Availability of Books in the Byzantine Empire, A.D. 750–850', in *Byzantine Books and Bookmen* (Washington, DC, 1975), pp. 29–46, esp. 30–1.
[31] N. Baynes, 'Idolatry and the Early Church', in his *Byzantine Studies and Other Essays* (London, 1955), pp. 116–43, esp. p. 141; J. McGuckin, 'The Theology of Images and the Legitimation of Power in Eighth-Century Byzantium', forthcoming. The iconophile argument in Germanos's *De haeresibus et synodis* (*PG* 98, cols 40–88) and elsewhere rests on the idea that images belong to the tradition' of the Ecumenical Councils, whereas Iconoclasm is a flagrant example of heresy. See also Leslie Brubaker, 'Byzantine art in the ninth century: theory, practice and culture', *Byzantine and Modern Greek Studies*, 13 (1989), pp. 23–93, at pp. 42–56, emphasizing the role of the florilegia, of which the *Sacra Parallela* attributed to John of Damascus is the most conspicuous example, and which was duly illustrated with approved miniatures: see K. Weitzmann, *The Miniatures in the Sacra Parallela* (Princeton, 1979).
[32] See also the stimulating article by G. Dagron, 'Le Culte des images dans le monde byzantin', in his collection *La Romanité chrétienne en Orient* (London, 1984), no. XI.

ICONS AND SOCIAL CHANGE

These arguments take various forms, with varying degrees of nuance and plausibility. Aside from the view of Iconoclasm as a purely theological quarrel, some theories focus narrowly on the contemporary context; thus it is often argued that Byzantine Iconoclasm took its impetus from contemporary Islam, sometimes with reference to the Syrian origin of the first iconoclastic emperor, Leo III. It is thus connected straightforwardly with imperial personalities. But it has also received broader explanations, being seen, for instance, as essentially puritanical; a reform movement within the religious life of Byzantium inspired by the sense that the recent problems of the Empire were a punishment from God as well as, perhaps, by a sense of justified criticism from Jews, Muslims, or traditionalist Christians. Alternatively, it has been interpreted as a social movement, or as a matter of the assertion of imperial authority, whether over and against an overly-independent Church, represented particularly by the monks, or, in political terms, after decades of danger and insecurity.[33] Lastly, this was a historical crisis of major proportions, which centred on questions of visual art; naturally, therefore, it has also been seen primarily as a problem in art history.[34]

In the case of the 'rise of icons', one version of what we might term the social explanation is represented by the persistent claim that devotion to icons represents a type of popular religion.[35] Peter Brown has argued to some extent against this view, by emphasizing the appeal of icons to 'human', not 'popular', needs: 'Rather than assume that the worship of icons rose like a damp stain from the masses, we should look into the

---

[33] See Cormack, *Writing in Gold*, pp. 106–18, for an excellent analysis of the range of explanations listed above. Muslim iconoclasm: see G. R. D. King, 'Islam, Iconoclasm and the declaration of doctrine', *Bulletin of the School of Oriental and African Studies*, 48 (1985), pp. 267–77.

[34] Discussion of the coins of Justinian II and their possible relation to contemporary Islamic coinage (Cormack, *Writing in Gold*, pp. 96–106) is part of the story. See also J. Moorhead, 'Byzantine Iconoclasm as a problem in art history', *Parergon*, ns 4 (1986), pp. 1–18. The style and development of icons themselves in the sixth and seventh centuries is still a controversial matter, being hampered by the paucity of surviving material and the lack of external dating criteria; see especially the works of E. Kitzinger, 'On Some Icons of the Seventh Century', in K. Weitzmann *et al.*, eds., *Late Classical and Medieval Studies in Honor of A. M. Friend* (Princeton, 1955), pp. 132–50; 'Byzantine art in the period between Justinian and Iconoclasm', *Berichte zum XI. internationalen Byzantinisten Kongress* (Munich, 1958), pp. 1–50; *Byzantine Art in the Making* (Cambridge, Mass., 1977), and for some discussion of the issues, J. Trilling, 'Sinai Icons: another look', *Byzantion*, 53 (1983), pp. 300–11. After writing this paper I found many parallelisms of approach with the valuable discussion of the later phase of Byzantine Iconoclasm by Brubaker, 'Byzantine art in the ninth century' (see esp. pp. 23–4).

[35] See Cyril Mango, *Byzantium. The Empire of New Rome* (London, 1980), p. 98 ('popular piety') and especially Kitzinger, 'The Cult of Images'; Herrin, *The Formation of Christendom*, p. 307.

needs which the piety of Late Antique men sought to satisfy in looking at them.'[36] Icons are also held to have a characteristically 'private' role—hence their tendency to be cited in stories about women, who are always seen as the denizens of the private sphere.[37] But their appeal was universal: a good deal of contemporary anecdotal evidence suggests that they were seen by high and low alike as offering the power of emotional solace and access to the divine. This might affect emperors and empresses as much as humble people; they too had their favourite icons, and displayed them in public as well as private life. The first major public icons, including the image of Christ 'not made by human hands' from Camuliana, appeared in the context of the wars against Persia in the late sixth century, when they were publicly paraded,[38] and in Constantinople, too, public images, like relics, were brought out at times of crisis, especially when the city was attacked; it is in this period that the Virgin, through her icon and relics, acquired her status as the protectress of the city.[39] Rich donors were also quick to associate themselves with images of Christ, the Virgin, and the saints in the decorative schemes which they financed.[40] Here, too, public and private merge. Robin Cormack emphasizes the role played by icons in the story of the life of Theodore of Sykeon; in only one of several such interventions, the saints Cosmas and Damian come out of their icon to cure him and to go off to Heaven for help on his behalf.[41] But the icons demonstrate the power of the saint to individuals: in their role as 'supernatural defenders' they also protected the state and society at large.[42]

It has generally been held that the disturbed social conditions which prevailed in the Byzantine 'Dark Age' fostered the popularity of religious images. In most of its forms such a view is not only functionalist (icons serve a useful purpose in assuaging anxiety), but also essentially reductionist

[36] 'A Dark-Age crisis: aspects of the Iconoclastic Controversy', *EHR*, 88 (1973), pp. 1–34, repr. in his *Society and the Holy in Late Antiquity* (Berkeley and Los Angeles, 1982), pp. 251–301, esp. p. 274; earlier, he had written of the 'democratization' of culture in Late Antiquity: see *The World of Late Antiquity* (London, 1971), pp. 74–180ff., on which see Averil Cameron, 'Images of authority: elites and icons in late sixth-century Byzantium', *PaP*, 84 (1979), pp. 3–35, esp. 24–5.

[37] See Herrin, *The Formation of Christendom*, pp. 309f. and other works cited there; *Christianity and the Rhetoric of Empire*, pp. 201–3.

[38] Ps. Zacharias Rhetor, *Historia ecclesiastica*, XII.4, tr. in Mango, *Art of the Byzantine Empire*, pp. 114–15.

[39] See further Cameron, 'Images of authority'.

[40] Cf. also the analysis of the *Miracles of S. Demetrios* and the mosaics of the church of St Demetrios at Thessaloniki: Cormack, *Writing in Gold*, pp. 50–94.

[41] *Writing in Gold*, p. 46; analysis of the *Life of Theodore of Sykeon*, pp. 39–47.

[42] See N. Baynes, 'The supernatural defenders of Constantinople', *AnBoll*, 67 (1949), pp. 165–77 and 'The icons before Iconoclasm', *HThR*, 44 (1951), pp. 116–43 (both in his *Byzantine Studies and Other Essays*, pp. 248–60 and 226–39 respectively).

Plate 9   Fresco with Virgin Enthroned between St Felix and St Adauctus, with Turtura, in whose honour the fresco was dedicated by her son, sixth century (Rome, Catacomb of Commodilla).

(icons are to be explained in terms other than religious ones). Whatever its merits, it does not do full justice either to the seventh-century developments or to the extraordinary persistence and eventual victory of the iconophiles in the ninth century, which ensured the centrality of icons in the Orthodox Church to this day. Nevertheless, it is possible to avoid these pitfalls while still focusing on the seventh to eighth centuries as a period of major change.

This change affected the very structure of Byzantine society, and thus the relationships within it, usually in drastic ways—between town and country, capital and provinces, civil and military. Especially after the death of Heraclius in 641, and the dismal times which followed for the Empire, imperial authority diminished, leaving more and more of a leadership role to the Church and the higher clergy. The latter should not be seen as an isolated sector of society; a substantial number of bishops in this period had also held civil office, and in the siege of Constantinople in 626 nobody found it odd for authority to be vested in the patriarch, nor for the military despatches later sent back from the Emperor Heraclius's campaigns against the Persians to be read out from the ambo in Hagia Sophia, also the scene of political demonstrations.[43] The interdependence in these events of civil and ecclesiastical authorities, and indeed personnel, is very striking; indeed, the responses to the military danger included actual liturgical innovation.[44] The early seventh century saw some important developments in the patriarchal liturgy of Hagia Sophia in Constantinople, which collectively can only have enhanced the position and authority of the patriarch himself.[45] The triumphal return of the Emperor from his Persian wars, when he was formally met at Hieria by his son and the patriarch Sergius, also combined liturgical features with traditional imperial ceremony.[46] The Church's position changed in other ways, too. Its wealth, if anything, had been increasing; even small and obscure Syrian churches in the seventh century owned vast amounts of liturgical silver, which continue to present us with surprises in relation to the overall economic picture (plate 10).[47] The Quinisext Council of 691–2 was

[43] *Chronicon Paschale, 284–628 AD*, ed. and tr. Michael and Mary Whitby (Liverpool, 1989), s.a. 626, 628.

[44] Ibid., s.a. 624, and cf. also s.a. 615; for all this account see the valuable translation and notes by Michael and Mary Whitby, esp. pp. 166ff., referring to further bibliography; the 626 siege marked an important moment in the formation of the idea of Constantinople as specially protected by God and especially the Virgin, although the famous icon of the Virgin at Blachernae (no longer surviving) is not securely attested at this date (see Averil Cameron, 'The Virgin's robe; an episode in the history of early seventh-century Constantinople', *Byzantion*, 49 (1979), pp. 47–8). The editors comment that the liturgical changes of 615 and 624 were 'intended to emphasise that God was present with the congregation, a reliable source of protection in troubled times' (p. 168, n. 454).

[45] See, e.g., H.-J. Schulz, *The Byzantine Liturgy*, Eng. tr. (New York, 1986), pp. 38–40, 164–72.

[46] Theophanes, *Chronographia*, ed. C. de Boor (Leipzig, 1883), I, anno mundi 6119, pp. 327–8; cf. Nicephorus, *Breviarum*, 19, and see Michael McCormick, *Eternal Victory* (Cambridge, 1986), pp. 70–2. On the chronological problems and the question of whether or not these two accounts refer to the same occasion, see Mango, *Patriarch Nikephoros*, pp. 185–6.

[47] See now Marlia Mundell Mango, 'The Uses of Liturgical Silver, 4th–7th Centuries', in Morris, ed., *Church and People in Byzantium*, pp. 245–62; cf. also M. Kaplan, 'L'Eglise byzantin des VIe–XIe siècles: terres et paysans', in ibid., pp. 109–23; according to Procopius, *De*

Plate 10 Silver Paten from Stuma Treasure, showing the Communion of the Apostles, Syria, late sixth century (Istanbul Archaeological Musem).

justifiably worried about the situation of bishops and clergy whose sees had been taken over by 'barbarians'; but even as these lands were lost, the growth of monastic holdings changed the balance of ecclesiastical to secular property in the territories which remained. While these major

---

aedificiis, ed. J. Haury, rev. G. Wirth (Leipzig, 1913), I. 1. 65, the original sanctuary furnishings of St Sophia in Constantinople amounted to 40,000 lbs of silver; the altar was of gold, with gold columns and a ciborium of silver (Paul the Silentiary, *Ekphrasis on Hagia Sophia*, ed. P. Friedländer, *Johannes von Gaza und Paulus Silentiarius* (Leipzig and Berlin, 1912), lines 720–54). The same period saw changes in the monetary and fiscal structure as basic as any of the military and administrative developments: see the contributions by C. Morrisson, J. Durliat, and R. Delmaire in *Hommes et richesses dans l'empire byzantin, IVe–VIIe siècle* (Paris, 1989).

changes were affecting the place of churches, monasteries, and ecclesiastics in Byzantine society, we see a parallel move towards the interpretation of the liturgy and the churches themselves. In several contemporary works the Church is interpreted as the image or microcosm of heaven, and the liturgy itself as a symbolic enactment which also implied the real presence of God. Church furniture, vestments, icons were all parts that made up the whole, as a series of writers pointed out.[48]

Why did images become so much more of an issue in the East than in the West? While not neglecting the inheritance of debate about Christian art, we must also place the rise of icons in its contemporary context. We have already noted the extent of general social change in the East in the seventh century, and the fact that icons also came to prominence simultaneously with an increasing splendour in the celebration of the liturgy, accompanied by a theoretical exposition in symbolic terms, and a focusing of attention on the meaning of the Eucharist and on all aspects of church decoration, furniture, and ceremony. We shall see that the opponents of icons were concerned not only with the Platonizing concepts of image and prototype, but also with questions of materiality and symbolism which arose in several other seventh-century contexts. Already in the sixth century the patriarch Eutychius had argued against a symbolic interpretation of the Eucharist,[49] and we shall see during the seventh century a shift away from the more symbolic interpretation of Maximus Confessor in the direction of literal realism, associated with Patriarch Germanos I (715–30). Thus the debate in which religious images were a part was both more immediate and more continuous in the Eastern context, where the history of Christian opposition to images combined with the particular circumstances of the seventh century to make them the focus of existing tensions between symbolism and realism.

---

[48] See Bishop Kallistos, 'The Meaning of the Divine Liturgy', and further below. Symbolic interpretations of church buildings: Corippus, *In laudem Iustini*, IV. 288–311, ed. with tr. and comm. Averil Cameron (London, 1976), with pp. 206–7; Paul the Silentiary, *Ekphrasis on H. Sophia*, on which see R. Macrides and P. Magdalino, 'The architecture of Ekphrasis: construction and context of Paul the Silentiary's Ekphrasis of Hagia Sophia', *Byzantine and Modern Greek Studies*, 12 (1988), pp. 47–82; Andrew Palmer, with Lyn Rodley, 'The inauguration anthem of Hagia Sophia in Edessa: a new edition and translation with historical and architectural notes and a comparison with a contemporary Constantinopolitan kontakion', ibid., pp. 117–67; Mathews, *The Early Churches of Constantinople*, and on the symbolism of church architecture in the ninth century and later, cf. also 'The Transformation Symbolism in Byzantine Architecture and the Meaning of the Pantokrator in the Dome', in Morris, ed., *Church and People in Byzantium*, pp. 191–214.
[49] Eutychius, *Sermo de paschate et eucharistia*, PG 86, 2.2400–1.

THE PROBLEM OF CHRISTIAN REPRESENTATION

But the immediate circumstances of the late seventh and early eighth centuries do not provide the whole explanation for the concerns voiced about religious images, for besides the traditional prohibition of figural art, the question of religious images also relates to longstanding problems which Christians had had with the verbal representation of religious truth.[50] The Iconoclasts claimed that only the human, not the divine, nature of God could be represented in visual terms.[51] A very similar difficulty had been felt in relation to language by Christian writers for centuries, especially by the Cappadocians; indeed, the representation of God in linguistic terms is still an issue today. One author who followed in the tradition of negative theology set by the Cappadocians was Pseudo-Dionysius the Areopagite, and, sure enough, during the period of the 'rise of icons' the Pseudo-Dionysius's works gained increasing importance. Several sets of scholia on his works were put together in the sixth and seventh centuries, culminating with the work of John Damascene in the eighth. In contrast to theologians, many historians have tended to neglect such works as peripheral to their concerns, yet the fact that the Pseudo-Dionysius, who posed in the sharpest possible way the central problem of Christian representation, and did so exactly as the rival secular culture was on the verge of yielding, rapidly became canonical for all parties is in itself surely significant.

In a famous passage Pseudo-Dionysius the Areopagite writes of the ultimate darkness of religious experience. Taking up themes from Gregory of Nyssa's *Life of Moses* and from Gregory of Nazianzus, he describes how, when Moses knows God, he plunges into the 'truly mysterious darkness of unknowing'.[52] His briefest work, the *Mystical Theology*, begins with a prayer to the Trinity:

> Lead us up beyond unknowing and light,
> up to the farthest, highest peak
> of mystic scripture,

---

[50] For discussion of earlier patristic views see Charles Murray, 'Art in the Early Church', *JThS*, ns 28 (1977), pp. 303–45; 'Le Problème d'iconophobie et les premiers siècles chrétiens', in F. Boespflug and N. Lossky, eds, *Nicée II 787–1987* (Paris, 1987), pp. 39–49.

[51] See P. Henry, 'What was the Iconoclastic Controversy all about?' *Church History*, 45 (1976), pp. 21–5.

[52] *Mystical Theology*, 1001A, tr. C. Luibheid and P. Rorem, *Pseudo Dionysius: the Complete Works* (London, 1987), p. 137; cf. V. Lossky, *The Mystical Theology of the Eastern Church*, tr. Members of the Fellowship of St Alban and St Sergius (Cambridge, 1957), p. 35.

> where the mysteries of God's Word
> lie simple, absolute and unchangeable
> in the brilliant darkness of a hidden silence.

This is the culmination of negative theology—one cannot describe but only experience in direct contemplation. The logical outcome should have been silence, an end to theology and to all attempts to describe the truth.

In practice, of course, churchmen continued to try to describe the divine. The Pseudo-Dionysius himself discusses the implications of the view that God can only be assessed through images. While he presents this as a linguistic dilemma, he also discusses the imagery commonly used of God in more visual terms. In letter 9, for instance, he describes how in the lost *Symbolic Theology* he had discussed the physical imagery used of God in the Old Testament, including the cruder forms of anthropomorphism; these are to be found, he argues, 'so that what is hidden may be brought out into the open and multiplied, what is unique and undivided may be divided up and multiple shapes and forms be given to what has no shape or form.'[53] Similarly, the ranks of angels are represented as creatures on thrones, not 'for the sake of art', but 'as a concession to the nature of our own mind',[54] for the real simplicity of the heavenly creatures cannot be depicted at all. The author is not concerned with religious images in the sense of icons, but rather with the much more basic question of how God can be apprehended in the first place. These images do not operate through likeness but because they are dissimilar, and this is, in the mind of the Pseudo-Dionysius, the superior form of representation since it does not pretend to portray what is actually transcendent and indescribable.[55]

But the author is indeed in a dilemma. He takes up the Pauline saying at Romans 1.20, according to which the invisible truth is to be understood through the visible world;[56] 'the visible is truly the plain image of the invisible',[57] even while, again like Paul, he emphasizes the mysteriousness of God, which cannot be expressed directly but only through signs, as in the case of the parables of Jesus.[58] The Pseudo-Dionysius was not writing about the religious images that we call icons, that is, direct representations

---

[53] Letter 9, 1105C, pp. 282–3.
[54] *Celestial Hierarchies*, 2, 137B, p. 148.
[55] Ibid., 140D, p. 149.
[56] Letter 9, 2, 1108B, p. 284.
[57] Letter 10, 1117B, p. 289.
[58] Letter 9, 1105D, p. 283.

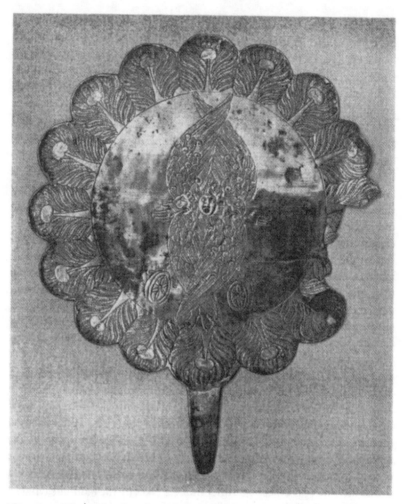

Plate 11   Silver-gilt Rhipidion (liturgical fan) from Riha, Syria, late sixth century, with cherub flanked by fiery wheels, as in the Vision of Ezekiel (cf. Ezekiel 1. 5–14) (Byzantine Visual Resources, © 1991, Dumbarton Oaks, Washington, DC).

of Christ, the Virgin, and the saints, but about the figural depictions of God and the cherubim to be found in the Old Testament. But the cherubim of Solomon and Ezekiel, like the brazen serpent of Moses, were to feature in the catalogues of Old Testament representations to which iconophiles turned for supporting evidence.[59] Indeed, his preoccupation with the general issue of representation of the divine made him a natural source for the iconophile writers, who selected the parts of his argument most congenial to their needs. As has been noted, Hypatius of Ephesus in the sixth century had already justified Christian art along the lines of inter- pretation laid down by the Pseudo-Dionysius.[60] But the Pseudo-Dionysius is not to be seen as wholly symbolist;[61] a more realist reading is also possible, which lays emphasis on the liturgy and the sacraments, and this approach was indeed taken up in the course of the greater emphasis on literalism in the late seventh century. Accordingly, the Iconoclasts were also able to claim his support at the Iconoclast Council of Hieria in 754, as the acts of the Seventh Council make clear: 'Since they put as a preface the patristic words of Dionysius the revealer of God, would that they had preserved his teachings, as well as those of all our holy Fathers, unbroken.'[62] But he was particularly cited by iconophiles: the account of the decoration of Hosios David at Thessaloniki, for instance, refers directly to the Pseudo- Dionysius's discussion of cherubim.[63] Iconophiles were able to find in the corpus a justification both for the double concept of the Eucharist as image and as the Real Presence, and were thus able to deny that the Eucharist was '*only* an image'.[64] In one sense, the thrust of the writings of the Pseudo- Dionysius led to the path of contemplation, mystical silence, and this was

[59] E.g. Joh. Dam., *Oratio* III.22, *De imaginibus*; Theodore Abu Qurrah, *De cultu imaginum*, ed. I. Dick, *Théodore Abuqurra, Traité du culte des icones* (Jounieh and Rome, 1986, ch. 15); see Sidney H. Griffith, 'Theodore Abu Qurrah's Arabic Tract on the Christian practice of venerating images', *Journal of the American Oriental Society*, 105 (1985), pp. 53–73. I am grateful to Sidney Griffith for his generosity in sharing his translation with me in advance of publica- tion, and for continued help in other ways.

[60] Kitzinger, 'Cult of images', pp. 137f., with Charles Murray, 'Artistic Idiom and Doctrinal Development', in Rowan Williams, ed., *The Making of Orthodoxy. Essays in Honour of Henry Chadwick* (Cambridge, 1989), pp. 288–308, at p. 298, and Baynes, 'The icons before Iconoclasm', pp. 226–8.

[61] As, for instance, J. Meyendorff, *Christ in Eastern Christian Thought* (Washington, 1969), p. 79; see, however, P. Rorem, *Biblical and Liturgical Symbols within the Pseudo-Dionysian Synthesis = Studies and Texts*, 71 (Toronto, 1984); A. Louth, 'Pagan theurgy and Christian sacramentalism in Denys the Areopagite', *JThS*, ns 37 (1986), pp. 432–8, and see his *Denys the Areopagite* (London, 1989).

[62] Mansi, 13, 212A, tr. D. Sahas, *Icon and Logos: Sources in Eighth-Century Iconoclasm* (Toronto, 1986), p. 54.

[63] Ignatius Monachus, *Narratio de imagine Christi in monasterio Latoni*, 6, tr. in Mango, *Art of the Byzantine Empire*, p. 155.

[64] See Bishop Kallistos, 'The Meaning of the Divine Liturgy', p. 17.

certainly a strong element in the theology of Maximus;[65] signs and symbols pointed the seeker of truth on his way, not logical argument.

Thus knowledge of God, if it cannot be adequately expressed in language, must come through signs. Pseudo-Dionysius was voicing an emphasis on the hiddenness of divine truth and the need for revelation through signs which had been present in Christian discourse from the earliest times. In the *Ecclesiastical Hierarchy* he understands the liturgy in this way. The language is difficult; the synaxis itself is said to be surrounded by 'symbolic garments of enigmas', yet the Sacrament can nevertheless show itself clearly and 'fill the eyes of our mind with a unifying and ineffable light'.[66] As the Pseudo-Dionysius insists, it is St Paul's emphasis on mystery and paradox that lies behind this thinking. Paul too lays heavy stress on the hiddenness of divine truth, how God's 'foolishness has confounded the wisdom of the world' by the paradox of the Cross and how now 'we see through a glass, darkly'.[67] Augustine, in his turn, had struggled to define the source and nature of divine knowledge, citing the same Pauline arguments in doing so;[68] he too arrived at the view that knowledge of God came through revelation, and spoke of the Scriptures as the 'fleshly wrappings' of the truth.[69] Following Paul, Christian discourse itself was essentially figural, and our consciousness of the long-standing conflict over biblical interpretation between Alexandrian allegorizers and Antiochene literalists should not be allowed to obscure the fact that all Christian writers alike, from Paul onwards, used a vocabulary of mystery and hidden meaning.

After all, Christian discourse appealed to faith: 'He that hath ears, let him hear', and 'It is given unto you to know the mysteries of the kingdom of heaven.'[70] Fundamental to it was the idea of a complex of signs and symbols requiring interpretation but capable of revealing the truth; despite the Old Testament prohibition on graven images, it was only a very short step from this figural discourse to the resort to actual visual images.[71] When Anastasius of Sinai preferred pictorial representations to

[65] Cf. R. Mortley, *From Word to Silence*, 2 vols, Theophaneia, 34–35 (Bonn, 1986), esp. 2, pp. 221–41; Maximus: see H. U. von Balthasar, *Kosmische Liturgie. Das Weltbild Maximus des Bekenners*, 2nd edn (Einsiedeln, 1961).

[66] *Eccl. Hier.* 2, 428C, p. 212.

[67] I Cor. 1. 18f.; 13. 12.

[68] *De doctrina christiana*, I.11.11, 12.11; see Cameron, *Christianity and the Rhetoric of Empire*, pp. 66–7.

[69] Cf. *De rudibus catechizandis*, 9.13.

[70] Mark 4. 9; Matt. 13. 43; Luke 14. 15; Matt. 13. 11.

[71] See on this Cameron, *Christianity and the Rhetoric of Empire*, ch. 2, esp. pp. 47–8, 56–7. For revelation by 'signs' and the view of creation as containing 'signs' of God's purpose in the Early Christian period see R. M. Grant, *The Letter and the Spirit* (London, 1957).

written ones, he was only voicing a version of the arguments by which earlier Christian writers had justified and praised religious pictures as a means of instruction.[72] His argument is the converse of the Iconoclast privileging of writing over pictures; by contrast, images and writing were often at this stage simply equated by iconophiles, for whom it was necessary to show that images had the same status as the Scriptures.[73] In the words of John of Damascus, the way was clear: depiction of God in human form was not merely allowable but even incumbent. 'How depict the invisible? How picture the inconceivable?' In his view pictures could help: 'When he who is without form or limitation . . . takes upon himself the form of a servant in substance and a body of flesh, then you may draw his likeness and show it to anyone willing to contemplate it.'[74]

REVELATION THROUGH SIGNS

At this point, however, a shift takes place. Images were not the only indicators of divine truth. Moreover, while symbolism was indeed an issue in this period, it is misleading to talk of symbols in relation to the signs which are the ways of revelation; rather, the signs which are often listed in seventh- and eighth-century authors as ways to an understanding of God are not symbols in the usual sense in which we use the term—when one thing stands for another—but, to quote Lossky, real 'material signs of the presence of the spiritual world'.[75]

These 'signs' by which God reveals himself are variously listed, but typically include the Cross, the Scriptures, the trappings of the liturgy—incense, candles, water, as well as, for instance, the Ark and the Burning Bush. The listing of signs had also begun early;[76] from now on, however, they begin to acquire the status of canonical lists, and holy images to figure as one of the items included.[77] Iconophile writers claim for images the same status as the Cross and the Gospels, deserving of veneration,

---

[72] See Cameron, *Christianity and the Rhetoric of Empire*, p. 150.
[73] See Brubaker, 'Byzantine art in the ninth century', pp. 70–5 for examples. In later versions of the iconophile argument the point is made that pictures are universal, whereas writing is circumscribed by having to use a specific language.
[74] *Oratio I de imaginibus*, 16, ed. B. Kotter, 3 (Berlin, 1975), pp. 89–90; *PG* 94, col. 1245.
[75] Lossky, *Mystical Theology*, p. 189; this judgement draws on contemporary statements, but cf. also D. Sperber, *Rethinking Symbolism*, Eng. tr. (Cambridge, 1975), p. 85: 'symbols are not signs'.
[76] See, e.g., Cyril of Jerusalem, *Catechetical Homilies*, 10.19.
[77] E.g. John Dam., *Oratio III de imaginibus* 22, Kotter, 3, p. 129, cf. *Or.* I.12 (the Burning Bush, the dew upon the fleece (Judges 6. 40), Aaron's Rod, manna, the brazen serpent (Num. 21.9), the sea, water, and clouds).

though not of worship; as icons are a 'sign', so the other 'signs' could be read as icons.[78] Again, the case of the Cross is instructive: the terms applied to it in the Christian apologiae against the Jews in order to rebut charges of idolatry, include both *typos* and *semeion* (sign);[79] during 'second Icono-clasm' debates about terminology reached a highly sophisticated level in the works of Nicephorus and Theodore the Studite, but in the early stages of the controversy the very ambiguity of the Greek terminology may have helped the equation.

The listings of signs indicates an authoritarian view of divine knowledge, based on revelation; it works on the premise that knowledge is not to be found through secular learning but by direct revelation. But this revelation is not arbitrary; on the contrary, it comes only through the channels which have been officially approved as orthodox by the Church. Thus the arguments about the nature of images, as about material and created signs in general, were indeed arguments about authority, about the licensing of signs. In our period, the learning of the world really does fall away, and as it does, holy images begin to claim the authoritative status of divine 'signs'. The argument on their behalf made large claims: Theodore Abu Qurrah's ninth-century defence of images argues that as Christianity is based on a mystery, to reject icon-veneration is to reject all the other mysteries of Christianity as well. He, too, invokes St Paul, this time for an answer to the accusation that icon-veneration is foolish: had not the Apostle said that Christianity itself was based on foolishness in the eyes of the world—'We speak of God's wisdom in a mystery' and 'The world's wisdom is foolishness with God'?[80] Religious images were a way out of this dilemma; they fell naturally into place as one of the signs by which the impossibility of understanding God through language could be circumvented.[81] But the repertoire of these images was potentially vast, and their doctrinal and other implications could be alarming if uncon-trolled. What we see therefore are progressive attempts by iconophiles and Iconoclasts alike to do just that, that is, to regulate the signs and define their meaning.

Miracle afforded another means by which to read the providence of God. As icons are not simply indicators of popular religion, so miracle can be read not just as a manifestation of popular credulity, but as providing

[78] The same idea transferred into Arabic: Abu Qurrah, *De cultu imaginum*, 15: 'the greatest, the most famous icon, the tablets of the Law'.
[79] See Déroche, 'L'Authenticité de l'"Apologie contre les Juifs"', p. 661; see further below.
[80] I Cor. 2. 7; 3. 19, cited by Abu Qurrah, *De cultu imaginum*, 3.
[81] Cf. Brubaker, 'Byzantine art in the ninth century', pp. 75–81.

direct access to knowledge of God, and as a further alternative to secular learning. The period of the so-called 'rise of icons' also saw a proliferation of miracle collections attached to shrines and a great increase in stories of miraculous intervention, often featuring the Virgin or with reference to icons.[82] Like our reading of the significance of icons, how we view the collections of such stories in the *Miracles of Artemius* or the *Miracles of S. Demetrius* (to name only two) is partly a matter of emphasis. While they do certainly testify in our terms to popular credulity, we are equally entitled to see them as yet another example of the impulse towards an authoritative codification of the signs which could lead to religious knowledge.

The Virgin, the Mother of God, is the agent in many of the miracle stories, typically as a beautiful lady dressed in purple or blue, and is frequently mentioned in iconophile argument. Of the surviving pre-Iconoclastic images, a high proportion depict the Virgin and Child, a fact which is indicative of her Christological importance, and which, in itself, illustrates the way in which visual art was being used to make doctrinal points. The period of the rise of icons also saw the establishment of the cult of the Virgin as the special protectress of Constantinople; the 'restoration of orthodoxy' took place in 843, but it was with the dedication by Photius in 867 of an image of the Virgin and Child in the apse of St Sophia that the ending of Iconoclasm was finally confirmed. In the West, from the sixth century onwards, we can see the beginning of the collections of 'Mary miracles' which continue into the medieval period.[83] But while there was nothing quite like this in the East, it was, indeed, precisely now that the icons of the Virgin leapt to prominence in the sieges of 626 and 717; indeed, the great Akathistos hymn was elaborated as a hymn of triumph to the Virgin after the city's deliverance in 626. Now, too, I believe, the Marian relics in Constantinople, the Virgin's robe and girdle, were equipped with their highly elaborated stories.[84]

The Cross, the Mother of God, miracles, the holy images—these must be taken together. I find it hard to separate consideration of icons either from consideration of the other 'signs' or from verbal representation. All were seen as ways of perceiving truth, and truth was seen as absolute and

---

[82] See Cameron, *Christianity and the Rhetoric of Empire*, pp. 208–13. For some examples, see Mango, *Art of the Byzantine Empire*, pp. 133–9.

[83] See Benedicta Ward, *Miracles and the Medieval Mind. Theory, Record and Event 1000–1215* (London, 1987), pp. 132ff.; Cameron, *Christianity and the Rhetoric of Empire*, pp. 212ff. (also associated with miracle stories focused on the Eucharist).

[84] Cameron, 'Images of authority', pp. 18–24.

objectively real. But such a conception of knowledge was, of course, also political. Again we turn to the Pseudo-Dionysius. Besides his emphasis on mystery and the need for revelation, his most striking characteristic is his insistence on hierarchy, as shown by the titles of his works known as the *Celestial* and *Ecclesiastical Hierarchies*. Being is constituted for him in an ascending hierarchy, from the natural world at the bottom to the divine truth at the summit; heaven and the Church are each similarly constructed. From this it follows that knowledge will be a matter of gradual ascent towards the ultimate. There is no need to labour the Platonic framework within which he writes, except to stress that like Plato he, too, was an advocate of the closed society. For the Pseudo-Dionysius, too, there is no logical way of dissent; it is knowledge, not opinion, about which he writes, *episteme* rather than *doxa*, and knowledge, like Plato's *episteme*, is only of truth. The codification of hierarchies, the marshalling of instances of divine intervention, the listing of patristic and scriptural citations were all striving for this certainty, for which the Pseudo-Dionysius taught that the soul longed with a natural desire (*eros*). It is no coincidence that both the great followers of the Pseudo-Dionysius, Maximus Confessor and John Damascene, each sought effectively to produce great syntheses of Christian knowledge, as though a complete listing of the routes to religious understanding would guarantee the eventual perception of truth.[85]

In such an intellectual climate the various components of the system locked together to form an overall coherence. I am suggesting that we should see icons as part of this complex. The importance of icons is not just a problem in Byzantine art, though, of course, it may be that too. Nor are they to be seen just in social terms, whether in relation to patronage or to private piety. Rather, they provided one of the answers to the problem of how God could be apprehended, a problem which had been inherent in Christianity from the very beginning and which only became more acute as time went on. They were the guarantors of truth;[86] while at the same time a way of controlling true belief. And as the classical alternative fell away, Christian knowledge *was* social knowledge.

---

[85] Cameron, *Christianity and the Rhetoric of Empire*, pp. 218–19. In John Damascene the defence of images went together with the exposition of the faith (cf. his *De fide orthodoxa*, ed. B. Kotter, *Die Schriften des Johannes von Damaskos*, 2 (Berlin, 1973). For John of Damascus and the idea of a hierarchy of images and approved ways to God, see also John Elsner, 'Image and Iconoclasm in Byzantium', *Art History*, 11 (1988), pp. 471–91, esp. pp. 477–91.

[86] Thus the iconophiles condemned iconophile 'innovation' and claimed their own obedience to apostolic, patristic, and ecclesiastical tradition: Mansi, 13, 208C, tr. Sahas, *Icon and Logos*, p. 52; see Brubaker, 'Byzantine art in the ninth century', pp. 48–9.

The Language of Images

This is not the old question of the theology of the icon, but an attempt to place the rise of icons in the context of a general intellectual realignment, in effect, the replacement of the remaining vestiges of classical culture by a codification of knowledge based on religious truth. It has the advantage for the historian that explanations for the rise of icons are neither detached from the general cultural context, as they often are, or too closely linked to particular external circumstances. For while if one could get away from functional explanations altogether, history would probably not be history, historical explanations are much more satisfying if they can embed the phenomena they are trying to explain in a really thick context.

REALISM AND TRUTH

Seeing icons in this way raises some other questions. One is that of realism; for if icons are to be seen not just as a specialized form of Byzantine art, but as having a connection with the sociology of knowledge, the old art-historical problem of realism as opposed to abstractionism has to be reopened. However, the reason why this should be a problem lies more with ourselves and with the way in which we frame the question than with the icons. Contemporaries did not doubt that they were true representations of actual reality, a conviction which explains the accusations of idolatry from Iconoclasts and Muslims alike. To us, Byzantine religious art usually appears anything but realistic.[87] Nor, on the whole, do modern historians share the contemporary beliefs either in the religious entities themselves (or at any rate, not in these objectified forms) or in the notion that language, verbal or artistic, represents objective reality. But the question of realism remains. Photius on the restored image of the Virgin in Hagia Sophia and the French realist painters of the nineteenth century alike claimed that art was a reflection of reality. Both had supreme confidence; neither would have tolerated for a moment the modern difficulty that 'realism' is itself relative.

But during the centuries before Iconoclasm—the period of the rise of icons—the conception of reality itself had changed. Confusingly for us, Erich Auerbach's famous book, *Mimesis*, made 'realism' the touchstone of Christian and medieval, as opposed to classical, representation. His classic

---

[87] On these issues see L. Brubaker, 'Perception and conception: art, theory and culture in ninth-century Byzantium', *Word and Image*, 5 (1989), forthcoming, with 'Byzantine art in the ninth century', pp. 24–6.

analyses of the Gospel account of Peter's denial of Christ and of the arrest of Peter Valvomeres in the history of Ammianus Marcellinus put forward an antithesis between the formalities of classical representation, with its emphasis on levels of style, and the contrasting realism of Christian and medieval description.[88] Christianity provided the touchstone: to quote from his epilogue, 'It was the story of Christ, with its ruthless mixture of everyday reality and the highest and most sublime tragedy, which had conquered the classical rule of styles.'[89] Christianity and Christianization are therefore made the keys to understanding changing types of representation in Late Antiquity generally. But this is the realism of Huizinga's late Western Middle Ages, with its earthy juxtaposition of opposites, and disregard for the unity of styles. It is not at all the same as the realism of Byzantine icons; indeed, the East, with its continuous theological tradition, went in quite another way. Auerbach's antithesis is embedded in the context of interpretation in which Late Antiquity is seen as demonstrating encroaching gloom, the descent into irrationality, 'something sultry and oppressive', a 'darkening of the atmosphere of life'—all the familiar spectres of old-fashioned history, and categories which, if they belong anywhere, belong to the fragmentation of the early medieval West rather than to Byzantium.

In contrast, the realism claimed for religious images by contemporaries in early Byzantium has to do with authority. The ultimate reality, God himself, cannot be represented directly, either in visual art or in language, and can only be known by entering the 'cloud of unknowing' described by the Pseudo-Dionysius. But the images of Christ in human form, and of the Virgin and the saints, function as guarantees, ways to perceiving truth.

Obviously the Christianization of society was indeed vital to the rise in importance of religious images, though not in Auerbach's sense, and although this process was slow, the sixth century can plausibly be seen as the critical stage in the East. From now on, social and economic circumstances also increasingly undermined the classical culture which had survived tenaciously for so long. What effect it continued to exert on Byzantium in later centuries is another story. Meanwhile, religious images represented one element in the necessary construction of an alternative world-view.

---

[88] E. Auerbach, *Mimesis. The Representation of Reality in Western Literature*, Eng. tr. (Princeton, 1953), pp. 40ff., 53f., 63, 74ff.; cf. *The Literary Language and its Public in Late Latin Antiquity and in the Middle Ages*, Eng. tr. (London, 1965), pp. 22, 60f.

[89] *Mimesis*, p. 555.

The Language of Images

MATERIALITY, CREATED OBJECTS AND LITERALISM

Yet some powerful counter-arguments existed, which we can clearly see in prototype during the seventh century. One of the charges made most often by the eighth-century Iconoclasts was that of idolatry: veneration of an image was simply veneration of a material object, and therefore constituted idolatry.[90] If indeed icons were considered as a 'real material sign' the charge was fully understandable. It was not, however, an argument brought against icons alone, but against the veneration of all created objects, and indeed the status of matter. It was, most notably, at the heart of Christian-Jewish argument, and it is very striking to note the degree to which an intensified Christian polemic against Jews is already apparent, in which the same argument was directed at Christian veneration of the Cross, well before images as such came under attack. Anti-Jewish arguments creep into a strikingly high proportion of the surviving theological writings of the period, not to mention the anti-Jewish polemic we hear of but which does not survive.[91] In the seventh-century context, the argument appears particularly in connection with Palestine, and especially with Jerusalem, after its capture by the Persians in 614 and surrender to the Arabs in 638.[92] The Jews were accused of assisting the Persians in their invasion, and after his triumphal return to Constantinople and the restoration of the True Cross (seized by the Persians in 614), the Emperor Heraclius (610–41) decreed forced baptism for Jews, a measure repeated according to Theophanes by Leo III in 721–2 on the eve of Iconoclasm.[93] In the several anti-Jewish polemical works which survive from the immediately following period, from the *Doctrina Jacobi nuper baptizati*, a

[90] See the letter of Germanos I to Thomas of Klaudiopolis, *PG* 98, cols 156C–D, 176D, on which see Herrin, *The Formation of Christendom*, pp. 331–2; Brubaker, 'Byzantine art in the ninth century', p. 34; see also Dagron, 'Le Culte des images', pp. 141–2.

[91] Rebuttal of supposed Jewish arguments is still a strong theme in Abu Qurrah's tract, which goes through the whole repertoire of created objects which receive veneration in the Old Testament; see Griffith, 'Theodore Abu Qurrah's Arabic Tract', pp. 59–62; also Sidney H. Griffith, 'Anastasios of Sinai, the *Hodegos* and the Muslims', *Greek Orthodox Theological Review*, 32 (1987), pp. 341–58, at pp. 345ff. For the importance of the theme in the seventh century see also Dagron,'Le culte des images', p. 143 ('cette nouvelle appréciation de l'héritage judaïque'). The hardening of Christian attitudes to Judaism is not so much a cause of Iconoclasm as a parallel development.

[92] See recently G. G. Stroumsa, 'Religious contacts in Byzantine Palestine', *Numen*, 36 (1989), pp. 16–42.

[93] See, e.g., A. Sharf, *Byzantine Jewry from Justinian to the Fourth Crusade* (London, 1971), pp. 48–57. Leo III: Theoph., *Chron.*, anno mundi 6214, p. 401, de Boor; according to Theophanes the iconoclastic edict of Caliph Yazid II which belongs to 722 was also inspired by 'a Jewish wizard'.

kind of Christian catechism for Jewish converts in the form of a dialogue, to the *Apology* of Leontius of Neapolis and the so-called *Trophies of Damascus*, the Christian worship of material objects, in particular the Cross, is represented as a major Jewish accusation to be rebutted.[94] It is answered by two strategies—resort to lists of citations from the Old Testament, indicating the material objects honoured by Jews themselves (the tablets of the law, the Ark, the Burning Bush, and so on), and the argument, also on the basis of Scripture, that the Cross is venerated for what it represents, not as a piece of wood.[95] The dramatic reversals in the fate of Jerusalem, and especially the vicissitudes of the True Cross in this period, made such a focus particularly apt, and also helped to stimulate an increased interest in Constantine the Great as the traditional discoverer of the True Cross and builder of Christian Jerusalem.[96] Both Christians and Jews had had brief periods of renewed hope in relation to Jerusalem, and both were disappointed. Doing their best to save the situation, the Christian anti-Jewish dialogues make much of the fact that the Temple had never been rebuilt, while the Christian Empire could still just about be said to have survived.[97]

The Christian apologiae for veneration of the Cross thus had a strongly political flavour. But they also fit into the wider context of Christian concern about materiality; when the examples chosen in the anti-Jewish literature broaden to include icons they do so in relation to their physical nature as images on wood or other materials. Were not Christians idolaters and worshippers of the material? The counter-argument followed the teaching of the Pseudo-Dionysius that the visible world signifies God; thus we read in Leontius of Neapolis how God is worshipped through creation and created objects, which embrace not only 'heaven and earth and sea', but also 'wood and stone ... relics and church-buildings and the cross'.[98] Creation itself, it is argued, is a sign and mirror of God; the material objects which he has created are the signs through which he is recognized and represented. A similar defence of

[94] On this genre and its main themes see Déroche, 'L'Authenticité de l'"Apologie contre les Juifs"', discussing its purpose at pp. 668–9.

[95] See N. Gendle, 'Leontius of Neapolis: a seventh century defender of holy images', *Studia Patristica*, 18 (1985), pp. 135–9.

[96] See Averil Cameron, 'Byzantium in the Seventh Century. The Search for Redefinition', in J. Fontaine and J. Hillgarth, eds, *The Seventh Century: Change and Continuity* (London, forthcoming).

[97] See, e.g., *Trophies of Damascus*, ed. G. Bardy, *Patrologia Orientalis*, 15 (1927), pp. 169–292, at p. 221.

[98] Leontius of Neapolis, *PG* 93, col. 1604B.

veneration of material objects such as the Cross is an important part of
John of Damascus's apologia for images; he links veneration of the Cross
explicitly with such material signs of the death and resurrection of Christ
as the rock of Calvary, the tomb, and the stone.[99] The Jews may have
accused Christians of idolatry, but the Christian argument itself was
about signification, what signified, and how.

Whatever else it may have been, Byzantine Iconoclasm was certainly an
argument about the correct representation of God. According to the
Iconoclasts, only certain signs were to be allowed, principally the
Eucharist, the 'one true image' of God.[100] They thus claimed it for themselves, while denying the legitimacy of other signs favoured by their
opponents. This is why actual icons and figural decoration in churches
were destroyed, whitewashed, or replaced. Needless to say, the Iconoclast
argument, including Constantine V's understanding of the Eucharist, was
hotly rebutted.[101] Both sides in the controversy, however, drew on the
arguments of the preceding century. One such was a renewed stress on the
suffering of Christ in the flesh, that is, in his human and physical form,
which constituted a major concern of late seventh-century Eastern
theology, and which now also began to manifest itself in the late appearance in Byzantine art of representations of the dead Christ on the Cross.[102]
Again, the emphasis is on materiality; Christ suffered in the body, not
symbolically. But this posed major Christological problems: in which
nature did Christ suffer? Theopaschites and others who wished to restrict
his suffering to one nature only were now again formally condemned.[103]
The two natures had to be realized somehow in every part of the divine
economy, and in every portrayal of it. It is obvious that any picture of
Christ would raise the issue of exactly what it was that was represented,

---

[99] Scorn for matter is represented as a Manichaean error: *Oratio* II.13, Kotter, 3, p. 104; *PG* 94,
col. 1300B, cf. 1245B (other material signs; see n. 77 above).

[100] As argued in the *Peuseis* of the Emperor Constantine V: see S. Gero, 'Notes on Byzantine
Iconoclasm in the eighth century', *Byzantion*, 44 (1974), pp. 23–42; 'The eucharistic doctrine
of the Byzantine Iconoclasts and its sources', *Byzantinische Zeitschrift*, 68 (1975), pp. 4–22.

[101] See, e.g., Nicephorus, *Antirrhetici*, II.2: *PG* 100, col. 333B–D, usefully tr. with notes M.-J.
Mondzain-Baudinet, *Nicéphore, Discours contre les iconoclastes* (Paris, 1990).

[102] See the discussion by Anna Kartsonis, *Anastasis. The Making of an Image* (Princeton, 1986),
pp. 33–60; Brubaker, 'Byzantine art in the ninth century', p. 39. Interestingly, a miniature in
the Chludov Psalter (ninth century) shows the figure of Pseudo-Dionysius as a witness to the
Crucifixion, illustrating the text of Ps. 45.7, 'Nations may be in turmoil and thrones totter';
see Cormack, *Writing in Gold*, p. 134.

[103] Theopaschism, condemned by the Fifth Ecumenical Council of 553, was also condemned in
691–2 (canon 81, see below), and at the Second Council of Nicaea, 787.

over and above the existing doubts about materiality in relation to the objects themselves.

These worries also showed themselves in other ways. The greatest theologian of the seventh century, Maximus Confessor, composed scholia on the writings of the Pseudo-Dionysius, and emphasized symbolism and mystery in his own work on the liturgy, the *Mystagogia*. The practice of commenting on and interpreting the liturgy was taken up again on the eve of Iconoclasm by Germanos I in his *Historia ecclesiastica*.[104] By this time, however, a new strain of realism is evident, with an emphasis on the human and physical aspects of the life of Christ signified in the Eucharist; undue emphasis on symbolism was reined in by stressing the realistic details of the Incarnation, as in canon 82 of the Council in Trullo, where symbolic representations of Christ are forbidden.[105] Behind this, there seems to have been something of a move in the direction of Antiochene literalism in reaction against an over-symbolic theory of interpretation. It was a long-standing difference; the theology of Theodore of Mopsuestia, condemned by the Fifth Council, nevertheless provided the basis for this more literal reading.[106] The Sixth Ecumenical Council of 680–1, which condemned Monothelitism, laid a heavy emphasis on the human nature of Christ and his existence on earth in the flesh, while the passage in Anastasius of Sinai already cited, insisting on material representations rather than mere words, may belong to the period shortly before.[107] In his *De haeresibus*, Germanos argued that the human representation of Christ was necessary in order to remember his life in the flesh, his suffering, and

---

[104] Germanos's exposition of the meaning of the Eucharist also follows in the tradition of the Pseudo-Dionysius, and draws on Maximus. The Migne text of his *Historia ecclesiastica* or *Historia mystagogica* (*PG* 98, cols 384–453) is late and interpolated, but the original can be reconstructed from other versions, including the Latin translation of Anastasius Bibliothecarius: see R. Taft, 'The Liturgy of the Great Church: an initial synthesis of structure and interpretation on the eve of Iconoclasm', *DOP*, 34–5 (1980–1), pp. 45–76, and on the Urtext, R. Bornert, *Les Commentaires byzantins de la divine liturgie du VIIe au XVe siècle* (Paris, 1966), pp. 125–42; for the extant versions see *CPG*, 3, 8023, and see J. Meyendorff, *On the Divine Liturgy* (*Historia ecclesiastica*), ed. and tr. (Crestwood, NY, 1984); for Maximus's *Mystagogia*, see J. Stead, ed. and tr., *The Church, the Liturgy and the Soul of Man: the Mystagogia of St. Maximus the Confessor* (Still River, Mass., 1982).

[105] On the development from Pseudo-Dionysius to Germanos see Taft, 'The Liturgy', p. 58, and cf. pp. 67ff., with p. 71 on Maximus; see also Barber, 'The Koimesis Church, Nicaea'. Cf. also the similar emphasis in the Acts of II Nicaea, Mansi, 13, 288C–E: the coming of Christ in the flesh justified the place of the material in the divine economy against the Iconoclast view that matter was evil (280D).

[106] For a brilliant short exposition of the implications of Antiochene literalism versus Alexandrian allegory see H. Chadwick, 'Philoponus the Christian Theologian', in R. Sorabji, ed., *Philoponus* (London, 1987), pp. 42–6.

[107] Sixth Council: see Barber, 'The Koimesis Church'; Anastasius: above, n. 28.

his death, and maintained that rejection of the Sixth Council implied rejection of all the rest,[108] while the argument of his *Historia ecclesiastica* contains an emphatic reading of the Eucharist as a memorial of Christ's passion and death, and the gifts at the Great Entrance as signifying the body of the dead Christ, and employs a realism which Father Taft compares to the realism of visual art.[109] This was certainly a political as well as a religious dispute: the Sixth Council, with its emphasis on the humanity of Christ, had been emphatically rejected by the Emperor Philippicus (711–13), who had even removed a depiction of it from the imperial palace, provoking the Pope to set up an image of the Six Councils in St Peter's.[110] It is a sign of the twists and turns of ecclesiastical and political life in the period that the same Germanus who now supported the Sixth Council so warmly is listed by Theophanes as being among Philippicus's supporters.

But the issue of symbolism versus literalism was a real one. It was not a matter of mutually exclusive alternatives, but rather of achieving the right balance; the symbolic interpretation of church buildings and of the liturgy itself, which is characteristic of this period, did not preclude an emphasis on the materiality of the buildings or the divine elements. The iconophiles indeed rested part of their case for images on the argument of the Pseudo-Dionysius about the efficacy of material aids towards religious understanding.[111] The attention paid by writers of this period to the interpretation of the elements of the Eucharist, also material signs until transformed into the Body and Blood of Christ, is part and parcel of the debate. Thus when the Iconoclasts claimed the Eucharist as the only true image of Christ, they were paradoxically appropriating a eucharistic emphasis which was already a major feature of the thought of the supporters of images and the sources on which they depended; both Iconoclasts and iconophiles alike had to find ways of explaining the eucharistic elements in relation both to materiality and to representation.

It is not surprising that Byzantines of the same period were also worried about what was actually represented by the classical statues which still survived, especially in Constantinople itself.[112] When the exact nature of

---

[108] *PG* 98, cols 80A, 81B.

[109] Taft, 'The Liturgy', p. 58.

[110] Theoph., *Chron.*, anno mundi, 6203, pp. 381–2, de Boor; *Liber Pontificalis*, ed. L. Duchesne, 2 vols (Paris, 1886–92), *s.v.* Constantine I (708–15); Herrin, *Formation of Christendom*, p. 312.

[111] See Bishop Kallistos, 'The Meaning of the Divine Liturgy', pp. 12–15; Brubaker, 'Byzantine art in the ninth century', pp. 65–7.

[112] See Mango, 'Antique Statuary'; Cameron and Herrin, *Constantinople in the Eighth Century*, intro., pp. 31–4.

what was depicted in religious pictures had become such a matter of attention and controversy, it was only natural that representations of pagan gods and mythological characters should become a major anxiety, especially when their very identification had often been forgotten. It was tempting to ascribe magic powers to them, or to believe that they had been bewitched.[113] Lurking behind this fear of ancient statues is the same suspicion of idolatry which was directed at religious images; thus in the eighth-century *Parastaseis* Christian emperors are credited with destroying pagan statues, and the pagan Emperor Julian with tricking people into venerating idols in the guise of imperial images.[114] Whatever powers that ancient statues might possess, nobody imagined that they could be beneficent. The historical past, even the reign of Constantine, had receded into half-remembered fantasy.[115] As for classical statues, if a picture of the Virgin and Child, or someone's favourite saint, was now suspect, how much more suspect were Apollo and Aphrodite? The story of a mosaicist whose hand was struck by a demon as he tried to remove a depiction of Aphrodite exactly expresses how people felt.[116] If nothing else, Iconoclasm demonstrated that the representation of Classical Antiquity no longer had a place in medieval Byzantium.

IMAGES AS GUIDES TO TRUTH

The 'rise of icons' and the attack made on them by the Iconoclasts have received a vast amount of attention in histories of Byzantium. I have tried to show that one way of reading both is in relation not just to 'society', or to theology, or to the disasters of the seventh century, but in relation to the intellectual and imaginative framework of contemporary society. A massive intellectual adjustment was necessitated by the final demise of the classical world and the new circumstances of the early medieval one.[117] As

---

[113] Cameron and Herrin, *Constantinople in the Eighth Century*, intro., p. 33.

[114] *Parastaseis Syntomoi Chronikai*, chs 53, 57, 47, ed. Th. Preger, *Scriptores Originum Constantinopolitanarum*, 1 (Leipzig, 1901, repr. New York, 1975); cf. Cameron and Herrin, eds, *Constantinople in the Eighth Century*, p. 33.

[115] See ibid., pp. 34ff. But not only as the discoverer of the True Cross but also as the founder of Constantinople as a Christian city, contrasted with another imperial builder, the pagan Emperor Septimius Severus, Constantine also acquired a new prominence; see also Cameron, 'Byzantium in the Seventh Century'.

[116] Eustratius, *Vita Eutychii*, 53, PG 86.2.2333, tr. Mango, *Art of the Byzantine Empire*, pp. 133–4.

[117] Cf. Dagron, 'Le culte des images', p. 143: 'un long processus d'acculturation, au cours duquel la Byzance chrétienne apprend ce qu'elle eut revendiquer de son passé romano-hellénique et ce à quoi il lui faut renoncer.'

the traditional systems crumbled, the nature of truth and the foundations of knowledge were themselves called into question. We can see this sharply confirmed by the extreme concern for the citation of genuine texts and authorities shown at the councils of 680–1 and 787. Which authorities one should accept was precisely the issue.[118]

Truth being redefined as religious knowledge, images were seen by many as one, though only one, of the ways by which access to this truth was possible (see colour plate 2). They occupied this privileged position not least because of the long struggle in Christian thought to find a language by which God could be represented and in relation to the emphasis placed by writers such as the Pseudo-Dionysius, Maximus, and Germanos on symbolic interpretation and revelation through signs. But they also raised fundamental issues about matter and about what they could actually be held to represent, in a period concerned about charges of idolatry and still dominated by basic Christological issues. The same Quinisext Council which sought to regulate the visual representation of religious subjects also laid down stricter principles for the celebration of the Eucharist, condemned surviving pagan practices, and anathematized those who upheld the addition of the words 'who was crucified for us' to the Trisagion as implying that God could suffer on the Cross.[119] The regulation of images ran parallel to the regulation of behaviour and doctrine as part of the closer definition of the truth. As the Christological arguments of the seventh century centred on the exact definition of the physical life and suffering of Christ, so religious images began to be seen as a means of demonstrating doctrine even more exactly than could be done in words; their potential in this regard is explicitly defended in the powerful argument put by Anastasius of Sinai to which I have already referred, according to which pictures are a more effective way of convincing people of true doctrine than quotations from the Scripture and the Fathers.[120]

The Iconoclastic movement in Byzantium is a perfect illustration of how history proceeds by the convergence of multiple factors, all of which

---

[118] For a similar process at work in the late sixth century see Cameron, 'Models of the Past'.

[119] Canons 73 (Cross not to be used to decorate floors), 82 (Christ not to be represented as a lamb, but in human form, so as to remember the physical suffering of Christ in the flesh); 23, 28, 29, 31, 32, 58, 70 (women must be silent during the liturgy), 83, 101 (Eucharist); 57, 61, 62, 65 (pagan practices; many other canons regulate custom, dress, and entertainment); 81 (Trisagion). On canon 81, condemning Theopaschism, see Kartsonis, *Anastasis*, p. 37.

[120] Above, n. 28; Anastasius's argument also appears in the context of an attack on Theopaschism.

must be given their due. One can read post-Iconoclastic Byzantine art as the vindication of the sign-system which images implied.[121] But I hope to have shown that we must overlook either the place of images in the intellectual framework which had evolved as a replacement for the secular tradition, or the fact that they were seen as representing truth. 'Icons are equivalent to writing';[122] they claimed to be part of the grammar of Byzantine representation. It was hardly surprising that this flight to icons created as many problems as it seemed to solve, but one is sometimes inclined to forget that in the long run the defenders of icons won out, and the system of which icons formed a part was confirmed.

King's College London

---

[121] Brubaker, 'Byzantine art in the ninth century', deals mainly with the art of the ninth century in this light.
[122] Abu Qurrah, *De cultu imaginum*, 13.

CELIA CHAZELLE

Memory, Instruction, Worship: "Gregory's" Influence on Early Medieval Doctrines of the Artistic Image

The influence of Pope Gregory the Great reached into virtually every corner of medieval Christian thought in the West. As a result, his teachings helped shape almost the entire range of Western medieval Christian imagery, for the creators of this art moved in an intellectual environment steeped in Gregory's work. Historians and art historians who analyze the relationship of intellectual developments to medieval artistic production most often focus on only a few, relatively short writings from the vast corpus for which Gregory was responsible. These are letters in which he comments on the significance of Christian artistic images and on how Christians should relate to them, and they are the most widely cited sources in medieval Latin literature for explaining proper Christian views on those issues. Indeed, on the basis of the countless surviving medieval references to the two best known of the letters, written by Gregory to the iconoclast, Bishop Serenus of Marseilles, in 599 and 600 (= Serenus 1 and Serenus 2),[1] the justifications that Western churchmen of the Middle Ages offer for the presence of artistic depictions of Christian themes in churches have been characterized as "Gregorian" at their core. For Ernst Kitzinger, who described Gregory's letters to Serenus as the "classical expressions of the western attitude" toward religious art,[2] and for other scholars, the teachings outlined to the bishop of Marseilles encouraged later Western clergy to reject both iconoclasm and all forms of image-worship, and they prompted a consistent emphasis on the value of images in instructing illiterate or ignorant viewers.[3]

It is not hard to understand why Gregory and particularly his letters to Serenus are so frequently invoked in later Western writings that defend Christian artistic imagery. Here was an authority of doctrine, a pope recognized as a Father of the Church, who provided, for a Latin clergy conscious of the problem of turning pagan converts away from idols, solid reasons why Christian images were useful in that task and deserved respect. While the writings of Augustine, for example, contain numerous ambivalent and sometimes overtly hostile references to artistic imagery, pagan and Christian,[4] Gregory's two letters to the bishop of Marseilles make it clear that the images that filled Christian places of worship in his own day and after should remain there, protected from iconoclastic attacks, and that the Christians who desired to preserve the images were not necessarily, for this reason, idolators.

Although Gregory is the authority to whom Latin medieval texts defending Christian images most often appeal, it is not enough simply to name him as the source of a comment on Christian imagery without also exploring precisely how his thought is used there. Thus, while it has been observed that William Durandus, for one, quotes from Serenus 2 to explain the value of images in churches, William goes on to declare, in words that have no parallel in either letter to Serenus, "we do not adore [images], nor call them gods, nor put hope of salvation in them, since that would be idolatry; but we venerate them in memory and recollection of things done in the past." Elaborating on this, William suggests that Gregory embraced essentially the same doctrine as that expressed by a poem describing an image of Christ: "Anyone who passes the effigy of Christ, honor [it] by prostrating yourself. Yet do not adore the effigy, but that which it signifies . . . For it is not God or man, the image which you presently see; but he is God and man, whom the sacred image figures."[5]

William and other medieval theologians may have derived their knowledge of Gregory from mediating sources, such as florilegia, rather than directly from his writings; but whether or not they were responsible for all the departures they make from the pope's statements, it is evident that merely to identify later comments as Gregorian, as scholars regularly do, does not tell us everything about the thinking they present. Transmitting Gregory's teachings on images to later generations sometimes involved imparting new colors to his ideas.[6]

The range of beliefs about images with which Western medieval writers might connect Gregory's name is especially apparent in the eighth and ninth centuries. Several Latin tracts that deal with the role of Christian artistic images have survived from this period, most of them by Carolingian churchmen working outside papal circles in Rome.[7] The majority of these texts openly acknowledge Gregory as one of their sources, yet that does not mean they all set forth the same doctrines or even that those they defend necessarily come from Gregory. One of the striking characteristics of the writings to be discussed in this essay is how most of them find support in Gregory not simply for different views concerning imagery's function, but even for conflicting attitudes toward image worship. Certain texts draw on Gregory to support the view that images can be worshiped, so long as the reverence is distinguished from the adoration owed to God, but others do so to contend that all image worship must be avoided. To some extent the differing notions of the role of images and of image worship that are associated with Gregory reflect the vagueness of some of his own comments on these issues. In addition, they are indicative of the availability to early medieval churchmen, alongside authentic writings by Gregory, of a forged text attributed to him that had been prepared in Rome in the eighth century, to defend iconodulism against Byzantine iconoclasm.[8] How far Gregory could be brought to bear in supporting dissimilar doctrines of images is evidence, too, of the flexibility with which early medieval churchmen regularly handled their sources—not just Gregory but others as well—as they selected material from older texts and shaped it into their own, often quite distinctive teachings.

The writings by Gregory that are most often noted in eighth- and ninth-century Latin discussions of images, the letters to Bishop Serenus of Marseilles, accuse Serenus of destroying images, probably frescoes or mosaics, in churches in his diocese to prevent people from "adoring" them.[9] Against Serenus, Gregory insists that iconoclasm and the "adoration" of artistic representations are equally wrong. Images of holy persons should neither be destroyed nor adored, Gregory tells Serenus, but instead should be preserved for the benefits they bring to the illiterate or ignorant *(ignorantes, idiotae)*—words that Gregory, like other early medieval writers, uses to denote people with little or no knowledge of Latin and therefore unable to learn Christian doctrine from written sources.[10] Through images, according to Gregory, such viewers gain knowledge of the stories depicted in the works of art, because they are able to "read" in the depictions what they cannot read in books.[11] As Serenus 2 also notes, sight of the images leads viewers to adore God rather than the images themselves, to imitate the virtues of the holy persons represented, and to feel a compunction that again encourages them to prostrate themselves in adoration not of the images but of the Trinity.[12]

Early medieval discussions of artistic imagery occasionally refer, as well, to a letter sent by Gregory to Bishop Januarius of Cagliari, where Gregory briefly comments on an image of Mary with Jesus and on a cross that had been forcibly placed in a synagogue, and advises Januarius that both objects should be removed "with such veneration as is deserved."[13] More often mentioned is the forgery noted above. Added to a letter sent by Gregory to the hermit Secundinus of Gaul, and first recorded in relation to the Lateran Council of 769, the forgery was most likely composed sometime in the eighth century to reinforce Roman iconodulist arguments against Byzantine iconoclasm. In the interpolation "Gregory" encourages Secundinus to contemplate a picture of Christ sent by the pope—the words indicate that the writer had in mind a small image useful for private devotion, such as an icon—because

> with every effort you seek in your heart him whose image you desire to have before your eyes, so that, every day, what your eyes see brings back to you the person depicted, so that while you gaze at the picture your soul burns for him whose image you so carefully contemplate . . . We know that you do not want an image of our savior in order to worship it as though it were a god, but in order to recall the Son of God and thus warm in love of him whose image you take care to behold. And certainly we do not prostrate ourselves before that image as if before a deity, but we adore him whom we remember through the image, at his birth or passion or seated on his throne.[14]

Gregory's letters to Serenus indicate that the pope thought Serenus's iconoclasm was directed primarily against large-scale images of Christian themes—holy persons and events—placed in public view on church walls. The letters seek to make Serenus aware of the value of these artistic representations for leading uneducated viewers to better knowledge of Christian teachings, by arguing that the images have an impact on the uneducated similar to that of written texts on literate, educated Christians. Where the letters refer to image worship, they do so only in negative terms, through denunciations of the "adoration" of images, though it is not certain whether the term is used to express opposition only to the idolatrous worship of images in the manner owed to God, allowing for the possibility that other forms of image worship exist and are permissible, or whether it indicates opposition to the veneration of images in any sense.[15] The letters' vagueness on this issue left an important opening for later Western writers who wanted both to base their teachings on Gregory and to defend image worship.

Certain features of Gregory's comments to Serenus have no known precedents in earlier Christian writings that discuss the role of artistic images. In particular, as I have argued elsewhere, this is true of his assertions that images can be "read" by illiterate viewers just as books are read by the literate, a concept that represents Gregory's adaptation of comments by Augustine on the Christian's relationship to miracles.[16] In comparing images to books, in objecting both to iconoclasm and to idolatrous behavior toward images, and in affirming that images help teach the illiterate, however, the letters to Serenus echo the teachings of other authorities of the fifth and sixth centuries from the East and the West.[17] The interpolation, on the other hand, reflects arguments employed by seventh- and eighth-century defenders of images when it emphasizes the benefits that smaller pictures, such as icons, bring to Christians like Gregory and Secundinus who are trained in Christian doctrine. For the author of the interpolation, as for other seventh- and eighth-century iconodulist writers, these smaller images of Christian subjects can be objects of private contemplation, and they assist educated viewers to feel love for and recall already familiar prototypes. The viewer rightly bows in worship of the image or icon so long as he does not intend his reverence for the image alone, as though it were a deity, but as a means to honor God or Christ.[18]

Before turning to the Carolingian texts that discuss the role of artistic images and their worship, a few writings from eighth-century

Rome should be considered—works that deal with the same issues and, in doing so, draw on Gregory the Great. The first clear identification of Gregory as a source for a doctrine of images occurs in relation to the Lateran Council of 769, convened under Pope Stephen III to reaffirm the decisions against Greek iconoclasm of a council held in 731 under Pope Gregory III. According to Pope Hadrian I, writing to Charlemagne in 793,[19] Bishop Herulf of Langres, one of several Frankish bishops at the council of 769, had read the interpolated letter to Secundinus before the assembly as evidence of how images were properly venerated. Hadrian's letter to Charlemagne and other records of the 769 council[20] reveal that the synod, like the writer of the interpolation, distinguished image worship from the adoration owed to God, although the assembly evidently considered the term *adoration* acceptable for denoting the reverence given to images.[21] The worship paid to an image of a Christian event or holy person was recognized by the council to be an expression of the viewer's love for the image's prototype, a means to honor God, and the equivalent of the honors owed to relics of the saints, to basilicas dedicated to saints, and to the Cross.[22] The images deserved such reverence because they were holy, might work miracles or be miraculously made, led the viewer to remember and contemplate the holy beings they represented, and stirred compunction.[23]

The same letter by Hadrian, which is mainly a defense of the iconodulist Second Nicene Council (787) and a response to a list of chapter headings (the *Capitulare adversus synodum*) for the Carolingian treatise, the *Libri Carolini*, links Gregory with Roman iconodulist doctrine in other ways as well.[24] References to the letters to Serenus, for example, are used to support Hadrian's own claims that images are comparable to Scripture, that they allow the illiterate to read what they cannot read in books and help teach their viewers,[25] as well as his assertions that Gregory respected and venerated "holy images"[26] and that images, like Scripture, should be kept in memory and veneration of those depicted in them.[27] The letter to Januarius and the interpolation are also noted as evidence that Gregory believed images to deserve some form of veneration, and the interpolation alone is mentioned to defend the statement of Nicaea II, rejected in the *Capitulare,* that "through an image, which is formed with colors, his [Christ's] strength is adored and

glorified, and we will come to memory of his presence on earth."²⁸
The last section of Hadrian's letter brings all four Gregorian texts
together—Serenus 1 and 2, the letter to Januarius, and the interpolation—to uphold the doctrines that images of the saints demonstrate love of the saints and God and are legitimately worshiped,
"as Gregory taught," by being kissed and "humbly saluted [honora-
bilem salutationem reddere]."²⁹ Hadrian is careful to distinguish
the veneration of images from the adoration owed to God, despite
his occasional employment of the term *adoration* to describe
image worship.³⁰ In his belief, as he notes near the end of his letter
to Charlemagne, both Serenus 2 and the interpolation confirm that
such worship is valid: Christians may prostrate themselves before
images, not to adore them as if they were deities, but because the
images inspire adoration of God.³¹

By identifying Gregory with the iconodulist response to Byzantine iconoclasm, Hadrian and the Lateran Council of 769 effectively
linked him with doctrines and practices regarding images that had
taken shape mainly in the East after Gregory's death and gained
strength in Rome under Eastern influence. The bridge between Gregory's teachings, products of the late sixth century, and eighth-
century Roman iconodulism was built partly with the interpolation
to the letter to Secundinus. Added to the corpus of authentic Gregorian material, it provided a foundation in Gregory for almost every
practice and doctrine relating to images that the eighth-century
papacy defended against the Greek iconoclasts. In spite of the interpolation's importance to Hadrian and the 769 council, though, it is
clear that Hadrian, at least, also read the letters to Januarius and
Serenus through the filter of Roman iconodulist teachings. All the
Gregorian texts available by the late eighth century seemed to him
to reveal Gregory's agreement with the iconodulist doctrines promulgated in 731 and reaffirmed in 769,³² as well as with those
expressed in the decrees of Nicaea II: for Hadrian, Gregory, too, held
that artistic depictions of Christian themes stirred love and memory and taught the ignorant, that they were holy objects deserving a
worship equivalent to that given to relics and basilicas dedicated to
the saints, and that this reverence was distinguishable from the
adoration due to God alone and yet brought honor to God and the
subjects of the images. None of Gregory's writings appeared to
Hadrian to contradict these teachings. This is true even of Serenus

1 and 2, which might have been taken to reject the validity of worshiping images, but which Hadrian apparently understood only to
deny that images merited the honor owed to God.

When we move from eighth-century Rome to the *Libri Carolini*
(LC) completed for Charlemagne in 793, we confront a text that
uses Gregory to support a doctrine of images radically different
from that espoused by the council of 769 of Hadrian, one that
denies the propriety of any form of image worship and narrows
considerably the range of functions that images perform for Christians.[33] That the churchmen responsible for the *LC* interpreted
Gregory differently from Roman iconodules already emerges from
the *Capitulare*, sent to Hadrian in 790–92 while work on the *LC*
was under way, which provoked the pope's letter of 793 to Charlemagne. The only reference to Gregory in the *Capitulare* that is def-
initely part of the list of chapters originally sent to Hadrian, and
the only one that became part of the completed version of the *LC*,
occurs in the heading to chapter 50, which mentions Gregory's
opposition to the destruction and the adoration of images, but
emphasizes his rejection of the latter, and implies that all image
worship is wrong.[34] The *LC*, written primarily by Theodulf of
Orléans and revised by him with the help of other theologians
associated with Charlemagne,[35] quotes two passages from Serenus
2 in book 2, chapter 23, which corresponds to chapter 50 in the
Capitulare.[36] There is no mention in the *LC* of Serenus 1 or, more
important, of the letters to Januarius and Secundinus. Perhaps
Theodulf and his colleagues were unaware of these texts or did
not recognize their significance for assessing Gregory's doctrine
of images, at least until they received Hadrian's response to the
Capitulare, which reached Charlemagne only after the *LC* was finished.[37] But the most obvious factor behind the absence in the *LC*
of any references to the letters to Secundinus and Januarius is the
support they seem to offer for a cult of images, which the *LC*
emphatically rejects.

Not only the choice of Gregorian material but also the teachings
in Serenus 2 highlighted in the *LC* differ from what is seen in
Hadrian's letter to Charlemagne. Although the passages repeated
from Serenus 2 state that images teach the illiterate, the *LC* does
not openly discuss this notion in its own words; instead, the focus
is on Gregory's warnings that artistic depictions should not be

destroyed or adored. As in the *Capitulare,* the need to avoid the adoration of images is emphasized more than the error of destroying them, and the injunction against their adoration is associated with the concept that image worship in any sense is wrong.[38]

The Carolingians thought that Nicaea II had advocated idolatry, the bestowal on images of the adoration owed to the Trinity, when actually the Greek council, like the council of 769 and Hadrian, had distinguished between the adoration of God and the reverence paid to images. Since the *LC* rejects image worship in any form, however, and since it criticizes Nicaea II not only for its iconodulism but for also numerous other failings, it is unlikely that Theodulf and his colleagues would have accepted the decrees of Nicaea II even if they had understood them.[39] The total disapproval of image worship shown in the *LC,* the treatise's association of Gregory with this position, and the general antipathy toward images that is evident there suited the Carolingians' desire to distance themselves politically from the iconodulist government in Byzantium. The political advantages of the position that the *LC* adopts on images and on other issues, though, do not mean that Theodulf and his associates had failed to think through the theological dimensions of their attack on the Greek council. Although this is not an aspect of the *LC* that needs to be explored in depth here, it is important to reiterate a point I have argued at greater length elsewhere:[40] much of the attack on Nicaea II in the *LC* can be traced to a vision of the relationship of the material world to the spiritual that, I suspect, was grounded in Theodulf's interpretation of Augustine, possibly derived from a Spanish school of Augustinianism.[41] In the *LC,* apparently on the basis of Augustinian doctrine, the material world is perceived as something good, yet it is so completely separate from the spiritual realm that only when mortals turn away from material things can they hope to draw nearer to the spiritual or God. This conception of matter's relationship to spirit affected how Serenus 2 was employed in the *LC* as well as virtually every other element of the teachings in the *LC,* teachings that seek to demonstrate how all the many errors made by Nicaea II, not simply its defense of iconodulism, are indicative of the Greek council's failure to follow Scripture, orthodoxy, and Rome.[42]

The relationship of the material to the spiritual realm envisioned in the *LC* influenced the treatise's employment of Serenus 2

in two ways. First, it guided the interpretation of Gregory's warnings against both the destruction and the adoration of images.
These statements were understood to affirm, on the one hand, that
matter, represented by artistic images, is not evil and should not be
rejected, as it was by the iconoclasts, and on the other hand, that
the material world to which images belong exists totally separate
from the spiritual sphere. God alone deserves adoration, and the
saints in heaven deserve veneration, but images should never
receive Christian worship.[43] For Theodulf and his colleagues, the
material object can have no spiritual dimension unless it is specially consecrated by God, a blessing that will be revealed in Scripture, the word of God that records all sacred truth. The Bible never
indicates images to be consecrated things, and so they must be
nothing more than material objects, produced by mortal, fallible
craftsmen, with no connection whatsoever to the invisible, spiritual things of heaven.[44]

Second, the separation that the LC posits between the material
world and the spiritual affected the treatise's handling of Gregory's
advice to Serenus that images are comparable to books and teach
the illiterate. Although these concepts are expressed in the passages quoted from Gregory in LC 2.23, they are not reiterated or
reaffirmed when Theodulf and his associates comment on the passages in their own words, nor are they mentioned at other points in
the LC where the benefits of images are discussed. Indeed, rather
than defending the ability of images to teach or the parallel they
present to books, LC 2.23 implies that Serenus 2 supports the
belief, upheld elsewhere in the LC, that images are useful only as
decoration and as an aid to memory of the past.[45]

The approach to these aspects of Gregory's teachings is ambiguous, then, and for us to understand why, we must keep in mind a
few further elements of the LC that grow out of its conception of
the relationship between the material and spiritual realms. As
other portions of the LC indicate, Theodulf and his associates saw
images as objects divorced from the spiritual not only because they
are fabricated from matter but also because, as material *likenesses*,
they necessarily recall their subjects only to the extent that they
resemble those persons or things—and consequently only insofar
as the images' subjects, too, are material. An artist can never depict
something spiritual, and therefore artistic images are unable to

reveal anything to the viewer's eyes of the spiritual world.[46] This means that the image is inferior to the written word as a means of communication. Although writing is also a material creation, for Theodulf and his colleagues it operates as a system of signs that designate things, which the written letters and words do not have to resemble, and which therefore can encompass spiritual things.[47] God's choice to have his word recorded in writing rather than in painting is evidence of the superiority of the written word over the image as an instrument of communication; out of all written texts, Christians should turn especially to the Bible for insight into the spiritual realm. Blessed by God, Scripture is one of the few things that do exist on both a spiritual and a material level, and Christians who read the Bible or hear it read can gain insight into the vast treasure of wisdom revealed through a spiritual as well as a literal (that is, material) interpretation of its contents.[48]

To say that images serve as decoration and as reminders of the past conforms with this conception of their total imprisonment in the material realm. Something that is decorative is appreciated for its aesthetic value—for the quality of its components and the skill of its execution—and therefore for its material features. If what the image recalls is part of the past, that subject, like the image itself, necessarily lies within the temporal, material sphere. Like Gregory, the *LE* recognizes that images are particularly useful to viewers with little education in Christian doctrine, such as recent converts from paganism. The Carolingian treatise suggests that the faith of such people can be strengthened by artistic representations, because the images make them more aware of holy figures and events, and also because, unlike more "mature" Christians, the new converts may not yet be ready to take the final steps away from dependency on the material world that they must take in order to grasp the things revealed through attention to Scripture's hidden, spiritual meaning.[49] Yet it probably would have been difficult for Theodulf and his colleagues to give as much weight to the parallel that Gregory drew between images and books, or to the notion that images teach the illiterate, as they did to the doctrine that images are decorative and recall the past. Given the separation between the materiality of images and the spiritual sphere, envisioned in the *LC*, books—written words—are clearly superior to artistic representations, and whatever information the image imparts to its viewer has nothing to do with the unseen, spiritual realm revealed in Scripture, which should be the main focus of Christian study.

As Ann Freeman has observed, the LC never circulated widely after its completion, no doubt partly because of the discrepancy that Hadrian's letter to Charlemagne revealed between the pope's attitude toward Nicaea II and that espoused in the LC.[50] The length of the LC—228 pages in the current printed edition—may also have been a factor, since this must have made copying difficult.[51] Both circumstances likely explain why only two copies of the LC are known to have been produced in the ninth century[52] and why, even though a few other extant Carolingian writings on images espouse some doctrines similar to those of the LC, there is little if any evidence that the LC directly influenced later Carolingian thought. When later Carolingian writers turn to Gregory to defend their views on the role of images and on image worship, they tend to use him differently than the LC does, sometimes to the extent that their interpretations of his teachings fall closer to what is seen in Hadrian's letter to Charlemagne. Moreover, just as none of the later Carolingian writings presents doctrines that exactly mirror those found in the LC, no two of these texts express exactly the same thoughts. Certain themes and beliefs regarding images emerge in most (though not all) of them, above all the doctrine that artistic representations should neither be destroyed nor adored, yet otherwise there is considerable variation in the understanding they demonstrate of the functions that images perform for Christians and of how Christians should approach images.

The first extant, clearly datable Carolingian texts dealing with the role of images that postdate the LC are the documents produced in relation to the Synod of Paris (825).[53] The synod, possibly only a small assembly,[54] was convened to respond to a letter from the Byzantine emperors Michael and Theophilus, who were moderate iconoclasts, asking Louis the Pious to aid their campaign against iconodulism. The letter notes that the Greek emperors had ordered the removal of images from the lower portions of church walls in order to prevent the faithful from worshiping them, while permitting images higher on the walls because they served there as a form of "Scripture."[55]

The response of the Synod of Paris was initially outlined in a libellus prepared for Louis.[56] In certain respects the position taken in the libellus resembles that of the *LC:* both iconoclasm and Byzantine iconodulism are rejected; the latter error is associated with the adoration of images in the sense owed to God; Nicaea II is attacked for supposedly having advocated such behavior; and overall, less interest is shown in condemning iconoclasm than in denouncing the beliefs that the Carolingians linked with the Greek iconodules.[57] The libellus differs from the *LC* in its much greater emphasis on imagery's usefulness to Christians and its greater tolerance of image worship—differences that are linked with a different approach to Gregory. Selections from the letters to Januarius, Secundinus, and Serenus are quoted three times in the libellus, twice on the grounds that they provide evidence of what constitutes "discretion" *(discretio)* in the use of images. Although a precise definition of that term is not offered, the libellus suggests that its meaning is to be found particularly in Serenus 2, where it is connected with Gregory's doctrine that images should be neither destroyed nor adored: discretion means the avoidance of both errors.[58] The *LC,* too, makes this doctrine central to its teachings, yet the range of functions for images that is understood to fall between the two extremes of adoration and destruction is significantly larger in the libellus. The *LC* recognizes only imagery's ability to serve as decoration and to remind viewers of the past, but the libellus acknowledges that images decorate the places in which they appear, stir compunction, teach the ignorant, and (with an appeal to Gregory) encourage love as well as memory of the saints.[59]

Furthermore, turning to Gregory for support, the libellus asserts that the worship it condemns as the "adoration" of images consists of "undeserved" or "unfitting" forms of reverence *(indebitus cultus, superfluus cultus),*[60] implying that "deserved" veneration also exists. The libellus makes clear the council's beliefs that artistic representations have no inherent sanctity, cannot help the Christian approach heaven, and can be ignored without harming the Christian's soul,[61] and that no action should be performed for idolatrous purposes, such that the image is honored for its own sake as though it were a god; the last notion seems to underlie the disapproval expressed for the placing of incense and lights before images.[62] Images (by which is meant here artistic representations other than crosses) are therefore very different from the Cross and crosses, which are praised in the libellus as divinely consecrated objects filled with sacred power[63] that deserve "veneration," "exaltation," and "adoration," in an echo of the major liturgical rites in honor of the Cross.[64]

There is no direct admission that artistic imagery other than crosses should be revered. Nevertheless, the synod's willingness to accept reverential actions before images—actions presumably understood to differ from the "veneration, exaltation, and adoration" owed to crosses—and its conviction that this accorded with Gregory's teachings become evident from the testimonia of earlier authorities offered in the second half of the libellus to illustrate acceptable beliefs and actions involving works of art. These texts, as the introduction to this portion of the libellus states, demonstrate that images should be neither loved nor condemned "beyond what is fitting."[65] The section opens with excerpts from the letters to Serenus, Januarius, and Secundinus.[66] A few testimonia by authorities other than Gregory suggest that images lack holiness, dwelling on the need to adore God alone;[67] others deal mainly with the Cross, crosses, and their sanctity.[68] The majority of the sources quoted in the second half of the libellus, though—some of them originally written in Greek—contain positive references to Christian artistic depictions, their merits, and the respect Christians should show them. Some of the passages call upon Christians to "worship" and "adore" Christ, Mary, and the saints through their images; admit that true "adoration" is owed to God, but that the word can denote honors properly paid to creatures; and distinguish the worship legitimately paid to images from that rendered to God.[69]

The Synod of Paris probably would not have included this section in its libellus unless the participants had generally agreed that images may receive some veneration, even though the council insisted that its position had no connection with the one promulgated by Nicaea II and supported by Hadrian I.[70] Such a position on image worship is implied, too, by a passage near the end of the libellus discussing the letter to Secundinus. Despite "Gregory's" claim in the interpolation that he does not worship an image of Christ as if it were a separate deity, but rather adores Christ, whom sight of the image brings him to remember, the synod apparently believed that the text came dangerously close to implying that images should receive the adoration that God deserves and thus to contradicting Gregory's advice to Serenus. The synod endeavors to explain away the perceived contradiction by drawing an analogy between the behavior described in the interpolation and a subject's behavior before his king. The subject does not prostrate himself before the king as if the monarch were a god, the libellus argues, but rather he adores Jesus, whom sight of the king brings to mind, since Jesus possesses a human nature and since the enthroned ruler "imitates" the enthroned Christ in heaven.[71] The implication is that Christians may prostrate themselves before images, not to adore the images themselves but to express their reverence for the heavenly beings (Christ, the angels, the saints) represented in them.

It is possible, for several reasons, that theologians under Charlemagne and Louis the Pious may have disagreed less about image worship than the *LC* and the libellus would suggest. For one, while the *LC* was written against an iconodulist government in Byzantium, the Synod of Paris faced a Greek policy of iconoclasm.[72] The more flexible and tolerant attitudes toward images and their worship found in the libellus may stem in part from a perception in 825 that iconodulism was a less immediate threat than the iconoclastic policies of Michael and Theophilus. In addition, the libellus is mainly a hastily compiled collection of testimonia from different authorities.[73] Neither it nor the epitome that Jonas of Orléans and Jeremiah of Sens later made from the libellus to convey the synod's decisions to Pope Eugenius II[74] is a formal treatise, unlike the *LC*, where scriptural passages and references to patristic sources are integrated into a carefully organized and thorough critique of iconoclasm, of the iconodulism of Nicaea II, of major aspects of the Byzantine imperial government's claims to authority, and of still other failings attributed to the Eastern Empire. It is no wonder, then, that the writings of the 825 synod show no trace of the driving effort seen in the *LC* to make every argument conform to a single, rigid principle regarding the relationship of matter to spirit. The desire to bring each element of the *LC's* teachings into line with this one principle may have encouraged Theodulf and his colleagues to express stricter opposition to image worship and to deemphasize the value of artistic imagery beyond what they might have done under other circumstances. And finally, it must be remembered that the *LC* is primarily Theodulf's work: the treatise's doctrines may represent chiefly his views, and other Carolingian theologians at the time may have held quite different beliefs about the role of images and their worship, perhaps ones similar to those in the libellus.

At least under Charlemagne's successors, other Carolingian writings reveal the existence of a range of different attitudes toward artistic depictions and particularly toward their worship. These diverse views are regularly defended by appeal to Gregory I. Among the most radical teachings on image worship recorded in any Carolingian text—though apparently not based on Gregory— are those in the surviving fragments of a treatise written by Bishop Claudius of Turin between 824 and his death in c. 827, answering questions raised about his orthodoxy by Abbot Theutmir of Psalmody (Nîmes).[75] Claudius states that he had been appalled, on arriving in Turin in 817, to find that the city's churches were filled with "filthy images" and that Christians engaged in their "worship" *(colere)*—a sign, perhaps, that before his arrival the clergy of Turin had allowed practices before images similar to those the Paris synod appears to have tolerated.[76] The letter against Theutmir defends Claudius's destruction of the images on the grounds that artistic depictions must not receive any manner of worship; it also rejects crosses, asserts that pilgrimages to Rome and the cult of relics have no sacral value and that the saints cannot intercede with God after their deaths, and appears to scorn Rome and papal authority.[77] Claudius's disapproval of images—not merely of their worship but of their presence in churches altogether—is suggested to be based first on a very strict interpretation of the Second Commandment and second—underlying his negative attitude toward crosses, relics, and pilgrimages—on a denial of any spiritual worth to the material world.[78] His antipathy toward the material sphere may have extended even to Christ's human weakness and suffering, as suggested by the claim against Theutmir that, like unbelievers, worshipers of crosses find pleasing in Christ only "the shame of the passion and the mockery of [his] death."[79]

Claudius's comments against Theutmir depart from the *LC* both because the *LC* forbids iconoclasm and because Theodulf and his associates stressed the sanctity of the Cross and relics and the veneration of the saints.[80] The two documents share, however, the assumption of a sharp separation between the material and spiritual worlds. The surviving portions of Claudius's text are too brief to allow us much insight into the theological underpinnings of its dual-

ism, but since Claudius was from Spain,[81] as was Theodulf, one factor may have been a similar interpretation of Augustine, rooted
again perhaps in Spanish traditions.[82] As far as Gregory is concerned,
there is no reference to him in the extant portions of Claudius's
work, possibly because of the fragmentary state in which it has survived, although it does seem likely that Claudius would have considered Greogry's thought incompatible with his own iconoclasm.

According to both Claudius and Dungal the Scot, writing in 827,
news of Claudius's teachings spread throughout the Carolingian
Empire, and Dungal claims that support for Claudius was widely
found.[83] That Claudius did not stand alone in at least some of his
beliefs is also indicated by the tract attacking the cult of images—
chiefly a patristic florilegium—by Agobard of Lyons,[84] perhaps a
contribution to the Paris synod's effort to gather sources relating to
the function and worship of artistic representations.[85] The treatise
includes a passage from Bede asserting that artistic representations
help illiterate viewers and are comparable to books, and Agobard
comments in his own words on imagery's value for recalling the
past and for stirring love of the holy persons depicted.[86] Although
he does not actually quote from Gregory, he claims that Gregory
reproved the bishop of Frejus (evidently meaning Serenus) for
destroying images "of the apostles" after he found people adoring
them, when he should have kept them for later generations as
reminders of the persons they represent.[87]

Most of Agobard's treatise focuses on his opposition to image
worship, and here he leaves no doubt that he considered any such
acts unacceptable. His attitude seems to rest on a rigid dualism that
may reflect the same Spanish Augustinianism possibly behind the
dualism of the *LC* and Claudius. Agobard, too, was of Spanish origin,[88] and the vast majority of the sources quoted in his treatise are
passages from Augustine, carefully arranged with texts by a few
other authorities, such as Gregory (from writings other than his letters on images), to convey the doctrines that the material world
exists completely divorced from the spiritual, that there is therefore
nothing holy about images, and that to turn to images, things
rooted in the material sphere, is to turn away from spiritual
things.[89] Images are worthless in the Christian's quest to approach
God; any reverence shown to them is idolatrous, even when the
worshiper inwardly intends to honor Christ or the saints in heaven.

Consequently, following the Council of Elvira (305), it is better to do without images in churches entirely than risk that they be revered.[90] Agobard apparently did not perceive the conflict—or chose to ignore it—between this position and his reference to Gregory's letters to Serenus. After citing Gregory he goes on to remark, recalling Claudius's policy, that if people venerate images of the saints the images should be destroyed. The depictions are purely human creations that God never ordered to be made, Agobard declares by way of explanation,[91] but his call for the destruction of the works of art is also tied to his belief that the veneration of Christian images is always, by definition, idolatrous. Images that are revered are no better than pagan idols.[92]

No other Carolingian writing that openly supports iconoclasm appears to have survived, although Dungal's comment on the popularity of Claudius's attitudes may be a sign that others were written. Still, some ninth-century Carolingian theologians disagreed in other ways with the position enunciated at the Synod of Paris. Among them were Jeremiah of Sens and Jonas of Orléans, who attended the synod and prepared the epitome of its libellus.[93] The epitome follows the organization of the libellus and draws its sources from there, but the choice made from those sources and the comments added by Jonas and Jeremiah demonstrate that these two bishops held a different conception of proper Christian behavior toward images than that which the libellus suggests represented the consensus of the whole synod. The epitome agrees with the libellus in affirming the Carolingians' opposition both to the destruction of images and to their adoration or "undue worship."[94] Images are valuable because they show Christians' love and respect for the saints, aid memory, and are decorative,[95] it is stated. Yet, like the libellus, the epitome denies that images possess sanctity or that incense or lights should be placed before them,[96] and it insists that they are vastly inferior to the Cross.[97] The position taken in the epitome is declared to be grounded on Pope Gregory I, the spokesman of discretion and Eugenius's outstanding predecessor.[98] But the epitome recalls the LC more than the libellus. First, the only writings by Gregory quoted are excerpts from the letters to Serenus;[99] the letters to Januarius and Secundinus are not mentioned, even though these texts were in the libellus, from which Jonas and Jeremiah selected their own sources.[100] Second, like the

LC, the epitome avoids any hint that some acts of image worship are distinguishable from the "adoration" owed to God alone and are therefore acceptable. The implication throughout the epitome is that image worship in any sense should be opposed, a position clearly easier to link with Gregory when references to the letters to Januarius and Secundinus are avoided.

Jonas's opposition to image worship is also evident from his attack on Claudius of Turin. Although Jonas had not finished his treatise when Claudius died, he started to write again after the death in 840 of Louis the Pious because, Jonas contended, supporters of Claudius had resurfaced and the ideas about images they embraced—Claudius's teachings—were related to Arianism and Spanish Adoptionism.[101] Jonas holds that his own doctrine of images conforms with that expressed in Gregory's letters to Serenus, which he cites near the beginning of his treatise as evidence that images have traditionally been kept in churches and should not be adored or destroyed but rather should be preserved "only to instruct ignorant minds [solummodo ad instruendas nescientium mentes]."[102] Contrary to Claudius's belief, Jonas asserts, the Second Commandment does not forbid all artistic imagery but only images that receive the *cultus* and adoration owed to God. Just as God permitted the cherubim in the tabernacle and the decorations in Solomon's temple, he allows Christian images to be placed in churches as decoration and to evoke memories of the past.[103] Yet although Christians who "pray to images of the saints out of respect for them and in excessive and indiscreet love" are not necessarily idolators, their prayers to or worship of the images are still wrong.[104] As in the epitome and the *LC,* Gregory's injunction against the adoration of images is understood to encompass all forms of image worship. Hence, Jonas adamantly opposes the concept, to which Claudius, too, objects, but which recalls some of the testimonia quoted in the libellus that Christians may "adore" an image with "veneration" and "in honor" of the holy person depicted. Such actions, Jonas insists, give to a "weak and worthless *simulacrum* the honor owed to the Divinity" and so represent the same sin committed by "certain Greeks."[105] In this light, it is understandable that Jonas's treatise does not mention the letter to Secundinus, despite his familiarity with it from the Synod of Paris. His disapproval of image worship also illumines his one reference

321

to Gregory's letter to Januarius: Jonas quotes the passage in the letter where Gregory urges Januarius to remove, "with such veneration as is deserved," the image of Mary with Jesus and the cross
placed in the synagogue; but he remarks solely on the respect owed
to crosses, not on what the letter might imply concerning proper
behavior toward images of Mary or Christ.[106]

Claudius, Agobard, Jonas, and Jeremiah disagree on what the
clergy should do about image worship when they find the practice
occurring, but they agree in believing that the worship of images in
any sense must be opposed. This is probably why, unlike the Paris
synod in its libellus, none of them links his doctrine of images
with the letter to Januarius or mentions the interpolated version of
the letter to Secundinus.

One Carolingian text that expresses, much more clearly than the
libellus of 825, a favorable view of image worship is Dungal's tract
against Claudius. Dungal maintains that he opposes both those
who think that a part of creation deserves the reverence owed to
God—thus he rejects, for example, the offering of sacrifices to any
creature[107]—and those who would destroy something made "in
God's honor," such as an image of a saint. He identifies his position with the teachings of the Synod of Paris and of Serenus 2, from
which he quotes a passage,[108] and he probably has both that letter
and the synod's decisions in mind when he suggests that images
should be preserved because they "offer almost as much to erudi-
tion as do sacred letters."[109] The Second Commandment does not
outlaw all artistic imagery, Dungal contends; such objects mentioned in the Old Testament as the Ark's cherubim and the brazen
serpent show God's acceptance of images made "to his honor,"[110]
and artistic images of Christian themes similarly honor God by
assisting memory and love of the heavenly beings they depict.[111]
More interesting, however, is a statement implying that Christians
properly pray before images of the saints to gain the saints' intercession,[112] as well as Dungal's assertions that "holy pictures"
should be venerated just like crosses and relics. Although none of
these objects deserves the worship given to God, all are properly
revered or venerated "in God and on God's behalf . . . so that they
are honored and embraced in love, honor, praise of him and in his
glory, as separate, holy, and venerable signs and vessels, as it is
appropriate . . . with saving and not false faith."[113]

The libellus of the synod of 825 only tacitly admits that images may be worshiped, and it insists on the inferiority of images to crosses, while Dungal openly defends the veneration of images and implies that images have equivalent sanctity to crosses and relics, such that all these objects are equally "holy and venerable signs and vessels." Yet like the Synod of Paris, Dungal apparently saw no contradiction between his teachings and those of Gregory. Although he does not refer to Gregory's letters to Januarius or to Secundinus, he seems to have thought that his beliefs about images were compatible with the excerpt he does quote from Serenus 2. For Dungal, when Gregory rejected the adoration of images he meant to condemn only the bestowal on them of the adoration owed to God, while recognizing the existence of other, legitimate forms of image worship.

The chapter on images in Walafrid Strabo's *De exordiis*, written in the early 840s,[114] around the time that Jonas probably completed his tract against Claudius, does not mention Gregory directly, but it deserves notice because it again upholds a relatively positive doctrine of image worship. Claiming to reflect the decisions of the Roman council of 731 (reaffirmed in 769) and of the synod of 825,[115] the chapter attacks proponents of iconoclasm, including Claudius,[116] in part on the grounds that the Old Testament accounts of the tabernacle and temple show that the Second Commandment was not intended to outlaw all artistic depictions.[117] Any irreverence demonstrated toward Christian artistic images redounds to the injury of the persons depicted there,[118] Walafrid declares; such depictions are beneficial because they provide a manner of writing for the illiterate, stir memory and love for their subjects,[119] and arouse feelings of compunction, so that viewers show through their tears that the figures represented in the images "are impressed on their hearts."[120] Although it is wrong, according to Walafrid, to give "immoderate worship" *(cultus immoderatus)* or "spiritual worship" *(spiritalis cultus)* to images and other corporal things, or to revere them in the manner owed to God,[121] artistic representations can be shown "honest and moderate honors [honesti et moderati imaginum honores]"[122]—though precisely what such honors entail is not explained.

Finally, the *Opusculum LV capitulorum*, written by Hincmar of Reims against Hincmar of Laon in 869–70, should be mentioned, because Hincmar of Rheims again thought that his comments there on the function of images and on image worship accorded with Gregory's teachings.[123] Earlier in the treatise Hincmar quotes a passage from the LC discussing the nature of an ecumenical council,[124] and we know that he had a copy of the LC made for himself,[125] yet there is little evidence that the LC directly influenced his thinking about images. Like the LC and the libellus of 825, Hincmar's Opusculum condemns Nicaea II, calling it a "pseudosynod" held "without the authority of the apostolic see,"[126] where those who wanted to destroy images battled those who said that images must be adored.[127] The orthodox position, he states, was rather the one announced in the letters to Secundinus and Serenus, where those are reprehended

> who with the excuse that [images] should not be adored say that they must be destroyed, and those [are praised] who establish that [the images] must neither be adored nor destroyed but set up only for instructing ignorant minds; since one ought to prostrate oneself humbly in adoration solely of the omnipotent holy Trinity, and if anyone wishes to make images of God [i.e., Christ] and the saints for the purpose of instruction he should not in any way be prohibited from having them.[128]

Hincmar goes on to suggest that images of the saints, just like the saints' words, assist knowledge of their subjects[129]—a very different view of the relationship between words and images from that found in the LC, but one in keeping with Gregory's comparison of images to books and with Hincmar's clear affirmation that images teach the ignorant. While Hincmar's attitude toward image worship is uncertain, the approving manner in which he cites the letter to Secundinus probably indicates some acceptance of the practice. This is also implied by Flodoard's comment, in his *Historia ecclesiae Remensis*, that Hincmar had written a treatise (now lost) on "how images of our savior and his saints should be venerated [qualiter imagines Salvatoris nostri, vel sanctorum ipsius venerandae sint]."[130]

Modern scholarship tends to refer to Western attitudes toward images as though a single doctrine of the artistic representation runs in a straight line from Gregory the Great to Bernard of Clairvaux and beyond—one involving, in Gregory as in later medieval writers, a consistent emphasis on imagery's didactic value and a consistent effort to repress all worship of artistic depictions. Such attitudes were indeed strong in this period. Yet in the Carolingian realm and empire, particularly if we take Rome into account, we find that doctrines of images also could move in quite different directions, as Latin theologians selected texts by Gregory and other authorities, focused on certain "Gregorian" doctrines at the expense of others, and interpreted all their sources in different ways, even as they regularly claimed to base their teachings on Gregory's. The doctrine enunciated by Gregory that is most often mentioned in writings from the eighth- and ninth-century West, a concept clearly accepted by the majority of the theologians I have discussed here—by all of them except Claudius and Agobard—is that Christian images should neither be adored like God nor destroyed. Within this somewhat vague framework, though, the beliefs about the role of images and about image worship affirmed in the same writings represent varying developments on Gregory's thought, ones sometimes clearly influenced by other concerns and sources, while the positions expressed by writers like Agobard and Claudius perhaps reveal an equally deliberate rejection of some of Gregory's doctrines. Latin theologians frequently disagreed not only in their assessments of what constituted "Gregorian" thought on images but also in their broader judgments of how Christians should approach artistic representations. They were evidently willing to allow a certain amount of disagreement to exist. Only when a churchman such as Claudius *actively* followed a policy departing from the principle that images deserve neither destruction nor adoration—so that he went beyond the defense of iconoclasm to the actual destruction of Christian artistic images—did formal proceedings against him begin. But it should be noted that there is no certainty that these proceedings would have started if Claudius had not also rejected crosses; opposed the cult of relics, pilgrimages, and belief in the intercession of the saints; and possibly questioned papal authority.

It is an error to assume the existence in the eighth- and ninth-century West of a single, well-defined doctrine of the artistic image. Likewise, we would be wrong to assume that a description of teachings on images from this period as "Gregorian" is synonymous with declaring that they represent a single theory of art.

204 CELIA CHAZELLE

These errors perhaps reveal the need to reconsider, for other centuries of the Middle Ages as well, the extent to which the Western attitude toward Christian artistic imagery was monolithic. They also underscore a point to which Richard Sullivan has drawn attention: the importance of reexamining the traditional scholarly view of the Carolingian period as one in which the intellectual elite sought to create a society ruled by the principle of uniformity, and in this way to effect a "universal" and "unified" intellectual and cultural order in Carolingian regions.[131] As Sullivan has shown, much recent scholarship on the Carolingians calls this assessment of that era into question. A growing body of studies of social, intellectual, and artistic developments in Carolingian Europe has demonstrated the diversity, dissent, and tolerance for dissent found in numerous areas of intellectual and cultural activity, suggesting that Carolingian thought and culture were marked less by uniformity than by plurality.[132] From this perspective, the dissimilar views about Christian images, their role, and worship of them preached by Carolingian clergy by no means represent an exception to a normal search for unity. Rather, they reflect the creative energy, richness, and complexity of Carolingian society and culture as a whole, a complexity to which knowledge of the writings on images ascribed, correctly or incorrectly, to Gregory the Great contributed.

NOTES

My thanks to the University of Notre Dame, Department of Theology, and particularly to John Cavadini and Robert Markus, for the opportunity to present a version of this paper at their symposium on Gregory the Great. My thinking about Gregory has profited from the stellar work on the sixth-century pope by Robert Markus and other conference participants, espcially Markus's *End of Ancient Christianity* and Carole Straw's *Gregory the Great: Perfection in Imperfection*.

1. *Ep.* 9.209 (*CCSL* 140A:768); 11.10 (*CCSL* 140A:873–76). I have analyzed these letters in Celia Chazelle, "Pictures, Books, and the Illiterate: Pope Gregory I's Letters to Serenus of Marseilles," *Word and Image* 6 (1990): 138–53. For surveys of the numerous medieval references to the letters to Serenus, in particular to their assertions that images help teach the illiterate, see Lawrence G. Duggan, "Was Art Really the 'Book of the Illiterate'?" *Word and Image* 5 (1989): 227–51;

326

and the earlier work by L. Gougaud, "Muta praedicatio," *RvBén* 42 (1930): 168–71.

2. Ernst Kitzinger, "The Cult of Icons in the Age before Iconoclasm," *Dumbarton Oaks Papers* 8 (1954): 83–150, at 132.

3. As a few examples, Gerhart B. Ladner, "Origin and Significance of the Byzantine Iconoclastic Controversy," *Medieval Studies* 2 (1940): 127–49, at 147 and n. 116; William R. Jones, "Art and Christian Piety: Iconoclasm in Medieval Europe," in *The Image and the Word: Confrontations in Judaism, Christianity, and Islam*, ed. Joseph Gutmann (Missoula, 1977), 75–105, at 78; Michael Camille, "Seeing and Reading: Some Visual Implications of Medieval Literacy and Illiteracy," *Art History* 8 (1985): 26–49, at 26; Conrad Rudolph, *The "Things of Greater Importance": Bernard of Clairvaux's Apologia and the Medieval Attitude toward Art* (Philadelphia, 1990), 50–51. Cf. Duggan, "Art," 240–43.

4. E.g., pictures and statues "must be counted among the superfluous institutions of men" (Augustine, *De doctrina Christiana* 2.25.39; *CCSL* 32:61). Other passages can be found (translated) in Caecilia Davis-Weyer, *Early Medieval Art, 300–1150* (Toronto, 1986), 40–44.

5. William Durandus, *Rationale divinorum officiorum* 1.3; Gregory, *Ep.* 11.10 (*CCSL* 140A:874). Partially translated in Elizabeth G. Holt, *A Documentary History of Art*, 2 vols. (Garden City, N.Y., 1957), 1:121, using the translation by J. M. Neale and B. Webb, *The Symbolism of Churches and Church Ornaments* (Leeds, 1843; reprint, New York, 1973), 53. Duggan, "Art," 231–32, notes the problems in identifying William's thought with that of Gregory.

6. Cf. Duggan, "Art," 230–40, on the post-Carolingian period.

7. I will not discuss Bede's comments on this topic, since he does not directly tie his remarks to Gregory and it is unclear that Gregory was a source for them: Paul Meyvaert, "Bede and the Church Paintings at Wearmouth-Jarrow," *Anglo-Saxon England* 8 (1979): 63–77; Duggan, "Art," 229–30. Cf. Paul Meyvaert, "The *Registrum* of Gregory the Great and Bede," *RvBén* 80 (1970): 162–66 (reprinted in Meyvaert, *Benedict*, as no. XI).

8. *Registrum, Appendix*, 10 (*CCSL* 140A:1104–11; 1104 on the mss. containing the interpolation, and 1110–11).

9. *Ep.* 9.209 (*CCSL* 140A:768); 11.10 (*CCSL* 140A:873–75).

10. Chazelle, "Pictures," 142, and n. 19, with references to earlier scholarly literature.

11. E.g., *Ep.* 9.209 (*CCSL* 140A:768.8–14): "Praeterea indico dudum ad nos peruenisse quod fraternitas uestra quosdam imaginum adoratores aspiciens easdem ecclesiis imagines confregit atque proiecit. Et

quidem zelum uos, ne quid manufactum adorari possit, habuisse laudauimus, sed frangere easdem imagines non debuisse iudicamus.
Idcirco enim pictura in ecclesiis adhibetur, ut hi qui litteras nesciunt
saltem in parietibus uidendo legant, quae legere in codicibus non
ualent." And *Ep.* 11.10 (*CCSL* 140A:873.17–74.19, 21–26, 29–31): "Et
quidem quia eas [imagines] adorari uetuisses omnino laudauimus,
fregisse uero reprehendimus . . . Aliud est enim picturam adorare,
aliud per picturae historiam quid sit adorandum addiscere. Nam quod
legentibus scriptura, hoc idiotis praestat pictura cernentibus, quia in
ipsa ignorantes uident quod sequi debeant, in ipsa legunt qui litteras
nesciunt; unde praecipue gentibus pro lectione pictura est . . . Frangi
ergo non debuit quod non ad adorandum in ecclesiis sed ad instruendas
solummodo mentes fuit nescientium collocatum."

12. As above, note 11; and *Ep.* 11.10 9 (*CCSL* 140A:875.52–62): "Si
ad hanc instructionem, ad quam imagines antiquitus factae sunt,
habere uultis in ecclesia, eas modis omnibus et fieri et haberi per-
mitto. Atque indica quod non tibi ipsa uisio historiae, quae pictura
teste pandebatur, displicuerit sed illa adoratio, quae picturis fuerat
incompetenter exhibita. Atque in his uerbis eorum mentes demulcens
eos ad concordiam tuam reuoca. Et si quis imagines facere uoluerit,
minime prohibe, adorare uero imagines omnimodis deuita. Sed hoc
sollicite fraternitas tua admoneat ut ex uisione rei gestae ardorem
compunctionis percipiant et in adoratione solius omnipotentis sanctae
trinitatis humiliter prosternantur."

13. "[S]ublata exinde cum ea qua dignum est ueneratione imagine
atque cruce, debeatis quod uiolenter ablatum est reformare" (*Ep.*
9.196; *CCSL* 140A:750–52).

14. *Registrum, Appendix,* 1110–11.

15. See Chazelle, "Pictures," 141, on the types of images that concerned Gregory, and 143–44 on Gregory's use of the term "adoration"
(*adoratio, adorare*).

16. Ibid., especially 146–47.

17. Ibid., 144–47.

18. E.g., the acts of Nicaea II (787), citing Leontius of Neapolis
(d. c. 650), John of Salonica (first half seventh century), and John Damascene (d. c. 749): Mansi, 13.43–54, 164–67, 357–58. Also the anonymous seventh-century Armenian apology for images: Sirarpie Der
Nersessian, "Une apologie des images du septième siècle," *Byzantion*
17 (1944–45): 58–87, at 58–69. See also Kitzinger, "The Cult of Icons,"
passim; Norman H. Baynes, "The Icons before Iconoclasm," *Harvard
Theological Review* 44 (1951): 93–106; Leslie Barnard, "The Theology
of Images," in *Iconoclasm: Papers Given at the Ninth Spring Sympo-*

sium of Byzantine Studies, University of Birmingham, March 1975, ed. A. Bryer and J. Herrin (Birmingham, 1977), 7–13.

19. Hadrian, *Ep.* 2.5–57, at 20 (*MGH, Epistolae,* 5); *Concilium Romanum. 769, MGH, Concilia,* 2.1, 89–90. On the date of Hadrian's letter, see Ann Freeman, "Carolingian Orthodoxy and the Fate of the *Libri Carolini,*" *Viator* 16 (1985): 65–108, at 90.

20. *Conc. Rom.* 74–92.

21. *Conc. Rom.* 87; Hadrian, *Ep.* 2.19–20.

22. *Conc. Rom.* 87.

23. *Conc. Rom.* 89–92, cf. 77.29–38; Hadrian, *Ep.* 2.11, 15–16, 19–20, 23, 27–28, 32–33, 36, 41, 46, 47, 54.

24. Hadrian, *Ep.* 2.5–57. I omit here Hadrian's letter to Irene and Constantine VI, inserted into the acts of Nicaea II. Its complicated manuscript transmission makes it difficult to know precisely what the original said about Gregory: Luitpold Wallach, "The Greek and Latin Versions of II Nicaea, 787, and the *Synodica* of Hadrian I (*JE* 2448)," in *Diplomatic Studies in Latin and Greek Documents from the Carolingian Age* (Ithaca, N.Y., 1977) 3–26, esp. 13–14; Wallach, "The Testimonia of Image-Worship in Hadrian I's *Synodica* of 785 (*JE* 2448)," in ibid., 27–42.

25. Hadrian, *Ep.* 2.48; cf. 2.42–43, 55–56.

26. Hadrian, *Ep.* 2.37.

27. Hadrian, *Ep.* 2.42–43.

28. Hadrian, *Ep.* 2.43. Cf. 2.19–20 (quoting the interpolation); 2.37.31–32 ("Nequaquam sacras contempsit [Gregorius] imagines aliquando, sed magis constantissime observavit et eorum veneravit figuras"); 2.38 (letter to Januarius); 2.43.5–6 (to Januarius); 2.46.28–31 (interpolation).

29. Hadrian, *Ep.* 2.56.29–32; cf. 2.54–56. The section opens (54–55) by quoting what Hadrian claims is the last chapter heading in the *Capitulare,* though no such chapter appears in the completed *LC:* "Ultimum capitulum est, ut sciat domnus apostolicus et pater noster et cuncta simul Romanorum ecclesia, ut secundum quod continet in epistola beatissimi Gregorii, quam ad Serenum Masiliensem episcopum direxit, permittimus imagines sanctorum, quicumque eas formare voluerint, tam in ecclesia, quamque extra ecclesia propter amorem Dei et sanctorum eius. Adorare vero eas nequaquam cogimus, qui noluerint." As will be seen, the position suggested here—that the adoration of images should be avoided by those "who do not want" to engage in such practices—seems incompatible with the *LC* doctrine that good Christians always avoid image worship of any kind. Possibly the chapter heading reflects a line of thought about image worship that

208

circulated among Charlemagne's theologians but did not make its way into the *LC*, or possibly the heading was composed in Rome and inserted into Hadrian's letter to allow Charlemagne an opportunity to embrace a position closer to that of Rome, without seeming to abandon the *Capitulare* completely. Cf. Karl Hampe, "Hadrians I. Vertheidigung der zweiten nicaenischen Synode gegen die Angriffe Karls des Grossen," *Neues Archiv* 21 (1896): 85–113, at 89; Hadrian, *Ep.* 2.55n.1.

30. E.g., Hadrian, *Ep.* 2.15.34.

31. Hadrian, *Ep.* 2.56.3–7.

32. See above, notes 21, 22.

33. Hubert Bastgen, ed., *Libri Carolini sive Caroli Magni Capitulare de imaginibus*, MGH Conc. 2, suppl. (Hanover, 1924). A new edition is being prepared by Ann Freeman: *Opus Caroli regis contra synodum (Libri Carolini)*, MGH Conc. 2, Neuarbeitung. My references to Bastgen's edition indicate the corresponding folio numbers in the two manuscripts that both Bastgen and Freeman use for their editions: Paris, Bib. de l'Arsenal, MS 663 (= A), and Theodulf's autograph copy, Vatican City, Bib. Vat., MS Latinus 7207 (= V). Readers may thus refer to either edition, once Freeman's edition is available, since both indicate folio numbers. See Freeman, "Carolingian Orthodoxy," passim, citing earlier literature on the *LC*, including her own extensive work on the treatise, much of it devoted (successfully) to proving that Theodulf of Orléans wrote the initial draft. On the doctrine of the *LC*, see also Celia Chazelle, "Matter, Spirit, and Image in the *Libri Carolini*," *RechA* 21 (1986): 163–84; Chazelle, "Images, Scripture, the Church, and the *Libri Carolini*," *Proceedings of the PMR Conference* 16/17 (1993): 53–76; Chazelle, "'Not in Painting But in Writing': Augustine and the Supremacy of the Word in the *Libri Carolini*," in *Reading and Wisdom: The De doctrina christiana of Augustine in the Middle Ages*, ed. Edward D. English (Notre Dame, Ind.: University of Notre Dame Press, 1995), 1–22.

34. "Quod contra beati Gregorii instituta sit imagines adorare seu frangere et quia vetus et novum testamentum et poene omnes precipui doctores ecclesiae consentiunt beato Gregorio in non adorandis imaginibus, nec ut aliquid preter Deum omnipotentem adorare debeamus, in multis locis confirmat sanctus Gregorius papa" (Hadrian, *Ep.* 2.37).

35. Ann Freeman, "Additions and Corrections to the *Libri Carolini*: Links with Alcuin and the Adoptionist Controversy," in *Scire litteras: Forschungen zum mittelalterlichen Geistesleben*, ed. Sigrid Krämer and Michael Bernhard (Munich, 1988), 159–69.

36. *LC*, ed. Bastgen, 81–82 (V, fols. 88v–89v).

37. Freeman, "Carolingian Orthodoxy," 90–92.

38. *LC* 2.23 (ed. Bastgen, 82; V, fol. 88v). Adoration is owed to God alone and veneration to the saints, but neither to images: e.g., *LC* Praef. (ed. Bastgen, 6; A, fols. 5v–6); see also *LC* 3.15 (ed. Bastgen, 136.9–15; V, fol. 152v), where it is noted that some people worship images because they are overcome with joy at the likenesses of those they love (the saints and Christ), and that this is not idolatry; yet "reverentiores tamen et districtiores hanc consuetudinem perhorrent christiani." Cf. *LC* 3.6 (ed. Bastgen, 118–19; V, fols. 131v–32); 3.11 (ed. Bastgen, 124.14–15; V, fol. 138v). See also Chazelle, "Matter, Spirit, and Image," 165.

39. On the significance of the faulty Latin translation of Nicaea II available to the Carolingians, see Stephen Gero, "The *Libri Carolini* and the Image Controversy," *Greek Orthodox Theological Review* 18 (1973): 7–34, at 10–11; Gert Händler, *Epochen karolingischer Theologie: Eine Untersuchung über die karolingischen Gutachten zum byzantinischen Bilderstreit* (Berlin, 1958), 67–73.

40. Chazelle, "Images, Scripture, the Church."

41. John Cavadini, "Claudius of Turin and the Augustinian Tradition," *Proceedings of the PMR Conference* 11 (1986): 43–50, especially 47. On Theodulf's background, see Ann Freeman, "Further Studies in the *Libri Carolini*, I and II," *Speculum* 40 (1965): 203–89, at 274–78.

42. Discussed further in Chazelle, "Images."

43. "[Q]ui nos viam regiam tenere instituit, imagines in ornamentis ecclesiarum et memoria rerum gestarum habentes et solum Deum adorantes et eius sanctis opportunam venerationem exhibentes" (*LC* Praef.; ed. Bastgen, 5–6; A, fols. 5v–6). Cf. *LC* 1.9 (ed. Bastgen, 27–28; V, fols. 25v–26); 2.25 (ed. Bastgen, 84–85; V, fols. 90v–92v); Praef. (ed. Bastgen, 3 [vs. iconoclasm]; A, fol. 3).

44. Cf. *LC* 1.9 (ed. Bastgen, 26; V, fol. 24); 3.15 (ed. Bastgen, 135; V, fol. 151r–v). On Scripture as the repository of sacred truth, see *LC* 2.30 (ed. Bastgen, 92–100; V, fol. 101–10v). On the contrast between artistic images and the few things, in addition to Scripture, that the Bible reveals are specially blessed by God, see, e.g., *LC* 1.15 (ed. Bastgen, 34–37 [Ark]; V, fols. 34–37); 1.20 (ed. Bastgen, 45–48 [Ark]; V, fols. 47v–51); 2.27–29 (ed. Bastgen, 87–92 [Eucharist, Cross, holy vessels]; V, fols. 94v–100v); 3.24 (ed. Bastgen, 153–55 [saints' relics]; V, fols. 173v–75v). Cf. Chazelle, "Matter, Spirit, and Image," 165–70.

45. *LC* 2.23 (ed. Bastgen, 82.13; V, fol. 88v). Cf., e.g., *LC* Praef. (ed. Bastgen, 6; A, fol. 5v); 1.9 (ed. Bastgen, 29; V, fol. 27); 2.26 (ed. Bastgen, 85; V, fol. 93); 4.19 (ed. Bastgen, 209; A, fol. 223r–v); 3.15 (ed. Bastgen, 136; V, fol. 152v), suggesting that the memory images stir may be joined with love for the images' subjects.

46. I argue this more fully in Chazelle, "Images, Scripture, the Church." Cf. LC 1.8 (ed. Bastgen, 25–26; V, fols. 22v–23v); 3.16 (ed. Bastgen, 137; V, fol. 154r–v). An image cannot depict such invisible qualities as wisdom and eloquence: LC 1.17 (ed. Bastgen, 41–42; V, fols. 42–43).

47. Thus, many things mentioned in Scripture cannot be depicted: see, e.g., LC 1.17 (ed. Bastgen, 41–42; V, fols. 42–43). Written letters are noted to be signs in LC 2.30 (ed. Bastgen, 93.8–9; V, fols. 101v–2).

48. LC 2.30 (ed. Bastgen, 92–100; V, fols. 101–10v).

49. See, e.g., LC 4.15 (ed. Bastgen, 201 [concerning a statue erected by the woman with an issue of blood]; A, fol. 214r–v); and 2.13 (ed. Bastgen, 73; V, fols. 79–80): if Pope Sylvester ordered Constantine to adore the images that the pope showed the emperor, it could only have been in order to help him reach the level of mature Christians, who have abandoned "the milk of infants" for "solid food." Cf. LC 3.15 (ed. Bastgen, 136.12–15; V, fol. 152v).

50. Freeman, "Carolingian Orthodoxy," especially 96–99.

51. As pointed out to me by Thomas Noble (personal communication).

52. Freeman, "Carolingian Orthodoxy," 65–66, 96–99.

53. Concilium Parisiense. 825, MGH Concilia 2.1, 473–551. Discussed in Freeman, "Carolingian Orthodoxy," 100–105; Wilfried Hartmann, Die Synoden der Karolingerzeit im Frankenreich und in Italien (Paderborn, 1987), 168–71; Egon Boshof, Erzbischof Agobard von Lyon: Leben und Werk (Cologne, 1969), 140–43; Händler, Epochen karolingischer Theologie, 102–38, cf. 43–55.

54. Hartmann, Synoden, 169.

55. Conc. Paris., 475–80, at 478–79; translated in Freeman, "Carolingian Orthodoxy," 100.

56. Conc. Paris., 480–532.

57. See the introduction to the libellus, Conc. Paris., 481, and 484–502. The libellus also criticizes Hadrian I for his support of Nicaea II, though it diplomatically suggests that the pope erred only out of ignorance rather than knowingly, since he professed to follow Gregory (ibid., 482.1–6).

58. Ep. 11[10].874.32; Conc. Paris., 487–89, 507, 527–28; cf. 531.23–29.

59. Conc. Paris., 483–84 (images assist memory and love "sicut a beatissimo Gregorio satis catholice perspicueque dictum declaratur"), 487.5–7 (images assist memory and compunction), 499.13–14 (images aid memory and love), 526.6–12 (images teach, assist memory, and decorate), 531.30–33 (images teach and aid memory); cf. 529.7–10.

60. See *Conc. Paris.*, 489.18, 490.26, 507.6–8, 527.7, 531.24–25, 532.13–14.

61. *Conc. Paris.*, 481.14–17 (denouncing Hadrian and Nicaea II for the doctrine that images should be adored and called holy), 489.18–20 (against the belief that images are holy and sanctify Christians), 493. 12–15 (images cannot mediate between earth and heaven), 500.18–19 ("Contra illos etiam, qui imagines adorare se profitentur, quia sacra ab illis nuncupantur et sacris vasis eas aequiperant"), 524–26.

62. See *Conc. Paris.*, 494.14–16, 497.20–29.

63. *Conc. Paris.*, 502–6. Images are also inferior to sacred vessels and the cherubim of the Ark of the Covenant: ibid., 500. The *LC* discuss the cross's sanctity: *LC* 2.28 (ed. Bastgen, 89–91; V, fols. 97v–99v); 1.23 (ed. Bastgen, 51–52; V, fol. 55–55v); 4.16 (ed. Bastgen, 203–5; A, fol. 216–16v). They seem to deny, however, that manufactured crosses share this quality: *LC* 1.19 (ed. Bastgen, 44; V, fols. 45v–46).

64. *Conc. Paris.*, 506. The passage alludes to the three rites of the *Inventio crucis*, *Exaltatio crucis*, and the Good Friday *Adoratio crucis*. On the origin and development of the last, see Gerhard Römer, "Die Liturgie des Karfreitags," *Zeitschrift für katholische Theologie* 77 (1955): 39–93, especially 70–86.

65. *Conc. Paris.*, 507.6–7).

66. *Conc. Paris.*, 507–8.

67. *Conc. Paris.*, e.g., 516, 519 (Augustine).

68. *Conc. Paris.*, 514 (Leontius of Neapolis), 515 (Augustine).

69. *Conc. Paris.*, e.g., 510 (Pope Gregory III), 511 (Pseudo-Basil, Athanasius), 511–12 (Stephen of Bostra), 514 (Leontius of Neapolis), 518 (Patriarch Germanus).

70. *Conc. Paris.*, 481–83.

71. *Conc. Paris.*, 528–29.

72. Daniel J. Sahas, *Icon and Logos: Sources in Eighth-Century Iconoclasm* (Toronto: University of Toronto Press, 1986), 24–44; Judith Herrin, *The Formation of Christendom* (Princeton: Princeton University Press, 1987), 307–89, 406–75.

73. *Conc. Paris.*, 483.

74. *Conc. Paris*, 535–51. Discussed in the text at note 93.

75. Claudius, *Ep.* 12.610–13 (*MGH, Epistolae*, 4); see Dungal, *Liber adversus Claudium Taurinensem* (*PL* 105:457–530, at 459–64); Boshof, *Erzbischoff Agobard von Lyon*, 144–47, 157; L. Van Acker, ed., *Agobard: Opera Omnia* (*CCCM* 52:xxix); Alain Boureau, "Les théologiens carolingiens devant les images religieuses: La conjoncture de 825," in *Nicée II, 787–1987: Douze siècles d'images religieuses*, ed. F. Boespflug and N. Lossky (Paris, 1987), 247–62, at 247. Although Dungal implies

that Claudius had caused trouble almost from his consecration, Dungal's treatise, the first surviving against Claudius, is internally dated to 827. Claudius's teachings were probably not an issue much before then: see *Adv. Claud.* (*PL* 105:468B–C). Jonas of Orléans cut short his work on a treatise against Claudius when the latter died unexpectedly: *De cultu imaginum libri tres* (*PL* 106:305–88, at 307A). It is unlikely that Claudius wrote the treatise ascribed in the *PL* and *CCCM* to Agobard of Lyons (*Liber contra eorum superstitionem* [*PL* 104:199–228]; *De picturis et imaginibus,* ed. L. Van Acker [*CCCM* 52:149–81]; henceforth cited from the *CCCM* edition as *De picturis*), as proposed by Paulino Bellet, "El liber de imaginibus sanctorum bajo el nombre de Agobardo de Lyon obra de Claudio de Turin," *Annalecta sacra Tarraconensia (Barcelona)* 26 (1953): 151–94. Against Bellet's thesis, see especially Boshof, *Agobard,* 147–57; Acker, *CCCM* 52:xxiv–xxxiii; cf. Boureau, "Les théologiens carolingiens," 256–57. One indication of different authorship is that Agobard's treatise attributes holiness to relics and crosses, and the intercessory ability to the saints, ideas Claudius seems to reject: Agobard, *De picturis* 10.160–11.161, 19.168; Acker, *CCCM* 52:xxxi; Boshof, *Agobard,* 150, 154–55.

76. Claudius, *Ep.* 12.610.

77. Against the worship of artistic images, Claudius, *Ep.* 12.610–11; on crosses, 611–12; on pilgrimages to Rome, 612; on the cult of relics and his disbelief in the intercession of the saints and, possibly, in papal authority, 613.

78. On the Second Commandment, Claudius, *Ep.* 12.610. Claudius's general suspicion of material things is suggested by his comments on crosses and relics as well as on images (12.611–13).

79. "Sed dicunt isti falsae religionis atque superstitionis cultores: 'Nos ob recordationem salvatoris nostri crucem pictam atque in eius honore imaginatam colimus, veneramur atque adoramus'. Quibus nihil aliud placet in salvatore nostro, nisi quod et impiis placuit: obprobrium passionis et inrisio mortis" (Claudius, *Ep.* 12.611).

80. See above, notes 37, 43.

81. Jonas, *De cultu* (*PL* 106:305–6). Cf. Boureau, "Les théologiens carolingiens," 257; Edward James Martin, *A History of the Iconoclastic Controversy* (London, 1930), 263–64, on Claudius's relationship with Felix of Urgel.

82. Cf. Cavadini, "Claudius," passim, discussing the Augustinianism, conceivably Spanish, of Claudius's thought.

83. Claudius, *Ep.* 12.610; Dungal, *Adv. Claud.* (*PL* 105:465–66). This part of Dungal's treatise is also printed in *MGH, Epistolae,* 4:583–85, see 583–84.

84. Above, note 74.

85. *Conc. Paris.*, 483.18–25. See Boshof, *Agobard,* 156–57; Acker, *CCCM* 52:xxix.

86. Agobard, *De picturis,* 20.168–21.171; Bede, *De templo* 2 (*CCCM* 119A:212–13). See Meyvaert, "Bede and the Church Paintings," especially 68–69. Meyvaert translates Bede's text.

87. Agobard, *De picturis,* 22.171–72: "Foroiuliensem etiam episcopum beatus papa Gregorius arguisse legitur, ideo quod imagines apostolorum de sua basilica eraserit ob superstitionem uulgi eas contra regulam fidei adorantis, ac non potius rationabili auctoritate eiusmodi errorem correxit, pictura inlesa ad posterorum memoriam permanente."

88. See Cavadini, "Claudius," 50n.52. Cf. Boshof, *Agobard,* 150–51.

89. The first seven sources come from Augustine, followed by two passages from Gregory and four from Augustine: Agobard, *De picturis,* 1.151–9.159. Augustine, especially *De civitate Dei,* is the main source in the rest of the treatise. Agobard's dependence on Augustine to support the notion that Christians must abandon the material world to approach the spiritual emerges especially in the following comment: "Nemo igitur sapientum ignorat, quod homo fidelis, ut profitiat, ab exterioribus introrsus traendus est, non ab interioribus exterius proiciendus, ut defitiat. Transire enim debet de carne ad animam, de corpore ad spiritum, de uisibilibus ad inuisibilia, de mundo ad Deum. Et iste dicitur profectus, si ad meliora quis transeat, non ad deteriora. Melius uero esse animum, deterius corpus, eminentius spiritum, infimam carnem, nouit qui ea, que paulo superius sunt posita sancti Augustini uerba legit et intellegit" (Agobard, *De picturis* 16.165). See also, using excerpts from Augustine, 24.172–74 (God is venerated more chastely without images); 25.174–75 (nothing impedes reception of the truth more than libidiny and false images of sensible things); 26.175 (it is wrong to usurp anything divine for sacrilegious rites).

90. Agobard, *De picturis* 33.180: "nullum ab imaginibus, quas aspicimus, auxilium sperare debemus, quia nec male possunt facere, nec bene. Recte nimirum ob huiusmodi euacuandam superstitionem ab orthodoxis patribus definitum est, 'picturas in ecclesia fieri non debere, nec quod colitur et adoratur, in parietibus depingatur'." Cf. 3.154 (nothing can mediate between God and man except him who is both God and man); 15.164 (visible things are harmful for seeking invisible things, and love of corporal things impedes contemplation of the spiritual); 19.168 and 31.179 (to worship images is idolatry).

91. Agobard, *De picturis* 23.172.

92. Agobard, *De picturis* 23.172, 19.168, 31.179.

214   CELIA CHAZELLE

93. *Conc. Paris.*, 535–51.

94. *Conc. Paris.*, 536–39 (against iconoclasm), 540–49 (against the "undue worship" of images); cf. 541.20–21.

95. E.g., *Conc. Paris.*, 536.25–26 (images demonstrate love and respect), 537.12–13 (images help memory), 549.4–6 (images aid love and are decorative).

96. *Conc. Paris.*, 540.34–35, 541.9–10, 547.1–9.

97. *Conc. Paris.*, 549–50.

98. *Conc. Paris.*, 539.

99. *Conc. Paris.*, 539–40.

100. The two bishops also altered a statement from the libellus referring to Gregory's teachings. Where the libellus declares that discretion should be maintained toward images, "sicut eximius doctor beatus papa Gregorius docuit et in suis scriptis nobis tenendum sequendumque reliquit," the epitome states that discretion should be preserved, "sicut eximius doctor beatus papa Gregorius sermonem Massiliensi episcopo scribens et in eisdem scriptis tenendum sequendumque reliquit" (*Conc. Paris.*, 497.26–29 [libellus], 547.6–9 [epitome]).

101. Jonas, *De cultu* (PL 106:306–10).

102. Jonas, *De cultu* (PL 106:310D–11A; see also 332B–C).

103. Jonas, *De cultu* (PL 106:318A–C).

104. Jonas, *De cultu* (PL 106:326A–B; see also 329D–30A).

105. Jonas, *De cultu* (PL 106:325C–D). Cf. Claudius, *Ep.* 12.610–11.

106. Jonas, *De cultu* (PL 106:332C–D).

107. Dungal, *Adv. Claud.* (PL 105:472B).

108. Dungal, *Adv. Claud.* (PL 105:468–69).

109. Dungal, *Adv. Claud.* (PL 105:465B).

110. Dungal, *Adv. Claud.* (PL 105:471A–B).

111. Dungal, *Adv. Claud.* (PL 105:467D–68A, 470D, 471C).

112. Dungal, *Adv. Claud.* (PL 105:472B).

113. Dungal, *Adv. Claud.* (PL 105:527D, 467D–68A, 472A–B).

114. Walafrid, *Libellus de exordiis et incrementis quarundam in observationibus ecclesiasticis rerum*, MGH Legum sectio 2, Capitularia regum Francorum, 2.473–516, 473 on the treatise's date.

115. Walafrid, *De exordiis* 482–83.

116. Walafrid, *De exordiis* 483.4–9.

117. Walafrid, *De exordiis* 482.6–20.

118. Walafrid, *De exordiis* 484.12–14; cf. 483.9–10.

119. Walafrid, *De exordiis* 482.18–20 (images stir memory and love); cf. 483.35–36 (images encourage devotion and love of "invisible things"); 484.1–3 (images are literature for the illiterate).

120. Walafrid, *De exordiis* 484.5–8.

121. Walafrid, *De exordiis* 482.4, 23; 484.14. Iconodules venerate images "beyond what is acceptable [easdem imagines ultra, quam satis est, venerantur]" (482.31–35).

122. Walafrid, *De exordiis* 483.28–29.

123. Hincmar of Reims, *Opusculum LV capitulorum* (*PL* 126:282–494, at 389C–90A).

124. Hincmar, *LV capit.* (*PL* 126:360–61).

125. Freeman, "Carolingian Orthodoxy," 66, 96.

126. Hincmar, *LV capit.* (*PL* 126:360A). Translated in Freeman, "Carolingian Orthodoxy," 68, cf. 66–67. Hincmar diplomatically avoids any discussion of the papacy's acceptance of Nicaea II.

127. Possibly Hincmar confuses the iconoclastic council of 754 with the iconodulist Nicaea II: Freeman, "Carolingian Orthodoxy," 68.

128. Hincmar, *LV capit.* (*PL* 126:389C–D).

129. "[E]x verbis sanctorum, quasi ex eorum imaginibus, ipsos, videlicet corda et promulgationes eorum, cognoscere possumus" (Hincmar, *LV capit.*; *PL* 126:389D–90A).

130. Flodoard, *Historia ecclesiae Remensis* (*PL* 135:23–328, at 260A).

131. Terms from Richard Sullivan, "The Carolingian Age: Reflections on Its Place in the History of the Middle Ages," *Speculum* 64 (1989): 267–306, especially 272–78, with extensive footnotes citing the relevant scholarly literature.

132. Ibid., 287–97, especially 297: "Cultural plurality of a deep and pervasive nature seems much more characteristic of the period than does cultural unity and uniformity."

Journal of Ecclesiastical History, Vol. 42, No. 2, April 1991

A Reassessment of the Early Career and Exile of Hilary of Poitiers

by D. H. WILLIAMS

Exiled from his see in the year 356, Hilary of Poitiers suddenly emerges on the historical scene out of a shroud of undocumented silence. It is well known by students of Hilary and his times how few facts are available about the saint's early life and his first years as bishop.[1] The existence of such lacunae in the career of a person who would eventually become one of the West's major theologians and apologists created a vacuum too tempting not to fill. It comes as no surprise, therefore, to find later hagiographic accounts eager to trace Hilary's *virtus* and undefiled orthodoxy back to the earliest stages of his life. This is well exemplified by Hilary's sixth-century biographer Venantius Fortunatus, who locates signs of future fidelities in the very beginning. Despite the implications in the first book of *De Trinitate* that Hilary had been a pagan prior to becoming a Christian, Venantius confidently tells us how the saint took in Christian doctrine and true religion with his mother's milk.[2]

One of the most frustrating silences that surrounds the bishop's early career is the lack of information about the precise reasons for his exile at Béziers. And it is at this juncture, perhaps, that hagiography has made its most influential mark. Accounts by Sulpicius Severus, John Cassian, Gregory of Tours and others[3] have contributed to the development of a

CSEL = Corpus Scriptorum ecclesiasticorum latinorum; CCSL = Corpus Christianorum, series latina; *HE* = *Historia Ecclesiastica*; *RB* = *Revue Bénédictine*

[1] For an assembly of the available evidence for his early life and literary works see C. F. Borchardt, *Hilary of Poitiers' Role in the Arian Controversy*, The Hague 1966, 1–17.

[2] *Vita Hilarii* i. 3.

[3] See Sulpicius Severus, *Chron.* ii. 39, 'Hilarius...inter procellas persecutionum ita immobilis perstitit, ut per invictae fidei fortitudinem etiam confessoris ceperit dignitatem': Cassianus, *De incarnatione* vii. 24: PL l. 250–1. But it is in the writings of Venantius Fortunatus and Gregory of Tours (both sixth century) that Hilary's life becomes included among the hagiographic accounts of important saints in Gaul. In the *Liber primus* of Fortunatus' *Vita Sancti Hilarii Episcopi Pictaviensis*, PL lxxxviii. 439–54, it is told how Hilary was exiled on account of his faith and how he continued steadfast in the face of heresy. Gregory also notes that 'Hilary, blessed defender of the undivided Trinity and for its sake driven into exile, was both restored to his own country and entered Paradise': *Historia Francorum* prol. iii, trans. O. M. Dalton, *History of the Franks by Gregory of Tours* ii, Oxford 1927. Hilary having obtained the status of 'confessor' and saint, both Fortunatus, in *Liber secundo*, and Gregory, *De gloria beatorum confessorum*, PL lxxi. 830–1, record a

picture of an individual who stood in the vanguard of the defence of orthodox faith in the West amid Arian oppression and aggression. Hilary's courageous support of Athanasius, as well as his bold leadership of the Gallic bishops against heresy, is what ultimately led to his 'martyrdom' by banishment.

Surprisingly, the above caricature of Hilary is widely reflected in most modern assessments of his role in the later Arian controversy. Not untypically, the bishop is described as 'a champion of the orthodox party...in Gaul' and as being 'animated by one single idea which filled his life and constituted its unity: the fight against Arianism'.[4] There can be no question that Hilary was very active in opposing the defenders of Homoeanism in Gaul and North Italy, both politically and literarily, after his return from exile (probably in the spring of 360). But was his earlier career typified by such concerns as well? After all, Hilary himself states that he had never heard of the Nicene Creed until he was about to go into exile: 'Fidem Nicaenam numquam nisi exsulaturus audivi...'.[5]

The problem with this passage is determining exactly what it proves. Just how ignorant was Hilary of the theological and political issues of his day? Some have argued that his reference to the *symbolum* of Nicaea need not rule out previous knowledge on his part of the Eastern trinitarian controversies. And the degree to which the Nicene faith was known in the West prior to Hilary's exile is itself a matter of dispute. Paul Burns has concluded from his study of Hilary's commentary on Matthew that Hilary had some awareness of the content of Arian arguments. The commentary, which is generally considered to be one of Hilary's earliest works,[6] and precedes his exile, manifests specific polemical arguments against a subordinationist Christology.[7] But the basis for Burns's view rests on a two-pronged presupposition – that Hilary was exiled at Béziers

---

number of miracles that took place at his tomb. The bishop's reputation for fearlessly opposing the Arian heresy is especially revealed in Gregory's account of King Clovis's military exploits against the (Arian) Goths. When the Frankish army came to the neighbourhood of Poitiers and pitched camp, Clovis 'saw a fiery beacon issue from the church of the holy Hilary and come over above his head; it signified that aided by the light of the blessed confessor Hilary he might more surely overcome the host of those heretics against whom the saint himself had so often done battle for the faith': *Hist. Franc.* ii. 37.

[4] Respectively, T. S. Holmes, *The Origin and Development of the Christian Church in Gaul*, London 1911, 148, and J. R. Palanque et al., *The Church in the Christian Roman Empire*, trans. Ernest C. Messenger, New York 1953, 281. For similar conceptions, see E. C. S. Gibson, *Nicene and Post-Nicene Fathers* i, 617, 4n; S. McKenna, 'Introduction', *Fathers of the Church* xxv, New York 1954, p. vi; Nora K. Chadwick, *Poetry and Letters in Early Christian Gaul*, London 1955, 116. M. Meslin is one of the few to recognise that our depiction of Hilary has been misconstrued historically because of the influence of hagiography, 'Hilaire et la crise Arienne', in *Hilaire et son temps: Actes du Colloque de Poitiers 29 Septembre– 3 Octobre 1968 à l'occasion du XVIe centenaire de la mort de Saint Hilaire*, Paris 1969, 19.

[5] *De synodis* xci, PL x. 545 A.

[6] A catalogue of Hilary's works is found in Jerome's *De viris illustribus* c. Cf. J. Doignon, *Hilaire de Poitiers sur Matthieu* i, Paris 1978, 20.

[7] See the monograph by Paul Burns, *The Christology in Hilary of Poitiers' Commentary on Matthew*, in *Studia Ephemeridis 'Augustinianum'*, Rome 1981, 13–22, which briefly surveys

for his opposition to Arianism, and that he prepared his anti-Arian dossier *Liber adversus Valentem et Ursacium* in light of the controversies which were central to that council.[8] Since the 'Liber 1' of the *Liber adversus Valentem et Ursacium* (as organised by A. Feder in CSEL lxv) includes the *symbolum* of Nicaea (CSEL lxv. 150), it is concluded Hilary knew of the Nicene faith at the time of his council in such a way that he may well have used its authority against his 'Arian' adversaries at Béziers. The concern of this paper is not so much with the commentary on Matthew but with Burns's presupposition. For it is this presupposition which is basic to most reconstructions of Hilary's early life and exile. However, this paper will show that both parts of the presupposition are seriously flawed. As a consequence, we are forced to re-evaluate Hilary's role in the Arian controversy.

Why was Hilary of Poitiers exiled at Béziers? It is a question that continues to vex scholars of the late-fourth-century Arian controversies. Central to this inquiry is the widely held assumption that Hilary was exiled for refusing to condemn Athanasius and the Nicene faith. It will be seen that this is a view grounded in the belief that Hilary's condemnation at Béziers in 356 paralleled the course of events at Arles (353) and Milan (355).[9] There is, however, sufficient evidence to warrant the rejection of the above assumption: Hilary could not have been exiled on the same grounds (that is, for theological reasons) as the dissenting bishops at Arles and Milan.

Now it seems certain that the bishops condemned and exiled at Arles and Milan were judged according to the same criteria. Sulpicius Severus reports that an *edictum* was issued by the emperor that those who did not subscribe to the condemnation of Marcellus, Photinus and Athanasius should be sent into banishment.[10] This was duly enforced at the Synod of Arles, which resulted in the exile of at least one bishop, Paulinus of Treves.[11] Girardet has convincingly shown that the *edictum* presented at Arles is one and the same as the 'epistola synodica' from the Synod of Milan addressed to Eusebius of Vercelli,[12] who, along with several other bishops, was exiled by that synod. This 'epistola synodica' clearly

the broad spectrum of views on the subject – ranging from Galtier's position that the whole commentary was designed to refute Arianism to Doignon's attempt to depict the work more as an example of Western (Tertullianic) Christology. Burns concludes that Hilary had some awareness of Arianism and that it does seem to be an object of his commentary, which 'makes it easier to understand the speed of Hilary's reaction to Arianism between the Council of Milan and his own exile at the Council of Béziers in the very next year': ibid. 22.   [8] Ibid. 12–13; Cf. Borchardt, *Hilary of Poitiers*, 14, 26–7.

[9] This assumption can be observed at work in M. Simonetti's recent article, 'Hilary of Poitiers and the Arian crisis in the West', in *Patrology* iv, ed. A. di Berardino, Westminster, MD. 1986, 34–5.

[10] 'Edictum ab imperatore proponitur, ut qui in damnationem Athanasii non subscriberent in exilium pellerentur': *Chron.* ii. 39. 2; CSEL i. 92.

[11] *Chron.* ii. 37. 7; 39. 3. Prosper, *Chron.* 1090, and Jerome, *Chron.* 2370, include Rhodanius of Toulouse.   [12] CCSL ix. 119.

corresponds to the principal elements of the edict at Arles, specifically, demanding subscription against Marcellus, Photinus and Athanasius.[13] In his historical narrative, Sulpicius succinctly states when describing the transition of events from Arles to Milan that the same controversy was continued without any interruption of bitterness.[14] It is also known that an attempt was made by the 'orthodox' bishops at the two synods to engage their colleagues in a discussion about matters of true faith.[15] In both cases the attempts failed, and all in attendance were forced to sign or face the consequences.

The evidence for the Synod of Béziers is very blurry, and it is complicated by the fact that many ancient historians (only Prosper and Jerome are excepted)[16] think Hilary was exiled at Milan (355).[17] Practically the sole witnesses to what happened at Béziers come from two passages penned by Hilary several years after the event. These are as follows:[18]

1. As all of you are aware, brothers, either having heard me or through personal contact with me, that I, foreseeing long in advance the very great danger to the faith, separated myself with the Gallic bishops five years ago from the communion of Saturninus, Valens and Ursacius after the exiles of the holy men Paulinus, Eusebius, Lucifer and Dionysius…Being compelled afterwards to attend the synod of Béziers through the devices of these pseudoapostles, I presented a case which made manifest this heresy (*In Constantium* ii; spring 360).

2. I rejoiced in the Lord that you kept yourselves undefiled and unharmed from every contagion of detestable heresy, and as partakers of my exile, into which Saturninus had me thrust after having deceived the emperor and fearing his own conscience, you have denied him communion for the whole of three years unto now (*De synodis* ii; late 358 or early 359).

In accordance with the presupposition that Hilary was already a strong advocate of the Athanasian cause and/or Nicene orthodoxy, many

---

[13] K. M. Girardet, 'Constance II, Athanase et L'Édict d'Arles (353)', in *Politique et théologie chez Athanase d'Alexandrie*, ed. Charles Kannengiesser, Paris 1974, 72, 82.

[14] *Chron.* ii. 39 3, CSEL i. 92.

[15] Hilary, *Oratio Synodi Sardicensis ad Constantium Imperatorem* ii. 3 = 'Liber I ad Const.', CSEL lxv. 187; Sulpicius, *Chron.* ii. 39. 3.

[16] Prosper, *Chron.* 1096; Jerome, *De viris illust.* 100.

[17] Sulpicius, *Chron.* ii. 39. 7; Socrates, *HE* ii. 36; Sozomen, *HE* iv. 9; Rufinus (*HE* i. 20). Rufinus is somewhat ambiguous on the subject, for he writes after the exile of Eusebius, Paulinus, Rhodanius and Lucifer: 'Hilary also was joined to these others who were either ignorant or did not believe the fraud.'

[18] (*1*) 'Ego, fratres, ut mihi omnes, qui me vel audiunt vel familiaritate cognitum habent, testes sunt, gravissimum fidei periculum longe antea praevidens, post sanctorum virorum exsilia Paulini, Eusebii, Luciferi, Dionysii, quinto abhinc anno, a Saturnini et Ursacii et Valentis communione me cum Gallicanis episcopis separavi…Qui postea per factionem eorum pseudoapostolorum ad Biterrensem synodum compulsus, cognitionem demonstrandae huius haereseos obtuli': PL x. 578–9.

(*2*) 'Gratulatus sum in Domino, incontaminatos vos et illaesos ab omni contagio detestandae haereseos perstitisse, vosque comparticipes exsilii mei, in quod me Saturninus, ipsam conscientiam suam veritus, circumvento imperatore detruserat, negata ipsi usque hoc tempus toto jam triennio communione': PL x. 481 A.

scholars have seen in these passages the suggestion of a kind of conspiracy active in Gaul formed in opposition to the policies instituted at Arles and Milan. Especially the first passage from *In Constantium* is most frequently interpreted as indicating that, soon after the Synod of Milan, Hilary, along with other Gallic bishops, dissociated himself from Saturninus, Ursacius and Valens on account of their Arianising activities.[19] Moreover, Hilary has often been characterised as the ringleader of the supposed opposition movement and may even have called a synod to unify the movement as, for example, C. F. Borchardt, William Rusch and Joseph Emmenegger have speculated.[20] The deduction follows naturally that Hilary must have been called to Béziers and there deposed for his covert action against the anti-Athanasian policies being enforced in the West.[21]

Not all studies of Hilary support the above reconstruction. A recent, yet relatively ignored,[22] monograph by H. C. Brennecke has questioned many of the traditional assumptions, and a few of his arguments are worth considering in some detail. It will, however, become apparent in the proceeding analysis that the challenges which Brennecke has posed to the traditional scenario are perhaps more valuable than the conclusions which he has drawn.

With Brennecke, we may well wonder whether the general tendency to attribute a role of noteworthy prominence to Hilary at this stage in his otherwise obscure career is more the result of the influence of hagiography than simple exegesis of the main evidence. This becomes more conspicuous when no direct evidence can be discovered from a Gallic synod or a separatist movement in response to Arles or Milan. And the implication of a coalition from the *In Constantium* passage must be carefully weighed in light of Hilary's context and perspective in the spring of 360. There is also the question whether Hilary, bishop of a village on the periphery of Christian Gaul, would have possessed the authority to bring together such a representative gathering of bishops.[23]

[19] E. Griffe, *La Gaule chrétienne à l'époque romaine* i, Paris 1964, 224; G. M. Newlands, *Hilary of Poitiers: a study in theological method*, Bern 1978, 7.
[20] Borchardt, *Hilary of Poitiers*, 24–5; J. E. Emmenegger, *The Functions of Faith and Reason in the Theology of Hilary of Poitiers*, Washington 1947, 5; W. Rusch, *The Later Latin Fathers*, London 1977, 12. See A. Rocher's newly published commentary, *Hilaire de Poitiers: Contre Constance*, Sources chrétiennes cccxxxiv. 57, for the most recent adoption of this viewpoint.
[21] Griffe, *La Gaule*, 224–5; Borchardt, *Hilary of Poitiers*, 26.
[22] *Hilarius von Poitiers und die Bischofsopposition gegen Konstantius II*, Patristische Texte und Studien xxvi, Berlin 1984. I have been able to locate only two reviews of the book. One is by J. Doignon, 'Hilaire de Poitiers "Kirchenpolitiker"?', *Revue d'Histoire Ecclésiastique* lxxx (1985), 441–54, who (not surprisingly) finds Brennecke's attempt to diminish Hilary's anti-Arian role at Béziers unsatisfactory (see esp. p. 447); the other is a short, purely descriptive review by R. Klein in *Das Gymnasium* xciii (1986), 381–4. There is no notice of Brennecke's book in English-language periodicals with the exception of a brief review in *Patristics* xix.i (1990), 6–7 by M. Vessey.
[23] This point was brought out long ago by J. H. Reinkens, *Hilarius von Poitiers*, Schaffhansen 1864, 114, n. 2, who follows A. Viehhauser, *Hilarius Pictaviensis geschildert in*

In addition to these concerns, Brennecke has raised the question, if such a collected expression of resentment did exist against the policies of Constantius, why was this not demonstrated earlier at Milan?[24] It is a point that merits consideration. While it is true that no organised episcopal coalition against Constantius' policies as such can be detected at Milan, Brennecke's treatment of the events at this synod is hardly satisfactory. In particular, Brennecke assumes that there was no cognisance of the Nicene Creed in the West before 357 (i.e. before Hilary introduced it to the West).[25] He is too willing to reject reliable evidence that there was in fact an offensive plan enacted by pro-Athanasian participants at Milan in which the Nicene Creed was presented for signatures before any other action could be taken.[26] It is quite likely that Hilary was referring to this very episode when he tells us he had heard of the Nicene *fides* just before he was banished.[27] If there is no reason to question the historicity of this event then it permits the conclusion that the Nicene Creed was known in the West by 355 at the latest, and probably even earlier. The question at stake is not whether the creed was known at all in the West but, rather, who knew of it. It cannot be forgotten that in 343 Hosius felt obliged to reassure Julius of Rome that the purpose in issuing the Sardican Creed was not to replace the Nicene.[28] When Eusebius of Vercelli presented the Nicene Creed for signatures at Milan twelve years later, he was working on the assumption that those Western bishops would recognise the creed as an acceptable symbol of orthodoxy. The fact that Hilary was not aware of the creed until 356 does not so much prove that the creed was unknown in the West as betray how peripheral the creed had been in the task of theological definition over the last three decades. If anything, Hilary's ignorance of the creed underlines his remoteness from, and uninvolvement with, the actual issues of the controversy prior to his banishment at Béziers.

Since Hilary clearly says in *In Constantium* ii that he, along with a portion of Gallic bishops, separated themselves from Saturninus, Ursacius

---

seinem Kampfe gegen den Arianismus, 1860: 'Hilarius war nicht Metröpolit und konnte keine Synode versammeln; auch war die Situation einer solchen Versammlung gegen den Kaiser und gegen Saturnin keineswegs günstig.' Unfortunately, Reinkens does not mould his conclusions to his observation.   [24] Brennecke, *Hilarius von Poitiers*, 216.

[25] CSEL lxv. 187. See Brennecke's excursus, 'Zur angeblichen Vorlage des Nizänum auf der Synode zu Mailand durch Euseb von Vercellae': (*Hilarius von Poitiers*, 178–92). Brennecke tries to minimise the episode recorded by Hilary as unhistorical, given its polemical character. He does not reveal why he is so intent on denying the appearance of the *Nicaeanum* at this time, except to insist that Hilary, in his *Liber adversus Valentem et Ursacium*, was the first to introduce the Latin version of the *symbolum* to the West cf. ibid. 306.

[26] 'Liber i ad Constantium', viii, CSEL lxv. 187. Liberius' letters to Constantius, CSEL lxv. 93, and to Eusebius of Vercelli, CCSL ix. 122–3, demonstrate the existence of an offensive movement on the part of some Western bishops to reverse the decisions of Arles (353) and to instate the Nicene Creed as the basis of orthodoxy.

[27] A point also made by Meslin, 'Hilaire', 22.

[28] Sozomen, *HE* iii. 12. The brief letter is found in PL lvi. 839–40.

and Valens, we must ask when this happened. But before this question can be addressed, it is important first to examine the context of the *In Constantium* and then compare it with Hilary's other reference to his exile, in *De synodis*.

The *In Constantium*[29] is a vindictive and angry letter, in which the emperor, far from receiving the standard compliments of pious spirituality, is described as 'omnium crudelium crudelissime' (c. viii), 'lupe rapax' (x), 'sceleste' (xxv) and having a 'diabolici ingenium' (xvii). Much energy is invested by Hilary to show the extreme difference between the impiety which characterises the emperor and his followers and the true faith which Hilary and the pro-Nicene bishops represent. In the course of his argument, a pattern of solidarity is established among the supporters of orthodoxy, especially since all mention of *homoousios* or *homoiousios* had been recently outlawed by the Council of Constantinople in 360 (xxv). Hilary is eager to demonstrate to the apostate emperor how the advocates of the Nicene faith have maintained their unity and perseverance throughout his persecutions over the last seven or eight years (xi). This contrast between the persecuted but unified orthodox bishops and the

[29] Precision in the dating of this document is difficult to obtain. Jerome tells us that Hilary wrote a *libellus* to Constantius while living in Constantinople, and that he wrote another, 'in Constantium, quem post mortem ejus scripsit': *De viris illust.* c, PL xxiii. 699. Jerome's description corresponds to earlier MSS which establish the title of the work as *In Constantium* rather than the more commonly accepted *Contra Constantium*: Rocher, *Contre Constance*, 142–3. Rocher has developed an elaborate scheme in which Hilary wrote the work, not as a unitary composition, but on separate occasions from 359–61, ibid. 29ff. To take Jerome literally would place the *Contra Constantium* after 3 Nov. 361, the date of Constantius' death. According to Rocher, when Hilary learned of the death of the emperor, he assembled the different sections together and added a prologue (ch. i) around Dec. 361. While I cannot offer a critique of Rocher's redactional theory here, I am in agreement with T. D. Barnes's assessment that the scheme is overly and unnecessarily complex, seemingly intended to square Jerome's description 'with the evident internal indications of composition' during Constantius' lifetime, *JTS*, xxxix (1988), 610. It is not at all certain, however, that Jerome is correct. Internal features of *In Constantium* seem to demand an earlier date. It is clear that Hilary sees his treatise as a manifesto of revolt: 'The time has come for speaking for the time of keeping silent is past': c. i. His opposition to the policies of the emperor is now loudly voiced as he recounts the deeds which Constantius has perpetrated in alliance with the heretics. The treatise concludes by summarising the events at the Council of Seleucia (late 359), and their culmination at Constantinople (360), where the prohibition of *homoousios, homoiousios* and *substantiae* was ratified, c. 25. No other events of 360 are recorded. There is no mention of the pivotal Synod of Paris (summer 360) or any of the other counter-councils that met over the next two years in reaction to Rimini and Constantinople. This is particularly hard to understand as, if Hilary wrote the *In Constantium* after Nov. 361, he would have been in Gaul. Nor is there any hint in the treatise that Constantius has died. Instead, the work always treats him as a present threat and calls upon all who love the true faith to oppose him and his policies. A date of early 360 seems to fit this work best. Hilary's outspokenness is due in part to the fact that he has just returned from exile and now enjoys religious immunity from Constantius under the new Augustus of the West, Julian. It may also stem from Hilary's declared desire to be a martyr for the faith, which would have overridden any concerns for his own personal safety.

heretical bishops is readily discernible in chapter 2. Now, half a decade later, Hilary reflects on a specific period (353–6) when he and other Western bishops were exiled for their faithfulness. The phrase 'quinto abhinc anno' in chapter 2, therefore, cannot be referring to a single event, such as Milan, for he is obviously conflating the list of bishops who were exiled at both Arles and Milan. The *In Constantium* passage ought to be treated more as a reflection of theological hindsight which Hilary acquired in his struggles with the Homoeans. Furthermore, since the names of Valens and Ursacius appear nowhere else than here with regard to Béziers, it is tempting to think that the inclusion of these names is also a conflation. For now, after having been in exile and having achieved a certain insight into the intricacies of partisan politics, Hilary realises that Valens and Ursacius were in league with Saturninus all along.

The passage from *De synodis* presents a different picture. At the time of writing Hilary has been in exile for about three years.[30] Addressing his fellow bishops in Gaul and Britain,[31] he rejoices over the fact that they have refused communion with Saturninus for nearly three years and have also rejected the formula from Sirmium (357), which Hilary later designates as the 'blasphemia'.[32] But what is striking is that there is no clue in this passage, or elsewhere in *De synodis*, that Hilary, united with the Gallic bishops, had severed communion with Saturninus, Ursacius and Valens immediately after the Synod of Milan. In fact, as Brennecke has rightly pointed out, the united posture of a portion of the Gallic bishops against Saturninus comes as a great and welcome surprise for Hilary.[33] This seems to indicate that there could not have been any kind of episcopal coalition with Hilary as its leader or else Hilary would surely have known his colleagues' position before he went into exile.

Brennecke goes a step further by ruling out any possibility that Hilary may have enjoyed the support of some sort of network of bishops prior to his banishment.[34] But his assessment is surely overdrawn since the language in both *In Constantium* and *De synodis* undeniably assumes some measure of co-episcopal sympathy for Hilary's position. What specific form this might have taken is very difficult to tell. It must have been more tenuous than the traditional scenario allows. Two much-neglected

[30] The dating of *De synodis* is based on Hilary's knowing that the earthquake which struck Nicomedia on 28 Aug. 358 caused a change of location of one of the two forthcoming councils announced by Constantius: *De syn.* viii. But Hilary does not know that Seleucia was finally chosen as the alternative sometime early in the following year.
[31] *De syn.* i. [32] Ibid. x, xi. [33] Brennecke, *Hilarius von Poitiers*, 219.
[34] Brennecke shows himself to be aware of the problem but offers a wholly unsatisfactory answer. He proposes that, while Hilary was in exile, he kept such close contact with fellow bishops ('ist so eng') that there was a 'geistige und sakramentale Gemeinschaft' between him and them, ibid. 221. Contrary to this explanation, Hilary, in *De syn.* i, complains to his fellow bishops about their 'prolonged silence' since he has been in exile, even though he has written to them on several previous occasions. This hardly substantiates the kind of close contact of which Brennecke speaks while Hilary was in exile. It seems inescapable that Hilary must have had some kind of bond with his fellow bishops in Gaul before his exile and he is reflecting upon in *De syn.* ii.

passages from *De synodis* seem to indicate that Hilary was worried about being misunderstood by his fellow bishops. In the introduction, Hilary requests his readers not to prejudge him nor to draw their conclusions until they have finished reading the entire treatise.[35] His concern is echoed again, this time more strongly, in the conclusion: 'I do not know, now that I have expounded the faith, whether it would be as pleasant to return to you in the Lord Jesus Christ, as it would be to die carefree.'[36] The very ambiguity of these remarks reveals that Hilary's relationship with his fellow Gallic bishops prior to his exile cannot have been characterised by the unity of mind so often attributed to it by modern scholarship, or even by Hilary himself in his later attack, *In Constantium*.

We are now in a better position to ask whether the events at Beziers followed a similar course as the events at Arles and Milan. M. Meslin believes there are striking resemblances between the actions of Hilary at Béziers and Eusebius of Vercelli at Milan (355). Like Eusebius, Hilary wants to discuss doctrinal matters with his opponents but is forced to condemn Athanasius. Also like Eusebius, he refuses and is condemned.[37] It has already been noted that the evidence is too inconsistent to sustain this view; besides, Hilary nowhere mentions Athanasius in this respect. In addition, there are at least two important points that must be taken into consideration. First, in a letter which Hilary sent to the emperor (early 360) in order to appeal the grounds of his exile, he claims that he was condemned on the basis of false charges and lies reported by the synod to the emperor.[38] Secondly, in this same passage Hilary says that both the emperor and his caesar (Julian) had been deceived.[39] In *De synodis* ii Saturninus is specifically said to have thrust Hilary into exile having deceived ('circumvento') the emperor.[40]

Now if Hilary had refused to subscribe the condemnation of Athanasius and was subsequently exiled, he could have hardly claimed that he was condemned on account of false charges.[41] None of those banished at Arles and Milan because of their solidarity with Athanasius claimed they had been condemned on the basis of false charges. Indeed, no other charges were necessary at Arles and Milan for those bishops who defied the *edictum* of the emperor. Nor do we hear of those bishops attempting to file an

[35] C. 6.

[36] C. 92: 'Nescio an tam jucundum est ad vos in Domino Jesu Christo reverti, quam securum est mori': c. 6, PL x. 546.   [37] 'Hilaire et la crise', 23-4.

[38] 'Exulo autem non crimine, sed factione et falsis nuntiis synodi ad te imperatorem pium, non ob aliquam criminum meorum conscientiam per impios homines delatus...falsa autem eorum omnia, qui in exilium meum procurauerunt, non in obscuro sunt': *Liber II ad Constantium* ii. 1, CSEL lxv. 198; 'cuius ministerio exulo, usque ad confessionem falsorum, quae gessit': c. 3.

[39] 'Circumuentum te Augustum inlusumque Caesarem tuum ea confidens conscientiae meae condicione patefaciam': *Liber II* ii. 2.

[40] 'Saturninus, ipsam conscientiam suam veritus, circumvento imperatore detruserat': PL. x. 481. Cf. Jerome, 'factione Saturnini Arelatensis episcopi': *De viris illust.* c.

[41] See Brennecke, *Hilarius von Poitiers*, 237-8. I regard this as one of the most convincing sections of his argument.

appeal with the emperor as Hilary does when he is in Constantinople in 360. It can be concluded, therefore, that Hilary was not condemned at Béziers for the same reasons as were the bishops at Arles and Milan.

Why then was Hilary, after being forced to come to Béziers, condemned and banished into exile? Unfortunately the bishop never tells us the exact reasons. In light of the fact that Hilary has referred to false charges as the basis of his exile, and that, four years after his banishment at Constantinople, he is still adamantly seeking audience with the emperor in order to confront his accuser directly with these charges, it may be that the reasons for his exile were not theological, but political in nature.

In his letter to Constantius, which was cited earlier, Hilary is quick to point out that Julian is sympathetic to his cause, referring to him as his 'witness' and 'pious lord'.[42] Seeking a personal audience with the emperor, Hilary is in no position to give false information, and his words, however baffling, should be taken literally. Intrigued by his attachment to Julian, Meslin thinks it makes the most sense if Hilary is seen trying to de-activate an accusation of a political nature.[43] This hearkens back to a proposal made by Henry Chadwick over three decades ago which suggested that Hilary may have been accused of supporting the revolt of Silvanus,[44] who proclaimed himself Augustus on 11 August 355.[45] Now, most recently, Brennecke has adopted the idea, claiming that the turbulent aftermath of Magnentius' and Silvanus' usurpations makes such a denunciation of treason very probable – and sure to receive Constantius' immediate attention.[46]

In support of this scenario, we know such denunciations are not unique. A similar accusation was aimed at Athanasius for his correspondence with Magnentius.[47] And if Kopecek is correct, an accusation (by Basil) of a treasonous alliance with Gallus led to the initial downfall of Aetius, Eudoxius and Theophilus.[48] On the other hand, there is no direct evidence to sustain a revival of Chadwick's thesis as Brennecke tries to do. All that can be said is that, for reasons unknown, Saturninus was successful in convincing the emperor that Hilary was guilty of charges severe enough to warrant a speedy hearing and banishment. Hilary describes these as 'false charges' and requests a new hearing before the

---

[42] *Liber II* ii. 1.

[43] 'Hilaire et la crise', 24. Meslin concludes, 'Donc, mesure de police et non sanction canonique, la sentence d'exil fut rendue au plus tard dans l'été 356', 25. Meslin does not seem to see the implications of this conclusion for his later arguments; see n. 57 below.

[44] 'Hilarius von Poitiers (*ca* 315–367)', *Die Religion in Geschichte und Gegenwart* iii, 317. Chadwick regards Hilary as the leader of opposition against Constantius, who saw a favourable opportunity in Silvanus' revolt. But Silvanus was murdered and Hilary was condemned for high treason.

[45] A. H. M. Jones, *The Later Roman Empire, 284–602*, i, Oxford 1964, 116.

[46] Brennecke, *Hilarius von Poitiers*, 239–40.   [47] *Apol. ad Const.* vi.

[48] Thomas A. Kopecek, *A History of Neo-Arianism*, i, Cambridge, Mass. 1979, 174; based on Philostorgius, *HE* iv. 8.

emperor to have them reviewed. We are left with the insinuation that the condemnation at Béziers had little to do with theological controversy as witnessed at Arles and Milan, and was founded perhaps upon political reasons. But the mystery remains why Hilary, who was a relatively unimportant bishop, had to be removed in 356. As a Western traditionalist, Hilary may have posed an obstruction to the attempts of Saturninus to create a common front among the Gallic bishops in support of the new religious policies of Constantius. Certainly the enforced banishment at Arles (which was the see of Saturninus) of Paulinus, who probably presided at the synod, cannot have been popular among the Westerners. It is likely that the Arian bishop was present and supported the banishments at Milan as well.[49] But whatever the reasons, there was a personal quality to this inter-episcopal strife; Hilary's request to Constantius in the 'Liber II' to review his case bespeaks a harsh intimacy between the two Gallic bishops. Unfortunately only suppositions remain as to how Hilary might have become involved and incurred the hostility of Saturninus.

If correct, the above reconstruction has major implications for the dating of Hilary's now fragmentary work described by Jerome as a 'liber adversus Valentem et Ursacium, historiam Ariminensis et Seleucensis synodi continens'.[50] Scholarly opinion has generally been content to follow Wilmart's and Feder's conclusion that the work was probably compiled in three stages, the first of which Hilary prepared in reaction to his condemnation at Béziers.

In 1907, Wilmart established that the so-called 'Ad Constantium liber primus' was in fact part of a letter addressed to Constantius by the Western bishops at the Synod of Sardica.[51] This document, along with an explanatory narrative by Hilary, is included in a dossier of documents which Feder has entitled in his critical edition 'Liber I'.[52] Wilmart

[49] M. Meslin, in Les Ariens d'Occident 335-430, Paris 1967, 34, states that Saturninus was a co-signataire with Ursacius, Valens, etc., at Milan, based on the evidence of a surviving synodical letter, CCSL ix. 119. However, the text of the letter yields no names, a fact which Meslin does acknowledge in a footnote, ibid. 35 n. 15.   [50] De viris illust. c.

[51] A. Wilmart, 'L'Ad Constantium Liber primus de Saint Hilaire de Poitiers et les fragments historiques', RB xxiv (1907), 159-60. Most intriguing is his idea that this section was part of the letter which Vincentius of Capua and Euphrates of Cologne presented to Constantius in Antioch, 167-8.

[52] See CSEL lxv. 191. According to the arrangement of Feder, this dossier consists of the so-called 'Ad Constantium Liber primus', CSEL lxv. 181-7; the letter from the Eastern bishops of the Sardican council with the names of heretics and subscribers, 48-78; a letter from the Western bishops at Sardica to all churches, 103-26; a letter from the Western bishops at Sardica to Julius, 126-30; two letters of Ursacius and Valens, one to Julius, 143-4, the other to Athanasius, 145; a copy of the symbolum from Nicaea with a detailed explanation, 150-4; and a preface with information about the events at Arles, 98-102. The rest of the Adversus Valentem et Ursacium was compiled in two later stages. See Simonetti's brief but helpful summary of the editorial progression of this collection, 'Fragmenta historica', in Patrology iv. 46-8.

believed that Hilary took the Sardican document out of its original context and included it in his own survey of synods up until the time of Milan (355). A *terminus ante quem* for the letter 'Ad Constantium liber primus' is established by the fact that it was already exercising literary influence by the end of 357 or 358, since Phoebadius of Agen uses several segments from it in his *Contra Arrianos*.[53] It is generally agreed that Phoebadius wrote against the Sirmium Declaration of 357, but before the Council of Rimini (359). Thus, Phoebadius' work can be roughly dated to the end of 357 or 358. It may be safely assumed, therefore, that the 'pamphlet historique', or early 'Liber I', of Hilary is dated sometime before Phoebadius' work.

In another article a year later, Wilmart concluded that Hilary, who directed the contents of the *Adversus Valentem et Ursacium* against the agents of the Arian cause in the West, must have published the 'Liber I' in 356 as a result of the synod of Béziers.[54] Likewise, Feder proposed that Hilary had not been able at Béziers to present his defence against the accusations of Saturninus, Valens and Ursacius and subsequently wrote the 'Liber I' before he left Gaul for exile.[55] Both he and Wilmart believed Hilary was condemned at Béziers on the same anti-Athanasian grounds as were the bishops at Arles and Milan. It is not surprising, therefore, that they believed that Hilary prepared this series of anti-Arian documents in his defence.

This proposed dating and historical context of 'Liber I' of the *Adversus Valentem et Ursacium* has been widely accepted by patrologies and studies on Hilary.[56] A variation on the same theme is revived by Borchardt, who contends that Hilary probably prepared this dossier of documents to use in dispute with his opponents at Béziers.[57] This idea has found reinforcement in Paul Burns's recent article 'Hilary of Poitiers' confrontation with Arianism'.[58]

[53] Wilmart, 'L'Ad Constantium', 159–60. In checking the citations which Phoebadius is said to have borrowed from the 'Liber I' (also annotated in Feder's notes in CSEL lxv), I find only three of six occasions convincing: *Oratio syn. Sardicensis* iii, CSEL lxv. 183. 12–16, and *Contra Ar.* xv, PL xx. 23D; *Oratio syn. Sardicensis* vii, CSEL lxv. 186. 16–17, and *Contra Ar.* xv (Feder wrongly cites *Contra Ar.* xvi, PL xx. 24B; 'Incipit Fides apud Nicheam' v, CSEL lxv. 154. 1–3, and *Contra Ar.* vii, PL xx. 17C).

[54] 'Les fragments historiques et le Synode de Béziers en 356', *RB* xxv (1908), 226.

[55] 'Studien zu Hilarius von Poitiers I. Die sogenannte "fragmenta historica" und der sogenannte "Liber I ad Constantium Imperatorem" nach iher Überlieferung, inhaltlicher Bedeutung und Entstehung', in *Sitzungsberichte Acad. Wien* clxii/4 (1910), 114–15.

[56] E.g. Altaner, *Patrology*, 426; D. J. Chapman, 'The contested letters of Pope Liberius', *RB* xxvii (1910), 328; Emmennegger, *Functions of Faith*, 21; Meslin, 'Hilaire et la crise', 25; M. Figura, *Das Kirchenverständnis des Hilarius von Poitiers*, Freiburg 1984, 263; Simonetti, 'Fragmenta historica', 45.

[57] Borchardt, *Hilary of Poitiers*, 33–4. The origination of the argument goes back to B. Marx, 'Zwei Zeugen für die Herkunft der Fragmente I und II des sogennanten *Opus historicum* s. Hilarii', *Theologischen Quartalsschrift* xxviii (1906), 403–6.

[58] In *Arianism: historical and theological reassessments*, ed. R. C. Gregg, Philadelphia 1985, 288.

However, if it is true that Hilary was not exiled at Béziers for anti-Arian sentiments, then there is no necessity for the 'Liber i' to have been directly related to the events at Béziers. Nor is there any compelling reason why Hilary had to have compiled the work before his exile. Indeed, it seems more reasonable that he would have learned of the Sardican letters only in exile, particularly the *Epistula synodi Sardicensis Orientalium*, a document with which he clearly shows familiarity in another exilic work, *De synodis*.[59] Another document that looks suspiciously out of place in a collection of pre-exilic materials is the Nicene Creed. Hilary wrote that he had heard of the Nicene *fides* just before going into exile. But in the 'Liber i' he not only quotes the creed in its entirety but is able to expound on its meaning as well.[60] This can only be explained by the theological education Hilary received once he was in exile,[61] an education which eventually enabled this receptive bishop to produce his *magnum opus*, the *De Trinitate*. Lastly, if it is correct to assume that Valens and Ursacius were not at Béziers, then it is most unlikely that Hilary would have compiled a polemical broadside entitled 'Adversus Valentem et Ursacium' in preparation for, or in reaction to, Béziers.

If not Béziers, what then was the occasion for the *Adversus Valentem et Ursacium liber i*? The probable answer is the publication of the Sirmium Declaration in 357 by Valens and Ursacius, which Hilary soon afterward scorns as the 'blasphemia'.[62] It was the unveiling of this 'Manifesto' (as Gwatkin called it), which ruled out any discussion of *ousia* as unscriptural, that so horrified and angered the West. And it was this formula that called forth Hilary's indignant response, moving him to write *De synodis*[63] in order to alert his Western episcopal colleagues to the threat which lay before them. The documents of the 'Liber i' and their intent seem to fit this context best.

Of course, for Phoebadius to have utilised some material from the 'Liber primus' in his own response to the Sirmium formula, Hilary would have had to have sent his *Adversus Valentem et Ursacium* to the West very soon after the publication of the 'blasphemia'.[64] But is the timing for this

---

[59] *De syn.* xxxiv–xxxvii.   [60] B ii. 10, 11, CSEL lxv. 150–4.

[61] He appears to have spent much time with Basil (of Ancyra) and Eleusius (of Cyzicus); see *De syn.* xc. He also appears to have absorbed from them a great deal of his perspective of the contemporary theological controversies. 'Nam absque episcopo Eleusio et paucis cum eo, ex majori parte Asianae decem provinciae, intra quas consisto, vere Deum nesciunt...Sed horum episcoporum dolor se intra silentium non continens, unitatem fidei huius quaerit': *De syn.* lxiii, PL x. 522–3. By the time he writes *De synodis* (see above n. 29), Hilary is fully able to criticise the positions of *homoousios* and *homoiousios*. The insight required to frame together the documents of the 'Liber i' also seem to bespeak such intellectual exposure to the theological world.

[62] *De syn.* xi, a view also taken by Brennecke, *Hilarius von Poitiers*, 311, 326–7.

[63] See *De syn.* viii.

[64] The assembly at Sirmium (there is no reason to assume it was actually a council) met in either the summer or autumn of 357. Older studies (e.g. H. M. Gwatkin, *Studies in Arianism*, London 1889, 89) tend to prefer the earlier date. Since Constantius does not

scheme too tight? It is probably not the case. Unlike the solitary confinement imposed upon many ecclesiastical exiles,[65] Hilary enjoyed a surprising degree of freedom of movement and was allowed to fraternise with whomever he wished. Being in the company of men like Basil and Eleusius, chief standard-bearers for the doctrine of *homoiousios*, the report of the 'Declaration' would have been readily accessible to Hilary. He was well aware of the impact which the document had on this group, since it was in part directed against their confessional position. For the purposes of his own later work, *De synodis*, Hilary lists twelve of the nineteen anathemas from the synodical statement of Ancyra (358) immediately following his citation of the 'blasphemia'.[66] It is reasonable, therefore, to assume that Hilary's state of exile not only did not impede his learning of the Sirmium Formula but, rather, made it possible for him to receive it all the more quickly. In fact, there is evidence in *De synodis* i that Hilary had already sent to his Western *fratres* certain documents and elaborations of the affairs of the Eastern bishops.

> For since I had frequently informed you from many cities of the Roman provinces what was the faith and the efforts of our religious brethren, the eastern bishops, and how the devil, profiting by the discords of the times, spewed out his deadly doctrine with poisonous lips, I was afraid that your silence was indicative of a polluted and impious conscience, especially given that so many bishops are involved in such disastrous impiety or error. Ignorance I could not attribute to you; you had been too frequently warned.[67]

It is entirely possible that some parts or all of what is now referred to as the 'Liber I' were included in those things that Hilary transmitted to his Western colleagues for their illumination. The character of the synodical dossier well suits the context of the above passage, and it is known that his readers were already aware of the Sirmium Declaration

---

return to Sirmium until 17 Oct. (O. Seeck, *Regesten der Kaiser und Päpste für die Jahre 31 bis 476 n. Chr.*, Stuttgart 1919, 204), the latter is more likely. On the other hand, nowhere in the citations of the formula is the emperor said to be present. See Athanasius, *De syn.* xxviii; Hilary, *De syn.* xi; Socrates, *HE* ii. 30.

[65] For the treatment of Eusebius of Vercelli (exiled at Milan) and Liberius of Rome, see M. Goemans, 'L'exil du pape Libère', in *Mélanges offertes à Mlle. Christine Mohrmann*, Utrecht 1963, 184–9.

[66] Hilary's transition statement from discussing the Sirmium formula in *De syn.* xii to the Ancyran council gives the reader the impression that the latter was mostly anti-Sirmium in its intent. 'His itaque et tantis impietatis professionibus editis, has rursum e contrario Orientales episcopi in unum congregati sententiarum definitiones condiderunt': PL x. 489–90. In fact, however, the Ancyran council was an attempt to derail Aetius' proselytising activities in Antioch, Sozomen, *HE* iv. 13, even though the stress on *homoiousios* must surely have represented a rebuttal to Sirmium's ban on the term.

[67] 'Nam cum frequenter vobis ex plurimis Romanarum provinciarum urbibus significassem, quid cum religiosis fratribus nostris Orientis episcopis fidei studiique esset, quantaque, sub occasione temporalium motuum, diabolus venenato ore atque lingua mortiferae doctrinae sibila protulisset; verens ne in tanto ac tam plurium episcoporum calamitosae impietatis vel erroris periculo, taciturnitas vestra de pollutae atque impiatae conscientiae esset desperatione suscepta (nam ignorare vobis frequenter admonitis non licebat)': PL x. 479–80.

before Hilary sent the *De synodis*.[68] Moreover, the striking similarities between the *Adversus* and the *De synodis* – a cataloguing of and commenting on credal confessions and synodical letters – suggests a similar purpose and context for the publication of both.

If it is the case that the 'Liber I' was compiled in reaction to the Sirmium Declaration of 357, then the date of its publication ought to be pushed forward from the traditional date of 356 to the end of 357 or early 358. No reason prohibits the transfer. But this may have the added implication that the list of documents which Feder includes in the 'Liber I' has to be expanded to include, for instance, certain letters of Liberius.[69] Thematically, these letters might serve to illustrate in the 'Liber I' Hilary's intent by demonstrating the centrality of the Nicene Creed in the attacks of the heretics.[70] But the inclusion of Liberius' letters in the 'Liber I' is fraught with problems. For example how would Hilary have had access to the letters, especially the personal correspondence, such as the letter to Vincentius ('Non doceo') or to Valens, Ursacius and Germinius ('Quia scio'), whereas an encounter with Liberius on the way home from exile (360) could easily account for his having the whole collection in his hands? More important is the issue of timing. Could Hilary have had enough time to receive copies of the letters and send the 'Liber I' to the West for Phoebadius to have relied on them in early 358? The fact that most scholars believe Liberius did not return to Rome until 2 August 358[71] allows for the possibility that his letters, written in exile, may have been almost as late. If so, Hilary could never have had access to them in time.

Even if the Liberian correspondence was not available to Hilary at the time of writing, it does nothing to detract from the argument that he compiled the 'Liber I' in reaction to the Sirmium Declaration of 357. Indeed, the argument still stands whether Phoebadius was dependent on the 'Liber I' or not. Once faulty presuppositions about the purpose of the 'Liber I' are removed, as was attempted above, the internal evidence of the 'Liber I' and its comparison to *De synodis* suggest both the later date and purpose.

In sum, whatever set of circumstances lay behind the motive for plotting Hilary's exile in 356, it cannot be concluded that the grounds for

[68] 'Meministis namque in ea ipsa scripta proxime apud Sirmium blasphemia': *De syn.* x, PL x. 486.

[69] These letters of Liberius are placed by Feder in 'Liber II' of the *Adversus Valentem et Ursacium*; see CSEL lxv. 192.

[70] See Brennecke, *Hilarius von Poitiers*, 311–12. Brennecke argues that these letters of Liberius, datable to 353–7, thematically suit the 'Liber I' better than the 'Liber II', which is concerned with the Synods of Rimini and Seleucia. The letters categorised in 'Liber II' (Feder's enumeration) are as follows: A vii ('ad Constantium'), B iii ('ad Orientales episcopi') and B vii ('Quamvis sub imagine', 'Nolo te', 'Inter haec', 'Pro deifico', 'Quia scio' and 'Non doceo').

[71] The *Liber pontificalis*, ed. L. Duchesne, 2nd edn, Paris 1955, 208, provides only the day and the month (2 Aug.) of Liberius' re-entry into Rome.

his exile and the context of Béziers were parallel with the events of Arles and Milan. This should serve as a warning against too readily attributing to Hilary an assumed anti-Arian role at this early stage of his career. On the contrary, removal of the hagiographic veneer reveals a little known Gallic bishop who may have been relatively ignorant of the theological and political complexities which had grown out of the early Arian controversy. In harmony with this conclusion we were also led to regard Hilary's 'Liber I' of *Adversus Valentem et Ursacius* as a product of his exile rather than a reaction to (or in preparation for) it. This, too, would confirm the development of Hilary's convictions about the Nicene Creed and its opponents after 356. And while it still may be accurate to bestow upon the bishop of Poitiers the title 'Athanasius of the west',[72] such an appellation is justified only after the exile had begun and this Western bishop had his eyes opened in the East.

[72] F. L. Cross and E. A. Livingstone (eds), *The Oxford Dictionary of the Christian Church*, Oxford 1974, 649. The phrase seems to have originated with Karl A. Hase, *Kirchengeschichte*, Leipzig 1836², 137: 'durch Thaten, Leiden und Schriften der Athanasius des Abendlandes' (Borchardt, *Hilary of Poitiers*, p. vii).

POLEMICS AND POLITICS IN AMBROSE OF MILAN'S *DE FIDE*

THERE are surprisingly few specialized studies which address the historical-theological context of Ambrose's earliest anti-'Arian' writing, namely, the *De fide*. Books I–II of this treatise are manifestly a single production, and have been the main object of scholarly inquiries. Attention has centered around their purpose and date,[1] while more recent publications have begun the necessary task of integrating *De fide* I–II with our increasing knowledge about Latin 'Arianism', or Homoianism, and its response to pro-Nicene theology.[2] No such treatment has yet been given to Books III–V. Apart from the useful introductory notes provided by O. Faller in his critical edition of *De fide* I–V in CSEL 78, Books III–V are still in need of a contextual analysis which would explain their particular content and occasion in distinction from those of the earlier books. The fulfillment of that task would shed further light on Ambrose's early episcopacy, a period about which we possess little reliable information. This essay attempts to provide a remedy for that deficiency, albeit a preliminary one. Considering the historical and religious environment that gave rise to *De fide* III–V, I wish to suggest that Ambrose had not intended to add three more books to his initial polemical effort and that he did so only under the duress of his ecclesiastical struggle with Homoian opponents in Milan.

I

The publication of *De fide* I–II, probably at the end of 378, marked the bishop's formal entry into the half-century conflict

---

[1] G. Gottlieb (*Ambrosius von Mailand and Kaiser Gratian* (Göttingen, 1973), 49 f.) wants to place the work in 380, following Gratian's April meeting with Ambrose in Milan. But P. Nautin has rightly criticized the reasoning of Gottlieb ('Les premières relations d'Ambroise avec l'emperor Gratien. Le *De fide* (livres I–II)', in Y. M. Duval (ed.), *Ambroise de Milan: XVI* Centenaire de son election épiscopale* (Paris, 1974), 229–44) and returns to the more traditional date which is soon after the battle of Hadrianople on 9 August (cf. Palanque, *Saint Ambroise et L'Empire Romain: Contribution à L'Histoire des Rapports de L'Eglise et de L'Etat à la Fin du Quatrième Siècle* (Paris, 1933), 498; H. Von Campenhausen, *Ambrosius von Mailand als Kirchenpolitiker* (Berlin und Leipzig, 1929), 279; O. Faller, CSEL 78, 5*–7*).

[2] N. McLynn, 'The "Apology" of Palladius: Nature and Purpose', *JTS*, NS, 42 (1991), 52–76; D. H. Williams, *Ambrose of Milan and the End of the Nicene-Arian Conflicts* (Oxford, 1995). Gryson's edition of the 'scholia ariana' in *Scolies ariennes sur le Concile d'Aquilée*, Sources Chrétiennes 267 (Paris, 1980) has greatly facilitated a renewed interest in Homoianism and its attacks on Ambrose.

© Oxford University Press 1995

[Journal of Theological Studies, NS, Vol. 46, Pt. 2, October 1995]

between pro-Nicenes and anti-Nicenes. Prior to this time Ambrose had said nothing about 'Arians'[3] or about the social and religious tensions that had continued to plague Milan since his Homoian predecessor, Auxentius, held that bishopric (355–374).[4] But once Ambrose began his attack, 'Arianism' became the worst of heresies (I.6.46), another form of pagan polytheism (I.1.16), a religion of philosophical disputation or dialectics (I.5.42; 13.84), and that of the antichrist (II.15.135).

No one 'Arian' seems to be the subject of his assault; in fact, Ambrose does not seem to have a clear idea about what the 'Arians' teach. His diatribe is relegated to using a rhetorical strategy of attacking his opponents that was already common in the fourth century—that of classifying opposing opinions and persons in relation to previously condemned positions.[5] Thus he conflates popularized heretical ideas taken from Arius, from the Eunomians, and from Homoians, such as Palladius of Ratiaria, whom he names along with Demophilus of Constantinople and Auxentius, the former bishop of Milan. (I.6.45). Such evident confusion on his part drew stinging criticism from Palladius who wrote a riposte against *De fide* I–II, part of which is preserved in the 'scholia ariana'.[6]

Despite these handicaps, *De fide* I–II is a systematic tour de force which argues against six propositions attributed to its opponents.

(1) They affirm that the Son is unlike (*dissimilis*) the Father.

(2) They affirm that the Son had a beginning in time.

(3) They affirm that the Son was created.

(4) They deny the goodness of the Son.

(5) They deny the omnipotence of the Son.

(6) They deny that the Son is of the same substance as the Father.

As Ambrose marshalled his case against each of these, his overriding concern was to defend the divine unity of the Father and the Son who, he argued, are one in *potestas* (sometimes *virtus*), one in *operatio*, and the same in substance. This unity is affirmed

---

[3] Correctly noted by Angelo Paredi, *Saint Ambrose: His Life and Times*, trans. M. J. Costelloe (Notre Dame, 1964), 176.

[4] Rufinus, *HE* ii.11 (*PL* XXI.521B). The exegetical tracts, *De paradiso* and *De Cain et Abel*, and the funeral sermon for his brother Satyrus, precede *De fide* I–II chronologically but tell us nothing about theological conflicts in Milan.

[5] J. R. Lyman, 'A Topography of Heresy: Mapping the Rhetorical Creation of Arianism', in M. R. Barnes and D. H. Williams (eds.), *Arianism After Arius: Essays on the Development of the Fourth Century Trinitarian Conflicts* (Edinburgh, 1993), 45–62.

[6] 'Contra De fide', Scholia, 336[r], 1–337[r], 49.

to its utmost extent so that no multiplicity (*multiplex*) exists in the Father and the Son because they are *indifferens*. Nor is the term *persona* used as a means of distinguishing Father and Son in Books I–II, despite its inclusion in De Romestin's English transla- tion (NPNF X) (cf. *De fide* II.1.18; 3.33). The overriding polem- ical agenda was that no possible wedge of inequality should be driven between the Father and the Son. As a result, Ambrose says almost nothing about the internal dynamic of trinitarian relations, and even less about the Holy Spirit, not addressing issues con- cerning the consubstantiality of the Spirit until 381.

It is of prime importance that *De fide* I–II be understood as a document penned in response to imperial instigation. In the pre- face Ambrose states that the emperor Gratian wrote to him requesting a *libellum* explaining his faith: *Tu quoque, sancte imper- ator Gratiane ... fidem meam audire voluisti.*[7] But why would the Western emperor, whose usual place of residence had been in Trier, have sought such a declaration from the bishop of Milan? Older scholarship, such as the work of Homes-Dudden, interprets Gratian's request as evidence of a prior relationship of religious sympathy between the emperor and the bishop. On this reading, Gratian was seeking theological instruction from a spiritual mentor. Such an approach can easily be discounted. In the first place Ambrose himself makes it clear in the beginning of *De fide* that the two books explicating his faith were written not for the emperor's instruction, but for his approval.[8] Secondly, Gratian continued to maintain a political policy of religious toleration toward the 'Arians' at least until early 381, so that while the emperor knew Ambrose and may have been partial to the bishop's pro-Nicene position,[9] imperial dialogue also extended to Homoian bishops.[10] Thirdly and most importantly, a strong case has been made by Pierre Nautin that the reason Gratian demanded a written statement from Ambrose was because the latter had been accused of heretical teaching, perhaps by Palladius[11] or, more likely, by Homoians in Milan.

We must not minimize the religious unrest that vexed the north Italian city. Just two or three years after Ambrose's accession to the episcopate (*c.* 376/7), he faced a wall of opposition fuelled by local Homoians who had been bolstered by new leadership. There

---

[7] *De fide* I. praef. 1 (CSEL 78.3–4).
[8] *De fide* I. prol. 1 (CSEL 78.4.6–7).
[9] As Gratian's letter to Ambrose, 'Cupio valde', indicates.
[10] Just before the council of Aquiliea (September 381), Palladius claims to have discussed with Gratian the terms and purpose of the council (see n.48).
[11] 'Les premières', 239–40.

is evidence that a certain Julian Valens, former bishop of Poetovio and known Gothic sympathizer, established himself at the head of the Homoian community in Milan and carried on a kind of clandestine operation through ordinations and the propagating of anti-Nicene doctrine.[12] Nor was Valens alone in his agitations; he received an unlikely ally in the person of Ursinus, the arch-rival of Damasus for the Roman see, who suddenly appeared in Milan and joined Valens in the task of covertly nurturing anti-Nicene sentiments.[13]

Even more problematic for Ambrose was the imperial support which the Milanese Homoians received. By the autumn of 378 the court of the boy emperor Valentinian II had taken occupation of the imperial residence of Milan, having been granted temporary refuge by Gratian during the aftermath of the battle of Hadrianople. According to the Latin historian Rufinus, Justina, the infamous 'Arian' empress and domineering mother of Valentinian II, began to manifest her 'Arian' sentiments openly after the death of her husband (Valentinian I), that is, by the time she arrived in Milan.[14] Undoubtedly her patronage was enthusiastically received by the Milanese Homoians who had been denied access to a basilica by Ambrose and were now relegated to meeting in their own homes. Justina is said to have fomented discord within the church in Milan by inciting attacks against Ambrose and the pro-Nicene clergy. The cumulative effect of such carefully directed agitation could easily have included formal objections raised against the homoousian theology of the bishop. We know that more than once anti-Nicenes accused the homoousian position of teaching that the Father and the Son were two equal and eternal *ousiai*, or three equals with the Holy Spirit, thereby advocating a pagan-like tritheism.[15]

Whatever affinities Gratian may have shared with Ambrose, a charge of gross heresy against a metropolitan bishop could not be

---

[12] *Ep.* 2.10 (CSEL 82.3.323.119–21). Valens' presence posed a threat to Ambrose's position strong enough for him to ask the emperor at the Council of Aquileia in 381 to take legal action against Valens by banning him from the city ibid. (CSEL 82.3.323.117–19).

[13] Another synodical letter from the Council of Aquileia accounts for Ursinus' activities: 'he was in league and joined with the Arians at this time with whom, along with Valens, he tried to throw the church of Milan into confusion; holding detestable assemblies sometimes before the doors of the synagogue, sometimes in the homes of the Arians, hatching secret schemes and uniting their followers' (*Ep.* 5 [extra coll.].3 (CSEL 82.3.183–84.33–37).

[14] *HE* ii.15 (*PL* xxi.523C).

[15] See Scholia, 345ᵛ, 128–29; 303ᵛ, 36; Ambrose, *De fide* I.1.10; Hilary, *De trin.* i.17.

ignored. Ironically, the same manoeuvre had been tried by Hilary of Poitiers fifteen years earlier against Ambrose's 'Arian' predecessor, Auxentius, in order to dislodge him from the Milanese see.[16] By directing an accusation of doctrinal *impietas* against Auxentius, the emperor had been compelled to investigate, for such a charge carried with it the potential threat of public disturbance. Now in 378 Ambrose faced a similar situation which necessitated a written statement in his defence. Not surprisingly, he offers a prayer at the end of Book I of *De fide* that God would cleanse the ears of the emperor from all the slander of his opponents.

II

How did Gratian respond to Ambrose's declaration of faith? Sometime in the spring of 379,[17] the emperor sent a letter to Milan signalling his favourable receipt of the work by requesting the bishop to 'hurry to me, religious priest of God, so that you might teach me the true doctrine which is to be believed'.[18] In that same letter, Gratian asks that Ambrose would enlarge his arguments by writing something further about the Holy Spirit.[19]

We also possess Ambrose's reply to Gratian's letter, written that same year, in which he sounds obviously relieved: he 'whom you piously believe, [knows how] my strength is refreshed by your faith, your salvation, your glory'.[20] The precariousness of Ambrose's situation is implied by his words at the close of the letter, 'because Your Clemency has approved the two books I sent, I do not fear [any] danger'.[21] The bishop then proceeds to promise that he will soon hasten to the emperor's presence (which he has not yet done for reasons that are far from clear), and that he will seek from the Spirit the necessary grace for further writing, presumably to fulfill Gratian's request for pro-Nicene arguments on the divinity of the Holy Spirit. However it was not until February or March of 381—almost three years later—that Ambrose finally honoured the emperor's petition by completing *De spiritu sancto*,[22] a work in three books which is dedicated to

[16] *Contra Auxentium* 8 (*PL* X.614C). Hilary appended Auxentius' written confession to the end of his treatise, 'Exemplum Blasphemiae Auxenti' (*PL* X.617–18).

[17] While Gratian was still in Sirmium. O. Seeck, *Regesten der Kaiser und Päpste für die Jahre 311 bis 476 n. Chr.* (Stuttgart, 1919), 250.

[18] 'Cupio valde' 1 (*PL* XVI.913A).

[19] *Ibid.* 3 (914A).

[20] 'Non mihi affectus' 2 (CSEL 79.6*).

[21] *Ibid.* 7 (CSEL 79.7*).

[22] The completion of *De spir. sancto* can be dated with some certainty to February or March of 381 (Faller, *CSEL* 79.15*–16*).

Gratian. One might ask why it took Ambrose so long to comply
with the wishes of one whose goodwill he was so anxious to secure.
Just as curious is the unannounced appearance in the meantime
of three more books *De fide*, which are clearly not addressing the
doctrine of the Holy Spirit, and seem at first sight to be superfluous since the emperor had already approved the first two. What
need was there for this second effort of polemical self-defence?

The fact that Books III–V are an expansion of the arguments
presented in I–II, and that they are linked by common theological
concerns, gives the appearance that these two separate works are
parts of a single whole, as some scholars have assumed.[23] Such an
assumption is easily derived from Ambrose himself. In the prologue of Book V, the bishop twice states that he is commencing
the 'fifth book', and compares his five books analogously to the
five talents of faith in Matthew 25.[24] It is obvious that he wanted
his readers to believe that *De fide* I–V was an unbroken literary
unit. It can nonetheless be shown that Books III–V have a completely distinct historical occasion and literary structure that not
only distinguishes them from I–II as an individual treatise, but
also reveals valuable information about the Homoian reaction to
Ambrose's first polemic.

If we return to the letter which Ambrose sent in reply to
Gratian, it is evident that Books III–V are not yet written. We can
likewise agree with Faller that the letter shows no indication of a
plan for the continuation of *De fide*.[25] Not until a year and a half
later will Ambrose decide to add further material to his first efforts.
In the prologue of Book III he states the reason for these additions:

Sed quoniam mens prava quorundam serendis intenta quaestionibus stilo
lacessit uberiore confici, tuae quoque pia me cura clementiae ad cetera
vocat volens in pluribus experiri, quem in paucis probasti, ea quae
perstricta paucis superius sunt, placuit paulo latius exsequi, ne ea
quasi diffidentia adsertionis deseruisse potius quam securitate fiduciae
proposuisse videamur.[26]

[23] E.g. R. P. C. Hanson, *The Search for the Christian Doctrine of God*
(Edinburgh, 1988), 669–75.
[24] *De fide*, prol. 7. In writing his *Commonitorium* (AD 434), Vincentius of Lérins
knows of *De fide* only in its expanded form, citing passages from Books I and III
as 'of the same work' (*Comm.* v.12).
[25] CSEL 78.9*.
[26] III.1.2 (CSEL 78.108): 'Because certain depraved minds, fixed on the sowing
of disputes with their pen, are arousing even further labors to be done, and also
the pious concern of Your Clemency invokes other matters wishing for demonstration in many things which you approved in a few, it is necessary for me to describe
somewhat more fully those issues which I only lightly touched upon earlier lest
we seem to have abandoned these views, as if carelessly asserted, rather than
proposed in the assurance of fidelity.'

The Italian scholar Maria Grazie Mara interprets this passage as evidence that Books III–V were answering another request of the emperor for further labours.[27] But it can be shown that just the opposite is true, namely that Ambrose is offering the emperor an explanation why he embarked on this expansion of his first treatise independent of imperial direction. While the wording of the passage is admittedly abstruse, it seems that Ambrose is making a distinction between the pious concern of the emperor that 'calls me to other matters', namely a treatise on the Holy Spirit, and the necessity of the moment in which Ambrose feels obliged to complement his earlier work against the continued disputings of a 'depraved mind'.

This interpretation is easily vindicated when one turns to the prologue of Book V where Ambrose addresses the emperor and states that in this last book he discusses the divine indivisibility of the Father, the Son, and the Holy Spirit which has caused him to put aside (*sequestrata*) a fuller disputation on the Spirit.[28] Elsewhere in the same prologue, Ambrose defends the priority of answering his opponents: 'If we are silent we will seem to be giving way', and 'it was necessary to write something so that … our writings might answer the impieties of the heretics'.[29] It appears then that Ambrose was not fulfilling an imperial injunction by writing Books III–V, but was under some other compulsion to defend his pro-Nicene position against 'Arians'.

Such a conclusion naturally raises the question: what happened after the publication of *De fide* I–II that prompted Ambrose's decision to compose a sequel? There are at least two identifiable factors.

First, the mention of 'depraved minds' by Ambrose in the beginning of Book III is almost certainly a reference to Palladius of Ratiaria, a Homoian bishop in Illyricum,[30] who was little known prior to 379 when he appears suddenly as a spokesman for Western Homoianism and as the arch-opponent of Ambrose. Palladius moved to the centre of the theological stage when he published a withering polemic against *De fide* I–II. Only a fragment of this polemic is extant among the corpus of the *scholia* found in the

---

[27] *Patrology* iv.169. Cf. Faller, CSEL 78.9*.

[28] V. prol. 7 (CSEL 78.218).

[29] V. prol. 5 (217–18).

[30] This is probably the same Palladius who is addressed, along with other Homoian bishops, by Germinius of Sirmium in a letter (*c.*366) extant in the *fragmenta historica* of Hilary of Poitiers (CSEL 65.160–64).

526   D. H. WILLIAMS

Paris manuscript latinus 8907, now edited by Gryson.[31] In what remains of this anti-Nicene work, a number of Ambrose's criticisms about 'Arians' are utterly rejected, such as his insistence that his opponents teach the doctrine of *dissimilis*. Palladius writes, 'If we believe that the Son said, "Whatever the Father does the Son also does similarly" [John 5: 19], how can we claim he is "unlike"?'[32] Ambrose is said to accuse them of teaching *dissimilis* for the simple reason that they say the Son is not coexistent and coeternal with the unbegotten Father. And yet, says Palladius, even Ambrose admits that the Son is begotten and thereby differs from the Father.

Palladius then accuses the doctrine of *homoousios* of obviating the personal qualities (*propriaetates*) of the Father and the Son, thus leading to the denial of both, since the properties peculiar to the Father and to the Son are run together and lost. Such a view also does violence to the integrity of the Father–Son relationship. If the Son is pleased to be subject to the Father in all things, why does Ambrose insist that the Father must beget him as an equal? For this wicked blasphemy Ambrose is urged to beg favour from God 'against whom you sinned by impiously denying the character of both. For you acknowledge neither the Father nor the Son ...'.[33]

Towards the end of the fragment, Palladius sternly admonishes Ambrose with a series of imperative verbs to put away any 'unconstructive and superfluous report of a subtle deceit',[34] and to cease from 'monstrous comparisons'; a reference to Ambrose's analogy in *De fide* I between his opponents and the mythical Hydra and Scylla—a comparison which seems especially to have irked Palladius, and which Ambrose restates in *De fide* III.1.3, as if only to exasperate his Homoian detractor further.

Palladius' 'Contra *de fide*' offered a formidable counter-defence, not only in attacking the pro-Nicene theological platform, but in

[31] Gryson, *Scolies*, 264–74. Gryson believes that the scholia are a conflation of several separate anti-Nicene works, Palladius being the author of two: the polemic against *De fide* I–II and a longer *apologia* opposing the disgraceful treatment which the Homoian bishops received at the Council of Aquileia, (fos. 337ʳ, 50–349, 4). Neil McLynn has recently shown that the 'Contra *De fide*' was issued twice by Palladius; the first time in opposition to Ambrose's Books I–II, and then again after 381, appended to the apology against the Aquileian council ('The "Apology" of Palladius', 57f.). That Ambrose published three more books against Palladius's arguments seems to underscore McLynn's arguments. There remains only the question why Palladius, who should have been aware of Ambrose's additional books, would not have incorporated a rebuttal or made some reference to them in his re-issue of the 'Contra *De fide*'.
[32] *Ibid.* 337ʳ, 10–14 (Gryson, *Scolies*, 272).
[33] *Ibid.* 337ᵛ, 48b–49 (Gryson, *Scolies*, 270).
[34] *Ibid.* 337ʳ, 32–34 (Gryson, *Scolies*, 272).

asserting the distinctiveness of post-Ariminum theology. Its potential effectiveness was not lost on Ambrose. Unlike *De fide* I–II, Books III–V entail a much more careful refutation of specific scriptural interpretations or objections put forward by the Homoians. Throughout there is a serious recognition that the 'Arians' possess quite a number of exegetical arguments in their arsenal to defend the differences between the Father and the Son, and these Ambrose considers at length. No longer can Palladius charge Ambrose with not knowing the writings of his opponents. Theologically, Books III–V reveal several significant changes in emphasis or argumentation from that of Books I–II. For instance, it seems that Palladius' criticisms about divine unity in homoousian doctrine hit home, since in III.15.126–127 Ambrose takes up for the first time a discussion about the 'distinction of persons and unity of nature' as a true explanation of the word *homoousios*.[35] It is especially fascinating that the proper interpretation of *homoousios* should be broadened to include divine *distinctio* as well as unity of substance! In a later book, Ambrose acknowledges an internal distinction in the divine relations by stating that *generatio* is a unique property (*proprietas*) of the Father, just as the Son, who is 'the wisdom of God', is generated according to his true property (*proprietas*).[36] From this he concludes 'we know the fact of distinction' (*distinctionem scimus*, 8.91), yet without resorting to the division or sundering apart of the essential unity of the two.

Another recognition on Ambrose's part is his awareness in Book III that one's doctrine of the incarnation is absolutely central to the preservation, or dissolution, of an essential unity between the Father and the Son. This direction in Ambrose's thought prognosticates his treatise *De incarnationis domenicae sacramento*. Palladius' teachings are again targeted by Ambrose when he asks the question: 'Why do you attribute the calamities of the body to divinity, and connect the weakness of human pain with the divine nature?'[37] As his own insistence about the complete separation between the human and divine natures in the incarnate Son shows, Ambrose has no toleration for the Homoian view that God the Son truly suffered in the incarnation since it necessitated the

---

[35] CSEL 78.152: *Recte ergo homousion patri filium dicimus, quia verbo eo et personarum distinctio et naturae unitas significatur.* The only other use of *persona* appears in V.3.46 though is not used as a reference to divine internal relations.

[36] IV.8.77–95. 8.81: *Generatio enim paternae proprietatis est ...*; 8.87: *Proprietatem autem generationis esse oracula divina declarant* (cf. 8.88: *ut proprietatem verae generationis ostenderet*).

[37] *De incarn.* V.41. Cf. Palladius' second known work against the decisions of the Council of Aquileia, also in fragmented form, Scholia, 340ᵛ, 32–41 (Gryson, *Scolies*, 292).

subordination of the Son to the Father. He never changes his stance on this subject.

Ambrose's dependence on caricature as a means of undermining the position of his opponents is much reduced as his theological skills have sharpened. Interestingly we hear no more in *De fide* III–V about Eunomius, nor is it claimed a priori that the 'Arians' teach the Son is unlike the Father, with the exception of III.1.15, where Ambrose contends that *dissimilis* is the logical result of their doctrine.[38] It is also admitted at one point that his opponents deny they are 'Arians' (IV.9.96), though Ambrose ignores this grievance, not hesitating to refer to them as 'Arius' disciples' (IV.10.130). Obviously Ambrose had not relinquished all his rhetorical-polemical devices.

III

While the 'Contra *De fide*' of Palladius supplies us with the probable primary object of Ambrose's invective, it does not provide the whole context and rationale behind the publication of *De fide* III–V. Palanque proposed that increased agitation on the part of Julian Valens and the 'Arians' in Milan was the reason for the additional books. He is partially correct. No doubt the Milanese Homoians welcomed Justina's patronage in their struggle to maintain their ecclesiastical identity. As the influx of refugees streamed into the city from the Illyrian provinces besieged by Gothic incursions, the number of non-Nicenes was considerably augmented, creating new needs for religious accommodation in the Homoian community.

The literary structure of *De fide* III–V offers some suggestive corroboration for the scenario proposed above. It can be demonstrated that Books III–V are, in fact, a compilation of sermons or addresses which Ambrose delivered against the 'Arians' in Milan. One can cite several instances, such as at the end of Book III, where Ambrose is evidently finishing a church service: 'Let us bring today's discourse to a close and sing the praises of the holy martyr'.[39] Or, in the beginning of Book V, Ambrose commences his address with the statement, 'You who hear or read these words ...'.[40] A passage in the *De incarnatione* also lends support to the sermonic nature of Book IV in that Ambrose's opponents

[38] In V.1.27 Ambrose also used the word *dissimilis* as if to imply that the 'Arians' teach this about the differences of divinity between the Father and the Son (CSEL 78.226).

[39] III.17.142.

[40] V. prol. 9.

are said to have 'listened' when anti-'Arian' arguments were preached.[41]

The lack of internal organization in Books III–V underscores the likelihood that the work (or more properly, works) is an edited series of polemical arguments which were later prepared for the emperor Gratian. Book III has no prologue, the first chapter expressing only a justification for the lengthiness of the present treatise. As chapters unfold, no scheme is announced or readily discernible by the reader, except the reviewing and refuting of 'Arian' exegetical arguments one after another. A standard prologue is also lacking in Book IV, although a brief (1.1–2.26) discourse about the christological identity of the 'Lord' in Psalm 23 (Latin Bible)[42] has been utilized to act as an introduction. It bears no relation to the arguments of subsequent chapters, whereas the opening words of chapter 3 make a more accurate announcement: *Itaque discutiamus eorum alias quaestiones* (3.27). In contrast, Book V begins with a lengthy prologue addressed to the emperor and exhibits a concerted attempt to show that the preceding and present arguments are meant to be a literary unit. Ambrose calls it a *libellus*, and for the first time he refers to the 'earlier books' (V.2.27). The editorial seams of Book V in particular are noticeable when one compares the prologue (chapters 1–8) with chapter 9 and following. The prologue invokes the emperor (*imperator auguste*) as the intended audience, stating the necessity for prolonging the discussion beyond the content of the previous book. In chapter 9 we sense an audience change: Ambrose is addressing 'You (*vos*) who hear or read these things', and we encounter (chs. 9–10) a repeated use of the plural pronoun (*vos, vestris, vobis*) with the description of his listeners as *fratres* (ch. 11). We are left with the impression that, in contrast to Books I–II, the material in III–V was not originally intended to be a unified treatise, but soon after was compiled and hastily edited to look like one. The acknowledgements to the emperor in the beginnings of Books III and V and the honorable mentions of 'Your majesty' located at different intervals within the text[43] were also added afterwards, probably by Ambrose himself, indicating that Gratian was the intended reader for the collection.

We have yet to answer the question why Ambrose would have wanted to send such a compilation of anti-'Arian' arguments to the emperor after the latter had already approved his earlier treat-

[41] *De incar.* VIII.79.

[42] B. Studer, 'Die anti-arianische Auslegung von Psalm 23, 7–10 in *De fide* IV, 1–2 des Ambrosius von Mailand', in *Ambroise de Milan*, 245–66.

[43] III.1.1; 14.108; IV.1.1; 8.78; V. prol. 6; 7.88; 13.153.

530		D. H. WILLIAMS

ise. Why not address his three books as a rebuttal to Palladius or to his antagonists in Milan?

The answer can be found by considering the reaction of the Latin Homoians to *De fide* I–II. Despite Gratian's warm acceptance of this first treatise of Ambrose, the attacks against the bishop did not abate but continued to increase in intensity, as is demonstrated by Palladius' critical response to the anti-'Arian' content of *De fide*. To secure the emperor's sympathies was a step in the right direction for Ambrose, although it did not reap any changes in imperial policy regarding religion for the years 379–380.[44] The Homoians had no less access to the emperor's ear through Justina's influence as exemplified in the episode of the Homoians receiving a basilica for worship.[45]

Still further precision is possible in explaining the conditions which induced Ambrose to compile and send *De fide* III–V. While Gratian remained in the West for the first half of 380, the early summer months found him journeying to the Balkans for a joint military campaign with the newly appointed Augustus of the East, Theodosius.[46] On 2 August, Gratian is known to have been in Sirmium,[47] and it is there that Palladius and his episcopal confederates met with him. Evidence for this interview is derived from Palladius' own remarks in the recorded proceedings of the council of Aquileia, that 'the emperor himself spoke to us' at Sirmium. Twice Palladius makes reference to this discussion during which he was concerned to secure a just hearing for the Homoian position by adequate representation of Homoian bishops at the forthcoming council.[48] It was evidently a favourable interview for Palladius since he insinuates in the minutes of the council that he was satisfied with the emperor's decision.

Ambrose surely knew of Gratian's journey to Sirmium, and was probably informed of the interview with Palladius after the fact. Such news was not welcome. In light of his current conten-

[44] The three anti-heretical laws which Gratian allegedly issued (*CTh* XVI.2, 23 (Cf. XVI.2, 12); XVI.5, 4; and a rescript issued in Sirmium known to us only by implication in XVI.5, 5) are not anti-'Arian' but directed against the Donatists. See Gottlieb, *Ambrosius von Mailand*, 77 f. and 'Gratian's Religious Politics' in chapter five of *Ambrose of Milan and the End of the Nicene-Arian Conflicts*. Not until the early months of 381 did Gratian change the legal status of 'Arianism' as a sect condemned in the west on a par with the Photinians, Manicheans, and Donatists.

[45] See 'When Did the Emperor Gratian Return the Basilica to the Pro-Nicenes in Milan?', *Studia Patristica* XXIV (1993), 208–15.

[46] Zosimus, *Historia Nova* IV.33.1; Piganiol, *L'Empire chrétienne (325–395)*, (Paris, 1972²), 233.

[47] *Regesten*, 254.

[48] *Gesta* 8 (CSEL 82.3.330); 10 (331–32).

tions with Palladius and the Milanese Homoians, Ambrose felt the need to maintain his favourable initial reception with the emperor by flooding him with another series of anti-'Arian' arguments. It is therefore reasonable to suppose that Ambrose prepared and sent his edited collection as a continuation of *De fide* I–II under the same title, counting on the fact that the first two books had been well received. Such a move was intended to keep Palladius and his kind from gaining any further ground in the accord which they achieved with the emperor. The politically astute Ambrose was fully aware of the fragility of his own position, and that an accord between the Homoians and Gratian threatened to railroad any hopes of dealing his opponents a decisive blow at the forthcoming Western council.

In sum, we have seen that the success of *De fide* I–II in establishing Ambrose's favour with Gratian or ensuring the security of his position in Milan was much more limited than the textbook picture allows. The need to produce a substantial addendum of material, which took the shape of three additional books, reveals that Ambrose's struggle with the Homoians seriously troubled his early episcopate. Not until the council of Aquileia, September 381, was Ambrose able to wield the kind of controlling dominance over contrary situations for which he is so characterized by later writers. Even then his conflicts with Milanese Homoians did not end.

As an entirely separate production from the first two books, *De fide* III–V demonstrates a progression both in Ambrose's knowledge of his enemies and in his own theological abilities. That he was compelled to refute the arguments of the 'Arians' with a greater sophistication before the watching eyes of the emperor indicates more than paranoia on Ambrose's part. He had discovered that the controversy was indeed complicated, requiring superior skills than the mere throwing of rhetorical darts at one's opponent. The 'Arian controversy' was not yet over, at least in Milan, and Ambrose would have to spend the first decade of his episcopate engaged with much more than straw men who could easily be knocked down.

D. H. WILLIAMS

1996 NAPS Presidential Address
On The Brink: Bede

JOSEPH F. KELLY

The venerable Bede (673–735) occupies a unique place in the history of Christian scholarship. A Germanic barbarian, descendant of those warriors who overran Christian, Roman Britain, he spent his life preserving the culture his ancestors almost destroyed. Indeed, so identified is he with that culture, that many scholars consider him a church father. The *Clavis Patrum Latinorum* has canonized him by inclusion and others continue to ratify that decision,[1] but *The Oxford Dictionary of the Christian Church,* edited by two leading students of Early Christianity, dissents, identifying Isidore of Seville (d. 636) as the last of the fathers.[2] This paper will not focus on that question, except to note that only one person could have said with confidence whether or not Bede was a father, and that was Bede, who would have said no.

This paper will focus instead on Bede as a scholar on the brink between two worlds, an ancient one he knew only from books but which he still loved dearly, and a modern one, which he frequently criticized,[3] but whose inhabitants, the English, the newest of God's elect peoples,[4] he

1. For a recent work, cf. Richard W. Pfaff, "Bede among the Fathers? The Evidence from Liturgical Commemoration," *Studia Patristica* 28 (1993): 225–29.
2. F. L. Cross and E. A. Livingstone, eds., *The Oxford Dictionary of the Christian Church,* 2nd ed. (Oxford, 1974), 504.
3. His letter to Egbert, written in 734, complains of the ignorance and greed of the clergy; cf. Charles Plummer, *Venerabilis Bedae Opera Historica* (Oxford, 1896), I, 405–23; English translation in *English Historical Documents, c. 500–1042,* ed. Dorothy Whitelock (New York, 1955), 735–45. In the *Historia Ecclesiastica Gentis Anglorum* (hereafter *HE*), and in his prose *vita* of Cuthbert, he frequently points out how "in those days" the clergy had the respect of the people. *HE* will be cited in the edition of Bertram Colgrave and R. A. B. Mynors, *Bede's Ecclesiastical History of the English People* (Oxford, 1969).
4. On the English as the New Israel, cf. Robert W. Hanning, *The Vision of History in Early Britain* (New York, 1966), 70. The notion of the election of the English

Journal of Early Christian Studies 5:1, 85–103 © 1997 The Johns Hopkins University Press also loved dearly. Bede struggled for a lifetime to bridge the gap between those two worlds, earning a compliment from his fellow Anglo-Saxon, the great missionary Boniface, who called him a *candela ecclesiae*.[5] This was indeed a light which shined brightly, enlightening the study of early Christianity to our own day.

That last sentence sounds startling, but a survey of Bede's legacy will validate it. His *Historia Ecclesiastica* provides the only reliable data on the career of the Romano-British missionary Ninian,[6] and it preserves an important work of Gregory the Great, his *libellus responsionum* or "little book of replies" to the queries of Augustine of Canterbury about how to deal with the newly converted English,[7] an essential witness to Gregory's missionary policy.

Like all Anglo-Saxons, Bede admired Gregory the Great. Not only did he make him a central figure of the early part of the *Historia Ecclesiastica*, he also made extensive use of the pope's exegesis and even cited him in his works on grammar and writing, hardly a common practice in the middle ages.[8] Given the amount of modern scholarship on Gregory, interest in him does not seem remarkable, but, in Bede's day, Gregory was not popular in his own city. After his death in 604, the Roman clergy did not elect another monk as pope for more than four centuries, choosing instead from their own ranks.[9] The *Liber Pontificalis* has a "scrappy and grudging" biography of him which is shorter than those of many other popes, and the first full Roman biography was commissioned by Pope John VIII (872–882) and then only after he had learned of the great reverence for Gregory among the northern Christians, a reverence spread by English missionaries and Bedes writings.[10] Bede knew that Gregory had "by his efforts (converted the English) from the power of

---

appears throughout his commentary on Genesis; cf. Charles W. Jones, "Some Introductory Remarks on Bede's *Commentary on Genesis*," *Sacris Erudiri* 19 (1969–1970), 129, with references to the original.

5. *Epistola* 91, ed. M. Tangl, *Die Briefe des heiligen Bonfiatius und Lullus*, MGH, *Epist. Sel.* I, 207, line 17.

6. *HE* iii.4; pp. 220–22.

7. *HE* i.27; cf. Paul Meyvaert, "Bede's Text of the *Libellus Reponsionum* of Gregory the Great to Augustine of Canterbury," in *England before the Conquest*, ed. Peter Clemoes and Kathleen Hughes (Cambridge, 1971), 15–33.

8. Martin Irvine, "Bede the Grammarian," *Anglo-Saxon England* 13 (1986): 15–44; citation at p. 38.

9. Boniface IV (608–15) and Honorius I (625–38) both established monasteries in Rome but after their elections; Agatho (678–81) was a former monk at the time of his election.

10. Jeffrey Richards, *Consul of God: The Life and Times of Gregory the Great* (London, 1980), 260.

Satan,"[11] and that God had worked through such a man. He may have been biased, but Bede made the Western world take Gregory seriously as a scholar.

He also did the same for Primasius, whose Apocalypse commentary became known in the West because Bede used it for his own commentary.[12]

When Paul the Deacon, a late eighth-century Carolingian, prepared a standard homilarium, he included more of Bede's homilies than those of even Augustine and Gregory, and many medieval homilists learned patristic preaching through Bede's use of it.[13] Bede's *opera exegetica* were so popular that the Anglo-Saxons had to invent a new type of minuscule to meet the demands for his works on the continent.[14] He became the first writer to place together Ambrose, Jerome, Augustine, and Gregory as the four great doctors of the Church.[15] Because Bede preferred the Vulgate to the various *Vetus Latina* versions in circulation, he employed it in his chronological and exegetical works, thus increasing its popularity. No less an authority than Henri deLubac called Bede the "l'esprit le plus scientifique du haut moyen âge" and the one "qui a frappé la formule définitive du quadruple sens [de l'Écriture]."[16] Bede did not establish the fourfold formula—John Cassian did—but he convinced medieval scholars to use it, thus influencing biblical exegesis until the Reformation.[17]

So high was Bede's reputation for chronology and computistics, that as late as 1537 his *opera de temporibus* were published for their technical rather than historical value.[18] Bede disagreed with the chronology of

11. *HE* ii.1; p. 123.

12. Gerald Bonner, *Saint Bede in the Tradition of Western Apocalypse Commentary,* Jarrow Lecture 1966 (Jarrow, 1966), 7. The wide distribution of manuscripts of Bede's commentary helped spread Primasius' reputation; cf. W. F. Bolton, *A History of Anglo-Latin Literature 597–1066,* I (Princeton, 1967), 107.

13. G. H. Brown, *Bede the Venerable* (Boston, 1987), 98.

14. Ibid., 97. More than 160 manuscripts just of *HE* survive on the continent; cf. L. W. Barnard, "Bede and Eusebius as Church Historians," in *Famulus Christi,* ed. Gerald Bonner (London, 1976), 106–24, citation at p. 116. For a dated but still valuable survey, cf. M. L. W. Laistner and H. H. King, *A Hand-List of Bede Manuscripts* (Ithaca, N.Y., 1943). Also, the MSS lists for the CCSL critical editions would provide information for individual books.

15. J. N. Hart-Hasler, "Bede's Use of Patristic Sources: The Transfiguration," *Studia Patristica* 28 (1993): 198, n. 5.

16. *Exegese Médiévale* (Paris, 1959), I, ii:664.

17. Jones, "Introductory Remarks," 140.

18. Gerald Bonner, "Bede and Medieval Civilization," *Anglo-Saxon England* 2 (1973): 82.

Eusebius and Rufinus, and his chronology prevailed. After he decimated the computistical works of Pseudo-Anatolius, that author ceased to be an authority.[19]

Although Alcuin, Boniface, and others called the new barbarian inhabitants of Britain *Saxones,* Bede considered the term appropriate only for the pagans still on the continent, and his writings guaranteed that the name *Angli,* used by his beloved Gregory the Great, would prevail.[20]

This humble monk, by the power of the pen, single-handedly changed the western view of time. He preferred the new chronological scheme of Dionysius Exiguus, and so he employed it in both his chronological and historical works; it is because of Bede, not Dionysius, that the western world uses a calendar based upon the birth of Christ.[21]

If this were not enough, Bede's influence actually extended into heaven. He is the only Englishman whom Dante placed in Paradise. (*Paradiso* x.131)

The larger situation of western Christendom contributed to the depth of Bede's influence. When he wrote his most important works in the 720s, the Saracens[22] had conquered North Africa, almost all of Spain, and, until the battle of Tours in 732, sizeable parts of France. Latin Christianity flourished only in Italy, part of France, Britain, and Ireland, with pagan survivals in the last two. Bede had few colleagues and no equal. Little wonder that his works had such large and, significantly, immediate impact. Many continental manuscripts of his works date to the eighth and ninth centuries.[23]

It would be erroneous to imply that the fathers influenced medieval writers primarily because Bede cited them. Although we can name no great Italian scholars contemporary with Bede, Italy continued to furnish manuscripts of the fathers. The Irish also studied the fathers, but much

---

19. Bolton, *Anglo-Latin Literature,* I, 157.

20. Michael Richter, "Bede's *Angli:* Angles or English?" *Peritia* 3 (1984): 99–114.

21. Brown, *Bede,* 84.

22. Bede used this term for the Arabs; he found it in Jerome's *Hebraicum quaestionum in Genesim,* xvi.12 and cited it in his *Libri Quatuor in Principium Genesis,* I:246–49, ed. C. W. Jones, CCSL 118A (1967), 201. (Hereafter cited *In Genesim.*)

23. Bolton, *Anglo-Latin Literature,* 107, 125.

24. For the Irish use of the fathers in their exegesis, cf. Joseph F. Kelly, "A Catalogue of Early Medieval Hiberno-Latin Biblical Commentaries (I)," *Traditio* 44 (1988): 537–71, and "A Catalogue of Early Medieval Hiberno-Latin Biblical Commentaries (II)," *Traditio* 45 (1989–1990): 393–434.

of their influence on the larger culture occurred after Bede's death,[24] while the Franks awaited the Carolingian Renaissance. Furthermore, Bede's intellectual integrity demanded that he use the fathers. In his commentary on Genesis, for example, he relied very heavily on Augustine to interpret the Garden of Eden narrative—a simple recognition that the African father had provided the most brilliant interpretation available, and Bede the scholar could not help but use it. Finally, there is something of a circular argument to consider, that is, that Bede was Bede precisely because he read the fathers; had he not, he would never have been such an imposing scholar. But, even allowing for these considerations, his work did determine much of the future of patristics in the Latin West.

Scholars who study Bede and the fathers have concentrated on two themes, Bede's knowledge of them and his use of their works. For the former, the pioneering work of M. L. W. Laistner still has great value,[25] but the best places to look are the *indices auctorum* of the *CCSL* editions. Although this theme still demands study, this paper will concentrate on the second one, but with a difference.

Its concern is to portray Bede as someone trying to bridge the gap between two ages and two worlds. One can do this by showing how Bede relied on the fathers for his work, but that would convey only part of the story. The fathers represented far more than resources for his scholarship; they represented a *Weltanschauung,* a way of life, an entry to a better and more authentic life. Bede wanted to pass along their values, those deeply held beliefs and practices that informed every word they wrote. Their great scholarship presumed those values and flowed from them. Bede transformed scholarship not because he could accumulate patristic footnotes, but because he made the fathers' values his own.

The personal importance of the fathers to Bede cannot be overestimated. The names of only five of his students are extant. Although learned men, they did not approach him as scholars.[26] Bede tells us that Theodore of Canterbury trained English students who knew "Latin and Greek just as well as their native tongue,"[27] but the names of just five survive, only one of whom, Aldhelm, left any writings, and none of these

25. "The Library of the Venerable Bede," in *Bede: His Life, Times, and Writings,* ed. A. H. Thompson (Oxford, 1935), 237–66; reprinted in M. L. W. Laistner, *The Intellectual Heritage of the Early Middle Ages* (Ithaca, N.Y., 1957), 117–49. Bede knew more than 200 patristic works, including Greek writers in translation. Scholars still debate if he knew any Greek writers in the original.

26. Dorothy Whitelock, "Bede and His Teachers and Friends" in *Famulus Christi,* 19–39, at pp. 33–34.

27. *HE* iv.2; p. 335.

five resided in Bede's monastery.[28] Bede clearly had learned friends who supported and encouraged his work,[29] but he did not interact with other scholars on a routine basis. Indeed, he tells us that *ipse mihi dictator simul notarius et liibrarius existerem.*[30] He also mentions some annoying demands (*perterritus et obstrepentium caursarum*), known to his correspondent, which kept him from his scholarly work.[31] That he turned to the fathers and found solace there should be no surprise. When he opened his books, he found his brothers in the spirit.

The patristic values which Bede appropriated were preceded by his personal values, which interpenetrated and interacted with the patristic ones, thus forming a unique, western approach to the fathers. A leading Bede scholar, Arthur Holder, tells us that "If we want to understand Bede's exegesis in the context of his life and culture, we will do well to keep in mind three aspects of his identity: Bede was a Northumbrian by birth, a monk by profession, and a teacher by vocation."[32] This wise observation also applies to Bede's non-exegetical writings.

Bede was born while the Syrian Theodore of Tarsus held the archbishopric of Canterbury (668–90) and less than ten years after the Synod of Whitby had determined that the Northumbrians would follow the Roman calculation of Easter rather than the "Celtic" one.[33] He tells us he was born on the lands of Wearmouth monastery. At an age of seven, he was entrusted by his kinsfolk to the monastery, although scholars do not know if this was a form of fosterage or if Bede's family, tenant farmers,

---

28. Michael Lapidge, "The School of Theodore and Hadrian," *Anglo-Saxon England* 15 (1986): 45–72, at p. 46. Lapidge and Bernhard Bischoff, *Biblical Commentaries from the Canterbury School of Theodore and Hadrian* (Cambridge, 1994) have reclaimed some works of that school, but this would not alter the argument that Bede worked largely on his own.

29. Cf. Whitelock, "Teachers and Friends," for a survey.

30. *In Lucae Evangelium Expositio, prologus*: 95–96, ed. D. Hurst, CCSL 120 (1960), 7.

31. *Expositio Actuum Apostolorum, praefatio*: 10–12, ed. M. L. W. Laistner, CCSL 121 (1983), 3.

32. "The Venerable Bede on the Mysteries of Our Salvation," *American Benedictine Review* 42 (1991): 140–62; citation at p. 140.

33. The misleading terms "Roman" and "Celtic" suggest that the Roman missionaries were on one side and the Irish and Britons on the other. In fact, southern Ireland had a strong Romanist party, and Bede says that the events which led up to Whitby were initiated by an Irishman named Ronan (*HE* iii.25; p. 294). For the views of an Irish Romanist, cf. *Cummian's Letter De Controversia Paschali and the De Ratione Conputanid*, edited by Maura Walsh and Dáibhí O Cróinín, Studies and Texts, 86 (Toronto, 1988).

had too many mouths to feed and gave their bright young boy to the monks.[34]

Bede never forgot his roots, which would have been reinforced in the monastery, where, initially at least, he carried his own weight in the field work and where he worked with simpler, English-speaking brothers. This attachment shows up in much of his writing. For example, in his prose *vita* of Cuthbert, Bede followed patristic conventions: a child miraculously recognizes the future bishop of Lindisfarne,[35] just as a child had recognized the future bishop of Milan. But when Bede wrote his history of the abbots of Wearmouth and Jarrow, he delighted in telling how Abbot Eosterwine, disdaining the trappings of office, milked ewes and cows, ploughed the field, and hammered iron like a blacksmith.[36] (Significantly, Bede never tells such homely stories about the Roman missionaries.)

Commenting on Genesis 1.20, the creation of the winged creatures, Bede wrote about sea-birds, and on 1.21–22 he wrote about fish;[37] unlike most patristic Genesis commentators, he probably fished at the sea for food for the brothers. Although Bede knew the mystical significance of the number eight,[38] when he interpreted the eight people on Noah's ark, this Germanic peasant asked a question which would never have occurred to the urbane Augustine and the aristocratic Gregory: how did so few people take care of all those animals?[39]

Bede's interest in his roots also led him to record some valuable information about English paganism, for example, that in times of famine "forty or fifty men, wasted with hunger, would go together to some precipice or to the seashore where in their misery they would join hands and leap into the sea" in order to extend the food supply for others.[40] His great work on chronology, *De Tempore Rationum*, has a

34. *HE* v.24, p. 566.

35. *Vita Cuthberti*, i, ed. Bertram Colgrave, *Two Lives of Saint Cuthbert* (Cambridge, 1985), 154–58.

36. *Historia Abbatum* (hereafter *HA*) 8, edited by Charles Plummer, *Opera Historica*, I.371–72.

37. *In Genesim*, I:585–95, 653–60; *CCSL* 118A, 20, 22.

38. Jones, "Some Introductory Remarks," 171.

39. *In Genesim*, I:1412–35; *CCSL* 118A, 113. Elsewhere Bede did give the eight people an allegorical significance, for example *In Epistolas Septem Catholicas* (*I Petri*), iii.20–21:263–66, ed. D. Hurst, *CCSL* 121 (1983), 250, where they symbolize the day on which Christ rose; ibid. (*II Petri*), ii.5:86–96, 270–71, where they symbolize the eighth age in which the general resurrection and last judgment will occur.

40. *HE* iv.13, pp. 372–74.

chapter *de mensibus Anglorum* which includes *Eosturmonath, qui nunc paschalis mensis interpretatur, quondam a dea illorum (Anglorum) quae Eostre vocabatur et cui in illo festa celebrabant nomen habuit,* the first appearance in print of a word irrevocably associated with Bede.[41]

The second element in Holder's trio is Bede the monk. He entered Wearmouth but was soon transferred to a new foundation, Jarrow,[42] although the two foundations were as one.[43] Benedict Biscop, the first great English bibliophile, founded both houses and stocked them with books obtained by five trips to Rome. He studied different monastic rules and decided upon a *regula mixta* but with "as concentrated a dose of Benedictinism as was available anywhere in the seventh century."[44]

Except for one trip to Lindisfarne and a second to York,[45] Bede spent the rest of his life in Jarrow. Even allowing for his genius and the quality of the Wearmouth-Jarrow library, it is a tribute to monastic education that Bede spent fifty-five years in one monastery and still became the most learned person in Latin Christendom.

This paper can only consider some of Bede's Benedictine values. He constantly encouraged humility. This appears most in the *Historia Ecclesiastica* where repeatedly he praises Aidan, Oswald, Hild, and Cuthbert *inter alios* for this quality. Following—and establishing—an early medieval hagiographical trope, Bede emphasized how Hild had lived the first part of her life as a noblewoman, but she abandoned that life for the monastery, where this once rich woman lived with others "after the example of the primitive church, no one was rich, no one was in need, for they had all things in common and none had any private property."[46] Bede gave a picturesque and unforgettable portrayal of Oswald, the Northumbrian king who took refuge in Iona for a while and

41. *De Tempore Rationum* (hereafter *DTR*), 15:36–38, ed. C. W. Jones, *CCSL* 123B (1977), 331.

42. In the introduction to a new translation of the *Historia Ecclesiastica*, Judith McClure and Roger Collins argue that Bede never lived at Jarrow, *Bede—The Ecclesiastical History of the English People* (Oxford, 1994), xiii, but the traditional view is supported by Ian Wood, "The Most Holy Abbot Ceolfrith," *Jarrow Lecture 1995* (Whitby, 1995), 34 n. 5.

43. Bede says (*HA* 7) that brotherly love united the two houses (*fraterna societate coniuncta*) just as it had united their patrons, Peter and Paul; Plummer, *Opera Historica*, i.371.

44. Patrick Wormald, "Bede and Bendict Biscop," *Famulus Christi*, 141–69, at p. 144.

45. Lindisfarne: *Vita Cuthberti, prologus,* p. 144; York: *Epistola ad Ecgbertum,* Plummer, *Opera*, i.1, p. 405.

46. *HE* iv.23; p. 409.

there learned the Irish language. When, at the king's request, Aidan came from Iona to evangelize the Northumbrians, he did not speak their language, so he preached while the king humbled himself to be the monk's translator. Bede called this a *pulcherrimum spectaculum,* "a most beautiful sight."[47]

His awareness of being a barbarian reinforced his monastic humility. In the preface to his *Commentary on the Canticle of Canticles,* he explained that he relied on ancient authorities for information about the various aromatic plants in the biblical book not to display his learning, but because he and his people live at the end of the world *in insula maris oceani,* and they knew what happened *in primis orbis partibus* only by the writings of those who have been there.[48]

His monastic humility appears everywhere, for example, in a discussion of rhetoric. A good stylist, he appreciated rhetorical devices and flourishes but feared they could be abused. After all, the heresiarch Julian of Eclanum was *rhetor peritissimus.*[49] Jerome had spoken for many fathers when he bragged "that the 'whole world' had come to speak in the style of 'our fishermen.'"[50] Bede followed his patristic exemplars and employed this piscatory style in his exegesis and histories. He had no doubt of the scriptural sanction for the *sermo simplex,* since he believed that the Holy Spirit came in the form of a dove specifically to teach Christians to be simple.[51] This also made him value peasant narratives, sources rarely quoted before him but which he trusted precisely because of their rustic simplicity.[52] This trait resonated with one of his countrymen. The twelfth-century historian William of Malmesbury characterized Bede as *vir maxime doctus et minime superbus.*[53]

Bede also showed a great respect for *auctoritas.* He never criticized those in authority by name, and he "had no wish to be original,"[54] in the sense that he did not wish to depart from a grand tradition. He knew

47. *HE* iii.3; p. 220.

48. *In Cantica Canticorum, praefatio,* 508–13, ed. David Hurst, *CCSL* 119B (1983), 180.

49. *In Cantica Canticorum, praef.*:12; *CCSL* 119B, 168.

50. *Commentariorum in Epistolam ad Galatas, PL* 26, 401BC; also Roger Ray, "Bede, the Exegete as Historian," in *Famulus Christi,* 125–40, at pp. 133–36.

51. *Exp. Act. Apost.,* viii:40–41; *CCSL* 121, 40.

52. Bede, *Vita Sancti Cuthberti,* iii; p. 164.

53. *De Gestis Regum Anglorum,* ed. W. Stubbs, Rolls Series (1887–1889), I.1.

54. Brown, *Bede,* 17, 20; he goes on to defend Bede by defining originality as "a quality authors and public have seen as praiseworthy since the nineteenth century." But he does see Bede as original "within the exegetical tradition" by his ability to adapt and synthesize materials (p. 42).

that he would never be the *vir trilinguis* Jerome had been, that he could not theologize like Augustine, that he could not match Gregory's pastoral insights. He firmly believed that God had aided their work which he should thus take most seriously. He knew that Josephus had seen the Temple, so when Cassiodorus cited Josephus, Bede thought it only sensible to follow Cassiodorus.[55] Since Bede could never put himself on the fathers' level, he would have considered differing from them, except for compelling reasons, not as originality but as foolishness.

Yet he did not follow his *auctoritates* slavishly. He routinely chose to cite some and not others, and the sources he did use, he used selectively. Although Augustine determined his understanding of the Garden of Eden, Bede put a more naturalistic interpretation upon the Hexameron. Furthermore, he realized that even Scriptural authors could be humanly fallible. The patriarch Shem could not have been born when Noah was 500 (Genesis 5.31), entered the ark when Noah was 600 (7.11–13), and still be 100 when he fathered Arfaxad two years after the flood (11.10). Bede concluded that Moses, like Homer, must have nodded.[56]

His monastic interests appear in diverse ways in his works. He thought that the book of Tobit offered much on the literal level for the moral life,[57] and his *vita* of Cuthbert was read for two days *coram senioribus ac doctoribus* in the hopes they would consider it for the monks at Lindisfarne.[58] Since "some knowledge of number was needed for a life which depended on the regular observance of the monastic horarium,"[59] Bede's interest in numbers had a partially monastic base. When he interpreted the moral teaching of the Catholic Epistles, he found monastic values such as restraint of speech and obedience.[60] So completely did he identify with the monastic life that, according to Alcuin, Bede believed that angels visited monasteries during the canonical hours, and he never missed the Divine Office for fear that they would wonder where he was.[61]

The final element of Holder's trio deals with what made Bede great.

---

55. *De Templo,* II:448–52, ed. David Hurst, *CCSL* 119A (1969), 193.

56. *In Genesim,* III.710–60; *CCSL* 118, 162–63.

57. *In Librum Beati Patris Tobiae* (hereafter *In Tobiam*), *praefatio,* 1–3, ed. D. Hurst, *CCSL* 119B (1983), 7.

58. *Vita Cuthberti, prologus*; p. 144.

59. Peter Hunter Blair, *The World of Bede,* rev. ed. (London, 1991), 260.

60. *In Epistolas Septem Catholicas* (*Iacobi*), iv.17:180, *CCSL* 121, 216; ibid. (*I Petri*) v.5:45–49, 257.

61. *Ep.* 16, *MGH Epp.* IV.443.

Not all Northumbrians were monks and not all monks were teachers, but he was, and his teaching duties brought him to the Fathers.

Teaching undergirded his whole life. Bede's pedagogical career began on a low but significant note. He taught young boys how to count on their fingers,[62] the likely genesis of his lifelong interest in numbers.[63] His pupil Cuthbert portrayed him on his deathbed, still concerned about his students, trying to finish a translation of parts of John's gospel and worrying that the students might follow Isidore of Seville's *De Rerum Natura,* be misled, and waste their labor on that book *post meum obitum.*[64] Although patristic values certainly influenced the monk and the Northumbrian, the teacher passed them along to the world at large.

Although we shall concentrate on scholarship, we must recall that for Bede this was useless without a good life; teaching objectively taught nothing. Cuthbert, Aidan, Hild and all good teachers taught primarily by their lives *primo facere, postea docere, quia Iesus bonum doctorem instituens nulla nisi quae fecit docuit,* and his apostles followed his lead.[65]

The most significant value Bede received from the fathers was a reverence for Scripture. Reading him reminds one of reading Augustine. Bede genuinely loved the Bible. He considered it the center of Christian life in all its forms—spiritual, intellectual, cultural, and moral. Scripture dominated every phase of his life, gave him comfort in difficult times, explained God's plan for the English people, allowed the natural scientist to rejoice in God's creation, challenged the scholar, and pointed the path to salvation. As Douglas Burton-Christie demonstrated for the Egyptian ascetics,[66] Bede lived the Scriptures, quoting them at will and viewing the world through their lenses. He worked diligently on all his books, but a sense of joy at living with God's word pervades them.

One can see his biblically centered *Weltanschauung* in many places, but perhaps best in the *Historia Ecclesiastica.* Bede tells the historical tale

---

62. For a medieval manuscript illustration of the procedure, cf. Peter Hunter Blair, *Northumbria in the Days of Bede* (London, 1976), figure 13 opposite p. 161.

63. He devoted the first chapter of *DTR* to *De Computo vel Loquela Digitorum;* CCSL 123B, 268–73.

64. *Epistola Cuthberti de Obitu Bedae,* in Colgrave and Mynors, *Bede's Ecclesiastical History,* 580–87; citation at p. 582. Although scholars accept the authenticity of Cuthbert's accounts, it can easily mislead one about Bede's genuine respect for much of Isidore's scholarship; cf. William McCready, "Bede and the Isidorian Legacy," *Mediaevel Studies* 57 (1995): 41–73.

65. *Exp. Act. Apost.,* i.10–12, iii.32–36; CCSL 121, 6, 24.

66. *The Word in the Desert: Scripture and the Quest for Holiness in Early Christian Monasticism* (Oxford, 1993).

of Augustine of Canterbury's mission to England, but he knew that the significance of the event lay beyond the facts. Christianity had been born again among the English, and to prove that, he deliberately portrayed the Roman mission as *ecclesia primitiva renovata*.[67]

Augustine of Canterbury and the other missionaries, like the Apostles, proved the truth of their word by matching preaching and miracles. Massive conversions occurred. Initially there were diverse practices, including Jewish ones, until the church moved toward unity, partially via regularizing the observance of Easter. Just as some recalcitrant Jewish Christians resented Paul, the apostle to the Gentiles, so the Romano-Britons resented Augustine and his desire to spread the faith to the English.[68] Lest anyone miss the point, Bede said outright that the Roman missionaries *coeperunt apostolicam primitivae ecclesiae vitam imitari*.[69]

So deeply had Bede imbibed the identification of the Roman mission with the *ecclesia primitiva* that he even turned it around. In his commentary on Acts, he observed that when Paul was in Athens, he smartly refrained from initially destroying the idols so that the angry gentiles would not reject his teaching.[70] Gregory the Great advised Augustine of Canterbury to follow a similar course, leaving pagan places of worship alone but reconsecrating them and filling them with altars and relics to replace the idols which should be destroyed.[71] Gregory believed that familiar surroundings would make Christianity more palatable. How wise of Paul to follow Gregory's practice.[72]

Relating the "modern" English to the Bible also had spiritual value. In a homily for his monastic brothers, Bede saw in Benedict Biscop the rich young man of the gospels, but one who accepted the Lord's challenge

---

67. On Bede's general view of the *ecclesia primitiva*, cf. Glenn Olsen, "Bede as Historian: The Evidence from his Observations on the Life of the First Christian Community at Jerusalem," *Journal of Ecclesiastical History* 33 (1982): 519–30.

68. The account of Augustine's mission is in *HE* i.23–33; parallels to Acts are *passim*. In addition to the work of Olsen just cited cf. his "From Bede to the Anglo-Saxon Presence in the Carolingian Empire," in *Angli e Sassone al di qua e al di là del mare nell'alto medioevo, Settimane di studio del Centro italiano di studi sull'alto medioeve*, no. 32 (Spoleto, 1986), 306–82, esp. 366–82. Also, cf. C. B. Kendall, "Imitation and the Venerable Bede's *Historia Ecclesiastica*," in *Saints, Scholars, and Heroes*, I, ed. M. H. King and W. M. Stevens (Collegeville, Minn., 1979), 161–90, esp. 182ff.

69. *HE* i.26; p. 76.

70. *Exp. Act. Apost.*, xvii:49–50; CCSL 121, 72.

71. *HE* i.30; p. 106.

72. Bede wrote *HE* after the Acts commentary, but he knew about Gregory long before writing *HE*.

and for the right reason, unlike Plato and Diogenes who abandoned riches *pro inani . . . mortalium laude captanda.*[73]

Since the Bible is the word of God, Bede rightly understood that to make the most of it for his life, he had to study it as completely as possible, thus embracing a patristic value almost as important as reverence for the text. With admirable consistency, he turned to the greatest of the fathers to learn how to study the Bible. "[F]ollowing the program put forth by St. Augustine in *De Doctrina Christiana,* Bede viewed all his work in relation to its usefulness for shedding light on the scriptures."[74] Thanks to Augustine, he came to view the fathers primarily as exegetes, no matter what they wrote about. To phrase it in a more Augustinian manner, for Bede the *opera patrum* became the *spolia Aegyptiorum.*

The Augustinian value of endless study opened new worlds for Bede. To discover the meaning of the biblical words, he studied grammar, rhetoric, tropes, and verse. He soon encountered the same difficulty the fathers had—what to do with pagan literature? He did find value in it. For example, he liked Vergil, and he relied heavily on pagan grammarians and on Pliny the Elder for geographical details.[75] But he still worried, pointing out that *nobiles magistri ecclesiae* read pagan literature and one of them enjoyed it so much that the Lord warned him in a vision that he was *non christianus sed Ciceronianus.*[76] This would not happen to Bede.

From these ancient pagan writers he cautiously collected the ideas which would result in *De Schematibus et Tropis, De Arte Metrica,* and *De Orthographia.*[77] But the wary Bede worried about his students. If he took his examples from pagan literature, might they not think less of the Scriptures as literature? To counter that he told his students: *sancta Scriptura ceteris omnibus scripturis non solum auctoritate, quia divina est, vel utilitate, quia ad vitam ducit aeternam, sed et antiquitate et ipsa*

73. *Homeliarum Evangelii,* i.13:1–10, ed. D. Hurst, CCSL 122 (1955), 88.

74. Lawrence Martin, *The Venerable Bede: Commentary on the Acts of the Apostles,* Cistercian Studies, 117 (Kalamazoo, Mich., 1989), xvi.

75. On the grammarians, cf. Irvine, "Bede the Grammarian." Thanks to Pliny, Bede knew that Candace (Acts 8.27) was not a proper name but the style of the female rulers in Ethiopia; cf. *Exp. Act. Apost.,* viii.27:72–75, CCSL 121, 41, to cite just one of many examples.

76. *In Primam Partem Samuhelis* (hereafter *In Sam.*), ii.xiv:2173–79, ed. D. Hurst, CCSL 119 (1962), 120.

77. The first two titles were edited by C. B. Kendall and the third by C. W. Jones for CCSL 123A (1975).

praeeminet positione dicendi, placuit mihi collectis de ipsa exemplis ostendere quia nihil huiusmodi schematum sive troporum valent praetendere saecularis eloquentiae magistri, quod non in illa praecesserit.[78] Bede kept his word, producing a grammatical work which used no pagan examples but only, except for three references to Christian poets, scriptural examples. He was the first to do this, but subsequent Christian grammarians largely followed his example.[79]

The impracticality and delight of poetry presented a special problem, but, observing that the metrical art *divinis non est incognita libris,*[80] Bede studied poetry and wrote his own, albeit with debatable success.[81]

From words Bede turned to numbers. No exegete, excepting perhaps Augustine, has loved numbers as he did. He recognized their theological and mystical value, but, unlike most other exegetes, he took a very practical approach to them, and not just because he had to teach boys how to count. He grew up while the Easter controversy still raged and saw at first hand the harm innumeracy could do. The entire Christian liturgical year depended upon the date of Easter. "What did the unity of Christians mean if they could not even agree about the date on which their main festival should be celebrated? . . . The whole lengthy dispute about the dating of Easter represents a struggle by man to orient himself in time, no less significant than his struggle of the present day to orient himself in space."[82] Bede always took numbers seriously.

With a practical background and Augustine as a guide, Bede eagerly sought out numbers in Scripture. It was not a difficult search. Indeed, he often had to decide which of many interpretations to use, so he employed several for the same number. For example, in *De Tabernaculo,* he interpreted four rings as the gospels, four table corners as the four ways to interpret Scripture, and four pillars of acacia wood as the four cardinal virtues.[83] Bede never developed a metaphysics of number, but he made the interpretation of numbers a central theme of his exegesis. He was especially fond of the ages of the world, which fit in with his

78. *De Schem. et Trop.,* ii.1:13–19; CCSL 123A, 142–43.
79. Bede's grammatical work has spawned considerable literature; cf. Irvine *passim*; Brown, *Bede,* 31–36; also Roger Ray, "Bede and Cicero," *Anglo-Saxon England* 16 (1987): 1–15.
80. *De Arte Metrica,* xxv:30–31; CCSL 123A, 141.
81. F. J. E. Raby, *A History of Christian Latin Poetry,* 2nd ed. (Oxford, 1966), 148, patronizes Bede; Brown, *Bede,* 76, 128 n. 39 defends him.
82. Henry Mayr-Harting, *The Coming of Christianity to England,* 3rd ed. (University Park, Penn., 1991), 104–5.
83. *De Tabernaculo,* I.419–20, 776–84, II.1157–61; CCSL 119A, 15, 24–25, 71.

compustistical studies and historical writing, and "which clearly appealed to his orderly mind. . . ."[84] Charles Jones has prepared a masterful guide to Bede's number symbolism.[85]

Mathematics represented only one aspect of Bede's ventures into the natural sciences in order to understand Scripture. For example, in order to understand the meaning of the stones of Revelation 21, he searched both Christian and pagan sources for lapidary information.[86] He tried to understand the composition of the various woods and fabrics associated with the Mosaic tabernacle in order to determine their exegetical significance.[87]

Numbers fascinated Bede, but unity obsessed him. Modern New Testament scholarship may stress the diverse forces and groups in earliest Christianity, but he accepted the patristic view that first there was unity and only the heretics and schismatics introduced diversity. He accepted unquestioningly the value of church unity. Although no real heresy threatened the English church, the "faith of the Fathers was as his own and their enemies were to be regarded as his."[88] His works catalogue heresies, and his refutation of them shows how well he understood the issues involved, such as the persons of the Trinity or the natures of Christ.[89] One heresy Bede did have some reason to fear was Pelagianism, known among the Britons and Irish and thought to have been associated with the Easter controversy,[90] but the powerful Romanizing movement in both Britain and Ireland brought with it Augustinian notions, and Pelagianism never became a serious threat to the English church.

Bede did not view church unity in a simplistic way. He recognized that

84. Brown, *Bede*, 38.

85. "Some Introductory Remarks," 166–74.

86. Peter Kitson, "Lapidary Traditions in Anglo-Saxon England: Part II, Bede's *Explanatio Apocalypsis* and Related Works," *Anglo-Saxon England* 12 (1983): 73–123.

87. *De Tabernaculo et Vasis Eius ac Vestibus Sacerdotum*, ed. D. Hurst, CCSL 119A (1969), *passim*. The situation is much the same for his work *De Templo*.

88. Gerald Bonner, "Bede and Medieval Civilization," *Anglo-Saxon England* 2 (1973): 71–90; citation at p. 74.

89. Plummer provides a valuable list of all the heresies Bede cites and where he cites them; *Opera Historica*, i.lxii–lxiii.

90. For the Britons, cf. David Dumville, "Late Seventh- or Eighth-Century Evidence for the British Transmission of Pelagius," *Cambridge Medieval Celtic Studies* 10 (1985): 39–52; for the Irish, cf. Joseph F. Kelly, "Pelagius, Pelagianism, and the Early Medieval Irish," *Mediaevalia* 4 (1978): 99–124; for the Easter Controversy, cf. Daíbhí O Cróinín, "'New Heresy for Old': Pelagianism in Ireland and the Papal Letter of 640," *Speculum* 60 (1985): 505–16.

the primitive church did change and develop and that in its earliest stages it observed Jewish practices.[91] This enabled him to see historical progress as something gradual; even retrogressions to paganism did not halt the progress of Christianity among the English.

Although Bede accepted and transmitted many patristic values, the last we shall consider is that all exegesis should tend to charity, a value known to many fathers but formulated by Augustine.[92] For Bede charity meant simply love of others, and the exegete showed love for others by making the treasures of Scripture available to them. He knew Gregory's *Pastoral Rule,* which recommends adapting the message to the hearer, and Bede used this approach to reach the goal of charity. He set out to be a popularizer, not in the modern, pejorative sense of the term, but in the Gregorian sense, one who brought the message to the people, rather like a preacher.[93] The church grows through preaching; "both preacher and hearer are nourished by the word."[94]

To the practical Bede, this meant he should adapt his message in whatever way he could. Scholars have long noted how Bede wrote commentaries on biblical books (Tobit, Acts, Ezra and Nehemiah, Mark) or topics (Tabernacle, Temple) for which there were no or few patristic exemplars. He did not comment upon these books because they provided, so to speak, a wide open field to demonstrate his scholarship, but because he wanted to make biblical treasures available. Any book left unstudied represented a spiritual loss. As for heavily treated books like Genesis and Luke, he wrote about the first largely in order to validate some of his historical and computistical researches and also to demonstrate the election of the Gentiles, no small concern to the English. He wrote about Luke because his friend bishop Acca[95] pointed out that

---

91. *Exp. Act. Apost.,* xv.21:41–46; CCSL 121, 67. For a general discussion, cf. Olsen, "Bede as Historian," 522–24. Proof of the importance of this notion is its appearance in unexpected places, for instance, the five pillars of acacia wood in the Tabernacle represent the five books of Moses which the primitive Christian teachers used until the gospels and epistles had been written; *De Tabernaculo,* II.1285–91; CCSL 119A, 74.

92. *In Genesim,* iv.715–17; CCSL 121, 214, following *De Doctrina Christiana,* I.xxvi.

93. Paul Meyvaert, *Bede and Gregory the Great,* Jarrow Lecture 1964 (Jarrow, 1964), 1–26; citation at p. 15.

94. Edward Echlin, "Bede and the Church," *Irish Theological Quarterly* 40 (1973): 351–63; citation at p. 358.

95. Acca was not the only friend who made such a request. Bede wrote *Expositio in Canticum Abacuc Prophetae* for an anonymous *dilectissima in Christo soror; praefatio:* 1–2, ed. J. E. Hudson, CCSL 119B (1983), 379.

Ambrose's commentary could be *a doctoribus solum intellegi* and not *a rudibus . . . lectoribus quales in praesenti aevo plures invenies.*[96]

Bede believed that allegorical exegesis best suited his English audience, but he never took a strict line, varying his exegetical method to suit the point he wished to make.[97] If illustrations would aid the presentation, he recommended their use;[98] his admirer Boniface followed his lead, wryly observing that worldly minded people were impressed by gilded, illustrated bibles.[99]

Bede complained to Bishop Egbert that there were monks who did not know Latin, but he urged that they be taught in their own tongue.[100] He knew and enjoyed vernacular songs (*doctus in nostris carminibus*), he translated part of John's gospel,[101] the Lord's prayer, the Creed,[102] and he praised the vernacular, biblical songs of Caedmon.[103] Bede studied languages constantly, gaining a solid knowledge of Greek only later in life but one good enough to revise his commentary on Acts using three Latin and two Greek manuscripts, one of which survives.[104] He literally did whatever he could.

One striking example best illustrates the difficulties Bede faced in meeting the demands of charity and making the Scriptures available to the newly converted English. In his commentary on Acts, he relied upon Isidore of Seville for a definition of the word *theatrum,* something which neither he nor any of his readers had ever seen.[105]

This scholar on the brink between two worlds established himself as the bridge between them, as the conduit and shaper of patristic values to the middle ages and beyond. But why did he particularly play such a crucial role? Why did his approach to scholarly questions enjoy such

96. *In Lucam, prologus:* 35–37; CCSL 120, 6. Brown, *Bede,* sums up his approach: "His purposes were therefore either to furnish traditional commentary derived from established sources but put in a simplified form for his English students or to fill for them the gaps in which no commentary yet existed" (p. 21).

97. Olsen, "Bede as Historian," 529.

98. Paul Meyvaert, "Bede and the Church Paintings at Wearmouth-Jarrow," *Anglo-Saxon England* 8 (1979): 63–77.

99. Hunter Blair, *The World of Bede,* 226.

100. *Ep. ad Ecgbertum,* 5; Plummer, *Opera historica,* i.408–9.

101. Cuthbert, *De Obitu Bedae,* pp. 580, 582.

102. *Ep. ad Ecbertum,* 5, Plummer, *Opera historica,* i.409.

103. *HE* iv.24; pp. 414–20.

104. Kevin Lynch, "The Venerable Bede's Knowledge of Greek," *Traditio* 39 (1983): 432–39. The extant MS is Oxford Bodleian Library, Laudianus Graecus 35.

105. *Exp. Act Apost.,* xix.29:98–101; CCSL 121, 80, with note to Isidore.

success that it sometimes obscured even the patristic sources upon which he relied?

Several answers are possible. First, as a monk, Bede took the same approach to Scripture as almost all the leading medieval exegetes of the pre-scholastic period. Knowing who would have to carry on his work, he wrote his commentaries and histories in such a way that they were suitable for monastic *lectiones,* thus immeasurably increasing their usefulness. Typically, he found a biblical foundation for the practice since "the biblical narratives were similarly episodic"; did not Luke have "within the larger *historia* many small *historiae*"?[106] Only when the scholastics supplanted the monks would his influence wane, but never completely.

Second, from the seventh to the ninth century, the new converts in Britain and on the continent were almost all Germans, and Bede spoke their language, both literally and figuratively. The fathers had greater appeal to these new peoples because Bede translated for them.

Third, Latin was Bede's second language.[107] He mastered it but never with the range of a native speaker. He wrote a Latin medieval scholars could access easily, a Latin they wrote themselves. Furthermore, his emphasis on the *sermo simplex* had a spiritual and moral appeal to monastic scribes and exegetes.

Fourth, Bede used the Vulgate. That does not sound like a major point, but the Vulgate was the Bible of the Carolingian age and the scholastics; even the Renaissance humanists who turned to the Greek and Hebrew still referred to the Vulgate. Bede commented upon the Bible which scholars read. Since the Codex Amiatinus was produced at Wearmouth-Jarrow in the early eighth century, he probably worked on it, thus influencing the very text of the Vulgate.[108]

Fifth, Bede was simply more interesting to read than many other Latin writers. People who do not recall Gregory the Great's exegesis still savor Bede's vivid account of the pope's seeing English slave boys on sale in Rome and making a pun on *Angli* and *angeli.*[109] This vividness appears not only in the *Historia Ecclesiastica* but also in his hagiography (Eosterwine at the plough) and exegesis (the sea birds, caring for the animals on the ark).

It is thus fitting to close this account of Bede with two of his best narratives, both *historiae* suitable for the monastic *lectio.* The first is

106. Ray, "Bede, the Exegete, as Historian," 133.
107. A point emphasized by Bonner, "Bede and Medieval Civilization," 76.
108. Hunter Blair, "The Northumbrian Bible," *The World of Bede,* 221–36.
109. *HE* ii.1; pp. 132–34.

famous and a standard in many anthologies. The English King Edwin wished to convert to Christianity, but, by tradition, he had to consult with his nobles. An anonymous thegn gave this advice:[110]

> O King, this is how the present life of man on earth appears to me in comparison with that time which is unknown to us. You are sitting feasting with your ealdormen and thegns in winter time; the fire is burning on the hearth in the middle of the hall and all inside is warm, while outside the wintry storms of rain and snow are raging. Then a sparrow flies swiftly through the hall. It enters in at one door and quickly flies out through the other. For the few moments it is inside, the storm and wintry tempests cannot touch it, but after the briefest moment of calm, it flits from your sight—out of the wintry storm and into it again. So this life of man appears but for a moment; what follows or indeed what went before, we know not at all. If this new doctrine brings us more certain information, it seems right that we should accept it.

This presents a classic, even unforgettable picture of Germanic pagans inspired to embrace Christianity via a sign from the natural world. The reader shares the sparrow's momentary feeling of warmth as it escapes temporarily from a northern winter.

The second tale, not so well known, gives an equally classic picture, this time of Christian asceticism's finding a new home among the English, a theme dear to Bede. Drycthelm, a monk, obtained permission to pursue the life of a hermit.[111]

> [Drycthelm] received a more secret retreat in the monastery where he could freely devote himself to the service of his Maker in constant prayer. As his retreat was on the banks of the river, he often used to enter it in his great longing to chastise his body, frequently immersing himself deep in the water. He would remain there motionless, reciting prayers and psalms for as long as he could endure it, while the water of the river came up to his loins and sometimes even to his neck. When he came out of the water, he would never trouble to take off his cold, wet garments but rather let them dry on his body. In winter months, when the river froze, he would break a hole in the ice and stand in the frigid water while broken pieces of ice floated about him. Those who saw this would say to him, "Brother Drycthelm, how can you endure such bitter cold?" To which he, being a man of simple disposition and few words, would reply, "I have known it colder."

Joseph F. Kelly is Professor of Christian History at John Carroll University, Cleveland.

110. *HE* ii.13, pp. 183–85.
111. *HE* v.12; pp. 497–99.

Acknowledgments

Norris, Frederick W. "Black Marks on the Communities' Manuscripts." *Journal of Early Christian Studies* 2 (1994): 443–66. Reprinted with the permission of Johns Hopkins University Press.

Moriarty, Rachel. "'The Faith of Our Fathers': The Making of the Early Christian Past." *Studies in Church History* 33 (1997): 5–17. Reprinted with the permission of the Ecclestiastical History Society.

Kaufman, Peter Iver. "Tertullian on Heresy, History, and the Reappropriation of Revelation." *Church History* 60 (1991): 167–79. Reprinted with permission from *Church History*.

Studer, Basil. "History and Faith in Augustine's *De Trinitate.*" *Augustinian Studies* 28 (1997): 7–50. Reprinted with the permission of *Augustinian Studies*.

Eno, Robert B. "Radix Catholica." *Revue des Études Augustiniennes* 43 (1997): 3–13. Reprinted with the permission of Institut d'Études Augustiniennes.

Edwards, M.J. "Origen's Two Resurrections." *Journal of Theological Studies,* n.s. 46 (1995): 502–18. Reprinted with the permission of Oxford University Press.

Hennessey, Lawrence R. "Origen of Alexandria: The Fate of the Soul and the Body after Death." *The Second Century* 8 (1991): 163–78. Reprinted with the permission of Johns Hopkins University Press.

Bynum, Caroline W. "Images of the Resurrection Body in the Theology of Late Antiquity." *Catholic Historical Review* 80 (1995): 215–37. Reprinted with the permission of the Catholic University of America Press.

Barclift, Philip L. "Predestination and Divine Foreknowledge in the Sermons of Pope Leo the Great." *Church History* 62 (1993): 5–21. Reprinted with permission from *Church History*.

Norris, Richard A., Jr. "Theology and Language in Irenaeus of Lyon." *Anglican Theological Review* 76 (1994): 285–95. Reprinted with the permission of the Anglican Theological Review, Richard E. Wentz, Editor-in-Chief.

Ando, Clifford. "Augustine on Language." *Revue des Études Augustiniennes* 40 (1994): 45–78. Reprinted with the permission of Institut d'Études Augustiniennes.

Barclift, Philip L. "The Shifting Tones of Pope Leo the Great's Christological Vocabulary." *Church History* 66 (1997): 221–39. Reprinted with permission from *Church History*.

Ferreiro, Alberto. "'Frequenter Legere': The Propagation of Literacy, Education, and Divine Wisdom in Caesarius of Arles." *Journal of Ecclesiastical History* 43 (1992): 5–15. Reprinted with the permission of Cambridge University Press.

Cameron, Averil. "The Language of Images: The Rise of Icons and Christian Representation." *Studies in Church History* 28 (1992): 1–42. Reprinted with the permission of the Ecclesiastical History Society.

Chazelle, Celia. "Memory, Instruction, Worship: 'Gregory's' Influence on Early Medieval Doctrines of the Artistic Image." In *Gregory the Great: A Symposium*, edited by John C. Cavadini (Notre Dame: University of Notre Dame Press, 1995): 181–215. Reprinted with the permission of the University of Notre Dame Press.

Williams, D.H. "A Reassessment of the Early Career and Exile of Hilary of Poitiers." *Journal of Ecclesiastical History* 42 (1991): 202–17. Reprinted with the permission of Cambridge University Press.

Williams, D.H. "Polemics and Politics in Ambrose of Milan's *De Fide*." *Journal of Theological Studies*, n.s. 46 (1995): 519–31. Reprinted with the permission of Oxford University Press.

Kelly, Joseph F. "On the Brink: Bede." *Journal of Early Christian Studies* 5 (1997): 85–103. Reprinted with the permission of Johns Hopkins University Press.